For

Ezenwa Ohaeto

Phanuel Egejuru

Tijan M. Sallah

Ngozi Okonjo-Iweala

for enriching biographies of Chinua Achebe

Emerging Perspectives on Chinua Achebe

Vol. II. *ISINKA*: The Artistic Purpose
Chinua Achebe and the Theory of African Literature

Edited by

Ernest N. Emenyonu
and
Iniobong I. Uko

Africa World Press, Inc.

P.O. Box 1892
Trenton, NJ 08607

P.O. Box 48
Asmara, ERITREA

Copyright © 2004 Ernest N. Emenyonu
First Printing 2004

Book design & Typesetting: S. Kim Glassman, Jerusalem Typesetting

Cover design: Roger Dormann
Cover photograph: Patricia T. Emenyonu

Library of Congress Cataloging-in-Publication Data

Emerging perspectives on Chinua Achebe / edited by Ernest N. Emenyonu and
Iniobong I. Uko.

  p. cm.
Includes bibliographical references and index.
  ISBN 0-86543-877-3 (v. 2) -- ISBN 0-86543-878-1 (v. 2 : pbk.)

1. Achebe, Chinua--Criticism and interpretation. 2. Nigeria--In
literature. I. Emenyonu, Ernest, 1939- II. Uko, Iniobong I., 1964-

PR9387.9.A3Z655 2003
823'.914--dc22

                                2003015791

Table of Contents

Part One: Art and Aesthetics

Chapter 1

Chapter 2

Chapter 3

Chapter 4

Chapter 5

Table of Contents

Preface

THE 24TH ANNUAL CONFERENCE of the African Literature Association (U.S.A.) held in Austin, Texas (March 25–29, 1998) was the key catalyst in the inspiration for the production and publication of two seminal volumes of critical essays on Chinua Achebe, Africa's master storyteller and pioneer literary philosopher of the 20th Century. The volumes: OMENKA: The Master Artist and ISINKA: The Artistic Purpose seek to establish the impact of the place of Chinua Achebe in the development of both African creative writing, and the criticism of African Literature in the 20th Century.

Some weeks before the conference, Bernth Lindfors, the co-convener and a good friend of mine, had contacted me and requested that I introduce the Keynote Speaker, Chinua Achebe in "the most befitting manner of the Igbo tradition." This got me thinking about the traditional Igbo society about which Achebe himself had written, that age was revered but achievements were respected. Chinua Achebe had both age and achievements. He had taken the highest title in his hometown, Ogidi, and achieved universal fame in World Literature. I thought also about orators in the traditional Igbo society, about whom Achebe too, had written that verbal dexterity was enriched by the use of proverbs which for them had become "the palm oil with which words are eaten." In the traditional Igbo society, if a famous and great man were to be presented to an audience, a skilled orator would begin with special praise names reminding the gathering that the pre-eminent person before them had gone to battle and brought home human heads; he had crossed seven rivers and climbed seven mountains and returned home safely; he had gone to the land of the spirits and wrestled the hydra-headed spirit to the ground and returned to the human world unscathed. Chinua Achebe is the great man whose fame has spread all over the globe like the impestuous harmattan fire. Armed with all these facts and fore-knowledge, I proceeded to prepare a nine-page introduction for the occasion. A few days later, the advance copy which I had sent to Bernth Lindfors was returned with a cherry note:

Dear Ernest,

Here's my hatchet job on your introduction. I was trying to reduce it to 2 ½ pages (about 5 minutes reading time) and almost succeeded but there was too much good material in it. But do keep it brief.

Best wishes.
Bernth.

The introduction, when it was presented on March 27, 1998 before a crowded auditorium at the University of Texas, Austin, was precise. It portrayed Chinua Achebe as a Nigerian-born novelist, who at the young age of twenty-eight, and only five years after obtaining a Bachelors degree in Arts (English, History, & Religion) at Nigeria's premier university (Ibadan), had produced a first novel (1958) which was to change the course of World Literature in English, and define for future generations of mankind, the African novel – its character, its function, its tongue, and its unique features. That introduction is reproduced here as still appropriate for introducing Chinua Achebe to the wider literary world of the 21st Century.

The Igbo people have a cryptic way of articulating the dilemma of a person who has been given a "burden", though pleasant, much above his status. He is like a child of humble circumstances who suddenly sits face to face with an enormous plate of food, the like of which he had never before encountered in his life. No matter how hungry or tempted he might be, he does not pounce on the food immediately. He tries to find out from the host, who else would be sharing the food with him. "Nobody", the host would reply with an understanding twinkle of the eye, "it's all yours." The subsequent reaction of the child comes with a mixture of joy and fear. I am this evening facing a prodigious mound of pounded yam, the like of which I have never before encountered.

In the Igbo pantheon, there is a hierarchy of deities with varying degrees of aura and reverence. It is said that, during a ritual performance, there are deities who can be carried with just a few fingers, some within one palm, some with one full hand; but there are deities who require two or more hands to carry. In our act of worship tonight we are invoking the deity of deities who requires not two hands, not four hands but indeed eight hands and more, to carry.

My job has been made relatively easier by the fact that every member of the African Literature Association sitting here tonight, can legitimately claim and assert to be a friend of our speaker, Chinua Achebe. Now, you do not introduce a friend to his friends. You only present him, reminding his friends of a few things which might have transpired since the last get-together. It is a great honor for me to be asked to present Chinua Achebe to his friends.

In 1978, when the then University of Ife became the first Nigerian University to award you an honorary doctorate degree, the university orator, Professor Wole Soyinka, praised you for "making the life of your fellow men (and women) better through literature," for which we salute you. In 1985, when the university of Nigeria,

Nsukka, appointed you Professor Emeritus, you were described as a man whose humility, transparent honesty, inner peace, and yet keen sense of humor have fascinated colleagues and friends; a man whose pen has edified and inspired peoples the world over by producing clear and eloquent ideas which have endeared you to millions of readers; a man who has always performed the noble role of a teacher, a seeker of truth, whose exemplary leadership the community has fully recognized and appreciated," for which we are proud of you.

You have through your works touched and changed many lives. You have been a caring frontiersman and a generous brother's keeper both in Africa and the African diaspora. Nuruddin Farah says that he and many of his contemporaries "owe a great deal to you, many having learnt the craft from you," as "Africa's best novelist and craftsman, and one of the world's greatest, living or dead." Mariama Ba told you in 1980, before her tragic death in 1981, that she "started writing after reading *Things Fall Apart.*" Toni Morrison has thanked you for "doors which you figuratively opened for her." To Jerome Brooks you are the "necessary angel who restored for us (Africans in the diaspora) something that slavery took from us." James Baldwin held you in such high esteem that at his death his family presented to you his most priceless possession as a writer, his briefcase, believing that "he would have wanted you to have it."

Distinguished ladies and gentlemen, I find nothing more appropriate to present our noble speaker to you tonight, than the words of Professor Ola Rotimi, Orator of the University of Port Harcourt, Nigeria in February 1991, when the University bestowed on Chinua Achebe an honorary doctorate degree.

Chinua, son of Achebe, let me from this point on, address you in the style of traditional African Oratory... Speaker in proverbs, we salute you. Exponent of the values of Africa's cultural heritage I say it is you we greet. You who ventured into the forest of world literature and came back a hero.

> *If danger aims its arrow at you again,*
> *The arrows will never fly.*
> *If they do fly,*
> *They will not hit you.*
> *If they do hit you,*
> *They will not wound you.*
> *If they do wound you,*
> *You will not weaken.*
> *If you do weaken,*
> *You will not fall down.*
> *If you do fall down,*
> *You will not faint.*
> *If you do faint,*
> *You will not... die!*

Distinguished guests, please welcome the immortal Akwa Akwuru I of African

Literature, the Ugo N'abo of Ogidi, "the man of letters, the man of ideas, the man of words,' Professor Chinua Achebe.

Hours after that introduction, I was approached by Mr Kassahun Checole, President/Publisher of Africa World Press, with a request to edit essays on Chinua Achebe for their *Emerging Perspectives on African Writers Series*. By the existing format of the series, a writer is chosen and a volume of critical essays devoted to all aspects of his or her writing. But in the case of Achebe, the publisher requested two volumes, and left the nature, organization, and contents entirely to me. After consultations with some colleagues, I decided to focus the first volume on Achebe's creative works and the second on his non-fictional writings which buttress his concept and philosophy of art and the artist in the African situation. Professors Emmanuel N. Obiechina and Clement A. Okafor lent their expertise in Igbo thought and wisdom in the wording of the titles of the two volumes.

There are altogether sixty-seven essays in the two volumes, contributed by scholars from various parts of the world, with an impressive number coming from scholars based on the African continent. In addition, volume II ends with an Epilogue, which probes Achebe's vision of writing in the Igbo language. A considerable number of publishable papers were unfortunately, because of space constraints, left out. Even after the volumes had gone to press, scholars from all over the world were still making inquiries about submitting their papers. Chinua Achebe seems never to have a shortage of readers of his creative works as he never seems to lack erudite commentators on his literary and theoretical ideas. These readers, teachers, and research scholars speak eloquently about Chinua Achebe's unprecedented impacts on the World Literature in English, and the art of the novel in global second language situations since the second half of the 20th Century. In his fictional explorations of the colonial encounters with indigenous non-European races, and in his indigenization of the English language to suit local sensibilities, Chinua Achebe seems to have no rival in contemporary world literature. The contributors to these two volumes have provided ample evidence to support these declarations.

It is, therefore, strange and baffling to literary scholars around the globe that Chinua Achebe has to date not been honored with a Nobel Prize for Literature. We have in him more than any other writer in the second half of the 20th Century, an artist who has influenced for the better, the course of World Literature in English not only for his generation, but for eternity; a writer who, through his works, has touched and changed many lives; an African novelist who has "provided a renewed sense of African heritage, history, and tradition." The two volumes, OMENKA and ISINKA establish Chinua Achebe's legacy as a creative and philosophical genius whose pen has touched and changed a large portion of humanity regardless of race, color, tongue, or creed. The literary world continues watching!

Ernest N. Emenyonu
Chair, Department of Africana Studies
University of Michigan-Flint
Flint, Michigan, February, 2004

Acknowledgments

THE EDITORS AND PUBLISHERS of this book of essays are very grateful to Patricia T. Emenyonu for the front and back cover photos. The Editors acknowledge and thank Dr. Sally Harris, Director , Office of Research, University of Michigan-Flint, for financial assistance which facilitated the typing and production of the manuscript.

Introduction

Ernest N. Emenyonu

CHINUA ACHEBE'S REMARKABLE INFLUENCE on contemporary African
Literature is as much in the establishment of the art of the African novel in
his fiction, as it is in the articulation of African poetics and aesthetics in his extra
fictional pronouncements. He is as much the father of the modern African novel,
as he is the forerunner-theoretician of African literary criticism. Such philosophical and theoretical articles as *The Role of the Writer in a New Nation*, *The Novelist
as Teacher*, *English and the African Writer*, *Thoughts on the African Novel*, *Colonialist
Criticism*, *The Black Writer's Burden*, and *The African Writer and the Biafran Cause*,
among others, read like blueprints for both creative writers and critics of African
literature. They are as imaginatively versatile as they are theoretically profound. In
his role as Philosopher-critic, Achebe has bequeathed to critics of African literature,
a legacy of ideas and theories, which has helped to shape the trends in contemporary
African literary criticism.

ISINKA, comprises 30 dynamic essays, which explore and analyze in depth, as
has never been done before, Chinua Achebe's ideas and visions of art as they relate
to his fiction in particular, and African Literature in general. It is organized in six
parts. Part I contains seven essays which comprehensively address the issues of *art
and aesthetics*. Part II has six essays, which explore with diligent thoroughness the
issues of *Igbo Worldview and Christianity*. Part III has five essays that deal with
the issue of "*The Artist in Society*" an issue which has become quite problematic in
the African setting. Part IV examines in three erudite essays the "*Visions of History*"
in Achebe's fiction. Part V comprises seven essays which address from revealingly
contrasting perspectives, the controversy of the depiction of "*African Womanhood*"
in Achebe's novels. Part VI has two intricate essays. One discusses the influence
of Achebe on other African writers, using one typical Nigerian novelist for lucid

illustration. The second reviews a personal experience in the complex issue of tracking Achebe's life through a biography. The Epilogue which concludes the book, examines Achebe's ideas about writing in an indigenous African language beset with complex multiple dialects. The center of the discourse is the problem of writing in the Igbo language.

An interesting general observation in many of these essays is the attempt by the scholars to assess how much Chinua Achebe's extra fictional ideas about African literature or Literature in general are justified in his own creative fiction. In a few cases, statements have been sifted from Achebe's fiction and analyzed in the light of contemporary socio-political ideologies. Many of the essays on *Anthills of the Savannah* for instance, center the discourse about characterization on prevailing feminist ideas about womanhood. Their major point of view is that Achebe has finally been compelled by the outcries of feminist critics of his earlier works, to write *Anthills* with a heavy bent towards extolling the attributes of an independent and liberated womanhood. They argue that the dominant male chauvinism evident in the earlier novels is missing in *Anthills*, and that is an indication that Chinua Achebe was consciously atoning for the misdeeds against womanhood in his earlier novels especially *Things Fall Apart*. Their verdict, therefore, is that in *Anthills* Achebe has done a good job and deserves to be acquitted of all feminist charges of denigration of womanhood in his fiction. One excited scholar goes so far as to declare Chinua Achebe a feminist! Beatrice, the aggressive female protagonist in *Anthills* is seen more as the result of popular feminist reaction and protest than a character that historically evolved in Achebe's creative imagination. In effect, they assert that in the novel, Achebe's primary concern is to address "the womanhood question" rather than (as clamored by some other critics) provide answers to the perennial problem of bad political leadership so ably articulated in his petite polemical treatise, *The Trouble with Nigeria* (1983), which preceded *Anthills*. Interesting as this feminist theory about Achebe's motive for writing *Anthills* may be, one must observe that well known authoritative social/cultural anthropologists (v.C. Uchendu, Simon Ottenberg, etc) who have written persuasively on the pre-colonial Igbo society, have not contradicted Achebe's portrait of womanhood in his earlier novels, as indeed, the way things really were.

Of the seven essays on African womanhood in ISINKA, six are by female scholars. Four of them argue passionately that Chinua Achebe had come a long way in his fictional depiction of the African woman from *Things Fall Apart* to *Anthills of the Savannah*. The other two essays (by Sophia O. Ogwude and Grace Malgwi) differ very strongly from this feminist viewpoint, and argue instead, that Achebe's portrait of the female image in *Anthills* is consistent with his vision in the earlier novels. They maintain that it would have been false for Achebe to portray the female characters in *Things Fall Apart* and *Arrow of God* differently from what and how they appear in those novels. They further argue that their feminist colleagues do not seem to have taken enough time and trouble to understand the realities of gender roles in pre-colonial African societies. Achebe's function as a writer depicting the society of that era, was simply to hold a mirror up to that society and describe the reflection faithfully. To do otherwise would have devalued his artistic integrity. The only article written by a male scholar (Tanure Ojaide) on this issue, quite symbolically entitled "In Fairness: The Female in Two of Chinua Achebe's Novels" agrees with the position taken by Ogwude and Malgwi. Ojaide proceeds to show with empirical evidence and careful historical analysis that Achebe's portrait of womanhood in *Things Fall Apart* and *Anthills of the Savannah* is a manifestation of his skills as a creative artist with a proper sense of history consistent with his repeated description of himself as a "conscious artist."

Whatever position one takes on this issue, it must be remembered that Achebe's depiction of Africa and Africans in his novels is informed by his unique vision of history. His creative works seem organized to follow patterns of African historical development from the pre-colonial to post-colonial. His imaginary characters act true to their times, settings, and environments. The self confident and emancipated Beatrice of *Anthills*, who seductively steered a Head of State from a dance floor to an outside balcony just to fearlessly reprimand him for succumbing too cheaply to an attractive visiting female American journalist (possibly a spy), would have been out of place in the setting of *Things Fall Apart* and *Arrow of God*, constricted as they were, not only by traditional masculinity in the culture, but also by the unbending officialdom of the colonial presence. Similarly, Uzowulu, the obnoxious wife-battering husband in *Things Fall Apart* (who beats and abuses his wife on any pretext, and is himself beaten up by his wife's brothers who also take back their sister) would, in the setting of *Anthills*, have perhaps faced charges of domestic violence in a court of law. Achebe's self declared mission as a committed African writer is to explore "the human condition in depth." A conscious artist would always draw a good balance between entertainment and realism. It would appear that in his portrait of Africa and Africans in his fiction, Achebe has not digressed from his position as "a concerned and informed insider," whose guiding principle is to show things and people the way they really were then, and are now.

In their total essence the essays in ISINKA show the diverse and lively discourse on how Achebe's theoretical ideas and literary techniques have helped to shape the forms and manners of the criticism of African Literature since the middle of the 20th Century.

On June 11, 2000 my wife and I visited Chinua Achebe at his home at Bard College, Annandale-on-Hudson in New York State where my wife Patricia, took the photographs for the covers of both OMENKA and ISINKA. I seized the opportunity to pose two questions to Chinua Achebe on some positions he had taken four decades earlier on critics of African Literature in particular and the criticism of African Literature in general. I thought it would be of interest to the literary world to get a glimpse of his perspectives on the development of the criticism of African Literature from the ancestral times of *Things Fall Apart* to the liberated era of *Anthills of the Savannah*. The two questions and his responses are reproduced below.

1. Nearly forty years ago, in an article, "Where Angels Fear to Tread," you decried the "special criticisms which have been designed for us (African writers) by people whose knowledge of us is very limited." And in 1980 in an interview with Kalu Ogbaa, you decried the "complacent attitude" of many indigenous (African) critics, maintaining that "there is not enough dedication and diligence among our critics…" and you looked forward to a change. Now, at the end of the 20th Century, how do you assess the criticism of African Literature by (a) African critics and (b) Western or non-African critics?

     I wouldn't be talking about criticism if things were well. My advice to our critics is to be seriously dedicated. Well meaning people can have divergent views on the same issue and still advance the cause of scholarship. One hopes that flourishing creative works so evident now on the contemporary African literary scene will go on side by side with lively criticism. We have come a long way from when one could say that our critics were not good. We now have a number of serious minded and committed literary critics, Africans and non-Africans alike, who take criticism very seriously and are not in it for extraneous reasons.

     But there should be increased activity such that no African writer has cause to complain that no critic is paying attention to his/her works. A writer who produces even one work alone deserves no less attention by critics. There are many African writers (e.g. T. Obinkaram Echewa and others) who have done a lot of impressive creative writing but nobody seems to take critical notice. No palm nut in African creative writing should be allowed to get lost in the fire of African literary criticism. For the benefit of our readers, all creative works should receive critical attention and evaluation. That is a challenge for African literary critics in the 21st Century.

2. In the years after the Nigerian independence (1960), you decried the little attention paid to African writing by African (Nigerian) intellectuals who hardly read novels for pleasure. Now at the end of the 20th Century, have African Literature and the African writer achieved the honorable status that each deserves and which you hoped for on the African continent?

     No, the situation has not changed much. It will require a longer period of time. The reading habit has to be acquired and inculcated in Africans and African cultures. This can best be done in the schools. Educated parents can start off their children at home. The goal must be to instill the reading habit from a young age. Inculcation of the reading habit presupposes working economies, well equipped schools, and stable educational systems etc. The 80's and 90's have not been good decades for Africa with particular reference to strong economies and stable educational and political systems. We hope that things can stabilize in the 21ˢᵗ Century and that the reading habit would have the chance to develop. How the new technologies will impinge on reading in general, one is not sure. But one hopes that no matter what, the reading of books will not ever be lost, not the least in African societies.

The essays in ISINKA (Igbo term for "the artistic purpose") demonstrate the dimensions of vigor and versatility in African literary criticism which has been evolving since Chinua Achebe's outcry four decades ago, against biased criticism by Western critics of African Literature, and shoddy criticism by indigenous African literary critics. Individually and collectively, the thirty essays in this volume bear testimony to Chinua Achebe's direct and indirect impacts on the development of the criticism of African Literature over half a century. They establish definitively Chinua Achebe's legacy to African literary criticism at the end of the 20ᵗʰ Century, and thus provide for teachers, students, and researchers a defining approach to the criticism of African Literature in the new millennium. It is a legacy by one who is not only an incomparable Master Artist, but also a fore-runner theoretician who defined for his age and future generations, the appropriate directions for objective literary criticism, as well as the foundation for a better understanding of the theory of African Literature.

Prologue
Eagle on Iroko: For Chinua Achebe at 70

Osita Ezeliora

I wrap this song in the silhouettes of your tales;
I sing in this twilight of songs the cadence
Of your common tones;
I sing of the sublime Eagle perched on the giant tree;
The tenor of the rendering plucked from the rhythms of Idemili.
I stand on the rock of our forebears
To dispense kolanut radicles to known deities;
My mug of palm-wine filled to the brim,
I pour libations to unseen spirits
Even as the living sludge to unknown destinations.
I have traversed the terrains of Nri regal slopes: Amichi to Ogidi;
Aguleri through Umuleri: feasted with Chike
At the bank of the river; and listened to monotonous cackles of
    demented voices.
Has the giant tree fallen: do we live on hopes or impediments?
Why have birds of the air flown to unknown abodes?
On every tree and every clime:
See the children of iroko fingering ice
And spiders make palace of our wisdom's citadels.
Ugo beelu n'orji tell me: how do we trudge through
The fragmented terrains of the rising sun?
We had risen for a toast of your songs
But even at dawn, the songs were awry; sour to
The tongues and deadening to the nerves.
Things had shattered apart, fallen to the
Baboons at the belts of our bleeding eyes.

The doves sing of peace; the cats seek fraternity of rats,
Even as the goats choose guardianship of the barn;
But what acolyte is there for the lion and the goat?
We had toiled at the peak of sunny moons
Dreamt of happy days of timeless joy;
You had seen the trouble with the union,
Long when your elders were in slumber
How can there be peace when
The living are mere trumpeters to rogues and scorpions?
A child who flaunts insomnia to its mother
Surely leaves its hours of slumber in the winds;
What woman is scared of her husband's
Nakedness in the privacy of her connubial chamber?
Ugo beelu n'orji tells me: they are no longer at ease.
Yes! I heard your wailings: no one climbs the
Pepper stem; one only walks about it. I heard it
Of the bedbug who summons its scions to taste a mug
Of chilled endurance, for the scary oven is on
Pilgrimage to the abode of the lifeless ash.
We heard your proddings: and we vowed not to lift our
Fists: for there's abundant bearded meat for the living penis.
A lone kernel does not disappear in the fire: where are the messengers of God?
Since when have divine arrows missed their spots?
Must elders stare as mother-goats give birth on tethers?
The cock has suddenly grown teeth, and the chick
Celebrates ownership of its progenitors.
The lanterns are dry:
The bearers have flown to unknown abodes, and our kin
Loiter on the margins of Ochanja, Nkwo-Nnewi
And Idumota for a crumb of stock-fish.
But Ugo beelu n'orji tells me: Echi di ime, taa bu gboo:
Morning yet on creation day.
This is the dancing ground.
We are in the arena.
We dance in the savannah of the living; we dance
The dance of our forebears, and the anthills remain transfixed.
I wrap this song in the canticles of your tales
I sing in this twilight of songs the cadence of your common tones:
Your embalmed voice echoed from the shells, telling lasting tales of
sublime thoughts.
I sing of Ugo beelu n'orji who warned of mere anarchy
Blanketing a drunken world;
We recall this day your prophetic calls:
We invoke this day a certain man of the people
Whose brutal frankness stung more painful than wasp's.

Prologue

I sing this day of Ugo beelu n'orji who whispered
To us from where the rains beat us.
Yes, we sing indeed the lasting songs of the EAGLE ON IROKO.

OSITA EZELIORA,
School of Literature and Language Studies,
The Discipline of African Literature,
University of the Witwatersrand,
Private Bag 3,
Wits 2050,
Johannesburg, South Africa.

Part One

Art and Aesthetics

Chapter 1

The Art of the Word in Achebe[1]

John Douthwaite

ONE SIGN OF A GREAT WRITER is his/her ability to write simply about simple things, and yet proffer deep messages through doing so. Mundane and apparently superficial matters may be discussed at an inordinate length compared to the importance we would attribute in our daily lives to actions such as doing the washing and the cleaning, dressing and undressing, walking down a road or through a park, or taking some refreshment in a café. In normal circumstances, such subjects would not seem to herald the advent of exalted literature, as would a type of work which, on the other hand, began with a birth or a death (natural or violent) or a novel which had such august topics as religion, the struggle for survival, justice and freedom as its explicitly avowed theme.

Such an impression would turn to a strong conviction if the language used in our "simple" novel were modest in range and complexity, and the style informal or neutral. The text would seem to have little to say and neither art nor charm in its telling.

Yet such a description, of seemingly belittling paltriness with regard to both content and form, is applicable to some of the greatest creations of literature. If the reader goes over the actions listed above s/he may recognize the material appearing in several highly rated short stories and novels by Mansfield, Woolf and Joyce, to restrict the roll call to three major virtuosos with the pen.

The hallmark of these great writers is that they are allusive, indirect, subtle, meaning far more than what they actually, i.e. literally, say. They are deliberately ambiguous and multifunctional, operating at a variety of levels of meaning simultaneously to convey a complex message. Surface simplicity of language may thus contrast starkly with deep meaning, to borrow Chomskian terminology. In exactly the same way, elementary concepts, run-of-the-mill events and actions, and attention to minute detail concerning ordinary affairs, may mask the more profound workings of the human psyche and of social mechanisms and social structure influencing the individual. The stature of many eminent writers thus lies in the fact that they delve the depths of human experience without ever making it appear so.

Achebe, in my opinion, belongs to this class of writers. I will try to demonstrate my thesis by offering a close reading of a short extract from his first novel, *Things Fall Apart* which on the surface exhibits those features of simplicity, explicitness and mundaneness to an extreme degree, masking both depth and importance of content as well as an extremely refined linguistic technique.[2]

The extract comes from chapter eight, when Okonkwo is beginning to recover from his "illness" following his active participation in the ritual killing of his adopted son Ikemefuna.

1. 'Go and bring me some cold water,' he said.

2. Ezinma rushed out of the hut, chewing the fish, and soon returned with a bowl of cool water from the earthen pot in her mother's hut.

3. Okonkwo took the bowl from her and gulped the water down.

4. He ate a few more pieces of plantain and pushed the dish aside.

5. 'Bring me my bag,' he asked, and Ezinma brought his goatskin bag from the far end of the hut.

6. He searched in it for his snuff-bottle.

7. It was a deep bag and took almost the whole length of his arm.

8. It contained other things apart from his snuff-bottle.

9. There was a drinking horn in it, and also a drinking gourd, and they knocked against each other as he searched.

10. When he brought out the snuff-bottle he tapped it a few times against his knee-cap before taking some snuff in the palm of his left hand.

11. Then he remembered he had not taken out his snuff-spoon.

12. He searched his bag again and brought out a small, flat, ivory spoon, with which he carried the brown snuff to his nostrils.

First, the language. Simplicity is the keynote. The passage is written in a paratactic style, cohesion is elementary, sentences are short, and rankshifting is neither extensive nor deep.

Of the twelve sentences in the extract, four sentences (1, 6, 8, 11) contain only one main clause, five sentences are realized by two main clauses. This represents 75% of the passage. Of the other three sentences, one (2) is composed of two main clauses and a subordinate clause, another (10) is constituted by two subordinate clauses and a main clause, and one sentence (9) is realized by three main clauses and a subordinate clause.

Confirmation of the lack of complexity comes from cohesion. As befitting a paratactic style, logical links and referential links (bar pronouns) between sentences are scarce. Where they do occur, they are realized by grammatically and conceptually simple coordinating and subordinating conjunctions (and, when, then), indicating (at a surface level) addition and uncomplicated linear temporal progression. Conceptually more complex logical links between utterances, such as cause-effect, are not explicitly signaled by the language. The main form of inter-sentential reference is pronominal cohesion – one of the simplest devices for achieving cohesion. The abundance of this phenomenon (he occurs eleven times) reinforces the sense of the repetition achieved in other ways, and thereby helps create the impression of the depiction of a mundane life.

Rankshift, one important indicator of complexity, occurs at the level of clause in only four of the sentences. Significantly, three of the examples (1, 5, 11) are more marginal instances of rankshift as an indicator of complexity for the clauses realize the function of direct object of verbal processes. By definition this class of verb constrains rankshift. Complexity in such cases is semantico-grammatically forced – it is not a deliberate complicating choice on the part of the writer. Furthermore, the verbal process of saying (explained below) determining the rankshift poses no particular problems of conceptual difficulty requiring special cognitive processing. Only sentence 9 contains a *bona fide* instance of rankshift. But even in this case, the realization of rankshift comes in the form of a relative clause – a standard occurrence in English.

Phrases also tend toward simplicity. Many consist of a single word. Modifiers and qualifiers are generally simple as well as infrequent. Indeed, lengthy modifiers are generally limited to a postmodifying prepositional phrase.

Sentence length, another measure of complexity, is also limited here. Even where sentences are longer, their complexity is belied by the simplicity of the construction. The longest sentences (9, 10, 12) can hardly be classified as complex, as a comparison with a prototypical sentence by a writer such as Henry James will immediately bear out.

Grammatical range is minute. Verbs are massively concentrated in the past simple – twenty-five out of twenty-eight. There are two gerunds, one past perfect and no modals. Direct speech is in the imperative form.

Lexis is also simple. Let us consider the verbs. The lexeme bring appears five times, take four times and search three times. Stated differently, repetition accounts for 43% of the verbs. This simplicity is echoed on other lexical planes. First, if one employs Halliday's (1975) classification of verbal processes, then 22 of the verbs (79%) convey material processes (concrete actions), and extremely simple processes at that (bring, take, eat). Three are relational processes of being (be, twice and contain), again concepts which are not particularly profound, and three (said, asked, remembered) are processes of saying, these too being elementary acts, (with the exception of remembered, which will be commented on later). In sum, conceptual content is restricted to concrete acts of doing and saying related to the humdrum here-and-now. Second, semantic field analysis confirms that simplicity of deed constitutes the content of this extract. Simple movements account for 68% of the verbs (a) moving objects: bring, carry, take, push, knock and tap – a set of synonyms almost; (b) bodily movement: go, rush, return). Ingesting food (chew, gulp, eat), verbs of saying (say, remember) and copulas (be, contain) all account for 11% each.

The analysis of the nouns yields parallel results. Repetition is again prevalent water, hut, bag, snuff, snuff-bottle all occur three times, bowl occurs twice, and drinking horn and drinking gourd create patterning. Repetition thus accounts for 61% of the nouns employed in this extract. In addition, virtually all the items are concrete, common nouns. Semantic field analysis again underscores simplicity. The vast majority of the terms (70%) convey the general concepts of home, food and utensils. Six items (20%) refer to parts of the body. External, physical, concrete, here-and-now reality, limited to the home, is being talked about. Metaphors and other tropes are patently absent, again suggestive of simplicity.

The passage is written as third person narrative, without any intrusion on the part of the narrator. No emotions, attitudes or evaluations, no social, psychological or philosophical reflections appear on the surface of the text. With one exception (he remembered...), no thoughts of the characters or the author are explicitly conveyed. The passage appears to be neutral, almost empty. To conclude with a sweeping generalization, this style is fairly typical of the entire novel. Yet if we scratch below the surface, we will see that this outer state masks an inner complexity. This inner depth may be identified through close reading employing the tools of literary stylistics.

The illocutionary force of the first sentence is that of issuing an order. That the utterance does convey an order is underscored by the exploitation of the Gricean maxims of quantity and relevance. Very few words are pronounced (quantity), and all those words are functional to the communicative needs of the sentence (relevance). The sentence contains no other type of information (quantity), whether this be ideational, psychological or social. With regard to the latter dimension of meaning, there are, for instance, no softners or downtoners (please, or a conditional, e.g. would you…), no preparatory move, no follow up. Stated differently, the sentence is short and curt. The implications of the former quality reinforce those of the latter feature, thereby underlining the illocutionary force of the utterance. The order thus appears to be peremptory.

There is, however, one significant exception to this social-attitudinal dimension of the message, and the peremptoriness signaled by this dimension. This lies in the lexical choice of the verb said. In one sense, said is literally true. The sentence recounts the words uttered by Okonkwo. But saying is not exactly the same as ordering, denotatively speaking. While it may be objected that the order is conveyed by ideational content of Okonkwo's utterance and not by the verb reporting the utterance, and that therefore said pragmatically implies ordered, or that the use of said is consequently irrelevant to the issuing of the dictatorial order, this interpretation ignores the information furnished by context and co-text, namely by those dimensions which enable an utterance to pragmatically take on an illocutionary force which may diverge from its locutionary force.

First, Okonkwo is normally authoritarian. One would expect terse orders from him. In this sense, if said actually meant ordered, the deployment of the former term would be out of character. Second, Okonkwo's being ill might produce a less aggressive form of behavior, making said more appropriate than ordered. Third, ideationally and interpersonally, the entire extract centers on the simple execution of role-appropriate actions without hint of conflict. Both parties willingly accept their situations in life, as I shall demonstrate in the following two paragraphs. Assertiveness is not required-said is more than sufficient to imply the order. Fourth, the general tone of the entire passage is one of calmness. Hence, the fact that the author opts for the lexeme said, avoiding the more explicit and aggressive possible choice of ordered, may be taken as deliberate and significant, justifying the mapping onto the written signal of a neutral phonological pattern, bereft of anger or of the exercise of authority for purposes of manifesting one's power. In fact, the particular lexical choice tones down the illocutionary force of Okonkwo's utterance, the issuing of an order.

Significantly, the girl makes no reply. She simply complies with the command. This is an implicature based on the supposition (for which the text offers no evidence to the contrary) that Achebe has respected the Gricean maxim of quantity and that therefore the girl said nothing. If perchance she did say something, the reader must suppose it was of no importance, otherwise, on the basis of the maxim of relevance, Achebe would have been honor-bound to inform us. Clearly, this supposition must also be taken as valid if we are to argue that Achebe is a skillful author as well as a reliable one. What this amounts to in terms of message is that the girl's individuality is, in one sense, cancelled out, or, if one wishes to take a less extreme view is subaltern. In other words, the imparting of the order and the appropriacy to context of the linguistic exponent employed to this communicative end focus principally on the social identity of the participants, (the contextual component which gives rise to the referential function, in Jacobson's model of communication), with a minor component of the message focusing on the sender which gives rise to the emotive function (again in Jacobson's terms).

The precious hypothesis is borne out by contextual knowledge, for the two participants are father and daughter in a traditional society. This explains, for example, the lack of Leechian-style politeness norms acting as softeners in Okonkwo's directive to Ezinma.

Indeed, in addition to the fact that the girl makes no reply but simply executes the order, the second sentence contains further indications which bolster the hypothesis that a stark order has been issued by a parent to a child from whom obedience is socially expected. First, lexical choices indicating alacrity: rushed and soon. Ezinma could have gone or walked or sauntered to get the water. Instead she rushed. Second, we presume that an obedient child receiving an order for drink from a father who is undoubtedly thirsty in a social context where blind obedience is demanded of children would not go out and play with her friends, and then go and chat with her mother before returning with the water. Instead, she would carry out the request without any intermediate interruptions. Since no information to the effect that Ezinma dawdled is included in the text, and since no verbal signal is offered that may be construed as setting up an implicature to this effect, then we may deduce that the Gricean maxim of quantity has been respected on this matter, hence no procrastination has occurred.

We might also add the observation that co-textual information throughout the novel informs the reader that Okonkwo has a fiery temper and resorts to physical violence, including wife beating, apparently without great qualms. One may thus infer that a modicum of fear incurring Okonkwo's wrath will be felt by those socially committed to obeying him.

Stated differently, soon is made redundant by the context, for it conveys precisely how we would have expected or predicted Ezinma to act. If Achebe has not opted out of Grice's cooperative principle, (and not only is there no evidence of his having done so, but to do so would be a contradiction in a novel), then the inclusion of redundant information must be taken as a deliberate signal that the surface violation of the maxim of quantity has indeed been respected at some deeper, non-literal, thereby setting up an implicature, in this case that of underlining Ezinma's obedient nature.

Such a hypothesis would also explain another instance of seeming redundancy or irrelevance – that of informing the reader that Ezinma was chewing fish while she carried out her father's request. Per se, such information would not appear to be furthering plot, nor would it seem to provide psychological, emotional or attitudinal insight into aspects of the novel. If, on the contrary, the maxim of relevance has been respected at some non-literal level, then we draw from the mundane inference that the girl does not wait to finish her mouthful of food before complying with her father's wish.

Unconditional obedience might also lie behind yet another example or redundancy in such a short space of time – the inclusion of cool. Again, one presumes that if the father asked for cold water, then that is what a normal, obedient child would bring his/her parent. So why tell the reader what is obvious, if not to underline through indirect hints the social relationships between the characters in the novel?

In this particular instance, however, the inclusion of redundant cool sets up a second, and more important, implicature. Previous co-text has established that Okonkwo undergoes a terrible illness (three days, like the resurrection of Christ) after having killed his adopted son Ikemefuna. His present request for water is therefore to be interpreted as a sign of "resurrection," of recovery, of his return to normality following his (symbolic) illness. It should be noted in passing that this parallel with the Christian resurrection is ironic, for where Jesus receives vinegar to quench his thirst and later lives, Okonkwo obtains the water he requested but later dies without achieveing the new life, which is historically apt, for his suicide symbolizes defeat and not victory over "death," for traditional Ibo society.

If to the context we add the fact that cool is not simply a stylistic variant of cold employed by the writer to avoid literal repetition and prove he is "a good writer," then it will be noted that the connotations of the two synonyms are unmistakably different. Where cold has harsh, potentially harmful, overtones, cool conveys a sense of the soothing, healing power of water. To take the previous analogy one stage further, water is the substance used to baptize people into the church, another "curative" process. Such a reference underscores the irony in Okonkwo's "resurrection" for another end result is the loss of his other, biological, son. This is doubly ironic for he loses his son to the Whiteman's church.

However, the implicature does not end here. The referents are also crucial. The daughter does not bring her father the restorative liquid simply out of a sense of filial duty. The story has already made it clear that Ezinma loves her father, worships him even. Hence the offer of a "medicine" contemporaneously symbolizes an act of love.

This interpretation receives support co-textually through parallelism. When Okonkwo returns home after being released following his detention, fine and whipping for having burned down the church (with its intertextual reference to Christ's arrest and journey to Golgotha?) (Chapter 24), Ezinma prepares food for Okonkwo as soon as she hears he is about to be released. Again she takes it to his *obi*, again her father is recovering from an illness (both physical and mental), again he has no great appetite because of the strings and arrows of life. Nevertheless, Okonkwo ate, but only...to please her [Ezinma]... Ezinma's love is reciprocated by Okonkwo.

There is a third implicature, one that the preceding quotation from nearer the end of the book confirms. Okonkwo returns his daughter's love. This is indeed no one-way relationship. When the priestess Chielo takes Ezinma off to the cave, terrorizing mother and father as to their daughter's destiny, Okonkwo keeps vigil over the cave without informing anyone, proving both his love as husband and father, and his lack of ostentation in this sphere of human life.

However, the parallelism set up by the use of synonyms linking father and daughter also has an antithetical, contrastive effect. For Okonkwo is a hard person, one who embodies the male principle of mother earth. Hence the differing connotations of the two lexemes reflect the antithetical personalities of the two characters, who in their turn reflect two contrasting, though complementary, principles in Igbo philosophy. Clearly, a simple play on cohesion through lexical repetition (Halliday and Hasan) has deep ramifications at the level of implicature.

At this point we may return to the beginning of the analysis and explain what might then have appeared as a contradiction. After asserting that the choice of said toned down the illocutionary force of the utterance it referred to, I then emphasized the harshness and totality of the chain of command, of the socially-defined parent-child relationship. The analysis that ensued however, brought to light the fact that other linguistic choices conveyed the idea of a strong bond of affection tying the two protagonists. This helps account for why Achebe should have selected the verb said rather than ordered in that particular circumstance. It tones down the order and allows the order and compliance with it to signal not simply the social relationship but also, and importantly, the positive emotional relationship between the two interactants which a harsh order might have appeared to contradict. This dual message is conveyed indirectly, subtly, through the deployment of such linguistic mechanisms as lexical cohesion and implicature.

One standard method of supporting this type of linguistic argumentation is to consider possible alternative modes of expression. In this particular instance, Achebe could have produced a sentence as Okonkwo ordered Ezinma to bring him some water, which she did immediately. The conceptual essence, (at level of illocutionary force and ideational content), of the two original sentences and the synthetic alternative would have been identical. What would have been lost, however, through concise rephrasing between the two protagonists, their individual personalities, as well as the philosophical principles they embody in the story, and, finally and more specifically, the nature of the specific event being referred to (Okonkwo's recovery), together with its ironic Biblical intertextuality. Stated differently, Achebe's version sets up a series of implicatures, many of which have global as well as local relevance. In sum, a lot is happening below the surface of ordinary, concrete everyday actions. A simple external world stands for a complex internal one, through implicature.

If we take up our analysis of redundancy, we will note that we have by no means exhausted the surface violations Achebe commits of the Gricean maxim of quantity in this short paragraph. Why should it be important to inform the reader that Ezinma goes out of the hut to get water for her father, that she should bring the water in an earthen pot, and that the provenance of the water is from her mother's hut? After all, who cares where the water came from? The important point, one would imagine, is that the water is fetched is earthen, wooden or metal? What Okonkwo wants is water, not a pretty or an expensive bowl!

Thinking along these lines, one would be fully justified in inferring that the mention of the mother's hut must in some way be abnormal, otherwise it would not have been included, (the principles of quantity and relevance), and that its inclusion consequently sets up some for of implicature. But the text offers no clue as to a possible hidden message. If, on the contrary, it is standard social practice for the child to go to its mother's hut for food and drink, then one concludes Achebe is furnishing additional details of traditional Ibo social life.

That this might be so emerges from the entire novel, as well as from this extract, since the quantity and quality of the detail provided show clearly that in this work Achebe wishes to bring back to life (at least in virtual terms, to keep abreast of the times) a dead society. Nevertheless, the detail is so elementary, and so detached from plot, characterization, emotion and other realms which are important to a novel as to seem verge on narcissism or infantilism.

Such a dire attack is readily countered. The answer may be sought in Achebe's vision of the role of the "novelist as teacher," as the title of his famous 1965 essay makes clear. In this essay, Achebe underlines that in the previous year *Things Fall Apart* had sold 250 times the number of copies in Nigeria than it had in England, and that the vast majority of his readers were young people whose knowledge of traditional Nigerian society was virtually non-existent! Despite the fact that this might have been in part a defence against the vicious accusation leveled against Achebe that he wrote in English for financial gain or for political propaganda, since this language offered a much larger market, and although this mathematical relationship was soon to be inverted, there can be no doubt that Achebe sincerely believed (and still believes) his role was to instruct.

Such a vision of the social function of the artist does not however, automatically protect Achebe from the accusation of narcissism or infantilism or, quite simply, incapacity as a writer, for having included details such as those discussed four paragraphs above. Stated differently, the fact that material is functional to the work is not a criterion which turns that text into a work of art. There are, however, two additional, deeper or more global, levels of implicature which derive from the basic stance that a social portrait is being offered that account for the importance of such details and render them vital... Both of these implicatures emerge from the continuation of the argument Achebe outlines in his essay on the novelist as teacher.[3]

The first high level generalization is that such details portray a given class (if such a term be legitimate) and a given culture:

[2] In those days – when I was growing up – I also remember that it was the poor benighted heathen who had any use for our local handicraft, e.g., our pottery. Christians and the well-to-do (and they were usually the same people) displayed their tins and other metalware.

Hence, in the extract we are scrutinizing, social identity and social mores are established through apparently banal details such as earthenware pots. Equally importantly, the social group identified is pitted against those members of its community will be instrumental in bringing about its downfall by siding with the British and adopting their value systems, the two main behavioral patterns being Christianity and trading (namely the two key institutions of religion and economics), as emerges clearly late on in the novel – penetration by imperialist forces, the consequent loss of Nigerian independence accompanied by the destruction of traditional Igbo society, replaced by a different economic structure and social organization.

This implicature leads to an even deeper level of implicature. Nigerian independence, one might argue, put paid to foreign domination, restoring freedom and dignity to the country. Not so, Achebe counterattacks. For postcolonial independence did not wipe out at tone blow the problems caused by a disrupted society beset by problems of underdevelopment in a global economy. In his second novel, *No Longer at Ease*, Achebe shows that independence did not bring about the solution of all of Nigeria's dire problems. Poverty, corruption and interethnic conflict, for instance, remained rife.

The colonial heritage has left an even deeper and more preoccupying wound on Nigeria, Achebe's argument continues. One of the most harmful effects of British rule was the creation of an inferiority complex in the Nigerian psyche which continues to prevent total recovery from the evils of colonialism which Nigerians can legitimately expect from independence.

Nevertheless, the most unfortunate aspect of this psychological condition is that the blame cannot be laid entirely at the door of the invader, as Achebe makes clear in his previously quoted essay on the novelist as teacher:

> [3] Needless to say, we do have our own sins and blasphemies recorded against out name. If I were God I would regard as the very worst our acceptance – for whatever reason – of racial inferiority. It is too late in the day to get worked up about it or blame others, much as they may deserve such blame and condemnation. What we need to do is look back and try to find out where we went wrong, where the rain began to beat us.

Let me give one or two examples of the result of the disaster brought upon the African psyche in the period of subjection to alien races. I remember the shock felt by Christians of my father's generation in my village in the early 1940's when for the first time the local girls' school performed Nigerian dances at the anniversary of the coming of the gospel. Hitherto they had always put on something Christian and civilised which I believe was called the maypole dance. In those days – when I was growing up – I also remember that it was the poor benighted heathen who had any use for our local handicraft, e.g., our pottery. Christians and the well-to-do (and they were usually the same people displayed their tins and other metalware. We never carried waterpots to the stream. I had a small cylindrical biscuit-tin suitable to my years while the older members of our household carried four-gallon kerosene tins.

Today, things have changed a lot, but it would be foolish to pretend that we have fully recovered from the traumatic effects of our first confrontation with Europe. Three or four weeks ago my wife, who teaches in a boys' school, asked a pupil why he wrote about winter when he meant the harmattan. He said the other boys would call him a bushman if he did such a thing! Now, you wouldn't have thought, would you, that there was something shameful in your weather? Bit apparently we do. How can this blasphemy be purged? I think it is part of my business as a writer to teach that boy that there is nothing disgraceful about the African weather, that the palm tree is a fit subject for poetry.

Here then is an adequate revolution for me to espouse – to help my society to regain belief in itself and put away the complexes of the years of denigration and self-abasement. And it is essentially a question of education, in the best sense of that word...

The writer cannot expect to be excused from the task of re-education and regeneration that muse be done. In fact he should march right in front...

I for one would not wish to be excused. I would be quite satisfied if my novels (especially the ones I set in the past) did no more that teach my readers that their past – with all its imperfections – was not one long night of savagery from which the first Europeans acting on God's behalf delivered them. Perhaps what I write is applied art as distinct from pure. But who cares? Art is important, but so is education of the kind I have in mind. (my emphasis)

The quotation is long because this allows the intensity of Achebe's feelings to emerge and because it covers a wide range of crucial points. All of these points help to illuminate the hidden function of what may at first glance appear to be superficial, irrelevant material and details in *Things Fall Apart*.

The feeling of racial inferiority impedes the modern Nigerian from facing the enormous problems of postcolonialism with the necessary serene, confident and determined attitude required to deal competently with the situation and the "right" decisions. This inferiority complex derives from having had his culture denigrated and having succumbed to such denigration. Hence, the task of the writer is to recover the past in order to demonstrate that the African was not a savage, that society was ordered, that such an order was functional to survival in the environment the African inhabited, and that the African's values were worth those of any other "civilization," since the goal was social survival and prosperity for the entire community, an ethos which was guaranteed by a communalistic attitude to and organization of society, namely a society exhibiting integration and solidarity, in the sense of the term used by British writers and critics from Coleridge through Arnold and on to Leavis, to present the same concept from a literary ideological standpoint. The type of wrong decisions caused by the ignorant rejection of the Nigerian past and the negative effects this brings about on Nigerian progress are effectively illustrated by Achebe in *No Longer at Ease*.

This interpretation brings out one of the most significant aspects of the closing chapter of *Things Fall Apart*. Symbolically, the chapter is dominated by the District Commissioner, for he represents the triumph of the colonial power. He is the protagonist of the chapter, he is the first and last person to be mentioned, and the book ends with his thoughts regarding his planned anthropological work significantly and ironically entitled *The Pacification of the Primitive Tribes of the Lower Niger*. The point of view from which the chapter is written is his, hence the implicit value judgments are those of the white man: he had toiled to bring civilization to different parts of Africa…The story of this man who had killed a messenger and had hanged himself would make interesting reading. Western civilization is one of Achebe's main targets. Irony is deftly achieved by the deployment of toiled on two counts. First, it infringes the praise and modesty maxims of Leech's politeness principle through denying them the status of civilization; this contemporaneously infringes the modesty maxim by maximizing instead of minimizing self-praise. The second piece of irony is a behavioral extension of the latter social dimension of language, for in the novel we see little evidence of "toiling" on the part of the Commissioner. He has his administrators, messengers and soldiers do that. In true imperialist fashion, he commands, they execute. And of course, he takes the kudos!

Such self praise is ironic, for the Commissioner's book fails to understand the natives. Even worse, he does not even try to understand them. The Commissioner does not ask himself why Okonkwo committed the act. He simply dismisses it by branding it as a killing.

A final, fiercely ironic thrust is delivered through the adjective *interesting*. In the face of violent, tragic death signaling the destruction not only a single human being but of a people, the Commissioner's only reaction is that of recording an *event* which will be interesting to his readers. No concern, no sympathy, no commiseration are shown. The callous lack of humanity this reaction implies negates his self-made claim to being the bearer of civilization. Okonkwo (namely Nigeria) is simply an object, an object of interest, of study, of conquest because different, a historical event in the progress of civilization, his civilization.

Achebe's overriding concern with civilization may be documented in other ways. Wren notes that although the Commissioner's book is fiction, in actual fact other books like it do exist, and Achebe was acquainted with them or had read them as a boy. Such works were produced by representatives of the two main institutions Achebe sets out to criticize – government and religion.

On the government side is District Commissioner Talbot's In the Shadow of the Bush (1912), and on the religious side works by the missionary G. T. Basden. Wren quotes both men to demonstrate they held views akin to those of the District Commissioner in *Things Fall Apart*. Both men failed to comprehend what they saw and described. Indeed, given the numerous parallelisms between the works of Talbot and Basden and those of Achebe, Wren posits that Achebe wittingly or unwittingly set out to provide a refutation of their standpoint.

Another sector representing the same type of opinion which Achebe consciously set out to reject is that of other novelists. Wren points out that Achebe single out Joyce Cary's highly praised novel *Mister Johnson*. Achebe judged it "a most superficial picture…not only to the country and even of the Nigerian character" given from the outside, hence "someone ought to try and look at this from the inside".

Achebe's attitude to Conrad's *Heart of Darkness* is far less tender. In *An Image of Africa: Racism in Conrad's Heart of Darkness,* Achebe takes Conrad to task for painting the portrait of the African as a savage, a cannibal, a purely physical being (a whirl of black limbs, a mass of hands clapping, of feet stamping, of bodies swaying, of eyes rolling), no brain, no culture, with at best a rudimentary soul (quotes from *Heart of Darkness* included in Achebe's essay). Such a picture, says Achebe, "projects the image of Africa as 'the other world', as the antithesis of Europe and therefore civilization, a place where man's vaunted intelligence and refinement are finally mocked by triumphant bestiality...(Africa is merely a) setting and backdrop which eliminates the African as human factor. Africa is a metaphysical battlefield devoid of all recognizable humanity, into which the European enters at his peril." Thus, Achebe concludes, "Conrad was a thoroughgoing racist". That Achebe is irremovably entrenched in this political position of 'criticism as a prerequisite to rebirth' is borne out by the fact that he forcibly reiterated this view in his address to the 24th Annual Conference of the African Literature Association which took place at Austin, Texas at Easter 1998.[4]

The foregoing analysis confirms two vital points regarding Achebe's technique and material. First the Empire is writing back through dense intertextuality (the Bible and documents by religious authorities, anthropological text and bureaucratic documents, literary texts), as critics such as Lindfors and Said have noted. Here is Said's comment from Culture and Imperialism (91):

> [4] On the one hand, when in celebrated essay Chinua Achebe criticizes Conrad's racism, he either says nothing about or overrides the limitations placed on Conrad by the novel as an aesthetic form. On the other hands, Achebe shows that he understands how the form works when, in some of his own novels he rewrites – painstakingly and with originality – Conrad.

Second, what might on the surface seem to be empty material, conveying concepts of trivial importance from any standpoint (no contribution to theme, to plot, to characterization and so forth) may in fact hide deeper layers of meaning. One important level of meaning that such material conveys is the high-level dimension blending the historical with the socio-political and cultural depiction of Igbo society. Such a portrait is tied to Achebe's view of the social function of the African writer, namely that of recovering the African heritage not only to demonstrate the falsity of the traditional Western view of the African as a primitive savage, but also to combat the African's inferiority complex which was the result of the gradual penetration of the African worldview by Western ideology which was then transmitted to the younger generations through the process of socialization. Such a stance has been advanced, among others, by Edward Said in his critical work Orientalism. Cultural texts, by which is intended political, sociological, religious and economic as well as literary tracts, (hence Talbot and Basden, as well as Conrad and Cary), moulded a discourse "by which European culture was able to manage – and even produce – the orient politically, sociologically, militarily, ideologically, scientifically, and imaginatively during the Post-Enlightenment period". Achebe's desire to revive the African psyche is functional to his people gaining independence in the personal as well as in the purely politico-geographical sphere in order to be in a better position to improve their own society.

Some of the messages I have read into the superficially bitty material analyzed so far relate to the highest level of generalization in the novel – its global political aim. However, the very same messages, as in all good literature, are multifunctional – they operate contemporaneously on middle and low levels of generalizations.

Killam has pointed to various "accusations" leveled at *Things Fall Apart* that are comparable to those I launched in the introduction. Achebe's prose has been labeled "leisurely" and "stately". "A casual reading of the book", Killam comments, "especially the first part, supports such a judgment". Though Killam employs analytical tools which are different from the ones employed here and to different ends, he too reaches the conclusion that the "casual approach and style quite belie the intensity of the life the novel evokes." He supports his contention with several arguments which are at a high to middle level of generalization. I will reformulate the relevant ones in methodological terms which are pertinent to the discussion.

First "in his evocation of his grandfather's generation, Achebe achieves concreteness and convincingness through strict precision and control". Precision and control are the other side of the coin to the wealth of detail employed by Achebe (Gricean quantity) and the functions I have tried to demonstrate such detail may realize (Gricean relevance). Second, Achebe is able to view objectively the forces which irresistibly and inevitably destroyed traditional Ibo social ties and with them the quality of Ibo life. In showing Ibo society before and after the coming of the white man he avoids the temptation to present the past as idealized and the present as ugly and unsatisfactory". Both these points are quite clearly functional to Achebe's global aim of recovering Africa's past and hence her pride.

Another point many critics make concerns the three part structure of the novel and, more precisely, the far greater text length (or Gricean quantity at a macro-level, which comes out at approximately 60% compared to 20% each for the remaining two parts) of the first part, the part that has been classified as leisurely. Indeed, given the limited role of action advancing plot and the concentration on description of physical and social affairs, the resultant staticness justifies the appellation of leisureliness. Two reasons are generally offered for Achebe's lengthy presentation. First, the need to draw an accurate and complete picture of traditional Igbo society in order to fully and convincingly recover the past. Second, the speed with which Igbo society collapses under Western penetration, due to its inability to react culturally to the Western power and, above all, ideology, is reflected in the limited number of pages devoted to the process – acceleration in contrast to the deceleration of the first part of the novel. In other terms, the rapid disintegration of Igbo society is comprehensible only through the extreme precision and comprehensiveness with which social structure and social psychology are documented, (hence the leisureliness of the first part of the novel) for the picture created brings out the contrast in mind and society between blacks and whites, pinpointing those aspects which cause things to fall apart.[5]

However, I believe that the relative duration of the three parts of the novel serve further functions. Most importantly, the staticness of the first part symbolizes the leisureliness and stability of a social system which is able to enjoy the cultural solution it has worked out to the problem of survival. Although there are periods of intense, hard agricultural work, the Igbo also indulge extensively in pleasurable activities, as the various ceremonies described in the novel show. The neuroses of our fast-paced, rapidly changing modern society with its constant geographical, economic, social and political upheavals are in the main absent from the Igbo world, which is therefore to be valued.

The second point regarding the decelerated description of Igbo society allows us to return to our local level of analysis. Symbolic in this sense is the simplicity of the amply documented Ibo customs, which together with the Igbo's unfailing adherence to those customs account for what would otherwise appear to be gullibility, translatable into primitiveness and mindlessness, for people who hold views akin to those of Basden.[6] The social belief in the power of the *egwugwu*, the ancestral spirits of the clan, as the village leaders, the most powerful and the most secret cult in the clan, is a cogent instantiation of legitimated simplicity. Chapter Ten shows quite clearly that the *egwugwu* are a farce from the standpoint of reality – everyone knows they are not spirits, but their own kinsmen in flesh and blood: Okonkwo's wives, and perhaps other women as well, might have noticed that the second *egwugwu* had the springly walk of Okonkwo. And they might also have noticed that Okonkwo was not among the titled men and elders who sat behind the row of *egwugwu*. But if they thought these things, they kept them within themselves. The constant and delicate use of implicature is a hallmark of Achebe's writing: contrast the mild, aristocratic indirectness of might, perhaps, if, etc. with the heavy-handedness of conveying the real illocutionary force of the excerpt quoted by deploying a linguistic exponent such as "any fool could have seen that it was Okonkwo dressed up as an *egwugwu*".

Yet when the white man engages in essentially identical activity types, he does not for one moment classify himself as primitive, savage or gullible, as when he plays Father Christmas, practices black magic, or carefully avoids walking under a ladder. The strength and stability of Igbo social structure is highlighted indirectly through the respect given to the cult:

> [5] One of the greatest crimes a man could commit was to unmask an *egwugwu* in public, or to say or do anything which might reduce its immortal prestige in the eyes of the uninitiated. And this is what Enoch did. (Chapter 22)

Despite the surface directness of this paragraph, it is more complex than it seems, for it is this linguistic complexity which helps convey the complexity and stability of Igbo society.

First, the paragraph makes use of a number of foregrounding devices to enhance the power of the message it conveys: a short paragraph; the key sentence is even shorter and occupies final position in the clause – two graphological indices of prominence; the key sentence is couched as an emphatic pseudo-cleft construction. The linguistic construction warmly invites the reader to hunt for implicatures.

Second, the final sentence illustrates one of Achebe's most skillfully deployed techniques – speech and thought presentation. Although both sentences could be claimed as being in third person narrative (extradiegetic narrator), the grammatical form of the second sentence also justifies the view that it is written in free direct speech. Note, for instance, the sentence begins with colloquial And, the entire construction and lexical choice is colloquial, as well as reduced in explicitness (as will emerge from the third point), demonstrative this is not transformed to more deictically distant that, and the main verb is in the present tense and not backshifted as it would be in indirect speech. All of these linguistic features contribute to creating the impression that the mode of narration has switched to a homodiegetic narrator directly addressing the listener. In other words, Free Direct Speech is being used. The ease with which Achebe slips unobtrusively from one narrative plane to another, from one form of speech/thought presentation to another, and the extra meaning such changes produce, are another hallmark of Achebe's artistry with the pen.

Third, the illocutionary force of reporting an infringement is not the sole function performed by the second sentence of [5]. If its superficial simplicity does not induce the reader into treating it as a neutral report, and if its colloquial nature persuades the reader that it is indeed written in Free Direct Speech, then one can supply the relevant phonological features to a would-be oral production of the utterance (for this is, after all, a story being recounted) to show that the tone is far from emotionally and attitudinally neutral. What the emitter is simultaneously conveying together with the description of the monstrous deed is not simply his moral condemnation of that deed, but, more importantly, his shock that such a thing could ever have happened.

Shock as a reaction is crucial to the social canvass, for it is based on the presupposition that an act of this nature is inconceivable on the part of a member of the community. It is just not done. Enoch had killed an ancestral spirit, and Umuofia was thrown into confusion. Confusion regarding social behavior in such an elaborately-regulated society is almost a contradiction in terms, which is what gives this lexical item its tremendous implicational force. What it conveys is that society is so sure of itself that it has no-prepared cultural solution to the problem, (namely a sanction such as banishment or a heavy fine), as it has to most problems, for the simple reason that it has never foreseen that this kind of problem could ever arise. Fearing for the lives of his community, the Christian missionary asks himself what the Igbo are going to do about Enoch's crime. No one knew, because such a thing had never happened before.

It is significant that the second sentence of [5], reporting Enoch's crime, employs simple words, of a high generality, and a simple construction. Without context to clarify the nature of the referents, those words would signify nothing. This contrasts with the preceding sentence where a complex structure is bolstered by formal lexical choices indicating precise concepts, an utterance which is far less context-bound compared to the utterance following it. Is the parallelism which sets up an antithesis (black = complex, precise, context-free, while white = simple, vague and context dependent) a piece of linguistic irony directed against white civilization?

The same sociological and historical point is also made through a preceding violation of another fundamental norm of Umuofian society committed by Enoch: "thou shalt not kill the royal python", the most revered animal in Mbanta and all the surrounding clans. It was addressed as "Our Father". The social reaction is identical to Enoch's having unmasked an *egwugwu* in public: If a clansman killed a royal python accidentally, he made sacrifices of atonement and performed an expensive burial ceremony such as was done for a great man. No punishment was prescribed for a man who killed the python knowingly. Nobody thought that such a thing could ever happen.

Fourth, the first sentence is based on the presupposition that heinous crimes are punished. This causes the following sentence to generate the expectation (by implicature) that not only will punishment be meted out, but also that this event will be recounted.

Fifth, another staple weapon in the well-equipped Achebe linguistic armoury is brought to bear on the story telling – analepsis and prolepsis. Here interruption in linear order occurs and the reader is taken back in time (analepsis) to recount the entire scene of the horrendous act, instead of forward (prolepsis) to tell the reader what punishment was inflicted on Enoch, as expectations of linear order created by sentence two (point 4 above) would have demanded.

Why should Achebe make this time shift? The episode recounted in the analepsis contains significant recurrent features on both a linguistic and conceptual level: simple language, simple events, so simple indeed that the accusation of primitive gullibility could again be launched by the die-hards. This may be illustrated, for instance, by the fact that when the elders go to Enoch's compound to "deal" with him, which actually means "face" him, for they are at a loss as to how to "deal" with him (!), they are wearing heavy protections of charms and amulets. This will bring a smile to the "civilized white", a smile which, the critical reader will point out, betrays the white man's incomprehension. For the crisis faced by the Umuofians is serious, both because it strikes at the heart of their system of beliefs and behaviors and because they do not know what to do about the problem. Indeed, in the episode, Achebe provides the real answer for the uncomprehending whites: It seemed as if the very soul of the tribe wept for a great evil that was coming – its own death.

And this episode, together with the rest of the novel, both on a conceptual and on a linguistic level, works up to the central message: simplicity, a stable, orderly society which has the allegiance of its members, in which conflict is minimal and functional (i.e. it does not endanger social structure), and which takes place in a physical environment which is relatively constant, is incapable of the type of understanding of structure and motive necessary to comprehend the white man, with his acquisitive, domineering society which is in a state of constant flux. The Umuofian social mentality is therefore incapable of the kind of forward planning required to meet the problems set by a changing environment presenting external threats of the type posed by a radically different (imperialist, non-agrarian) culture. Umuofia's consolidated cultural responses being unable to furnish a solution to novel problems, indeed, being incapable of even beginning to understand there is a problem and the nature of that problem, explains precisely why Umuofia was thrown into confusion, to lay bare the import of an early quotation.

In parallel fashion, comprehension not only of Africa's past but also of our own history,[7] is equally difficult for the modern Eurocentric man, used to social mobility, tax evasion, murder, violent and organized crime, terrorism and ethnic cleansing and bombing as solutions to problems – all civilized solutions, of course! And our faith in justice, both that farmed out by our own national courts and by those international organisms that determine our lives is not comparable to the faith the Umuofians held in theirs, novels such as *Things Fall Apart* and *No Longer at Ease* tell us.

For here we have reached the crux of the matter. Two cultures meet. The nature and objectives of the two cultures are very diverse. The result is that they come into headlong conflict and the weaker one goes to the wall. Put this way, the thesis is extremely simple. But proving it to those who do not understand or refuse to understand, together with the other aims Achebe set himself in the novel, such as recovering the validity of African culture and healing the psychological wounds inflicted in the process of domination, is quite another matter. Achebe takes an entire book to do so, donating a world striving for multiculturalism a marvelously appropriate book teaching humane lessons in the process. Seen in the light of Achebe's objectives and with a knowledge of the context, the material, which previously seemed to be presented in little bits and pieces, of microscopic importance and even less relevance, lacking in any form of cohesion, can now be seen as fitting comfortably and significantly into place.

We can now understand, without imposing our western ideology of the other's inferiority and backwardness on macro episodes and micro details. Thus, at a macro level the sudden collapse of the Igbo society is clearly inevitable. What to unweaned western eyes would appear to be the stupidity with which Okonkwo and the five elders answer the District Commissioner's summons, believing he will actually listen to them fairly turns out to be realistic, given the painstakingly accurate picture Achebe has painted of his society, for Umuofians respect the norms of the society they adhere to. Instead, the District Commissioner tells the six men that "I have invited you to come …because of what happened during my absence. …Let us talk about it like friends and find a way of ensuring that it does not happen again". His way… like friends is that of then arresting the men. He does not play the social game the Umuofians expect him to play – he breaks the rules. Their rules, for the Umuofians do not realize the DC's rules are different.

Essentially, the DC then tells the Umuofians that "We have brought a peaceful administration to you and your people so that you may be happy. If any man ill-treats you we shall come to your rescue." Apart from the fact that he is again treating the Umuofians as if they were savages, with no form of social organization of their own, we have argued that this is not only the opposite of the truth, but that, ironically, the justice of the white man is sadly lacking. One simple example, the graft the messengers demand for their "free" services in helping the "ill-treated"!

What this analysis has demonstrated, I hope, is the constant and complex interplay between micro-level and macro-level. Apparently simple utterances are in actual fact multifunctional, full of hidden implicatures, which resound through-out the novel. And the linguistic devices Achebe employs to convey his complex messages cover the entire range the language makes available to the language user. And this is the note I would like to end on – an emphasis on the linguistic artistry exhibited by Achebe. To do so I will return to the original passage I was examining.

The second paragraph again centers on deeds and not words. Okonkwo simply took the bowl from his daughter. He offers no words of thanks. He gulped the water down. The choice of gulped to describe the way Okonkwo drinks is significant. It sets up lexical cohesion, for it continues the concept of speed set up by rushed and soon. Besides recalling the hierarchical role relationship emerged from the use of words pertaining to this semantic field in the previous paragraph, it contains further allusions. Gulping down food and drink has connotations of childlike behavior, inelegance, lack of manners. This aspect of Okonkwo's behavior is echoed in the next sentence when, after eating a few more pieces of plantain, Okonkwo did not "place" his dish in the requisite location but pushed his dish aside. Alliteration together with the harshness of the alliterated /p/ and /d/ sounds combine with the connotations of push to reiterate the suggestion of an aggressive character as well as a person who expects to be served. Okonkwo is a man of action, and he is characterized through his actions.

There is, however, a second possible implicature set up by lexical choice and alliteration, an interpretation which is additional rather than alternative. Gulped could create a sense of urgency. Okonkwo has been "fasting" for three days. He is "at the end of his tether" and desperately requires sustenance for his "resurrection". Extending this implicature further yields the interpretation that performing actions such as gulping and pushing demonstrate that Okonkwo is not yet fully fit and in control of his mental faculties. He has not fully overcome his dejection. Such actions are "instinctive", physically less functional to efficient survival (for gulping can be dangerous) and socially unaware (since pushing is socially inept).

The sense of brusqueness and starkness is underscored grammatically and graphologically. This second paragraph is short, and therefore emphatic. It is composed of two parallel sentences: each sentence consists of two main clauses coordinated by and. Indeed, the second main clause in each sentence consists of four words all belonging respectively to the same word class. The subject of each sentence is identical, as is the subject matter, the first referring to ingesting drink, the second to ingesting food. The short paragraph is thus broken up into two shorter sentences which in turn are subdivided into two shorter clauses. The effect is to underline the terseness of the action, symbolizing Okonkwo's mental and physical states as well as his social behavior.

The important high level generalization here concerns Achebe's technique. The analysis of this paragraph lends further support to the contention that external physical descriptions of actions which seem devoid of any great significance are made to convey internal moods and emotions, mental and social action. Achebe does not report Okonkwo's suffering at the death of his adopted son and his part in it. He alludes to it by describing Okonkwo's actions in his physical environment. The reader is invited to fill out the mental and social text him/herself from the actions, much as do Hemingway in The Killers and Joyce in Eveline.

The third paragraph provides further evidence sustaining the arguments outlined so far. Okonkwo characterizes his social relationship to Ezinma as well as his current mental and physical state by issuing another curt order: Bring me my bag. The entire argument advanced regarding legitimacy of the social structure and the existence of a strong bond of affection between Okonkwo and his daughter which I centered on the deployment of the verb said in the first paragraph finds confirmation in the parallel use of the verb asked when Okonkwo imparts his second command. Again, Ezinma does not speak, again Ezinma obeys instantly.

This paragraph is also characterized by extreme redundancy, hence superficially open to the accusation of having violated the maxims of quantity and relevance. Of what relevance is telling the reader that the goatskin bag was at the far end of the hut, that it was a deep bag and took almost the whole length of his arm? The sentences It contained other things apart from his snuff-bottle. There was a drinking horn in it, and also a drinking gourd, and they knocked against each other as he searched could have been conflated into one sentence, with the omission of the last clause which seems pointless. The same motives furnished here with regard to detail, namely the higher level ideological and psychological operations Achebe is out to achieve with regard to his reading public are equally valid here.

There is, however, more than meets the eye yet again. The quantity and precision of detail, together with sequencing (the Gricean equivalent of this term being the maxim of order) suggest that the extract is not the product of extradiegetic narration with external focalization, although in formal terms the passage does exhibit the linguistic features of such a form. Instead, starting from sentence seven, It was a deep bag…, (if not from the sentence before it), we move inside Okonkwo's head through his body, so to speak – we experience directly what he experiences, as if a homodiegetic narrator with internal focalization has taken over, though such focalization continues to be mediated linguistically through the standard description of actions. [8]Here Achebe's indubitable indebtedness to Joyce emerges most clearly. In Eveline, Joyce moves imperceptibly from an external description of Eveline in the opening paragraph to her internal mental acts in the second paragraph, though the content and linguistic form appear to remain unchanged.

Thus Okonkwo puts his hand into the bag and realizes its depth by seeing his arm disappear almost entirely into it. Once his arm is in the bag, he feels around inside (unstated, implicit) and finds several objects in it (explicit information). The fact that these are identified one by one, in a random fashion in a series of clauses (the randomness being signaled by the diversity of grammatical structures of the clauses in the relevant sequence, It contained…knocked against each other), instead of being listed in a single clause as a tidily organized group of objects, together with the fact that the noise of the objects knocking against each other is related (the implicit result of Okonkwo moving his hand around inside), confirm the hypothesis that we are perceiving the episode internally, as Okonkwo perceived it, and not as a pure external physical description.

Such an interpretation accounts for a variety of other linguistic features of the paragraph, all of which center on the function of snuff. The first main observation here is that snuff is the most important object for Okonkwo at this particular moment of for a variety of reasons. The first is conceptual. We induce snuff is the reason why Okonkwo asks Ezinma to fetch him his bag, for there is no conjunction such as because linking sentence five to sentence six which makes the point explicitly. The deployment of the verb searched, in contrast to looked, implies greater determination and a very precise will in carrying out the act. Second, on the general symbolic principle that first is most important, then snuff must be foremost among Achebe's concerns, for it is the first of the list of contents to be mentioned. Third, snuff-bottle occupies emphatic end focus position in sentence eight. This must be deliberate. Since the snuff bottle has been mentioned previously, in sentence six (where there too the item occupies end focus), then its pragmatic status in sentence eight is that of given information. Hence it would have been more normal to present the item earlier in the sentence, as in the synthetic version: "Apart from the snuff-bottle, the bag contained other things".

These three points must be connected to the more general consideration that snuff recurs constantly throughout the novel. It is taken regularly on ceremonial occasions. It thus represents a substance with a dual function – it is taken for relaxation and it has the value of a "peace offering". It is comparable in the wine regions of Northern Italy to the uncorking of a good bottle when guests arrive, no matter whether they are alcoholics or tea-totallers! In other words, taking snuff is an act of identity.

The fact that snuff taking is ritualistic helps explain the seemingly extravagant detail with which the scene is described, right down to microscopic facts such as Okonkwo taking the snuff in his left hand and taking the snuff through his nostrils (is there, unbeknown to me, another inlet for snuff?)! The text reads like a Piagetian psychologist describing a baby clumsily learning to grasp an object. In other words, from a simple information-imparting viewpoint, the way snuff is taken forms part of our knowledge of the world and it is therefore redundant to describe the process to a knowledgeable adult. From an adult standpoint, sentences 10 to 12 could have been reduced to a sentence such as "He remembered he had not taken his snuff and proceeded to do so". This would have reduced the number of words by half and eliminated the "obvious" and apparently extraneous detail. Had Achebe done so, however, the middle and high level objectives of the novel would have suffered seriously, for the various implicatures Achebe creates through the description of daily physical routines would have been lost.

However, the second main observation regarding snuff is locally far more important and testifies to the intricacy of Achebe's technique. Rituals are acts of identity. Rituals consist of set actions executed in a set order. This aspect of the nature of ritual bolsters its function as an act of identity. Sentence 11 thus sets up the implicature that taking snuff in the palm of one's hand is contrary to the standard (personal or social) routine, both because the information is given to the reader (respect of the maxims of quantity and relevance) and because from the point of view of the real world, there is no physical reason preventing a human being from taking snuff from the palm of his hand. If Okonkwo insists on doing so from a spoon, the motive must be social and/or psychological. And in this case it is both. Okonkwo, we will remember, is beginning to come out of his depression. He has just eaten and drunk that little amount which will begin to restore him physically. Following this act comes the social ceremony of relaxation – the taking of snuff. Okonkwo is still not yet in the full control of his mental faculties. Hence he seems to go blindly through the ritual. He calls for his bag, knowing his snuff bottle is inside, reaches in and pokes around, slowly realizing what other objects the bag contains. When he brings the bottle out he automatically, unthinkingly puts some snuff in his palm, for such an act would indeed be sufficient to take snuff. At that point, his gradually re-dawning consciousness makes him realize that he is on the point of violating his ritual. He is not taking snuff with his spoon. He thus consciously sets out to restore order and through this, his own identity: he searched his bag again (note the deliberate verbatim repetition of the significant lexical item searched). Religiously observing the ritual of snuff-taking thus demonstrates both Okonkwo's allegiance to his society and the process of his regaining his sanity.

And this is the crux of the matter. One key characteristic of Achebe's art, one he shares in common with other great writers mentioned at the outset of this essay is the ability to portray social and psychological reality, together with its moral and political implications, through the external description of mundane objects and events, the things one normally takes for granted. The fact that one does take such events for granted means that they lie below the surface of common consciousness, hence they are not attributed importance, hence their real significance escapes people in their daily routine. Achebe thus obliges us to reflect on this fact, to rediscover the significance of such objects and events. Clearly, he is implicitly inviting us to recover what is important in them. This is one aspect of Achebe's work which makes him universal, rather than local, despite his being clearly situated historically, geographically and ethnically.

The third and final observation regarding snuff confirms another aspect of Achebe's technique, as well as the complexity of his writing. The taking of snuff is an act of identity. As such, it re-affirms Okonkwo's stability. This parallels an event which takes place in Conrad's short story, Typhoon. During the lull in the middle of the frightful storm, when the ship has been battered by the sea and when the crew have lost their self-control and are on the verge of despair, the most staid character in the story, Captain MacWhirr, takes a short break to go to the chart-room, his living quarters, for a brief respite from the tension of command on the deck. There was no light there; but he could feel the disorder of that place where he used to live tidily. He gropes in the dark looking for a matchbox, finding it where he expects it to be, given he is an extremely orderly person – in a deep ledge from which the storm has not managed to shift it. On lighting up a match he sees the havoc wreaked by the typhoon:

> [7] all the things that had their safe appointed places – they were gone, as if a mischievous hand had plucked them out one by one and flung them on the wet floor. The hurricane had broken in upon the orderly arrangements of his privacy. This had never happened before, and the feeling of dismay reached the very seat of his composure. And the worst was to come yet!

He then turns his mind to the return of the typhoon once the ship has gone through the centre of the storm. His mind is filled with terrible premonitions for he realizes the ship and all the lives on board will very probably be lost. Yet, these somber thoughts of hopelessness are accompanied by the following "instinctive" action before he returns to his proper station on deck:

> [8] He extended his hand to put back the matchbox in its corner of the shelf. There were always matches there – by his order. The steward had his instructions impressed upon him long before. "A box...just there, see? Not so very full...where I can put my hand on it, steward. Might want a light in a hurry."

There are numerous parallels between Okonkwo taking snuff and MacWhirr replacing the box of matches in its proper place. Both men are under severe duress; both men react unconsciously; both men perform a ritual or routine which is emblematic of their character and of their fidelity to the society they are members of; in each case the act involves an elementary physical operation; the entities involved (snuff and a match) are in some way comparable physically and functionally (both being chemical substances which aid the actor in restoring his identity). In other words, both men carry out an act of re-affirmation of identity in comparable circumstances and in a comparable fashion.

This parallelism has two principal functions. First, Achebe adds complexity and extra meaning to the extract through intertextuality. Second, Achebe is writing back to Conrad. MacWhirr represents the staid, unheroic, middle of the road Englishman who comes through thick and thin, a symbol in one sense of an indomitable conquering spirit. A captain, moreover. This contrasts ironically with the heroism of Okonkwo, (he too a leader), who, instead succumbs to the forces of adversity precisely because he is heroic. To return to extract [1], I leave it to the reader to decide whether the fact that Okonkwo's spoon is made of ivory is an intertextual reference to that symbolic substance in *Heart of Darkness*.

It will be noted that my treatment of *Things Fall Apart* has been extremely partial. On the content side, I make sparse mention of the religious dimension, for instance. On the technical side I do not analyze Achebe as the inheritor of the African oral tradition. I make no apologies for my manifold omissions, for the main objective I set myself was the highly circumscribed one of trying to prove Achebe's artistry with words, that he is such a skilful deployer of language that he can deceive the unwary reader into believing that his text is simplicity itself, when in point of fact it is extremely complex, multifaceted and multifunctional, one in which the major themes of life are debated indirectly through the simple affairs of everyday life. The fact that his texts are also highly readable and entertaining is no drawback. Thank you Chinua.

Notes

1. Invaluable thanks go to my dear friend, Claudio Gorlier, who provided me with a variety of stimuli during the writing of this article. Very warm thanks also go to two new friends I made at the recent EACLALS conference in Tuebingen, where I read a short extract from this paper in order to test out some of my ideas: Syd Harrex and Janet Wilson. Syd gave me further examples of Achebe writing back to Conrad, and Janet made the point that my analysis of Achebe's heavily implicit and flat style was also reminiscent of Hemingway. Achebe's links with Joyce, Mansfield and Woolf are, I feel, stronger and more extensive. As is true and not just standard practice, any mistakes are mine.

2. That this extract is not idiosyncratic is demonstrated by the fact that almost verbatim parallels may be found in other novels by Achebe. Compare with the following extract from *Arrow of God*:

    'Keep quiet there, you too.' Ezeulu rolled the yam out of the fire with the stick and quickly felt it between his thumb and first finger, and was satisfied. He brought down a two-edged knife from the rafters and began to scrape off the coat of black on the roast yam. His hands were covered in soot when he had finished, and he clapped them together a few times to get them clean again. His wooden bowl was near at hand and he cut the yam into it and waited for it to be cool. (p. 5)

3. It should be noted that the ideas Achebe expresses in this essay are voiced constantly in his non-fictional writing. They may be found in newspaper articles and interviews, as well as in his essays.

4. Achebe's essay attacking Conrad was an address made as part of The Chancellor's Lecture Series, 1974–75 at the University of Massachusetts, Amherst. *Things Fall Apart* was first published in 1958. Nevertheless, it is interesting to note with regard to the European vocation to bring civilization to Africa that Achebe' use of the verb toiled to refer to the District Commissioner's view of his own work, which I analyzed earlier, echoes a key sentence in *Heart of Darkness: The steamer toiled along slowly on the edge of a black and incomprehensible frenzy.* I have not as yet had the time to apply modern computer technology to making a word count and comparing connotations, characters and contexts and their correlation with word counts, but this appears to have a promising line of enquiry.

5. In order to avoid misunderstandings, it should be noted that contrasts in mind are

socially determined, as a sociologist reading will hold and as the novel clearly illustrates, and not a question of biological innateness. Hence, no notion of superiority/inferiority of any kind is either stated or implied in the present discussion.

6. Clearly, I am referring to the majority of the characters, those who maintain their allegiance to Igbo society. The exceptions that do exist come under two headings and prove the generalization. On the one hand there is Okonkwo. He exceeds the bounds for psychological reasons. He is not an ideological rebel. In contrast, his son does rebel. Although his rebellion is also psychological in origin (ironically, it parallels his father's reaction against the latter's father's character), the form that rebellion takes is ideological, for he rejects Igbo society, adopting the historically available model which constituted a counter-culture – that of the white invader.

7. The present article is written by a European white, to clarify my "objective" (?) position.

8. The only exception to this latter point is he remembered in sentence eleven, which, significantly, comes with Rimmon-Kenan's sub-category of an external focalizer granted "the privilege of penetrating the consciousness of the focalized (as in most nineteenth century-novels). When the focalized is seen from within, especially by an external focalizer, indicators such as 'he thought', 'he felt', 'it seemed to him', 'he knew', 'he recognized', often appear in the text."

Works Cited

Achebe, Chinua. *Things Fall Apart*. London: Heinemann, 1958.

———. *No Longer at Ease*. London: Heinemann, 1960.

———. *Arrow of God*. London: Heinemann, 1964.

———. "The Role of the Writer in a New Nation." in *African Writers on African Writing*. Ed. G.D. Killam. Evanston: Northwestern UP, 1973.

———. "The Novelist as Teacher." in New Statesman. Jan 29, 1965. Reprinted in Chinua Achebe. *Hopes and Impediments: Selected Essays*. New York: Doubleday, 1989.

———. "An Image of Africa: Racism in Conrad's *Heart of Darkness*" in *Hopes and Impediments: Selected Essays*. New York: Doubleday, 1989.

———. *Hopes and Impediments: Selected Essays*. New York: Doubleday, 1989.

———. In interview with R. Serumaga. *African Writers Talking*. Ed. D. Duerden and C. Pieterse. London: Heinemann, 1972.

Austin, J.L. *How to do Things with Words*. Oxford: Clarendon Press, 1962.

Douthwaite, J. *Teaching English as a Foreign Language*. SEI: Torino, 1991.

Gikanda, S. *Reading Chinua Achebe*. London: James Currey, 1991.

Grice, H.P. "Logic and Conversation." in *Syntax and Semantics Vol 3: Speech Acts*. New York: Academic Press, 1975.

Griffiths, G. "Language and Action in the Novels of Chinua Achebe" in *Critical Perspectives on Chinua Achebe*. Ed. C.L Innes and Bernth Lindfors. London: Heinemann, 1978.

Halliday, M.A.K. *Functional Grammar*. London: Edward Arnold, 1975

———. and Hasan, R. *Cohesion in English*. London: Longman, 1976.

Innes, C.L. and Bernth Lindfors Eds. *Critical Perspectives on Chinua Achebe*. London: Heinemann, 1978.

Killam, G. *The Writings of Chinua Achebe*. London: Heinemann, 1969.

Leech, G.N. and M.H. Short. *Style in Fiction*. London: Longman, 1981.

Lindfors, Bernth. Ed. *Conservations with Chinua Achebe*. Jackson: University of Mississippi Press, 1997.

Mey, J. *Pragmatics*. Oxford: Blackwell, 1993.

Moore, G. *Twelve African Writers*. London: Hutchinson, 1980.

Moore-Gilbert, B. *Postcolonial Theory*. London: Verso, 1997.

Ojinmah, U. *Chinua Achebe: New Perspectives*. Ibadan: Spectrum Books, 1991.

Omotoso, Kole. *Achebe or Soyinka? A Study in Contrasts*. London: Hans Zell Publishers, 1996.

Riddy, F. "Language as a Theme in *No Longer at Ease*." in *Critical Perspectives on Chinua Achebe*. Ed. C.L. Innes and Bernth Lindfors. London: Heinemann, 1978.

Rimmon-Kenan, S. *Narrative Fiction: Contemporary Politics*. London: Routledge, 1983.

Said, E.W. *Culture and Imperialism*. London: Chatto and Windus, 1993.

———. *Orientalism*. London: Routledge and Kegan Paul, 1978.

Wren, R.M. *Achebe's World*. Burnt Mill: Longman, 1981.

Chapter 2

Didactic Aesthetics:
Achebe the Griot and the Mbari Artist

Omar Sougou

I must create a system or be enslaved by another man's.
William Blake

The story is our escort; without it, we are blind. Does the blind man own his escort?...
Like fire, when it is not blazing it is smouldering under its own ashes or sleeping and
resting inside its flint-house.[1]
Chinua Achebe

LIKE THE TRADITIONAL GRIOT Achebe defends and celebrates the African world and its art. Very much like the Mbari artists with whom he identifies and constantly refers to as an inspirational aesthetic source, he serves society by way of his art. Both Achebe's exemplars, the Mbari craftsmen and women and the griot, are the sensitive points of their community to paraphrase Ezekiel Mphahlele whose words Achebe quotes in *The Novelist as Teacher* to emphasize the role of the literary artist in society.[2]

This paper proposes to discuss Achebe's artistic achievement in the light of the two concepts: the griot and the Mbari artist. They are central to his theory and practice of creativity and reflect his vision of didacticism and commitment. This implies a look into the effects of his work on readers. The use of myth and the critical reception of the novelist's work will also be considered here.

The term "griot" is used extensively but its real meaning has not been duly conveyed in respect of its social and literary implications. No doubt that Achebe is fully aware of these as shown by his identification with this figure who is a repository of art and a medium of social consciousness, conscience, and memory. In most West African societies, the griots and associated castes have been the most resilient custodians of traditional values.[3] The social status of the griot needs to be better encapsulated, but this is not the place to do it. The focus will rather be on the role of a writer as new griot using literature instead of orature, unlike the griot of old, or combining both forms. Ousmane Sembene, another West African griot, a version of Ngugi's Gicããndi player in *Devil on the Cross*, gives us an idea of the writer as a griot which aptly describes Achebe's function. Sembene prefaces his novel *L'harmattan* with these significant words:

> Far from me is any intention of theorizing on the African novel. Yet I remember that long ago in that Africa usually seen as classical, the griot was not only the dynamic element of his tribe, clan, or village, but also the patent witness to every single event. He was the one who recorded everyone's deeds, and laid them out under the palaver-tree for all to see. The motive behind my work rests on this teaching: to be most close to reality and the people.[4]

He applies this principle in this novel set on the eve of the independence of the French West African colonies. The fictional representation of the role of the griot is even better mediated in the stand, outspokenness, and attentiveness of Gnagna Guisse and Dethye Law, in his short story, *White Genesis*, one of incest in a noble family.[5] They are not only protectors, their house is a safe haven for fugitives, but Dethye Law remains the uncompromising voice of truth in the village, an honest and rigorous judge. Of course, the griot in Sembene's story is no celebrant of anything. The story exposes depravity, false social assumption, cunning and mean dealings.

In happier circumstances, the griot is an organizer, entertainer and performer of music and other recreative arts. Yet, even while entertaining there is always for the griot an opportunity to highlight the ills of the individual or the community by means of a composite genre which can be both satirical and laudatory and well suited to expose facts. It is these attributes of the griot that are found in Chinua Achebe's writings, as he has asserted them in a lecture:

> It is inevitable, I believe, to see the emergence of modern African literature as a return of celebration. It is tempting to say that this literature came to put people back in Africa. But that would be wrong because people never left Africa except in the guilty imagination of Africa's antagonists. I must now emphasize one final point. Celebration does not mean praise or approval. Of course praise can be part of it, but only a part.[6]

This clearly evokes the question of aesthetics, didacticism, and commitment, all of which are at the core of Achebe's concern as can be seen in the position he expresses in such essays as *"Africa and her Writers"* and *"The Novelist as Teacher"* and gives form in his fiction. The first essay vindicates the democratic exercise of art by all and for all the community as in the Igbo Mbari festival. It involves all and sundry regardless of skill and status in a collective creative enterprise where individual expertise is encouraged to blossom out. By contrast, the production of art in some areas of Africa tends to be confined to particular castes, such as those in which the griot operates, for the consumption of other classes in society. It is noteworthy that in the coupling of these (the griot and the Mbari artist) art spiritually and socially becomes significant, while retaining its entertaining value. Then one can understand the reference to the roles of the griot, a historian and social critic, and to the Mbari iconographers as signifiers for Achebe's view of literature. Moreover, his artistic perspective recalls what Hegel wrote:

> The historical is only then ours…when we can regard the present in general as a consequence of those events in whose chain the characters or deeds represented constitute an essential link…For art does not exist for a small, closed circle of the privilegedly cultured few, but for the nation as a whole. What holds good for the work of art in general, however, also has its application for the outer side of the historical reality represented. It, too, must be made clear and accessible to us without extensive learning so that we, who belong to our own time and nation, may find ourselves at home therein, and not be obliged to halt before it, as before some alien and unintelligible world.[7]

Achebe's novels do the same thing, namely, *Things Fall Apart* (1958), *Arrow of God* (1964), and *Anthills of the Savannah* (1987) which are the foci of this discussion. The body of his work reflects a considerable dialectical outlook rooted in a will to educate. Achebe thus abides by the principle he stated in *The Novelist as a Teacher* (1965) He would not – as literary creator – wish to be excused from the tasks of addressing the problems of Africa as African scientists, historians, and political scientists do in their fields. In this respect he writes:

> I would be quite satisfied if my novels (especially the ones I set in the past) did no more than teach my readers that their past with all its imperfections – was not one long night of savagery from which the first Europeans acting on God's behalf delivered them. Perhaps what I write is applied art as distinct from pure. But who cares? Art is important but so is education of the kind I have in mind. (45)

Things Fall Apart offers reliable referents on account of the subjacent historicity which informs it, as does *Arrow of God*. The embedding of the colonial question in the social and cultural backdrop in both novels constitutes their impact. By means of this device Achebe achieves texts that show and teach. The novels are both pieces of literature and useful anthropological and historical reflectors of Igbo experience which is to a large extent paradigmatic of the African predicament at some point in history. *Things Fall Apart* is a seminal work which has impressed on many readers the idea that even if the white man had put a knife on the things that held them together, Africans have still much in common in terms of culture. The West African readers of *Things Fall Apart* and *Arrow of God* recognize themselves easily in these works not only in the customary social interactions, the beliefs, but also the linguistic and rhetorical features of the Igbo language which Achebe adroitly renders in a coherent sampling of maxims, sayings or proverbs.[8] Most of the figures of speech are the same as in readers' own language or have equivalents.

African readers other than those of West Africa share a similar experience as evidenced by the experiment conducted in a project by a group of students at the department of English of the University of Oran (Algeria). Their work does not claim to be ambitious but is nonetheless, very useful, because it was impelled by the concern to make profitable the teachings of African literature; it was carried out with a view to applying by way of analogy the knowledge acquired through the works that have been studied to the Algerian cultural context. They meant to initiate and encourage the collection of elements of regional popular oral culture that are in danger of extinction.[9] For this purpose they found *Things Fall Apart* a most essential tool owing to its didactic virtue residing in the tales, myths, and legends woven in the narrative. Such elements function as a semiotic system and are a key to the philosophy of the people whom Achebe describes. The force and the vitality of the culture incarnated by Okonkwo who is proud to a fault, is forcefully projected in a spectrum wider than his individual self. While Okonkwo stands for the rugged principle of manly dignity, it is through the community at large and their encounter with the colonial order that Achebe's teachings are carried out.

He gives an illustration of how erroneous the assumption that literature can do nothing to alter our social and political condition can be. He discovers in the late eighties that reading *Things Fall Apart* dissuaded an eminent German jurist from settling in Namibia in 1961 and accepting an offer to become a constitutional consultant to the regime. The novel killed his enthusiasm because "he had never seen Africa in that way and that after having read that book he was no more innocent." This work opened his eyes in giving him a picture different from the papers' clichés. He needed, as Achebe says, to hear Africa speak for itself after a lifetime of hearing Africa spoken about by others.[10] Although Achebe does not entirely subscribe to Negritude which he conceives of in "*The Novelist as Teacher*" as one of the "props fashioned at different times to help us get on our feet again" (42), like Aime Cesaire in attempting to challenge the world view that colonialism and slavery have engendered, he has been constrained by his education to forge weapons out of the adversary's adrenal.[11]

Things Fall Apart transcends the limit of the ethno-linguistic text with which it might be tempting to assimilate it; it embraces and codifies via a single entity, the Igbo, a larger range of experience. A number of critics and reviewers have interpreted this novel as pure atavism underlining Achebe's glorification of the past. Others like Omafume F. Onoge have seen Achebe as a "non-Negritude realist." Onoge even points in relation to Soyinka and Achebe to a transition to a pan – African, proletarian-internationalist in their theoretical outlook.[12] Lewis Nkosi senses an underlying pathos in Achebe's portrayal of the conflict between African traditional society and European colonialism in both novels. This finds expression particularly in *Arrow of God* in Ezeulu's perception that the new order "spells the collapse of everything", but "the necessity for change is hinted at; there is a rueful recognition that these are not the times we used to know and we must meet them are they come or be rolled in the dust."[13]

It is significant that the same critic admits to what he calls Achebe's achievement in a complex task, "which is the dramatization of African history in such a way that we can extract meaning from it without losing sight of the living drama in which real men and women were involved." Nkosi notes also that Achebe's judgement of the colonial administration and Christian missionaries has been found "unnecessarily harsh and frequently a distortion of what were after all benign intentions" Most important to this discussion is Nkosi's thesis:

> This is hardly borne out by any careful reading of the novels…In both *Things Fall
> Apart* and *Arrow of God* there is constant shift in the amount of blame assigned
> to either of the two sides in the confrontation. Achebe is more of a "realist" in
> his treatment of African history than some rigorously trained historians. (39)

These testimonies are a recognition of Achebe's "objective" outlook which makes him expose such aspects of tradition and harm the individual or affect the community in general. The novelist does not try to justify the killing of Ikemefuna, or the throwing away of corpses in the bush, and least of all the taboo about twins in *Things Fall Apart* for instance. Speaking of Achebe's treatment to the past, Ravenscroft makes a point worthy of note:

> Many commentators have stressed the "charm" of this evocation of the past, as
> if Achebe's chief concerns were to make a genuflection to departed African
> glories, and show only that the coming of the white man and his paraphernalia
> destroyed a finely wrought indigenous culture. Such a view is too limited. It
> implies that Achebe has sentimentalized the setting of his story, whereas the
> greatest strength of *Things Fall Apart* is the tragic "objectivity" with which
> Achebe handles a duel theme"[14]

This "objectivity", perhaps conditioned by the Igbo concept of dualism: "Wherever something stands, there something else will stand" to which Achebe refers very often, is a principle he strives to maintain. Such an attitude is perceptible in his lecture where he questions Eurocentric notions as manifested in Conrad's *Heart of Darkness* by insisting on the politics of negating the presence of the other, the African, which is concomitant with colonial dispossession.[15] In his argument Achebe states: "It is not simply true that the English forced us to learn their language. On the contrary, British colonial policy in Africa and elsewhere emphasized time and again its preference for native languages." As can be expected this remark has shocked many and has spurred a debate in *West Africa*.[16] Let it suffice to consider this statement as an illustration of the point made earlier about his care for objectivity which is found in *Things Fall Apart* and *Arrow of God*.

A similar philosophical attitude is discernible in the rationalism which prompts the failure of Achebe's protagonists, Okonkwo and Ezeulu. Both Okonkwo and Ezeulu embody the predicament of a number of community leaders in their encounter with colonialism in other parts of the continent.[17] In the apparent fall of both men transpire lessons of history, and that is what Achebe has aimed to highlight in his aesthetics of resistance with all the sensitivity of an artist aware of his relationship to his material.

Ezeulu is a paragon through whom Achebe's touch for character depiction appears. In the complexity of this protagonist one sees a deft rendering of the human predicament. (A term used with care here bearing in mind Achebe's phrase "human condition syndrome" as in his essay *"Africa and Her Writers"*.) He himself cautions us not to read a character like Ezeulu in a simplistic manner, and as an observer of society he notes that life and history are very complex:

> What we try to do when we encapsulate perhaps, is merely to help us in our understanding of life; it is not to delude us into thinking that this is a final answer. I am fully convinced that the Igbo tradition was very sophisticated in its appreciation of this complexity of life....Therefore then, having accepted the complexity of reality, to attempt to interpret Ezeulu in a simplistic manner is bound to be problematic....He believed in his priesthood; he was not going to overthrow it in order to be considered advanced or in order to make things convenient for anybody.[18]

The final sentence of this remark is consonant with the tone of Achebe's answer with respect to current contentious issues around literature. "I can see no situation in which I will be presented with a Draconic choice between reading books and watching movies; or between English and Igbo. For me, no either/or, I insist on both. Which, you night say, makes my life difficult and even a little untidy. But I prefer it that way."[19]

Achebe further points out that he is not attempting in the novel to create "the perfect ideal society," that he writes stories which he hopes are credible, but which have overtones and suggestions of change. In the stories "there will be a balance between things as they are, and as they ought to be;" he further writes:

> I think one has to be careful (depending on one's ideological position and one's concept of the role of art) how much you can interfere in a story in the name of reconstructing the world. The purpose of art of course is to change the world, but in my view you do not do it in too obvious fashion.[20]

There appears an aesthetic perspective without which implementing the notion of "no art for art's sake" might result in producing pamphlets or chronicles of events. There also lies Achebe's strength apparent in the imaginative impulse behind his novels, especially those set in the past. In this regard, what Lukacs said of Walter Scott can apply to Achebe even if his are not historical novels:

> He is a patriot, he is proud of the development of his people. This is vital for the creation of the real historical novel, i.e. one which brings the past close to us and allows us to experience its real and true being. Without a felt relationship to the present, a portrayal of history is impossible.[21]

Achebe digs deep down into the culture of the world which he describes to sustain his aesthetics. In the tradition of the Mbari artists and the griot he moulds his pieces with the tools and materials that the culture of the land provides: proverbs, folktales, and myths. Both the fiction and expository writing of Achebe bear a singular hallmark given them by what one may call the deliberate authentication of his language. He is fully aware of "the usefulness of myths, of metaphors, of figures of language and of thought, of analogies and irony, humour and a sense of drama"; and also that the Nigerian/African mind is "attuned to the powerful suggestions of rhetorically organized language."[22]

* * *

Both the hearer and readers of Achebe are familiar with his use of the Igbo pantheon in his rhetoric. This can have diverse effects on his addressees as shown by the accounts of his London lecture given by *West Africa* and the *Newstatesman and Society*. If both magazines have had to be selective for editorial reasons, the African reader of both versions notices the glaring absence of the Mbari institution in the *Newstatesman and Society*. Mbari is important enough for the speaker to dwell on it as an illustration of, as Achebe puts it, "My pre-colonial inheritance – of art as celebration of my reality; of art in its social dimension." The description of Mbari, and even the word itself is reduced to a mere "this", a deictic which deprives the reader of substantial referential codes. There clearly appears the problem of target audience; the implied readers of this magazine are assumed to be Europeans in their majority, hence the Editor's choice. In return, this impairs the effect intended by the author. All the more so as this device which consists of referring to myths, legends and folktales is a cardinal one for Achebe because just like the proverbs; profound meanings lie in them. Such textual constituents are therefore a significant dimension of his craft. Again, the Mbari ceremony which he has also employed prior to this talk in *"Africa and her Writers"* (1972) can hardly be dispensed with. Neither can the many other mythological figures like the mischievous Yoruba deity Eshu whose deed in the folktale Achebe uses in the same essay as a parable for "the recrimination between capitalist and communist aesthetics in our time" (21). Other examples are the Fulani myth of creation from Mali and that of the Wapangwa people of Tanzania which he employs in *"Language and the Destiny of Man"* (1972).

One can add to these that other Hausa folktale which Achebe tells in his London address (which the reader of *The Newstatesman* misses as well) to illustrate how stories can be made to foster the status quo in a class society. The Snake, an aristocrat, owns a horse but does not know how to ride it, whereas the Toad, a commoner, is skilled in horsemanship by dint of hard work but does not possess a horse. Achebe imagines the peals of laughter of the Emir and his court from hearing such an entertaining story. But mark his concluding remark which is central to his argument and metonymical above all:

> In the fullness of time the same story will stand ready to serve a revolutionary purpose using what was already there: an unattractive, incompetent and complacent aristocracy, exposing it not to laughter this time but to severe stricture.

Myth similarly acts as a conveyer of messages in Achebe's imaginative works. Of course, in accordance with his vision of art they do not serve as adorning paraphernalia. And unlike modernists like Yeats to whom he owes the title of *Things Fall Apart*, and perhaps T.S. Eliot who supplies that of *No Longer at Ease*, he does not need to construct a mythopoeic language. It is all there in his Igbo background and he capitalizes on it with a twofold purpose. In the first place to authenticate his discourse and style, second, to fix graphically such components of traditional oral culture. "Myth is language: to be known, myth has to be told; it is part of human speech. In order to preserve its specificity we must be able to show that it is both the same thing as language, and also something different from it."[23]

It may be useful to study just two instances of myth used in Achebe's novels and poems before moving further, both are related to the deity Idemili. The first is of totemic order in that it is informed by the Sacred Python, the next rests on the goddess herself. These mythical elements become signs whose referential realm Achebe considerably extends as he does with the Sacred Python by way of analogy and parable. The Idemili/Python mythical imagery becomes replete with meaning and assumes a greater scope each time it occurs. In *Things Fall Apart* the python undergoes the first assault from a Christian convert, Okoli, who kills it. In *Arrow of God* the same totemic animal confirms the symbolic function it suggests in the first novel. The python works figuratively as a symbol of the state of convulsion in which the community is as a result of the choking grip of the new religion and colonial power. This is apparent in the plight of the python that Oduche, Ezeulu's son, imprisons in an airtight wooden box. This also reflects Ezeulu's own circumstances: his personal struggle against his rival priest, his suspecting the new order yet wanting to know its secret, and sending there his unwilling son, knowing that a "man who brings home ant-infested faggots should not complain if he is visited by lizards" (72). Besides, the python epitomizes the colonial situation, the defeat of the old ways. Like the elders forced to submission in *Things Fall Apart*, the world of Ezeulu retreats, in the eyes of the python, before the "strange bell [that] has been ringing a song of desolation." Thus, the once revered messenger of Idemili now "must scuttle away in haste" to avoid the children's taunts (278).

The significance of Idemili and *Ala* (the Earth goddess who commissions Mbari festivals) for Achebe is enhanced by the presence of both deities in his poetry, respectively in *"Beware Soul Brother"* and *"The Lament of the Sacred Python"*[24] These poems were seemingly written during the Biafra war, a time when he found this kind of writing more suited to his mood: "something short, intense." In his own words he could write essays and even lecture. "All this," he said, "was creating in the context of our struggle." He could not write a novel then, even if he wanted to.[25]

In *"Beware Soul Brother"* Achebe evokes *Ala*, the tutelary deity of art, to caution this son of his mother to stand firm on the ground, and urge him to be aware of "the lures of ascension day," "for others there will be that day/ lying in wait leaden-footed, tone-deaf/ passionate only for the deep entrails/ of our soil;…

> *Our ancestors, soul brother, were wiser*
> *than is often made out. Remember*
> *they gave Ala, great goddess*
> *of their earth, sovereignty too over*
> *their arts for they understood*
> *so well those hard-headed*
> *men of departed dance where a man's*
> *foot must return whatever beauties*
> *it may weave in the air, where*
> *it must return for safety*
> *and renewal of strength.*

The advisory tone on the brother's or teacher's voice imposes a measured pace on the poem, which echoes the control and restraint *Ala* demands from the most skilled artist.

In *"The Lament of the Sacred Python"* the pitch is higher and anger more perceptible in the condemnation of the betrayal of Idemili, the land, in other words, by the corrupt nationals. These "empty men suborned with the stranger's tawdry gifts" offered father Idemili to an errant cannibal god "tooth-filed to eat his fellows." In the poem the python's lament seems to have moved to a higher temporal level, from the colonial setting of *Arrow of God* to the neo-colonial one. These poems are important in that they are a transition between Achebe's pre-civil war novels and the most recent one. Also of great significance is what Achebe said at the time of the war: "Well, let's not waste too much time explaining what we were and pleading with some people and telling them we are also human. Let us forget that; let's map out what we are going to be tomorrow."[26] Years after that Achebe is still telling the Western world about dispossession, witness the London lecture. To the Africans and his compatriots he tells something else in the manner he does in *Anthills of the Savannah* (1987). In the novel steeped in modern political quagmire, myth finds room, Idemili is under focus and basically supports a paramount part of the allegorical discourse. Idemili suggestively exercises a role similar to *Ala*'s, working for restraint.

Wole Soyinka, discussing deities in African literature, notes that when the gods die, new ones come to life from the carver's work. The discarded one rots in the bush and is eaten by termites, the new inherits the powers of the old and may acquire new powers. The act of the termites in likened to the attitude of the writer who either aids the process of desuetude by acting as the white ants or by ignoring the old deities and creating new ones. Some African writers belong to this school. Beside them, Soyinka identifies a school of iconoclasm that facilitates and complements the process by what he calls the simple method of secularizing old deities. "In African literature this is an organic step; the gods themselves, unlike the gods of Islam and Christianity, are already prone to secularism; they cannot escape their history." But what interests us even more is his accurate placing of Achebe who, he says, "will serve as a bridge between the entrenchment of deities – indigenous and foreign – as mentors of social perspectives, and works of an assertive secular vision such as we encounter in Ousmane [Sembene] and others."[27]

Soyinka grounds his comments on *Arrow of God*. However, years later *Anthills of the Savannah* substantiates them in the resurgence of Idemili, a motif by way of which potent literary effects are performed. The myth of Idemili is made into an elaborate language within which is wrought the semantics of power and the ethos of the novel. In this manner, it may be said that Achebe shifts myth from the status of a "depoliticized speech" which Ronald Barthes ascribes to a political one.[28] The Idemili literary figure is supported by two ancillary media of linguistic, textual, and contextual import, namely the speech of the elder of Abazon (a griot and a sage) and the various discourses of Ikem, the poet-journalist (a modern griot like the author himself). Both of these characters and the mythic figures of Idemili are outlets of "the running battle between the Emperor and the poet in Africa" which is not, as Achebe puts it, "a modern phenomenon either. Our ancestral poets, the griots, had their way of dealing with the problem, sometimes direct, at other times oblique."[29]

The multi-voiced and multi-focal narrative of *Anthills* combines these two aspects of rhetoric in the same way as it does Western poetics and an African mode of story-telling. At this point it is interesting to note the reaction of some Scandinavian readers in Granqvist's account of the reviews the novel fostered. It appears in them that the text's mosaic of discourses and narrative perspectives, its reference to Igbo aesthetics, its syncretism, and its post-modernist slant eventually distance the Western reader. They complicate and bewilder (53–54).

A number of conclusions can be drawn from this. The first and most obvious is done by the compiler of the reviews himself, his attitude testifies to colonial prejudice. Secondly, Achebe's painstaking task to weave all the material and contrive a pluri-dimensional fictional work is an important step towards a poetics of African literature even though Achebe thinks that the duty of defining it lies with others.[30] Thirdly, one has gone a long way since Nkosi underscored the almost classical serenity of Chinua Achebe's narrative style which he called a sort of "art which conceals art." In opposition to Achebe he names the "modernist" group in Africa, who, in some of their works, call attention beyond the narrated event "to the essential duplicity of form itself, to the strained artificiality of language, to the uncertainty of the ground modern art tries to imply." Yet, while pointing to a certain similarity with modernist movements in other parts of the world, Nkosi stresses that to see the trend in African fiction as a mere extension of what is occurring elsewhere "is to seriously misjudge the African phenomenon, its roots, its ideological compulsion." On the other hand, it is this critic's analytical insight which astonishingly reverberates in *Anthills*, that is when he emphasizes that this "modernist movement" both faces forward to the latest innovations in fiction as well as backwards to the roots of African tradition. He propounds:

> Indeed, some of the experiments being carried out in African fiction owe nothing to European and American examples, but achieve their queer effects by returning us to African traditional sources and by exploiting certain properties of native languages (54).

Finally, one can contend that Achebe retains a progressive and forward-looking creative impulse that partakes both of the philosophy of constant artistic renewal that underlies the Mbari institution, and of the traditional story-teller and moral censor that the griot is. *Anthills* is a repository of all this. The novel is bound to be a significant item in discussions of the aesthetics of African literature. The book presents all the questions that concern the criticism of African literary texts: arts and politics, gender, and poetics for example.

Achebe is today one of the writers who compels respect even from adverse critics. This, on the part of Achebe, pertains to a consciously cultivated attitude of personal integrity and obstinate disregard for dogmatic prescriptivism, even from society itself at the service of which he places himself as an artist. Critics would have wanted him to be more committed as part perhaps of the burden of a great writer who rejects "art for art's sake" but to this *Anthills* provides answers. His commitment to Africa's future is obvious in his homage to Agostinho Neto, and even more so in his tribute to the murdered President of Burkina Faso, Thomas Sankara, as one of the few hopeful examples of leadership in Africa. A young man whom, he says, a veteran socialist like President Mitterand regarded as "a disturbing person…who does not leave your conscience alone."

> I have no doubt that Mitterand meant his comment as a praise for his young impatient host. But it was also a deadly arraignment and even conviction. Principalities and powers do not tolerate those who interrupt the sleep of their consciences.[31]

One remembers Achebe seeing writing a novel as not agreeing with his mood, and inappropriate with the civil war context. The statement has provoked the comment of a sharp critic who has seen in it the vivid illustration of the dilemma of "applied art" when it is faced with political revolution. Pointing out that Achebe's reputation has essentially rested on a cultural revolution against colonial stereotypes, which is rooted in the rediscovery of African past in a style marked with detachment, irony and fairness. But the difficult problem then, he inquires, "is how can these same qualities be used to best effect in the political realities if the present. Can the novelist as social reformer allow himself the luxury of acknowledging that whenever something stands, something else will stand beside it?"[32] It would be wrong to see the last statement as a monolithic principle of Achebe's aesthetics. He asserts in *Anthills* as well as in other writings that even though he believes that writing can change the world, the artist should not be looked upon as a provider of solution to concrete political and economic problems, his or her task is to make people alert, to make them think, and act. That is what didacticism implies as shown herein.

Notes

1. Chinua Achebe, *Anthills of the Savannah* (London: Heinemann, 1987), p. 124. Other novels dealt with here are *Things Fall Apart* (1958) and *Arrow of God* (1964). Page references are based on the Heinemann AWS publications and appear in the main text.

2. "The Novelist as Teacher" in *Morning Yet on Creation Day* (London: Heinemann, 1975), p. 45. All other essays by Achebe herein cited are from this edition unless otherwise indicated.

3. See Roy Dilley, "Performance, Ambiguity and Power in Tukulor Weaver' Songs" in *Discourse and its Disguises: The Interpretation of African Oral Text*, edited by Karen Barber and F.P. de Moraes Farias (Birmingham, England: Birmingham University African Studies Series 1, 1989).

4. (Paris: Presence Africaine, 1980; first published, 1964). My own translation.

5. *The Money Order with White Genesis*, translated by Clive Wake (London: Heinemann AWS, 1972; first published 1965).

6. The Sixth South Bank Show (London Weekend Television) annual lecture, 4 February 1990. See "Literature of celebration," extracts of this talk, in West Africa 5–11 February 1990 pp. 167–168; and "A Song of Ourselves," *New Statesman & Society* 9 February 1990, pp. 30–32. Both texts should be read for a full account of the literary content of Achebe's talk. This talk will be referred to hereafter as "London lecture/address"; passages quoted are from *West Africa*.

7. Georg W.F. Hegel as quoted by Georg Lukacs in *The Historical Novel* (Lincoln and London: University of Nebraska Press, 1983), p. 53.

8. Scholars have discussed this widely. See for examples Bernth Lindfors, "The Palm Oil with which Achebe's Words are Eaten" in *Critical Perspectives on Chinua Achebe*, edited by C.L. Innes and B. Lindfors (London: Heinemann, 1979), pp. 47–66; Emmanuel Obiechina, *Culture, Tradition and Society in the West African Novel* (Cambridge: Cambridge University Press, 1975), chap. 7; Chukwuma Okoye, "Achebe: The Literary Function on Proverbs and Proverbial sayings in Two Novels" in *Lores and Language*, 2, no. 10 (1979), 45–63 (University of Sheffield).

9. Lakhdar-Barka Sidi Mohamed, Introduction to "Essai de fixation par écrit d'unités culturelles orales" (monograph, University d`Oran ILVE, Department of English), p. 6.

10. "Travelling White" in the *Weekend Guardian*, G. Britain, 21–22 October 1989, p. 7.

11. A. James Arnold, *Modernism and Negritude: The Poetry and Poetics of Aime Cesaire* (Cambridge: Cambridge University Press, 1981), p. 70.

12. "The Crisis of consciousness in Modern African Literature: A Survey", in *Marxism and African Literature*, edited by Georg M. Gugelberger (London: James Currey, 1985), pp. 21–49 (p. 23).

13. *Tasks and Masks: Themes and Styles of African Literature* (Harlow, Essex: Longman, 1981), p. 46.

14. Arthur Ravenscroft, *Chinua Achebe* (Harlow, Essex: Longman, 1997) p. 9.

15. South Bank Show lecture (note no. 6 above). See Achebe's critique of Conrad in his essay, "An Image of Africa", *Research in African Literatures* 9, no. 1 (1978), 1–15; it also appears in his *Hopes and Impediments: Selected Essays 1965–87* (London, Heinemann, 1988) under the explicit title: "An Image of Africa: Racism in Conrad's *Heart of Darkness*".

16. Letters to the Editor: A.B. Bodomo in *West Africa* 19–25 February 1990, p. 262, and Dr. J.K. Mprah in *West Africa* 12–18 March 1990, p. 424; and finally the essay of C.M.B. Brown "Language and Power" *West Africa* 25 June–1 July 1990. See also Omar Sougou, "The Issue of Literatures in African Languages: A Survey", *Université, Recherché et Développement*, 1 (1993), 63–78. (Université, Gaston Berger, Saint Louis, Senegal).

17. In the history of West Africa there are instances of various individual responses to the colonialists comparable to Okonkwo's from secular leaders who killed the white man and killed themselves. Others preferred exile. Religious leaders also were subject to harassment. Robert M. Wren discussing the historical sources of *Arrow of God* in *Achebe's World: The Historical and Cultural Context of the Novels of Chinua Achebe* (Harlow, Essex: Longman, 1980) posits that there has been a case similar to Ezeulu's in the history of that Eastern Nigeria.

18. "An interview with Chinua Achebe", J.O.J. Nwachukwu-Agbada, The Massachusetts Review 28, no. 2 (1987), 273–285 (pp. 281–282).

19. "The Writer and His Community", *Hopes and Impediments*, p. 41. Refer to note no. 16 above.

20. Raoul Granqvist, Travelling: Chinua Achebe in Scandinavia (Umea, Sweden: Umea Papers in English no. 11, 1990, p. 46.

21. *The Historical Novel* (Lincoln and London: University of Nebraska Press, 1983), p. 53.

22. Emmanuel Obiechina, "The Writer and his Commitment in contemporary Nigerian Society", Okike, 27–28 (1988), 1–9 (p. 9)

23. Claude Levi-Strauss, *Structural Anthropology* (Harmondsworth: Penguin, 1972), p. 209.

24. *Christmas in Biafra and Other Poems* (New York: Doubleday, 1973), respectively pp. 46–47 and 72–73.

25. Bernth Lindfors, "Achebe on Commitment and African Writers", *Africa Report*, 15, 3, (1970), 16–18.

26. Bernth Lindfors, *Africa Report*, 15, 3 (1970), 16–18.

27. *Myth, Literature and the African World* (Cambridge: Cambridge University Press, 1976), pp. 86–87.

28. *Mythologies*, Transl. by Annette Lavers (London: Paladin Grafton Books-Collins, 1973), p. 141.

29. *West Africa*, see no. 8 above.

30. Achebe interviewed by J.O.J. Nwachukwu-Agbada, pp. 276–277, 280–281.

31. "Postscript: James Baldwin (1924–1987)", *Hopes and Impediments*, p. 120.

32. David Carroll, *Chinua Achebe* (London: Macmillan, 1980).

Chapter 3

Mbari versus Conrad: Chinua Achebe's Aesthetics

Claudio Gorlier

CHINUA ACHEBE'S ESSAYS DEFINITELY REPRESENT an impressive instance of critical and theoretical writing *per se*; nevertheless, they should almost necessarily be discussed in a strict connection with his fiction. I find it quite legitimate to assert that Achebe puts forth some fundamental paradigms of what can be defined as a literary theory, and that such a theory, "the Quest for an African Hermeneutics", as Simon Gikandi formulates it referring specifically to *Anthills of the Savannah*, consistently sustains and underpins his novels, becoming an elemental factor in the discourse. Suffice it to recall the memorable image of life as "a dancing mask" in *Arrow of God*, which offers a poignant, explicit view of the imaginative stance inherent in the creative process. Granted this, I intend to limit myself to a scrutiny of Achebe's essays, and I shall consider them in the light of a double, albeit complementary perspective: a *pars destruens* and a *part construes* (Gikandi 131 ff).

The first of those two parts undoubtedly borders a vigorous passionate and topical indictment of colonialism, with special emphasis on its mystifying portrayal of the African mind; of African history, tantamount to an actual non-history or sub-history; of African culture, tantamount to an actual sub-culture. It should be preliminary underscored that in his antagonistic analysis of the main featured of colonialism Achebe systematically crosses the boundaries of literature as such; never does he consider literature as an independent institution. The "colonialist rhetoric", as he calls it in *Colonialist Criticism*, the opening essay of *Morning Yet on Creation Day* (*MYCD*) (it is worth noticing the allusive valency of "creation" in the title of this book), accommodates itself in words once it has established its pseudo-anthropological and pseudo-historical premises. Abdul R JanMohamed aptly stresses that "Achebe's reaction against this kind of denigration… provides us with the sociological imperatives which influence him and other black writers." Again in *Colonialist Criticism*, Achebe, recalling his talk with A.D. Hope, insists, "every literature must seek the things that belong unto its place, must, in other words, speak of a particular place. Evolve out of the necessities of its history, past and current, and the aspirations and destiny of its people": categories – we should add

All misinterpreted or even viciously thwarted by the "colonialist rhetoric." Only in the final pages of the essay does Achebe revert to a specifically literary issue, when he castigates the western prejudice "of dismissing the African novel", because the novel "is a peculiarly western genre" (53).

Needless to say, the climax of Achebe's deconstruction of "the colonialist rhetoric" is reached in the seminal and controversial essay on Joseph Conrad's *Heart of Darkness*. I contend that a number of debates have missed a crucial point: Achebe is consciously and consistently playing the *pars destruens*, and consequently he is not indulging in a systematic exercise in "objective" literary criticism; on the contrary, *Heart of Darkness* conspicuously carries a challenge "he has to respond to." An image of Africa: Racism in Conrad's *Heart of Darkness* is provocatively biased and clearly objectionable. In the essay, a few central features are deliberately eschewed: the distancing of Marlow as first person narrator from the writer; Marlow's neurosis that forces him to leave and that ostensibly symbolizes the loss of a center, i.e. western civilization at the height of industrial revolution and of its colonialist overgrowth; Kurtz as the emblem of madness and self-destruction brought by colonialist exploitation of Africa. Terry Collits convincingly remarks that "Achebe's passionate misreading of *Heart of Darkness* aims at denouncing "the hegemony of western discourse", or "an overcoming of colonial discourse", and possibly to attack "the then pervasive New Critical practices in the United States academy."

The second point made by Collits (66) seems especially relevant in that Achebe chooses Conrad's book as the springboard for a putative profession of anti-formalistic criticism. Though Achebe does not explicitly brand *Heart of Darkness* as a literary failure, he exposes it even brutally ("an offensive and deplorable book") somehow undermining its potential objective and denying any possible neutrality of the work of art. In so doing, Edward said (91) warns, "he either says nothing about or overrides the limitations placed on Conrad by the novel as an aesthetic form."

At this stage, the *pars destruens* is welded together with the pars construens, and a significant profession of faith, the coherent sequel to *Colonialist Criticism*, emerges in the opening page of the second essay in *Morning Yet on Creation Day*, "Africa and her Writers": "… I will insist that art is, and will always, in the service of man". This peremptory statement follows a blunt repudiation of the notion of Art for art's sake, and anticipates the sheer rejection of the "idea", "somewhere in the history of European Civilization", that "art should be accountable to no one, and needed to justify itself to nobody except itself..." In this context, "good" becomes a key word, and it must not be taken as an ethical sign post, but rather as a conceptual standpoint, in the sense that art imparts values, or, more precisely, is imbued with values which substantiate any literary discourse. (*MYCD* 19 ff)

The "relationship between cultural norms and perceptual values" appropriately commented on by Lloyd W. Brown calls for a special place in an organic theory of literature as articulated by Achebe, and opens the way to the core of the theory itself, when it comes to systematize the coordinates of the creative process and the proper directions for a critical interpretation (22 ff).

A preliminary category is firmly established by Achebe in his essay "Thoughts on the African Novel": "The first is that the African novel has to be about Africa. A pretty severe restriction, I am told. But Africa is not only a geographical expression, it is also a metaphysical landscape – it is in fact a view of the world and of the whole cosmos perceived from a particular position." (*MYCD* 50) Let us complete this peremptory principle with the previously quoted passage from *Colonialist Criticism* on the relevance of place and of history, and with another, almost confessional statement in "The Novelist as Teacher": "I would be quite satisfied if my novels (especially the ones I set in the past) did no more than teach my readers that their past – with all its imperfections – was not one long night of savagery from which the first Europeans acting on God's behalf delivered them." (*MYCD* 45)

Achebe is ostensibly formulating two inescapable tenets, place and history, and reinforcing them in his interview with Anthony Appiah, when he has this to say, speaking of the writers role: to encourage the creation of an African identity." Place, history, identity, all subsume the "typicality" of African literature, and in this respect JanMohamed rightly observes that "Achebe wishes the African writer to undertake the awesome task of alleviating the problems of historical petrification and catalepsy"; furthermore, he perceptively points to the availability of Georg Lukacs's theory of realism. I would add that "typical" is the conceptual term which Lukacs depends on when defining his aesthetic credo (155).

Achebe's "typicality" stems from further theoretical pronouncements: the relationship between the writer and his community; the principal of truth in fiction; the role of the novelist as teacher; the indigenous character of the creative process vis-à-vis the Western Models. "The Writer and His Community" owes its singular relevance to Achebe's literary theory mostly for the resolute dismissal of the role of the individual hero in fiction, "the very angel and paragon of creation", in the mainstream of Western fiction. The non-Western hero "is still in a very real sense subordinate to his community. But even more important, he is subject to the sway of non-human forces in the universe... I call them sometimes the *Powers of*

Event....To powers inhabiting that order of reality the human hero counts of little."
(*Hopes and Impediments* (*HI* 57)). While Achebe adopts a literary genre, the novel,
whose Western origin is generally taken for granted, he pre-empts one of its major
paradigms, the overwhelming function of the individual hero.

Truth acquires a multivalent significants and virtually includes the whole
range of literature. On the one hand, as C.L. Innes shows, "like Fanon he defends
the role of the writer (and intellectual) as cultural nationalist (104). In "The Role
of the Writer in a New nation", Achebe proclaims "the writers duty" to help the
African peoples to regain their lost dignity and, in short, their history. On the other
hand, truth in fiction amounts to conveying values not didactically, but by means
of imagination. Consequently, "the fiction which imaginative literature offers us...
does not enslave; it liberates the mind of man. Its truth.... Begins as an adventure
in self-discovery and ends in wisdom and human conscience." (*HI* 153). Finally,
truth permeates language: "For when language is disjoined from truth... horrors
can descend again on mankind" (*MYCD* 37).

"The Novelist as Teacher" reaffirms Achebe's unwillingness to deal with literature as a thoroughly independent, self-contained, unassailable realm; in other words,
separated from, truth, from reality, from history. A shamanic trait is discernible
when he looks at the novelist as teacher but also, largely as an intellectual leader who
shows the way and marches on the front. Curiously enough, here and elsewhere
in his essays he seems to appropriate some of the main arguments expounded by
Antonio Gramsci in his Marxist or neo-Marxist analysis: the attack on culture
hegemony and the revolt of subaltern culture; the quest for a "popular-national"
culture, the figure of the "organic intellectual", who allies himself with the masses
and commits himself, who speaks out, who voices their deepest aspiration. Literature
is tantamount to positive thinking. No wonder if Achebe aggressively pans Ayi
Kwei Armah's *The Beautyful Ones Are Not Yet Born*. Achebe's dictate on the African
specificity, the African "typicality", of genuine African novel: "there is enormous
distance between Armah and Ghana." In other words, Armah is "scornful", "cold and
remote" and implicitly unfair to his country, on the verge – one would be tempted
to conclude – of defamation. Armah's Ghana is unrealistic, and this infringes on
the loyalty and reality professed by Achebe. The second reason cuts deeper into the
issue; here Achebe is clearly an alienated writer, a modern writer complete with
all the symptoms." Armah becomes this privileged target of Achebe's unmitigated
rejection of the literature of alienation, of estrangement, of "ANXIETY" (written
in capital letters to emphasize his rebuttal). Camus's "outsider" cannot claim any
right of citizenship for Achebe, his widely accepted influence notwithstanding, and
"modern' must be read in this – for Achebe – despicable, even sick vaslency. Armah's
malaise is unacceptable, in so fat as it relates to Western models; furthermore, his

alienation "is a statement of defeat", a surrender, and actual self-annihilation: "A man is never more defeated than when he is running away from himself." (*MYCD* 26–7) In this context, we cannot help recalling Lukacs's stern rejection of Kafka, as un-realistic, un-historical, "modern" writer par excellence" Nevertheless, today African writers have almost necessarily to confront themselves with such burning issues as alienation and anxiety, or, for that matter, with "anomy" a cardinal and occasionally ambiguous, pregnant concept, which permeates Wole Soyinka's novel SEASON OF ANOMY from its very title. Incidentally, Soyinka has openly praised *The Beautyful Ones Are Not Yet Born*. In point of fact, it should be noticed that a characteristic malaise infiltrates Achebe's *No Longer at Ease* and above all, *Anthills of the Savannah*. I do not thoroughly share Kole Omotoso's unconditional opinion ("The ultimate comment of the novel is that life as it is lived in Nigeria has no meaning"), yet I find it hard to deny that anxiety or at least anomy comes out as interstitial in *Anthills of the Savannah*. Both *No Longer at Ease* and *Anthills of the Savannah* also display a gallery of female characters, and the latter resolutely enters the area of sexuality, an undisputable taboo in most contemporary African fiction (Ekwensi represents a peculiar exception), and a subject systematically dodged by Achebe in his essays (Omotoso 92).

The culmination and the quintessence of Achebe's literary theory are to be identified in the discussion of the phenomenology of the creative process. As we have already pointed out, Achebe's categorization of the African novel exacts an indispensable pre-requisite, that "it has to be about Africa." Language follows as the second imperative. When we approach the essay "Language and the Destiny of Man", we may be mislead into thinking that Achebe tends to marginalize the function of language in literature and/or to face it in a peripheral way only. The essay sounds didactic and even educational, so to speak, in its inception and its successive development, when it goes back to the origin and the scope of language, to the vari-ous functions of language, to its use and misuse or its corruption, ascribing a kind of redeeming quality to it: "... our remote ancestors who made and preserved language for us... crossed the first threshold from bestiality to humanness." (*MYCD* 35)

Quite appropriately Achebe paves the way for the equation between lan-guage and truth, eschewing any strict analysis of literary language at large, or of the language of its own fiction. Achebe never yields to the enticement of any kind of formalistic criticism, to the effect that language, no less than literature, funda-mentally conveys values albeit in the imaginative mode. The function of language materializes as substantially communicative and subject. When Achebe denies the objectivity of language and relatedly of the narrative voice, he reiterates his denial of one of the main tenets of the kind of modern that he consciously discounts.

The only pronouncement on language in literature is in regards of the choice of the language of the African writer. In "The African Writer and the English Language" we come across the memorable as well as controversial definition of the distinction between a national literature and an ethnic literature. In Nigeria, the national literature is the literature written in English, the national language. (*MYCD* 56) We are eventually taken into one of the crucial, genetic aspects of the creative process: "The real question is not whether Africans could write in English but whether they ought to. Is it right that a man should abandon his mother-tongue for someone else's? It looks like a dreadful betrayal and produces a guilty feeling." The rhetorical question finds a prompt and resolute answer: "But for me there is no other choice. I have been given the language and I intend to use it." (*MYCD* 62) However, Achebe turns disappointingly elusive on the kind of English he has elected to put to use and to re-create or to re-think: "But it will have to be a new English, still in full communion with its ancestral home but altered to suit its African surroundings." We can at least register an increasing process of hybridization in Achebe's fiction, up to *Anthills of the Savannah*, mostly by the recourse to a multilingual language where Nigerian pidgin claims a greater role. What actually matters is the deliberate subversion of hegemonic culture and the empowerment of a subaltern culture. The phenomenon also applies to the appropriation of a supposedly alien genre such as the novel, and to its re-creation." I have no doubt at all about the existence of the African novel. This form of fiction has seized the imagination of many African writers and they will use it according to their differing abilities, sensibilities and visions without seeking anyone's permission." (*MYCD* 54). Neither language nor fiction is a mere technique, and Lloyd W. Brown's comment ("he uses the literary traditions of the English tongue to liberate the African's identity and history from the ethnocentric images that have been enshrined in the psychopathology of the colonizer's language…") impeccably clarifies Achebe's theoretical assumptions no less than the way he applies them in his fiction. In his turn, James Snead effectively elaborates on Brown's remarks ("… in evoking Yeats's theme… the novelist has exploited the European's cultural criteria… in order to reverse the white man's exclusivist definitions of history and culture."): "Far more than merely borrowing the notion of historical cycles from Yeats, he is in fact reclaiming an age-old non-western cyclical conception that European writers had only recently annexed" (9).

The decks having been provisionally cleared, we are now in a position to tackle the most complex and original paradigm of Achebe's African aesthetics, the theory of *mbari*. Mbari is steeped in ethnic culture and society, precisely the one exhaustively and subtly investigated by Ernest Emenyonu in his book *The Rise of the Igbo Novel* (Ibadan: OUP, 1978). Mbari does not solely characterize a creative act, whose language is both verbal and visual, abstract and concrete, ephemeral and permanent, but incarnates a ritual worldview, a celebration performed as a festival. "A colorful ceremony...", Achebe writes in "Africa and her Writers", *mbari* is "a profound affirmation of the people's belief in the indivisibility of art and society." The "house of images" built "into seclusion in a forest-clearing", a work that "might take a year or even two... was often a miracle of artistic achievement." While "the making of art is not the exclusive concern of a particular caste or secret society...", it so happens that "... the greater community which comes to the unveiling of the art and then receives its makers again into its normal life becomes a beneficiary – indeed an active partaker – of this spiritual experience." (*MYCD* 21–2) The referential choice by Achebe of "... the visual and plastic arts and the drama of *mbari*..." makes sense in that "*mbari* manages to make its statements more comprehensively and compactly and perhaps more memorably than anything I can think of in our language arts" ("African Literature..." 10).

Mbari sanctions the relationship between the artist, the craftsman and the community who benefit from it; no elitist attitude on the part of the artist is conceivable. Above all, in its being decidedly affirmative, it does not allow any space to undecidability: it upsets the main canon of the Western metaphysics effectively summarized by Jacques Derrida as "limitation du sens de l'etre dans le champ de la presence" (37).

The artists and the performers of *mbari* must be accepted and accounted for as actual code-keepers, whose experience and whose permanence is translatable and should be translated "annexed", in a wider context, made available among the patterns of creative process. Mbari supplies some necessary instruments to validate an African aesthetics and at the same time to disambiguate Western aesthetics. The essay on Onitsha, "Onitsha, Gift of the Niger", complements Achebe's speculations on *mbari*; it enhances a fertile duality inherent in "the esoteric region from which creativity sallies forth at will to manifest itself" and "immediately" conjures Frantz Fanon's phrase on "a zone of occult instability". (*MYCD* 90)

This duality must discourage the critic from trapping Achebe's aesthetics and fiction into a sequel of facile labels ("realist" and "realism"; "historic") of superficial Western matrix, conducive to a risky misinterpretation. Along with this caveat, the critic and the scholar should conveniently adopt an almost proverbial sentence from the essay on Onitsha: "All we can do is to speculate."

Works Cited

Achebe, Chinua. "African Literature as Restoration of Celebration." In *Okike*, 30. Nov. 1990: 9–20

———. "An Image of Africa: Racism in Conrad's *Heart of Darkness*." In *Hopes and Impediments*. New York: Doubleday, 1989: 1–20

———. in Interview with Anthony Appiah, John Ryle and D.A.N. Jones *Times Literary Supplement*, February 26, 1982

———. *Morning Yet On Creation Day*. London: Heinemann, 1975.

Brown, Lloyd W. "Cultural Norms and Modes of Perception in Achebe's fiction." In C.L. Innes & Bernth Lindfors, eds. *Critical Perspectives on Chinua Achebe*. London: Heinemann, 1979: 22–36

Collits, Terry. "Theorizing Racism." In Chris Tiffin and Alan Lawson, eds. *De-Scribing Empire*. London: Routledge

Derrida, Jacques. *De la Grammatologie*. Paris: Les Editions de Minuit, 1967.

Gikandi, Simon. *Reading Chinua Achebe*. London: James Currey, 1991.

Innes, C.L. *Chinua Achebe*. Cambridge Univ. Press, 1990.

JanMohamed, Abdul. Manichean Aesthetics: The Politics of *Literature in Colonial Africa*. Amherst: The Univ. of Massachusetts Press, 1983.

Omotoso, Kole. *Achebe or Soyinka? A Study in Contrast*. London: Hans Zell Publishers, 1996.

Said, Edward W. *Culture and Imperialism*. London: Chatto & Windus, 1993

Snead, James. "Eurpean Pedigrees/ African Contagious." In Homi K. Bhabba, ed. *Nation and Narration*. London: Routledge, 1990.

Chapter 4

Artistic and Pedagogical Experimentations: Chinua Achebe's Short Stories and Novels

Iniobong I. Uko

CHINUA ACHEBE HAS BEEN CONSISTENT in making his literary works serve pedagogical purposes among the Igbo people, specifically, and other African people in general. He demonstrates the fact that being the "critical conscience" of his society, and a chronicler of events within that society; he has the duty of recreating the events in artistic forms. This preoccupation necessarily entails utilizing the real events as different colors of thread to weave a fictionalized fabric that is relevant to the people and gives them a sense of dynamic hopefulness and profound identity in history. Achebe's writings constitute a tremendously useful storehouse of cultural values in Igbo cosmology. It transcends the statis framework of "art-for-art's sake" within which some literary works are trapped, thereby not serving the socio-cultural, economic and political needs of the people. Many African writers function largely as intellectuals and teachers of the people, and are also impelled to provide ethical guideposts and moral signboards to reveal the hidden snares and the treacherous quick sands that constitute the hazards that people perpetually live in (Obiechina 32).

Achebe is a quintessential teacher with a rare commitment. He uses the particular case of his Igbo background to touch on the universal. This phenomenal teacher instructs artistically involving his own experiences, which are deeply embedded within African traditional mores. Little wonder then why his writings are an encapsulation of proverbs, unique traditional symbols, sophisticated rhythms, playful improvisations, witty double meanings, resonant repetitions and other folkloric elements. Achebe and his writings serve as the bridge between two opposing values: the Christian and the tradition. He asserts:

> On one arm of the cross we sang hymns and read the Bible night and day. On the other my father's brother and his family, blinded by heathenism, offered food to idols. …Those idols and that food had a strange pull on me in spite of my being such a thorough little Christian. … What I do remember is a fascination for the ritual and the life on the other arm of the crossroads… ("Named for Victoria, Queen of England" 35).

In his various writings, Achebe portrays the trajectory of a people/nation as a storyline in which a peaceful (even though intensely traditional) existence is lost at the throes of the incursion of a new dominating and arrogant culture. This debilitating contact justifies Achebe's argument that "… it would be foolish to pretend that we have fully recovered from the traumatic effects of our first confrontation with Europe" ("Novelist as Teacher" 44). This confrontation creates an unhealthy ambivalence, which the people/nation are ill equipped to deal with. It is from this backdrop that Achebe justifiably highlights the events and practices among the people, prior to the incursion. Having personally experienced events in his Ogidi home that were manifestations of the incursion of the Christian religion into the hitherto peaceful existence of the people, he recalls:

> I was born in Ogidi in Eastern Nigeria of devout Christian parents. The line between Christian and non-Christian was much more definite in my village forty years ago than it is today [1998]. … We tended to look down on the others. We were called in our language "the people of the church" or "the association of God". The others we called, with the conceit appropriate to followers of the true religion, the heathen or even "the people of nothing" ("Named for Victoria, Queen of England" 30).

Achebe's preoccupations serve numerous roles, summarized into these fundamental two:

- To retain, while simultaneously enlightening and teaching posterity the values of the people. Most of the values have become influenced by the alien culture or have been completely eroded; and,

- Offer a subtle means towards resolving the polemics over the validity of traditional life and practices in a global modern era.

Essentially, he explains in "Africa's Tarnished Name" that his writings address "the vast arsenal of derogatory images of Africa amassed to defend the slave trade and later, colonization, [which] gave the world not only a literary tradition that is now, happily, defunct, but also a particular way of looking (or rather *not* looking) at Africa and Africans that endures, alas, into our own day" (104) (Achebe's emphasis).

Achebe's thematic concerns conceptualized on the Igbo experience and worldview, are handled in ways that reach out and become testaments with which the non-Igbo, non-Nigerians can easily identify. According to him:

> Here then is an adequate revolution for me to espouse – to help my society regain belief in itself and put away the complexes of the years of denigration and self-abasement. And it is essentially a question of education, in the best sense of that word. Here ... my aims and the deepest aspirations of my society meet....

The writer cannot expect to be excused from the task of re-education and regeneration that must be done. In fact, he should march right in front.

> For he is ... the sensitive point of his community
> ("The Novelist as Teacher" 44–45).

Herein lies the framework that defines Achebe's roles as a writer and a teacher. It is evident that the dominant critical reactions to Achebe's works seem to focus on his novels, which undoubtedly deserve such attention, but his short stories seem comparatively to be in oblivion, even though they evince equally vital and fundamental themes as the novels. A close examination of many of Achebe's novels and short stories reveals that the latter serve as precursor to the former. Issues explored in the novels are treated with infused exactness considering the paucity of space in the short stories. This experimentation shows Achebe's ardent and consistent concern with his themes, techniques and characterization, but in all these, the focus remains on pedagogy.

In view of these and other factors, this study explores selected stories in Achebe's *Girls at War and Other Stories* and some of his novels within the context of experimentation without losing sight of their pedagogical relevance in contemporary Nigerian society.

The ebullience and dexterity with which Achebe captures the issues he examines, and his obvious closeness to those issues manifest in the authenticity of his themes, the effectiveness of his style, especially his careful manipulation of language to serve his purpose. In "The Madman", Achebe portrays a graphic picture of the madman, his mode of operation and how he is regarded and treated in the community. The story begins:

> He was drawn to markets and straight roads. Not any tiny neighbourhood market where *a handful of garrulous women might gather at sunset to gossip and buy ogili for the evening's soup*, but a huge, engulfing bazaar beckoning people familiar and strange from far and near. ... After much wandering he had discovered two such markets linked together by such a highway; and so ended his wandering. *One market was Afo, the other Eke.* ... He passed the night there putting right again his hut after a day of defilement by two fat-bottomed market women who said it was their market stall ... (3) (My Emphasis).

The above, constituting the opening of the story is doubly significant. It depicts the particular features that describe a person who is mad: drifting and aimless. All the emphases added specifically highlight issues in the narration that convey the way of life of the people: the madman chooses the market days, *Afo* and *Eke* to stay in the market, leaving the other market days for other people; and the common female stereotypes – gossipy, garrulous and fat-bottomed. All these make indelible impressions on the reader especially as the concise portrayal is sustained throughout the story.

This female image manifests later in the story in the relationship between Nwibe's wives, Mgboye and Udenkwo. Udenkwo, the younger wife, is very quarrelsome and abusive, and her target is usually Mgboye, the older wife, who is very quiet and self-respectful. Achebe inserts this story within a story not just to show female garrulousness, but, perhaps more importantly, to reveal Nwibe's ability to instill order in his family. He is the only one who successfully intervenes and stops Udenkwo's insolence:

> If Udenkwo is crazy must everybody else go crazy with her? Is one crazy woman not enough in my compound so early in the day?
>
> Shut your mouth, shameless woman, or a wild beast will lick your eyes for you this morning. When will you learn to keep your badness within this compound instead of shouting it to all Ogbu to hear? I say shut your mouth! (6, 7).

Thus, Nwibe is portrayed as firm and authoritative; he leaves no one in doubt that he is the man, a credible man who is in full charge of his household. It is this image that is contradicted later the same morning as Nwibe's cloths are taken by the madman while Nwibe bathes in the stream. Rather than seek the help of sane people for clothing, Nwibe runs stark naked after the madman into the market, answering the call of the market place and presenting himself as the actual madman. In consequence, he is no longer fit to take the *ozo* title. The story condemns irrational actions and reactions. Nwibe's mind was fixed on retrieving his clothing from the madman. His running stark naked after the madman is tantamount to irrational action and he accounts for that by the momentary insanity he suffers. By implication, if anyone takes an irrational action he has to account for it.

While "The Madman" explores traditional issues, "The Voter" uses the political context to teach important lessons. Achebe uses sarcasm to explain the political values in contemporary Nigeria: Chief the Honourable Marcus Ibe, of the People's Alliance Party is the Minister of Culture in the outgoing government. He is certain to continue in the incoming government as well:

> ...he had two long cars and had just built himself the biggest house anyone had seen in these parts. But ... none of these successes had gone to Marcus' head. ... He remained devoted to his people. Whenever he could he left the good things of

the capital and returned to his village which had neither running water nor electricity, although he had lately installed a private plant to supply electricity to his new house. ... Marcus had christened his new house "Umuofia Mansions" in honour of his village, and he had slaughtered five bulls and countless goats to entertain the people on the day it was opened by the Archbishop (14–15).

Evidently, these endeared Marcus to his Umuofia people. Rufus Okeke (Roof), his political campaign leader, is a vibrant and popular man in Umuofia. He recently won a land case "because, among other things, he had been chauffeur-driven to the disputed site" (16). It is through him that Marcus bribes the elders to curry election support.

However, in a dramatic twist of events, Roof succumbs to the luring by their opponent's agents who bribe him with five pounds:

> No words were wasted. He placed five pounds on the floor before Roof and said, 'We want your vote' ...
> Marcus will not be there when you put in your paper (17, 18).

Roof accepts and takes an oath to confirm it. Through this portrayal, Achebe satirizes as he highlights the consequences of a sell-out like Roof, because in the end, Roof votes for none of the parties since he invalidates his vote:

> He folded the (ballot) paper, tore it in two along the crease and put one half in each box. He took the precaution of putting the first half into Maduka's box and confirming the action verbally: 'I vote for Maduka' (21).

Roof's ambivalence here recapitulates the crossroads that underlie a clash of opposing interests, just as Achebe states, "We lived at the crossroads of cultures" ("Named for Victoria ..." 34). "The Voter" clearly reveals the deceit, intrigue and roguery that characterize the political system in Umuofia, a mythological Nigeria. Achebe ridicules the questionable character of Chief the Honourable:

> ... only the other day Marcus Ibe was a not too successful mission teacher. Then politics had come to their village and he had wisely joined ... just in time to avoid imminent dismissal arising from a female teacher's pregnancy (16).

Achebe also derides the pursuit of selfish interests by political leaders. In this story, this trend results in the people being neglected, public facilities and amenities not provided, yet the people are deceived and bought over by a huge party by Honourable Marcus Ibe, a practice that is still common in contemporary Nigeria and African societies:

> Besides Roof and his assistant there were five elders in the room. An old hurricane lamp with a cracked, sooty, glass gave out yellowish light in their midst. The elders sat on very low stools. On the floor, directly in front of each of them, lay two shilling pieces (15–16).

According to Nnolim, (167), politics enters literature when the writer's concern extends beyond destinies of nations or the masses. In this connection, Achebe is politically committed because of his concern with the fate or destinies of the Igbo in particular, and Nigerians and Africans in general in the collective encounter with Europe. Indeed, there are obvious connections between Achebe's *A Man of the People* (1967) and "The Voter"; both explore the themes of socio-economic corruption, moral decadence and degeneration in the post-independence Nigerian society. Chief the Honourable M.A. Nanga, M.P. is visible as Chief the Honourable in "The Voter", and both display diverse forms of intrigues, deceit and corruption in electoral campaigns, voting processes. However, the failed hopes of a new and hopeful leadership in *A Man of the People*, progresses to the opposite in "The Voter", with its implied victory of Maduka over Chief the Honourable Marcus Ibe. This is indicative of Achebe's vision of hope and eventual redemption of the degenerate Nigerian society and polity. To stress the importance of this theme, Achebe examines it in a more realistic form in the apparent poor governance in Nigeria in *The Trouble with Nigeria*, about which he asserts: "The trouble with Nigeria is simply and squarely a failure of leadership (1).

In another story, "Marriage is a Private Affair", Achebe condemns rigidity in human relationships. Nnaemeka and Nene Atang (of Igbo and Efik ethnic backgrounds respectively) get engaged and later married, against the consent, support and blessing of Nnaemeka's father, Okeke. He is firmly against the union because, as he notes in his letter to Nnaemeka:

I have found a girl who will suit you admirably – Ugoye Nwekwe, the eldest daughter of our neighbour, Jacob Nweke. She has a proper Christian upbringing. When she stopped schooling some years ago, her father (a man of sound judgment) sent her to live in the house of a pastor where she received all the training a wife could have. Her Sunday School teacher has told me that she reads the Bible very fluently. I hope we shall begin negotiations when you come home in December (24).

Nnaemeka apologizes to his father as he declines the kind gesture and offer:

"I don't love her"
"Nobody said you did. Why should you?" asked his father.
"Marriage today is different …"
"… Look here, my son, … nothing is different. What one looks for in a wife are a good character and a Christian background.".…
"I am engaged to marry another girl.… She is a good Christian and a teacher in a Girls' School in Lagos."
  "Teacher, did you say? If you consider that a qualification for a good wife, I should like to point out to you, Emeka, that *no Christian woman should teach*. St. Paul in his letter to the Corinthians says that women should keep silence" (24–25).

Generally, no man in Nnaemeka's community has ever married a woman from elsewhere: "It has never been heard" (26), and Nnaemeka's action confirms the Biblical prediction that "sons shall rise against their fathers ..." (26). In reaction, Okeke resolves to have nothing to do with his son. He resents the marriage, and especially Nene. The wedding picture of his son and wife sent to him is the object on which Okeke makes manifest his resentment: he cuts off Nene from the picture and returns it to Nnaemeka because he has nothing to do with her. For eight years, Okeke does not relate with them. Nene also faces different forms of prejudice and discrimination from other women in their village meeting in Lagos.

However, Okeke's rigid position becomes modified – unwillingly though – by his knowledge that Nnaemeka and Nene have two sons who desire to see their grandfather. By these developments, Achebe addresses such issues as the mysterious bonding between grandparents and grandchildren, ethnicity and the outmoded status of women in traditional society as well as parental control of their children's choice. Achebe expounds a similar issue in *No Longer at Ease* (1960). Obi Okonkwo, a *been-to*, graduate, a *senior service* in Lagos, son of Nwoye and grandson of the powerful, brave and self-made Ogbuefi Okonkwo in *Things Fall Apart*, wishes to marry Clara, a Britain-trained and hard-working nurse, but who, unfortunately, is *osu*. Obi's parents are opposed to the idea, regardless of the facts that Obi's father is a devoted Christian, and a Catechist, and his mother a faithful believer in God. Obi's attempt at rationalizing the situation is futile. He asserts to his father that the fact that Clara is *osu* does not matter, after all:

> "We are Christians ..."
> "We are Christians [his father] ... said. "But that is no reason to marry an *osu*"
> "The Bible says that in Christ there are no bond or free".
> "My son, ... I understand what you say. But this thing is deeper than you think".
> "What is this thing? Our fathers in their darkness and ignorance called an innocent man *osu*, a thing given to idols, and thereafter he became an outcast, and his children, and his children's children forever. But have we not seen the light of the Gospel?"
> "I know Josiah Okeke [Clara's father] very well ... and I know his wife. He is a good man and a great Christian. But he is *osu*" (151–152).

Obi's father parallels *osu* and leprosy; he refers to the great Syrian warrior, the Biblical Naaman, whose valor did not change the contemptuous attitude towards him because of the stigma from leprosy. Obi's father pleads with Obi to realize that *osu* is like leprosy in the minds of the people; if he should marry *osu*, he injects the mark of shame and leprosy into the family, thereby condemning his children unto the third and fourth generations to scorn, rejection, curse, without no one condescending to marry his daughters: "We are Christians, but we cannot marry our own daughters" (152–153).

On her part, Obi's mother reacts to Obi's idea of marrying *osu* thus "if you want to marry this girl, you must wait until I am no more. If God hears my prayers, you will not wait long" (154) (My emphasis). This speaks volumes, reverberates in Obi's mind, shatters all his hopes and dreams, crumbles his idea of marrying Clara and empowers him to effect the termination of Clara's pregnancy by him, for which he borrows thirty pounds, further complicating his financial situation.

Obviously, Obi's eventual failure to marry Clara because she is *osu* is indicative of the severity of the issue involved. This is unlike the ethnic factor that underlies "Marriage is a Private Affair", Achebe seems to argue that the privacy one may feel about marriage does not make marriage overlook or transcend such traditional considerations as the status and extent of acceptability of the two people involved. He indicates that the graveness of this factor in Igbo cosmology defies resolution and is incomparable to the ethnic factor in "Marriage is a Private Affair". Obi's parents in *No Longer at Ease* are adamantly indisposed to Obi's idea of marrying *osu*, as opposed to Nnaemeka's father's initial stiff resistance to Nnaemeka's marriage to Nene, an Efik lady. It is the old man's love for, and desire to meet with his grandchildren by Nene that make the difference.

The *Osu* caste system is also the focus of Achebe's "Chike's School Days". The story depicts the adverse consequence on the traditional system and people of the incursion of new, strange cultural norms. Amos is encouraged by the new religion in the community, Christianity, to marry "an *Osu* woman":

In the past an *Osu* could not raise his shaggy head in the presence of the free-born. He was a slave to one of the many gods of the clan. He was a thing set apart, not to be venerated but to be despised and almost spat on. He could not marry a free-born, and he could not take any titles of his clan. When he died, he was buried by his kind in the bad bush (38).

Strangely, the new religion debunks the above, accepts the *Osu* into its fold and advocates marriages between them and the free-born. That was how Amos, Chike's father, married Sarah, an *Osu*. This union automatically makes him and all their children *Osu*. Achebe's position in this matter in this story signifies his recognition of contemporary realities that insist on changes, thus questioning and invalidating his previous notion in *No Longer at Ease*. This is a very important stage in the discourse of the thorny issue of the *osu*, which has defied reason and rationale in generations in Igbo cosmology. In fact, Achebe in this story opens an interesting vista, a new trend in this discourse. He highlights the possibility of accepting this class of people; he endows them with self-esteem and pride regardless of their despised status in the society. Indeed, "Chike's School Days" gains utmost relevance within this context.

The bonding of grandparents-grandchildren portrayed as the factor that resolves the conflict in "Marriage is a Private Affair", is also expounded in "Akueke". This story portrays Akueke, whose illness defies all forms of treatment. She is the village beauty, yet refuses all the suitors who approach her for marriage. Her brothers are worried because "proud girls who refused every suitor often came to grief" (33). Akueke feels safe in her maternal grandfather's love for her. She knew that while in Ezi, "she could get away with anything; her grandfather forbade anyone to rebuke her" (32); "he was very fond of [her as she] …was the image of his own mother. He rarely called her Akueke by name; it was always Mother. She was in fact, the older woman returned in the cycle of life" (32). As Akueke's health constantly deteriorates, with no hope from the medicine men consulted:

> Neighbours came in and warned the brothers of the grave danger to which they were exposing the nine villages of Umuofia.
> In the evening, they (Akueke's brothers) carried her into the bad bush. They had constructed a temporary shelter and a rough bed for her (34).
> Akueke ends up with her grandfather in Ezi, who, believing that she is his mother reincarnated, has returned into the family. He immediately adopts her and changes her name to Matefi, insisting that when she marries, her bride-price will be his, not her brothers' (35).

Achebe, in this story deals with issues of the sacred position and regard for the mother, the bride-price and the traditional African belief in reincarnation.

The need for flexibility in life is explored in "Dead Men's Path". Michael Obi, the over zealous school headmaster of Ndume Central School:

> …accepted the responsibility with enthusiasm. He had many wonderful ideas and this was an opportunity to put them into practice. He had had sound secondary school education which designated him a "pivotal teacher" in the official records and set him apart from the other headmasters in the mission field. He was outspoken in his condemnation of the narrow issues of these older and often less-educated ones (70).

With this enthusiastic background, Mr. Obi strives to make his school a model by drastically transforming it physically and otherwise, because "Ndume School was backward in every sense of the word." Thus, he closes an essential footpath that runs through the school premises connecting the village shrine and the cemetery:

> Heavy sticks were planted closely across the path at the two places where it entered and left the school premises. These were further strengthened with barbed wire (73).

Mr. Obi's resolve to beautify the school premises and set a high standard of teaching cannot yield to the advice and plea of the village, especially the village priest of Ani, who explains that the "… path was here before you were born and before your father was born. The whole life of this village depends on it; our dead relatives depart by it and our ancestors visit us by it. But most important, it is the path of children coming in to be born ... (73). The priest's articulation of the spiritual essence of the path, and Mr. Obi's defiance and obstinacy, lead to unprecedented calamities within the community and Mr. Obi's career:

> Two days later a young woman in the village died in childbirth. A diviner ... prescribed heavy sacrifices to propitiate [the] ancestors insulted by the fence.
>
> Obi woke up next morning among the ruins of his work. The beautiful hedges were torn up not just near the path but right round the school, the flowers trampled to death and one of the school buildings pulled down. ...That day, the white Supervisor came to inspect the school and wrote a nasty report on the state of the premises but more seriously about the 'tribal-war situation developing between the school and the village, arising in part from the misguided zeal of the new headmaster' (74).

Here, Achebe clearly condemns obstinacy. The futility of all of Mr. Obi's efforts stresses that Mr. Obi should have considered the validity of other people's opinion and values. Success and fame elude him as his hard and negative stand on issues relating to the traditional and spiritual becomes his undoing. His failure derives from his ignoring the advice (or challenge) of the priest expressed in the proverb: "let the hawk perch and let the eagle perch" (74), but Mr. Obi refuses to let the eagle perch as he refuses to reopen the footpath.

Mr. Obi is reminiscent of Ezeulu's in Achebe's *Arrow of God*. Both men, leaders in their respective rights: Mr. Obi is a school headmaster and Ezeulu is the Chief Priest of Ulu, the founding and principal deity of the six-village clan called Umuaro. Ezeulu's spectacular testimony against his people in the land case with Okperi renders him liable to be crushed. He is crushed by the centripetal forces that symbolize the people he represents and serves; he is also crushed by the centrifugal forces denoted as the extraneous being, Ulu, the god he serves. The complex imperatives involved in this process imply that for being so uncompromising and inflexible, Ezeulu must of necessity be crushed by circumstances which require adjustment rather than firmness (Ola 100). On the other hand, Mr. Obi's bright hopes for Ndume Central School are similar to Ezeulu's sincere concern for the clan. Palmer's description of Ezeulu's personality is appropriate for Mr. Obi's as well: spiteful, ill-tempered, contemptuous, over-bearing, tactless, proud, haughty, uncompromising and even vindictive (94). That each man is consequently crushed in and by the system he cherishes, but that does not believe in isolation, emphasizes Achebe's thesis that the individual is only an aspect of the society and has to be subject to the community that enlivens and empowers him.

Clearly, the plot of each of the stories examined in this study is complex largely because of the different stories that Achebe compresses into one. Set at different historical periods in Nigeria, Achebe highlights the trends that characterized each period. "The Madman" and "Akueke" are set in pre-colonial Nigeria when the people lived harmoniously, observing the rites and upholding the values of their tradition, which have not been subjected to any foreign influence.

"Chike's School Days" and "Dead Men's Path" recount the people's lives in colonial Nigeria. Obiechina holds that "by the nineteen fifties and sixties and with the approach and actual arrival of political independence, the need for Africans to re-define themselves and to re-establish their identity in the world had become very pressing. There was the need to re-assess the past and evaluate the present" (32). These two stories, therefore, fit into the framework of re-assessing the people's values to establish their authenticity and acceptability given operative contemporary realities.

"The Voter" and "Marriage is a Private Affair" capture the post-independence Nigerian society in which the people grapple with the problem of creating an affinity between communal and individual interests. By these diverse portrayals, Achebe serves contemporary Nigeria as a teacher of events, trends, values and concepts that prevailed among the people at different times in the past. Within this praxis, therefore, Achebe displays commitment – to keep alive what would otherwise have been lost, thereby teaching contemporary Nigerian people (especially the youth) the traditional essence of the past. Achebe's effort at, and insistence on recapturing in his writings a past that should not be lost, is explained and justified by de Certeau in his concern with the "unknown other". In explaining this phenomenon evolved by de Certeau, Okafor states that:

> This 'other' usually takes the form of absence, silence, or void, and historiography
> begins with the location of this absence or past, and with separating it from
> the present (179).

Identifying Achebe's writings to be conditioned by history, Obiechina highlights that "as a keen student of history, [Achebe] … was aware of the part played by the slave trade, colonial domination and racism in damaging the African psyche and in loading Africans with self-denigrating attitudes and negative self-perceptions" (31).

Achebe wrote the stories and novels between 1952 and 1971, a crucial period in Nigeria's political history – the period of transition from the status of British colony to an independent nation, and after independence, the widespread tribalism, nepotism and political bigotry that led to the senseless civil war between Nigeria and Biafra from 1967 to 1970. This constitutes the backcloth on which Achebe stitches together different layers of meanings that relate to the devastating war that Nigeria experienced. He also demonstrates the post-independence class-consciousness, self-absorption, greed, uncontrolled pursuit of wealth and power that prevailed in Nigeria. These social malaise arouse Achebe's concerns for posterity, thus he determines to return to the virtues, which were drastically being eroded.

In "The Madman", the madman (symbolizing Nigeria) runs away and adorns himself with Nwibe's clothes. Nwibe unthinkingly pursues him, and in the process is mistaken as the actual madman. Clearly, Northern Nigeria dominated the national polity and marginalized the people from the South East so brutally that the latter sought to secede, and called their new entity Biafra. However, Nigeria overpowered Biafra in the war because the latter was ill-prepared and ill-equipped to handle the demands of the war. Biafra received subtle criticisms just as Nwibe receives in "The Madman". This political critique reveals the more dominant Nigeria as the real madman, while Biafra's insanity, like Nwibe's, was instigated by the former's. Biafra's enormous losses are manifested in Nwibe's loss of the opportunity to join the dignified *ozo* society of reputable men.

Within this context of the Nigerian civil war, Achebe's "The Voter" ridicules the powerful, deceitful and selfish Chief Honourable Minister Marcus Ibe, who takes advantage of the poor, ignorant elders and other Umuofia people, who voted for him "free of charge five years ago." While he symbolizes Nigeria on the one hand, the underdeveloped, deprived, yet wise and well-endowed elders and other Umuofia people on the other hand, represent the cheated, oppressed and marginalized Biafran people. Even though the latter are vulnerable, there are prospects of their rebelling and seeking recognition, better treatment and a place in the larger socio-political schema. The treacherous Roof represents other ethnic groups that were happily serving Nigeria's interests, rather than teaming up to demand for their rights. These political undertones demonstrate Achebe's sense of commitment about which he asserts:

> If an artist is anything he is a human being with heightened sensitivities; he must be aware of the faintest nuances of injustice in human relations. The African writer cannot therefore be unaware of, or indifferent to, the monumental injustice which his people suffer (*Morning Yet on Creation Day* 99).

Achebe skillfully grafts the different meanings of the political (war) undertones on to the stories without losing the consistency of the outer meanings, which are equally useful in teaching about the people's lives and values. This is in consonance with his contention that:

> It is clear to me that an African creative writer who tries to avoid the big social issues of contemporary Africa will end up being completely irrelevant like that absurd man in the proverb who leaves his burning house to pursue a rat fleeing from the flames (*Morning Yet on Creation Day* 78).

In spite of the brevity of the short story form as juxtaposed with the novel, Achebe has carefully adjusted the language to suit his intentions. His use of the proverb, transliteration, local color, myth and other folkloric elements makes for a celebration of the Igbo (and Nigerian and African) identity, with which his writings are always associated. In "The Madman", the first medicine man describes Nwibe's insanity as the condition of:

> ...a man who has sipped the spirit-waters of ani-mmo. It is the same with a madman who of his own accord delivers himself to the divinities of the market-place.
>
> They have already embraced him. It is like a man who runs away from the oppression of his fellows to the grove of an *alusi* and says to him: Take me, oh spirit, I am your *osu*. No man can touch him thereafter. He is free yet no power can break his bondage. He is free of men but bonded to a god (10, 11).

Achebe essentially explains the belief of his Igbo people in the potency of the supernatural. He fully explores the *Osu* caste system in "Chike's School Days", thus emphasizing his people's recognition of this class system. These have been made manifest through his dexterity in the use of language to capture the nuances of the people's ways of life. Significantly, Achebe does not use the stories to uphold any ideology. The portrayals are so apt and realistic as to be relevant to both the young and adult. The stories generally derive relevance from the African folkloric tradition, which involves conveying messages through story-telling, and his messages span from the sociological to the economic as well as the political, and sometimes, more than one of these concerns occur in one story. His art, through which he teaches in the stories, seems a part of the process of atonement with his past, the ritual return and homage of a prodigal son, which was begun in *Things Fall Apart* ("Named for Victoria ..." 38).

In conclusion, Achebe's background and sense of commitment account for the contiguity between his writings and the Igbo cultural essence; where the former is conceived in terms of the historicity as well as the recreation of the religious values of a people. His writings resonate with the folktales he was exposed to at childhood. From then, Achebe's mind vigorously (even if unconsciously) internalized and processed the skills. These were enhanced by his strict Christian background, which luckily, did not abhor story-telling as some extreme cases did at that time. The apparent consanguinal relationship between the novels and the short stories is highly significant. Apart from showing his adeptness in handling similar issues successfully across the boundaries of genres, it emphasizes the relevance of the issues he explores, which actually transcends time and space within the Igbo cosmic world. The pedagogy in these issues is apt and elaborate as it spans from the spiritual to the secular.

Works Cited

Achebe, Chinua. "Africa's Tarnished Name". Another Africa: Photographs, Essays and Poems. Robert Lyons and Chinua Achebe. New York: Anchor Books, 1996

———. *The Trouble with Nigeria.* Enugu: Fourth Dimension, 1983.

———. *Morning Yet on Creation Day: Essays.* New York: Doubleday, 1975.

———. *Girls at War and Other Stories.* New York: Doubleday, 1972.

———. "Named for Victoria, Queen of England". *Hopes and Impediments: Selected Essays.* New York: Doubleday, 1989: 30–39.

———. "The Novelist as Teacher". *Hopes and Impediments*: 40–46.

———. *A Man of the People.* London: Heinemann, 1966.

———. *Arrow of God.* London: Heinemann, 1964.

———. *No Longer at Ease.* London: Heinemann, 1960.

de Certeau, Michael. *Heterologies.* Trans. Brian Massumi. Linneapolis: University of Minnesota Press, 1986.

Nnolim, Charles. "Achebe As A Social Critic". *Eagle on Iroko: Selected Papers from the Chinua Achebe International Symposium 1990.* Ed. Edith Ihekweazu. Ibadan: Heinemann, 1996: 166–177.

Obiechina, Emmanuel. "In Praise of the Teacher". *Eagle on Iroko*: 22–41.

Okafor, Dubem. "History and Ideology in *A Man of the People*". *Eagle on Iroko*: 178–193.

Ola, Virginia U. "The Conflict of Genius and Discipline in *Arrow of God*. *Eagle on Iroko*: 95–104.

Palmer, Eustace. *The Growth of the African Novel.* London: Heinemann, 1979.

Sofola, Zulu. "The Bogey of African Writer's Language Limitations in the Creative Process: The Core of the Matter". *Literature and Society: Selected Essays on African Literature.* Ed. Ernest Emenyonu. Owerri: Zim Pan African Publishers, 1986: 168–178.

Chapter 5

Archetypes and the Quest for Excellence in Chinua Achebe's Early Novels

Jasper A. Onuekwusi

EVERY INDIVIDUAL, ESPECIALLY THE CREATIVE ARTIST, has certain events, ideas, objects or images which by education, experience or impression are fixed on his recurrent repertoire. He may have taken these from his cultural group or race, but they are always significant in determining his actions and expressions even when he seems to have forgotten them. Carl Jung in Holman explains this better when he states that "behind each individual's Unconscious" – the blocked-off residue of the past – lies the "collective unconscious" of the human race – the blocked off memory of our racial past even of our pre-human experiences" (34).

However the creative artist usually the knowledgeable, highly and perceptive person, reminds the society of these images, patterns, plots and ideas as he elevates them in various creative efforts to archetypes. Holman defines an archetype as:

> an image, a descriptive detail, a plot, a pattern or a character that frequently occurs in literature, myth, religion or folklore and is therefore believed to evoke profound emotions in the reader because it awakens a primordial image in his unconscious (34).

T.S. Eliot in Holman emphasizes the primacy of the creative artist as the sustainer of the "collective unconscious" (and therefore of archetypes) when he asserts that the "prelogical mentality" persists in civilized man, but becomes available only to or through the poet, and that the "primordial image which taps this pre-logical mentality is called the archetype" (34) Leslie Fielder opines that recent interest in archetype and mythological studies emanate from critics' sense that "the deepest meanings, meanings which extend beyond the single work to a whole body of books, are to be sought in archetypal symbols to which writers compulsively turn" (249).

This paper affirms that Achebe's use of the novel as a means of creative expression was a response to the grave need to rectify a race that was given a most superficial picture. It was a defense for a people whose essence was reduced and who needed to regain confidence in themselves. It was therefore necessary for Achebe to return now and again to those patterns, character types, plots and indeed images that were significant to his people in order to achieve "the deepest meanings that extend beyond the single work" for his society.

A reading of Chinua Achebe's *Things Fall Apart* and *No Longer at Ease* reveals the author's persistent interest in "great" men in quest of excellence who are often overwhelmed to the point of fatality by uncontrollable forces in themselves and in their societies. They are men whose efforts to epitomize excellence are finally scorned and rejected by their societies.

Although earlier studies of these novels hurriedly put their protagonists into the mould of the classical Aristotelian tragic hero, this study posits that the explorations of these antagonists transcend a writer's mere quest for conventionalism. Undeniable as the classical tragic hero interpretation may seem, these protagonists are rather emanations from the "civilized" writer's effort to preserve, perhaps unconsciously, those prehistorical areas of knowledge articulated in his culture which have great meaning and appeal and which feature ever so often in the narratives of his people.

Charles Nnolim writes about the protagonist of *Things Fall Apart* thus:

> Many a critic has pointed out Okonkwo's resemblance to Aristotle's tragic hero, and the construction of the plot in the manner of Greek tragedy. I see the work as sharing many things with the classical epic – the warrior-hero, the temporary exile of the hero, the hero's embodiment of his national cultural aspirations, the glorification of the national heritage and so on (28).

It may be observed that Okonkwo Unoka in *Things Fall Apart*, Ezeulu in *Arrow of God*, Obi Okonkwo in *No Longer at Ease* are complex modern equivalents of simple man-on-a-journey archetypal protagonists whose destinies are tied up with those of their societies and who often feature in Igbo oral narratives. Whether as animal or human heroes or even gods, many protagonists in Igbo oral narratives often undertake journeys of one kind or another in quest of excellence in the form of recognizable social, moral or ethical ideals with which to enhance their dignity or valorize their communities.

Emmanuel Obiechina suggests in his study of the journey motif in Igbo narratives that the popularity of this mode arises from widespread conception of life itself as a journey. He explains thus:

> The journey motif is well-developed in Igbo narrative whether in traditional narrative text or texts written and oral that refer to more recent experience. Characters are engaged constantly in journeys of one kind or another, real and imagined, terrestrial and cosmic, physical and metaphysical, literal and symbolical, historical and mythical, external and internalized. Journeying to them is a mode for working out individual destinies, controlling realities and clearing up contradictions and ambiguities that beset life from birth (27).

Whether the journeys take the protagonists across "seven hills and seven seas" and last seven days and seven nights as formularized in some mythical Igbo narrative tales or across vast lands and waters in steam boats, aeroplanes or cars as in the modern novel, the journey remains for the protagonist a means of dispelling insularity and "inexperience." It is veritable means of expanding his consciousness, and his boundaries of knowledge, of broadening his cognitive potentiality and adding some more to his repertoires of ready experience with which he confronts the vagaries of life. Indeed, the journey becomes the protagonist's means of seeking excellence. How well he handles the overwhelming internal and external forces he confronts while on this journey determines his success in his quest for excellence and indeed his success in upholding or ruining his vital interests and those of his community and culture.

My analysis of the journey-and-quest-for-excellence archetypal protagonist in this paper is restricted to Achebe's three early novels because of two reasons. In addition to their publications being close to the transition from oracy to writing, a remarkable phase in the development of African literature, Chinua Achebe gives consanguinal links to prominent characters in *Things Fall Apart* and *No Longer at Ease* which deepen our appreciation of archetypes.

Secondly, the journey motif is for the protagonists of these early novels a means of trying out their moral positions on which their excellence and survival depend in a way it is not in the later novels.

The protagonist in *Things Fall Apart*, Okonkwo Unoka begins his life as a prodigious teenager who at eighteen throws a renowned wrestler in a most remarkable contest. He soon becomes one of the greatest men of his time. His prominence is even more remarkable because he is a foil to his indolent and romantic father, Unoka. He is born into a society where one's fame and indeed excellence rest on solid personal achievements. He starts off every life on a mental and physical journey in quest of various indices of excellence in his society. These include ownership of a large family of many wives and children, large yam barns, and many titles. It also includes occupation of a respectable position in the social hierarchy of the people and being a leader of the people whose words and actions count in the scheme of things.

Okonkwo goes to Nwakibe to borrow seed yams. Soon after, he becomes an expert farmer and owns large yam barns, three wives, children and three titles of the land. He becomes a revered elder, a great warrior who brings home five human heads, a member of the council of masquerades and a man who can be trusted with weighty responsibilities. Very early in Okonkwo's quest for excellence, a concerned elder and kinsman finds it pertinent to caution him about his rigidity, brusque impatience and lack of regard for less successful men like Osugo whom he called a woman. The caution was in the proverb: "Those whose palm kernels were cracked for them by a benevolent spirit should not forget to be humble".

In the words and essence of this proverb are found some of the factors that predispose Okonkwo to his inability to successfully complete his journey and his quest for excellence. He is proud, in fact, arrogant. He is altruistic, in fact foolhardy. He is rash and often tactless. Ernest Emenyonu rightly concludes that Achebe's preoccupation in *Things Fall Apart* is with the fate and destiny of a large section of humanity and not necessarily the rise and fall of this one man (47). This is because Okonkwo's destiny is inextricably tied to that of his community and his crude decimation of his larger-than-life posture is indeed the decimation of his community. In fact, he is representative of a people whose quest for excellence as defined by them is destroyed partly by flaws in their personalities and partly by a belligerent and arrogant group that mindlessly arrogates to itself the position of judge of cultural excellence.

Driven by an obsession for excellence, Okonkwo early in his journey determines to shun anything that suggests that he is weak. He struggles hard to hide some feelings of love he has for his wives and children. His extreme rigidity and rashness drive him into trying unsuccessfully a "male Ochu" by pulling the trigger at his own wife in the "weak of peace".

Although the later killing of a kinsman at a funeral is inadvertent, the possibility of the act lies more at all times with the rash and the careless; with the man who finds fulfillment only when he is noticed; with the man who can slash off the head of a "son" so as not to be called a weak man. Be that as it may, this "female Ochu" and subsequent exile reduce Okonkwo's worth. It is a physical, social and economic misfortune to the archetype in quest of excellence. It is an unfortunate hiatus in a rising graph of successes. Bernth Lindfors captures the fortunes of Okonkwo in simple language:

> *His entire life has been a struggle to achieve status; he*
> *has almost attained a position of pre-eminence when*

he accidentally kills a kinsman. For his crime, he must
leave his clan and live in exile for seven years.

When he returns at the end of the seventh year,
he finds that things have changed in his home village.

Okonkwo tries to rouse his clan to take action against
these foreigners and their institutions. In a rage he kills

one of the District Commissioner's messengers. When his
clan dose not support his action, he commits suicide. (6)

But Okonkwo is on a journey that determines personal and group excellence. While living in exile, he loses his premier position in the traditional schema. On his return to Umuofia, he is unable to redefine the indices of excellence in the new dispensation. He relies on old strategies and old yard-sticks such as show of brute force and rashness, fiery temper, resistance to change and rigid show of 'manliness complex' to acquire excellence in the new environment. He becomes a victim of tragic possibilities open to extreme tendencies. Achebe aptly expressed this in an interview when he says:

life just has to go on and if you refuse to accept changes,
then tragic though it may be, you are swept aside (14).

Okonkwo is swept aside. He hangs himself and is buried like a dog. It is ironic that in spite of his quest for excellence, Okonkwo does not ultimately rise above his father. He is an "outsider" to his people especially on his return from exile. He is unable to understand his new environment and to apply reason to his obsessive quest for excellence. These are the personality traits that predispose him to the fatal fall. But also important are the overwhelming forces in his environment. Okonkwo therefore dies a lonely man, a subject of scorn and a father of a weak son. He is buried by strangers perhaps in the "bad bush" like his father. This is a final show of revulsion from the clan, which is unable to accommodate Okonkwo's inability to change with the times.

Obi Okonkwo, the protagonist in *No Longer at Ease*, is the grandson of Okonkwo Unoka, the protagonist in *Things Fall Apart*. Achebe's indication of this consanguinal relationship helps our contention on his use of archetypes in his early novels. Unoka, the romantic artist, is ultimately an outsider to his society. He hates blood and violence. He is indolent by his people's assessment but strives unsuccessfully after excellence in the way of being a master artist and a benevolent epicurean. He is stopped on his journey to excellence by his inability to control his epicureanistic tendencies and to live within the values of his clan. He dies of the *swollen disease* and is given a dog's burial in the *bad bush*. Also, Okonkwo's unwillingness to be guided by the "new" values of his clan at a particular time in the clan's historical evolution causes Okonkwo's ignominious end. But it is in the lives of Isaac Okonkwo who is also Nwoye, the indolent, weak and good-for-nothing son of fiery Okonkwo in *Things Fall Apart* and the former's son, Obi Okonkwo that we find most vividly illustrated, the tragedy of the life of an outsider in quest of excellence defined outside the areas of acceptability of his clan.

One of the early recipients of Christianity, Isaac Okonkwo becomes a church teacher and is obsessed with the preaching of the gospel. Averse to violence and rashness like his grandfather Unoka, his father brands him a failure early in *Things Fall Apart.* One kinsman intimates the others with the fact that Isaac Okonkwo fails to attend the burial of a parent, a shameful act which is repeated by his grandson, Obi Okonkwo, the protagonist in *No Longer at Ease.*

Even in these, we see "a pattern or a character type, indeed an archetype that occurs frequently" in Achebe's early novels. Shatto Gakwandi describes Obi Okonkwo as:

> ...a patriotic, but in some ways, naïve young
> graduate who aspires to rid his country of moral and
> social ills which he attributes to backwardness. Slowly,
> as his enthusiasm becomes eroded by the temptations of
> privilege and the stresses of living in a decaying social
> system, he succumbs to a deep pessimism and acknowledges
> the inadequacy of his generation in providing answers
> to the complex dilemmas of modern Africa (27).

The above again illustrates the initial contention of this paper which is that Achebe's protagonists in his early novels are men whose quests for excellence are ruined by their inability to survive the throes of personal flaws and the overwhelming forces in their environments. While Unoka unsuccessfully tries to reach excellence in art especially music, poetry and dance, Okonkwo in warfare and protection of cultural values, Isaac Okonkwo in Christianity, Obi Okonkwo fails to reach excellence in moral regeneration and social engineering.

All archetypes fail, for the greater part of their quests are antithetical to the prevailing mood and values of their times. Like his forbears on the journey to excellence, Obi Okonkwo, the representative of the African intelligentsia ever ready to lead in a new post-independence Africa, the pride of his people, loses his bearing and ends up pathetically and ignominiously as a convict and a prisoner. He is unable to understand the contradictions of his life style. He is too weak and sentimental to continue in his quest and does not dare to rise to any social commitment. He gets into conflicts with his fiancée, his own family, his kinsmen, his own ideals and the law. When Obi Okonkwo returns to Nigeria, he tears the euphoristic and sentimental poem he wrote on Nigeria while in Britain. In fact, his destruction of the poem symbolically shows his inability to uphold the ideals and values he acquired in his journey in quest of excellence. It is the highest point of his disillusionment and a final resignation from the arduous task of educating his people and cleaning, the augean stable that is his social environment.

If we can find this archetypal pattern running in the Unoka lineage, it is unquestionably the case in the life of Ezeulu in *Arrow of God*. At the beginning of his quest for excellence, Ezeulu is a good priest of his god, Ulu who dutifully mediates between this great deity and the people of Umuaro.

He is a cultural enthusiast and indisputably a dignified lover of his community. The pumpkin leaves festival during which he carries with dignity and altruism the annual sins of his people, the strictness with which he keeps the community's agricultural, religious, economic and political calendar, his readiness to part ways with his community in defense of truth are undeniable qualities of a man in quest of excellence. He is fortified in his bid by his annual recapitulation of the mythic journey that established the almightiness of his god and its priesthood. Part of Achebe's credit in *Arrow of God* lies in the reader's diverse understanding of Ezeulu. To some, he is a headstrong priest who overreaches himself in his selfish protection of his power and self esteem. To others, he is an uncompromising votary of his god and an avowed defender of the sanctity of his people's culture. To others still, he is a little minded avenger who is ready to destroy his people for neglecting their priest. Each position raises questions and answers. Whatever one's stand is, one fact is indisputable. Ezeulu fails in his quest for excellence like Unoka, Okonkwo, Isaac and Obi Okonkwo because of personal and social problems. The intrigue of lesser priests of lesser god tasks his ego and makes him unleash bitterness into the politics of Umuaro pantheon.

Secondly, his obstinacy, a purely personal trait, his inability to choose between the new and old and indeed a latent ambition to be priest, king and all blind him to the limits of social reality. When he refuses the pleas of all Umuaro that he eat the remaining ritual yams, he seeks excellence outside the limits of acceptability in his society. He challenges the very basis of his existence and that of his deity.

But excellence in any time and place is socially defined, socially adopted or socially repudiated. Umuaro therefore takes liberties with Ulu and ultimately abandons Ezeulu. The death of Obika and subsequent insanity of Ezeulu are Achebe's attempts to emphasize the failure of Ezeulu's quest for excellence.

Perhaps, Ezeidemili's sober reflection on the tragedy of Ezeulu is the deepest meaning to which Achebe *compulsively turns* in the *whole body of books* discussed. On hearing of the death of Obika, this priest of a rival god says that *this should teach him* (Ezeulu) how far he could dare next time (228). Generally, cautious realization of limitations is necessary for the African's quest for those values that define his essence. This fact is prominent in Achebe's early novels and is the ultimate lesson that "the novelist as teacher" reinforces through the use of archetypes. It stresses the "deep meaning" in the explicit concluding statements in *Arrow of God*:

> *no man, however great was greater than his people;*
> *no one ever won a judgment against his clan (228).*

Indeed, Achebe's early novels will remain the unparalleled classics of our time because of the serious, fundamental issues they raise.

Notes

1. Unoka in *Things Fall Apart* is Okonkwo's father and Nwoye's Grandfather. Nwoye, Okonkwo's indolent son and one of the first recipients of Christianity in *Things Fall Apart* is Isaac Okonkwo who is Obi Okonkwo's father in *No Longer at Ease*.

Works Cited

Achebe, Chinua. *Things Fall Apart.* London: Heinemann, 1958.

———. *No Longer at Ease.* London: Heinemann, 1960.

———. *Arrow of God.* London: Heinemann, 1964.

———. in *African Writers Talking.* Ed. Cosmo Pieterse and Dennis Duerden. London: Heinemann, 1972.

Eliot, T.S. Quoted in Hugh Holman. *A Handbook of Literature.* 4th Ed. Indianapolis: Bobbs Merrill, 1980.

Emenyonu, Ernest N. *Studies on the Nigerian Novel.* Ibadan: Heinemann, 1991.

Fielder, Leslie. Quoted in Wilbur Scott. *Five Approaches of Literary Criticism.* New York: Collier Books, 1962.

Gakwandi, Shatto. *The Novel and Contemporary Experience in Africa.* London: Heinemann, 1977.

Jung, Carl. Quoted in Hugh Holman. *A Handbook of Literature.* 4th Ed. Indianapolis: Bobbs Merrill, 1980.

Lindfors, Bernth. "The Palm Oil with which Achebe's words are Eaten" in *African Literature Today* 1–4. Ed. Eldred D. Jones. London: Heinemann, 1972.

Nnolim, Charles. *Approaches to the African Novel: Essays in Analysis.* Port Harcourt: Saros International, 1992.

Obiechina, Emmanuel. *Ahiajoku Lecture.* Owerri: Ministry of Information and Social Development, 1994.

Chapter 6

"Saturday Nights": Pidgin English as a Stylistic Element in Chinua Achebe's Fiction

Nicholas Pweddon

Introduction

On the role of pidgin English in African literature today, Chinua Achebe declares:

> I have used pidgin. I think that pidgin has a possibility in a particularly limited sense. I do not think it has enough flexibility to carry all that I want to say. I can see its possibility on the stage. I can see its possibility in certain forms of dialogue, not just the dialogue of any particular class of people, because it goes through all classes of Nigeria. A man who spoke standard English would use pidgin for a certain purpose, and I think it can be used in that way in literature. (In Morell 45).

From the point of view of this paper, the last sentence is the most relevant: the use of pidgin for a particular purpose in African literature. The main body of this paper will be devoted to the analysis of the use of pidgin in Achebe's tetralogy, his first four novels and shorter fiction. Meanwhile, we shall look at one or two aspects of Achebe's use of language which are also germane to this study.

Achebe is a sensitive user of the English language. His belief is that African writing in English should attempt to secure "verisimilitude by rendering African speech literally into the metropolitan language (Quoted by Young, 72). He contends that language should not only be correct grammatically; it must also be accurate geographically. He, however, warns that before a writer can bend the grammatical rules of English, he must do so through his command of it and not out of ignorance or innocence. Since the African artist has an experience which is peculiarly African, it behoves him to find a medium through which his thought-patterns can be adequately expressed. This is what Achebe has in mind when he talks of "a serious writer" looking "for an animal whose blood can match the power of his offering" while discussing "The English Language and the African Writer." In the same article, Achebe answers a number of questions on the role of English as a medium of communication and as a vehicle for literary expression. Can the African writer effectively convey his peculiar experience in English? Should he try to speak and use English like a native English speaker? Achebe insists that on no account should the value of English as "a medium of international exchange" be compromised. But because he has something new to impart to his fellow Africans and the world, it is neither necessary nor desirable for him to be able to use it like a native speaker. He goes on:

> The African writer should aim to use English in a way that brings out his mes-
> sage best without altering the language to the extent that its value as a medium of
> international exchange will be lost. He should aim at fashioning out an English
> which is at once universal and able to carry his peculiar experience. I have in
> mind here the writer who has something new, something different to say ... A
> serious writer must look for an animal whose blood can match the power of his
> offering ("The English Language and the African Writer" 21).

To enable the English Language to retain its international currency in his art, Achebe confines to dialogue the use of proverbs and tales, translated from Igbo. It is also for that reason that he restricts the use of pidgin to dialogue. Moore correctly points to how Achebe's "judicious mixture of translation and authentic invention produced a conversational style which walked through his pages with all weight of formality, precedence and tradition, yet never stumbled over itself through in-eptitude" (152). The Nigerian critic, John Pepper Clark, attributes most of Achebe's literary achievements to the ingenious use to which he has put that graded speech, a peculiar literary device that has enabled him to define "the relative superiority of social stations among characters" and to find "for himself a voice of balanced tones, adequate for his purposes, faithful to the facts, and fair to all sections of his reader-ship." The language is thus inextricably woven into the texture of his fiction and in harmony with his themes. That is what distinguishes Achebe from the ordinary run of African writers. His remarkable use of these various speech patterns in his creative writing makes his fiction reflect the African environment and ground his art in contemporary reality.

Having looked at what constitutes Achebe's philosophy of language and how language as a tool should be utilized, it is relevant to examine the status and stylistic purposes of pidgin in Africa. The linguistic origins of pidgin appear to be shrouded in obscurity, and historical linguists do not appear to agree on the provenience of the name. Mihalic maintains, for instance, that "this language began amongst the New Britain peoples who were working as indentured labourers in the plantations of Queensland about a century ago (1). Robert Hall disagrees with that view and sees Canton, China as the place where "business English" was turned into "bishin" to give rise to the present term "pidgin". This corruption of "business", according to Hall, was completed in 1843 (30). Ramson has a slightly different theory. While not completely discounting a possible Chinese corruption of "business", Ramson thinks that the origin of "pidgin" can be linked to "Pidian", an archaic word for the Indians on the border between Brazil and French Guiana (102–103). The acrimonious debate raging on its ultimate origins is absent on the factors which gave rise to its emergence.

Pidgin came into being on the West Coast of Africa to satisfy a desperate and urgent desire to trade. It became a *lingua franca* "for African workers who have no first language in common, for white men of various ethnic and language backgrounds and for the coastal traders and transient peoples (Schneider 46). Over the years, people's attitudes to pidgin as a means of communication have evolved through diverse stages, and more extra linguistic and social factors have been considered in discourse on pidgin. Pidgin is regarded in some areas today as a rude "barbaric" perversion, "suitable for use only to natives" (Hall 46). Specifically, in West Africa, pidgin

> was frowned upon by the schoolmaster and swept under the carpet by almost
> all colonial educationists. Many Africans who made use of it were also made
> ashamed of it... (Spencer 5).

The emphasis is usually on the universally accepted formal written registers of conventional English as this is the medium for all scientific, literary and legal writings. It is also argued that pidgin is incapable of the highest cultural expression because it lacks abstract nouns and has limited vocabulary, and deficiencies which render it "unsuited for lofty artistic endeavour" (Hall 134) and aesthetic expression. Its proponents, naturally, have a different point of view.

They think that all the arguments against pidgin are culturally biased. Their experience is that despite the limited resources and heavy dependence on its base language, English, pidgin does have a grammatical and semantic structure of its own, but one which differs radically from that of English. They believe it is unfair to regard pidgin as a symbol of status, a caste language. My experience seems to bear out what the opponents of pidgin have been saying. Language is a tool man uses to communicate with his fellow men and pidgin English is not sufficiently sharp to convey all one wants to say on the human condition which is supposed to be one of the central concerns of any major literary work. One quality of it that usually frustrates attempts to use it for serious writing is its tendency to make people laugh. Achebe himself was asked at a class discussion to spell out the limitation of pidgin English. He notes that a

> version of a book of the Bible…was translated into pidgin in the Cameroons long ago. All that it did was make you laugh, … Now this is not the intention of the Bible (In Morell 46).

It is inadequate to insist that the range of meaning that pidgin conveys is wide enough in the milieu in which it is used. It will have to show that it has the capacity to give expression to literary and abstract truths. On the basis of present available evidence, it seems impossible to sustain a novel or a short story that really seeks to explore all aspects of human existence in pidgin English. It is apparent that the most important role of pidgin in African creative writing is to serve the "certain purpose" to which Achebe referred in his Seattle appearance (In Morell 45). That means that pidgin can be used as a symbol to represent whatever the artist wishes to convey to his readers.

Achebe's Use of Pidgin

As Schneider's quotation has explained, pidgin satisfied a desperate desire on the part of the various coastal traders and other groups in West Africa to communicate with one another in the past. That need still exists in different parts of the newly independent states of Africa. In Nigeria particularly, some two hundred indigenous languages are spoken, the people have to find a means of communicating with each other, a *lingua franca*. Recognizing that the ability to speak English is consequent upon attendance at school, in big urban Nigerian cities like Lagos, Jos, Enugu, and Kaduna, pidgin English is the common language of most people. In Achebe's *Arrow of God*, Nwodika's switching to pidgin when Clarke's non-Igbo speaking servant visits them is connected with this factor of linguistic heterogeneity (174–175). This is consistent with the structure of social reality in contemporary Nigeria. To stick to Igbo under that condition may be considered antisocial and unhealthy as far as communal harmony is concerned. This also explains why Chief Nanga is made to speak pidgin in the company of people like Mrs. John and the journalist who covered his speaking engagement to the staff and students of Anata Grammar School (*A Man of the People* 13). The use of pidgin as a contact language authenticates Achebe's art because that is the way people behave in Lagos, Port Harcourt and other big cities especially in the Southern States. The use of pidgin to indicate the absence of a common national language is just one aspect of pidgin as a literary symbol.

Achebe sometimes uses this speech pattern to exemplify his sense of humor. There is humor, for example, in the advice Chief Nanga gives Odili and other aspiring, ambitious young men on ministerial work. He has just declared that he is determined to "Do the right and shame the Devil" by respecting people who were senior to him in age despite his high position. From there he moved to:

> Minister de sweet for eye but too much katakata de for inside. Believe me yours sincerely. (*A Man of the People* 14).

We recognize that the "shame the Devil" sentiments mean practically nothing. It is the usual speech gilded with idealistic verbiage. "Katakata" is the corrupt form of the English "scatter", and means "trouble" or "problems" in its new pidgin environment. This is humorous because if a minister's job is so difficult, why does he remain in office and continue to molest those who dare to dissent? Why does he regard legitimate political opposition and other forms of dissidence as treason? Why has he not curbed the excesses of his political supporters? The advice is capable of arousing visible responses from his audience because of the hypocrisy involved. A situation normally amuses us when it assaults our logic and contradicts our perception of the natural order of things. That supposedly fatherly advice does just that. The humoristic element in "Believe me yours sincerely" lies in the inappropriate choice or mixing of registers. The phrase "yours sincerely", is a stylized expression normally used to end semiformal letters. The Minister's calculations are that the therapeutic effect of this humor should be such that his listeners, who are angry because of the repression they suffer would feel content with their current condition. But as Josiah puts it:

> I no kuku mind the katakata wey de for inside. Make you put Minister money for my hand and all the wahala on top. I no mind at all (14).

Translated into standard English as:

> I do not mind the problems involved. Just give me the minister's money plus all the trouble. It will not bother me.

It should be observed that Josiah's remarks are directed at Chief Nanga and not at ministers in general. In *A Man of the People*, "the Minister", spelt with a capital M, is specific; it always refers to Chief Nanga. Equally humorous is the use of the word nyarsh, pidgin English for arse, in the exchanges between Odili and the Local Council Policemen that come to arrest his father on the grounds of tax evasion. The arrest derives from the fact that Odili's father seems to support his son's opposition party, the CPC. The extensive reference to sex in this novel is significant and humorous. Sex is a primary source of most human conflicts and tensions, which can be released by humor. Our being asked to consider its relevance to a possible defeat of Chief Nanga is also humorous. Odili threatens to report them to their superior officers on the matter:

"Na only up you go take am?" asked their leader. "If I be you I go take am down too, when I done finish take am up. Turn your back make I see the nyarsh you go take fight Nanga." "Foolis-man," said one of the others as they left (126).

The use of nyarsh is not the only humorous element in that passage. Several other incongruous ideas are contained in it. One possible interpretation is that they have deliberately tried to be funny by asking him not to forget to take the matter down also with those in authority. Another view, which seems more valid because of what should be the educational background of Local Council Policemen, is that they have taken his statement literally. On the other hand, they seriously tell him not to forget in his calculation those of them who are the dregs of the society. In this sense, the humor remains because a reversal is portrayed in the proper bureaucratic channel of airing grievances. The juxtaposition of "up" and "down" is not only a distortion of the bureaucratic procedure; it is also an ingenious way of exposing what the people think and how they feel. This element of incongruity brings about aesthetic unity in that the opposed or contradictory elements need and supplement each other. It is like the genuine unity between contrasting colors that appear to contradict each other whereas in reality, they are a unified whole. Other instances of this phenomenon can be found elsewhere in Achebe's work. The reunion between Odili and Andrew is a case in point. Odili initiates the dialogue:

"How the go de go?" I asked
"Bo, son of man done tire."

Odili then inquires about a girl both of them know and Andrew feigns hostility to the subject:

"Why na so so girl, girl, girl been full your mouth."
"Wetin? So person no fit talk any serious talk with you. I never see."
"O.K., Mr. Gentleman," I said, pumping the lamp. "Any person wey first mention about girl again for this room make him tongue cut. How is the weather?"
He laughed (19).

This exchange of ideas is, of course, much more relaxed and informal than the one which took place between Odili and the Local Policemen. This is a meeting between friends who have not seen each other for some time. *Na so so* is *it is always* and Andrew's complaint is that Odili always talks about girls and leaves serious matters untouched. Odili labels him Mr. Gentleman because a *gentleman* is expected to be circumspect with women. Women are believed to be a "corrupting" influence that should be avoided. Odili reinforces his position with *How is the weather?* This is an obvious reference to Europeans, notably the British, who are said to have more pleasure discussing the weather than anything else. In the Nigerian context, it is a social formula that has no significance. Its application to the Nigerian situation where it is not usually employed can generate a humorous response from a reader. In *Girls at War*, humor of a slightly different nature is evident. This is not strange as most of the stories deal with the traumatic experience of the Nigerian Civil War. A friend of Nwankwo's house-boy expresses his ambivalence over the Nigerian bombers hovering over their bunkers:

> "I see dem well well," ...
> "If no to say de ting de kill porson e for sweet for eye. To Good (119).

He is thrilled by the sight of the raiding planes and the expressive nature of that sight gives him an aesthetic satisfaction. There is another element in his observation that is noteworthy: the last two words. Chief Nanga's "To God" (14) is parodied in the pidgin "To Good" which reverses normal expectations and evokes laughter. The multi-layered use of language here enables Achebe to realize several literary truths. Chief Nanga's interview of the cook he wishes to employ reveals Achebe's dexterous deployment of pidgin. The cook admits that although his food is African, he does not know how to cook African food because, as he asks rhetorically:

> "How man wey get family go begin enter kitchen for make bitterleaf and egusi? Unless if man no get shame" (44).

This cook's dilemma is, in a sense, the problem that faces Bori and the entire national leadership of the country: hypocrisy and a false sense of self-importance. This manifests in Chief Nanga's efforts to convince Odili, Josiah and others about his moral stature in his determination to *do the right and shame the Devil*. He feels that merely stating ideals should be sufficient to prove the purity of his intention. It does not occur to him that promises are in themselves meaningless unless they are redeemed. Having reneged on his promises, it is unrealistic for him and other national leaders to expect the people to believe that the ministers are espousing their cause. The cook, to maintain his dignity as a man is determined not to allow his name to be associated with the traditional kitchen. It is *infra dig* for him to learn how to cook African food. That is his wife's job. It is sometimes a job of monumental proportions to be able to say, in a particular situation or utterance, what is humorous or funny for the simple reason that taste is largely a personal experience. But the cook's pidgin illustrates what Achebe had in mind when he told his audience in Washington that pidgin had the tendency to make people laugh all the time. It is not implied here that what is humorous is necessarily so for the other characters in the novels or in the short stories because many of the characters lead a wretched form of life and are too busy with survival struggles. The fact still remains, however, that the use of pidgin has enabled Achebe to be austere in the use of language and this no doubt has increased the literary and aesthetic value of his tetralogy and shorter fiction. Using pidgin as a *lingua franca* and for humoristic and aesthetically satisfying purposes are two of the reasons why Achebe uses pidgin in his art.

A character sometimes chooses out of his total armory of linguistic competence, a speech style other than the pidgin that he should be speaking. This is done in order to enable him to distance himself from other characters. When this situation is created, it is usually the characters with superior social status that are made to speak conventional English or their mother tongues. There is, of course, nothing new in this device. One of the requirements of the canon of literary propriety is that all characters should speak according to the dialect of their class and education. Some writers employ "English foreigner talk" to indicate either their characters' imperfect command of the language or possibly also their attitudes of superiority towards others (Ferguson 3). Mrs. Emenike's refusal to communicate with her Small Boy in pidgin is a reflection on her superiority complex. To speak her servant's pidgin will put her on the same social wavelength with him. She orders him to reveal the source of his information about his father's reported sickness:

> "My broder come to tell me."
> "When did your brother come?"
> "Yesterday for evening time."
> "Why didn't you bring him to see me?"
> "I no no say Madam go wan see am" (55).

It may have been this supercilious attitude that makes her lose several of her servants to her neighbors. By sticking to standard English, she is able to keep a good distance from them. This subtle use of pidgin to suggest conflicting levels of social relationships and meaning is also evident in the encounter between Odili and Mrs. Nanga when they are discussing the Minister's proposed visit to the United States to receive an honorary doctorate degree. The main debate is hinged on Mrs. Nanga's qualifications for the trip. Her belief is that she is *too old and too bush* to accompany her husband. She feels that Edna should be in the Minister's company. The reference to Edna prompts Odili to ask who Edna is:

> "Don't you know about Edna, our new wife?"
> "Oh, that girl. Nonsense. She doesn't know half as much book as you."
> "Ah, she does o. I no go Modern School."
> "But standard six in your time was superior to senior Cambridge today," I said
> in our language, refusing to be drawn into one levity of pidgin (83).

Unlike Mrs. Emenike in the previous case, Odili switches from pidgin to his first language, not to orthodox English, to avoid being *drawn into the levity of pidgin*. Alternatively, if he chooses regular English as Mrs. Emenike does in the example above, Mrs. Nanga would not understand him since she speaks very little or no standard English (30). The technique here is to let actions speak louder than words.

When one character makes the change from the expected medium of communication, the hope is that the other character will be able to make his own deductions. The idea is to stylize speech and thought to reveal a distinctive quality of attitude or moral vision. Closely related to that is the use of pidgin to define what J.P. Clark calls "the relative superiority of social stations among characters, and perhaps their geophysical locations (*The Example of Shakespeare* 24).

Achebe employs pidgin to indicate the social attitudes and distinctions in mixed urban life. For convenience, this study adopts *class* as a descriptive term for J.P. Clark's social stations because the phenomenon is essentially class. In Achebe's *No Longer at Ease*, the encounter between Obi and the waiting patients at the clinic where his girlfriend is admitted in connection with her pregnancy, is a case in point. Obi jumps the queue and the doctor reports to him Clara' state of health. As he leaves the doctor's office, one of the patients decides to confront him openly and twit him with his transgression of the first-come-first-served code of ethics or etiquette. In doing so, she attacks his most visible social status symbol: the car. She calls him *beast of no nation* and declares:

> You tink because government give you car you fit do what you like. You see all of we de wait here and you just go in. You tink na play we come play? (*No Longer at Ease* 143).

Obi is not to think that because the government has given him a car he can trespass, and with impunity infringe on the rights of others. Contrary to the belief of the privileged, educated few, their society does not owe them a living and it is certain in Obi's own interest that he keeps that constantly in mind. This attitude dominates the interview between Chief Nanga and the man who seeks a cooking position in his house. Not only do they question the authenticity of his credentials, they label him an *idiot*. The atmosphere is one of condescension and there is no doubt that the applicant suffers mental anguish:

> "Wetin you fit cook?" asked Chief Nanga as he perused the young man's sheaf of testimonials, probably not one of them genuine. "I fit cook every European chop like steak and kidney pie, chicken puri, misk grill, cale omolett ... (43).

Apart from underlining the causes that eventually lead to the military coup at the end of *A Man of the People*, these conflicts between social classes are valuable from the aesthetic point of view in that the contrasts of character they present clearly create a balanced unity. John's complaint that he has worked at the supermarket is ignored despite his representations to the manager on *dis monkey work* (54). The driver who carries Obi to Umuofia has no reason to be diplomatic in his denunciation of educated people and others of similar higher social status. He blames Obi for having meddled in the discussion between him and the policeman and content that if Obi did not do that the policeman would not have found anything wrong with his documents. The driver believes that too much "book" knowledge is detrimental to the development of the society and that is why he does not like to carry such people in his *God's Case No Appeal*. He states that *too know na him de worry una.* (47). The privileged and the educated are too legalistic and unrealistic in their approach to life and he does not like anyone to tell him how to run his truck. This scene lends authenticity to the discourse because the exchanges are a common feature in commercial vehicles in Nigeria. Most drivers believe that attempts by so-called progressive elements to stamp out bribery and corruption do not alleviate the suffering of the masses. On the contrary, the attempts anger the police and make lorry owners lose more money than necessary.

Furthermore, part of the problem involved in the lack of communication between Obi and his house-boy is largely class. If Obi has explained to his servant why he plans to effect strict economic measures in his budget, perhaps the steward would have been more understanding. For Obi such an explanation would have been socially degrading on his image as a senior civil servant. All Obi tells him is:

"No need to buy plenty meat at once."
"Yes, sir."
"Buy small today; when he finish buy small again."
"Yes, sir. Only I tink you say I go de go market once every week."
"I said nothing of the sort. I said I would only give you money once." (98).

Obi's stratagem is to present a façade of financial and economic independence. This financial stringency is designed to preserve his social prestige. This is indicative of Achebe's subtlety in technique and it enables him to put views in counterpointed rhythm to demonstrate the disparity in living standards and world views in general.

In the dialogue between Odili and his political agents, some relevant issues emerge. Boniface and his co-thug believe that unless they have more money it would be impossible to defeat Chief Nanga and his party at the polls. They also need money to pay those who would burn the Minister's car. Their thought is that Odili's opposition cpc has an inexhaustible source of income like the governing pop and he has to choose his words with great care in explaining the position:

No be Government de give us money, ... We na small party, cpc. We wan help poor people like you. How Government go give us money ...? (108).

Odili condescends to speak pidgin with them and they try to socialize with each other. But there is no doubt that he is talking to his social inferiors whom he describes as "poor people." The policy of the cpc is to "help" them. That is why cpc has decided to espouse its cause against the pop. The thugs are exasperated and tell Odili:

> if you no wan serious for this business make you go rest for house … Dem
> tell you say na gentlemanity to give other people minister …? … Na you sabi?
> (109).

Boniface and his colleague condemns Odili's detestation of the Machiavellian tactics they are recommending. Once the end is attained, the means used becomes inconsequential. Gentlemanity here means to be constitutional and legal, the approach that will not defeat the Chief, because the fight against the Chief is like fighting a "tiger with empty hands." They want Chief Nanga removed by all means because they also would like to "chop", to enjoy the ease and comfort that the Minister and his colleagues have been enjoying before the military putsch at the end of the novel. This is admittedly not class in the Marxist sense. The people in this novel are not organized on an ideologically polarized and antagonistic basis with one another. The use of pidgin in Achebe's fiction does, in some respects, suggest the emergence of social classes among the populations now living in urban centers like Okperi Government Hill and Lagos.

Minor Characters' Use of Pidgin

Instead of using pidgin to expose the emerging social groups, Achebe makes minor characters use pidgin, like the Greek chorus, to comment on the conduct of the protagonists in order to give expression to the counterpoint of their superiors' leading melody of attitudes and mores. Their comment draws attention to the moral aberrations from the code of ethics and etiquette to which they should have appealed. For example, Elsie, having seen the *shiny famous Cadillac*, wants to know whether Chief Nanga and other ministers of state *go go another heaven after this* (55). She might have taken literally the biblical insistence that it is as difficult for a rich man to go to Heaven as it is impossible for a camel to pass through the eye of a needle. Her remark punctures attempts by the rich to inure public opinion to the existing state of affairs because, as Mrs. John advises the poor *when poor man done see with him own eye how to make big man e go beg make e carry him property de go je-je* (14). In other words, the wretched poor should be content with their present lot because that way they would not have to face the problems of being rich. Josiah corrects Chief Nanga's fantastic mis-statement of facts when he (Nanga) avers that ministers and other public figures gain nothing personally by being in office. Josiah believes that all ministers are in office for personal enrichment, not for altruistic reasons as the Minister says. The aesthetic aspect of this debate is that since it involves a struggle, it appeals to the fighting spirit and protective impulses. The precise nature and scope of one's empathy will depend on one's general world view. However, observations like the ones made by Josiah inject sober reality into the action and help illuminate the major character's moral blindness, folly, and other weaknesses or miscalculations. In fact, Chief Nanga's shrewdness in getting his thugs to make him acceptable to the public does not succeed. Dogo's reference to the Minister's supposed urbane conduct in: "How many minister fit hanswer sir to any Tom, Dick and Harry we senior them for age? I hask you how many?" (10), implies respect for old age, and stresses the extent to which the leaders of the country have deviated from the values that ought to guide them in their conduct of public affairs. The difference between promise and performance discredits the leaders. Their public behavior is not conducive to the promotion of genuine public interests, and the realization of this fact by the people is indicative of the hopelessness of the future of their country. Lest it be supposed that the bribery and corruption that Obi's lorry driver talks about is limited to the Police and the politicians, a case should be taken from *Girls at War* to show that the decline in public morality complained of by Odili and others pervades all facets of government.

In "Vengeful Creditor", for example, a minor character's experience reveals that not even the courts are free from corruption. Mr. and Mrs. Mark Emenike's gardener, who is twenty years or more, wants to go to school under the then newly-introduced free primary education in his area, but Mark Emenike warns him that if, for any reason, he fails to get admitted into a school, he should not hope to return to the job. The gardener, in an obvious positive spirit, expresses hope regardless of his age, revealing the case of a man (older than the gardener's father) who was admitted because he bribed court officials and obtained the school age stipulated in the statute. The gardener declares:

> I no go fail, oga, … One man for our village wey old pass my fader sef done register everything finish. He just go for Magistrate Court and pay den five shilling and dey swear-am for Court juju wey no kill porson; e no fit kill rat sef (57).

The servant is talking, of course, about the money one pays for a statutory declaration of age. His statement shows how decisively corruption has reached areas normally regarded as invulnerable to bribery and corruption. The generality of the people, crippled by the realization that not even the highest echelon of their society is clean, consequently lapses into despairing resignation. None, it would appear is prepared to work for the common good of all. The magistrates would only perform their legitimate constitutional duty when the promise of financial pay-offs is given to them. This significantly amounts to a repudiation of the guiding principles of their profession and responsibility to the people.

Pidgin as Imagery.

Pidgin, in Achebe's art is not just a language, but a device of imagery deployed to restrict the reader's observation and levels of awareness to a limited field of consciousness so that he can appreciate with more clarity the artist's literary and aesthetic world. In other words, it is more than a language used on "Saturday Nights" (107) in beer halls. Achebe's success in the use of pidgin both as a language and as a medium of literary expression lies in the consistency with which he uses it.

Joyce Cary's use of pidgin in *Mister Johnson* seems inconsistent. For example, when Budbeck refuses to grant Johnson's request for "a small small advance," "Johnson's despair is extreme." Johnson indulges himself in an interior monologue, describing his master as "de bes' man in de worl' ..." in pidgin. That speech style quickly gives way to another because after that description still in despair – Johnson switches to standard conversational English:

> I'm a fool. I'll take a knife and split myself up – that's all I'm worth. I'm a bad fool – I'm tired of myself (61, 62).

His conversation with Ajali on robbery also shows this inconsistency as the following piece indicates:

> "He my money," Johnson laughs at him. "He my sotre, Mister Benjamin – because I got de key to him!"
>
> "But, Johnson, if all people did so ... there would be nothing but bad trouble everywhere!"
>
> "Did you sell plenty cloth today, Mister Ajali? Did you buy me some good hides? Did you make plenty money for me? I go see now. Perhaps if plenty money no live, I give you de sack" (193).

Achebe's use of pidgin as a stylistic device is free from that irregularity. Something somewhat similar to that situation is found in Achebe's *A Man of the People* only when a character is speaking to other characters in one utterance. Chief Nanga does so while addressing Odili and the taxi-driver who conveys Odili to the Minister's quarters (29–30). When Max Kulamo misunderstands the reference Odili makes to the phone, he responds in both pidgin and standard English. The first part is in regular English because he thinks his friend is implying that he is not a successful lawyer. The second portion is in pidgin because he now realized that his reputation as a barrister is not in question. After that, they engage in intimate conversation in pidgin.

Another African writer who has made use of pidgin in his novels is Vincent C. Ike. In his *Toads for Supper*, he seems to be using a different technique. The protagonist, Amobi is not interested in pidgin English. Unlike Achebe's Christopher or Odili, he speaks standard English to everybody. He speaks impeccable English to the Porter at Oliaku Hall where his girlfriend, Miss Olowu, is residing although the Porter talks to him in pidgin. It is in standard English that he defends himself against Sweetie and her mother over Sweetie's pregnancy. In other words, Ike's pidgin serves as *lingua franca*, spoken mainly by people who are not literate in English. In *People of the City* Ekwensi shows the inconsistency that characterizes

Cary's *Mister Johnson*. For instance, Amusa Sango speaks pidgin only when his landlord, Lajide, informs him that his girlfriend, Aina, is arrested by the Police for stealing (10). In *Jagua Nana*, the reader is specifically told why Jagua uses pidgin at home and in Tropicana:

> Like Freddie she was an Ibo from Eastern Nigeria, but when she spoke to him she always used pidgin English because arriving in Lagos City they did not want too many embarrassing reminders of clan or custom. (10).

This survey shows the effective use of pidgin in African literature. In *Jagua Nana* when the two rivals for the Obanla constituency, Freddie and Uncle Taiwo, "began speaking in what Jagua regarded as "grammatical" ... she felt immediately excluded (150). But on closer examination, this impression is soon contradicted as Jagua herself begins to externalize her feelings in the same "grammatical English" she indicated lack of knowledge of. There is, in fact, abundant evidence that proves that she speaks that variety of English. When she returns late to Freddie and when she meets her brother, Funso, she uses "grammatical English". There is no suggestion anywhere that her speeches are translations from Ibo. That is inconsistency. It is from the dialogue between Jagua and Freddie that evening:

> "Freddie ..." came the low voice. "Anyone in de room wit' you?" He looked about him in the darkness. "Answer me, my loving Freddie! ... Anyone in de room wit' you? ... "I beg you: I want to come inside, Freddie. Is Jagua here – your woman" (48–49).

Jagua continued in that vein when her friend wanted to know the nature of her visit as they had quarreled before that visit. That is not what we have been made to expect with regard to her language. In fact, much of the encounter between her and Chief Ofubara is in orthodox English. Pidgin English is underscored in the following passage:

> I don' come here to sleep, Your Highness ... I come to beg for some favour.
> "You are very fair, my lady."
> "It is a big favour. And I am afraid to start."
> "Go on." He took her hand ...
> "My home town is Ogabu," Jagua smiled. "I be Ogabu lady."
> "All the women in Ogabu fine like you ... (98).

The episode in which Jagua withdraws into herself in an interior monologue on her attractive qualities is characterized by the same irregularity. Our final example for this portion is at the end of the novel when Jagua and her mother reminisce over the past and examine options for the future. Jagua thinks that Onitsha is the most strategic place for her business and her mother's fears that she would be forsaken by her daughter were quickly dispelled by Jagua in both conventional and pidgin English:

> "Mama, I don't know yet. But I wan' some place – not too far to Ogabu. Dere I kin trade. I kin come here when I like for look you. Ah wan' try Onitsha whedder I kin become Merchant Princess. I already got experience of de business ... (206).

It is largely on account of these internal inconsistencies in the use of pidgin in these other novels that the degree of integration with the chosen themes achieved in Achebe's fiction is sadly missing. Consequently, their use of pidgin does not seem to lend itself to as many levels of meaning and interpretation as Achebe's appears to do. Their use of pidgin dialogue is not great enough to generate what Moore, referring chiefly to the use of pidgin in *A Man of the People*, characterizes as:

> the humour and inventiveness of popular speech, its capacity for irreverence and deflation ... its capacity for registering reactions as naïve and potentially dangerous as those of Odili and Elsie faced with a shiny car and a uniformed chauffeur ... (55).

Unlike Achebe, they do not appear to have successfully "domesticated the English language" to the extent that it can "carry the full weight of what" (Lindfors 45) they want to say.

Pidgin, then, enables Achebe to realize a multiplicity of literary and aesthetic objectives. Its use reflects not only the linguistic heterogeneity of his world when he makes it serve as *lingua franca*, it also helps place his characters in relaxed situations and create an informal "Saturday Night" atmosphere that gives the reader an opportunity to see them in their natural state. Furthermore, pidgin, as used by the minor characters in Achebe's fiction is a vehicle for indicating the extent to which the leaders of their society have deviated from the definitions by which all ought to live. In this respect, their comments constitute not only an indictment of the lords of the land, but also a warning that their public conduct is prejudicial to public safety and communal survival. In that role, these otherwise socially inferior people become persons of superior insight, telling their compatriots how perilously close they all are to disaster as a national entity. Whether the dispute is between Chief Nanga and Odili or between Obi and his servant, minor characters, using pidgin as their weapon, show the leaders that their public statements lack both logic and moral strength. The leaders are then urged to abandon bogus reasoning and work for the good of all by subsuming their private vision under that of the state. Through that device, Achebe is able to expose the lineaments of that corrupt society and render more intelligible, the subtle differences that exist at various levels of the land. The conflicts between social classes and parties, like contrasting colors, cohere to make a unified, aesthetic whole in process. His use of pidgin, as a medium of literary expression, is able to take on this decisive significance because of the consistency with which it is used in the novels and the short stories studied for this paper. More significantly, and, from the point of view of art, pidgin has been kept within the fringes of international comprehension. By restricting its use to dialogue, Achebe does no violence to the natural syntax of the English language and leaves the structure of Nigerian social realism intact while its multilayered use adds extra dimensions to his fiction, a narrative technique that creates most of the tension in his fiction and promotes a high degree of verisimilitude while enabling characters such as Christopher to come "to terms with a double heritage" on "Saturday Nights" (106–107).

Works Cited

Achebe, Chinua. *A Man of the People*. New York: Doubleday, 1966.

———. *Arrow of God*. New York: Doubleday, 1964.

———. *Girls at War and Other Stories*. New York: Doubleday, 1973.

———. *No Longer at Ease*. Connecticut: Fawcett, 1960.

———. "The English Language and the African Writer." Insight. October/December, 1966.

Carry, Joyce. *Mister Johnson*. London: Michael Joseph, 1967 edn.

Clark, John Pepper. *The Example of Shakespeare*. Evanston: NUP, 1970.

Ekwensi, Cyprian. *Jugua Nana*. Fawcett, 1961.

———. *People of the City*. London: Heinemann Edition, 1963.

Hall Jr., Robert A. *Hands Off Pidgin*. Sydney: Pacific Publications, 1955.

Ike, V.C. *Toads for Supper*. London: Hawill Press, 1965.

Lindfors, Bernth. *Folklore in Nigerian Literature*. New York: Africana Publishing Company, 1973.

Mihalic, S.V.D. Father F. *Introduction to New Guinea Pidgin*. Camberra: The Jacaranda Press, 1970.

Moore, Gerald. *The Chosen Tongue: English Writing in the Tropical World*. New York: Harper & Row, 1969.

Morell, Karen L. ed. *In Person: Achebe, Awoonor, and Soyinka*, Seattle: Oxford University Press, 1972.

Ramson, W.S. ed. *English Transported: Essays on Australian English*. Canberra: ANUP, 1970.

Schneider, Gilbert D. *West African Pidgin English*. Ohio UP, 1967.

Spencer, John. ed. *The English Language in West Africa*. London, 1971.

Chapter 7

The Survival of Oral Speech Patterns in Modern African Literature: The Example of Chinua Acehebe's Fiction

Angela F. Miri

Works of art, much less works of literary endeavor, do not issue out of nothing; they are not created out of a historical vacuum, without any proper regard for the accumulated examples of the past. Modern African literature as has often been said was borne in adversity, as an instrument of protest against colonial exploitation and cultural domination. As such, African writers have written extensively not only to bring to general attention the plight of their people, but also, after independence they have continued to play a significant role in the process of nation-building. They have done so by reconstructing for their readers in the novels, plays and poems of outstanding beauty and merit, an image of a lost or vanishing Africa. Writers such as Chinua Achebe, Ngugi wa Thiong'o, Camara Laye, the Nobel Laureate Wole Soyinka, Elechi Amadi, and the poets Okot p, Bitek, Mazisi Kunene, Dennis Brutus, Kofi Awoonor, to mention only a few, by linking their works firmly to the sources of a viable African tradition have not only created fiction and poetic works memorable for their freshness, creative energy and originality but have also given us works which are in themselves acts of restitution of the "smashed up" African cultures.

The new poets, novelists and dramatists have had to begin by hacking away at the thick overgrowth of European legends, popular misconceptions and distortions of African history. They have had to destroy and to throw away in order to build again from the leveled ground up. The result of this was the creation of their own freshly conceived characters, heroes and villains cut out from the authentic cloth of human character and behavior in place of the stereotype and the caricature. It is as the renowned Kenyan novelist, Ngugi wa Thiong'o says, "What the African novelist has attempted, is to restore the African character to history" (Lewis Nkosi, 1977).

Critics have often referred to this attempt by African writers ("to restore the African character to its history") as being busily engaged in some form of window-dressing in which the past is idealized and the poverty of African history, where such a poverty exists, is conveniently down-played or outrightly concealed. This is an understandable reaction to centuries of European imperialist aggression which denied all semblance of dignity to the African past.

In fact, what distinguishes the new writing from Africa is its insistence on realism. Some writers seem even prepared to take more liberties with history than European outsiders would have thought proper to do. A writer like Yambo Ouologuem of Mali, in his prize-winning novel, *Bound to Violence* (Le devoire fe violence) goes further than any European chronicler, writing about Africa, would have considered proper or legitimate to go. Instead of the usual notion of Africa before the Fall, an innocent Africa before the white men came, Ouologuem gives us a picture of "hunger, sickness and privation," of bloodlust and greed when "under the lash of necessity a father sold his son, a brother his brother" and cannibalism "was one of the darkest features of that spectral Africa." Ouologuem is not an isolated example. The Ghanaian poet, Kofi Awoonor (*This Earth, My Brother*), has produced in his work another example of an uncompromising personal testament, full of the awkward allusions to the present state of African politics. Awoonor's novel is of a type which has become quite familiar in the post-independence Africa. Its deepest emotions are disgust, anger and despair at the corruption of ideals that has become a feature of post-independence African politics. Ayi Kwei Armah another remarkable Ghanaian novelist, has given a vivid expression to this sense of disillusionment in his first novel which, despite its many virtues and accomplishments, continues to attract criticism for the extreme sense of alienation it expresses. Other examples abound.

From the early 1960s to the present, African literature has grown in quality and output so that it has now become possible to stand back and take stock of this achievement. It has rightly been observed that the transition from speech to writing, from the spoken to the written word was not merely a technical change for it signaled also a major transition in modes of apprehension itself (Roy and Kirpal, 1989:9). However, specimens of African literature in English have revealed that oral forms do doubtlessly survive despite the adoption of the written medium in communicating literature.

In the light of the foregoing discussion, we can say very positively that Chinua Achebe, Africa's prolific teller of tales has exploited oral speech patterns in the expression of the African communal ethos and pathos as part and parcel of the people's tradition. Our task in this paper therefore, is to demonstrate how Chinua Achebe has employed writing as a means of presenting an oral or fluid culture specifically the African-Igbo traditional culture in some of his most outstanding novels.

Achebe has unarguably succeeded through his art in not only reconstructing African history but also his evocation of a traditional culture with a predominantly oral sensibility – a structure of feeling that is still in existence in the contemporary Nigerian society – which ironically employs the written mode for the narration of his tales. His works are among the first few written documents on the Ibgo of South Eastern Nigeria.

Achebe represents the Igbo traditional ways systematically compared to European ways without apology and consistently found to be better. There are critics, however, who would rather see this act of transmitting an oral culture through writing differently. Some view it as evidence of the writer's active participation in the process of the destruction or obliteration of that pre-literate world (Grifiths, 1971:89). Chris Wanjala (1980:xv) is also one of them. He believes this attempt is "alienation" of the writer shown in idyllic, picturesque depictment of the past, which he claims, is symptomatic of the writer's own alienation from reality. But Lewis Nkosi (1981) has also observed that this attempt by modern Africa writers (especially the "oral tradition school") represents an innovation that deserves applause.

Therefore, given the survival of the oral speech patterns and modes of perception in Nigeria and Africa as a whole (with a tradition that is essentially oral) despite the undermining influence of literacy and modernism (Obiechina, 1975 & 1980:27), it is possible and sensible to consider Achebe's fiction, namely *Things Fall Apart* (1958) and *Arrow of God* (1964) as oral accounts of Igbo life and culture. Achebe's other novels, *No Longer at Ease* (1960) and *A Man of the People* (1966) do not seem to function in the Igbo narrative tradition as explicitly or overtly as the aforementioned two texts. But, they too, conceal strikingly oral patterns and habits in their respective linguistic structures. Although the aforementioned four texts deal illuminatingly well but in varying degrees with matters of central importance for contemporary Africa, Achebe, nevertheless, does so using authentic African imagery, proverbs, laments, invocations and curses to mention only a few, thereby successfully rooting the modern in the tradition. There are instances in his fiction where clichés are rejuvenated, re-animated and re-contextualized to draw new meanings. Several examples of these will be seen in due course. Achebe goes about the business of presenting the Igbo traditional, cultural life in the following manner:

1. The Narrator

He employs first, the services of the traditional raconteur, the narrator or the oral teller of tales. In this regard, the legends of Okonkwo and Ezeulu, of Umuofia and Umuaro, are recounted by the oral artist whose conception of history is very different from those of the literary traditions. For the traditional African storyteller (herein engaged) takes into cognizance not only what has happened but also what is claimed to have taken place. He reconstructs the history of his people largely by drawing on myth and legend. While the unlettered narrator has the freedom to distort historical facts if need be (Okpewho 72), Achebe is unmistakably though painstakingly accurate and precise in recording the colonial infiltration of the Igbo bushland. Despite the absolute fidelity to historical truth, the colonial experience is presented from the perspective of the Igbo. The storyteller who undoubtedly represents the Igbo voice or the *vox populi* of the novels perceives and recreates this colonial experience in the popular language of myth and legend.

It is a well known fact that oral forms, including African myths and legends usually draw heavily on the repertoire of communal, traditional formulae. It is not surprising therefore that a commentary on the Igbo colonial experience in *Things Fall Apart* commences as follows:

> That was many years ago twenty years or more, and during this time Okonkwo's
> fame had grown like a bush fire in the harmattan (3).

The phrase – "many years ago" is a very familiar opening of many traditional tales and myths and this occurs several times in the course of the novel. It is also an indication of the proclivity of the local people to hark back to the past in order to clarify a present event. "Many years ago" reinforces the impression of "long ago", an uncertain, vague indefinite past in the manner of folk tales. As well, the elucidation "twenty years or more" underlines only an approximate rather than a precise number of years because, unlike modern man with his obsession for the minute segmentation of time, the unlettered man makes only broad divisions to mark time.

It is a characteristic feature of traditional African societies represented here by the Igbo culture that the history of the group is reconstructed not by naming and identifying dates and years but by stating time in relation to the phenomena and events that have significantly affected communal life. When Africans reckon time, it is for a concrete and specific purpose in connection with events but not just for the sake of mathematical correctness.

Savor the flavor of the following lines from *Things Fall Apart*:

> The year that Okonkwo took eight hundred seed yams from Nwadike was the
> worst year in living memory ...
> > That year the harvest was sad ...

> And that was also the year Okonkwo broke the peace and was pun-
> ished ...(26).

However, in *Arrow of God*, the time scheme seems to be more elaborately worked
out in terms of years. But the phrase "five years ago" occurs more as a refrain or
chorus. The emphasis here is on the events that distinguished that particular year
rather than on the exact date:

> On the day, five years ago, when the leaders of Umuaro decided to send an
> emissary to Okperi with white clay for peace or new palm frond for war, Ezeulu
> spoke in vain (15).
>
> In the five years since the white man broke the guns of Umuaro ... (38).
>
> It was five years since Ezeulu promised the white man that he would
> send one of his sons to church. But it was only two years ago that he fulfilled
> the promise (45).

In the traditional African-Igbo culture, time seems to move in a much more leisurely
way than in urban industrialized societies. No monumental event appears to have
taken place during those intervening years. The memory of hurts and enmities
incurred "five years ago" is still fresh and pressing. Even though the years are being
numbered, the traditional "phenomenal calendar" is in operation here rather than the
western "numerical calendar" (2). In traditional African society, time is still reckoned
in relation to calendrical or specific events as in the case of the Igbo culture – the
war between Umuaro and Okperi, the breaking of the guns by the white man, the
hostility between Ezeulu of Umuaro and Nwaka of Umunneora. Five years here
denote as do the "twenty years or more" already quoted in *Things Fall Apart*. Still,
in pre-literate societies, time seems to be fairly flexible, not necessarily confined to
an actual mathematical division of time. If "twenty years or more" are sufficient to
convert a living person (Okonkwo) into a legend, "five years" indicate a span whose
events still possess an immediacy with respect to the community's life.

Again, the propensity to mythicize every significant event is aptly expressed
in the formula, "the story was told."

> 'Abame has been wiped out,' said Obierika. 'It is a strange and terrible story'
> (*Things Fall Apart*, 124).
>
> The story of what these soldiers did in Abame was still told with fear.
> (*Arrow of God*, 28).

Situationally speaking, Achebe is making an actual historical reference to the
resistance offered by the natives of Abame during the Igbo-British encounter in
the interior of the African territory. Here again, even everyday events pertaining
to the members of the community become part and parcel of the common stock
of the communal repertoire:

> The story was told in Umuofia of how his father Unoka had gone to consult the oracle of the Hills and the Caves to find out why he always had a miserable harvest. (*Things Fall Apart*, 15).
>
> The story that the white man had whipped Obika spread through the villages. (*Arrow of God*, 87),

Although the communal cyclic consciousness of time has been replaced by the clock-time of the western industry and the office of the world of Obi and Odili, the old perception still asserts itself every now and then. For example, in *A Man of the People*, Odili combines a minute numerical awareness of hours with traditional leisureliness in dissecting time:

> I had not always disliked Mr. Nanga. Sixteen years or so ago he had been my teacher ... (2).
>
> The story had it that many years ago when Mr. Nwege was a poor, hungry elementary school teacher ... (13).

The traditional method of relating information still persists in Odili's style,

> They said this woman was a very close friend of the Minister's ... (15).
>
> A common saying in the country after independence was that it didn't matter what you knew but who you knew (17).

2. Repetition

Repetition, a glaring feature of African oral art is also in Achebe's fiction. It is correct to observe that the degree of repetition present in oral works if employed in writing would be tedious. It is in the light of the above that one can understand Marjorie Winters who has taken pains to explain that repetitiveness in written texts often leads to redundancy (Winters, 1981:62). But redundancy in oral art goes together with clarity. Redundancy or repetition in oral modes clarifies, underlines and reinforces. The significance of the rhythmic element in traditional African oral art can be seen in the use of repetitive devices by Achebe's narrator. The garrulous narrative voice of Achebe's fiction abounds in repetition or redundancy. The use of repetition is basically the product of the sort of emotional excitement that music in the traditional setting inspires.

Chinua Achebe, as a modern African writer is as conscious as the traditional oral artist of the emphatic value of repetition, but when he uses it (as he often does in his fiction), he is frequently more anxious to lend to his art a certain musical quality which reflects the rhythmic basis of the traditional literature. This is quite true of him (Achebe) and other African writers where a strong musical tradition has continued to survive. Anyone who is not familiar with the predominance of repetitive drum rhythms in, for example, Ghanaian culture will probably dismiss Atukwei Okai's Elvanyo Concerto or Soyinka's and Clark's "Abiku" as monotonous in their use of repeated sounds (alliteration, rhyme, assonance, etc). But for one who understands that tradition, Okai or Soyinka or Clark or Achebe for that matter is basically transferring to the printed page the kind of sounds that he grew up hearing (Okai, 1985:24).

The idea is that, although they accept to continue to use the European language to reach a wider audience even within Africa, they would wish to hear the rhythms of the native speech within the texture of their words. In fact, the desire to be closer to the language has driven many western educated African writers, especially poets to try their hands at writing poetry or fiction in their indigenous languages. Earlier generations had of course, done the same. In the late nineteenth and earlier twentieth centuries, a great deal of indigenous poetry was written especially in southern Africa, by writers like the Zulu B.W. Vitakazi and the Sotho B.M. Khaketla. Writing in the local language has indeed become, since the colonial era, a way of reasserting African culture. Both Gladys Casely Hayford in the 1940s and the Nigerian Frank Aig-Imoukhuede in the late 1950s used the West African pidgin in writing poetry. In 1981, the Nigerian novelist, Chinua Achebe, put together a volume of poems that he and his colleagues had written in Igbo under the title *Aka Weta*. Achebe's contribution to that volume is a dedicatory poem to the late poet Christopher Okigbo, written with phrases and structure taken from a well-known Igbo folk song. Such an effort on the part of an established writer like Achebe illustrates the strength of the modern writer's attraction to the oral tradition. Therefore repetitions in Achebe's fiction are not mere ornamentations but used for emphasizing a very significant point or a pressing need. It provides many details where one would suffice. It repeats and recapitulates at every opportunity.

Witness the following lines:

> The drums were still beating, persistent and unchanging. Their sound was no longer a separate thing from the living village. It was like the pulsation of its heart. It throbbed in the air, in the sunshine, and even in the trees, and filled the village with excitement (*Things Fall Apart*, 40).

One other way in which the modern African/Nigerian writer tries to return to his roots (the Igbo culture) is by achieving the musical basis of the traditional oral art. Many kinds of oral modes use music in one form or another: whether in the actual singing of songs, or in the meaningful control of tonal accents (as we find in Idoma, Igbo, Mernyang, Yoruba, etc), or else in the playing of musical instruments to provide background rhythm (Okpewho, 1985:24).

Achebe, the modern African writer is aware of how incapable writing is of achieving these ends, but he makes an effort to come close to them nevertheless. As it is evident, the opening of this passage introduces an idea which is repeated in the following two sentences. The drum beat, indissoluble from the living village in the first, is defined as "the pulsation of its heart" in the second. Its oneness is demonstrated by the way it permeates every "living" aspect of the village – "the air" "the sunshine", even "the trees".

Repetition, as used here serves the function of defining and explicating. It simplifies, it lessens the task of comprehension in the listener's mind. It also provides several examples to reinforce an idea and attempt to explore it from every possible perspective. Here is yet another example of the use of repetition:

> Perhaps in his heart Okonkwo was not a cruel man. But his whole life was dominated by fear, the fear of failure and weakness. It was deeper and more intimate than the fear of evil and capricious gods and of magic, the fear of the forest, and of the forces of nature, malevolent, red in tooth and claw. Okonkwo's fear was greater than these. It was not external but lay deep within himself, lest he should be found to resemble his father (*Things Fall Apart*, 13).

The listing of the various fears, "the fear of evil and capricious gods"… forces of nature: accentuates the shared, communal phobias. Against these are placed the personal, internal anxieties of Okonkwo spelt as the "fear of failure and weakness". Okonkwo's isolation is emphasized by defining first, the communal framework and then by underlining the private nature of Okonkwo's insecurity. The passage no doubt, illustrates the process by which the oral artist communicates with his audience, repeating for the sake of making his meaning clear, citing repetitious analogies to drive home his point. Again, this is a manner eminently suited to the bard and to the novelist who desires to educate the "alien" as well as the "alienated" in the grandeur of the African past.

3. Use of Etiological Formula

Achebe also transmits orally the culture of his people through the use of etiological kind of tale. Here, the predilection for elaboration and explanation in the traditional bard is associated with his pedagogic function. The etiological ending, "That was how" underlines the bard's responsibility to answer the unvoiced queries in his audience's mind, to transmit the wisdom of his race, to explain the reason and motives for happenings. Achebe's resort to the etiological formula, reflects a desire to leave very few questions unanswered, to explain motives and compulsions that give rise to certain action or behavior:

> That was how Okonkwo came to know that "*Agbala*" was not only another name for a woman, it could also mean a man who had taken no title (*Things Fall Apart*, 13).
>
> The man who had contradicted him had no titles. That was why he had called him a woman (*Things Fall Apart*, 24).

He must go on treating his grown children like little boys, and if they ever said so there was a big quarrel. This was why the older his children grew the more he seemed to dislike them (*Arrow of God*, 91).

4. Digression

As stated earlier, repetition, in oral narrative, is justified as a mnemonic aid. But redundancy and digressiveness are also related to the general expansive disposition of the oral narrative. The same digressive pattern is typical of Achebe's fiction:

> Okonkwo did not have the start in life which many young men usually had. He did not inherit a barn from his father. There was no barn to inherit. The story was told in Umuofia of how his father, Unoka had gone to consult the oracle of the hills and the caves to find out why he always had a miserable harvest (*Things Fall Apart*, 15).

In modern times especially in Christendom, this may probably be said to be the reason for the giving of tithes. It is necessary and emphasized. One can safely say in the light of the above quoted passage that as typical with the oral tradition, the traditional gods or oracles consulted by Okonkwo's father Unoka were not pleased with him which resulted in his usual poor harvest. A couple of pages later, the narrator resumes the same theme almost with the very word with which he had left off:

> With a father like Unoka, Okonkwo did not have the start in life which many young men had. He neither inherited a barn nor a title, nor even a young wife (17).

Isidore Okpewho explains this method as the "ring composition" in his *The Epic in Africa: Towards a Poetic of the Oral Performance* (Okpewho, 1979:194). The natural inflationary impulse of the bard, he asserts, leads him to inflate and expand. Typical of the oral artist that Achebe's narrator is, he employs improvisation, use of stock phrases and digression as his devices. In the passage above for example, the narrator, while recounting the tale of Okonkwo's career, makes a winding deviation which focuses not on Okonkwo but on his father Unoka. So the narrative first digresses into a description of the oracle Unoka had consulted and then goes on to give a detailed account of Unoka's converstion with the priestess of the oracle. But despite his fondness for digressing, the "bard" cannot afford to lose the train or thread of his main narrative thought. Therefore, he must return from Unoka to Okonkwo again. The "ring" – the resumptions of the theme with a repetition of the previous utterance – ensures and brings about stabilization and control. This is a miniature depiction of the grandeur of the oral performance of traditional African oral art. Also, the digressive structures flow over into the urban scene of Achebe's *No Longer at Ease*. Witness the following lines:

Mother's room was the most distinctive of the whole house, except for father's. The difficulty in deciding arose from the fact that one could not compare incomparable things. Mr. Okonkwo believed utterly and completely in the things of the white man and the symbol of the white man's power was the written word ...

Mother's room, on the other hand, was full of mundane things. She had her box of clothes on a stool. On the other side of the room were pots of solid palm-oil with which she made black soap (114–5).

The prospect of describing "Mother's room" leads to a digressive account of father's as well. A few paragraphs later the narrative returns to mother's occupations. The "ring composition" observed in the earlier novel is seen in this section as well.

5. Use of Annexions and Conjunctions

The recurrence of annexions in Achebe's work relates him to the oral storytelling traditions of Africa and Nigeria in particular which carried on its narratives in an "adding style". The paratactic construction of the texts, ostensibly in conformity with the spontaneous, improvised procedure of oral composition, is designed to produce clarity.

Commenting on the high incidence of connectives in Achebe's *Things Fall Apart*, Majorie Winters (62) asserts that these connectives account for the lucidity of his style. There is great variety in the manner in which the connective is employed:

Unoka loved it all, and he loved the first kites that returned with the dry season, and the children who sang songs of welcome to them (5).

And what made it worse in Okonkwo's case was that he had to support his mother and two sisters from his meager harvest. And supporting his mother also meant supporting his father (21).

Arrow of God reveals a larger occurrence of the connective "but":

But many people trembled for him that night in his compound when he had all but threatened Ulu ... But it did not follow that Ulu would also allow himself...(39).

More interesting, however, is the employment of the double connective "and so", Achebe finds in this combination an ideal way of summarizing the context of an elaborate argument or for underlining the effect of a certain action:

And so Okonkwo was ruled by one passion – to hate everything that his father Unoka loved ... (13).

And so Nwoye was developing into a sad-faced youth (13).

6. The Employment of a First-person Narrator

This archaic tradition or method of carrying on narratives in an "adding style" surprisingly can be traced in Achebe's urban novels as well.

The use of the first-person narrator in *A Man of the People*, who is so obviously "telling" his story) permits the introduction of paratactic structures:

> ... And when I got to the ward and was told with pointless brusqueness by a girl-nurse that my patient had been discharged yesterday I felt really downcast. ... so I drove from the hospital to Edna's place, although her father had told me three days earlier never to set foot in his house again. And for the first time since my return from Bori my luck was on. Edna was in and her father was out (104).

These similar structures can however, be seen in *No Longer at Ease* as well:

> After this there was another long silence. Then his father spoke, but not about the thing that was on their minds (125).

Evidently, oral linguistic style had been adapted in the delineation of the contemporary Nigerian milieu in the urban novels as well.

The distinction between the referential – denotative language of prose and the poetic, figurative, oral idiom seems to have been blurred in the modern poetic fiction. However, Emmanuel Obiechina appears to have seen a difference between the two. He demonstrates that the poetic language of a western writer in the literary tradition is merely an imposition of a "personal pattern of linguistic expression on life" through the medium of his "art" whereas the metaphoric style of African prose writers is the "reproduction of a social linguistic reality" (Obiechina, 170–1). In other words, the concrete, metaphoric idiom or oral literature is not a poeticization of reality but a distinct mode of perception. For the purpose of illustration, the following two descriptions of African rains are cited, one by Karen Blixen in *Out of Africa* and the other by our raconteur, Achebe:

> But when the earth answered like a sounding board in a deep fertile roar, and the world sang round you in all dimensions, all above and below – that was the rain. It was like coming back to the sea, when you have been a long time away from it, like a lover's embrace (*Out of Africa*, 41).
>
> And so nature was not interfered within the middle of the rainy season. Sometimes it poured down in such thick sheets of water that earth and sky seemed merged.
>
> In one grey wetness
>
> It was then uncertain whether the low rumbling of Amadiora's thunder came from above or below (*Things Fall Apart*, 31).

Each passage captures the rain in dual images, one visual and the other aural. Whereas Achebe's account is accurate and precise ("It poured down in such thick sheets of water"), Karen Blixen's analogy of the visualized long awaited meeting with the lover is highly subjective and personalized. Achebe also extends the literal – "poured down in such thick sheets of water" – with the allusive and metaphoric – "earth and sky seemed merged in one grey wetness." The analogy here is heightened by the reference to the traditional, folk theme of the relationship between the sky and the earth. He repeats this method while describing the sound of rain. He visualizes rain as the "rumbling of Amadiora's thunder" reflecting thereby the traditional African's propensity to apotheosize elemental forces and to regard natural phenomena as manifestations of divine wishes or desires.

Achebe's is no personal metaphor, but a part of the shared poetic tradition. Karen Blixen, on the other hand is inventing as it were, a poetic analogy.

7. Use of Personification

Achebe, also invests natural objects with human qualities. That is, he uses personification as well. The following lines illustrate the use of the device common in oral poetic renditions:

> Yam, the king of crops, was a man's crop (21).
> Yam, the king of crops, was a very exacting king (31).

The reverence towards planting yam can never find expression in a temperate and lifeless statement like for instance, "coffee growing is a long job" (*Out of Africa*, 18).

This is because the oral mind does not search for appropriate, catchy embellishments. Rather, it displays a natural inclination for analogical explanation:

> His power was no more than the power of a child over a goat that was said to be his. As long as the goat was alive it could be his, he would find it food and take care of it. But the day it was slaughtered he would know soon enough who the real owner was (*Arrow of God*, 3).
>
> Perhaps Akuebue was the only man in Umuaro who knew that the chief priest was helpless; that a thing greater than 'nte' had been caught in 'nte's' trap (*Arrow of God*, 219).

This is authentic oral poetry, pure and simple. While Baroness Karen Blixen's memoirs (*Out of Africa*) belongs to the genre of "belles-lettres", the above quoted passage from Achebe is the typical African art of conversation – It is that art laced with apposite proverbs so highly regarded among Africans in general and the Nigerian Igbo in particular from among whom Chinua Achebe derives most of his oral or folkloristic materials for his works.

Notes

1. See for example, the dramatic works of Ola Rotimi and the Nobel Laureate Wole Soyinka especially *The Gods Are Not to Blame* and *A Dance of the Forest* respectively for their unique and profuse uses of Yoruba proverbs (a traditional African speech mode) in drama. Examples from the writings of other African writers also abound.

    As well, see Abdul Jammohammed's article entitled "Sophisticated Primitivism: The Syncretism of Oral and Literate Models in Achebe's *Things Fall Apart* in Ariel 15, 4, 1984.

2. According to the African traditional calendar, the day, the month, the year, one's lifetime or human history, are all divided up or perceived in terms of their specific events for it is the phenomenal calendar that makes them meaningful.

3. Atukwei Okai uses an indigenous exclamation "Hi" to lament Galilo's plight; and although he gives us the English translation for "Elavanyo" once (line 52) he uses the word, nevertheless, four times, obviously because he feels that its peculiarly African sound works better for his kind of poetry (Okai enjoys reading his poetry aloud before audiences) than the English.

    Even, the very "modern" Nobel Laureate Soyinka, in an abuse or satirical poem called "Malediction", uses Yoruba words quite happily, although he uses English to shower curses on his adversary in most of the poem, at one point he breaks into Yoruba to give his abuse greater sauciness and bite.

    Some other African poets/writers have followed this practice.

Works Cited

Achebe, Chinua. *Things Fall Apart*. London: Heinemann, 1958. Reprinted 1982. Subsequent references are to the reprinted edition and cited in the essay.

———. *No Longer at Ease*. London: Heinemann, 1960. Reprinted 1981. Subsequent references are to the reprinted edition and cited in the essay.

———. *Arrow of God*. London: Heinemann, 1964. Reprinted 1982. Subsequent references are to the reprinted edition and cited in the essay.

———. *A Man of the People*. London: Heinemann, 1966. Reprinted 1982. Subsequent references are to the reprinted edition and cited in the essay.

Blixen, Karen. *Out of Africa* and Shadows on the Grass. Harmondsworth: Penquin, 1985.

Grifiths, Gareth. "Language and Action in the Novels of Chinua Achebe." *African Literature Today*, 5. Ed. Eldred D. Jones. Oxford: James Currey, 1971.

Nkosi, Lewis. *Tasks and Masks*. Essex: Longman, 1981.

Obiechina, Emmanuel. *Culture, Tradition and Society in the West African Novel*. Cambridge: Cambridge University Press, 1975. Reprinted 1980.

Okpewho, Isidore. *The Heritage of African Poetry*. London: Longman, 1985.

———. Ed. *The Epic in Africa*... New York: Columbia University Press, 1979.

Roy, Anjali and Viney Kirpal. "Oral Rhythms of Achebe's Fiction". ACLALS Bulletin in Eight Series. No. 1: *Contemporary Commonwealth Fiction*. Ed. John Thieme. Aarhus: Dangano Press, 1989.

Wanjala, Chris. *For Home and Freedom*. Nairobi: Kenya Literature Bureau, 1980.

Winters, Marjorie. "An Objective Approach to Achebe's Style". *Research in African Literatures* 12, 7. Spring 1981.

Part Two

Igbo Worldview and Christianity

Chapter 8

Achebe and Christianity

Augustine C. Okere

A CHEBE'S PIONEERING ROLE IN THE fictional portrayal of early Christian-mis-
sionary activity in Nigeria is well known to all scholars of African literature.
Other Nigerians who have addressed the theme include T.M. Aluko (*One Man One
Wife*, 1959), Onuora Nzekwu (*Blade Among the Boys*, 1962), John Munonye (*The Only
Son*, 1966). All these can be said to have trailed after Achebe, none of them catching
the fine, intricate relationships and complexities of the issues involved as Achebe
does especially in *Things Fall Apart* (1958), (*TFA*), and *Arrow of God* (1964), (*AG*).

Like these writers, Achebe is a nationalist writer, in his own case, avowedly
so. In his essay, "Named for Victoria, Queen of England" Achebe says that he
wrote his novels "especially those set in the past" to correct the distorted accounts
of Africa given by European explorers, missionaries and administrators and writers
(*Morning Yet on Creation Day*, 70). Of *Things Fall Apart* he says: "I now know that
my first book, *Things Fall Apart* was an act of atonement with my past, the ritual
return and homage of a prodigal son ("Named for Victoria", 70).

In spite of this nationalist outlook Achebe's treatment of the colonial-missionary encounter with African (Igbo) traditional culture does not take the subjective stance of a nationalist having it back on the European castigators of his race.
Militating against his adult, patriotic impulse is his background and upbringing.
In the essay mentioned above he says that he "was born of devout Christian parents" who gave him "a rigid and guarded Christian upbringing (67), including an
early Christian education. In this way he was exposed to reading that was Western, Christian-oriented. Although Achebe protested against this upbringing by
dropping his Christian name, Albert, Christianity has so much hold on him that

issues of the colonial missionary encounter dominate his first three novels. In these novels, Achebe explores the encounter as a historical event, and makes an objective appraisal of the colonial-missionary experience. It may be said that Achebe, like Ezeulu the hero of his third novel, is, in spite of himself, aware of the attractions and advantages of the new religion to his people. The significance of the title of his first novel, *Things Fall Apart*, must be taken into account in any serious discussion of Achebe's attitude to the colonial missionary experience.

The title is believed to have been taken from W.B. Yeats' poem, "The Second Coming," which is concerned with the catastrophic climax and collapse of the Christian era and the uncertain situation between it and the era succeeding it. Yeats' poem appears in *A Vision* (1925) in which he propounds his theory of the cyclic movement of history. What Achebe takes from the Yeatsian theory is the idea of the inevitability of change.

In *Things Fall Apart*, he portrays the events of the late 19th and early 20th centuries Igboland as marking the end of traditional Igbo civilization and the ushering in of another civilization, the Christian-oriented civilization of Western Europe. In his treatment of the encounter in both *Things Fall Apart* and *Arrow of God* Achebe seems to suggest that the indigenous system had reached the catastrophic climax of Yeats' formulation. He emphasizes the weaknesses inherent in the traditional system that predisposed those disadvantaged in the existing order towards embracing the new order.

The greatest shortcoming of the traditional order according to Achebe's portrayal was its failure to provide for the safety and welfare of all citizens. One example was the discrimination against the *osu* and mothers of twins and their babies. The traditional order also endorsed the killing of Ikemefuna because it had been "decreed by the Oracle of the Hills and the Caves" (TFA 51, 60). Achebe makes it clear that it was the feeling of insecurity and the distress of such victims of traditional religious sanctions like Enoch (an *osu*) and Nneka (mother of twin babies) as well as their sympathizers like Nwoye that predisposed them to embracing the new religion. Nwoye's alienation from his father and the traditional order starts after he knows that his father has killed Ikemefuna:

> As soon as his father walked in that night, Nwoye knew that Ikemefuna had been killed, and something seemed to give way inside him, like the snapping of a tightened bow (TFA 55).

The imagery here suggests both the jolt and trauma which the event causes Nwoye. Achebe does not miss any opportunity to remind us that the killing of Ikemefuna and the throwing away of twins are always associated with Nwoye's consciousness. Referring to Nwoye's feeling when he realizes that Ikemefuna had been killed, Achebe says:

He had the same kind of feeling not long ago, during the last harvest season...
Nwoye had felt for the first time a snapping inside him like the one he now
felt. They were returning...from a distant farm... when they heard the voice of
an infant crying in the thick forest...Nwoye had heard that twins were put in
earthen-ware pots and thrown away in the forest, but he had never yet come
across them. A vague chill had descended on him and his head seemed to swell...
Then something had given way inside him (*TFA* 55–56).

In the above passage Achebe is describing a humane impulse which was beginning
to vibrate in the minds of many people in Umuofia. Among the custodians of the
traditional religious order doubts and questions were also beginning to emerge
which suggest an element of dissatisfaction with the existing order. In *Things Fall
Apart* Obierika raises fundamental issues as he thinks of, and mourns Okonkwo's
calamity:

Why should a man suffer so grievously for an offence he had committed
inadvertently? But although he thought for a long time he found no answer.
He was merely led into greater complexities. He remembered his wife's twin
children, whom he had thrown away. What crime had they committed? The
earth had decreed that they were an offence on the land and must be destroyed ...
(*TFA* 113–114).

For a person in this frame of mind resistance to the in-coming order can hardly be
whole-hearted. Although he does not join the Christians his reaction to Okonkwo's
call to arms at the end of the novel (181–184) lacks enthusiasm and although he
blames the District Commissioner for Okonkwo's suicide he seems to be reconciled
to the situation of a new order.

By stressing that Okonkwo's exile is "decreed by earth" Achebe is also insinuat-
ing that the earth-goddess inadvertently facilitated the implanting of Christianity
in Umuofia by removing the rallying point of resistance to the new order. It will
be recalled that the killing of Ikemefuna and the throwing away of twins, both
inhuman acts, are said to be "decreed by earth."

This situation of an ailing social order making possible the implanting of
Christianity is also evident in *Arrow of God*. The jealousy and rivalry between
Ezeulu and Ezeidemili contributes to the weakening of the cohesion and stability
of the traditional social order in Umuaro. The rivalry between the priests of the
two deities (and their gods) is such that can only end in the destruction of one or
both of the cults. This is made clear in Ulu's rebuke of Ezeulu:

Go home and sleep and leave me to settle my quarrel with Idemili whose
envy seeks to destroy me that his python may come to power. ... as for me and
Idemili we shall fight to finish and whoever throws the other down will strip
him of his anklet (*AOG*, 192).

In *Arrow of God* Achebe also points out that the nature of the traditional deities makes it possible for the people to discard them whenever there was an occasion to do so. Ogbuefi Nwaka tells the people of Umuaro:

> And we have all heard how the people of Aninta dealt with their deity when he failed them. Did they not carry him to the boundary between them and their neighbours and set fire on him? (*AOG* 28).

There is evidence that the turbulence in Umuaro brings a situation of unease between the priest and his deity. Ezeulu saw the death of his son, Obika, in the midst of the struggle between him and Umuaro as a betrayal by his God. It is significant that he interprets the betrayal as pointing to "the collapse and ruin of all things" (*AOG* 229).

Although the people of Umuaro claim that "their god had taken sides with them against his headstrong and ambitious priest" (230), Achebe's comment is intended to show that the defeat of the chief priest also means the defeat (and death) of Ulu. As he puts it, if the claim of Umuaro were correct:

> Then Ulu had chosen a dangerous time to uphold that truth for in destroying his priest he had also brought disaster on himself, like the lizard in the fable who ruined his mother's funeral by his own hand. For a deity who chose a moment such as this to chastise his priest or abandon him before his enemies was inciting people to take liberties (215).

The moment referred to is the moment of the advent of Christianity in Umuaro. It is at such a moment that the people can defy traditional sanctions and try the advice of Goodcountry, the catechist of St. Mark's CMS Church, "that if they made their thank-offering to God they could harvest their crops without fear of Ulu." At the critical moment Ezeulu seems to have reconciled himself to the situation. As he contemplates his misfortune we get the impression that he does realize that the game is up. This is the implication of his last utterance in the novel:

> What could it point to but the collapse and ruin of all things? Then a god finding himself powerless might take flight and in one, final, backward glance at his abandoned worshippers cry: if the rat cannot flee fast enough let him make way for the tortoise (229).

Achebe's portrayal of the traditional set up in both *Things Fall Apart* and *Arrow of God* suggests that change became inevitable and desirable because of the weaknesses inherent in that set-up. But he is also interested in the performance of the missionaries and their converts. He distinguishes between two types of missionaries and converts and points out the shortcomings of each. The type of missionary represented by the Reverend Mr. Brown is prepared to dialogue with the existing traditional order. Achebe does not fail, however, to point out that the insights into traditional religion gained through such dialogue are misapplied by the missionaries.

Corresponding to this type of missionary are the moderate and less fanatical converts like Moses Unachukwu (*Arrow of God*). These types of converts are willing to respect the norms of traditional religion in the practice of their newly acquired religion. Moses is opposed to Mr. Goodcountry's insistence that killing the sacred python is the way to show the convert's belief in Christianity. Moses "told the new teacher quite bluntly that neither the Bible nor the catechism asked the converts to kill the python" (*AOG* 48). Moses Unachukwu advises the catechist:

> If you are wise you will face the work they sent you to do here and take your hand off the python ... nobody here has complained to you that the python ever blocked his way as he came to church. If you want to do your work in peace you will heed what I have said, but if you want to be the lizard that ruined his own mother's funeral you may carry on the way you are doing (*AOG* 50).

Moses Unachukwu's position is based on the Igbo philosophy of "live and let live." Achebe shows approval of such a stance and gives Moses the glory of getting Umuaro over to the Christian God at the end of the novel.

Achebe condemns the method of evangelism practiced by the Reverend Mr. Smith (*Things Fall Apart*) and Mr. Goodcountry (*Arrow of God*) which insists on the total eradication of the traditional order. The Reverend Mr. Smith, as we are told, "sees things as either white or black, and black is evil." Achebe considers as tragic a situation where the traditional religion is willing to let Christianity prove itself but the Christian missionaries and some of their converts fail to adopt the same attitude towards traditional religious practice.

One of the converts, Enoch, unmasks the *egwugwu* (*TFA* 68), an assault considered by the people of Umuofia as a most serious travesty of their custom. In *Arrow of God* Mr. Goodcountry encourages his converts to kill the totemic python and one of them, Oduche, actually attempts to kill it, although secretly, by suffocation. Achebe contrasts Oduche with Moses Unachukwu and makes the point that respect for the customs of the people does not necessarily vitiate the faith of the Christian converts.

Achebe illustrates the ideal relationship between the converts and the non-converts in his account of the situation in his own family. His great grandfather, Udo Osinyi-Udo, allowed the earliest missionaries to operate from his compound. He decided to eject them only because the "eerie songs they sang might make his neighbors think it was his funeral dirge ("Named for Victoria ..." 66). According to Achebe, the parting was "without rancour", and the old man did not raise "any serious objections" when Achebe's father joined the missionaries (66) and although he resisted the latter's attempt to convert him, it did not bring about a quarrel. The old man's disposition is summarized as follows:

> I don't know for certain but I think the old man was the very embodiment of tolerance insisting only that whatever a man decided to do he should do with style ("Named for Victoria ..." 66).

The essay, "Named for Victoria ...," must be taken seriously in any discussion of Achebe's attitude to Christianity as portrayed in his fiction. Critics who feel that Achebe is critical of Ezeulu's performance in *Arrow of God* may do well to read it. The spirit of tolerance is underscored in Achebe's description of his family:

> We lived at the crossroads of cultures. On one arm of the cross we sang hymns and read the Bible night and day. On the other arm my father's brother and his family ... offered food to the idols. That was how it was supposed to be anyhow ("Named for Victoria ..." 67).

He goes on to describe how, in spite of the fact that he was deep in the practice of Christianity, "those idols" had a "strange pull on" him. His account of the effect on this pull is worth quoting in full:

> ... despite those delusions of divine destiny (as a Christian) I was not past taking my little sister to our neighbour's house when our parents were not looking and partaking of heathen festival meals. I never found their rice and stew to have a flavour of idolatry. I was about ten then. If anyone likes to believe that I was torn by spiritual agonies or scorched on the racks of my ambivalence, he certainly may suit himself. I do not remember any undue distress. What I do remember was a fascination for the ritual and the life on the other arm of the cross-roads. And I believe two things were in my favour – that curiosity, and the little distance imposed between me and it by the accident of my birth. The distance becomes not a separation but a bringing together like the necessary backward step which a judicious viewer may take in order to see a canvas steadily and fully ("Named for Victoria..." 68).

The advantage of this vantage position manifests in all his works. He, more than any other Igbo novelist of English expression, shows an in-depth knowledge of both traditional and Christian religious practice and although he proclaims that he has renounced the latter, he cannot divest himself of the internalized tenets which his birth, upbringing and education impose on him. Thus, we find in his works not only chronicles of the colonial-missionary encounter but also ample evidence of the effects of this background. His subtle manipulation of biblical material demonstrates the excellence of his craftsmanship even better than his generally acclaimed manipulation of the English language.

Biblical material in his fiction are in the form of echoes, casual references, deliberate quotations used for analogies and comments. There are casual references to, and echoes of the Bible which are merely a manner of thinking or speaking. In *No Longer at Ease* (*NLAE*) for example, Isaac Okonkwo calls his daughters the foolish virgins (*NLAE* 56). The phrase "foolish virgins" is obviously taken from the parable of the Ten Virgins in Matthew 25, 1–13 but there is nothing in the novel to suggest that it has the implications of the biblical original. In the same manner, commenting on the permanence of the written word, Isaac Okonkwo quotes Pilate in John 19, 22: "what is written is written" (*NLAE* 115). And in *Arrow of God* the chief messenger tells John Nwodika, "you have already done what you were sent to do; the rest is for me. So put your tongue into its scabbard." We recall that in John 18, 11 Jesus tells Peter: "put your sword into the scabbard." This kind of use is common in Nigerian literature and is accounted for by the fact of the author's western missionary education.

In Achebe's fiction, however, the utterances acquire significance in the context of the novels as a whole. Isaac Okonkwo's "what is written is written" assumes the status of a prophecy when combined with what Odogwu says later about Obi: "As it was in the beginning, is now, and ever shall be…" The effect is to give the reader a deeper insight into the nature of Obi's tragedy and we pity him as we watch him struggling against forces that have been predestined to crush him.

In the same way, the chief messenger's words combine with the recurrent motif "everything has a season." John Nwodika himself is aware of this. He abides by it and succeeds. If we apply the motif to Ezeulu's situation, we see his alliance with Christianity as resulting from his deeper insight and he becomes even greater than a mere chief priest of Ulu.

Achebe's typical references and allusions to the Bible often operate at this deeper level of significance. In *A Man of the People* Odili refers to how Chief Nanga comes to him "in the dark like Nicodemus" and offers him "two fifty pounds" (143). This is an illusion to John 3, 1 where the Pharisee, Nicodemus, who was a member of the Jewish Sanhedrin went secretly at night to learn the truth of the ministry of Jesus. There is in the allusion an implication of the hypocrisy of Chief Nanga. It also brings out the relationship between Nanga, as a member of the ruling class, and Odili the idealist reformer. Like Nicodemus of the Bible Nanga is, on one occasion, during the political rally, in a group where Odili's popularity is on trial (156–157). Nanga judges, condemns and punishes Odili whereas in John 7, 50 Nicodemus pleads for a fair hearing for Jesus. The climax of the contrasts is that Nicodemus became so committed to the cause that Jesus espoused that he joined Joseph Arimathea to bury the body of the crucified Jesus. The allusion to Nicodemus makes the point that the ruling class of the society of *A Man of the People* is hypocritical and unregenerate, a situation that makes the collapse of their government inevitable and welcome. The novel states that "some political commentators have said that it was the supreme cynicism that inflamed the people and brought down the government" (161).

Often Achebe's biblical echoes, allusions or quotations give authenticity to what is said thus instilling confidence in, and eliciting belief from the person or persons addressed. This is the effect achieved by the catechist, Kiaga, when encouraging his converts to ignore the banter of the non-converts he quotes Psalm 2, 1; 4:

> Why do the nations race and the people imagine vain things ... he that sitteth in the heavens shall laugh. The lord shall have them in derision (*TFA* 143).

The quotation is in itself appropriate in the context where it appears. Psalm 2 is regarded by Bible scholars as a messianic Psalm in which "the psalmist depicts the revolt of the nations against God and his anointed son" as well as God's answer "and warning given to the rebels" (New American... Edition 4, 95). By quoting the psalm, Kiaga also puts himself entirely into the original biblical context and becomes one with the prophets, a transfiguration which is made complete by his speaking in character when Nwoye joins the converts:

> Blessed is he who forsakes his father and his mother for my sake (*TFA* 139) (Luke 14, 26: Matthew 10, 37–38).

This mode of perception makes the missionaries see events of the present as a fulfillment of biblical prophecies and their role as missionaries a continuation of the ministry of Jesus. Thus, the Reverend Mr. Brown expresses his satisfaction with the progress of his mission in Umuofia in a metaphor that clearly recalls Luke 8, 11:

> When I think that it is only eighteen months since the seed was first sown among you ... I marvel at *what the Lord has wrought* (*TFA* 146).

"Seed" represents here, as it does in the Bible, the word of God. The preachers of this word are described in the biblical metaphor of "labourers in the vineyard" (Matthew 20, 1). There is also a link with the Old Testament through the echo of Numbers 23, 23: I Marvel at "*what the Lord has wrought*" (my emphasis). It will be recalled that Numbers is a book of the Bible that deals with the preparation of the Israelites to be witnesses among the nations.

In *No Longer at Ease* Reverend Samuel Ikedi refers to Obi's going to study abroad as the fulfillment of the words of the prophet Isaiah 9, 2:

> The people which sat in darkness saw a great light and to them which sat in the region and shadow of death. To them did the light spring up (*NLAE* 7).

In Matthew 4, 16, this prophecy is seen as being fulfilled in the ministry of Jesus. The people "which sat in darkness" whom Reverend Ikedi refers to are the people of Umuofia and Obi is the light that has sprung up. Reverend Ikedi also refers to "the days of darkness from which we have been delivered by the blood of the lamb of God" (9). Having been delivered it becomes Obi's duty to heed the advice "that the fear of the Lord is the beginning of wisdom" (Proverbs 1, 7; NLAE 9). The rest of Obi's story hinges on this. It is ironic that in spite of his attempts to live according to the principles that Reverend Ikedi prescribes for him he gets into the tragic muddle that culminates in his imprisonment.

When Obi takes delivery of his new car, Green tells him: "you will do well to remember ... that at this time every year you will be called upon to cough up forty pounds for your insurance" (NLAE 87). Achebe likens Green's words to the apocalyptic warning of the coming of the "day of the Lord" in Joel. The underlying theme of preparing for the day of reckoning applies to Obi as later events show. By the analogy, Achebe gives Green's words all the eschatological weight of Joel's prophecy.

Achebe may appropriate a biblical reference, metaphor or symbol to define a situation or comment on an issue. At the reception organized for him by the Umuofia Progressive Union in Lagos, Obi says: "did not the psalmist say that it was good for brethren to meet together in harmony" (NLAE 73). This is a close but not exact quotation of Psalm 133, 1, which has the word "dwell". By quoting the Psalm Obi shows that he is aware of the "benefits of brotherly concord," which is the subject of the Psalm. Ironically, he is the first to break the "harmony" for he walks out on the Union when they introduce the subject of his association with Clara. There is here an implicit satire on the well-known divergence between ideals and practice which is an important theme in *No Longer at Ease*. In the novel, the only phrase Ogbuefi Odogwu appropriates from the Christians is the concluding portion of the prayer which says, "As it was in the beginning, is now and ever shall be world without end" (47). He applies this his favorite phrase to Isaac Okonkwo's family. As he puts it:

> As a man comes into this world ... so will he go out of it. When a titled man dies
> his anklets of title are cut so he will return as he came. The Christians are right
> when they say that as it was in the beginning so it will be in the end (47).

Later he applies it specifically to Obi: "He is Ogbuefi Okonkwo come back. He is Okonkwo *kpom kwem*, exact, perfect" (49). Although Obi's father, Isaac Okonkwo, protests that "dead men do not come back," Odogwu insists that they do, using the authority of the Christian prayer: "as it was in the beginning so it will be in the end. That is what your religion tells us" (49).

Taken as a whole Odogwu's speech has crucial implications for Obi Okonkwo's story. Literally, he is referring to the physical resemblance between Obi and Obi's grandfather. There is also a suggestion in the latter part of his speech that Obi will achieve greatness like his grandfather. But there is a further ironic implication of his sharing his grandfather's ultimate disgrace. The speech also defines the pattern of consequences of the contact with Christianity in the three generations from Okonkwo through his grandson Obi, and gives structural unity to the two novels, *Things Fall Apart* and *No Longer at Ease*, which span these generations.

Obi's grandfather, Okonkwo in *Things Fall Apart* dies trying to prevent Christianity from taking root in the clan. At his death, he is alienated from the very tradition he had labored so much to uphold. Okonkwo's son Nwoye (Isaac) defies him and embraces Christianity. Even if we agree that Achebe is yet to write a novel on Isaac Okonkwo's generation, we can infer from his reaction to Obi's proposal to marry Clara (an *Osu*) that he capitulates before the very tradition from which he is running away.

Odogwu's "as it was in the beginning" also links Obi with his father in another interesting way. When Obi refuses to go home for his mother's funeral, one member of the Umuofia Progressive Union in Lagos remarks:

> This story that we are all talking about, what has he done? He was told that his mother died and he did not care. It is a strange and surprising thing, but I can tell you that I have seen it before. His father did it ... when this boy's father – you all know him, Isaac Okonkwo – when Isaac Okonkwo heard of the death of his father he said that those that kill with the matchet must die by the matchet (NLAE 145).

Isaac Okonkwo himself confirms the story as he tries to tell Obi the sufferings he "went through ... to become a Christian":

> When they brought me word that he [his father Okonkwo] had hanged himself I told them that those who live by the sword must perish by the sword. Mr. Bradley, the white man who was our teacher, said it was not the right thing to say and told me to go home for the burial. I refused to go ... (125).

Expectedly, Isaac Okonkwo's is an accurate quotation from the Bible. It is ironic that he condemns his father using the language of the Bible and is in turn condemned, in the Clara debate, by his son, Obi, who reminds him that "the Bible says that in Christ there is no bond or free" (120). This story establishes the link between Obi, his father and his grandfather, and their three generations represent Odogwu's "was", "is" and "shall be".

Obi's reaction to the news of his mother's death can only be understood by him in terms of the story in 2 Samuel 12, 15–21 "of King David who refused food when his beloved son was sick but washed and ate when he (the son) died" (149). Achebe comments that Obi too must have felt this kind of peace. "The peace that passeth all understanding (Philippians 4,7). This peace marks the final resolution of all Obi's heartaches. He "had been utterly prostrated by the shock of his mother's death." When, after weeping, he goes to bed that night, and "he did not wake up even once in the night," unlike what had been his experience "in the last few months" when "he had hardly known any sleep at all" (146).

It is peace resulting from his reconciling himself with forces that he can neither control nor surmount. As Achebe observes, Obi's thoughts about his circumstances give him "a queer kind of pleasure" (151):

> They seemed to release his spirit. He no longer felt guilt. He, too, had died. Beyond death there are no ideals and no humbug, only reality. The patient idealist says, 'give me a place to stand and I shall move the earth.' But such a place does not exist. We all have to stand on the earth itself and go with her at her pace. The most horrible sight in the world cannot put out the eye. The death of a mother is not like a palm tree bearing fruit at the end of its leaf, no matter how much we want to make it so. And that is not the only illusion we have (151).

From this we can see that Obi realizes that his ideals have been an illusion. His mother's death has brought him face to face with reality. Coming to terms with this reality has brought him peace. He has to move with the earth at her own pace. He becomes a new Obi, to use his own words, "a brand new snake just emerged from its slough" (150). The snake image here is significant. Coming to terms with the world as he sees it also means the death of the idealist in him. He is now in the world in which he can think of himself as a snake with all the satanic implications. His first action after this "reformation" is to accept bribes and compromise his position by seducing the girl who is a candidate for scholarship – a course of action that leads to his tragic fall. The biblical analogy thus works in reverse for Obi. David came to terms with God, and the peace which he found was lasting peace because, as we are told, he had a son, Solomon, who was beloved by the Lord. Obi's peace, on the other hand, is only a brief interlude before the final catastrophe.

The impression one gets after reading Achebe's novels is that of an author addressing a society in which the Christian ethic has become a dominant factor in shaping the thinking and actions of the people. But Achebe seems to be saying that the acceptance of the Christian ethic must be seen in the context of the realities of life.

In *No Longer at Ease*, Isaac Okonkwo has four daughters before Obi is born. Because of the premium which Igbo culture places on male children, Isaac Okonkwo is, as Achebe tells us, "naturally becoming a little anxious." However, we are also reminded that he would not adopt the traditional mode of solution to his problem:

> ... Being a Christian convert – in fact a catechist – he would not marry a second wife ... he would not let the heathen know that he is unhappy (6).

The conflict within him is implied in the name "Nwanyidimma" (girl is good) which he gives to his fourth daughter. Although Achebe comments that Isaac Okonkwo's "voice did not carry conviction" there is an implication of a struggle to adopt the Christian attitude to his dilemma.

The distinction between acceptance of the Christian ethic and the practice of the demands of that acceptance is also implicit in the story of Elsie and Odili in *A Man of the People*, Odili meets the promiscuous Elsie "at a party organized by the students' Christian Movement" (27). This organization is one that claims for its membership a higher level of religiosity. The irony of the ease with which Elsie moves from the "prayerful" party to a sexual orgy is Achebe's criticism of the depravity of the age. It may also be his cynical suggestion that people like Elsie exist in spite of the ideals of the Students' Christian Movement.

Achebe's knowledge of, and involvement with, the Bible shows best in his exploration of characterization. Sometimes he deliberately models his characters on Biblical archetypes of either the Old or the New Testament. Indications of the Biblical connection are sometimes given through the characters' names. Thus Isaac in *Things Fall Apart* and Moses in *Arrow of God* are seen to perform in the novel the roles of the biblical archetypes.

A character does not need to be a Christian to function as a type. A close examination of the circumstances of Ezeulu reveals parallels with Old Testament figures and by figuration, with Jesus. Like the Old Testament prophets, Ezeulu is gifted with mystical insight. He tells his friend Akuebue, "I can see things where other men are blind" (*AOG* 132). He uses this deeper insight to guide his people although they always disobey him and suffer as a result. He does not hesitate to assert his superior status:

> But you cannot know the thing which beats the drum to which Ezeulu dances. I can see tomorrow; that is why I can tell Umuaro: 'come out from this because there is death there or do this because there is profit in it.' If they listen to me, o-o; if they refuse to listen, o-o. I have passed the stage of dancing to receive presents (132).

He displays this insight in his decision to send his son Oduche "to learn the secrets of the white man's magic." The people of Umuaro rightly point out that this is part of Ezeulu's pact with the white man. Although he does not see his action in this way he is in-fact unconsciously allying with the new forces, (religious and governmental), which eventually overthrow the very order of which he is the custodian. He does this because it has been given to him mystically to know that the "disease" which is afflicting his clan is one "that has never been seen before." Such revelation is comparable to God's manifestation of himself to such Old Testament figures as Abraham. Although Ezeulu interprets his own visions in terms of the traditional Igbo religion which he knows, he is always pointing to the "end of things" a phrase which he uses three times in his discussion of the subject of Oduche joining the Christians. He tells Akuebue:

> Shall I tell you why I sent my son?... A disease that has never been seen before cannot be cured with everyday herbs. When we want to make a charm we look for the animal whose blood can match its power ... but sometimes even a bull does not suffice, then we must look for a human. Do you think it is the sound of the death-cry gurgling through blood that we want to hear. No ... we do it because we have reached the very end of things... and our fathers have told us that it may even happen to an unfortunate generation that they are pushed beyond the end of things, ...When this happens they may sacrifice their own blood ...That was why our ancestors when they were pushed beyond the end of things by the Warriors of Abam sacrificed not a stranger but one of themselves and made the great medicine which they called Ulu (133–134) (my emphasis).

If we apply Ezeulu's philosophy to his situation we can conclude that sending Oduche to a missionary school is an act of sacrifice. This raises two points. In the first place, it reminds us of the sacrifice of Isaac by his father, Abraham (Auden 100). Ezeulu thus becomes a figure like Abraham, willing to sacrifice his son to God. But the more important point is that Ezeulu, the Chief Priest of Ulu, a deity of Igbo traditional religion, is offering the sacrifice as a result of the type of revelation normally associated with Old Testament prophets. Ezeulu's "end of things" is obviously a reference to the end of the traditional, pre-Christian order because at the climax of his agony he does not say that his betrayal by Ulu only points to "the collapse and ruin of all things." At that point we feel, in retrospect, the impact of the phrases and it becomes clear that Ezeulu has all along had, even if unconsciously, a foreknowledge of the collapse of the traditional order.

Obika's death marks the beginning of a new era when Umuaro is converted to Christianity. Without his knowing it, Ezeulu is both a prophet of this new era as well as the instrument ("the arrow of God") used by the Christian God for the conversion of Umuaro. In this regard, he becomes what Auden has described as a "doer of the word who has never heard the word" (100). This is a very important aspect of his complex personality. He is Man-God, "known" and "unknowable," a fact acknowledged both by custom which stipulates that he paints one part of his body white and the other black during rituals, and by Akuebue who says of him:

> I am your friend and I can talk to you as I like; but that does not mean I forget that one half of you is man and the other half spirit (133).

The duality places Ezeulu at a higher level than the Old Testament figures. There is an immediate reference to the cardinal doctrine of Christianity that Jesus Christ is "true God and true man."

Although one cannot think of Ezeulu as a Jesus figure in the usually accepted sense, the parallels with aspects of the story of Jesus are remarkable. For example, the dream in which he confronts the elders of Umuaro echoes the experiences of Jesus before the Jewish populace. There is the same community of opposition by the elders who shout together, "He shall not speak, we will not listen to him," (*AOG* 159). They also revile him in words that echo those used by the Jewish populace to deride the hanging Jesus: "He saved our fathers from the warriors of Abam but he cannot save us from the white man" (159). As in the case of Jesus, "some spat in his face and called him the priest of the dead God" (159).

Achebe gives significance to Ezeulu's death by linking it with an event that marks the triumph of Christianity in Umuaro. Although he lives and dies upholding the traditional order, his career is also inextricably bound up with the story of Christianity in Umuaro. Ezeulu's death is an ending, "the end" of the beginning of the Christian epoch in Umuaro.

The duality of Ezeulu's personality and the significance of his career in the history of Christianity in Umuaro make the comparison between him and the Christian Jesus inescapable. His unique position is emphasized even in his fall. His last days have the tragic grandeur, which is denied Okonkwo. The novel says that "in his last days" he lived "in the haughty splendor of a demented high priest ..." (229). "High Priest" is a deliberate echo of Jesus as High Priest in Hebrews, 9.

In Achebe's poetry, the use of biblical material is a bit more complex. Christian analogues are juxtaposed with traditional Igbo equivalents as Achebe is trying to demonstrate the validity of the latter. For example, in the poem "Mango Seedling" (5), the fate of a mango seedling sprouting on a concrete canopy is reminiscent of both the widow of Zarepath, "the widow/of infinite faith," and the traditional Igbo fable of the old tortoise and his "dot of cocoyam." Because of its limited source of food the seedling is compared with the widow, but it is also contrasted with her because the widow's meager store was miraculously replenished by God after she had provided for Elijah (1 Kings, 17, 12–16). In the same way the seedling is compared and contrasted with old Tortoise:

> Old Tortoise's miraculous feast on the ever recurring dot of cocoyam set in a
> large bowl of green vegetables – this day beyond fable, beyond faith (5).

The seedling, like the bat of Igbo folklore does not belong to earth or sky. It belongs neither to the religious tradition of the Jews nor to the tradition in which the Tortoise survived. So it dies in spite of its "passionate courage":

> Dry, wire-thin in sun and dust of the dry month headstone on the tiny debris
> of passionate courage (6).

The seedling is denied a thunderous and disastrous end "in delirious waterfall/

Toward earth below." Rather its end is uneventful, saddening but stubborn and courageous, as if nature would not let it down:

> ...every rainy day little playful floods assembled on the slab danced, parted round its feet united again, and passed ... (6).

The "primordial quarrel of Earth/And sky" between which according to the poem, the seedling is "poised in courageous impartiality" is the quarrel which, in Igbo folklore, led to the sky withholding rain for several months (*TFA* 48). Although the ensuing drought may have contributed to the death of the seedling, its problem is, specifically, its lack of rootedness in *ala*, to which, as Achebe has pointed out in "*Beware Soul Brother*":

> A man's
> Foot must return whatever beauties
> it may weave in air, where
> it must return for safety
> a renewal of strength ... (29).

The seedling is "striving bravely to sink roots/into objectivity, mid-air in stone." If it had been rooted in *ala* (the soil) it would, according to the argument of the poem, have survived.

The juxtaposing of the biblical and the contemporary is sometimes so subtle that Achebe's intention is not immediately obvious. In "Non Commitment":

> ...Pontius Pilate openly washed involvement off his white hands and became famous

And

> Judas wasn't such a fool either ... He alone in that motley crowd had sense enough to tell a doomed movement when he saw one and get out quick, a nice little pocket bulging his coat-pocket into the bargain (31).

Here Achebe is pointing out the irony implicit in a situation where those who will not commit themselves and traitors in issues of grave moral dimensions become celebrated characters. The biblical story of the betrayal of Jesus by Judas and Pilate's hypocritical washing of his hands in the matter of the condemnation of Jesus are taken by Achebe as analogues of the contemporary situation that he is describing. The word, "white" which qualifies Pilate's hand is a clue to the Pilates that Achebe has in mind. If we interpret the poem in terms of the Nigerian situation Judas would be a symbol of the local traitors. Of greater significance, however, is Achebe's reinterpretation of the Pilate-Judas situation which is a radical departure from the orthodox Christian interpretation.

In "Lazarus" Achebe contrasts the orthodox Christian interpretation of the raising to life of Lazarus by Jesus with the social implications of such a miracle in contemporary society. The resurrection of Lazarus is marked by:

The breath-taking joy of his sisters when the word spread: he is risen (37).

In contemporary society, there cannot be this unqualified joy because:

... a man who has lived a full life will have others to reckon with beside his sisters.

Resurrection in the modern social context will be an embarrassment to the officer who has been promoted to take the position left vacant by the dead person.

Achebe's poem is based on a contemporary event. The people of Ogbaku (in Owerri, Imo State of Nigeria) killed "the barrister" for apparently killing their kinsman (in a car accident). For this killing there could be "justification". When it turned out that their kinsman was not dead, the people then killed him to retain their plea. Achebe likens his revival to a resurrection. It brings joy to his sisters but it is a source of grave anxiety for the "luckless people" because "their kinsman avenged in murder" stirring "in wide eyed resurrection" would turn:

Away from them in obedience to other fraternities, would turn indeed their own accuser and in one breath obliterate their plea and justification! So they killed him a second time that day on the threshold of a promising resurrection (37–38).

Achebe's "Lazarus" has affinity with the ghost scene in Shakespeare's *Macbeth* III, IV, 77 ff where, in his distress over the appearance of Banquo's ghost *Macbeth* says:

The time has been that when the brains were out the man would die, and there an end; but now they rise again, with twenty mortal murders on their crowns and push us from our stools.

In both Shakespeare and Achebe resurrection is not treated in terms of orthodoxy, that is, the resurrection of all the dead on the Last Day, but resurrection particularized and coming before the Last Day, thus constituting an embarrassment to the living.

The treatment of a biblical theme in a contemporary context is also evident in the poem, "1966". This poem casts a backward look on the thoughtlessness and indolence of Nigerian rulers that led to the political turmoil in Nigeria in 1966. Because of their misrule:

A diamond-tipped drillpoint crept closer to residual chaos to rare artesian hatred that once squirmed warm blood in God's face confirming his first disappointment in Eden (31).

The fratricidal confrontations in Nigeria are likened to the killing of Abel by his brother, Cain. Both crimes have their origin in "residual chaos/… rare artesian hatred." God had been disappointed with the fall of Adam and Eve. The killings in Nigeria, like the crime of Cain, heighten this disappointment.

This poem is, however, weak in its logic. If, as Achebe implies, sin is inherent (residual chaos…) the events of 1996 in Nigeria cannot be incidental on the absent-mindedness or the thoughtlessness of Nigerian rulers, but should be seen as part of God's design.

Not only is Achebe influenced by the Bible he is fascinated by Christian religious practice and ritual. In "Christmas in Biafra" he looks closely at, and carefully describes a Christmas crib set up by Catholic nuns working in a hospital in war-torn Biafra:

> Beyond the hospital gate the good nuns had set up a manger of palms to house
> in fine plastercast scene at Bethlehem. The holy Family was central, serene, the
> child Jesus plump, wise-looking and rose-cheeked; one of the magic in keeping
> with legend of black Othello in sumptuous robes. Other figures of men and
> angels stood at well-appointed distances from the heart of the divine miracle
> and the usual cattle gazed on in holy wonder…(13).

This description emphasizes the beauty of the crib. There is implicit in it the awe and reverence of a poet who knows the full import of the mystery represented by the crib. Nevertheless, he is also mindful of its irrelevance in war-torn Biafra. The reader is directed from the "Child Jesus, plump wise-looking and plump-cheeked" to the "infant son" of the woman worshipper:

> flat like a dead lizard
> on her shoulder his arms and legs
> cauterized by famine was a miracle
> of its own kind. Large sunken eyes
> stricken past boredom to a flat
> unrecognizing glueyness moped faraway
> motionless across her shoulder…(14).

The figure in the crib, like the "faraway sounds of other men's carols" appears to the poet to mock the worshippers. Achebe's comments are implied in the reaction of the child when his mother:

> turned him round and pointed
> at those pretty figures of God
> and angels and men and beasts –
> a spectacle to stir the heart
> of a child (14).

The child, who, like most children in Biafra, is doomed to the slow-grinding death by kwashiorkor, represents the spirit of the Biafran nation. All he does is to cast:

> one slow deadpan look of total
> unrecognition and he began again
> to swivel his enormous head away
> to mope as before at his empty distance (24).

The "empty distance" is symbolic of the hopelessness of the child's situation, and his reaction amounts to a rejection of this gesture of the nuns; it is an expression of "pure transcendental hate" (13).

Achebe's somber description shows that neither the crib nor the faraway sounds of other/men's carols floating on crackling waves arouses the usual festive emotions associated with Christmas.

"Christmas in Biafra" is unlike "Lazarus". Whereas "Lazarus" uses the biblical story for what it is worth "Christmas in Biafra" actually comments on the Christian situation itself. As in the poignantly ironic reference to "Madonna and Child" in the poem, "Refugee Mother and Child," Achebe seems to be saying that what the child needs in his present circumstances is not a well-laid out crib. In fact, for him, the whole idea of Christmas is rejected in Biafra, the "death-calls of the moment":

> this sunken-eyed moment wobbling
> down the rocky steepness on broken
> bones slowly fearfully to hideous
> concourse of gathering sorrows ...

Achebe's despair is comparable to that of Mycerinus (Arnold 2–5) as the latter contemplates the decree of the oracle from the city of Buto that he had only six years more to live, in spite of his just rule. Achebe is in effect asking the Christian nuns the same questions that Mycerinus asks of the gods:

> O wherefore cheat our youth, if thus it be...
> stringing vain words of powers we cannot see,
> blind divinations of a will supreme;
> lost labour! When the circumambient gloom
> but hides, if Gods, Gods careless of our doom?

For Achebe the problem is not the question of believing or not believing in the meaning of Christmas, but of there being no need at all to believe in a God who is apparently unconcerned with the suffering of the people. It should be recalled that for the people on the Biafran side, the Nigerian civil war was a war of survival. Theirs was the "just position" and to many, God did not seem to have appreciated the justness of their cause. "Christmas in Biafra" is thus an eloquent expression of the resultant despair.

Achebe is a prominent writer of the conflict-protest tradition of African literature. This is literature that aims at showing Africans where the rain started to beat them; to trace the origins of an encounter that has exerted so much influence on their history and individual lives. Achebe's portrayal of the Christian missionary experience carries the message that there is need to retain what is best in both Christianity and traditional religion, a message he exemplifies in his portrayal of a character like Moses Unachukwu in *Arrow of God*. Achebe himself embodies the conflict situation which is played out in the individual writer who is aware of the benefits of the Christian missionary presence but who must also show a commitment to validating his cultural past. He is an intellectualized appraisal of the situation often through analogical use of biblical material to comment on and sometimes interpret events in contemporary Nigerian society.

Note

I am indebted to T.R. Henn's discussion of *A Vision in The Lonely Tower*. London: Methuen University Paperbacks, 1965: 191–219.

Works Cited

Achebe, Chinua. *Things Fall Apart*. London: Heinemann, 1958.

——. *Arrow of God*. London: Heinemann, 1964.

——. *No Longer at Ease*. London: Heinemann, 1960.

——. *A Man of the People*. London: Heinemann, 1966.

——. "Named for Victoria, Queen of England." In *Morning Yet on Creation Day*. London: Heinemann, 1975.

——. *Beware Soul Brother*. Enugu: Nwamife Publishers Ltd., 1971.

Arnold, Matthew. "Mycerinus" In *Selected Poetry and Prose*. New York: Holt, Rinehart and Winston, 1962.

Auden, M.H. *The Enchanted Flood or The Romantic Iconography of the Sea*. London: Faber & Faber Ltd., 1951.

New American Catholic Bible. Fireside Edition.

Chapter 9

Achebe and Duality in Igbo Thought

Anthonia C. Kalu

ACHEBE'S INTERPRETATION OF IGBO LIFE places him among the artists and philosophers of Igbo tradition. Claiming to be an ancestor worshipper, he uses aspects of Igbo religious life and practice to delineate the importance of traditional Igbo religious objects as art objects. In his *African Oral Literature: Backgrounds, Character, and Continuity* (1992), Okpewho, in discussing the reevaluation of the relationship between African oral and contemporary literature, asserts:

> There has, indeed been an increasing tendency on the part of modern African writers to identify with the literary traditions of their people in terms both of content and technique…when these African nations won their independence from foreign domination, they undertook to reexamine and overhaul not only the institutions by which they had been governed but also the image of their culture that had long been advertised by outsiders. The aim was to demonstrate that Africa has had, since time immemorial, traditions that should be respected and a culture to be proud of…[t]hat…African culture is not obsolete but relevant for the articulation of contemporary needs and goals (293).

Although, most of the work done since independence has focused on the question of image retrieval, the effort that has gone into the exploration of content has been largely ignored. Consequently, it has been difficult for contemporary African communities to find in these retrievals, "a culture to be proud of" (293). This work posits that although the level of cultural pride that the nationalist envisioned at independence is possible, it can only be achieved through a conscious reexamination and application of African cultural content.

But, such reexamination must move beyond the structural, engaging cultural content by searching for meanings in ways that will shape that immanent "expression-continuum" (Eco: 1979, 157) that African scholars recognize long before independence. In his discussion of a "Theory of Codes", Umberto Eco looks at the extent to which early linguistics research simplified and rigidified the relationships between *reference, symbol* and *referent*. He reaches the conclusion that:

> Within the framework of a theory of codes it is unnecessary to resort to the notion of extension, nor to that of possible words; the codes, insofar as they are accepted by a society, set up a 'cultural' world which is neither actual nor possible in the ontological sense; its existence is linked to a cultural order, which is the way in which a society thinks, speaks and, while speaking, explains the 'purport' of its thought through other thoughts. Since it is through thinking and speaking that a society develops, expands or collapses, even when dealing with 'impossible' worlds (i.e. aesthetic texts, ideological statements), a theory of codes is very much concerned with the format of such 'cultural' worlds, and faces the basic problem of how to touch contents (61–62) (Italics in original).

In light of the above, using semantics *to touch content*, as opposed to focusing on the referent, is significant to this work's project of excavating relevant meaning from contemporary African literature. Here, the main assumption is that a significant number of writers work from an African oral narrative base, whose framework is constructed from a recognizable "cultural world".

Achebe's understanding of Igbo society and thought parallels him to the traditional elders of the land in their capacity to re(create) order from familiar cultural worlds in conflict and transition. The relationships between these worlds constitute the explanatory bases for significant aspects of Igbo worldview. The explanations emphasized the transitional/reference points that Igbo thought provides for the emergence of a viable future.

As with the traditional priest/artist's religious objects, Achebe's works demonstrate the contemporary artist's commitment (Kalu: 1994) to the well being of Igbo (African) society and its dynamic role in the contemporary discourse on political and socio-economic development. By extending the boundaries of Igbo cultural practice through the form of the novel, the contemporary Igbo writer acknowledges similarities and differences between the Igbo and the vast terrain of African thought. So far, the degree of congruence has shown that Africans have a great deal in common beyond the oppression of colonialism and western domination.

Using selected works by Achebe, it is possible to begin to understand how he uses cultural references to evoke an Igbo (African) epistemological congruity that traverses all aspects of social and political interaction. The role then, of the scholar/activist, is to articulate the path toward an African Renaissance, a reassertion of an intrinsic integrity predicated on a dynamic ancestral legacy. If, as most scholars of African literature have established, African arts have always been in the service of the people, then an African literary criticism should be able to re-establish those significant relationships that were obvious to traditional African artists. Given that one of the aims of Independence "...was to demonstrate that Africa has had...traditions that should be respected and a culture to be proud of... (Okpewho, 293) the relevance of such relationships to contemporary African issues in the "expression-continuum" is self-evident.

Beginning with *Things Fall Apart* (1958) Achebe's works maintain a conscious-ness of duality, the relationship between the natural and the supernatural, the real and the metaphysical worlds, as manifested in all aspects of Igbo thought. An understanding of this relationship is important to comprehending Igbo arts. Briefly, one of the explanations based on the Igbo myth of the origin of the yam (Isichei: 1978, 22; Henderson: 1972, 59–61) asserts a relationship between the Igbo and the *Nri* people. The discussion between *Eri* and Chukwu culminated in *Eri's* and his children's mediation between the people and Chukwu on the one hand, and the people and Ani, the Earth Goddess, on the other. In executing their duties on behalf of the society, *Eri's* descendants became diviners of the wills of both Chukwu and *Ani*. This made them both priests in charge of the people's religion and medicine men who cleansed the land and people of abominations. This linkage between the physical and the spiritual persists in a majority of African socio-cultural relations.

Throughout Igboland, priests of other deities, oracles and nature spirits performed functions similar to those executed by the *Nri* priests. They all needed specific objects like carved figures and dishes made from metal or clay for sacrificed and other religious activities. The people specialized in the making of these objects, which became important in the Igbo art tradition. The priests themselves, adorned in their priestly regalia, were part of this art tradition, which translated abstract Igbo thought into concrete forms. Consequently, the priests bridging the two worlds became important to the community because while they more perceptively interpreted principles of the society, they became part of those interpretations themselves. Contemporary examples include scholar/activists like Nigeria's Wole Soyinka and Flora Nwapa; Senegalese poet/president Leopold Sedar Senghor; South Africa's Bishop Desmond Tutu; Kenya's Ngugi wa Thiong'o; Egypt's Nawal el Sadaawi; Ghana's Ama Ata Aidoo and others whose searches for collective liberation and relevance reflect the duality embedded in traditional concepts of service and community.

Erroneous interpretations resulted in chaos between the two worlds and this was felt immensely by the community. In such a situation, an abomination could be declared and the priests had to purify the people and/or the land. In most parts of Igboland, *Nri* priests were called upon to perform such purification (Isichei, 23, 41) as part of the effort to maintain this relationship across Igboland. Some Igbo groups saw them as blood relations (Isichei, 41) while others looked on them as associates with the responsibilities to cleanse the land when crimes like homicide, murder, suicide were committed (Isichei, 112). Thus, problems were perceived as the results of disharmonious relationships between the community and the supernatural realm. Equilibrium between the two worlds was established through sacrifices and rituals, which aimed at warding off evil spirits that were believed to invade the community during periods of disharmony. In essence, traditional priests or contemporary scholar/activists serve as mediators between the masses and that which stands between their communities and progress. The most recognizable of these obstacles to progress in recent memory are colonial oppression and the misguided leadership of the post-independence era.

On the individual level, priests were also required to offer sacrifices for people who were experiencing imbalance in their lives. An extremely sick person, for instance, would seek the help and intercession of priests or medicine men. Analogously, sick communities, as are common in many African states, look to the scholar/activist for guidance toward progress.

In his role as mediator, the priest became both man and spirit. The people and himself perceived him as such when he performed the duties of his office (Basden: 1938, 132–133). The priestly duality is part of a broader Igbo concept of the existence of things in pairs. Other pairs are good and evil, earth and firmament, and past and present. Balancing of such complementary opposites forms the basis for a continuous maintenance of harmony between two worlds:

> ... [the] Igbo look forward to the next world as being the same as this... [and] picture life there to be exactly as it is in this world. The ground there is just the same as it is here; the earth is similar. There are forests and hills and valleys with rivers flowing and roads leading from one town to another... [P]eople in Spiritland have their ordinary occupations, the farmer his farm (Leonard: 1906, 185–186.

On the level of Igbo religious belief and spirituality,

> ... Chukwu owns all
> And Sundry:
> He and Ana.
> Chukwu and *Ana* own all (Isichei, 171–177).

The relationships between *Ana*, the earth, and *Ana*, the Earth Goddess, and between them and Chukwu offer explanations that deal implicitly with duality. Out of *Ana*, the earth, on which the Igbo tread and from which they get life giving food grew the venerated *Ana*, the Earth Goddess. The Igbo saw this as a closer relationship than the one maintained with Chukwu, who, though powerful, was more abstract and therefore distant, and was not as directly involved in the affairs of humans as *Ana*. In traditional Igbo life, these relationships gave rise to the pervasiveness of religion in other areas and from them emanated Igbo relationships with other gods and spirits. In Igbo thought, these parallel universes allow the careful observer to draw from one universe to enhance and/or complement the other.

On the individual level, Chukwu was seen as the creator in charge of all, but everyone had his or her own *chi*, personal god, which also had creative qualities and endowed each person with creative talent and skills (Aniakor: 1974, 1). This created "a world order in which contrasting opposites within a unity len[t] harmonious creative tension to [Igbo] society and its culture" (Aniakor, 2). Individuals were encouraged to reconcile their creative talents to the community as this ensured conformity to society's standards. This need for conformity remains obvious in the Igbo art tradition which itself grows out of Igbo religion.

Originally, Igbo art is functional. However, the society also requires that beauty and elegance in art objects balance their utilitarian qualities. This balancing concept, although not always explicitly expressed among the Igbo, is still practiced with much vigor. It can be found in myths, poetry and other artistic modes of expression. It is a perception that holds as true for the carving of an *Ikenga* (Aniakor, 6) as it does for the performing of an oral narrative performance, the protagonist is portrayed as having to balance his personality and activities with that of the community. These narratives reflect part of this concept in their portrayals of the constant traffic between the natural and spirit worlds in which each protagonist searches for and find personal wholeness.

Authors of early written Igbo narratives used the concept of duality in their works. In Achara's *Ala Bingo* (1954) the king, living one year on earth and the next year in the sky, reflects this dualism. Later in the story, he has to balance his arrogance with humility, his individualism with a sense of community and using an awareness of the worth of others. In Pita Nwanna's *Omenuko* (1933) the man, Omenuko, years after selling his apprentices, seeks the help of medicine men to mediate between him and the spirits and the whole community. Only after the re-establishment of harmony between Omenuko and these two groups can he return peacefully to his home of birth. The individual, already aware of and practicing this concept in his life like Elelea in Achara's *Elelea Na Ihe O Mere* (1952), implicitly endorses individual and communal advancement and progress. Thus, Elelea reflects the ideals of traditional Igbo priesthood. Perceiving the priest as possessing this awareness of duality, the people vested in him the power to mediate the concept of duality in their lives. The figure of the half-man, half-spirit priest symbolized the extent to which the concept of duality was realizable in the real world. In Achebe's *Things Fall Apart*, this figure is concretely portrayed by the *egwugwu* and by the priestess, Chielo, on a more abstract level. This last point remains one of the most difficult in the transition from an oral to a written African verbal art. The problem is this: while the *egwugwu* is a practical and visual part of Igbo life and art, Chielo is an inherent discourse celebrated on a metaphoric level. Although she does not appear in priestly regalia in *Things Fall Apart*, she is cloaked by the night darkness when she takes Ezimma to the Oracle of the Hills and Caves and, by the mystery of ordinariness by day. This mystery of the ordinary informs Achebe's exploration of women. Chielo, the priestess of *Agbala*, is introduced as one of the women in the crowd during the wrestling match that takes place on the second day of the New Year when she stands, "shoulder to shoulder" (48) with Ekwefi. Achebe explores this relationship between the ordinary and the sacred further in *Arrow of God* (1964) when all the women of Umuaro (e)merge during the festival of the Pumpkin leaves as dancers "...stamping [their feet] together in unison...[until] the pumpkin leaves...had been smashed and trodden into the dust (83–84). Like Chielo, the women of Umuaro are ordinary women who, without visible priestly regalia, are co-participants with Ezeulu in his celebration of the annual cleansing ritual. This capacity of traditional African art to merge the concrete with the abstract remains problematic for contemporary African literature's efforts to transcend the colonial legacy of Roman script.

Among Igbo authors writing in English about Igbo life and experiences, Achebe recognizes the priest figure as a major participant in Igbo ontology. Before Achebe, Cyprian Ekwensi, like the writers of Igbo fiction, uses the concept but offers little explanation regarding its existence or practice in Igbo life or art tradition. His first novel, *People of the City* (1954) deals with life in the squalid, crime-ridden city of Lagos. Ekwensi's characters and their environment reflect little of Igbo beliefs. His works portray the corruption and fast-life of the new, exciting, but unfriendly city. The diversity of people and cultural backgrounds make the harmonious living which characterize traditional societies seem alien. *Jagua Nana* (1961) a novel which is also about city life, ends with the protagonist, Jagua, seeking and finding wholeness, through motherhood at the shrine of her village's major deity. Later, Buchi Emecheta (1979) explores these plots further using motherhood as the major downfall of the Igbo woman in the emerging brutality of city life. Ekwensi does not explore in great depth the traditional Igbo relationship with the other world. *Jagua Nana's* experience of peace and harmony is presented but not explained or explored. His other novels, *Beautiful Feathers* (1963) and *Iska* (1966) also address the problems of life in the city and contemporary issues. Among writers working from a traditional Igbo narrative viewpoint, Ekwensi and Emecheta work the most from the culture's surface structure, giving scant attention to the relevance of emerging contents to Igbo people's existence.

Achebe goes beyond other contemporary interpreters to explore Igbo social, political, economic and religious realities but stays within the Igbo art tradition by couching Igbo thought in the "metaphor of myth and poetry" (Achebe: 1975, 161).

Viewed against the Igbo art traditional background, his interpretations of traditional and contemporary Igbo life and experience are authentic in its reconciliation of personal creative talent to the society's concept of beauty and functionalism and aestheticism of the traditional mask carvings and *Ikenga*.

Achebe's early short stories reveal his first attempt to achieve this unity. "Dead Men's Path" (Achebe: 1973, 73–78) depicts the importance of the relationship between the natural and the supernatural, while "Akueke" (Achebe: 1973, 109–129) demonstrates the balance between traditional wisdom in the elderly and the ignorance of youth. The themes of these brief portrayals are developed in *Things Fall Apart*, which explores the complexities of the relationship between the male and female principles, among others. In *Arrow of God* (1969) the descriptions and interpretations are more explicit and intricate. Here, Achebe sets recognized pairs within the Igbo duality concept against each other and also looks at a new pair, the Igbo world and that of the British colonial administration. Where earlier Igbo authors focus on the second half of this new pair as an independent unit, Achebe works it into the tensions of Umuaro life. He compares Ezeulu and Winterbottom, and Ezeulu's intemperate son, Obierika, to the adventurous Mr. Wright. Ezeulu's involvement in Umuaro's politics reflects the functions of the traditional priests and the *okpala*, the heads of families, whose duties were to maintain harmony between individual families and the society.

Achebe's interpretations mediate the priest and artist's functions, linking the past and the present (Taiwo: 1976, 114) and harmonizing contemporary Igbo existence. He achieves this by disposing of the wrong interpretations that characterized colonial perceptions about Igbo (African) life and experience. His basic premise hinges on the tensions between the axiomatic pair, the individual and the community. The relationship between the two and their significant references in Igbo life cannot be overstated. In pre-colonial Igbo life, an individual who sought harmonious relationships with the spirit world had to be in good moral standing with the whole community. Thus, an *ofo*, staff or justice, holder had to be upright in every sense of the word (Ogbalu: 1979, 20–21). A man's *Ikenga*, the symbol of the strength of his right hand, had to have the *aka ikenga*, right hand, thrusting upwards. This upward thrust shows that the hands of *Ikenga* are clean and [that] one's thrusts in life are ethically sanctioned by society's codes of moral behavior: *Lee m! Akam di ocha* – "Look at me! My hands are clean!" (Aniakor, 5).

An individual's "clean hands" ensured the progress, good health and wealth of himself and his community. They indicated the maintenance of balance between the two worlds. In some areas, the upward thrust of the *Ikenga* was interpreted as a ram's horns, defining one's moral and physical strength (Aniakor 3–4). Whatever the interpretation, a viable *Ikenga* revealed an individual from whom his kin could expect fairness, justice and great achievements because of his awareness of the duality principle. When a man suffered regressions in life, his *Ikenga* was blamed and he could abandon it to make a new one (Udechukwu: 1971, 90). Traditional Igbo society disposed of fractious individuals, oracles or gods who threatened its well being, thereby creating new avenues for success and the maintenance of individual and societal harmony. But such disposal was only as a last resort, because the perception that everything and everybody contributed in some way to the maintenance of balance ensured that individuals were aware early of a tightly knit system of relationships. All worked to keep their places in each system until they fulfilled the requirements for moving up to the next. Most of these systems, like title taking and marriage, became synonymous with stages of social achievement. Movements between stages were determined more by individual ability than age. However, people tended to move to successive stages or social ranks in groups which were directly proportional to their ages. For example, young men or women of a certain age group would get married within three years of each other. The same was true of title taking. This led to a situation in which the ruling elders of a given community belonged in a certain age range. In this way, consensus democracy among the elders was possible because members did not feel threatened by each other.

In addition to this working together of the elders, the leader of each household was responsible for the activities of its members, directing and guiding their social behavior. This meant that a person's behavior in a household was subject to appraisal by his family and the community. However, one was first accountable to the immediate and extended family, as this ensured allegiance to *ora* or *oha*, the general community. The supremacy of *ora* remains a strong force in contemporary Igbo life and is demonstrated in Achebe's novels.

In *Things Fall Apart*, Okonkwo, as head of the family, is able to put Nwoye and Ikemefuna to work on the fence. Ezeulu, in *Arrow of God*, asks his sons to help him once every four-day market week. When he wants them to help complete the work on Obierika's homestead and Oduche declines, offering the excuse of having been chosen by his Christian group to go to Okperi, Ezeulu intervenes:

> Listen to what I shall say now... It is I who sent you to join those people because of my friendship to the white man, Wintabota... I did not send you so that you might leave your duty to my household...Tomorrow is the day on which my sons and my wives and sons' wives work for me. (Achebe: 1969, 14–15).

Group solidarity is simplicity maintained with the help of elders who check and balance individual participation within the group and their alliance to it. Individual involvement in family or village events emphasizes the role of the individual in the community. After the women who are cooking for Obierika's wife have fined the owner of the stray cow, for instance, there is a head-count to help them determine absentees the women's actions demonstrate that one does not have to be invited to participate in issues that threaten community welfare. Achebe emphasizes this by commenting after the incident: "Those women whom Obierika's wife had not asked to help her with the cooking returned to their homes and the rest went back in a body, to Obierika's compound" (Achebe: 1958, 80).

In his book, *Omenala Igbo* (1967) Ogbalu records many Igbo customs, telling when they take place, what and who are involved and what purposes they serve the people. Although there are no detailed comments or explanations, the emphasis on the relationship between the individual and the group is obvious in the descriptions. Connections between the community and the supernatural world are also seen in the activities of the family. The heads of families are usually the eldest sons. These are called the *okpala* or *okpara* (Olisa, 19). Traditionally, they held the family *ofo*. Olisa refers to the *ofo* as "the physical medium for the invocation of the powers of *Ala* and the ancestors" (Olisa, 22). The man who held it for the family had the right to carry out rituals or sacrificial rites that involved the family or its individual members. He also led the family in decision making. Since all such activities among the Igbo were in some way connected with their ancestors or gods, the *okpala* with the *ofo* were closer to both. Ezeulu, in *Arrow of God*, stood in such stead for his family as well as for the clan. Okonkwo's uncle, Uchendu, in *Things Fall Apart*, also had this role in their family.

The concept of maintaining a balanced relationship with the spirit world was more visible at the community level. The community's staff of justice, *nne ofo*, was held by chief priests like Ezeulu (Achebe: 1969, 19). Ulu is not, however, representative of the nature gods, the permanent gods of Igboland. According to Nwoga, "Ulu, in many ways, is not a characteristic Igbo god" (Nwoga: 1981, 19–20) because he did not survive confrontation like the other gods of "unknown" origin. Achebe created Ulu for the purposes of his artistic vision much as the traditional oral performers created spirits and human characters from their narrative visions. However, both Achebe and the traditional artist build their characters from aspects of well-known and accepted Igbo thought and belief systems. In creating an Ulu who is known and yet unknown, Achebe works within the traditional oral narrative technique of creating stories whose nameless characters his audience can only partly identify in the sense that their behavioral characteristics are familiar but their physical features are not. This technique allows the audience to identify in the sense that their behavioral characteristics are familiar but their physical features are not. This technique allows the audience to identify with the character, which in turn facilitates the major didactic function of oral narrative performance. Ulu has enough characteristics to identify him as one of the gods. Using this narrative technique frees Achebe from theological or mythical perspectives on religion (Nwoga: 1981, 20), Ezeulu, therefore, holding the Nneofo, the Mother of all the *ofo* in Umuaro, becomes the focus for the narrator's art which works on the assumption of shared experiences, including religious beliefs, between the narrator and the audience.

A juxtaposition of two incidents, one from *Things Fall Apart* and the other from *Arrow of God* clarifies this relationship between man and spirit at the community level. In the latter, when the elders meet to discuss issues (28–31) there is no need for them to invoke the presence of the ancestors by the donning of ritual regalia. This is because, as titled men and elders, they understand more than the average Igbo the operating concepts and relationships in the society's life and culture. They are the initiated. In *Things Fall Apart*, the situation is portrayed differently. Here, the elders of Umuofia have to settle the problems of some members of the community in public (63–66). The elders, therefore, reinforce for the uninitiated the fact that they depend on the wisdom of the ancestors for the maintenance of community harmony. They must wear *egwugwu* regalia, symbolizing for them and the rest of the people the source that balances and upholds their decisions. These become ratified because the ancestors have a hand in their creation. This may be seen in the comment of one of the elders after Uzowulu's case has been settled:

> "I don't know why such a trifle should come before the *egwugwu*" said one elder
> to another. "Don't you know what kind of man Uzowulu is? He will not listen
> to any other decision," replied another (66).

Uzowulu's insistence on the participation of the ancestors in the form of the *egwugwu* stems from the people's belief that societal harmony emanates from their awareness and application of the concept of duality. He takes back his wife after both men and gods endorse the act. Individuals like Uzowulu who need constant, overt expression of the duality principle make institutions like the *egwugwu* necessary. Their aggressive insistence on the balancing of perceived pairs in the duality principle endorses societal maintenance of the system. Significant in this regard is the balancing of the male/female principle on which *Things Fall Apart* places much emphasis.

Harmonizing the male and female principle is reflected in the place and function of men and women in the society. On the surface, Igbo society seems predominately patriarchal; however, women wield a considerable amount of influence. The idea of woman as counterpart to man is strongly emphasized. The female principle is revered. In the Igbo pantheon, the most revered and feared deity is *Ala*, the Earth Goddess. Shrines are built for her, and special priests, the Ezeala, are in charge of these. In the Owerri area a special art event, the Mbari is declared in her honor during intensive shortage of food crops or infertility in women. This event is supposed to help enhance the goddess' goodwill and a showering of her blessing on the community thereafter (Basden, 99–109; Udechukwu, 91). In *Things Fall Apart*, Achebe portrays how the Week of Peace is held to "honor our great goddess of the earth without whose blessing our crops will not grow" (22). Oracles are referred to as *agbala*, another name for woman. Potent medicines are believed to be female, like the *agadi nwanyi*, old woman, Umuofia's potent war medicine (9), or the ancient deity, *Nwanyieke*, the mythical old woman is said to be in charge of the great market at Okperi (21).

On the other hand, men who have not shown their valor in war or taken any titles, like Okonkwo's father, Unoka, are also called *agbala*. This is because they cannot demonstrate the existence of the male principle in their lives. However, mere demonstration is not enough. All individuals have to be able to balance both the male and female principles in themselves to maintain their positions in the society. As Achebe demonstrates in his works, men like Unoka fail because they manifest only the female principle, while the Okonkwos fail because they cannot maintain the balance between the two principles. Achebe uses the characters of Ogbuefi Ndulue and Ozoemena (47), his wife, to emphasize this. Before his death, Ogbuefi Ndulue, the greatest warrior in his day and the oldest man in his village, had lived in such harmony with his wife that they were said to have one mind. The people acknowledged his greatness by letting him lead Umuofia in wars. He was a great man because in will and physical strength he could be depended on to maintain a balance between the two demonstrable aspects of human existence.

Another aspect of the participation and place of the female principle in Igbo life is portrayed in the festival of the First Pumpkin Leaves in Umuaro. This festival is not held in honor of *Ala* as that which is held during the Week of Peace in Umuofia. Umuaro's aim is to cleanse its people and ask Ulu for abundance in all aspects of their lives. It is significant that pumpkin leaves – a woman's crop – is used and that women go to the village square carrying bunches of these leaves, symbolizing the sins of the people. The image of the women ritually throwing the leaves at the priest who later buries the sins of the people in the earth demonstrates the balance achieved when the male and female principles work together. The priest – philosopher, scapegoat and male – representing the male principle, works together here with the women, the female principle, to expiate ritually the evil, which have taken place in the community during the previous year. The leaves that the priest does not bury are stomped into the earth by the women. In this way, the people are able to crystallize the concepts, which they acknowledge and recognize in the abstract.

Although men are the major participants in the politics of the traditional Igbo community, women also wield considerable influence in this area. As Olisa says:

> The *Umuada* or *Umuokpu* (daughters of the family married outside, or, in some areas all the women of the kindred) are perhaps the most powerful of the organized women groups...Occasionally the *Umuada* could step in to settle long-standing kindred disputes which the male members have been unable to settle. They could also compel of them, for example, to conform to any measures

decided on the town level which measures they might have opposed (Olisa, 24–25; see also: Isichei, 74).

Achebe provides brief glimpses of the *Umuada* and their activities when the youngest son of Uchendu, Okonkwo's maternal uncle, gets married, and also, when the women who had been making music at a funeral go into Obi Okonkwo's father's compound to sing their welcome to Obi. Women's involvement in such matters that concern the individual or group shows the various ways in which their participation maintains communal harmony.

Maintenance of balance in the traditional Igbo concept of duality did not stop with the individual or with groups of people in a community. The entire community was subject to the operation of this concept. Like the individual, the community also had its male and female aspects; for instance, kinsmen of one's father and mother. Each checked and balanced the activities of the other. For the individual, this had notable advantages, especially in times of stress. One could always, as Okonkwo did, take refuge with one section if the other was wronged. In *Omenuko*, neighboring communities went out of their way to establish such relationships with each other (Nwanna: 1933, 10–11) to ensure that their members would have a place of refuge in times of conflict. However, if the threat came from the outside, the society would try to remain as one unit. This was one of the reasons why colonial occupations upset Igbo solidarity and rifts occurred first within the communities. The people found it difficult to fight the white man after their own people had joined the new religion. They could not fight them because that would have meant fighting and possibly killing their own. As Obierika observes to Okonkwo:

> Our own men and own sons have joined the ranks of the stranger. They have joined his religion and they help to uphold his government. If we should try to drive out the white man in Umuofia we should find it easy. There are only two of them. But what of our own people who are following their way and have been given power? (Achebe: 1958, 124)

But Okonkwo, lacking full understanding of what maintained communal balance and harmony, fights and resists both the strangers and his people. He disowns Nwoye and kills the court messenger. Achebe's portrayal of Okonkwo's lack of ability to advocate balance between the two principles demonstrates the necessity for the complex system that maintains societal order and harmony. Although a titled elder, his dependence on the external manifestations of the system is similar to Uzowulu's discussed above. Unlike Obierika who knows when it is appropriate to ask questions that will lead to consistent upholding of societal and individual harmony, Okonkwo kills Ikemefuna because the oracle orders his death. Having carefully considered potential sources for the excoriation of the things within the society itself, the people devise a system to ensure that the Okonkwos, though capable of achieving the conspicuous requirements for admission into the group of elders, would not be allowed to lead them toward self-destruction.

Where the concept of duality can not be easily perceived, explained or implemented in Igbo society, the people consciously establish new and concrete relationships. This is demonstrated in the creation of new village groups, like Umuaro in *Arrow of God*. In real life, initiated elders maintain this potential through the use of ritual language. For example, there is the normal, everyday language spoken by everybody, and the language of spirits, which only the ancestors or their representatives in the world of the living can use. Others only use the second kind of language in the context of artistic expression like oral narrative performances. Situations where people have to impersonate spirits, as in certain festivals requiring the display of masks, also provide further opportunities for the expansion of boundaries. Igbo thought and philosophy therefore have a built-in egalitarian outlook in terms of government, freedom of artistic expression and other freedoms. The elders who speak in the language of the spirits when they assume ancestral roles can not easily or even willingly stop their children from learning the ways of the strangers who came to live among them. In the new dispensation, the Igbo cultural world has expanded to include the new worldview and its effort to introduce ideas about *Unfreedom* incompatible with the society's socio-political and other realities.

Achebe's use of the English language fits into traditional Igbo thought, which allows the development of new solutions in times of conflict and transition. Such attitudes enable the society to change without experiencing the kind of violence that Okonkwo demonstrates in *Things Fall Apart*. In his use of the metaphor of "Things fall apart, the center cannot hold," Achebe, the artist of the new dispensation foresees the imbalance in African communities, a consequence of the emerging postcolonial reality, independence and subsequent acceptance of alienating notions of individuality over community. When things fell apart, communities could no longer grant their staffs of justice to individuals because in the new dispensation, the main character is the individual who holds the staff rather than the characters of justice, harmony and peace as inviolable responsibilities of Community.

Works Cited

Achara, D.N. *Ala Bingo*. London: Longmans, 1954.

———. *Elelea na Ihe Omere*. London: Longmans, 1952.

Achebe, Chinua. *Arrow of God*. New York: Doubleday & Company, 1969.

———. *Girls at War and Other Stories*. New York: Doubleday & Company, Inc., 1973.

———. *Morning Yet on Creation Day*. New York: Anchor Press/ Doubleday, 1975.

———. *No Longer at Ease*. London: Heinemann, 1960.

———. *Things Fall Apart*. London: Heinemann, 1958.

Aniakor, Chike. "Structuralism In *Ikenga*: An Ethno-Aesthetic Approach to Traditional Igbo Art," *Conch*, VI: 1 & 2 (1974).

Basden, G.T. *Niger Ibos*. London: Frank Cass & Co., Ltd., 1938.

Eco, Umberto. *A Theory of Semiotics*. Bloomington: Indiana University Press, 1976.

Ekwensi, Cyprian. *Beautiful Feathers*. London: Hutchison and Co., 1963.

———. *Iska*. London: Hutchinson and Co., 1966.

———. *Jagua Nana*. London: Hutchison and Co., 1961.

———. *People and the City*. London: Andrew Dakers, 1954.

Emecheta, Buchi. *The Joys of Motherhood*. London: Heinemann Educational Books, 1979.

Henderson, Richard N. *The King in Every Man*. New Haven: Yale University Press, 1972.

Isichei, Elizabeth. *Igbo Worlds*. Philadelphia: Institute for the Study of Human Issues, 1978.

Kalu Anthonia. "The Priest/Artist Tradition in Achebe's *Arrow of God*," *Africa Today*, 41, 2 (1994).

Leonard, A.G. *The Lower Niger and Its Tribes*. London: Macmillan, 1906.

Nwanna, Pita. *Omenuko*. London: Longmans, 1933.

Nwoga, Ibe D. "The Igbo World of *Arrow of God*," *Research in African Literatures*, 12, 1 (Spring 1981).

Ogbalu, F.C. *Omenala Igbo*. Onitsha: University Publishing Company, 1979.

Okpewho, Isidore. *African Oral Literature: Backgrounds, Character and Continuity*. Bloomington and Indianapolis: Indiana University Press, 1992.

Olisa, M.S.O. "Political Culture and Stability in Igbo Society," *Conch*, III, 2 (September 1971).

Taiwo, Oladele. *Culture and the Nigerian Novel*. London: Macmillan Education Limited, 1976.

Udechukwu, Obiora. "Functionalism, Symbolism and Decoration: Some Aspects of Traditional Igbo Art," *Conch*, III, 2 (September 1971).

Chapter 10

Igbo Humor in the Novels of Chinua Achebe

J.O.J. Nwachukwu – Agbada

The Nature of Humour

HUMOUR MAY BE CONSIDERED as that which we behold or perceive and it tickles or amuses us. It is the underlying thrilling feeling which we earn as a result of a sudden comprehension or from a striking realization immanent in what is uttered, in an activity, a pattern or a web of actions. Paul McGhee remarks that "when we speak of a person having a sense of humour, we mean that the person is especially likely not only to perceive such events, but also to derive special enjoyment from them" (6). At the turn of the century, Sigmund Freud was to argue that the pleasure which is achieved from humour results from exercising the intellect in a bid to appreciate a joke. Freud further remarks that adults engage in humour formulation and enjoyment because of the level of social constraints which compel man to occasionally abandon rigorous and logical thinking. In other words, Freud considers humour as a way of escape, a means of retreat into playful feelings, actions and thoughts. Bateson and Fry have advanced views closely related to those of Maier. They suggest that a series of paradoxes is characteristic of humorous situations and that we only see the humour when a punchline or other key information unexpectedly resolves these paradoxes. The resolution of a paradoxical complex is probably what Arthur Koestler refers to as 'bisociation'. Biosociation, states Koestler, is "the perceiving of a situation or idea ... in two self-consistent but habitually incompatible frames of reference." In the case of humour, bisociation

> causes an abrupt transfer of the train of thought from one matrix to another governed by a different logic or 'rule of the game'. But certain emotions, owing

to their greater inertia and persistence, cannot follow such nimble jumps of
thought; discarded by reason, they are worked off along the channels of least
resistance in the form of laughter (95).

Through bisociation, two domains of thought that have never before been considered to have any meaningful relationship are suddenly observed to have a common
thread of similarity or connection. A biosociative insight is relatively more creative
than others when this relationship is not initially easy to see but is obviously appropriate once it is realized.

Background to Achebean Humour

The humour in Chinua Achebe's novels is largely an Igbo event. This is because the
context of his humour is mostly realizable in the Igbo matrix. But more importantly,
the sources and resources of his humour are essentially Igbo in origin. Achebe likes
to say that the world-view that informs his works is Igbo.[1] His use of idioms and
proverbs, folktales, acecdotes, myths, songs, rhetoric and humour attests to his
debt to the Igbo tradition. In all these uses, Achebe has at the back of his mind
the biosociative relationship which must be resolved for purposes of enlightment
and a new awareness.

Igbo humour, from which Achebean humor is derived, is located in a number
of Igbo oral forms such as those already listed in the preceding paragraph. In addition, there are found in Igbo conversational styles satire, sarcasm, irony, invectives
and altercations, prayers, analogies, jokes, insults and abuses, sexy vignettes, taunts
and puns. These varied forms as employed by Achebe in his novels are meant to
prickle and fascinate the reader, and to shed some pleasure. He has carefully chosen
the variants of the oral forms which will ensure some personal enjoyment of his
works. One may wonder why a tragic novelist such as Achebe equally invests his
fiction with so much pleasure and entertainment mostly realized through jokes and
humorous contexts. Occidentalist scholarship will quickly point to one Western
classic writer or the other as the source of his influence, but the truth is that the
Igbo in real life accept the coexistence of play and pathos such that deaths are often
marked by dances and entertainment of various kinds.

Traditionally, adult Igbo enjoy a joking relationship such as exchange of aliases
(*aha ntu-ntu*)[2], weather greetings, prayers and wishes and the general jocose game
called *njakiri*. A.R. Radcliffe-Brown defines a joking relationship as:

> a relation between two persons in which one is by custom permitted, and in
> some instances required to tease or make fun of the other, who in turn is re-
> quired to take no offense ... The joking relationship is a peculiar combination
> of friendliness and antagonism (195).

Njakiri is an old Igbo joking relationship. As far back as the 1930s C.K. Meek had observed that "one may often see two Igbo reviling each other in the strongest language for several minutes and then bursting into laughter as they walk away" (230). *Njakiri*, notes Ebeogu, possesses two essential rhetorical ingredients namely, sarcasm (*iko onu*) and curse (*Ikpo iyi*). He further avers that, "when these two shades of the rhetorical art, in combination with relevant literary instruments are given informal dramatic situation, then an *njakiri* context emerges" (29).

Just as an *njakiri* session may involve more than two persons at the same time, *njakiri*, makes use of more than the two rhetorical tools of sarcasm and curse; it also employs mockery, noisy laughter, raillery, parody, exaggeration and understatement of image. It is the context of application of these rhetorical modes that determines whether what emerges is *njakiri*, obvious insult (*iko onu*), downright abuse (*mkpari*) or a quizzical play (*egwuregwu*). *Iko onu* among Igbo children is a playful act but this is not so among adults. Among Igbo adults, "it is neither a game nor a play nor a sally of words. It is profound abuse (*mkpari*), an affront which could lead to fighting or poisoning or outright murder" (Nwachukwu-Agbada 1995). However, in the proper context in which a joking relationship has been established *iko onu*, in combination with the other rhetorical forms, is transmuted from a pompous act to a jocose event.

Njakiri is the softer side of Igbo satire. The typical Igbo satire is punitive or corrective depending on the context. *Njakiri* is a lighthearted session of interpersonal jokes although it could hurt as much as satire. It is a by-product of satire because whereas satire is a literary attack on one who has committed a moral or material slip, *njakiri* directed at someone may not always result from an obvious inadequacy. In *njakiri*, "there is no intention to injure feelings or attack an offence either way, which is what satire aims at doing" (Egudu, "Social Values" 77).

Resources of Humor in Achebe's Novels

From the foregoing observations, it is clear that Achebe, once described by Donatus Nwoga as "a wise Igbo leader,"[3] must have gone into writing with a possession of the Igbo heritage of humor which is occasionally misunderstood by other Nigerians.[4] In order to invest his writing with enough humor, Achebe employs amusing proverbs, ironies, folktales, verbal rhetoric, anecdotes, invectives, gossips, prayers, superstitions, mirthful conversational styles and ludicrous exemplifications. He equally infuses his works with direct authorial humor through authorial intervention and the conscious creation of ironical situations. All these imbue his works with a tone that is vintage Achebe.

i. Ticklish Proverbs and Comparisons

Achebe's use of proverbs had been extensively discussed (Lindfors 1968; Seitel 1969;

Shelton 1969; Yankson 1990; Ogbaa 1992; Nwachukwu-Agbada 1993). However, there is need to emphasize his penchant for using those sayings that instantly excite one's sense of humor. Each of his witty sayings has equivalences which could have been used if he so desired. But it seems that most of the ones in his texts are so chosen because such proverbs contain glee and ensure some pleasure. This category of proverbs exercises the intellect until a striking realization emerges from the utterances. For instance, "an old woman is always uneasy when dry bones are mentioned in a proverb" (*TFA* 15). An old woman is bound to be uncomfortable at the mention of dry bones since her gums must have lost quite a number of teeth. The coiner of this proverb arrived at his/her decision through some assumptive poise since his/her inference is only by conjecture.

Ezeulu urges one of his sons, Oduche to join the Christian faith, even as he is himself a strong custodian of traditional Igbo religion with the following proverb – comparison: "I am like the bird *Eneke-nti-oba*. When his friends asked him why he was always on the wing he replied: 'Men of today have learnt to shoot without missing and so I have learnt to fly without perching'" (*AOG* 45 and *TFA* 16). Humor is derived from this saying in three ways: one, a bird is ascribed with speech: two, the Wellerism celebrates acute intelligence and the need for survival in a hostile setting; and three, man is tickled because it is man that is responsible for the bird's new posture. The bird *Eneke-nti-oba (Eneke* the flabby-earred) belongs to the swift family which fills the sky and is difficult to be seen perching on trees whenever it is in season.

Some of the proverbs are also utilized in jocular contexts in the novels as is the case in *Anthills* where Beatrice urges the taxi-driver not to worry about returning the empty bottle with which she gave him some water. The driver asks in Pidgin: "I be monkey wey dem say to give im water no hard but to get your tumbler back?" (182). It is the Igbo proverb which says "giving palm wine to a monkey is not a problem, it is retrieving the cup from him." At Osodi's address to the University of Bassa students, he employed a proverb which caused some laughter: "our proverb says that the earthworm is not dancing, it is only its manner of walking" (*Anthills* 157). Another of his proverbs attracts loud laughter from his audience: "If you want to get at the root of murder, they said, you have to look for the blacksmith who made the machete" (*Anthills* 159). A little while later he employs a contradictory proverb and there is "loud laughter and applause, catching even the severe young man off his guard" (*Anthills* 159–60). The contradictory proverb reads: "... it is like going to arrest the village blacksmith every time a man hacks his fellow to death" (*Anthills* 159).

Three proverbs found in the Speeches of two men in *No Longer at Ease* are quite humorous. Two of the proverbs are by the President of Umuofia Progressive

Union in Lagos namely, "if you want to eat a toad you should look for a fat and juicy one" (5) and "He told the proverb of the house rat who went swimming with his friend the lizard and died from cold, for while the lizard's scales kept him dry the rat's hairy body remained wet" (5). The third proverb is by Ikedi while advising Obi Okonkwo: "Do not be in a hurry to rush into the pleasure of the world like the young antelope who danced herself lame when the main dance was yet to come" (10). A toad is not a popular source of meat for the Igbo, hence the need for "a fat and juicy one" should it be eaten at all. Obi Okonkwo obtains only a small amount of money as bribe for which he will be sent to jail, yet he had all the opportunities previously to have received larger sums. Other people saw it as a mockery of his folly, for in doing what he has no mastery of. The third proverb pre-empted Obi's later acts of stupidity in the novel. It was said to him as he was about to leave for England in pursuit of higher education.

ii. Comic Ironies

Muecke remarks that irony constitutes ways of speaking, writing, acting, behaving, painting etc., in which real or intended meaning presented or evoked is intentionally incompatible with the ostensible or pretended meaning. By implication, irony is a source of humour, especially when Muecke insists that its definition "must likewise be allowed to include not only saying one thing and meaning another but also saying two things and meaning neither" (53). Achebe's mastery of the use of irony is comparable to those of Fielding, Sterne, Gibbon, Swift and Orwell although his ironical contexts differ from those of these Western classic writers. Hence, "to fail to consider the place of irony in his *Things Fall Apart* is like missing a crucial step as one climbs a high-rise building." This is because "the entire architecture of the narrative structure of the novel is built around this figure of thought, giving hint at once to the world-view of the Igbo whose philosophy and experience it imitates" (Nwachukwu-Agbada, "A Model" 41).

Okonkwo is a victim of irony in *Things Fall Apart*, he declares: "since I survived that year ... I shall survive anything" (18). That year refers to the year he lost several of his yams to vagrant weather. His father, Unoka also says encouragingly to him: "You have a manly and a proud heart. A proud heart can survive a general failure because such a failure does not prick its pride. It is more difficult and more bitter when a man fails alone" (18). Ironically Okonkwo does not survive everything as it is evident at the end of the story. Again he fails to "survive a general failure" as his father had thought. Moreover, Okonkwo fails alone because his community members blame him for acting against the interest of the white colonialists. The humorous dimension becomes clearer when one realizes that events take place which contradict initial thinking and supposition. This is further illustrated when the people of Umuofia accede to the missionaries' request for a parcel land. The people are convinced that if given the Evil Forest, the visitors would abandon it after a while. But this does not happen: "Everyone was puzzled. And then it became known that the white man's fetish had unbelievable power" (*TFA* 106).

Ezeulu's fate in *Arrow of God* is to a large extent a function of irony. His testimony at the Umuaro-Okperi land case brings him recognition from the white administration because he is a witness of truth. However, it is this truthful testimony that eventually brings him face-to-face in a collision course with the colonial administration. His refusal to accept the chieftaincy stool offered him by Captain Winterbottom is an embarrassment to the colonialists. Never before had the white administration suffered such humiliation. Ironically Winterbottom falls sick as Ezeulu is detained and this is interpreted to mean "the priest had hit him with a potent charm" (*AOG* 155). But the truth is that the Captain's ailment at this period of misunderstanding with the Ulu priest is only a coincidence.

iii. Delightful Anecdotes

Egudu defines an anecdote as "a brief story which often embodies witticism or a ludicrous situation, and which is used to embellish speech, reinforce or illustrate an argument, or convey moral lessons" ("Nature" 77). Each of Achebe's acecdotes contains a witticism or celebrates a ludicrous situation meant to cause laughter. Two of such anecdotes in *No Longer at Ease* are noteworthy. Christopher relates the incident of a woman who refused to be comforted over her children's death in a well. For three days she wept uncontrollably, insisting that she be allowed to commit suicide in the pit. Tired of her antics, her husband ordered that she be allowed to do her wish. She ran to the well "but when she got there she first had a peep and then she put her right foot in, brought it out and put her left" (131). This is the moment of decision. She has realized that the suicidal enterprise demands a lot of courage. The other anecdote is one in which Tortoise is the main character. Tortoise suspects that his mother is about to die and in order to shirk the responsibility of burying her he decides to leave home, instructing that he be invited home only when an unusual thing under the sun happened. Soon after his mother died. It was not a new thing. In order to bring him home, his people tell him that his father's palm tree had borne a fruit at the end of its leaf. "When tortoise heard this, he said he must return home to see this great monstrosity" (148–49). The acecdote is a satire on irresponsibility. Tortoise's attempt to abdicate his responsibility is served by a communal solution to his puzzling exit from personal duty.

The anecdote of the hunter in *A Man of the People* who shoots vultures feeding on the game carrying his bullet bespeaks of rashness since vultures are inedible birds. Max then says: "You may say that he was foolish to waste his bullet on them (the vultures) but I say no. He was angry and he wanted to wipe out the dirty thieves fighting over another man's inheritance" (140). The anecdote reminds one of another Igbo folkstory of a hunter who went into the forest to hunt games with a loaded gun. After his effort to hunt down some animals failed, he became so tired that he slept off under a tree. While in a deep slumber a tse-tsefly perched on his scrotum and sucked his blood until he suddenly leapt into consciousness. He grabbed his gun and watched the fly in question re-perch on a distant twig. Out of intense anger he shot the insect, certainly to smithereens.

Achebe's anecdote in *Arrow of God* (26) refers to the Ojaadili folkstory in Igbo orature although Ezeulu who uses it in the novel does not reveal his source. It is the story of a great wrestler who is declared a champion, he having defeated all his human opponents. Then he moves into the spirit realm and equally throws all the sprits that show up. Rather than be contented with such an achievement he continues "to challenge the spirits to bring out their best and strongest wrestler." The spirits play him a trick by presenting him with his own personal god, "a little wiry sprit who seized him with one hand and smashed him on the stony earth" (27).

These anecdotes are a mockery of the human personality and its attributes and values. The story of the woman who can not be comforted on the death of her children is a lampoon on recalcitrance. We earn our laugh when she is hesitant to end her life upon being given the opportunity to do so, a wish she had sought for three days. Tortoise in the Tortoise anecdote is not human, yet its wiles are of human proportions. The puzzle it leaves at home is matched with an equally puzzling solution. The champion wrestler is a case of *hubris* and his conquest is due to uncontrolled arrogance. In each case there is a reversal of what was initially expected or thought about. The result is that the story incident draws out a deep-throated laughter from the reader or listener.

iv. Mirthful Myths

All narratives of the oral tradition qualify as myths, but Okpewho insists that myth must emphasize "fanciful play." This is because it is the "quality of fancy which informs the creative or configurative powers of the human mind in varying degrees of intensity" (69). Fanciful play is at the centre of the story of a wealthy man in *Things Fall Apart* (26) who presents his guests with a mound of foo-foo yam which is so high that those who sit on one side of the food can not know what is going on the other side. It is later in the evening when the height of the foo-foo is reduced that guests can exchange greetings across the left-over. The myth exercises our imagination through exaggeration. Laughter is achieved through surprise and bewilderment.

There are also myths about non-Umuofia customs. Although they are possible cultural behaviors in some other parts of Igboland, and the world, they are dismissed in Umuofia as funny events of mythological import. The myths centre on the area of domestic activities, bride-price, the ownership of children, and about the colour of white men. In Abame and Aninta it is said that "titled men climb trees and pound foo-foo for their wives" (TFA 51). This is unbelievable to Umuofians. Equally in Abame and Aninta, they haggle and bargain over bride price "as if they were buying a goat or a cow in the market" (51). Obeirika's eldest brother mentions Umunso where there is no bargain over a girl's bride-price. "The suitor just goes on bringing bags of cowries until his in-laws tell him to stop" (51). Disbelief is expressed about Okokwo's example of some tribes in which "a man's children belong to his wife and her family" (51). This is the matrilineal system of inheritance in parts of Igboland which the Umuofians see as an abomination. The strangeness of the custom is underscored by Machi's riposte: "You might as well say that the woman lies on top of the man when they are making the children" (51). Obierika's notion of the white man's colour is mythical and funny: "It is like the story of white men who, they say, are white like this piece of chalk" (51). Moreover, "these white men, they say, have no toes" (52). White men were said to be toeless because they wore shoes. Each of the informants swoop yarns about other lands or people as hear-says. Just as the tit-bits sound funny to the listeners, the reader enjoys himself from the expressed ignorance of the Umuofians about other places and customs.

The Mosquito story in *Things Fall Apart* possesses mythopoeia.

> Mosquito... had asked Ear to marry him, whereupon Ear fell on the floor in uncontrollable laughter. 'How much longer do you think you will live?' she asked. 'You are already a skelton.' Mosquito went away humiliated, and any time he passed her way he told Ear that he was still alive (3).

Mosquito and Ear are not only raised to the status of human beings, they are gender classified. Mosquito is male and Ear is female. In the Igbo milieu, it is acceptable to refer to the ear as a female since it bears a woman's earring. Because Mosquito and Ear are given human attributes, they are also imbued with the power of speech, laughter, memory and retaliation. We are meant to willingly suspend disbelief by believing that it is the same mosquito whose marriage proposal was turned down by a particular ear that continuously disturbs all human ears during periods of rest, especially at nights.

v. True Humorous Incidents

We assume that a humorous incident in Achebe's novel is true when it is given to us as if it is a true life event. In Nwakilie's story about Obiako, the latter is mentio-ined to the former's listeners as someone who is well-known to them. According to Nwakibie, Obiako had gone to consult the Oracle on an issue when the oracle revealed that his dead father needed a sacrifice of a goat. Obiako retorted: "Ask my dead father if he ever had a fowl when he was alive" (*TFA* 15). This incident is also recalled in *Arrow of God* (217), showing how the author values it as a source of humor. The humor is that the "gods" are here beaten in their own game by an agitated human mind who questions the oracle's sense of justice.

The incident of the killing of the first white man that visited Abame in *Things Fall Apart* must have taken its cue from a true life incident in Igbo history.[5] The Abamians who saw the first white man in their territory ran away because they hed not seen a human being with such a weird pigmentation before. But the white man continued beckoning on them to come to him. They consulted their oracle and it proclaimed that the visitor be killed because "the strange man would break their clan and spread destruction among them" (97). Subsequently they killed the white man and had his bicycle (iron horse) tied to the sacred tree "because it looked as if it would run away to call the man's friends" (97). The ludicrous aspect of the story is the belief by the murders that a bicycle could on its own return to inform the victim's friends about the fate of its rider. His friends knew all the same.

Achebe's reference to an incident in the life of Mr. Nwege, the proprietar of Anata Grammer School in justified by Mr. Nwege's stilted behavior during Mr. Nanga's visit to the Anata Community. A tough young man's rude reference to "push me down and take three pence" demands that the narrator should relate the incident in full. Many years before, Nwege was riding an old rickety bicycle when suddenly he entered a steep slope. Unfortunately, the brakes were faulty. Soon he feared that he might end up having a head-on with an oncoming lorry. In his anxiety, My. Nwege beckoned on passers-by to help. Apparently nobody offered to be of assistance and so "he added an inducement: 'Push me down and my three pence is yours.'" (*AMOP* 14). Another bicycle incident in *A Man of the People* (105–106) is equally humorous in the sense that Odili's conveyance of Edna on the cross bar of his bicycle is some victory for him *vis-à-vis* his formidable rival in the person of Chief M.A. Nanga. However, an accident soon occurs in which the food Edna is taking to her ailing mother in hospital pours away on the sandy road.

vi. Amusing Folktales

Two amusing folktales are found in *Things Fall Apart*. The first one refers to the quarrel between Earth and Sky in the dim past. For seven years there was no rain. Crops withered and the dead could not be buried (38). This was due to the inability of hoes to break the ground. Vulture was sent to plead with Sky to release some rain. This request was granted after a long period of plea through moving songs. At last Sky gave Vulture rain wrapped in cocoyam leaves. However, as Vulture was returning to Earth, its talon tore the cocoyam leaves and thereafter it rained cats and dogs. The rain was so heavy that Vulture was compelled to fly to a distant land where it found a man making a sacrifice and had to warm itself by the fire, and later eating the sacrificial remnants. This folktale is meant to castigate irresponsibility and carelessness. If Vulture had been more careful, its talon could not have torn the cocoyam leaves and the entire earth could not have been messed up by excess rainfall. The more amusing dimension is Vulture's irresponsible act of abandoning its sacred duty and concentrating on personal satisfaction.

The other folktale is of the trickster type. Birds were invited to a feast in the sky. Upon Tortoise's plea to go with them, the birds took him along. However, when their hosts wanted to know them by their names, Tortoise gave his as "All of you". Subsequently each of the food items brought before the visitor, meant for 'all of you', was received and controlled by Tortoise. At the end of the event, the birds leave the sky in anger, retrieving the feathers they had lent Tortoise which enabled him to go on the visit with them. Stranded, Tortoise pleaded with Parrott to inform his household members "to bring out all the soft things in my house and the compound so that I can jump down from the sky without very great danger" (*TFA* 69). Instead Parrot instructed that all the hard things in Tortoise's house be brought out: hoes, matchets, spears, guns and cannon. Tortoise looked down from the sky and thinking that his wish had been fullfilled fell down and broke into pieces. It was a great medicine-man in the neighborhood who gathered his shells and stuck them together, which is "why Tortoise's shell is not smooth" (70).

The humor in the second folktale is located in the two developments in the story. The first is Tortoise's adoption of "All of You" as his name and the misinformation by Parrot. Tortoise's resort to a name which would effectively sideline his benefactors is a deft, tricky plot. In the end, he now eats his fill while "the birds gathered round to eat wat was left and to peck at the bones he (Tortosie) had thrown all about the floor" (69). The second source of amusement is Parrot's deliberate falsehood to the Tortoise family. We derive our smirk from Tortoise's punishment for his greedy and inconsiderate behavior.

viii. Entertaining Verbal Rhetoric

Within the speeches of some of Achebe's characters are found witty remarks of observations that are likely to elicit raucous laughter from readers. Ibe has come to ask that his wife, Akueke return to him. Akueke's father (Ezeulu) is willing to allow his daughter go back to her husband "but not today" (*AOG* 63). Earlier he had sought to know from Onwuzuligbo, the leader of Ibe's party, their reason for wanting Akueke's return. Ezeulu enumerates the reasons why men marry: some marry for children, some for decent meals, some for farm-hands, and some others for someone they can beat. He then said: "What I want to learn from your mouth is wheather our in-law (Ibe) has come because he has no one to beat when he wakes up in the morning nowadays" (*AOG*) 63).

Moses' speech in *Arrow of God* (49–50) elicits fun and lightens the heart. He asks Mr. Goodcountry, a fellow Igbo, if he thinks he (Moses) is the kind of person "you can put in your bag and walk away" and accuses his antagonist of being an outsider who chooses "to weep louder than the owners of the corpse" (49) i.e. white men who brought Christianity to Umuaro. Turning to Oduche who Mr. Goodcountry calls Peter because of his zeal in locking up a python inside his school box, Moses says: "As for you they may call you Peter or they may call you Paul or Barnabas; it does not pull a hair from me. I have nothing to say to a mere boy who should be picking palm nuts for his mother" (50). Moses' slant of language use is certainly humorous for the reader or listener but not to him, the speaker. He has sought to approach the new religion with some sense of realism but the new local fanatics of Christianity will not let him. It is Mr. Goodcountry's mockery of his stance that is responsible for the satirical anger in his voice.

In *No Longer at Ease*, the Welcome Address presented to Obi Okonkwo upon his return from England by the Umuofia Progressive Union is written in a grand style: "Sir, we the officers and members of the above-named Union present with humility and gratitude this token of our appreciation of your unprecedented academic brilliance..." (28). The address is full of cliché and highfalutin expressions: "polished irredentism", "march of progress", "nothing short of axiomatic", "momentous epoch in our political evolution", "to drink at the Pierian Spring of knowledge" etc. However, Obi's response is an anticlimax and the people are disappointed: "Obi's English, on the other hand, was most unimpressive. He spoke 'is' and 'was'" (*NLAE* 29).

In *Arrow of God*, Nwaka and Ezeulu are mutual antagonists. When Ezeulu has finished informing Umuaro that he is being invited by the white men at Okperi, Nwaka's response tries to hide the intense hatred he nurtures for this enemy. He begins by referring to Ezeulu as "a father" and assures him that his apology for not being able to present the Umuaro audience with palm wine is unnecessary. "Rather it is they who should bring palm wine to him (Ezeulu)", Nwaka pursues further. He greets Ezeulu for having thought it useful "to call us and tell us these things" because it "shows the high regard in which he holds us" (143). But the truth is that the Umuaro people still consider Ezeulu's testimony against them during the land case with Okperi as an act of treachery.

Nwaka's anger and distaste for Ezeulu is gradually revealed which is likely to post a crease of smile on a reader's face. The effectiveness of rhetorical passages is often due to the slow but deliberate unfolding of the speaker's actual intent as in Nwaka's case. He mentions the main information given by Ezeulu, namely that "the white ruler has asked him to go to Okperi" and wonders what is strange in the request. Nwaka asks: "When we have a feast do we not send for our friends in other clans to come and share with us, do they not also ask us to their own celebrations?" He goes on to show that Ezeulu's consultation with Umuaro people because the white man has invited him is a cowardly act, for after all he is the white man's friend, he having earned the white man's respect during the Umuaro-Okperi land tussle. Nwaka's listeners are amused by the sheer brilliance of his speech for which they laugh and call him "Owner of words". But Nwaka returns: "If laughter presses you you can laugh; as for me it does not press me" (AOG 144).

viii. Authorial Humour

Without reference to Achebe's direct witty remarks by which his own private sense of humour can be assessed, it would seem as if he made little contribution towards the level of lilt and lurch evident in his fiction. Although it takes a humorous writer to deploy borrowed whimsical acts from folkloric and realistic events in his/her works, there is a need to show that Achebe is himself an original creator of humour. We have already referred to the kind of proverbs, folktales, myths, anecdotes etc. he employs as a deliberate act of sourcing for humour. In conversations, for instance, the humour exchanged by the interlocutors is certainly Achebe's. So also are the earthy invectives and altercations, the sexual vignettes, the uproarious taunts, and the creation of such absurd figures as Unoka, Isaac Okonkwo, Odogwu, Nanga and Sam.

However, in addition, there are quite a number of cases of direct authorial humour in the novels. Ezeulu, having watched Umuaro at the brink of war with Okperi over a piece of land he believes does not belong to his own people, "sprang to his feet like one stung in the buttocks by a black ant" (AOG 18). Achebe's picture of a gluttonous dog called Nwanku that "made straight for the excrement which disappeared with four or five noisy flicks of its tongue" is imagistic and urgent. When Amoge's ailing child leaves "a tiny green drop" on the ground and Nwanku feels it is not worth the trouble getting up from where it is squatting "it merely stretched its neck and took it up with the corner of the tongue and sat up again to wait" (AOG 91). Here Achebe shows that he is indeed a child of the traditional Igbo home in which each nursing mother owns a dog for the maintenance of a clean, sanitary environment.

In *No Longer at Ease*, Achebe refers to an encounter between a boy selling *akara* (bean cakes) and a night-soilman. Anyone who has lived in a West African urban town will know about he quaint behavior of night-soilmen who bear drums of excrement on their heads and enjoy spilling some of it on anyone who complains about the stench of their ware. Says the narrator: "as soon as the night-soilman passed swinging his broom and hurricane lamp and trailing clouds of putrefaction the boy quickly sprang to his feet and began calling him names" (14).

Achebe's description of Mr. Omo or the picture he casts about Mr. Jones' fate in the hands of Simeon Nduka, the headmaster of a local primary school, is memorable. About Mr. Omo, he remarks:

> He had very bad teeth blackened by cigarettes and kola nuts. One was miss-ing in front, and when he laughed the gap looked like a vacant plot in a slum (*NLAE* 60).

Mr. Jones, the European inspector is held in awe by the natives because of his frequent acts of intimidation. On this occasion, Mr. Nduka is trying to explain something to him when he suddenly asks the headmaster to shut up, and thereafter follows it up with a slap. According to the author-narrator, "one of the things he (Nduka) had learnt in his youth was the great art of wrestling. In the twinkling of an eye Mr. Jones was flat on the floor and the school was thrown into confusion" (*NLAE* 58).

Achebe's strength as a writer equally resides in his quizzical, sometimes un-expected remarks about figures and events as well as his interpretations and acts of mimicry. Each of these compels the reader to laugh. Mr. Nwege's educational level and his stereotype are vividly highlighted by his description as one who "regularly read such literature as 'Toasts-How to Propose Them'" (*AMOP* 8). The Senior Tutor at Anata Grammar School is said to have "traces of snuff as usual in his nostrils" (*AMOP* 8). The various cliché employed by Chief the Honourable M.A. Nanga, M.P. and Minister of Culture show that he is a funny figure: "Do the right and shame the Devil" (12); "... no one is perfect except God" (75); "uneasy lies the head that wears the crown" (68). Although Nanga is cheating the people all the time, he calls himself "a man of the people". In *Anthills*, the author interprets what a bird says in this way: "Is the king's property correct? ... Is the king's property correct? ... The king's property... The king's property ... Is the king's property correct?" (108). There are two underlying forces in the interpretation of the bird's song: one is that the bird is virtually a security personnel; and secondly, an Igbo bird's utterance is not in the Igbo language, but in English.

Conclusion

A would-be reader of Achebe's fiction who has been told that Achebe is a tragic writer would expect to meet somberness in his novels. But this is not the case. Achebe's novels are laced with facetious incidents, witty remarks, amusing occasions, funny characters, salty sayings and entertaining rhetorical situations. As mentioned earlier, Igbo life simultaneously admits gloom and frolick. Tragic situations do not mean that if a laughable incident occurs nobody would laugh, for the Igbo say that "a pitiable incident draws laughter" (*Ihe ojoo n'akpa achi*). No wonder then that funerals are probably the best occasion to display lightheartedness. Apart from the fact that this is meant to lighten the grief of the bereaved, it equally shows that "wherever something stands another thing stands beside it" (*NLAE* 145).

The sources and resources of Achebe's humour are quite varied. This study does not pretend to have exhausted them. For instance, we have not discussed his taunts, prayers, songs, altercations and sexy, titillating titbits. His humorous Pidgin English contexts in *AMOP* and *Anthills* are omitted largely because of space. However, we have touched at its heart and essence by showing that Achebe's humour is interlaced with his thematic posture, rhetorical aims and character design. The texture of his humour is traceable to his folk culture to which he is very familiar. Much of the amusement we derive from reading his novels has its origins in the slant of Igbo proverbs, folktales, ironies, satires, rhetoric, anecdotes, myths and stories that he utilizes for purposes of an effective writing.

Notes

1. At an interview he granted me in October 1985, Achebe had said that "our tradition, the Igbo tradition... can claim 90% of it (i.e. his work) because that is the tradition that created the framework in which this sort of thing can happen." See J.O.J. Nwachukwu-Agbada, "A Conversation with Chinua Achebe" (122).

2. See J.O.J. Nwachukwu-Agbada, "Aliases among the Anambra Igbo: The Proverbial Dimension."

3. See D.I. Nwoga's introductory comment in *Rhythms of Creation* (1982).

4. As observed by Afam Ebeogu, an attempt by the Igbo to export their humour to other parts of Nigeria, they being an itinerant group, has led to their being accused of arrogance, indiscretion and boastfulness: "what would have been acceptable behaviour within their own culture is deemed evidence of insensitivity by some other ethic groups in the country (Nigeria)." See his essay, "*Njakiri*, The Quintessence of the Traditional Igbo Sense of Satire" (45–46).

5. The killing of Dr. Stewart, a British medical officer in Ahiara Imo State of Nigeria in 1905 and the reprisals that followed have been amply discussed in J.U.J. Asiegbu's *Nigeria and Its British Invaders 1851–1920* (1984); E.A. Isichei, *History of the Igbo People* (1976); A.E. Afigbo, "Patterns of Igbo Resistance of British Conquests" (1973); S.N. Nwabara, *Iboland: A Century of Contact with Britain 1860–1960* (1977) etc. etc.

6. According to D.I. Nwoga, "... the Igbo see the world as operating within a system of intrinsic dualities such that good and evil can come from the same universe." See his *Nka na Nzere: The Focus of Igbo World View* (45) for elaboration.

Works Cited

Acebe, Chinua. *Things Fall Apart*, London: Heinemann, 1976.

———. *No Longer at Ease*. London: Heinemann, 1960.

———. *Arrow of God*. London: Heinemann, 1974.

———. *A Man of the People*. London: Heinemann, 1966.

———. *Anthills of the Savannah*. London: Heinemann, 1987.

Afigbo, A.E. "Patterns of Igbo Resistance to British Conquest." *Tarikh* (Ibadan) 4.3 (1973).

Asiegbu, J.U.J. *Nigeria and Its British Invaders 1851–1920*. New York and Enugu: Nok Publishers, 1984.

Bateson, G. "The Role of Humour in Human Communication." In H. von Foerster. Ed. *Cybernetics*. New York: Macy Foundation, 1953.

Ebeogu, Afam. "*Njakiri*, The Quintessence of the Traditional Igbo Sense of Satire." In Gillian Benneth. Ed. *Spoken in Jest*. Sheffield: Sheffield Academic Press, 1991: 29–46.

Egudu, R.N. "Social Values and Thought in Traditional Literature: The Case of the Igbo Proverb and Thought". *Nigerian Libraries* 8 (1972): 63–84.

Freud, Sigmund. *Jokes and Their Relation to the Unconscious*. New York: Norton, 1960.

Fry, W.F. Jr. *Sweet Madness: A Study of Humor*. Palo Alto, California: Pacific, 1963.

Isichei, E. *A History of the Igbo People*. London: Macmillian, 1976.

Koestler, A. *The Act of Creation*. New York: Dell, 1964.

Lindfors, Bernth. "The Palm Oil with Which Achebe's Words are Eaten." *African Literature Today* 1–4 (1968): 3–18.

Maier, N.R.F. "A Gestalt Theory of Humour." *British Journal of Psychology* 23 (1932): 69–74

McGhee, P.E. *Humor: Its Origin and Development*. San Francisco: W.H. Freeman and Co., 1979.

Meek, C.K. *Law and Authority in a Nigerian Tribe*. London: Oxford University Press, 1937.

Muecke, D.C. *The Compass of Irony*. London: Methuen, 1969.

Nwabara, S.N. *Iboland: A Century of Contact with Britain: 1860–1960*. London: Hodder and Stoughton, 1977.

Nwachukwu-Agbada, J.O.J. "*Things Fall Apart*: A Model for the Teaching of Irony to African Students." *Ngoma* (Lusaka) 3.2 (June–December, 1998): 41–51.

———. "A Conversation with Chinua Achebe." *Commonwealth: Essays and Studies* 13.1 (Autumn, 1990): 117–124.

———. "Aliases Among the Anambra – Igbo: The Proverbial Dimension." Names: *Journal of American Name Society*. 39.2 (1991): 81–94.

————. "Chinua Achebe's Literary Proverbs as Reflections of Igbo Cultural and Philosophical Tenets." *Proverbium: Yearbook of International Proverb Scholarship* 10 (1993): 215–235.

————. "*Iko Onu*: The Tradition of Poetic Insult Among Igbo Children" *International Folklore Review* 12 (1995): Forth coming.

Nwoga, D.I. ed. *Rhythms of Creation: A Decade of 'Okike' Poetry*. Enugu, Nigeria: Fourth Dimension Publishers, 1982.

————. *Nka na Nzere: The Focus of Igbo World View (Ahiajoku Lecture* Series). Owerri: Culture Division Ministry of Information, Imo State, Nigeria, 1984

Ogbaa, Kalu. *Gods, Oracles and Divination: Folkways in Chinua Achebe's* Novels. New Jersey: Africa World Press, 1992.

Radcliffe-Brown, A.R. "On Joking Relationships". *Africa* 13 (1940): 195–210.

Seitell, Peter. "Proverbs: A Social Use of Metaphor." In *Folklore Genres*. Ed. Dan Ben-Amos. Austin: University of Texas Press, 1976 (1969): 127–143.

Shelton, Austin. "The Palm Oil of Language: Proverbs in Chinua Achebe's Novels." *Modern Language Quarterly* 30 (1969): 86–111.

Yankson, Kofi E. *Chinua Achebe's Novels: A Sociolinguistic Perspective*. Obosi, Nigeria: Pacific Publishers, 1990.

Chapter 11

The Igbo Home in Achebe's Fiction

Afam Ebeogu

THE MAIN ARGUMENT OF THIS ARTICLE is based on the premise that literature is not merely a product of society, but also an institution in that society, and can therefore be used to study society. This approach is different from the usual "sociological approach" that lays emphasis on the use of a known society as a reference point for assessing a literary work of art. It acknowledges this fact, but goes beyond it to recognize that an insight into the nature of society can be gained through the study of some literary works of art. This is an argument that has been the main prop of Marxist literary criticism (See Eagleton 1976), and has become so entrenched in the polemics of that aesthetics that the impression is created that it is exclusive to it.

But the premise is legitimate even when the study in question is a departure from Marxist literary scholarship, as is illustrated in Joan Rockwell's study (1974). A society can be interpreted on the basis of a literature based on it, and this proposition remains valid even when a writer is apparently not writing about his own society of the present, but about his society of the past. A writer who prefers to draw the materials of his art from the past is really projecting his own consciousness, conditioned by his contemporary society, into that past, and is extracting from that past materials that can help in the interpretation of the present.

When related to African literature, we find that some of the established novelists in the continent reveal a great deal about their society, past and present, in their writings. It is not surprising that some sociologists and anthropologists tend to quote some African novels as authentic sources of sociological and anthropological studies, even to the extent of prescribing such novels as reading texts for the social sciences.

This practice is by no means a total credit to these novelists, for there is a danger in the appropriation of a work of art, expected to assert its authenticity first and foremost through its aesthetic appeal, for the less subtle, more "scientific" purposes of a subject like Sociology or Anthropology. One can understand the feeling of some critics of a writer like Chinua Achebe who wonder whether he is a novelist or a sociologist,[1] but this kind of criticism arises when the reader misconceives the uses which the creative artist has made of sociological and anthropological materials as if these source materials of literature in themselves constitute the finished product. When a reader's attention becomes overly engrossed with the sociological and anthropological details which a novelist has very vividly painted, then that reader may be taking into the area of literature, with little restraint, a sensibility that is rather more sociological than aesthetic.

Of all the African novelists, Chinua Achebe probably paints the most vivid picture of the anthropological and sociological life of an African community (Palmer 100). But he does so "without sacrificing the unity of theme or cohesion of narrative" (Turkington 15). This is a point which the earlier critics of Achebe had tended to ignore, and gladly no less perceptive a critic of Achebe than G.D. Killam, quoted in Wren (ix) had had to complain that:

> so much has been written about the anthropological and sociological significance of *Things Fall Apart* and *Arrow of God* – their evocation of traditional nineteenth – and earlier twentieth-century Ibo village life – ... that the overall excellence of these books as pieces of fiction, as works of art, has been obscured.

We have decided to examine very closely one aspect of Igbo culture and life which Achebe x-rays in very great details in some of his fiction – the Igbo home. Our argument is that a reading of most of the fiction of Achebe reveals to us all the essentials that constitute the traditional Igbo home, and that Achebe neatly dovetails this sociological and anthropological picture of the Igbo home into a mainstream of sensibility that remains essentially literary.

We begin our argument by quoting what a scholar of Igbo language and culture has said of the Igbo home:

> *Mkpuke* is the name of a wife's house in distinction from the man's called *obi*. It is usually built behind a man's *obi*. Each wife has her own *mkpuke* where she spends most of her life with her children especially the girls. The husband eats in his *obi* and gives audience to visitors there. The close attachment of children to their mothers in polygamous families makes the father almost a stranger and of less importance to the children than the mother and where the man is unable to exercise effective control over rivalry and competition between the

mkpukes chaos is the usual result. The success or failure of a polygamous life depends to a considerable extent on the ability of the husband to be just and dispense love and care equally to all his wives and children to obey and respect him (Ogbalu 11).

The Igbo man often refers to his home as his *ezi na uno* "outside relations and those in the house" (Ogbalu 11). The Igbo family or home would imply the physical structures that constitute a compound, the members of that household, and the household's relationship with its immediate and remote environment; that is, the society. The Igbo home is therefore not limited to the anthropologist's elemental family. Such a home would include the man of the house (who is the *pater familias*), the wife, their child or children, and possibly, their wards. It would also include grandchildren (*umu di ala*), in-laws (*ndi ogo*), grand mothers and fathers (*ndi ikwu nne na nna ochie*). Achebe's presentation of Igbo homes in his novels has been so near the Igbo home that anthropologists and sociologists may not resist the temptation to cite such novels as authoritative source of information.

Perhaps the first thing that strikes one about Achebe's portrayal of an Igbo home is the pains he takes to erect a clear physical structure of the home. His layout of the physical structures in an Igbo home in *Things Fall Apart* (13–14), is an echo of the anthropological extract we have quoted. The passage is an adequate testimony to G. T. Basden's statement that an Igbo compound "may contain a miniature village" (Basden 47). It is a "village" with complete paraphernalia not only for autonomous existence in the mundane world but also for the incessant communion with the supernatural world. There is the *obi*, "the hub of the little universe" (Basden 153), which commands the only entrance to the compound. The *obi* is a kind of sanctum for the head of the house, and it is there that he does most of his reflections about life, as Okonkwo does after the killing of Ikemefuna in *Things Fall Apart*, or Obierika on why a man must suffer "so grievously for an offence he had committed inadvertently" (113). Then there are the three huts where Okonkwo's wives live behind the *obi*. The position of the huts, standing like a "half-moon" behind the *obi*, the center of the universe, symbolizes the protective role of Okonkwo over, and his headship of, his wives and the children. At one end of the compound is the barn where the yams – the king of crops – are stacked. They represent the food on which the humans depend for existence. Then there are the shelters for livestock, which denote that domestic animals are an inevitable part of the household. The "medicine house" is of course the shrine where Okonkwo keeps contact with the unseen forces that rule their world. Lastly, there is mention of the children for which main purpose the wives are part of the household. The household, then, physically, is a symbolic unit of Igbo traditional universe. It should be noted that on his exile to Mbanta, Okonkwo gets "the help of his mother's kinsmen [to] build himself an *obi* and three huts for his wives. He then installs his personal god and the symbols of his departed fathers.

Each of Uchendu's five sons contributes three hundred seed-yams to enable their cousin to plant a farm ..." (117–8). The physical nature of the traditional household is thus a constant, irrespective of situation and circumstance.

Ezeulu's compound in *Arrow of God* is similar to Okonkwo's except that Ezeulu has two married sons who own their own huts. His *obi* acquires some extra sacredness because, as a priest, Ezeulu "watches that part of the sky where the moon had its door" (*Arrow of God*, 1) from there. The home of Ezeulu derives its status in the society from the moon since Ezeulu's chief function as a priest of Ulu is to spot out the arrival of the new moon and then announce it to the whole of Umuaro. In other words, from his *obi*, Ezeulu calculates and keeps the calendar of the clan, which activity ensures the place of the clan in the universal order. It therefore becomes obvious how Ezeulu's absence from Umuaro; from his *obi*, while in prison, implies a standstill in the dynamics of both terrestrial and celestial activity. Ezeulu's tragedy springs in the main from this dilemma over how to restore this cosmic order of his society. We can then understand why *Arrow of God* begins with an introduction of Ezeulu's household in relation to the moon.

One of the most prominent characteristics of Achebe's home is the polygamous nature of most of such homes. "Polygamy", says Victor Uchendu (49), "a symbol of high social status, is the idea [among] the Igbo." Since polygamy involved very many people living in one compound, there were bound to be very many conflicts in that home. The polygamous home therefore needed a man – the head of the house – strong, wealthy, intelligent and firm enough to keep such a large household together:

> No matter how prosperous a man was, if he was unable to rule his women and his children (and especially his women) he was not really a man. He was like the man in the song who had ten and one wives and not enough soup for his foo-foo (*Things Fall Apart* 48).

Most of Achebe's male characters are presented in the light of their ability to rule their homes. But, more importantly, the author has, in the process, built up the character of such individuals in such a way that the over-all literary value of the novels can only be properly appraised in the light of the characters created. Okonkwo's heavy-handedness, his disgust for gentleness, his resilience, his hot temper and impatience, all mould him into a character that cannot tolerate any bickering between his different household units. The relationship between his wives is almost exemplary in its degree of understanding and cooperation (*Things Fall Apart* 27, 35, 37–8, 149). This impression of a decorous household in *Things Fall Apart* is in tune with the thematic concern of Achebe to portray as graphically as possible a traditional system that worked harmoniously, even if imperfectly, before a major disorder emerged with the coming of the white man. And that household continued to experience its own portion of disorder occasioned by the pressure of Christianity.

In *Arrow of God*, the situation is different. We have a lot of bickering between co-wives, and Achebe takes pains to paint vivid pictures of various incidents that illustrate conflicts built around co-wives' jealousies (9–10, 62, 67, 73, 129). Achebe, through his regulated introduction of these scenes of discord succeeds in building up a rather unpleasant picture of Matefi, Ezeulu's most senior wife, as one of those intolerant, nagging co-wives one comes across often in Igbo traditional homes. But more important to the artistic status of the novel is that those scenes reveal Achebe's deep understanding of the divisive forces that are always latent in polygamous households. They contribute in no small way in providing the local color and atmosphere characteristic of traditional Igbo environment, making the pages of the novel full of the kind of conflicts that remind us that the novel as a genre thrives on the life drama of human relationships.

A similar scene as those shown in *Arrow of God* is seen in the short story "The Madman" where a quarrel between Nwibe's two wives enables Achebe to introduce the main motif of the short story: madness. In the course of the co-wives' invectives, Nwibe accuses his second wife of being crazy; a few hours later Nwibe is mistakenly but seriously acknowledged by everyone in the community as suffering from that type of acute madness that makes the madman "deliver himself to the divinities of the market-place," an obvious reference to the Igbo proverb which says that the kind of madness that drives its victim to the market-place is beyond cure (*Ara pua ahia, adighi agwota ya agwota*). The irony of the passage is thus a reflection of the bigger, and tragic irony of the whole story whereby a completely sane man is compelled by circumstances and forces beyond his control to exchange places with a madman who considers himself normal and every other person – or, in fact, the rest of humanity – as "little beasts" and "vagabonds" who oppress him.

In *A Man of the People*, Mrs. Nanga is not happy that her husband is taking a second wife. To her, Edna is just a mercenary girl who wants to "eat Nanga's wealth" after she (Mrs. Nanga) had "toiled and starved when there [was] no money" (*A Man of the People* 88). The world of *A Man of the People* is of course a perverse world. In traditional Igbo society, few women would dare oppose their husbands marrying more wives. But the Igbo society of Anata in *A Man of the People* has lost much of its traditional base. Besides, the Nangas are not really part of that society. Mrs. Nanga's reason for not wanting a co-wife is characteristically a perversion of Igbo traditional marriage system. She thinks that Edna would help squander Chief Honorable Nanga's wealth. We are reminded that the world of this novel is a perverse world where emphasis is on how best to "eat" money and the people's notion of acquiring wealth a negation of the traditional Igbo emphasis on hard work and judicious expenditure.

Despite, however, the misunderstanding and family feuds which Achebe presents in his polygamous homes, polygamy does not, in the final analysis, acquire any potential for disaster. The much that can be said against it is that "in a big compound there was always something to spoil one's happiness" (*Arrow of God* 190). What Odili has to say about this is instructive:

> There were too many of us in the family for anyone to think of loneliness or unhappiness. And I must say this for my father that he never tolerated any of his wives drawing a line no matter how thin between her own children and those of others. We had only one Mama. The other two wives (at the time – there are more now) were called Mother by their children, or so and so's mother by the rest (*A Man of the People*, 28).

This passage reminds one very readily of Okonkwo's home in *Things Fall Apart*. As for Ezeulu, polygamy has not rendered him any bit ineffective as the dominant authority in his home. Much of the grandeur and dignity defining his personality is achieved through his activities at home. The dignified, unhurried, contemplative and sagacious posture he adopts in his dealings with the people of Umuaro and the white administration is, among other things, a result of his competence as head of a very large home. He is chief priest of his home as well as of his god. As one, he faces many conflicts that are largely external and mundane; as the other, his conflicts are internal and spiritual. Both conflicts find common alliance when, for Ezeulu's failure to resolve his internal, spiritual conflict judiciously, Ulu punishes him with a death in his home.

We can now easily appreciate the image of the father as created by Achebe in his works, bearing in mind what we have considered as Achebe's typical Igbo polygamous family set-up. "Okonkwo ruled his household with a heavy hand" (*Things Fall Apart* 12). All the strands that constitute Okonkwo's character manifest themselves in this one predisposition so succinctly expressed by Achebe in the above terse statement. *Things Fall Apart* is not unintentionally full of numerous instances of Okonkwo's heavy-handedness and hot temper (13, 24, 25, 27, 28, 30, 35). It is the hot temper in Okonkwo that leads him to kill the messenger from the white man, a climax that leads to the last tragic act of Okonkwo taking his own life. Okonkwo, then, as a father and head of a polygamous household, upholds a principle of violence and perverse masculinity. "It is possible," says Kate Turkington, "that Achebe is suggesting that Okonkwo's imbalance of strength and gentleness, the predominance of the male ethic in his character, reflects some of the severe elements in the society itself" (Turkington 42). Seen from this light, Okonkwo's disability as the head of his home, a disability which is also his tragic flaw, is a reflection of an aspect of Igbo manliness which the Igbo themselves find somewhat revolting, and which Achebe, who for artistic purposes is a representative of Igbo communal conscience, criticizes.

Ezeulu in *Arrow of God* is a departure from Okonkwo and certainly plays a more commendable role as the head of the home. He is much more understanding and tolerant than Okonkwo, even if he is as firm. Without the overbearing attitude one finds in Okonkwo, Ezeulu asserts his authority as the head of the home whose duty it is to guide (*Arrow of God* 5–6). The impression created is that of a man who controls his household effectively without having to bark too often, even though Edogo, his eldest son, accuses him of partisanship in family feuds. There may be some measure of truth in Edogo's well-meant criticism of his father of a policy of divide-and-rule. But Achebe succeeds in presenting Ezeulu as, in the words of Emmanuel Obiechina, "A quintessential paternalist" (Obiechina 94). It is Akuebue who verbalizes the intricacies of fatherhood in a large compound very appropriately when he says in the novel that:

> in all great compounds there must be people of all kinds – some good, some bad, some fearless and some cowardly; those who bring in wealth and those who scatter it, those who give good advice and those who only speak the words of palm-wine. That is why we say that whatever tune you play in the compound of a great man there is always someone to dance to it (*Arrow of God* 100).

Ezeulu seems to recognize the above view and that is why he gives a reasonable degree of freedom to his children and wives, without compromising his primary role as the *pater familias*. And therein lies the source of certain ambivalence in his overall character. For the liberal mind in Ezeulu – which predisposes him to adaptability – clashes with the rigid, and this clash, often dramatized in his household affairs, constitutes the dilemma in the novel: can a man of Ezeulu's social and spiritual stature afford to run with the hare and hunt with the hound? And this dilemma ultimately consumes him.

Having seen the position of fathers in Achebe's polygamous households, it is necessary to consider that of women, or mothers. As has been observed by many feminist critics of Achebe (Acholonu 40–41), his women in the home are always in the background, especially in the kitchen, which is also their hut (*mkpuke*), situated *behind* the center of the compound. Their role in the home, besides the cooking of meals, is essentially to bring up the children, especially the girls, in strict keeping with the female ethic in the society. They organize folktale sessions for the children, thereby inculcating in them through the medium of art certain cultural values. The women grow only women's crops like coco-yams, beans and cassava. In festival occasions, like Obika's marriage with Okuata in *Arrow of God*, they provide the songs and other noises of happiness that keep the occasions lively. Women are thus associated with the gentle and the feminine in Achebe's fiction. Their role in the home is subservient – for example, in *Arrow of God*, Oduche's mother has no hand in deciding that Oduche would join the Christian group.

But Achebe has made a great subtle use of the female essence in Igbo culture. As Ackley has pointed out about the two examples of marriage negotiations and celebration in *Things Fall Apart*,

> here Achebe is not digressing into interesting customs for the benefit of non-Igbo readers, but clearly showing the value attached to women as home-makers, help-mates, and potential mothers – children, after all, are the most valuable asset and the greatest blessing in a kinship-based society and the family is in the sacred, essential unit of organization (Ackley 2).

Ackley proceeds to argue that Okonkwo's tragic flaw is in fact a lack of the qualities of gentleness and softness which he considers feminine. Uchendu in *Things Fall Apart* gives a penetrating significance of motherhood in Igbo thought. Expatiating on why the Igbo cherish the name Nneka ("Mother is Supreme"), he says that "a man belongs to his fatherland when things are good and life is sweet. But when there is sorrow and bitterness he finds refuge in his motherland" (122). The point is hardly disputable, considering that Okonkwo and his family have just fled to Mbanta, his mother's place, for committing a "female crime" – we are reminded of an Igbo proverb which says that the wealthy man – he has so many yams to dig – should not forget to visit the land of his mothers, for when there is cause for him to flee his land, he cannot run into his bag of yams – his wealth cannot protect him ("*Onye gbukata ji, ya lue ikwunne ya nihi na oso chuba ya, o gaghi, agbaba n'akpa ji*"). In *Arrow of God*, Akukalia's rash act of destroying Ebo's *ikenga* – Igbo symbol of progress and dynamism – assumes a more heinous dimension when it is considered that he commits it in his mother's maiden home. It is true that in Igboland, a man can take a good number of liberties in his *ikwunne* he dares not contemplate taking in his own patrilineage, but the same social system which allows a man many liberties in his matrilineal home also demands from the man a large measure of reverence for his mother's people. Akukalia lacks the common-sense to realize this, and behaves like the man in the proverb who is not content to shake the hand offered him but must also grip the elbow for a pull. Akukalia did court his own death, a point Ezeulu was to make later in the novel.

Ackley provides a good summary on Achebe's women in Igbo home when he says that:

> Achebe clearly shows that the Igbo, like virtually every other African people, institutionalize make dominance and clear-cut social, economic, and religious roles for the men and women. But he goes to considerable lengths to show that the separation of the sexes does not mean the degradation of women or of their culturally defined personality. He fully acknowledges, in fact, that the valuable role of women and the positive nature of feminity is made sacred, is even ritualized (2).

Having thus far examined separately the husband and the wife in Achebe's novels, it is relevant to consider how the novelist handles the husband/wife relationship on a more philosophical level: as a relationship between people who are destined to live together and must give dignity and worth to that relationship. It is true that the society expects the woman to be subservient to the man, and makes humiliating remarks about the man who is being "ruled" by his wife. But what a couple makes of their marriage does depend on the individual characters of those involved. Okonkwo's dominance over his wives may be total, but the relationship between him and Ekwefi needs a closer look. There is an unsurfaced feeling of love and understanding between the two; unsurfaced because Okonkwo is not the man to show outward emotion, except it be that of anger. Ekwefi is the only person in the household who has dared throw words back at her husband, or have the "audacity to bang on his door." There is an evocative feeling of comradeship between the two as they stand before the mouth of the cave of *Agbala* into which Chielo has taken Ezinma. "As they stood there together, Ekwefi's mind went back to the days when they were young" (98).

The importance of this relationship between Ekwefi and Okonkwo to the over-all artistic unity of *Things Fall Apart* is that it testifies to the narrator's assertion that "perhaps down in his heart, Okonkwo was not a cruel man" (12). In spite of Okonkwo's determination not to show any emotion except that of anger, one has a feeling that he has a capacity for a depth of feeling that is not that of anger. It is this kind of feeling which Okonkwo tries to suppress that surfaces after his killing of Ikemefuna; it is also the same kind of feeling that makes him "deeply grieved" for his clan "which he saw breaking up and falling apart." This capacity for a feeling other than that of anger enhances Okonkwo's tragic stature; it enables the reader to see him also as a psychological character perpetually tormented by an inner conflict which can only find outward manifestation in the form of tragic action.

In *Arrow of God*, we find that though Ezeulu can browbeat his wives, he does not appear perturbed when they retort back. He does recognize their humanity, and shows a predisposition for tolerance. His attitude in the marriage relationship with his wives echoes the feeling of his younger brother, Onenyi, who tells their in-law, Akueke's husband that:

> my in-laws ... different people have different reasons for marrying. Apart from children which we all want, some men want a woman to cook their meals, some want a woman to help on the farm, others want someone to beat. What I want to learn from your mouth is whether our in-law has come because he has no one to beat when he wakes up in the morning nowadays (63).

Onenyi has his tongue in his cheek of course, for what he does is sound the general view of his culture in condemning wife-beating. As Evil Forest tells Uzowulu in

Things Fall Apart, "it is not bravery when a man fights with a woman" (85). It is Ezeulu himself who gives a resume of what he considers as the right relationship between a man and his wife. He quotes his father who had told him that

> in our custom a man is not expected to go down on his knees and knock his forehead on the ground to his wife to ask her forgiveness or beg a favour. But, a wise man knows that between him and his wife there may arise a need to say to her in secret: 'I beg you'. When such a thing happens nobody else must know it, and that woman if she has any sense will never boast about it or even open her mouth and speak of it (172).

If such an understanding as Ezeulu prescribes exists between a man and his wife, then the chances of a marriage break-up will be very slim. As Akuebue puts it, he would not encourage his daughter to think that because she is from a prosperous family, she can flee to her paternal home each time her husband "says yah" to her.

The Igbo attitude of minimal interference in the affairs of a husband and his wife derives, paradoxically, from a recognition of the other relationships in the society which the marriage has established. As Victor Uchendu (50) puts it, "Igbo marriage is an alliance between two families rather than a contract between two persons." Undue interference in the affairs of a man and his wife is thus an anti-communal move. Where it happens, the reason must be very strong, as in the case in *Things Fall Apart* where Uzowulu has been acknowledged as a chronic wife-beater, or in *Arrow of God* where Obika and his brothers rescue their sister from a beating-prone husband.

Thus Achebe seems to suggest that the sanctity of the home must be respected. It is important to note that this respect for the sanctity of the home is in tune with Achebe's persistent emphasis on the home as a semi-autonomous unit within a communal system, and, by extension, an extensive exercise of the individual will within a community that demands a large measure of conformity from the individual. It is this peculiarity which Achebe bestows on the societies of Umuofia and Umuaro that makes the tragedy in which the individual is involved become a communal tragedy. Part of the dilemma in which Obi is caught in *No Longer at Ease* arises from his resolve to preserve the sanctity of his future home, as he finds it "preposterous" that the Umuofia Progressive Union – which in Lagos is not just a gathering of clansmen but of kinsmen – should interfere in his affairs. We also find this kind of crisis based on a man's choice of marriage partner dramatized in "Marriage is a Private Affair" (*Girls at War* 20–28). Both cases illustrate that respect for marriage sanctity among the Igbo can only be thrown to the winds when the mode of the marriage is not that prescribed by the culture. That Obi and Nnaemeka attempt to marry without the support of their kinsmen is possible in the first place because their Igbo world is no longer intact. The collapse of the traditional system is ominous for the home both of Isaac Okonkwo and Nnaemeka's father, and also the Igbo home of the future generation.

The relationship between father and son in Achebe is another area that attracts considerable interest. Uchendu (55) has pointed out that in traditional Igbo society, it is possible to have a three-generation family living in the same large compound where the father is the head, because it is "unfilial" for a son to live apart during his father's life-time. A son has to be attached to his father as much as possible because fathers are, by virtue of their age, nearer the ancestors whom they join at death, requiring ancestral worship from their sons. It should be recalled that the primary reason why, in *Things Fall Apart*, Okonkwo is very worried over Nwoye's apostasy is that such an act would amount to a severance of this link between the living and the dead; a severance that would threaten the continuity of the family line.

The tendency then is for the Igbo father to view his son in his own image. What Okonkwo desires Nwoye to be is no more than what Okonkwo himself is: a strong and prosperous man capable of controlling his home and keeping his head high in the clan. The reason Okonkwo likes Ikemefuna is that he sees in the boy what he wishes to see in Nwoye. Ikemefuna is to Okonkwo like a son, whose relationship to the man he calls father is more than putative. He "could hardly imagine that Okonkwo is not his father," and he rushes to the man for paternal protection against his killers, only to be cut down by Okonkwo himself; an action, says Obierika, for which the gods can wipe off a clan. For three days after the incident, Okonkwo could not taste any food – for once he is moved by something other than the emotion of anger. Literally and symbolically, Okonkwo is mourning the death of a son. Weinstock (27) puts it very adequately when he points out that Nwoye and Ikemefuna are "dual aspects of a single son-figure"; that both are "literary doubles." This is true in the sense that what Ikemefuna has is what Nwoye needs to become a son after his father's heart. The physical death of Ikemefuna, Weinstock points out, is thus the symbolic death of Nwoye. In this connection of father/son relationship, it might be pointed out that Okonkwo regrets that Ezinma is not a boy; thus Ezinma is a female equivalent to Ikemefuna. We are told that she alone understands her father most. Okonkwo has no justification blaming Christianity for having snatched his son (Nwoye) from him – the religion only assumes responsibility for that which has been spiritually and physically rejected.

In *Arrow of God*, Obika is very much like his father, a likeness that is symbolized by their physical resemblance. It is not surprising that it is only Obika, of all Ezeulu's children, who is shown to have understood the plight of his father when Ezeulu refuses to name the day of the New Yam Festival, and that Ezeulu should consider the death of Obika as the greatest punishment Ulu could have inflicted on him. In the pathetic scene where Obika's body is brought into Ezeulu's compound, Ezeulu "slumped down on both knees beside the body ... [and] hid his head on Obika's chest (228). This gesture of unbounded sorrow symbolizes Obika's soul escaping the body in company of the man that is in Ezeulu. The tragic sense in the novel stems not so much from the fact that Ezeulu spends his last days "in the haughty splendour of a demented high priest" as that this state is caused by the death of Obika, a father-figure and a typical Igbo *nwokolobia* in every sense in which the world connotes fearlessness and admirable masculinity. It is a communal loss which "shook Umuaro to the roots; a man like him did not come into the world too often."

The relationship between Oduche and Ezeulu can best be appreciated only on the symbolic level. There is not much to indicate that Oduche is a favorite son of Ezeulu, and Edogo in fact does raise the doubt as to whether Oduche had ever attracted his father's affection, even as a toddler. One wonders with Oduche's mother and Edogo why it has to be Oduche that Ezeulu sacrifices to the Christian religion. Edogo and Akuebue think that the reason is in order to clear the way for Nwafo to become priest at Ezeulu's death. Ezeulu does not deny the charge, but argues that it is for Ulu to decide whom to make his priest. He does, however, make one important point which shifts emphasis from *who* to be sent to the white man's church to *why* someone must be sent there (45–56). It is an often quoted passage used to argue that Achebe uses the relationship between Ezeulu and Oduche to illustrate the Igbo spirit of adaptability; the relationship is not just an expose of a father/son relationship, but rather a kind of anecdote on the values of adaptability to change.

Nwafo, on the other hand, is Ezeulu's favorite. He has a particular position where he sits always in his father's *obi*. He watches his father offer the traditional prayers to Ulu after the sighting of the new moon. He sweeps Ezeulu's hut every morning and is always around to execute minor tasks like passing the bowl of kola round to visitors. Not surprisingly, Ezeulu talks to him as he would to an adult. There is a strong suggestion that there is something Ezeulu has found special in Nwafo, and Edogo and Akuebue think that Nwafo has been earmarked for succession to the priesthood of Ulu, an allegation Ezeulu does not deny. Nwafo himself seems to have believed in this priest-becoming role of himself. His relationship with his father is not merely filial; it acquires some quality of the professional – Nwafo is undergoing an apprenticeship under his father. It is this belief existing in the depth of his subconscious that makes him so very worried over the absence of his father from Umuaro while the latter is in detention at Okperi. "What would happen to the new moon?", Nwafo wonders, and, in one of the most imaginative passages in the novel, as the dusk brings along with it the new moon,

> ... Nwafo took position where his father always sat. He did not wait very long before he saw the young thin moon. It looked very thin and reluctant. Nwafo reached for the *ogene* and made to beat it but fear stopped his hand (166).

Had Nwafo beaten that *ogene*, then the almost intractable conflict that arose later would have assumed a new dimension, for Nwafo would have been taking over the spiritual function of his father as a high priest of Ulu.

But a system that encourages individualism at the same time as it demands considerable communal conformity and filial obedience is likely to create occasions for disagreement between father and son. The relationship between Ezeulu and Edogo illustrates this fact well. Early in the novel, this conflict is indicated in its latency, and as the novel progresses, the conflict is shown to grow deeper and more fundamental. While Ezeulu comes to regard his first son as "cold ash", the son considers his father as dictatorial and biased.

It is not easily explicable why there should be this strong disagreement between the two. Edogo is an artist – a carver – a work similar to Ezeulu's in the sense that both carving and priesthood require the use of the imaginative and reflective minds. Ezeulu's poor impression of his son does not seem to be justified; instead the impression one forms is that Edogo is an artist who is able to judge rather perceptively. Inevitably he condemns those attitudes in his father he thinks are unworthy of the head of a large family and the priest of a god. But, by and large, he does submit to his father's authority. Ezeulu's wrong judgment of his son may well be a fore-runner to the wrong judgment he is later to make in the conflict between him and his clan. The element of strong personal bias is present in both cases. For, in spite of his attempt to convince us that it is Ulu punishing his people for irreverence, it can hardly be denied that there is that element of personal vendetta in Ezeulu's refusal to name the New Yam Festival.

We see then that the Igbo home in Achebe is not without its feuds. Most of these feuds are fundamental and, in one way or the other, either literally or symbolically, related to the over-all artistic conception of the novels. Of *Things Fall Apart*, Irele (26) has written that Achebe carefully constructed "the cracks in the edifice where the falling apart begins." The statement can also be applied to Achebe's other fictional writings, since the falling apart that begins with *Things Fall Apart* is a process which continues in the other novels. It can therefore safely be said that a good number of those "cracks in the edifice where the falling apart begins" can be found in the relationship between Achebe's fathers and their sons.

A consideration of Igbo home in Achebe would be incomplete without an examination of Achebe's ability to paint vividly those apparently inconsequential incidents in the home which really make the home the theatre of activity it is expected to be. These apparent trivialities of the home help to make Achebe's scenes and incidents very credible. In *Things Fall Apart*, for instance, there is the scene where Ekwefi and Ezinma are together on the second day of the New Yam Festival. We are confronted with vivid details of how Ekwefi is preparing a fowl. Then there is Ezinma wanting to know how true it is that grown-ups are immune from fire-burns. From there mother and daughter soon begin to discuss the implication of the twitching of eyelids. Then soon Nwoye's mother comes shouting for some fire from across her own part of the compound.

There is nothing forced about the narrative, and the lively scene being painted has a relaxing effect on the reader. As one reads the passage, one thinks of the preceding incident where Okonkwo had beaten up his third wife and one is likely to come to the conclusion that Okonkwo's home is not all heavy face, roaring voice and over-spilling temper.

In *Arrow of God*, the children of Ezeulu echo the arrival of the new moon following Ezeulu's *ogene*-beat announcing the event. The women begin to discuss the moon and Ugoye says that, from the way it is sitting, it is a bad moon. Little Obiageli, tugging her mother's clothes, wants to know whether the moon kills people. A moment later, the children improvise a song about the moon being a killer. It is a particularly important passage, though it appears trivial, in the sense that here the moon metaphor is introduced again. The moon of course is a very important symbol in the Ezeulu household. The tragedy of *Arrow of God* is the tragedy of a moon that has turned malevolent. Ezeulu's inability to announce to his people the appearance of the moon for three consecutive times arrests, and later distorts, the progress of the seasons in the community. Harvesting cannot be done and crops perish in the hard earth. Famine sets in. In that traditional Igbo society, the period of the moon is a period of hilarity, joy, love-making and play-acting in the village square; in other words, the moon becomes a symbol for the comic mode of life. But the appearance of the moon is also associated with intensified insanity in those minds that are not very stable; the moon therefore also has its sad signification. It is this malevolent significance of the moon that triumphs in *Arrow of God*; the children are right in their song, for the moon does kill.

When Akukalia is at Okperi with his war ultimatum, he and his companions discuss the grave issue that made Akukalia not to accept kolanut hospitality in his mother's clan. Then a little girl suddenly interrupts the man in order to report to her father that she has been slapped. She is gently dismissed while the men continue with their grave discussion. Again this trivial incident serves as a kind of comic wedge inserted in order to mellow down the tension of the scene. Many of such scenes, serving a similar purpose, appear at significant points in Achebe's narratives. They are stylistic devices whereby the artist gives validity to his fictional world by drawing materials from the social and anthropological environment of his people.

Lastly, the Igbo home in Achebe needs to be considered in relation to the society in Achebe of which it structurally forms a part. In as much as the home in Achebe is organic and semi-autonomous, it is still part of a larger society that thrives on communal co-existence. Achebe's Igbo society is very close-knit; a corporate society very alive with ant-hill activity. Families act and react with outside forces to maintain the corporate nature of that society. As Echeruo (157) puts it,

> without that inner communal conscience – the ultimate veracity of his under-
> standing of Igbo society and of the traumas and conflicts it has – Achebe would
> have had no worthwhile truth to relate, no essential theme to express.

Achebe's novels are thus filled with incidents and metaphors that link the home with the society. Most of these incidents and scenes usually involve a household and its marriage relations to some other exogamous unit. In *Things Fall Apart*, Okonkwo invites his in-laws during the Feast of the New Yam Festival and his household is a scene of great joy and celebration. "Obierika's compound was as busy as an ant-hill" during the marriage of his daughter. The atmosphere of marriage celebration, occupying almost six pages of the novel, is a micro-cosmic enactment of commu-nal hilarity mixed with serious transaction. In *Arrow of God*, during the arrival of Okuata into Ezeulu's compound as Obika's wife, "the three compounds of Ezeulu and his sons were … full of relatives and friends … . The whole scene is a classic example of the traditional Igbo socio-economic system whereby the community always has a way of sharing in the wealth of its prominent members. Other such feasts include Okonkwo's valedictory feast at Mbanta in *Things Fall Apart* during which the old man who passes the vote of thanks says that "a man does not call his kinsmen to a feast to save them from starving; he does so because it is good for kinsmen to gather together just as people gather in the moon-lit village ground in spite of the fact that every man can behold the moon from his house" (152). What the old man upholds is the fact that the home is only a unit; a social component of the community.

There are also some rituals in Achebe's Igbo home which symbolically link the home in mystic identification with the universal forces that uphold the cor-porateness of the community. It is in such a light that Chielo's intrusion into, and temporary abduction of Ezinma from, Okonkwo's house in *Things Fall Apart* can properly be appreciated. Chielo tours the whole villages of Umuofia with Ezinma on her back before both of them finally disappear into the cave of *Agbala*, the goddess to whom Chielo ministers as priestess. *Agbala* is a protective deity of the clan, and in the novel we find Okonkwo three times committing offences that are a disrespect to the gods. The abduction of Okonkwo's daughter – whom he loves dearly – by the priestess of the goddess may therefore be seen both as a warning and a reminder to Okonkwo of his obligations to his clan-gods, however, prominent he may be in the community. It is a recognition by the gods that Okonkwo's personal disposition are a danger to the peace of the clan.

Another family ritual that assumes communal dimensions appears in *Arrow of God*. It is the purification rite of Okuata which is an exercise a new bride must undergo before she finally "goes in" to her husband; a kind of renunciation with spinsterhood. Before the burial of the sacrifice, the medicine-man intones:

> Any evil which you might have seen with your eyes, or spoken with your mouth, or heard with your ears or trodden with our feet; whatever your father might have brought upon you or our mother brought upon you, I cover them all here (119).

It is significant that the bowl containing the sacrifice is buried in such a way that "its curved back showed a little above the surface of the road" (120). This implies that innumerable human feet are likely to brush over the bowl for a long time. Symbolically then, this ritual makes the marriage between Obika and Okuata no longer only a household affair, but a sacred institution witnessed by the whole community both physically (as during the feast) and mystically (by the contact between the human feet and the buried bowl of sacrifice). Achebe's home is thus so much intertwined with the society it is part of that most of what happens in it assume communal significance.

In conclusion, Achebe's Igbo home is in fact a basic infrastructure which the author uses to present a comprehensive picture of his Igbo society, both in its mundane and spiritual manifestations. The home not only presents us with the polygamous nature of these homes, their physical structures, their organization, conflicts and trivialities, but also the bond between the homes and the society, and the spiritual forces that influence the affairs of the community. Achebe also portrays these diverse elements of the home in such a way that they have some relevance to his themes and the over-all artistic quality of his works.

Note

When Chinua Achebe published his *Arrow of God* in 1964, a then aspiring novelist of Achebe's own ethnic origin, I.N.C. Aniebo – he has now published a few novels and many short stories – asked if Achebe was a novelist or a sociologist (Aniebo 1964, 149–150).

Works Cited

Achebe, Chinua. *Things Fall Apart*. London: Heinemann, 1962.

———. *Arrow of God*. London: Heinemann, 1964.

———. *A Man of the People*. London: Heinemann, 1966.

———. *Girls at War and Other Stories*. London: Heineman, 1972 and 1977.

Acholonu, Rose. "The Female Predicament in the Nigerian Novel." *Feminist Criticism in African Literature*, ed. Helen Chukwuma, Enugu: New Generation Books, 1994, 38–52.

Ackley, Donald. "The Male Female Motif in *Things Fall Apart*". *Studies in Black Literature* 5:1 (Winter 1976).

Aniebo, I.N.C. "Novelist or Sociologist?" A Review of *Arrow of God*." *Nigerian Magazine* 81 (June 1964), 149–150.

Basden, G.T. *Niger Ibos*. London: New Franc Cass Edition, 1966.

Eagleton, Terry. *Marxism and Literary Criticism*. London: Methuen, 1976.

Echeruo, M.J.C. "China Achebe" *A Celebration of Black African Writing*, eds. Bruce King and Kolawole Ogungbesan. Ahmadu Bello University Press and Oxford University Press, 1976.

Irele, Abiola. "The Tragic Conflict in Achebe's Novels." *Black Orpheus* 17 (June 1975).

Obiechina, Emmanuel. *Culture, Tradition and Society in the West African Novel*. Cambridge: Cambridge University Press, 1975.

Ogbalu, F.C. Igbo *Institutions and Customs*. Onitsha: University Press Company, 1982.

Palmer, Enstace. *The Growth of the African Novel*. London: Heinemann, 1979.

Rockwell, Joan. *Facts in Fiction*. London: Routledge & Kegan Paul, 1974.

Turkington, Kate. Chinua Achebe's *Things Fall Apart* (*Studies in English Literature*). London: Edward Arnold, 1977.

Ucehdu, Victor. *The Igbo of Southeastern Nigeria*. Holt, Rinehart and Winston, 1975.

Weinstock, D.J. "Achebe's Christ-Figure". *Journal of New African Literature and the Arts* 5 & 6 (Spring/Fall, 1969).

Wren, Robert. *Achebe's World (The Historical and Cultural Context of the Novels of Chinua Achebe)*. London: Longman, 1980.

Chapter 12

Chinua Achebe and
Igbo (African) Traditional Religion

Odirin Omiegbe

CHINUA ACHEBE WAS BORN IN 1930 in Ogidi, in the present Anambra State of Nigeria. Chinua Achebe, whose father was an Evangelist and Teacher, grew up in a fascinating and challenging environment. It was in a time of transition when the technologically more advanced, imperialist European system was shattering the very foundation of indigenous Nigeria civilizations. Although he grew up under the shadow of his father who tried to shepherd him from the supposedly inimical influences of what Christians were taught to regard as a "pagan" community, young Achebe's curiosity could not be confined, as he made surreptitious contact with the traditional people in their work, their rituals and ceremonies, and their vigorous masking traditions. He observed the men in their assemblies in which rhetorical and forensic skills were exhibited. Against the wishes of his father, his mother and other relations told him stories from native folklore and history. All these influences were crystallized in his fiction.

In addition, Achebe (1975) states in his autobiographical essay "Named for Victoria, Queen of England," that he was christened Albert Chinualumogu. His father was an evangelist and church teacher, while many of his relatives and neighbors adhered to Igbo religion and customs. As a result, Achebe grew up at the crossroads of cultures. Achebe (1973) goes further to write:

> On one arm of the crossroads we sang hymns and read the Bible night and day.
> On the other hand my father's brother and his family, blinded by heathenism
> offered food to idols. That was how it was supposed to be anyhow. But I knew,

without knowing why, that it was too simple a way to describe what was going on … what I do remember was a fascination of the ritual and the life on the other arm of the crossroads. And I believe two things were in my favour – that curiosity and the little distance imposed between me and it by the accident of my birth. The distance becomes not a separation but a bringing together like the necessary backward step which a judicious viewer may take in order to see a convert steadily and fully.

The various comments on Chinua Achebe's works have made us have a background of Achebe and how these influenced his writings. Among his writings are *Things Fall Apart* (1958), *No Longer at Ease* (1960), *Arrow of God* (1964), *A Man of the People* (1966), *Girls at War* (1972) and *Anthills of the Savannah* (1987).

Ezirim (1987) has said that Achebe's main preoccupation as a writer has been to capture and interpret the momentous clash between the traditional African and technologically advanced European culture so that his people can make meaning out of the configuration of socio-political and historical forces. One of the consequences of this clash is the African's loss of identity, a loss which has resulted in a lack of sense of worth and self confidence. With the virtual destruction of the traditional African systems, the African has no cohesive value system to anchor his belief. In several interviews, essays and discussions, Achebe has stressed his concern as a novelist in very practical and graphic terms. In 1964, he wrote:

> The worst thing that can happen to any people is the loss of their dignity and self-respect. The writer's duty is to help them regain it by showing them in human terms what happened to them, what they lost.
>
> Those things that constitute the dignity and respect of the Africans are embedded in their culture, tradition and religion. This is what Achebe wants writers like himself to project through their writings so that the dignity and self-respect which the Africans used to have would be regained.

Ezirim (1987) explains further that one thing Achebe wants his readers to take very seriously is that African people did not hear of culture (including religion) for the first time from the Europeans, that their societies were not mindless but frequently had a philosophy of great depth and value and beauty, that they had poetry and, above all, they had dignity. The relevance of his statement becomes more evident today when we are striving to make the African people realize that Europeans have no monopoly of culture (including religion). Achebe has, therefore, set a task for himself and other African authors: the responsibility of liberating their people. However, the author liberates his people, not by sloganeering or idealism of their history, but by leading them through the positive, if painful, process of self-evaluation and criticism. Achebe considers it wrong for Africans to blame Europeans for "all our failings." But the colonial aggressors and Africans are implicated in the despoiling of Africa. Achebe also expects African writers to be involved in the reshaping of Africa, instead of thinking that all they need to do is to observe and describe.

How did Achebe use Igbo (African) traditional religion to restore the lost self-dignity and respect of the African people? How did he use his writings to show to the world of mankind that African people did not hear of religion for the first time from the Europeans? How did Achebe use his writings to liberate his people (the Africans) from religious inferiority? The following analysis of Achebe and his writings on Igbo (African) traditional religion depict how Achebe "liberates his people, not by sloganeering or idealization of their history, but by leading them through the positive, if painful, process of self-evaluation and criticism" (Ezirim 1987).

Belief in a Supreme Being

The Africans believe in the existence of God Almighty. They believe that he is the supreme Being to whom absolute worship should be directed. This idea is made known when Akunna in *Things Fall Apart* tells Mr. Brown, a British Missionary that:

> You said that there is one supreme God who made heaven and earth. We also believe in him and call him *Chukwu*; he made all the world and the other gods (126).

Belief in Intermediaries

Africans believe that there are intermediaries between the Supreme Being and man, and that He could be approached through such intermediaries. Achebe brought this belief out in *Things Fall Apart* in a discussion between Mr. Brown and Akunna, thus:

> 'There are no other gods,' said Mr. Brown. 'Chukwu is the only God and all others are false. You carve a piece of wood – like that one' (he pointed at the rafters from which Akunna's carved *Ikenga* hung) 'and you call it a god. But it is still a piece of wood.' 'Yes', said Akunna. 'It is indeed a piece of wood. The tree from which it came was made by Chukwu, as indeed all minor gods were. But He made them his messengers so that we could approach him through them. It is like yourself. You are the head of your church.' 'No', protested Mr. Brown. 'The head of my church is God Himself.' 'I know,' said Akunna 'but there must be a head in this world among men. Somebody like yourself must be the head here.'
> 'The head of my church in that sense is in England.' 'That is exactly what I am saying. The head of your church is in your country. He has sent you here as his messenger. And you have also appointed your own messengers and servants; or let me take another example, the District Commissioner. He is sent by your King.' 'They have a queen', said the interpreter of his own account, 'your Queen sends her messenger, the District Commissioner. He finds that he cannot do

the work alone and so he appoints Kotma to help him. It is the same with God or Chukwu. He appoints the smaller gods to help him because His work is too great for one person.' 'You should not think of him as a person', said Mr. Brown. 'It is because you do so that you imagine He must need helpers. And the worst thing about it is that you give all the worship to the false god you have created. That is not so. We make sacrifices to the little gods, but when they fail and there is no one else to turn to we go to Chukwu. It is right to do so. We approach a great man through his servants. But when his servants fail to help us, then we go to the last source of hope. We appear to pay greater attention to the little gods but that is not so. We worry them more because we are afraid to worry their master. Our fathers knew that Chukwu was the overlord and that is why many of them gave their children the name 'Chukwuka – Chukwu is supreme.' 'You said one interesting thing,' said Mr. Brown. 'You are afraid of Chukwu. In my religion, Chukwu is a loving father and need not be feared by those who do His will.' 'But we must fear Him when we are not doing his will,' said Akunna. 'And who is telling His will? It is too great to be known' (126).

Similarly, in *A Man of the People*, Achebe also writes:

My father was a District interpreter. In those days when no one understood as much as 'come' in the white man's language, The District Officer was like the supreme Deity and the interpreter the principal minor god who carried prayers and sacrifices to him (28).

Belief in Numerous Gods

The Africans believe in many gods. Achebe portrays this in most of his novels. Achebe in *Anthills of the Savannah*, writes:

Agwu (a god) does not call a meeting to choose his seers and diviners and artists ... (125).

There is the belief in *chi* – personal gods, and success and failure of man's life are ascribed to it. Achebe in *Things Fall Apart* notes:

If ever a man deserved his success that man was Okonkwo. At an early age he had achieved fame as the greatest wrestler in all the land. That was not luck. At most one could say that his *chi* or personal god was good. But the Ibo people have a proverb that when a man says 'Yes', his *chi* says 'Yes' also. Okonkwo said Yes very strongly; so his *chi* agreed (19).

When Okonkwo shoots his wife with a dane gun, her survival is attributed to her *chi*. A neighbor makes a remark in *Things Fall Apart*, to Ekwefi, Okonkwo's wife: "Your *chi* is very much awake." Achebe also makes it known that in African traditional religion a man's in-law is also seen as his personal god. In *No Longer at Ease* he asks:

Did not the elders say that a man's in-law was his *chi*, his personal god? (42).

In African traditional religion, there is the belief in *Ani* the earth goddess, and source of fertility. According to Achebe in *Things Fall Apart*:

> The feast of the new yam was approaching and Umuofia was in a festive mood. It was an occasion for all to give thanks to Ani, the earth goddess and the source of fertility. Ani played a greater part in the life of the people than any other deity. She was the ultimate judge of morality and conduct. And what was more, she was in close communion with the departed fathers of the clan whose bodies had been committed to earth. The feast of the new yam was held every year before the harvest began to honour the earth goddess ... (26).

A person's *chi* can be bad. According to Achebe in *Things Fall Apart*:

> Unoka was an ill-fated man. He had a bad *chi* or personal god and evil fortune followed him to the grave, or rather to his death, for he had no grave. He died of the swelling which was an abomination to the earth goddess ... (13).

Africans have the belief in the worship of *Ani* the earth goddess. Achebe in *Things Fall Apart* writes about Okonkwo's father Unoka, who went to meet the priestess of *Agbala* to find out reasons why he was not prosperous:

> Every year he (Unoka) said sadly: before I put any crop in the earth, I sacrifice a cock to Ani, the owner of all land. It is the law of our fathers – I also kill a cock at the shrine of Ifejioku, the god of yams. I clear the bush and set fire to it when it is dry.
>
> I sow the yams when the first rain has fallen and stake them when the young tendrils appear. I weed – 'Hold your peace!' screamed the priestess, her voice terrible as it echoed through the dark void. 'You have offended neither the gods nor your fathers. And when a man is at peace with his gods and his ancestors, his harvest will be good or bad according to the strength of his arm. You, Unoka, are known in all the clan for the weakness of your matchet and your hoe. When your neighbours go out with the axe to cut down virgin forests, you sow your yams on exhausted farms that take no labour to clear. They cross seven rivers to make their farms; you stay at home and offer sacrifices to a reluctant soil. Go home and work like a man' (12).

Lastly, to show how Africans attach importance to their numerous gods, Achebe in *Arrow of God*, writes about a prayer by Ezeulu, the priest, to Ulu, an important deity, thus:

> Ulu, I thank you for making me see another new moon. May I see it again and again. This household may it be healthy and prosperous. As this is the month of planting may the six villages plant with profit. May we escape danger in the farm – the bite of a snake or the sting of the scorpion, the mighty one of the scrubland. May we not cut our shinbone with the matchet or the hoe. And let our wives bear male children. May we increase in number at the next counting of the villages so that we shall sacrifice to you a cow, not a chicken as we did

after the last new yam feast. May children put their fathers into the earth and not fathers their children. May good meet the face of every man and every woman. Let it come to the land of the riverain folk and to the land of the forest peoples (6).

Belief in the Worship of Ancestors

The Africans believe in the worship of ancestors. They believe that the ancestors should be worshipped through music, dance, offering of sacrifices, keeping and having reverence for objects that represent the ancestors. They also believe that the ancestors protect and guide them in whatever they are doing. In most of his writings, Achebe brings such belief to the fore.

In *Things Fall Apart*, Achebe on Ancestor Worship writes:

As he (Unoka) broke the kola, he prayed to their ancestors for life and health, and for protection against their enemies (5).

In the same novel, Achebe writes about Okonkwo's zeal for ancestor worship:

Near the barn was a small house, the 'medicine house' or shrine where Okonkwo kept the wooden symbols of his personal gods and his ancestral spirits. He worshipped them with sacrifices of kola-nut, food and palm-wine, and offered prayers to them on behalf of himself, his three wives and eight children (10).

To show the importance that Africans attach to ancestor worship, when Okonkwo violates the week of peace, the priest rejects the kola-nut placed before him and says, in *Things Fall Apart*:

Take away your kola-nut. I shall not eat in the house of a man who has no respect for our gods and ancestors (21).

Similarly, Achebe also highlights Africans' worship of ancestors when he notes a comparison between throwing down a white man and unmasking an ancestral spirit. In *No Longer at Ease*, Achebe states:

To throw a white man down was like unmasking an ancestral spirit (58).

In this statement, Achebe shows that just as the white man viewed African's fighting and throwing them down as a very grievous offence so also the Africans viewed seriously the unmasking of an ancestral spirit.

In the celebration of the New Yam festival, in Okonkwo's household, there are indications of ancestor worship. According to Achebe in *Things Fall Apart*:

... the New Yam festival was celebrated with great joy in Okonkwo's household. Early that morning as he offered a sacrifice of new yam and palm-oil to his ancestors he asked them to protect him, his children and their mothers in the new year (28).

Also, to show the importance the Igbo traditional religion attaches to the worship of the ancestors, Achebe in *Arrow of God* discloses a conversation on the cause of the war between Umuaro and Okperi:

> This war between Umuaro and Okperi began in a rather interesting way. [it] ... started because a man from Umuaro went to visit a friend in Okperi one fine morning, and after he had one or two gallons of palm-wine – ... reached for his *Ikenga* and split it into two. I may explain that *Ikenga* is the most important fetish in the Ibo man's arsenal, so to speak. It represents his ancestors to whom he must make daily sacrifice. When he dies it is split into two; one half is buried with him and the other half is thrown away. So you can see the implication of what our friend from Umuaro did in splitting his host's fetish. It was, of course, the greatest sacrilege. The outraged host reached for his gun and blew the other's head off. And so a regular war developed between the two villages ... (37).

Lastly, Achebe shows Okonkwo's strong desire to leave ancestor worship as a legacy for his son:

> Okonkwo was inwardly pleased at his son's development and he knew it was due to Ikemefuna. He wanted Nwoye to grow into a tough young man capable of ruling his father's household when he was dead and gone to join the ancestors. He wanted him to be a prosperous man, having enough in his barn to feed the ancestors with regular sacrifices (37).

Belief in African Medicine

Achebe in his works shows that Africans believe in African medicine and its efficacy, and that priests, medicine-men and diviners are custodians of such a practice. In *Arrow of God*, Achebe portrays an incident of a child who has convulsions but is cured by the priest.

> Ezeulu rose from his goatskin and moved to the household shrine on a flat board behind the central dwarf wall at the entrance. His *Ikenga*, about as tall as a man's forearm, its animal horn as long as the rest of its human body, jostled with faceless *okposi* of the ancestors black with the blood of sacrifice, and his short personal staff of *ofo*. Nwafo's eyes picked out the special *Okposi* which belonged to him. It had been carved for him because of the convulsions he used to have at night. They told him to call it Namesake, and he did. Gradually, the convulsions had left him (6).

Akueke in Achebe's short story of the same title, is a young lady who is ill and whose relations consult medicine-men to cure her. In *Girls at War*, Achebe explains:

> Her protective spirit despairing of her had taken a hand in the matter and she was stricken with this disease. At first people pretended not to notice the swelling stomach. Medicine-men were brought from far and near to minister to her. But all their herbs and roots had no effect. An Ofa oracle sent Akueke's brothers in

search of a certain palm-tree smothered by a climbing vine. 'When you see it,' he said, to them, 'take a matchet and cut away the strangling climber. The spirits which have bound your sister will release her.' The brothers searched Umuofia and neighbouring villages for three days before they got such a palm-tree and cut it loose. But their sister was not released; rather, she got worse (31).

On the belief in medicine by the Igbo traditional religion, Achebe in *Arrow of God* observes:

> Things were so bad for the six villages that their leaders came together to save themselves. They hired a strong team of medicine-men to install a common deity for them. This deity which the fathers of the six villages made was Ulu. Half of the medicine was buried at a place which became Nkwo market and the other half thrown into the stream which became *mili ulu*. The six villages then took the name of Umuaro, and the priest of *Ulu* became their chief priest. From that day, they were never again beaten by an enemy (15).

The Igbo traditional religion attributes the large number of people coming to their market to a great medicine-man. In a conversation between two persons Achebe notes in *Arrow of God*:

> As the men of Umuaro passed company after company of these market women they talked about the great Eke market in Okperi to which folk from every part of Igbo and Ulu went. 'It is the result of an ancient medicine-man,' Akukalia explained. 'My mother's people are great medicine-men.' There was pride in his voice. At first Eke was a very small market. Other markets in the neighbourhood were drawing it dry. Then one day the men of Okperi made a powerful deity and placed their market in its care. From that day Eke grew and grew until it became the biggest market in those parts. This deity which is called Nwanyieke is an old woman. Every Eke day before cock-crow she appears in the market place with a broom in her right hand and dances round the vast open space beckoning with her broom in all directions of the earth and drawing folk from every land. That is why people will not come near the market before cock-crow; if they did they would see the ancient lady in her task. 'They tell the same story of the Nkwo Market beside the great river at Umuaro', said one of Akukalia's companions. "There the medicine has worked so well that the market no longer assembles only on Nkwo days.' Umuaro is no match for my mother's people in medicine, said Akukalia. 'Their market has grown because the white man took his merchandise there.' 'Why did he take his merchandise there' asked the other man, 'if not because of their medicine?' The old woman of the market has swept the world with her broom, even the land of the white men where they say the sun never shines (19).

Furthermore, in *No Longer at Ease*, Achebe through the conversation below depicts the religious phenomenon:

The old man ... said: you are not a stranger in Umuofia. You have heard our elders say that thunder cannot kill a son or a daughter of Umuofia. Do you know anyone either now or in the past who was killed? Okonkwo had to admit it that he knew no such person. 'But that is the work of God,' he said. 'It is the work of our forefathers,' said the old man. They built a powerful medicine to protect themselves from thunder, and not only themselves, but all their descendants forever. 'Very true,' said another man. 'Any one who denies it does so in vain. Let him go and ask Nwokeke how he was hit by thunder last year. All his skin peeled off like snake slough, but he was not killed. 'Why was he hit at all? That is a matter between him and his chi. But you must know that he was hit in Mbaino and not at home. Perhaps the thunder seeing him at Mbaino called him Mbaino-man at first (45).

African traditional religion also believes in sacrifice as part of their worship. In *Girls at War*, Achebe writes:

The moon was not up yet but there was a faint light in the sky which showed that it would not be long delayed. In this half-light he saw that he had stepped on an egg offered in sacrifice. Someone oppressed by misfortune had brought the offering to the crossroad in the dust. And he had stepped on it (46).

It is necessary that before a man takes a title in his clan, he offers sacrifices to appease the gods and solicit their assistance in taking such a title. Achebe in *Anthills of the Savannah* explains:

It is to this emblem that a man who has achieved wealth of crop and livestock and not wishes to pin an eagle's feather on his success by buying admission to the powerful hierarchy of Ozo must go to present himself and offer sacrifices before he can begin the ceremonies and again after he has concluded them (103).

The place of worship in African traditional religion is sacred. In *Girls at War*, when Obi, the headmaster closes the path leading to the people's sacred shrine, a clash ensues with severe consequences:

Three days later the village priest of Ani called on the headmaster. He was an old man and walked with a slight stoop. He carried a stout walking stick which he usually tapped on the floor by way of emphasis, each time he made a new point in his argument. 'I have heard', he said, after the usual exchange of cordialities 'that our ancestral foot-path has recently been closed' ... 'Yes' replied Mr. Obi. 'We cannot allow people to make a highway of our school compound.' 'Look here my son,' said the priest bringing down his walking stick. 'This path was here before you were born. The whole life of this village depends on it. Our dead relatives depart by it and our ancestors visit us by it. But most important, it is the path of our children, coming in to be born'... Mr. Obi listened with a satisfied smile on his face. 'The whole purpose of our school,' he said finally 'is to eradicate just such beliefs as that. Dead men do not require foot-paths. The whole idea is just fantastic. Our duty is to teach your children to laugh at such ideas.' 'What you say may be true' replied the priest, but 'we follow the practice of our fathers. If you re-open the path we shall have nothing to quarrel about. What I always say is: let the hawk perch and let the eagle perch.' He rose to go. 'I am sorry' said the young headmaster. 'But the school compound cannot be a thoroughfare. It is against our regulations. I suggest you construct another path, skirting our premises. We can even get our boys to help in building it. I don't suppose the ancestors will find the little detour too burdensome. 'I have no more words to say', said the old priest already outside. Two days later a young woman in the village died in child-birth. The diviner was immediately consulted and he prescribed heavy sacrifices to propitiate ancestors insulted by this offence. Obi woke up next morning among the ruins of his work. The beautiful hedges were torn up not just near the path but right round the school, the flowers trampled to death and one of the school buildings, pulled down ... (73).

Killings and Destruction of Property in African Traditional Religion are Justifiable

Achebe makes his audience know that some of the killings and destruction of property in African traditional religion are not barbaric but are justifiable. Such act is compared to a person who is killed if convicted for a capital punishment in countries where such an offence merits it.

In *Things Fall Apart*, Achebe explains that a pronouncement by the gods against those who have erred must be carried out. This was evident when Ogbuefi Ezeudu comes to Okonkwo to inform him about the fate of Ikemefuna as pronounced by the Oracle of the Hills and Caves. It could be recalled that Ikemefuna was brought into Umuofia as a ransom for the killing of a woman of Umuofia:

> That boy calls you father. Do not bear a hand in his death. Okonkwo was surprised and was about to say something when the old man continued. Yes, Umuofia has decided to kill him. The Oracle of the Hills and Caves has pronounced it. They will take him outside Umuofia as is the custom, and kill him there (40).

Similarly when Okonkwo's gun explodes and kills a sixteen-year-old boy, action had to be taken to appease the gods and cleanse the land. The penalty for such an act is for Okonkwo to go on exile have his houses and properties destroyed. According to Achebe in *Things Fall Apart*:

> As soon as the day broke, large crowds of men from Ezeudu's quarter stormed Okonkwo's compound, dressed in garbs of war. They set fire on his houses, demolished his red walls, killed his animals and destroyed his barn. It was the justice of the earth goddess, and they were merely the messengers. They had no hatred in their hearts against Okonkwo. His greatest friend, Obierika was among them. They were merely cleansing the land which Okonkwo had polluted with

the blood of a clansman. Obierika was a man who thought about things. When the will of the goddess had been done, he sat down in his *obi* and mourned his friend's calamity. Why should a man suffer so grievously for an offence he had committed inadvertently? But although he thought for a long time, he found no answer. He was merely led into greater complexities. He remembered his wife's twin children, whom he had thrown away. What crime had they committed? The earth had decreed that they were an offence on the land and they must be destroyed. And if the clan did not exact punishment for an offence against the great goddess, her wrath was loosed on all the land and not just on the offender. As the elders said, if one finger brought oil it soiled the others (87).

Correction of Some Erroneous Impressions

It is erroneously believed that the tradition of offering and eating of kola-nut is considered to be a sacrifice to an idol and as such Christians should not accept and eat kola-nuts presented to them by pagans. To correct this erroneous view, Achebe in *No Longer at Ease* portrays a conversation between Obi's father and his relatives who come to greet him on the arrival of his son to Umuofia:

> 'Zik' he called, meaning Isaac, 'bring us a kola-nut to break for this child's return.' 'This is a Christian house where kola-nut is not eaten,' sneered the man. 'Kola-nut is eaten here' replied Mr. Okonkwo 'but not sacrifice to idols.' 'Who talked about sacrifice? Here is a little child who returned from wrestling in the spirit world and you sit there blabbing about Christian house and idols, talking like a man whose palm-wine has gone into his nose.' He hissed in disgust, took up his goat-skin and went to sit outside (46).

Similarly, it is considered to be wrong when a man tells folk stories. In *No Longer at Ease*, the novelist highlights:

> ... in fact she (Obi's mother) used to tell her eldest daughters stories. But that was before Obi was born. She stopped because her husband forbade her to do so. 'We are not heathens,' he said. 'Stories like that are not for the people of church.' And Hannah had stopped telling her children folk-stories (52).

Accepting of food from neighbors and relatives who are not Christians is considered to be bad. In *No Longer at Ease*:

> Isaac Okonkwo was not merely a Christian; he was a catechist. In their first years of married life he made Hannah see the grave responsibility she carried as a catechist's wife. And as soon as she knew what was expected of her, she did it, sometimes showing more zeal than even her husband. She taught her children not to accept food in neighbours' houses because she said they offered their food to idols. That fact alone set her children apart from all others, for among the Ibos, children were free to eat where they liked. One day a neighbour offered a piece of yam to Obi who was then four years old. He shook his head

like his older and wiser sisters and then said: 'we don't eat heathen food.' His sister Janet tried too late to cover his mouth with her hand (53).

To establish the authenticity of Igbo traditional religion, and debunk the erroneous belief by Christian missionaries that it involves the worship of "false" gods, Chinua Achebe in *Things Fall Apart* puts the conversation between Akunna and Mr. Brown into good use:

> ... That is not so. We make sacrifices to the little gods but when they fail and there is no one else to turn to we go to Chukwu ... (127).

Achebe in *A Man of the People* makes a correction on an erroneous impression a British woman has on wooden figures. In the discussion between the British women (Jean) and Odili, Achebe holds that:

> One of our leading artists had just made an enormous wooden figure of a god for a public square in Bori. I had not seen it yet but had read a lot about it. In fact it had attracted so much attention that it soon became fashionable to say it was bad or un-African. The Englishman was not saying that it lacked something or other. 'I was pleased the other day' he said 'as I drove past to see one very old woman in uncontrollable rage shaking her fists at the sculpture' ... 'Now that's very interesting' said someone, '...Well it's more than that,' said another. 'You see this old woman, quite an illiterate pagan, who most probably worshipped this very god herself; unlike our friend trained in Europe art schools, this old lady is in a position to know ... Quite'. It was then I had my flash of insight. 'Did you say she was shaking her fist?' I asked. 'In that case you got her meaning all wrong. Shaking the fist in our society is a sign of great honour and respect; it means that you attribute power to the person or object.' Which of course is quite true. And if I may digress a little, I have since this incident, come up against another critic who committed a crime in my view because he transferred to an alien culture the same meanings and interpretation that his own people attach to certain gestures and facial expression. This critic, a freeman writing in a glossy magazine on African art said of a famous religious mask from this country. Note the half-closed eyes, sharply drawn and tense eyebrow, the ecstatic and passionate mouth ... It was simply scandalous. All that the mask said, all it felt for mankind was a certain superb, divine detachment and disdain. If I met a woman in the street and she looked at me with the face of the mask that would be its meaning (49).

African Traditional Religion has a Great Influence in Young Christian Converts More than Elderly Christian Converts.

Achebe's writings show that African traditional religion is deeply rooted in the minds of the elderly Igbo people more than the younger ones that such beliefs and practices can hardly be removed completely from the people. At times, such 'pagan' influences would be displayed when they are pushed to the wall.

To indicate that African traditional religion has an impact in the minds of young children in *Girls at War*, Achebe states that:

> Like his sisters Chike was brought up in the ways of the white men which meant the opposite of traditional religion. Amos had many years before, bought a tiny bell with which he summoned his family to prayers and hymn-singing first thing in the morning and last thing at night. This was one of the ways of the white man. Sarah taught her children not to eat in their neighbour's houses because 'they offered their food to their idols.' And thus she set herself against the age-old custom which regards children as the common responsibility of all, so that no matter what relationship existed between parents and their children, children played together and shared their food together. One day a neighbour offered a piece of yam to Chike, who was only four years old. The boy shook his head haughtily and said 'we don't eat heathen food.' The neighbour was full of rage, but she controlled herself and only muttered under her breath that even an *Osu* was full of pride nowadays, thanks to the white man (35).

Similarly, to portray that African traditional religion hardly has an impact on the minds of the elderly Christian converts, in *Girls at War*, Achebe writes about Elizabeth who converted to Christianity:

> A few days later he (Amos who was about to marry an *Osu* – outcast) told his widowed mother, who had recently been converted to Christianity and had taken the name Elizabeth. The shock nearly killed her. When she recovered, she went down on her knees and begged Amos not to do this thing. But he would not hear; his ears had been nailed up. At last in desperation, Elizabeth went to consult a Diviner. This Diviner was a man of great power and wisdom. As he sat on the floor of his hut beating a tortoise shell, a coating of white chalk round his eyes, he saw not only the present, but also what had been and what was to be. He was called the man of the four eyes. As soon as old Elizabeth appeared, he cast his stringed cowries and told her what she had come to see him about. 'Your son has joined the white-man's religion. And you too in your old age when you should know better. And do you wonder that he is stricken with insanity? Those who gather ant-infested faggots must be prepared for the visit of the lizards. He cast his cowries a number of times and wrote with a finger on a bowl of sand, and all the while his Nwifulu, a talking, calabash chatted to itself. 'Shut up' he roared, and it immediately held its peace. The Diviner then muttered a few incantations and rattled off a breathless reel of proverbs that followed one another like the cowries in his magic string. At last, he pronounced the cure. The ancestors were angry and must be appeased with a goat. Old Elizabeth performed the rites, but her son remained insane and married an *Osu* whose name was Sarah. Old Elizabeth renounced her new religion and returned to the faith of her people (37).

Similarly, when Obi's father (Isaac) a practicing Christian, who sometime before forbade his wife Hannah from telling their children folk stories because he considers such to be for heathens and not for people of the church, but surprisingly is against his son (Obi) marrying Clara, an *Osu* (outcast). This shows that despite Isaac's belief in Christianity, he still has some belief in African traditional religion. This indicates that Christianity is not deeply entrenched in his heart.

In *No Longer at Ease*, Achebe writes on the comment made by Obi's father to Obi when Obi expresses his intention to marry Clara, an *Osu* girl:

> *Osu* is like leprosy in the minds of our people, I beg of you my son, not to bring the mark of shame and of leprosy into your family. If you do, your children and your children's children unto the third generation will curse your memory (120).

In *Things Fall Apart*, Achebe also shows how the Igbo attach importance to their traditional religion despite their conversion to Christianity. This is evident when Reverend James Smith, Mr. Brown's successor condemns openly Mr. Brown's policy of compromise and accommodation of African traditional religious beliefs in the church and openly suspended a young woman from the church for "pouring new wine into old bottles."

In *Arrow of God*, a discussion between Mr. Goodcountry and Moses shows that some Christians still believe in the royal python. Achebe writes:

> He (Moses) told the new teacher (Mr. Goodcountry) quite bluntly that neither the Bible nor the catechism asked converts to kill the python, a beast full of illomen. Was it for nothing that God put a curse on its head? 'Today, there are six villages in Umuaro; but this has not always been the case. Our fathers tell us that there were seven before, and the seventh was called Umuama.' Some of the converts nodded their support. Mr. Goodcountry listened patiently and contemptuously: 'One day six brothers of Umuama killed the python and asked one of their number, Iweka, to cook yam pottage with it. Each of them brought a piece of yam and a bowl of water to Iweka. When he finished cooking the yam pottage, the men came one by one and took their pieces of yam. Then they began to fill their bowls to the mark with the yam stew. But this time only four of them took their measure before the stew got finished.' Moses Unachukwu's listeners smiled, except Mr. Goodcountry who sat like a rock. Oduche smiled because he had heard the story as a little boy and forgotten it until now. 'The brothers began to quarrel; Violently, and then began to fight. Very soon the fighting spread throughout Umuama, and so fierce was it that the village was almost wiped out. The few survivors fled their village, across the great river to the land Ulu where they are scattered today. The remaining six seeing what had happened to Umuama went to a seer to know the reason, and he told them that the royal python was sacred to Idemili; it was this deity which had punished Umuama. From that day, the six villages decreed that henceforth anyone who killed the python would be regarded as having killed his kinsman.' Moses ended by counting his fingers the villages and clans which also forbade the killing of

the snake. Then Mr. Goodcountry spoke. A story such as you have just told us is not fit to be heard in the house of God. But I allowed you to go on so that all may see the foolishness of it. There was murmuring from the congregation which might have stood either for agreement or disagreement. 'I shall leave it to your own people to answer you,' Mr. Goodcountry looked round the small congregation, but no one spoke. 'Is there no one here who can speak up for the Lord?' Oduche who had thus far inclined towards Unachukwu's position had a sudden stab of sight. He raised his hand and was about to put it down again. But Mr. Goodcountry had seen him. 'Yes?' 'It is not true that the Bible does not ask us to kill the serpent. Do not God tell Adam to crush its head after it had deceived his wife?' Many people clapped for him. 'Do you hear that, Moses?' Moses made to answer but Mr. Goodcountry was not going to give him another opportunity. 'You say you are the first Christian in Umuaro, you partake of the Holy Meal; and yet whenever you open your mouth nothing but heathen filth pours out. Today a child who sucks his mother's breast has taught you the scriptures. It is not as our Lord himself said that the first shall become the last and the last become first. The world will pass away but not one single word of our Lord will be set aside.' He turned to Oduche. 'When the time comes for your baptism you will be called Peter; on this rock will I build my church.' This caused more clapping from a part of the congregation. Moses was now fully aroused. 'Do I look to you like someone you can put in your bag and walk away?' he asked. 'I have been to the fountainhead of this new religion and seen with my own eyes the white people who brought it. So I want to tell you now that I will not be led astray by outsiders who choose to weep louder than the owners of the corpse. You are not the first teacher I have seen; you are not the second; you are not the third. If you are wise you will face the work they sent you to do here and take your hand off the python. You can say that I told you so. Nobody here has complained to you that the python has ever blocked his way as he came to church. If you want to do your work in peace you will heed what I have said, but if you want to be the lizard that ruined his own mother's funeral you may carry on as you are doing? He turned to Oduche. 'As for you they may call you Peter or they may call you Paul or Barnabas; it does not pull a hair from me. I have nothing to say to a mere boy who should be picking palm-nuts for his mother. But since you have also become our teacher, I shall be waiting for the day you will have the courage to kill a python in this Umuaro. A coward may cover the ground with his words but when the time comes to fight he runs away (48).

Similarly, in *Things Fall Apart*, when the issue of *Osu* joining the Christians in worship surfaces, the attitude displayed by some of the Christian converts towards the *Osu* (outcast) shows that they (the converts) still believe in Igbo traditional religion which forbade inter-social relationships between the *Osu* and the free born:

And the little church was at that moment too deeply absorbed in its own troubles to annoy the clan. It all began over the question of admitting outcasts. These outcasts or *Osu*, seeing that the new religion welcomed twins and such abominations, thought that it was possible that they would also be received. And so one Sunday two of them went into the church. There was an immediate stir; but so great was the work the new religion had among the converts that they did not immediately leave the church when the outcasts came in. Those who found themselves nearest to them merely moved to another seat. It was a miracle. But it only lasted until the end of the service. The whole church raised a protest and were about to drive these people out, when Mr. Kiage stopped them and began to explain. 'Before God' he said, 'there is no slave or free. We are all children of God and we must receive these our brothers.' 'You do not understand,' said one of the converts. 'What will the heathens say of us when they hear that we receive *Osu* into our midst? They will laugh.' 'Let them laugh,' said Mr. Kiage. God will laugh at them on the judgement day. Why do the nations rage and the peoples image a vain thing? He that sitteth in heavens shall laugh. The Lord shall have them in derision? 'You do not understand,' the convert maintained. 'You are our teacher and you can teach us the things of the new faith. But this is a matter which we know.' And he told him what an *Osu* was. He was a person dedicated to a god, a thing set apart – a taboo forever, and his children after him. He could neither marry nor be married by the freeborn. He was in fact an outcast, living in a special area of the village, close to the Great Shrine. Wherever he went he carried with him the mark of his forbidden caste-long, tangled and dirty hair. A razor was taboo for him. An *Osu* could not attend an assembly of the freeborn and they in turn, could not shelter under his roof. He could not take any of the four titles of the clan, and when he died he was buried by his kind in the evil forest. How could such a man be a follower of Christ?' 'He needs Christ more than you and I', said Mr. Kiaga. 'Then I shall go back to the clan,' said the convert. And he went (111).

Christian Missionaries Make Jest of African Traditional Religion and Christian Religion is Not Superior to African Religion

In some of Achebe's writings, the missionaries at one time or the other usually make jest of African traditional religion. They claim that Christianity is supreme. Logically, they explain the supreme Being and Christian teachings and practices. When converts try to explain some African traditional religious practices that cannot be divorced from the life of the Igbo man, the Christian missionary tends to make jest of them. Such is noticed in *Arrow of God* in the dialogue between Moses, a Christian convert and Mr. Goodcountry on the belief in the royal python.

In an effort to show that Christian religion is not superior to African traditional religion and that it can still be made jest of by African traditional religion believers, in *Things Fall Apart*, Achebe demonstrates how the Igbo traditional religious believers mock Christianity:

Okonkwo who only stayed in the hope that it might come to chasing the men out of the village or whipping them, now said: 'You told us with your own mouth that there was only one god. Now you talk about his son. He must have a wife, then?'The crowd agreed. 'I did not say he had a wife,' said the interpreter, somewhat lamely. 'Your buttocks said he had a son,' said the joker. So he must have a wife and all of them must have buttocks.'The missionary ignored him and went on to talk about the Holy Trinity. At the end Okonkwo was fully convinced that the man was mad. He shrugged his shoulders and went away to tap his afternoon palm-wine (103).

Conversion of Africans from African Traditional Religion to Christianity was a Difficult Task

The conversion of Africans from their traditional religion to Christianity was a very difficult task for the Christian missionaries. This is due to the fact that their traditional religion has deep influence in their life. Simply put, it is their way of life. It is noticeable in all their activities as in worship, dressing, festivals, occupation, music, dance, entertainment of visitors, moral values, work of art and craft, political organization and government.

To show how difficult it was for the Christian missionaries to convert the Africans from their traditional religion to Christianity Achebe in *Things Fall Apart* opines:

> He (Mr. Brown) came to the conclusion that a frontal attack on it (Igbo traditional religion) would not succeed. And so he built a school and a little hospital in Umuofia. He went from family to family begging people to send their children to his school ... He encouraged them with gifts of singlets and towels ... (128).

African Traditional Religion is Liberal and Tolerant

Christian missionaries portray African traditional religion as being hostile to Christianity. Achebe in his writings tries to explain that such an idea is not correct. He explains that African traditional religion is open-minded, having and showing a broad mind, free from prejudice against Christianity. He also demonstrates that Igbo traditional religion allows Christianity to be preached among its worshippers; but, the Christians would not show respect for the beliefs and practices of traditional religion. Achebe makes these views in *Things Fall Apart*, in the conversation between Ajofia and Mr. Smith, a missionary through an interpreter:

> Ajofia says: 'Tell the white man that we will not do any harm,' he said to the interpreter. 'Tell him to go back to his house and leave us alone. We liked his brother who was with us before. He was foolish, but, we liked him, and for his sake we shall not harm his brother. But this shrine which he built must be destroyed. We shall no longer allow it in our midst. It has bred untold abominations and we have come to put an end to it.' He turned to his comrades, 'fathers of Umuofia, I salute you' and they replied with one guttural voice. He turned again

to the missionaries 'you can stay with us if you like our ways. You can worship your own gods. It is good that a man should worship the gods and the spirits of his fathers. Go back to your house so that you may not be hurt. Our anger is great but we have held it down so that we can talk to you (134).

Conclusion

According to Booth (1977), an early Portuguese visitor to the southern coast of Africa, African "people are all Hottentots and they have no religion." He was wrong on both counts, but at least on the latter point his mistake was understandable. After all, he was from Europe where the presence of religion is manifested in church buildings, priests and sacred scriptures. Perhaps he was on his way from India where comparable phenomena would have been seen. In that part of Africa, the Portuguese visitor, however, saw no identifiable religious buildings, no distinctively religious functionaries, and certainly no scriptures. Therefore, he concluded that "they have no religion."

A parallel may be found in traditional China which has also been described as a country without religion. Yang (1967) has shown, however, that in China religion has been very important, not so much as a separate institution but as in "diffused" form with its theology rituals and organizations intimately merged with the concepts and structure of secular institutions. In this "diffused" form religion performs a pervasive function in an organized manner in every major aspect of the Chinese social life.

African traditional religion has been relegated to the background. It is described as being "fetish" and "primitive". According to Bitek (1977), it is important to avoid using terms such as "superstitions", "pagans", "fetish", "primitive" and "animism" in describing African traditional religion. Some of these terms may originally have had valid, non-judgemental meanings; today they have little clear content but strong suggestions of inferiority and are rightly resented by the African. In addition, he remarked that an African scholar says that "there are no animists in Africa; animism is a product of the western mind." Yes – it is indeed the product of the western minds that are swimming in the ocean of ignorance.

One can now see clearly the erroneous notions held by the Europeans about African traditional religion. To say that Africans have no religion is a serious mistake indeed. It is ignorance of the highest order and annoying to Africans. To say that African traditional religion is "pagan", "fetish", "primitive" and "animistic" is very unfortunate. From time immemorial, Africans indeed have a religion which has been handed down from parents to off-springs and from generation to generation. Their religion is a part of their life. It is held as a way of life. It is rich in many aspects of life as dance, music, songs, drama, poetry, dressing, folktales, moral values, works of art and craft, political organization and government which the Europeans can learn and benefit from.

One cannot wholly blame the Europeans for their ignorance and negative attitude towards African traditional religion. Had it been that the beliefs and practices of African traditional religion were in print, it would have made some sense and more impact and the Europeans would have appreciated it. This is precisely what Chinua Achebe has done. He brings out the beliefs and practices of African traditional religion in his writings so that the Europeans can have a better understanding and thereby be in a better position to "bail" themselves from ignorance, which indeed is a disease that urgently requires a cure.

When the Africans had their first contact with the Europeans, a kind of behavior better described as colonial mentality was observed among the Europeans. Such mentality made the Europeans look at African religion, culture and political organization as inferior to theirs. Some Africans themselves lost their self-respect and dignity in their religion, culture and political organization. In 1964, Achebe opined that:

> The worst thing that can happen to any people is the loss of their dignity and self-respect. The writer's duty is to help them regain it by showing them in human terms what happened to them, what they lost.

This is precisely what Achebe has done in his writings. He writes with the purpose of liberating Africans from an infested colonial mentality and helping to restore their lost dignity. History and posterity certainly would not forget him. No wonder, his writings "have endeared him to millions of readers all over the world. His impact is felt in at least fifty-five languages [worldwide] into which his novels have been translated. He is not merely the father of serious African fiction in English, he is also classed among the greatest writers in the world. His novels are read all over the world and are studied in universities, colleges and high schools in Africa, Britain, North America, India and Australia (Ezirim 1977) and he has received many national and international awards for his contribution to the development of African literature in the English language.

It is hoped that this essay would help to liberate the Europeans from ignorance about African traditional religion; liberate also the Africans from the colonial mentality which made them regard their religion as inferior and thus restore the dignity and respect of African traditional religion that was lost due to the contact with Christianity brought about by the white missionaries. Indeed Africans have a religion with many worshippers up till today. As children are born daily in large numbers into the world, so are many converts embracing the African traditional religion in Africa as well as in the Western world where people claim to be Christians. It is observed that one way or the other, directly or indirectly, many still believe and practice some of the beliefs of African traditional religion. African traditional religion cannot, therefore, be wiped out; for it is a legacy that has been handed down from parents to offsprings and from one generation to another.

Works Cited

Achebe, Chinua. *Things Fall Apart*. London: Heinemann Publishers, 1958.

——. *No Longer at Ease*. London: Heinemann, 1960.

——. *Arrow of God*. London: Heinemann, 1964.

——. *A Man of the People*. London: Heinemann, 1966.

——. *Girls at War*. London: Heinemann, 1972.

——. *Anthills of the Savannah*. London: Heinemann, 1987.

——. *Morning Yet on Creation Day: Essays*. London: Heinemann Press, 1975: 65–70.

Booth, N.S. *African Religions. A Symposium*. New York. Nok Publishers, Ltd. 1977.

Ezirim, C.C. *Chinua Achebe: Arrow of God, Revision, Hints, Summaries, Character Sketches, Notes and Questions and Answers – Aid to Students Series*. Onitsha, Nigeria; Tabansi Publishers Revised Edition, 1987.

Yang, C.K. *Religion in Chinese Society*. Berkeley: University of California Press, 1967.

Chapter 13

Chinua Achebe and Colonial Christianity: A Case of Subtle Ambiguity

Ebele O. Eko

To every man there openeth
A Way, and Ways, and a Way
And the High Soul climbs the High Way,
And the Low Soul gropes the Low
And in between, on the misty flats
The rest drift to and fro (Oxenham 31)

THE THEME OF RELIGION IN Achebe's works has not received the critical attention worthy of its centrality to the monumental Colonial encounter that has forever changed the destiny of Africa and the West. Critics have variously commented on the clash of cultures and religions without exploring adequately Achebe's "religion" and his perception of Colonial Christianity. G.D. Killam, Bernth Lindfors, Anna Rutherford and most Western critics emphasize the tragic vision of Achebe's novels, and like Innes, characterize his works as responses to events in Nigerian history. A host of excellent African critics like Donatus Nwoga, Charles Nnolim, Ernest Emenyonu, Clement Okafor, Virgina Ola, Romanus Egudu, Chidi Maduka and many others have also in their own ways focused on style, themes, use of oral tradition and the recreation of the Igbo world. Rare and far between are essays that focus on Achebe and Religion. This paper recognizes the need to fill that critical gap. Its premise is that Achebe's novels: *Things Fall Apart*, *Arrow of God*, and *No Longer at Ease* are the fruit of his religion, his "acts of atonement," and his mission.

This paper recognizes them as powerful emotions (not recollected in tranquility according to Wordsworth) but stirred up by Achebe's passionate hatred for injustice and hypocrisy, as well as determination to expose them wherever found. He hopes to stir up the conscience of the West and generate a return to the basic truth that all men are created equal and hence to eventual dialogue between Africa and the West. Achebe's novels are therefore the fictional exposition of his social vision and philosophy of life, which are made clear in his interviews, essays and talks. His novels are sharply critical of Colonial Christianity, and its zealous converts, but ambivalent as far as culture and tradition are concerned.

Achebe is a man of two worlds, two languages, two heritages: African and Western. He makes no qualms to express his great love and appreciation for his rich and dynamic African heritage, nor does he hesitate to recognize that he owes to the West, including ironically the tools with which to dismantle, to expose and to talk about what he disapproves of. Achebe strikes an enigmatic balance between two extreme schools of thought: those that would blame the West for every evil in Africa: past, present and future; and those who celebrate Colonialism as the magic wand that has saved the "darkest continent" from barbarism. For example, in a symposium organized in Dublin, Achebe says of his Western heritage: "We must in the manner of these incomparable artists of Mbari accord recognition to every grain that comes our way" (*Hopes and Impediments* 3). Thus he sees the mission and meaning of his earlier novels in their strong claims to the celebration of African humanity and its cultural contributions, which have been ignored, despised and maligned for so long by the West.

Achebe is deeply rooted in Christian religion as clearly evidenced by his allusions, quotations and numerous Biblical imagery. According to his biographer, Ezenwa Ohaeto, Achebe's father, Isaiah Okafor Achebe, was a church missionary catechist or evangelist, and his mother was not only a strong convert, but had lived with a white missionary lady as a domestic help while obtaining training and some education (Chapter 1). Once a zealous masquerader, Isaiah Achebe became an equally zealous convert, a "Nwoye" of *Things Fall Apart* in disguise. Like the proverbial lizard who weeps more than the owner of the corpse, Mr. Achebe raised his family with befitting strict adherence to the examples of Colonial missionaries in their attitude to non-Christians, by addressing them as "people of nothing" in the Igbo language. Despite their deliberate separation from all "heathen contamination," however, Achebe's mother still told him many Igbo stories and anecdotes, which the eager ears of young Achebe captured and treasured. The secret respect his father continued to show towards the traditions he had openly abandoned was certainly not lost on Achebe. As he confesses later, he and his younger sister deliberately break parental bounds to visit "heathen" relatives and partake of food and delicacies, as well as feast his eyes on festivals. Achebe's love for culture and tradition started very early and the depth of his roots is in the fact that his zeal has not diminished over time.

Clearly a man at ease in both worlds, young Achebe's artistic mind is greatly moved by the poetry of the Christian Bible in which he was nurtured and by the color and vibrancy of traditional religion which also left their indelible marks on him. His biography portrays him as a man in love and at peace with his environment, one who used to hang around traditional elders, soaking in their wisdom, their proverbs and their very balanced worldview of "let the kite perch, and let the eagle perch." It is a worldview that recognized hierarchy, achievement, titles and respect for age. Traditional way of life, as Achebe knows so well, is synonymous with the tenets of its religion. There is no distance between the living, ancestors and even the gods. Folktales like "The Flute" emphasize that fact, Achebe's favorite illustration of tradition's integrated and balanced worldview is the famous Mbari celebrations of life via art. Myriads of mud-sculptured gods take their due positions, on both sides of the supreme earth goddess. It is a world in which art and religion kiss and embrace, in which nothing pertaining to life and experience is excluded, not even the Colonial officer, "complete with his peaked helmet and pipe" (Peterson and Rutherford 3). Indeed Achebe takes pride in describing Mbari, because it represents for him the all-inclusiveness, the largesse and accommodative capacity of Igbo worldview and religion. I take liberty to quote Achebe extensively:

> Architecturally, it was a simple structure, a stage formed by three high walls supporting a peaked roof; but in place of a flat door, you had a deck of steps running from one sidewall to the other and rising almost to the roof at the back wall. This auditorium was then filled to the brim with sculptures in molded earth and clay, and the walls with murals in white, black, yellow and green. The sculptures were arranged carefully on the steps. At the center of the front row sat the earth goddess herself, a child on her left knee and a raised sword in her right hand. She is mother and judge. To her right and left, other deities took their places. Human figures, animals, figures from folklore, history, or pure imagination ... everything jostled together for space in that extraordinary convocation of the entire kingdom of human experience and imagination (2).

There is no doubt that Achebe loves his culture and empathizes with its survival strategies, nevertheless he does not in any way idealize it. He is very aware of the imperfections of that world, its harshness against women, its past history of blood sacrifice and destruction of twins as well as the dreaded *osu* caste system, whose victims gladly embrace the church for protection and for economic benefits. One could easily be misled by the verbal outrages of Okonkwo and the priestess Chielo into thinking that Achebe is anti-Christian. As if to lend support to that assumption, Achebe once described himself as "an ancestral worshipper." That is, however by no means the full picture, nor is there convincing evidence to support that view when statements of various characters are examined in context. Achebe is too tactful and sensitive an artist to be pigeonholed. He reminds one of a towering masquerade that wields a double-edged cutlass for slashing right, left, and center. On the one hand he exposes Colonial Christianity as a suppressive arm of Colonial administration; the inherent personal and collective weaknesses in the traditional system that lead to its collapse; and to the center, the disaster that results when both traditional and Christian religious moral bases are abandoned in the name of modernity, by educated Africans with neo-Colonial mentality.

Achebe sees his artistic role in unequivocal terms, as a teacher, a revealer of truth, and an arbiter between the West and Africa. His over-quoted mission of reeducating his people as to the viability, the quality and integrity of their culture tells only half of the story. He exposes through satire and irony, the duplicity of motive, the arrogance and the high handedness with which the West forced its presence on Africa. This first part of his larger mission will be dealt with in the next section.

Achebe does not recognize two separate Colonial powers, one secular and the other Christian. He sees them as intertwined and interlocked. Between Reverend Smith of *Things Fall Apart* (*TFA*), the Colonial administrator, Mr. Winterbottom of *Arrow of God* (*AG*) and Mr. Green, the Colonial civil servant and devout Christian of *No Longer at Ease* (*NLAE*), there is little difference in attitude and approach. All three are proudly "on His Majesty's service"; all three wear their superior attitudes like stiff white collars and all three treat Africans as inferior beings, and with paternalistic resignation they bear the white man's "burden". The way Reverend Smith despises the presence and significance of the "revered" masquerade is the way Mr. Winterbottom disregards Ezeulu's high office and Mr. Green mocks the "so-called educated African." The three see the world in two shades: black and white. Achebe's authorial statement in regard of Reverend Smith, the successor of the more tactful, liberal and successful Mr. Brown, can easily apply to them all: "He saw the world as a battlefield in which the children of light were locked in mortal conflict with the sons of darkness. He spoke in his sermons about sheep and goats and about wheat and tares. He believed in slaying the prophetess of baal (*TFA* 184).

As if to confirm this view of indistinguishable motive, attitude and method of approach between Missionaries and Colonial officers, Achebe's biographer supplies the reader with a historical example of a multi-purpose Colonialist; but one that was well-loved and respected like Mr. Brown in *TFA*. G.T. Basden, founder of the Mission College in Awka which Achebe's father attended, is described as missionary, amateur anthropologist, political counselor and teacher. His statement on relationships is a positive strategy for building mutual respect and friendship:

> A missionary has unique opportunities of becoming acquainted with village life,
> for from the very nature of things, the soundest policy is for him to live in close

communion with the people whom he seeks to influence. So it comes about that he enters freely into the life of the natives, their huts are always open to him and he goes in and out more or less as one of themselves. In like manner, they expect the missionary's house to be free to them to come and go as they please (Ezenwa-Ohaeto 3).

The evangelical success and fame of Basden is almost legendary in the area of his service and beyond. The many titles and costly gifts conferred on him by several Igbo communities attest to his political and religious astuteness as "an advocate, hard worker and responsible pioneer (Ezenwa-Ohaeto 5). His willingness to use dialogue rather than force or intimidation goes to the very heart of Achebe's quarrel with the West and constitutes his core insistence: For the West to recognize Africa as human, different but equal and worthy to engage in meaningful and fruitful dialogue. This message reverberates over and over through the novels and in many of his essays (*Hopes and Impediments* 1–5). In one of them, Achebe roundly condemns Conrad's highly acclaimed novel on Africa, *Heart of Darkness* as racist and therefore not worthy of greatness. In the essay titled "Impediments to Dialogue Between North and South," Achebe explains that dialogue implies communication between two equals but laments bitterly that: "equality is the one thing, which Europeans are consciously incapable of extending to others, especially Africans" (*Hopes and Impediments* 23). Achebe offers the example of a Rhodesian Governor who refers to the Colonial partnership as "that between the horse and its rider" (*Hopes and Impediments* 23). In this paper, Achebe reaches the height of impatience with the Colonial attitude that exempts neither Missionaries, nor administrators of purported Christian-based Western civilization. His stand is that Europe has either to accept the black man's total humanity and equality or reject it and so see him as a beast of burden. In his opinion: "no middle course exists except as an intellectual quibble. For centuries, Europe has chosen the beastly alternative, which automatically rules out the possibility of a dialogue" (*Hopes and Impediments* 23).

There certainly is no dialogue between Reverend Smith and his converts, nor between the Colonial administrator and Okonkwo's people who concede after Okonkwo hangs himself that he may be worth a reasonable paragraph of his proposed symbolic book: *The Pacification of the Primitive Tribes of the Lower Niger*" (*TFA* 209). The irony is complete, the satire unavoidable. Even Mr. Green in *NLAE* reminds Mr. Omo that he is not paid "to think", but to do as he is ordered to do (65). To further strengthen his argument, Achebe dissects Mr. Green's distrust of the protagonist, Obi, and all educated Africans, and his preference for those who know their place is ridiculed and his Christianity mocked:

> It is clear he loved Africa, but only Africa of a kind: The Africa of Charles, the messenger, the Africa of his garden-boy and steward-boy. He must have come originally with an idea – to bring light to the heart of darkness, to tribal

headhunters performing weird ceremonies and unspeakable rites. But when he arrived, Africa played him false ... In 1900, Mr. Green might have ranked among the great missionaries; in 1935 he would have made do with slapping headmasters in the presence of their pupils; but in 1957 he could only curse and swear (NLAE 106).

Achebe's message to the West is perhaps most effectively conveyed via the structure of his novels. The first half of TFA is fully devoted to chronicling the rich and complete rhythm and tapestry of traditional Igbo life. In this classic foil to Joyce Cary's parody in *Mr. Johnson* and the inhuman description of the Congo in Conrad's *Heart of Darkness*, Achebe's artistic triumph comes through in his characterization and language. The "ancestral worshipper" is echoed through Okonkwo's rage against his son Nwoye: "To abandon the gods of one's father and go about with a lot of effeminate men clucking like old hens was the very depths of abomination" (TFA 153). Chielo the priestess in TFA goes further to call the new converts "excrements" and Christianity "the mad dog [that] came to eat them up" (101).

Although Achebe empathizes with Okonkwo's dynamism, he is painfully aware of the silent sufferings of Okonkwo's wives under his heavy hands; the misery of mothers of twins and all the other oppressed in his community especially the *osu* outcasts. Achebe uses the voice of moderation like that of Obierika, to rebuke the excesses in Okonkwo, not only in beating his wives, putting a curse on his own son, Nwoye, but worst of all killing Ikemefuna his "son" with his own hands, just so he wouldn't be thought weak. His fear has roots in self-centered pride, which drives him out of step with his community into the tragedy of acting alone: "Okonkwo stood looking at the dead man [he cut down]. He knew that Umuofia would not go to war ... He heard voices asking, 'Why did he do it?'" (205).

In *Arrow of God*, Ezeulu is cornered into a noose in the power tussle between the chief priest of Ulu and Colonialism. As soon as he decides to test things out to their logical conclusion, even to the point of risking the starvation of his people, Ezeulu's pride would not let him back down. Faced with the choice between the Christian god who has defied their gods and starvation, the people convert *en mass* in order to fulfill a necessary rite before harvesting their yams. After all Ezeulu knows that no man can win a war against his people.

In comparison to those two, Achebe reserves his sting for overzealous converts like Enoch, the son of the Snake priest who kills and eats the sacred python. Achebe satirizes Enoch's arrogance, stubbornness and provocative utterances, which effectively destroy every chance for dialogue and peaceful compromise. In the same vein, Moses Unachukwu and Oduche, the son of Ezeulu, (sent by his father to be an eye for him in the mission) are shown to have ulterior motives for converting to Christianity. There is a double-edged satire against both the Missionaries' motive of "enlightening the natives" (who are deeply religious already) and the motive of

Ezeulu and Moses, who realize that: "the white man, the new religion, the soldiers, the new road" – are all part of the same thing. The white man has a gun, a matchet, a bow and carries fire in his mouth (*AG* 85). Truly, when one thing stands another stands beside it!

As a social realist, Achebe juxtaposes Mr. Brown's wise moderation and mediation through building schools and clinics with the irresponsible language of converts who refer to non-Christians as *efulefu*, people of nothing. Ironically and hypocritically, the devout Christian father of Obi in *No Longer at Ease* despises pagan gods as impotent yet he opposes his son's marriage to an *osu* from a very good Christian family. His mother's threatens to commit suicide, an abomination in both religions, proves a terrible dilemma. The seduction of materialism, the mixed motives, the hypocrites on both sides evoke the image of those drifting to and fro on the "misty flats" of Oxenham's poem. Achebe's ambivalence is perhaps most pronounced through this incident. Does he condemn or does he condone the action of Obi's parents? One feels Achebe's sympathy as well as his rebuke in what seems to be indeed a cultural vicious cycle and dilemma. Colonial Christianity poses a similar dilemma: "The white man had indeed brought a lunatic religion, but he had also brought a trading store and for the first time palm-oil and kernel became things of great price and much money flowed into Umuofia" (*TFA* 126).

Obierika's voice of counsel and deep reflection seems closest to that of Achebe in arbitrating between extremist traditional forces who wish death on the missionaries and mischievously allocate them the evil forest; and super zealots who overnight despise their heritage and adopt the offensive posture and language of their Colonial masters. Just like Achebe and Christianity, Obierika finds no easy answers but rather greater perplexities as he reflects on the negative aspects of tradition: the twins he had to throw away; (representing all other oppressed and innocent people) Ikemefuna, the *osus* and abused women ... "What crime had they committed?" he asks. The Christian in Achebe surely recognizes the powerful role of Missionaries in saving the Nwoyes and the outcasts, he recognizes the capriciousness of the oracle of the hills and caves which gives no reasons for ordering the death of Ikemefuna. With one single adjective, "terrible" Achebe admits to a dilemma: The Christian God has openly defied; "Amadiaoha, Idemili, Otakagu, Ekwensu (the devil) and all the terrible gods of the land which had held Umuofia together from time immemorial" (*TFA* 86).

The ending of his three novels is perhaps the most revealing of Achebe's ambivalence about Christianity and his seeing the protagonists as victims of Colonialism. Okonkwo and Ezeulu both fight to retain tradition but fail. Yet Obi who abandons both religions, fails also. Okonkwo is depicted as negative, aggressive and self-centered despite his heroic qualities, and Ezeulu, though a grand soul, is shown to be equally self-centered and proud. One commits suicide, the other ends in madness and both are abandoned by their gods and their people. Obi the educated secular man fails because he lacks a strong moral base; he violates secular laws, he is selfish and proud, and loses the sympathy and support of his people also. What is Achebe's saying in conclusion?

In *No Longer at Ease*, Achebe the social critic confronts the new generation of educated Africans essentially through the juxtaposition of Obi and Mr. Green. Most critics have interpreted *No Longer at Ease* as the failure of Colonial education for an African at the crossroads of cultures (Killiam, Babalola, Gakwandi). It is that and much more. In the light of Achebe's negative views on Colonial Christianity, Mr. Green, the "devout sidesman at the Colonial Church" is satirized for the disparity between his church position and his negative attitude and denigrating language. With a deft stroke, however, Achebe uses the impeccable work ethics of Mr. Green as a sharp sword to expose the false idealisms of educated Africans like Obi, the recipient of a collective sweat and tears scholarship of Umuofia Progressive Union members. Obi represents many Nigerian and African "been-tos", who like the young engineer of Soyinka's *The Interpreters*, have great dreams for their country but lack the patience and perseverance needed to pay the price or sacrifice in order to make impact. Mr. Green's complaints against Obi are no doubt motivated by his superiority complex, but they certainly reveal the practical problems facing modern African nations today – Neo Colonialism. It is having a too easy conscience when stepping into the "soft shoes" of Colonial amenities without modification or realistic changes as demanded by the relatively young and fragile economy of the individual nations. Obi for example does not question his entitlement to four months leave in a year (as opposed to two weeks in Britain) nor does Clara feel any guilt for her seventy days sick leave after her self-imposed abortion.

Achebe puts a sharp and justified rebuke in the mouth of Colonial Mr. Green to strike a resounding blow at the Neo-Colonial mentality of educated Africans. "…Education for what?" asks Mr. Green and then answers: "To get as much as they can for themselves and their families" (*NLAE* 116). He squarely accuses them of neglecting millions of their countrymen who die every day of hunger and disease. Ironically, Obi and Christopher, educated as they are, fail to appreciate Mr. Green's sense of devotion and commitment to duty. Obi mocks him, "He was like a man who has some great and supreme task that must be completed before a final catastrophe intervened" (*NLAE* 105). Rather than emulate Mr. Green's work ethics for the benefit of their very own country, Obi and his kind are at ease to exploit it by adopting a ready-made lifestyle that is so out of touch with the economic reality and so prone to corrupt the self-indulgent practices. Not only do they not question the Colonial structure, they are very defensive of it as their own share of what the Colonial Masters had instituted and enjoyed. Mr. Green may be satirized as a devout Christian with a Colonial attitude, but his commitment and self sacrifice, an echo of the Missionary's self abnegation in answering the call, raise a critical issue in retrospect about selfishness and pride in the new generation as in the old. Clara is not spared. She gets an authorial rebuke against her self-centeredness and lack of consideration: "You could tell a been-to not only by her phonetics, but by her walk … In company of her less fortunate sisters she always found an excuse for saying: 'When I was in England' …" (*NLAE* 93).

Between zealots for the power and money in the early days of Colonial Christianity like Moses Unachukwu and zealots for Colonial education like the typical been-tos, there seems to be very little difference in attitude. Achebe's point is that both groups betray their heritage by adopting without questioning, the same motives, attitudes and the same exploitative methods he accuses the West of having towards Africa. Betrayal of heritage is very central to Achebe's Mission and most sharply illustrated through the homecoming observations and reminiscings of Obi in chapter six of *No Longer at Ease*. This is perhaps the book's most critical chapter, which I believe comes straight from Achebe's heart, since it so closely mirrors his own childhood experiences. After four years of absence in England, Obi is shocked by his parents' physical appearance. His agonizing thoughts summarize for the reader Obi's and no doubt Achebe's appraisal of the quality, the attitude and the unsatisfactory results of a Colonial type of Christianity:

> It was scandalous, he thought, that after nearly thirty years' service in the church, his father should retire on a salary of two pounds a month, a good slice of which went back into the same church by way of class fees and other contributions. And he had his last two children at school, each paying school fees and church fees (55).

The zeal and commitment of Obi's father to the church, so evidence in his constant biblical allusions, imagery and direct quotes, and even in his docile acceptance of the blatant injustice of his situation, enrages Obi and justifies for him, his rejection of that religion. Out of respect and pity for his father, he merely wonders what would happen if he should say: "Father, I no longer believe in your God" (56). Through Obi, the educated "agnostic", Achebe reconstructs an explanatory past. Obi recalls that his father forbade his wife to tell folk-stories to their children because he considered them "heathen". Obi regrets his mother's submission to his father's will and her subsequent mistake in teaching her children not to accept food from neighbors, "because she said they offered their food to idols." Achebe's cutting satire comes through as he describes the Colonial mentality demonstrated so innocently but powerfully through a four-year-old Obi when he rejects a neighbor's offer of a piece of yam: "He shook his head like his older and wiser sisters and then said: 'We don't eat heathen food.' While his sister Janet tries too late to cover his mouth with her hand. It is very significant that Achebe takes time to narrate a critical childhood mishap of Obi, who cries for shame before his class because he could not tell a story. Recognizing his problem of rootlessness that early, little Obi persuades his mother to tell him folk tales behind his father's back, and thus regains his lost self image and dignity before his class: "Some weeks later, Obi was called up again. He faced the class boldly and told one of the new stories his mother had told him. He even added a touch to the end, which made everyone laugh" (59). The alienation of converts from their own people, teaching them to be ashamed of their wonderfully, rich heritage, to look down on others, to assume a superior pose and live in isolation from the life-giving socializatioin of extended family are in Achebe's view, the roots of tragedy in Africa's encounter with Colonial Christianity.

The rest of the novel is the end result of a Western education that merely reinforces a Colonial mentality that Obi imbibed in childhood. While acknowledging the great potentials of Western education, Achebe through the tragedy of Obi and other been-tos is pointing out with both hands raised, the bitter roots of potential tragedy: building one's personality on the false foundation of self hatred and self abnegation. Colonial mentality is the same in Achebe's view whether it is imbibed through Colonial Christianity that teaches the African that he is a child of darkness, or through Colonial higher education that "legitimately" prepares a few to exploit their less fortunate colleagues, through selfish inheritance of Colonial privileges. Achebe calls the vicious cycle a set up: "Quite simply it is the desire – one might indeed say the need – in Western psychology to *set Africa up* (emphasis mine) as a foil to Europe, as a place of negations at once remote and vaguely familiar, in comparison with which Europe's own state of spiritual grace will be manifest" (*Hopes* 2–3).

In conclusion, Achebe is ambivalent in his view of Colonial Christianity, though unequivocal in his condemnation of duplicity, arrogance and violence in Europe's dealings with Africa both through Colonial missionaries as well as through Colonial officers and merchants. He is equally pessimistic about Colonial education from nursery school to college, because of its alienating superior mentality, its tendency to produce rootless and therefore morally weak characters like Obi who can easily be shaken under great duress or pressurized into corruption. This is why he comes down so hard on zealous converts like Enoch and Obi's parents, who are misled into stifling creativity in children and negating wonderful African cultural values like proverbs, music, dance, respect for age, and hospitality: values that need to be maintained and integrated with other good values from other cultures for a richer and more dynamic modern mega culture.

Achebe is ambivalent in his relationship to traditional protagonists, traditional religion and culture in general. His deep love for festivals, masquerades, folk tales, anecdotes and good village fun is infectious. That love is no doubt instrumental in providing life and dynamic vitality to his art. The global success and growing popularity of *Things Fall Apart* attest to this. But what does Achebe the realist think of all the negative aspects of African tradition in a fast-paced world of global inter-relationships, civil rights, and feminism? What does he think of all the progressive ideas clearly championed by the Christian Bible, encapsuled in its command for unconditional love for all men? What does Achebe or any other African artist have to say about the perfect motive, attitude and method of the Missionary's Biblical mission: "to preach the gospel to the poor; to heal the broken-hearted, to preach deliverance to the captives and recovery of sight to the blind, to set at liberty those that are bruised"? (Luke 4:18).

The fault is not in the doctrine but in the vehicle of communication, which has been contaminated and corrupted by the men nurtured like young Obi by the imperialistic and exploitative motives and attitude of Colonialist Britain. And yet there are exceptions like Mr. Brown in *TFA* and Basden of Awka College. Achebe's personal convictions and soft spot for Christianity are evident in his creation of such good Missionary characters. These are the acknowledged liberators of the Nwoye's, the *osus*, twins and their heartbroken mothers, and all who are terrorized and exploited by "terrible" gods and "oracles of deceit." It is an open secret that such oracles, which demanded the death of beautiful Ikemefuna also enslaved or killed other innocent victims, like him. Achebe knows his Bible and must have contrasted Colonial Missionaries with St. Paul who "reasoned with heathen Greeks" without outright condemnation of their gods. He is familiar with the story of Evangelist Phillip, who witnessed to the Ethiopian Eunuch (the very first non-Jewish Christian, making Africa Christian even before Europe) with much grace and patience, explaining and teaching him from a platform of respect and love. Surely, there must be another way to initiate change! Michael Kirwen's book, *The Missionary and the Diviner*, recounts one such way. It tells of the atrocious crimes of Russian fur traders in Alaska against the natives until the arrival of the Russian Missionaries, who put a stop to the crimes. According to the record, they worked with Alaskans in a true Christian spirit honoring and integrating their language, local customs and spirituality (vii).

Colonial Christianity alienated most first generation educated Africans, who by reason of their education, urbanization and modernization are already cut off from the deep roots of their traditional culture. Their drifting on "misty flats" has continued unchecked as African writers (French and English speaking alike) have taken up as if in a relay race, the hue and cry against Colonial Christianity (Ngugi wa Thiong'o, Mongo Beti and Ferdinand Oyono, etc.). Achebe has shown the way to cultural chaos in Obi. However, the foibles of the protagonists in *A Man of the People* and the corruption of power in *Anthills of the Savannah* are enough internal indictment to make any sensible reader question the validity of continuing to blame Colonial Christianity of Okonkwo's days for the state of the nation over forty years after independence. Dreams of positive change require sincere action to make them reality.

Achebe's novels have demonstrated that the problems of Africa have long tap roots in Colonialism but they are also due to a lack of strong disciplined leadership, self disciplined enough to blast smugness, laziness and complacency in others. There is a dart of leaders that rule by example, men committed and devoted to duty like Mr. Green, patriotic like Winterbottom, courageous like Okonkwo, but with the sensitive heart of Nwoye, the intelligence of Ezeulu, the cordiality of Mr. Brown, the wisdom of Obierika and above all the humility and power of self-giving love.

Plato was right: "The visible is a shadow cast by the invisible" and so God is still around. All the fault-ridden human vehicles used to transmit love and compassion in Pre-Colonial, Colonial and Post-Colonial worlds cannot diminish His being one iota. Like Martin Luther King Jr., a contemporary and partner in the fight for Black man's recognition, Achebe has a dream. It is that one day, the scales will fall off the eyes of the West to recognize that indeed all men are created equal.

Works Cited

Achebe, Chinua. *Things Fall Apart*. London: Heinemann, 1994 edition.

———. *Arrow of God*. New York: Anchor, 1989 edition.

———. *No Longer at Ease*. London: Heinemann, 1983 edition.

———. *Hopes and Impediments: Selected Essays*. New York: Doubleday, 1989.

Brians, Paul Chinua Achebe. *Things Fall Apart Study Guide*. Homepage. Washington State University. 20 Nov 1999. <http:/www.wsu.edu: 8080/_brians_Anglophone/achebe.html>

Cary, Norman R. "Achebe's Novels and Their Religious Context: Missiological and Fictional Discourse." *Journal of the South Pacific Association for Commonwealth Literature and Language Studies*. 36 (1993) 20 November 1999.
<http://Kali.murdoch.edu.au/_continumm/litserv/SPAN/37/Cary.html>

Emenyonu, Ernest Ed. *Goatskin Bags and Wisdom: New Critical Perspectives on African Literature*. Trenton, NJ: African World Press, 2000.

Ezenwa-Ohaeto. *Chinua Achebe: A Biography*. Bloomington: Indiana UP, 1997.

Innes, C.L. *Chinua Achebe Studies of African and Caribbean Literature*: 1. Cambridge: UP, 1990.

Killiam, G.D. *The Novels of Chinua Achebe*. New York: Africana. 1969.

Kirwen, Michael C. *The Missionary and the Diviner*. New York. Orbis Books, 1987.

Peterson, Kirsten and Anna Rutherford, eds. *Chinua Achebe: A Celebration*. London: Heinemann, 1990.

Poem by Oxenham. Quoted in *The Measure of a Man* by Martin Luther King, Jr. Philadelphia: Fortress Press, 1988.

Part Three

The Artist in Society

Chapter 14

The Artist in Search of the Right Leadership: Achebe as a Social Critic

Charles E. Nnolim

THE TROUBLE WITH NIGERIA IS Achebe's non-fictional work written out of extreme frustration. It is a sort of last warning issued by Achebe to an audience that seems hard of hearing. The theme of poor leadership which takes centre stage in *The Trouble with Nigeria* may come as a surprise to scholars and literary critics who have spent two decades poring over various themes and techniques in Achebe's novels; but they needed not have been surprised for, from *Things Fall Apart* to *Anthills of the Savannah*, the one consistent concern exhibited by Achebe in each novel is the issue of leaders who, in time of crisis, fail their people. This study thus argues, that in *The Trouble with Nigeria*, Achebe the novelist, finally drops his mask and comes out in *propria persona* to address readers who, over the years, while correctly appreciating the felicities embedded in his story-telling techniques have failed to grasp his message; readers who seem to have come to a packed theatre in which great drama is being enacted, and decided only to watch the audience.

I will also try to demonstrate that before the publication of *The Trouble with Nigeria* in 1983, Achebe had tried, sometimes obliquely, to draw attention to the central concern of his novels – the issues of poor leadership – in his essays and public lectures, so that *The Trouble with Nigeria* was for him, a final summing up of an issue over which he thinks the last word could not be said. The leader that fails his people – what else is Okonkwo or Ezeulu or Obi Okonkwo or Chief Nanga or His Excellency, Sam all about? All else, for Achebe, are in the periphery not in the dead centre.

To begin with, politics enters literature through what we normally term the pragmatic theory of art, through literature's affective powers, for the pragmatic theory looks at art as an end because, according to the adage:

Some men wish to change men's minds,
Others wish to change the world men live in.

As we shall see, in all his creative works and in most of his non-fictional works, Achebe has demonstrated his political commitment in his works. Politics, as we know, enters literature also when the writer's concern with the public welfare is predominant, especially when the writer's concern extends beyond destinies of single individuals to encompass the collective destinies of nations or the masses. Achebe can thus be identified as a politically committed writer because of his concern with the fate of destiny of the Igbo in particular and Nigerians and Africans in general and their collective encounter with Europe. His commitment is further evidenced in his continued concern with the future of his people after independence: through his continued expression of disenchantment with the aftermath of independence (our "misgovernment" of ourselves) resulting in bribery and corruption, election rigging, poor leadership, and inequities in our body politic. It will be seen that Achebe, in the end, is a writer of the political novel whose end is utopian, because the goal toward which all his novels tend is that golden era when the intellectual elite will wrest politics from the illiterate politicians and the military and create an egalitarian society free from poor leadership, bribery and corruption; for that time when politics is played here, as in Europe and the West, according to the rules of the game; and for that time when African countries are free from all Neo-colonialist thralldom cushioned, of course by economic abundance and the absence of want. If this view of Achebe's works is sustained, a reappraisal of what has come to be known in critical circles as his philosophic pessimism will be in order, once we have established that far from being a nihilist, he holds out hopes for the future.

In this connection, in tracing the contours of the landscape of Achebe's creative and non-fictional works, we shall be obliged to constantly look from life to art and vice versa, for the two are inseparable in Achebe's thematic concerns. "The trouble with Nigeria" he asserts in *The Trouble with Nigeria* "is simply and squarely a failure of leadership." He continues: "The Nigerian problem is the unwillingness or inability of its leaders to rise to the responsibility, to the challenge of personal example which are the hallmarks of true leadership" (1). But before we get carried away we should understand what Achebe means by the word "leader". I personally understand a leader to be that person in a group to whom others look up for initiative in pursuit of group goal and one who must possess the following virtues in abundance: honesty, integrity, hard work, infectious enthusiasm about others and their welfare, strong moral character, humility, self-discipline, and patriotism for one cannot be the right leader in a society he does not truly love enough to be willing to die for. In Achebe's own words:

> Leaders are, in the language of psychologists, role models. People look up to them and copy their actions, behaviour and even mannerisms. Therefore if a leader lacks discipline the effect is apt to spread automatically down to his followers. The less discerning among these (i.e. the vast majority) will accept his actions quite simply as "the done thing" while the more critical may worry about it for a while and then settle the matter by telling themselves that the normal rules of social behaviour need not apply to those in power (31).

In examining the above, we must for the sake of argument look at Achebe's concept of the role of the leader under four broad headings:

1. Achebe, the writer, as leader
2. Leadership of his fictional characters in pre-colonial and colonial times
3. Leadership of his fictional characters in post-independence setting
4. Pronouncements on leadership in his essays and non-fictional works.

Achebe does not merely stand aside and preach about leadership. He does something about it as a writer by personal example. In "The Role of the Writer in a New Nation" he avers:

> It is inconceivable to me that a serous writer could stand aside from this debate, or be indifferent to this argument which calls his humanity in question – for me at any rate, there is a clear duty to make a statement (158).

And in "The Novelist as Teacher" he further says:

> Here then is an adequate revolution for me to espouse – to help my society regain belief in itself and put away the complexes of the years of denigration and self abasement ... Here, I think, my aims and the deepest aspirations of my society meet ... The writer cannot expect to be excused from the task of re-education and regeneration that must be done. In fact he should march right in front. For he is after all ... the sensitive point of his community (44–45).

In other words, Achebe tells us while at the same time admitting to himself that it is the duty of the writer to lead his people being "the sensitive point of his community." And in his statement below, he further argues that no writer worth his salt will refuse to be his society's gadfly, its social critic who must have the courage of his conviction to expose and attack injustice, social inequality, corruption in all its forms, and further be prepared to fight for all right and just causes. In "The African Writer and the Biafran Cause," Achebe states:

> It is clear to me that an African creative writer who tries to avoid the big social issues of contemporary Africa will end up being completely irrelevant – like that absurd man in the proverb who leaves his burning house to pursue a rat fleeing from the flames (78).

And

> If an artist is anything he is a human being with heightened sensitivities; he must be aware of the faintest nuances of injustice in human relations. The African writer cannot therefore be unaware of, or indifferent to, the monumental injustice which his people suffer ("The African Writer…" 79).

It can, therefore, be stated without equivocation or fear of contradiction that by sheer force of personal example, Achebe as a writer has carved out a leadership role for himself as "the sensitive point in the community" and determined to show his people "where the rain started beating them." It must further be stressed that as a writer, Achebe has given exemplary leadership not only to his people – the Igbo – but to Nigeria, Africa, and the entire third world. No scandal has ever touched his person; no odd quirks of genius for which others are infamous; no profligate or outlandish lifestyle both in dress and mannerisms (he does not even wear a beard); extreme restraint in the use of language both in his creative output and in debating issues close to his heart. Achebe, it is argued, is a shining example of the writer as leader who practices what he preaches. Achebe is a good family man, a great nationalist, a true patriot, a world-famous intellectual, a writer in a world class – in Igbo parlance, an eagle perched on an iroko. There is no higher heaven to conquer. And may his inkwell never dry!

From Achebe's idea and example of the writer as leader, we proceed to examine the fictional leaders he has created in his works reflecting the pre-colonial and colonial periods of our history. We have in mind Okonkwo of *Things Fall Apart*, and Ezeulu of *Arrow of God*. These are what I prefer to call the leaders of lost causes, tragic and heroic figures who represent the collective consciousness of their communities and whose end signifies the disintegration of the communities they represent. These were community leaders in the traditional setting who fail not because of indiscipline or inner depravity but because, caught in the vortex of inexorable historical changes, they read the signs wrongly or upside down, and held on a moment too long, to the status quo, and got swept away in the unrelenting eddies of history. These personages attain their leadership position in society not through the chicanery of the smart alec but "by the strength of their arm." They are members of the *Nze* and *Ozo* elite society, untouched by the corrupt practices that bring Obi Okonkwo and Chief Nanga so ignominiously low.

It is about these dignified personages that Achebe comments:

> A man's position in society was usually determined by his wealth. All the four titles in my village were taken – not given – and each had its own price. But in those days wealth meant the strength of your arm. No one became rich by swindling the community or stealing government money. In fact a man who was guilty of theft immediately lost all his titles. Today we have kept the materialism and thrown away the spirituality which kept it in check ("The Role of the Writer ..." 159).

For Okonkwo and Ezeulu, the ethic of traditional loyalties dictated that the people had control over their leaders and rulers through variously recognized sanctions. The communal nature of the traditional society was guided by what Mazrui calls "social collectivism":

> that complex of loyalties which tied the individual to his own specific society, which commanded his affections for his kith and kin, which aroused his protectiveness for the soil of his ancestors, which enabled him to serve and, very occasionally, to love his people (68).

So, why did they fail themselves and their people? Okonkwo's failure as a leader stems from the fact that he is not a man of the golden mean. Governed rather too much by his exaggerated notion of the masculine ideal, he kowtows to neither man nor the gods. Killed rather by too much action that is not tempered by reasoned dialogue with himself or his peers; too much in a haste to inquire into the why and consequences of things, too proud to show love and affection; too afraid of being thought weak, Okonkwo fails because he is not a leader of his people whose mores he breaks, whose wise counsel he does not seek, whose caution he squanders. A hero who lacks humility may be patriotic (and Okonkwo was greedy of things Umuofia) but his was a patriotism of the iconoclast, of the foolhardy. It is, in the final analysis, not the common good that Okonkwo dies for but in the pursuit of narrow selfish interests. Okonkwo finally fails in his inability to carry his people with him and in his too much stubborn adherence to the status-quo in a new world order that calls for adaptive suppleness of vision and temperament. Achebe thus blames the tragedy of Umuofia – by extension the Igbo – on bad leadership. When a leader like Okonkwo who is too strong, too proud to seek advice and compromise puts his own welfare and interests above those of the clan, the result is tragedy everywhere.

Achebe must have thought of Okonkwo as an undisciplined leader, especially in his violating the Week of Peace. And indiscipline is identified by Achebe as one of the causes of poor leadership. In *The Trouble with Nigeria*, Achebe describes indiscipline as:

> a failure or refusal to submit one's desires and actions to the restraints of orderly social conduct in recognition of the rights and desires of others. The goal

of indiscipline is self-interest, its action an abandonment of self-restraint in pursuit of the goal (27).

While Okonkwo's Achilles' heel was heedless action unsupported by philosophy or reasoned dialogue and compounded by indiscipline, Ezeulu's tragedy stems from too much philosophic rhetoric and reasoned dialogue ousted by the harassed course he steers between knowing what is right and doing the same. Here is a man who repeats *ad nauseam*, that a man must dance the dance prevalent in his life time" and that "the world is like a mask dancing. If you want to see it well you do not stand in one place." But when, under some sort of *situation ethics* ten elders demand that he eats two sacred yams at *their* collective peril for survival of the body politic, he bluntly refuses to do the dance prevalent in his time and becomes the proverbial rat that could not run fast enough and had to make way for the tortoise. Ezeulu fails as a leader because of stubbornness: the same stubborn resistance he exhibited in refusing the offer of paramount chieftaincy by the white man, and insisted upon when confronted by a delegation of ten elders who urge him to eat the two sacred yams to save Umuaro from mass starvation. The problem with Ezeulu is that he lacks tact; he has a poorly developed political instinct; and he lacks a proper sense of history as he strains after the gnat of personal power, swallowing in the process the camel of mass disaffection. He thus fails himself and fails Umuaro because he chooses to be blind to the limitations of his powers, forgetting that Ulu whose high priest he is, is not a nature-god but god over Umuaro by convention and compromise and could only retain its power by adjusting to the demands of the times. Ezeulu also ignores to his peril Nwaka's warning that unless Ezeulu trod carefully, what happened by Aninta might happen at Umuaro:

> And we have all heard how the people of Aninta dealt with their deity when he failed them: did they not carry him to the boundary between them and their neighbours and set him on fire (*Arrow of God* 31).

Thus Okonkwo and Ezeulu are two Igbo leaders of the old order who fail their people because, in times of crisis, they refuse to identify themselves with the plight of the people, preferring to pursue to the end their own narrow selfish interests: Okonkwo goes on to sign a "separate peace" through suicide; and Ezeulu abandons his people by discovering anew that he "was no more than an arrow in the bow of his god," thus losing grips on the issues of the moment and ending his days in demented dignity.

A close reading of *The Trouble with Nigeria* reveals that each chapter-caption reveals an aspect of the causes for the failure of leadership in Nigeria. They are:

Tribalism
Patriotism (or lack of it)

The cult of mediocrity
Indiscipline
Corruption

After examining each aspect listed above, Achebe lays at the door of the elite the duty of salvaging Nigeria from its leadership problems. First, he opines that part of the problem is the lack of intellectual rigor in the governance of Nigeria:

> In spite of conventional opinions Nigeria has been less than fortunate in its leadership. A basic element of this misfortune is the seminal absence of intellectual rigour the political thought of our founding fathers – a tendency to pious materialistic wooliness and self-centred pedestrianism (11).

Second, he calls on the elite to come out of their shells to shoulder the duty of intellectual leadership of the country or we all perish:

> What I am saying is that Nigeria is not beyond change. I am saying that Nigeria can change today if she discovers leaders who have the will, the ability and the vision ... But it is the duty of the enlightened citizens to lead the way in their discovery and to create an atmosphere conducive to their emergence. If this conscious effort is not made, good leaders, like good money will be driven out of bad (1–2).

With the above in mind, one can only imagine Achebe's disgust with a character like Obi Oknokwo of *No Longer at Ease*, an intellectual elite to whom the Umuofia Improvement Union looks up for leadership but who woefully fails them. Here is an educated young man clean ostensibly in limb and mind who is guilty of cowardice (why not challenge an effete custom like the *osu* system and marry Clara?); who is downright immoral (helping procure a dangerous abortion on his intended); whose high idealisms crumble like a cookie on the slightest test; who is guilty of bribery and corruption against which his public utterances are clear (and when he descends to the swamps of bribe-taking, he incurs the disgust and contempt of his kith and kin, that when he decided to eat a toad he did not have the high sense of eating a fat one!).

He does Africa further disservice by confirming Mr. Green's insulting utterance that "the African is corrupt through and through." Obi Okonkwo is thus Achebe's example of the modern intellectual elite who betrays trust, because he cannot cope with the demands of leadership which call for high discipline, for Obi Okonkwo is at heart morally bankrupt. "Here is the Nigerian intellectual for you" Achebe seems to be saying with utter disgust.

Chief Nanga (in *A Man of the People*) joins Obi Okonkwo as bastard sons of the new cities and the urban ethos created by the white man, both victims of the discontinuities of religious and ethical allegiance to the tribe, disoriented from the rural ethos, enmeshed in bribery and corruption, worshippers at the shrine of materialism with money as their god and material wealth as their new non-Sunday religion. After the shenanigans of the likes of leaders like Chief Nanga and Chief Koko, Achebe had said in an interview with Robert Serumaga:

> But I think the next generation of politicians, when we do have them, will have learned one or two lessons, I hope, from what happened to the First Republic. This is the only hope I have and if it turns out to be in vain, it would be terrible (11).

Chief Nanga and his ilk brought out into the open, a landslide of abuses of the privilege of leadership:

a. election malpractices – use of thugs, stuffing the ballot box, rigging of elections

b. politics of self-aggrandizement through blatant acts of bribery and corruption, contract inflation, etc.

c. ostentatious lifestyle

d. megalomania and abuse of power.

The despair of *A Man of the People* is that Odili, the intellectual on whom we hoped for deliverance, spoils his case by engaging in acts of personal vendetta and deviating from the rescue mission, which prompted his involvement into party politics. As some perceptive critics have pointed out, the two main protagonists of the novel are like the proverbial two knives in the house of a widow: the one that is sharp has no handle and the one that has a handle is not sharp. Odili with his worthwhile political ideas has no following, and Chief Nanga with a great political following is illiterate and is completely devoid of worthwhile political ideas.

The despair in *A Man of the People* stems from the fact that both the popular politician who is corrupt and the intellectual who cannot drum up enough following (with dark hints that both Odili and Max have descended to copy Chief Nanga's tactics) have all failed us. The only salvation, a cautious hope then by Achebe, was hope in the military to be our only solution, hence the suggested *deus ex machina* at the end of the novel through military intervention. But be this as it might, Achebe still pins his hope for the right leadership on the intellectuals.

In *The Trouble with Nigeria* Achebe makes this clarion call to the intellectuals:

> But arduous as the task is, Nigeria's educated elite must understand that they have no choice but to address themselves to it [the leadership issue] or receive history's merciless indictment. All those enlightened and thoughtful Nigerians who wring their hands in daily anguish on account of our wretched performance as a nation must bestir themselves to the patriotic action of proselytizing for

decent and civilized political values. We have stood too long on the sidelines and too many of us have adopted the cynical attitude that since you cannot beat them you must join them.

Our inaction or cynical action are a serious betrayal of our education, of our historic mission and of succeeding generations who will have no future unless we save it now for them. To be educated is, after all, to develop the questioning habit, to be skeptical of easy promises and to use past experience creatively (53).

Those who are familiar with the events of *A Man of the People* will easily confirm that the above cry from the heart is a fleshing out of the hints given in that novel. When Chief Nanga urges Odili to "take your money and take your scholarship to go and learn more book …" he adds intimidatingly and cynically, "and leave the dirty game of politics to us who know how to play it." Max had added as a postscript to so many things going awry in the body politic: "what else can you expect when intelligent people leave politics to illiterates like Chief Nanga?" (73).

I have stated earlier that Achebe wrote *The Trouble with Nigeria* to spell out correctly what he had all along obliquely touched upon in his fiction. In *Anthills of the Savannah*, he demonstrates that he has lost hope in the ability of the military to solve the political and economic problems in Nigeria. *Anthills of the Savannah* is a re-engineering in fictional form of the hopes he had placed in the ability of the military to save us at the end of *A Man of the People*. In *Anthills*, Achebe comes close to being cynical about the administrative and political ability of the military who are more interested in the props of power than in solving the nation's problems. And, in the end, Achebe expresses disgust at the ritual and cyclical method through which one military regime succeeds another. Achebe's solution: he re-pitches his tent with the intellectuals (whom the military has marginalized, intimidated and cowed) as the last hope for salvation. His hero: Ikem Osodi the fearless editor who was killed by agents of the military. His hope for the future: the intellectuals made up of the likes of Chris Oriko, the student leader, Emmanuel, and intelligent and educated women like Beatrice Okoh who takes charge of things on the death of Ikem Osodi. The era and mystique of the military, as far as Achebe is concerned, is gone forever.

In sum, throughout this study, we have looked from literature to life and vice versa in the works of Achebe on this issue of leadership and we have found no just man in a position of power. But he does profess a hope, not in the life of any of his fictional characters but in that of a leader from Kano whom he admires to no end – Mallam Aminu Kano. Achebe tells us in the concluding pages of *A Man of the People*:

I can see no rational answer to the chaotic jumble of tragic and tragi-comical problems we have unleashed on ourselves in the past twenty-five years, but the example of Aminu Kano – a self-less commitment to the common people of our land whom we daily deprive and dispossess and whose plight we treat so callously and frivolously ... When the late Prime Minister Abubakar Tafawa Balewa made the crack that if Aminu Kano were to become Prime Minister of Nigeria he would one day carry a placard and join a protest march against himself, he was paying a most profound and befitting tribute to a saint and revolutionary ... For it was indeed true that if for any reason Aminu Kano should discover that he had joined the ranks of the oppressor he would promptly and openly renounce his position and wage war on himself (62–63).

It is now evident that in all of Achebe's fictional and non-fictional output, he has all along been on a search for the right leader to lead us in our search for utopia – a utopia of reconstruction, of reinstitution, and healing the many wounds inflicted on us by the long years of colonialism and neo-colonialism, of the havoc wreaked on us and on the body-politic by our corrupt politicians and rapacious and power-drunk military leaders.

He finally pitches his hope for salvation on the intellectuals but only those intellectuals of the stamp of Aminu Kano – self-less, unassuming, not power-drunk, a true man of the people who in spite of the trappings of power will always consider himself, one with the masses.

Works Cited

Achebe, Chinua. *Anthills of the Savannah*. London: Heinemann, 1987.

———. *Arrow of God*. London: Heinemann, 1964.

———. *The Trouble with Nigeria*. Enugu: Fourth Dimension, 1983.

———. *Things Fall Apart*. London: Heinemann, 1958.

———. "The African Writer and the Biafran Cause." *Morning Yet on Creation Day*. London: Heinemann, 1975.

———. "The Role of the Writer in a New Nation." *Nigeria Magazine*, No 81. June 1964.

Mazrui, Ali. *The Trial of Christopher Okigbo*. London: Heinemann, 1978.

Serumaga, Robert. "Interview with Chinua Achebe." London: Transcription Center, 1962.

Chapter 15

The Idiom of a New Social Order in Chinua Achebe's Fiction

Isaac B. Lar

CHINUA ACHEBE'S LITERARY TECHNIQUE INVOLVES a unique symbiotic balance of two conflicting religious and socio-cultural values in certain narrative devices. In *Things Fall Apart* for instance, one of such devices is the famous inter-faith exchange between Mr. Brown and Akunna. Also in *Arrow of God* such techniques are reflected in three incidents: Ezeulu's flexibility in allowing Oduche to join the Christian fold, Unachukwu's personal decision to adopt the Christian faith and some aspects of Western culture; and Nwodika's unalloyed "conversion" to Western mercantilism and materialism as a survival strategy in a rapidly changing world.

It is through the same literary technique that in *No Longer at Ease*, Achebe blends (longer) biblical parlance with a traditional idiom to stress the reality about the inevitable convergence of opposite values. In *A Man of the People* the outing of a traditional masquerade to celebrate the Christmas festival is in fact a synthesis by which Achebe seems to create a paradigm for tolerance and accommodation in a multi-religious context.

In *Anthills of the Savannah*, the same theme of tolerance and accommodation is highlighted. In an episode in the novel, Ikem Osodi's child is born to his consort, Elewa. At the naming ceremony a Christian girl, Agatha takes up a praise song. Aina, a true Muslim, dances to the rhythm and Beatrice Buife, fondly perceived by Chris Oriko as the earth goddess of the traditional Igbo community, also responds to the music. To Achebe, this occasion which serves as a rallying point for people with different beliefs also shows that it is possible for people with different beliefs to coexist in the same society. This can happen when they emphasize the common elements in different religions which unite and bind humanity together in an ecumenical fraternity.

The discussion undertaken within this paper is based on Umezinwa's Semiotic Theory of African symbols, which signifies:

> flexibility, suppleness, renewal, growth, regeneration and reincarnation. The curvilinear theory thus attempts to refute, among other things, the popular saying in Western European Languages which erroneously associates the circle with viciousness. The theory hails the circle, as well as curves and spirals, as the African symbol of change and transformation (ix).

This semiotic theory, specifically the aspects that deal with flexibility, tolerance, accommodation and adaptation to changing situations, is used in analyzing Achebe's overall fictive technique, taking into consideration the earlier stated points about his fiction.

Brown-Akunna Inter-Faith Dialogue

As it is well known, Achebe's literary discourse adopts a neutral stance on issues, except where traditionalists or Christians have an obvious positive edge over each other. Only then does he manipulate our sympathies with great subtlety till he arrives at a resolution of the conflict in favor of the side he considers representative of his creative balancing. As a result of Achebe's apparent objectivity, Innes characterizes him as having a cold, dispassionate style, and his avoidance of the sensational has induced "him to achieve effects similar to those aimed at by Brecht" (169).

The originality of Achebe as an artist is essentially based on the fact that he focuses largely on episodes and incidents which subsume the concepts of mediation, tolerance, accommodation and a cosmopolitan outlook on life. This objective approach readily props up Achebe as an author who encourages inter-faith dialogue, mutual respect and understanding in a multi-religious setting. In *Things Fall Apart*, Achebe sets the tone for inter-faith discourse between the Christians and traditionalists through the famous Brown-Akunna dialogue in Chapter Twenty-One. To Chinua Achebe, both Mr. Brown the white Christian Missionary, and Ogbeufi Akunna the traditional elder, symbolize the best elements from both religious camps. The novelist therefore features both men and shows them engaged in a healthy dialogue in Akunna's *Obi* about their two belief systems.

In this healthy, verbal exchange, a realistic ambiance is created by the narrator through which Mr. Brown learns some sobering lessons about Akunna's traditional belief system. Mr. Brown is thus better enlightened and wisely concludes that "a frontal attack on it would not succeed" (126). This realization enables the British

Missionary to change tactics: one sees him trying to convince and win converts, not through preaching the superiority of Christian theology, but through materialism and the appeal of Western culture. For after building a school and hospital, he goes from family to family, imploring people to send their children to his school with the assurance that "the leaders of the land in the future would be men and women who had learnt to read and write" (128). He further encouraged them with gifts of singlets and towels. Within the framework of semiotic analysis, such concrete material signs and symbols as schools, hospitals and gifts of singlets and towels represent the attraction and enticement of Western material culture which have a special appeal to the natives. And accordingly, this strategy pays off with the passage of time.

That Achebe approves of this peaceful, logical and persuasive mode of evangelization which does not infringe on the people's religious sensibilities is evident through the results the narrator allows the church to achieve under Mr. Brown's leadership. In the first instance, Mr. Brown is able to win the love and admiration of the traditional community because "he trod softly on its faith" (126). Next, he restrains his members who have a tendency for "provoking the wrath of the clan" (126) through excesses in the fashion of Enoch, the newly converted son of the snake cult priest.

Then, as a practical demonstration of the respect Mr. Brown has won, elders of the clan choose to honor him with the gift of "a carved elephant tusk, which was a sign of dignity and rank" (126). Soon, products of the mission school like teachers, court clerks and evangelists begin to make their impact felt in the surrounding communities. Then, because of the mission's linkage "with the new administration it earned a new social prestige" (128). With all of these obvious benefits in view, the natives were compelled to rethink their attitude towards the new faith. Indeed, some came to change their opinion from regarding it as "a lunatic religion" (126) to one rooted in logic and method.

On a parallel scale, Lawrence Vambe (in his biographical and political book, *An Ill-Fated People* set in Colonial Zimbabwe) demonstrates how the Reverend Father Richartz with a similar disposition like Achebe's Mr. Brown, was able to win the hearts of the natives. He accomplished this feat by pursuing "a policy of persuasion and conviction, especially in the conversion of men and women to Christianity" (169).

But seen from a different perspective, however, it is quite apparent that Christian missionaries of goodwill like Mr. Brown and Reverend Father Richartz usually form a negligible minority. Achebe's works, in fact, dramatize at length how, in the name of pacification and Christianization, the Abame settlement was sacked, elders of Umuofia were disgraced, humiliated and imprisoned in *Things Fall Apart*. Similarly, in *Arrow of God*, the imprisonment of Ezeulu by forces of

Western imperialism is first symbolized by the literal imprisonment of the sacred python, the manifestation of the traditional religious god, Idemili. This sacrilegious act committed by Ezeulu's Christianized son, in turn, shows how the new religion was programmed to thrive and to destroy the influence traditional belief exerts on the local community of Umuaro.

By the end of the novel, Achebe shows convincingly the connivance of the Church, and the secular state in the decimation of the local African community and its ethos. This, the narrator ably dramatizes and embodies in the marriage of the white missionary doctor, Mary Savage to Captain Winterbottom, the colonial District Commissioner. This disintegration of the traditional society's cohesive structures is made possible through Christian opportunism. Taking advantage of an impasse created by Ezeulu's refusal to announce the time of the new yam festival, the church completes the rout of Umuaro. Headed by John Jaja Goodcountry, a veritable product of rigid Christian doctrine and orientation in the fashion of the Reverend James Smith of *Things Fall Apart*, the church capitalized on the situation to earn the harvest of the traditional society. It is this tendency of the church to ally itself with the secular colonial establishment in order to destroy local African institutions and values that informs Ojo-Ade's observation that:

> while preaching the sermon to the colonised, Europe set about pilfering and profaning, pirating and prostituting, all in the name of civilization (5).

This picture of rivalry and antagonism promoted by agents of Christianity, and implicitly by agents of colonialism is equally apparent in Achebe's *No Longer at Ease*. This is demonstrated in the rash action of Mrs. Hannah Okonkwo, wife of the village Catechist, who beheads the sacred Udo he-goat for eating her yams. And although the traditionalists ostracize her for a season, the narrator explains that her punishment cannot be sustained for long, owing to the emasculating work of the colonial dispensation on the clan.

Indeed, even in Achebe's *Things Fall Apart*, it is clear that the benign and tactful Mr. Brown adopts the posture of tolerance and dialogue, only because he wants to convert the Africans:

> But it is evidently clear that Achebe's Europeans, even the more liberal ones like Mr. Brown, will never dream that they have anything to learn from Africans – who may be studied but never imitated. That is part of the tragedy for the Africans, who find it almost impossible to comprehend the depth and consequences of the white man's arrogance (Innes 22).

From a historical standpoint, Ehusani notes that the scorn which white Missionaries had for African values can be attributed to the brand of Christianity that came to Africa during the colonial period. According to him, the whites brought a divided Christianity and imposed Western culture on Africans:

> But more than this, they brought a Christianity that had lost most of its cred-ibility to materialism. They brought the 'Enlightenment' Christianity which had consigned to near-independent compartments, the spiritual and the material, the sacred and the profane, science and religion. They brought 'the pie in the sky' religion (otherwise called 'spiritualism') which soothed the people as they were being drained of their humanity (Ehusani 21).

At the psychological level, the damage inflicted on Achebe's changing society is incalculable. This brought about a culture of self-denigration and the denial of the African's sense of self-worth. According to Achebe, "people accepted everything alien as good and practically everything local or native as inferior (Duerden and Pieterse 8). It is this phase of self-depreciation in the psychology of the colonized that is described as deriving

> From their internalization of the opinion the oppressors hold of them. So often do they hear that they are good for nothing, know nothing and are incapable of learning anything – that they are sick, lazy and unproductive – that in the end they become convinced of their own unfitness (Freire 38–39).

Indeed, it is this sort of self-denigration which propels Achebe's creative genius towards searching for ways of rescuing the African from this externally imposed tradition of self-abnegation. As a teacher to his society in this broad sense, Achebe sees himself as "historian, rescuing its past; as a critic, analyzing its present; as mentor, helping to guide it towards its future (Ojinma 4).

In *Things Fall Apart*, the inter-faith dialogue between Ogbuefi Akunna and Mr. Brown is used by Achebe as an artistic paradigm for bringing about peaceful coexistence in a multi-religious, multi-cultural context. This paradigm attains its fullest expression and consummation in *Anthills of the Savannah*.

The trinity of Western imperialism working jointly as commerce, Christianity and civilization – are clearly shown to have had adverse effects on the society of Achebe's fiction. This fact is revealed in structural binary oppositions: the truth that while the colonizing agents are identified with rigidity and violence, the African world is associated with flexibility, tolerance and adaptation to changing social realities. Indeed this fact is not unique to Achebe's fiction. The writings of Ngugi wa Thiong'o, Mongo Beti, Ferdinand Oyono, Stanlake Semkange, T. Obinkaram Echewa and Lawrence Vambe among others, all substantiate this claim.

Even when we go back to *Things Fall Apart*, it is observed that the famous Brown-Akunna discourse takes place in Akunna's *Obi*, not at the Christian mission station. The point being made here is that it is first and foremost the tolerance and accommodation of the African, as revealed by the narrative technique, which made for his conversion to Christianity. This, in effect, is the idiom and philosophy of the African world which allowed for the overall success of Christian proselytisation in Africa during and after colonialism. This is the truth that emerges from the fictional world of Chinua Achebe.

Ezeulu's Flexibility in Sending Oduche to School

The tolerance and flexibility of the African in adapting to changing realities in his environment, and which makes conversion of some Africans possible in *Things Fall Apart* is further sustained in Achebe's *Arrow of God*. Here, it is Ezeulu's willingness to adjust to the demands of a new era and to be relevant to it that cause the fetish priest to respond to the colonial administrator's appeal "to send one of his sons to the church" (45) after hesitating for three years. The chief priest of Ulu rationalizes his final decision in this way:

> The world is like a mask dancing. If you want to see it well you do not stand
> in one place. My spirit tells me that those who do not befriend the white man
> today will say had he known tomorrow (46).

Through this traditional oral art of self-expression laced with an idiom and trans-literation to bear the rich nuances and ethos of his native community, Achebe demonstrates convincingly how a pliant mind like Ezeulu's can accept and adjust itself to the requirements of a new dispensation.

Unachukwu's Willful Conversion to Christianity and White Civilizing Mission

In *Arrow of God*, Achebe dramatizes in detail how Moses Unachukwu of Umuaro comes to appreciate the reality of European presence, and to imbibe the new religion and the white civilizing mission. After more than ten years of sojourn outside the tribal setting of Umuaro, experience has taught him that "the white man was not a thing of fun" (46). On the strength of Unachukwu's services as a porter to the white invaders who conquered Abame, and also as houseboy to Hargreaves the carpenter – missionary, Achebe demonstrates to the reader why the combination of fear, awe and admiration compels Unachukwu to see the white man as invincible. He stresses the overwhelming extent of European power to his fellow villagers:

> The white man, the new religion, the soldiers, the new road – they are all part
> of the same thing. The white man has a gun, a matchet, a bow and carries fire
> in his mouth. He does not fight with one weapon alone (85).

With these words which support his earlier argument that "as daylight chases away darkness so will the white man drive away all our customs" (84). Unachukwu learns both to yield to the white man's presence and to justify and defend his own docile approach to foreign domination.

Nwabueze Nwodika's Conversion to Western Mercantilism

Nwabueze Nwodika is as flexible as Unachukwu in *Arrow of God*. He is quick to notice the necessity of adopting Western commerce as a basis for existence in a fast-changing world. This episode recorded in Chapter Fourteen of the novel, from the authorial perspective, is what the young African character thinks his "*Chi* planned it to be" (169). The incident is an initiation into Western culture as a whole, even if only through superficial trappings. His adoption of the name "John" at the instance of his white Master gives him an impressive Christian symbol, while his attempt at the mastery of the white man's "language and custom" (169) makes him an acolyte of the so-called civilizing mission. In short, while his ultimate aim is to prosper commercially, he imbibes in the process the three dominant aspects of Western civilization: Christianity, Commerce and Assimilation.

John Nwodika's response to Ekemezie's call during the full moon to renounce the tribal dance and to come in pursuit of the white man's money also reveals the basic truth about the African world of Achebe's fiction as a society that is "patient, tolerant and forebearing, entrenched in the wisdom of the ancients, yet flexible and adaptable, when necessary (Ojinma 13).

The Blend of Biblical Parlance with Traditional Anecdote

In *No Longer at Ease*, Achebe's idiom of a new order rooted in tolerance and accommodation is expressed through the blending of indigenous African and Christian values. As a novel of transition from traditional lifestyle to one in which African and European modes of living coexist, most of the novel's African characters demonstrate, in varying degrees, their mastery of the two ways of life. Western idioms and African proverbs are used conjointly in seasoning the speeches of most characters. One instance of such usage will suffice at this juncture to support the basic premise of this section. In the short paragraph quoted below, Achebe makes use of the novel's protagonist, Obi Okonkwo, to dramatize this admixture of values as a point of convergence for two cultures. As Obi rises to address members of the Umuofia Progression Union at a meeting, he emphasizes the need for unity and togetherness in these words:

> Did not the psalmist say that it was good for brethren to meet together in harmony? 'Our fathers also have a saying about the danger of living apart. They say it is the curse of the snake. If all snakes live together in one place, who would approach them? But they live everyone unto himself and so fall easy prey to man' (73).

The above blending of Christian thought with a traditional idiom is Achebe's way of saying his African characters are flexible enough and therefore can be converted into a new way of life when necessity demands it.

Masquerade Outing in Celebration of Christmas Festival

In *Things Fall Apart*, the unfortunate outing of the *egwugwu* coincides with the Christian day of worship. This resultant clash between Christian worshippers and the masked spirits leaves disastrous consequences in its wake. In *A Man of the People* however, Achebe ably balances the structure of his artistic creation. The result is quite salutary. He does this to show that the times have changed. And accordingly, what once resulted in violent confrontation is now working in reverse order. It is the masquerade that comes out to join in the Christmas celebration. Achebe's mode of expressing this concept of tolerance for corporate coexistence in a complex world of differing beliefs is through the paradigm of a dancing mask. The author allows us to witness this incident through Odili Samalu's narrative viewpoint. At Christmastime, children parodying a real dangerous masquerade had had one adult to act the role. They entertain the public and collect money. But the dancing mask is not violent because it is aware it must mediate between its traditional function and the Christmas festival of the Christian epoch. Contrary to its traditional role therefore, Achebe allows us to witness a situation where, even when it gained freedom from the restraining rope tied around its waist, the mask would "tamely put his matchet down, helped his disciples retie the rope, picked up his weapon again and resumed his dance" (97).

It is indeed this context of mediating with the demand of a new era based on tolerance and adaptation to the changing times that has made the erstwhile aggressive masquerade welcome company during the Christmas celebration. And from a historical standpoint, it was this willingness to accept new ways of life in the first instance that made the conversion of Achebe's traditional characters to Christianity possible at the beginning of the white man's presence in the community.

Naming Ceremony as Rallying point for Inter-Faith Exchange

In *Anthills of the Savannah*, Achebe's idiom of a new order has for its immediate context the naming of Ikem Osodi's baby girl he has with Elewa. The events at the occasion are arranged in the typical traditional way. After the ritual breaking of the kola comes the naming of the child. Then the traditional dance follows. But before these events, a joyful Christian girl, Agatha, takes up a chorus. Beatrice Buife, fondly regarded by Chris Oriko in the novel as the Igbo earth goddess, responds to the rhythm of the song by swaying her head from side to side" (224). And Aina, a Muslim woman joins in the seductive dance. The social gathering is an artistic device through which Achebe encourages tolerance, understanding and a certain type of ecumenical spirit among people of different cultural and religious backgrounds.

The choice of the name for the child itself is a synthesis of traditional Igbo and biblical names. According to David Carroll "the biblical name (the-remnant-shall-return) is translated into their [Igbo] version of eternal hopefulness, the indigenous Amaechina (may-the-path-never-close) (Carroll 183). In fact, the opening statement of the traditional elder after the ceremonial breaking of kola also sustains this motif of finding a common ground for the coexistence of different belief systems in *Anthills of the Savannah*:

> We have no quarrel with the church people; we have no quarrel with the mosque people. Their intentions are good, their mind on the right road. Only the hand fails to throw as straight as the eye sees. We praise a man when he slaughters a fowl so that if his hands become stronger tomorrow he will slaughter a goat (228)

Conclusion

From the discussion on the dialogues, episodes, personalities and festivities highlighted above, Achebe concludes his idiom of a new order by dramatizing that tolerance and accommodation are the essential ingredients that make for a peaceful and harmonious living in a multi-ethnic, multi-religious social context.

Perhaps it is pertinent to round off the discussion of this paper by quoting from a document which is deemed relevant to the study. It is a Communique issued in 1987 in the United States by a group of Catholic Bishops. According to them:

> Our first task is approaching another people, another culture, another religion, is to take off our shoes, for the place we are approaching is holy. Else we may find ourselves treading on another's dream; and more serious still, we may forget that God was there before our arrival (Ehusani 203).

Judging from the above statement, and taking cognizance of Achebe's polemical works, novels and critical essays, it does appear that the author is not averse to the conversion of the African to Christianity. Achebe's adoption of the inner-faith dialogue technique in his works appears to encourage responsible evangelism. This idea, in Achebe's conception, seems based on the need to study and understand African beliefs. And arising from the respect for, and mediation with these values, Achebe would seem to appreciate a situation whereby conscious attempts are made by African writers at finding appropriate idioms for literary expression of African cultures. The idiom of a new order, as perceived by Achebe, can serve as an apt medium for reaching the typical African. The creation of a healthy context of mutual respect may have minimized, if not eliminated some of the needless clashes and misunderstandings witnessed, especially in *Things Fall Apart* between the Christian Mission and traditionalists. Indeed, it is such a healthy context of evangelization which permeates Achebe's art and which shows his preference for flexibility, tolerance and adaptation to new situations.

Works Cited

Achebe, Chinua. *Things Fall Apart*. London: Heinemann Educational Books Ltd., 1958, 1980.

———. *Arrow of God*. London: Heinemann Educational Books, Ltd., 1964, 1992.

———. *No Longer at Ease*. London: Heinemann Educational Books, Ltd., 1960, 1980.

———. *A Man of the People*. London: Heinemann Educational Books, Ltd., 1966, 1980.

———. *Anthills of the Savannah*, Ibadan: Heinemann Educational Books, Ltd., 1987.

Animalu, Alexander O.E. *Ahiajoku Lecture*. Owerri: Government Printer, 1990.

Carroll, David. *Chinua Achebe: Novelist, Poet Critic*. London: McMillan Group, 1980, 1990.

Duerden, Dennis and Cosmo Pieterse Eds. *African Writers Talking*. London: Heinemann Educational Books, Ltd., 1972, 1978.

Ehusani, George Omaku. *An Afro-Christian Vision, Ozovehe!: Toward a More Humanized World*. New York: University Press of America. 1991, 1992.

Freire, Paulo. *Pedagogy of the Oppressed*. New York: Penguin Books. 1972, 1982.

Innes, C.L. *Chinua Achebe*. Ibadan. Heinemann Educational Books, Ltd. 1991.

Ojinma, Umelo. *Chinua Achebe: New Perspectives*. Ibadan: Spectrum Books. 1991.

Ojo-Ade, Femi. *On Black Culture*. Ile-Ife: Obafemi Awolowo University Press. 1989.

Vambe, Lawrence. *An Ill-fated People*. London: Heinemann Educational Books, Ltd., 1972, 1982.

Chapter 16

Achebe's Vision of Art and the Artist in Society

Sunday Osim Etim

T HIS PAPER PROPOSES TO stitch together snatches of Achebe's views and pronouncements which altogether approximate his vision of Art and the Artist in society. For purposes of illustration, it draws freely from Chinua Achebe: *Morning Yet on Creation Day* (*MYCD*), Duerden and Pieterse: *African Writers Talking* (*AWT*), *Chinua Achebe: New Perspectives* (*CANP*), and a number of other relevant works. A review of these extant literatures reveal that Achebe fundamentally conceives of Art as ideally sacrosanct, utilitarian and responsive, while the Artist – Writer, carver, composer, or even dancer – is not only the kibitzer and chronicler of fractured existences, but should as well be a catalyst to the reclamation of these existences.

Achebe's Vision of Art

To adequately appreciate Achebe's Vision of Art, it is pertinent to refer to an excerpt from *Anthills of the Savannah* which to my mind succinctly delineates the pre-eminence Achebe bestows on Art:

> To some of us the Owner of the World has apportioned the gift to tell their fellows that the time to get up has finally come. To others He gives the eagerness to rise when they hear the call; to rise with racing blood and put on their garbs of war and go to the boundary of their town to engage the invading enemy boldly in battle. And then there are those others whose part is to wait and when the struggle is ended, to take over and recount the story.
>
> The sounding of the battle drum is important; the fierce waging of the war itself is important; and the telling of the story afterwards – each is important in its own way. I tell you there is not one of them we could do without. But if you

ask me which of them takes the eagle feather I will say boldly; the story ... Why? Because it is only the story that can continue beyond the war and the warrior. It is the story that outlives the sound of war drums and the exploits of brave fighters. It is the story not the others that saves our progeny from blundering like blind beggars into the spikes of the cactus fence ... The story is our escort; without it, we are blind (123–124).

From the above pedestal therefore, it may be asserted that Achebe conceives of Art as essentially utilitarian; that Art should be purposeful, indeed, a veritable vehicle for social, political and economic reform. In one of his essays, "Africa and Her Writers," Achebe puts it very bluntly that, "art for art's sake is just another piece of deodorized dog-shit (*MYCD* 10). Obviously, Achebe's view of art is diametrically opposed to the 19th and early 20th century Western European paradigm of art as being accountable to no one, and needed to justify itself to nobody except itself, that art must be an end unto itself, making no prudish pedagogic statement about life, or acting as binoculars for the "criticism of life." On the contrary, Achebe holds that art should "minister to a basic human need, serve a down-to-earth necessity. "Art has to be responsive and relevant especially when viewed against the back-drop of the night-marish realities of the contemporary African milieu. Achebe reiterates:

> I will still insist that art is, and was always in the service of man. Our ancestors created their myths and legends and told their stories for a human purpose (including, no doubt, the excitement of wonder and pure delight); they made their sculptures in wood and terracotta, stone and bronze to serve the needs of their times. Their artists lived and moved and had their being in society, and created their works for the good of that society (*MYCD* 19).

As Iferenta (1989) notes, art is not supposed to escape. "Art has usually always been "good and useful." He goes on to explain what he means by "good". "I do not mean moral uplift although – why not? – that would be part of it, I mean good in the sense in which God at the end of each day's work of putting the world together saw that what He had made was good. Then, and only then, did he count it in a day's job (*MYCD* 19). Simply put, Achebe believes in and advocates for the sanctity of Art. This Art, according to Achebe, "exists independently of us, of all mankind. Man and his world may indeed pass away but not a jot from the laws of this Art (*MYCD* 19). Ideally, Art in Achebe's view should be pure, sacrosanct, incorruptible, immortal, imperishable transcending the ravages of time.

Achebe's Vision of the Artist in Society

For fear of terminological inexactitude, it will be academic and convenient to appropriately pigeon-hole the artist. Who in precise terms is an artist? He may be identified as:

   i.   Any professional public performer, as an actor, singer, etc.

   ii.   One who does anything particularly well, as with a feeling for form, effect, etc.

   iii.   A person who paints pictures, skilled in any of the fine arts, such as sculpture, music and literature.

A corollary to these definitions of the artist is that the term "artist" may be looked at generically, sub-summing the writer of imaginative literature, the painter on canvas, the critic, the musician, the theatre director, the television producer, etc. What role(s) then does Achebe assign to him in society? For purposes of convenience, I propose to consider the role(s) of the artist in society *inter alia* under the following sub-headings – the artist as custodian of regenerative wisdom, the artist as Teacher, and the artist as social crusader.

The Artist as Historian and Custodian of Regenerative Wisdom

For Achebe, the quintessential task of the artist is that of rescuing the African past from the colonial misrepresentation and biased stereotyping to which it had been subjected. The artist must mandatorily enlist in the unflinching effort to rehabilitate the disparaged image of the African past. This task cannot be compromised because in the eyes of Europe, to a very large extent, Africa is the "other world," the antithesis of Europe and therefore of civilization, a place where man's vaunted intelligence and refinement are finally mocked at by triumphant bestiality. As Achebe rightly observes in this essay, "The African Writer and the Biafran Cause":

> Whether we like to face up to it or not Africa has been the most insulted continent in the world. Africans' very claim to humanity has been questioned at various times, their persons abused, their intelligence insulted. These things have happened in the past and have gone on happening today. We have a duty to bring them to an end for our own sakes, for the sake of our children and indeed for the safety and happiness of the world (*MYCD* 78).

In an interview with Lewis Nkosi, Achebe stated that one of the things that "set me thinking was Joyce Cary's novel set in Nigeria, *Mr. Johnson*, which was praised so much, and it was clear to me that this was a most superficial picture of not only of the country, but even of the Nigerian character and so I thought if this was famous, then perhaps someone ought to try and look at this from the inside." (*AWT* 4). In this light therefore, Ojinmah (1991), quoting Kofi Awoonor writes that: "Achebe's *Things Fall Apart* seems to have been inspired by a deep-seated need to respond to what seemed to be Cary's sniggering laugh at Africa, whose image of filed teeth and bones stuck in the nose has scarcely receded in the Europe of Cary's colonial experience. Continuing, he notes that:

> To Achebe, the African World before the arrival of Europe was a well-in-tegrated one, with dignity and honour ... As a story of the tragic encounter between Africa and Europe, *Things Fall Apart* is an attempt to capture and restate the pristine integrity which has been so traumatically shattered by that confrontation.

According to Achebe, the artist like his historian counterpart has the necessary function of "replacing short, garbled, despised history with more sympathetic ac-count..." because we must begin to correct the prejudices which generations of detractors fabricated about the Negro. Achebe sees this as a necessary step before any meaningful progress:

> This is my answer to those who say that a writer should be writing about con-temporary issues ... about politics in 1964, about the last *coup d'etat*; of course these are all legitimate themes for a writer but as far as I am concerned the fundamental theme must first be disposed of. This theme ... put quite simply ... is that African people did not hear of culture for the first time from Europeans, that their societies were not mindless but frequently had a philosophy of great depth and value and beauty, that they had poetry, and, above all, they had dignity. It is this dignity that many African people all but lost during the colonial period, and it is this that they must now regain ("The Role of the Writer ..." 8).

Elsewhere again, Achebe notes that if an artist is anything he is a human being with heightened sensitivities; he must be aware of the faintest nuances of injustice in human relations. The African writer cannot therefore be unaware of, or indif-ferent to, the monumental injustice which his people suffer (*MYCD* 79). Reacting to a widespread sentiment in the years following the Nigerian Civil War, (1967–1970), that the recent past was best forgotten, Achebe replies:

> I do not agree, I believe that in our situation the greater danger lies not in remembering but in forgetting, in pretending that slogans are the same as truth; and that Nigeria, always prone to self deception, stands in great need of reminders ... I believe that if we are to survive as a nation we need to grasp the meaning of tragedy. One way to do it is to remind ourselves constantly of the things that happened and how we felt when they were happening.

The Artist as Teacher

In an interview with Donatus Nwoga, Achebe had asserted that: "I think we have a very important function – this is only one of the roles of the writer, as a teacher." He reiterates that "what I think a novelist can teach is something very fundamental, namely to indicate to his readers, to put it crudely, that we in Africa did not hear of culture for the first time from Europeans. Indeed the Writer has the responsibility to teach his audience that there is nothing shameful about the harmattan, that it is not only daffodils that can make a fit subject for poetry, but the palm tree and so on (*AWT* 8).

According to Ojinmah (1991) "For Achebe, the African novelist as teacher has three primary functions in relation to his society; as historian, rescuing its past; as a critic, analyzing its present; as mentor, helping to guide it towards its future." In the essay, "The Novelist as Teacher," Achebe posits that the artist cannot expect to be excused from the task of re-education and regeneration that must be done. In fact, he should march right in front (*MYCD* 44). This explains why Achebe contends that:

> I would be quite satisfied if my novels (especially the ones I set in the past) did no more than teach my readers that their past – with all the imperfections – was not one long night of savagery from which the first Europeans acting on God's behalf delivered them (*MYCD* 45).

In Achebe's view, it is the task of the artist as a teacher to recreate the past in the present in order to educate the reader and give him confidence in his/her cultural heritage, and also in order to enlighten the foreign reader and help him readjust the false impressions about the African culture acquired from centuries of cultural misrepresentation. In that same essay referred to above ("The Novelist as Teacher"), Achebe makes mention of a boy in his wife's class who was ashamed of writing about the harmattan because he was afraid that the other boys would ridicule him. Achebe retorts:

> It is my business as a writer to teach that boy that there is nothing disgraceful about the African weather, that the palm tree is a fit subject for poetry. Here then is an adequate revolution for me to espouse ... to help my society regain belief in itself and put away the complexes of the years of denigration and self-abasement.

It is the sublime task of the artist to restore to his people a good opinion of themselves because their association with Europe had visibly undermined their self-confidence. One of the results of this sort of attitude is what Achebe sees as manifest "self-contempt" which leads Africans into believing that they are inferior to all other races, and for which he states: "If I were God I would regard as the very worst our acceptance for whatever reason – of our racial inferiority" (*MYCD* 44).

The Artist as Social Crusader

It is Achebe's valued opinion that the artist must of necessity be a social crusader, in fact, a commentator on society's present course, a critic. Achebe believes that the writer has to be a free critic in a society lacking such criticism. Ojinmah (1991) quoting Rene Wellek says that literature is a "reflection of reality" and therefore, provides the truest mirror ... if the author shows an insight into the structure of the society and the future direction of its evolution. Ojinmah agrees that Achebe's social consciousness is heightened by this general belief, as noted by Maduka (1981), that literature can play a great role in straightening the patterns of social change in Africa. In an interview with Bernth Lindors, Achebe states:

> Yes I think by recording what had gone on before, they (the African writers) were in a way helping to set the tone of what was going to happen. And this is important because at this stage it seems to me that the writer's role is more in determining than merely reporting. In other words, his role is to act rather than to react ... Let us map out what we are going to be tomorrow. I think our most meaningful job today should be to determine what kind of society we want, how we are going to get there, what values we can take from the past, if we can, as we move along.

He further states that "a writer in the African revolution who steps aside can only writer footnotes or glossary when the event is over." Chinweizu, Jemie and Madubuike (1980), reinforce this Achebe's view when they opine that the function of the artist in Africa, in keeping with our traditions and needs, demands that the writer as a public voice should assume a responsibility to reflect public concerns in his writings, and not preoccupy himself with his puny ego. Therefore, " ... sense of social commitment is mandatory upon the artist ... He may choose to explore some of the values of his society, or some of the dangers in its path; or he may choose to lampoon its foibles or castigate its wrong doings."

Iferenta (1989) agrees with Achebe that the artist is the custodian of his society's conscience and that this should superfluously reflect in his work. Thus, the artist cannot write or sing about mushy love songs or scripts when his immediate surroundings are engulfed in a conflagration. The artist's sublime task is to put out the pillaging flames first. Then, later, as a form of catharsis, he can write queasy love ditties to his estranged heartthrob. As Achebe rightly puts it, "if writers should opt for such escapism, who is to meet the challenge? Indeed, ease and carelessness in our circumstance will only cause a total breakdown of communications" (*MYCD* 27). This again is reflected in Maduka's statement that: "The African writer cannot afford the luxury of withdrawing into the cocoon of creativity in the name of art for art's sake. As a participant in the drama of social change in Africa, he can use his skills to help shape the future of the society." This counteracts the European romantic perception of the artist living on the fringes of society – wearing a beard and a peculiar dress and generally behaving in a strange, unpredictable way, more often than not, in revolt against society, which in turn looks on him with suspicion if not hostility. In another essay, "Africa and her Writers," Achebe argues that:

> Certainly no artist reared within the Mbari culture could aspire to humiliate his community by hanging his canvas upside down in an exhibition and, with-

drawing to a corner, watch viewers extol its many fine and hidden points with much nodding of the head and outpouring of sophisticated jargon. It is really an appalling relationship. And the artist who so blatantly dramatises it has more to answer for than all those pathetic courtiers lost in admiration of the emperor's new clothes, desperately hiding in breathless garrulity the blankness of their vision (*MYCD* 32).

Elsewhere, Achebe notes that it is important to say at this point that "no self-respecting writer will take dictation from his audience. He must remain free to disagree with his society and go into rebellion against it if need be (*MYCD* 42).

Iferenta (1989), also shares this opinion that in a sadistic society where oppression, deprivation and dehumanization form the bulwark of society's super structure, it is balmy and distastefully defeatist for an artist to recoil into an indifferent shell of creative fantasy, celebrating Art-for-Art's sake. Ultimately for Achebe, the artist in a contemporary African situation must be seen at once as a social crusader, campaigner, preacher and advocate for socio-political and economic emancipation. In Achebe's view, that is the *raison d'etre* for being an artist, because:

"an African creative writer who tries to avoid the big social and political issues of contemporary African (society) will end up being completely irrelevant ...,
if he fails to espouse the "right and just causes" of his people, he is no better than "the absurd man in the proverb who deserts his burning house to pursue a rat fleeing from the flames (*MYCD* 78).

Conclusion

Interestingly, Achebe remains the colossus of African literature not only with his vast literary output, but his largeness of heart and profound philosophical thought-provoking positions on Art in general, and the Artist in particular. In fact, as a writer in contemporary Africa, Achebe has directed his artistic and creative arsenals towards perpetuating and ensuring the continuum of the society and the personal welfare of its members. In the same vein, our other artists will only be considered relevant as they fashion out an art that is at once socially relevant and committed to the education and awakening of the revolutionary consciousness of the down-trodden masses. As Ojinmah notes, Achebe's writings highlight the above commitments and motivations. Those set in the past espouse the African cultural heritage while his more recent writings have aimed at ascertaining "where we went wrong, where the rain began to beat us" as a prerequisite to "knowing where to begin to dry ourselves." One of Achebe's immortal dictums remains that "Art belongs to all, and is a "function" of Society. Therefore, let committed Art prevail. Not just perfunctory commitment to writing, painting or singing. In the words of Iferenta, "That commitment itself must be stubbornly committed to a culture of engagement ..."

Key to Abbreviations

AWT	–	*African Writers Talking*
AOS	–	*Anthills of the Savannah*
AWOAW	–	*African Writers on African Writing*
CANP	–	*Chinua Achebe: New Perspectives*
MYCD	–	*Morning Yet on Creation Day*

Works Cited

Achebe, Chinua. *Morning Yet on Creation Day: Essays*. London: Heinemann, 1982.

———. *Anthills of the Savannah*. Ibadan: Heinemann, 1988.

———. "The role of the Writer in a New Nation." *African Writers on African Writing*. Ed. Killam, G.D. North Western University Press, 1973.

Chinweizu, *et al. Toward the Decolonisation of African Literature*. Enugu: Fourth Dimension, 1980.

Duerden, D. and *African Writers Talking*. Ibadan: Heinemann, 1978. Cosmo Pieterse.

Iferenta, Ifemesia. "Art as a Custodian of Conscience." *The Guardian Sunday Supplement*. May 7, 1989. Lagos.

Maduka, C.T. "The African Writer and the Drama of Social Change". ARIEL, 12.3., 1981.

Ojinmah, U. *Chinua Achebe: New Perspectives*. Ibadan: Spectrum Books, Ltd., 1991.

Standard Dictionary: International Edition. Canada: Funk and Wagnall's.

World Book Dictionary. Vol. 1 A–K. Canada: Child Craft International Inc.

Chapter 17

The Dialectic of Power in Achebe's Novels

Barine Sanah Ngaage

THE DIALECTICAL TENSIONS IN ACHEBE'S *A Man of the People* and *Anthills of the Savannah* are caused by the quests made by civilians and military officers for power. Achebe in his earlier novel, *Arrow of God*, has shown the nature of power within the Igbo traditional society before the invasion of Western culture. The diachronic relevance of power to man in the traditional Igbo setting, the First Republic in Nigeria, the subsequent military intervention and the behavior of those controlling power are the things intended for careful study in this essay. The sociological approach which mediates between the social forces at work in the novels and the literary prowess of the author shall be adapted in the appraisal of the novels (Irele, *African Experience and Ideology* 23).

Access to power of any kind – feudalism, autocracy or militarism – gives authority to the possessor of power over his subjects. His exercise of authority over his subjects manifests in different modes as despotism, dictatorship and joint and free participation in the deliberations on the affairs of the state by the leader and his subjects. Bassey has listed the sources of political power as follows: authority, human resources, skills and knowledge and other factors as psychological and ideological factors which include attitudes towards obedience and submission; the absence or presence of a common faith (92). These factors play very important roles in the lives of the characters created by Achebe in his novels.

Anthills of the Savannah, Achebe's fictional narrative, is the story of the wrong application of power and the consequences for the power-drunk Sam, his cabinet and the entire country. Sam does not have any defined programme for the progress of his country. He is a military man trained to defend his country. He is suddenly

in government without preparing for governance. His administration is characterized by greed and power and refusal to seek advice from his civilian administrative
colleagues. Sam himself remarks:

> Soldiers are plain and blunt ... When we turn affairs of state back to you and
> return to barracks that will be the time to resume your civilian tricks. Have a
> little patience (4).

Sam has no useful programme to fulfill for public utility. He is a liar and his behavior is in sharp contrast with the civilians he accuses of holding discussions that
are diversionary. Democracy and militarism are compared in Sam's brief speech
above. The military, true to character, usurps power bluntly while civilians seek
power through elections.

The irony of the situation turns out to show the interest Sam has in becoming the President-for-life like President Ngongo. He tries to perpetuate himself in
office as Head of State by eliminating from his cabinet every voice of opposition
and reason. Ikem, a personal friend and editor of *National Gazette*, is taken out by
one o'clock at night and shot dead by security officers. Christopher Oriko, a former
primary school classmate made Commissioner of Education by Sam himself, is shot
dead on escaping from Kangan through Bassa in a confusing episode of attempted
rape of a female student by an armed policeman.

The behavior of those in power in the modern country of Kangan is expressed
through the myth of Idemili. Idemili is the female goddess that mediates between
the powerful and the powerless. Even the highly regarded persons in the land who
want to be recognized as title holders call at her shrine on the occasion of seeking
admission into the class of *Ozo* title holders. Idemili is the powerful goddess who
destroys those who use power to oppress others.

Colonel Johnson Osai, the masquerader of dark, nebulous and machiavellian
power, is destroyed in the process of exhibiting and misusing state power to suppress
and eliminate others. The functions of his office are questioned in the following
words of the author:

> Who or what were they securing? Perhaps they were posted there to prevent
> the hungry desert from taking its begging bowl inside the secure borders of
> the south (209).

Members of the delegation from Abazon are detained for demanding pipe borne
water. They cannot receive such an amenity except they support the candidacy of
Sam as President-for-life. The members of the delegation are framed up as agi-
tators who have caused instability in the country. Ikem is condemned as having
known about this framed plot against government. However, Ikem compounds
this situation of witch-hunting by delivering a lecture entitled: "The Tortoise and
Leopard – A Political Meditation on the Imperative of Struggle."

Ikem's lecture is about the behavior of power holders in the state, church or mosque, in party congress, in University and anywhere else. Controllers of power always use several devices to retain power. Ikem, therefore, does not succeed in his revolutionary mission against Sam, the dictator.

The wrong application of power gives birth to corruption and perpetuates it. The irony about the power of corruption is its silent continuity. The killing of armed robbers does not prevent armed robbery. This is described by the author of the following:

> For it was clear to me that the robber's words spoken with much power of calm-
> ness into the multitude's hysteria just minutes before his white lace reddened
> with blood and his hooded head withered instantly and dropped to his chest
> were greater than he, were indeed words of prophecy (42).

The words connotatively refer to the perpetual continuation of corruption. This is heightened by the vomit of a woman over the back of a man in the same scene. This physical act reinforces the social misdemeanor of the populace.

Dictatorship which is the forceful seizure of the power of state is like armed robbery. Dictatorship and smuggling are bedfellows. This fact offers an insight into the friendship existing between Sam, the Head of State and Alhaji Abdul Mahmond, a Kangan millionaire, who owns eight ocean liners, two or three private jets and fifty companies. He is the greatest and most dreaded smuggler in Kangan, whose businesses are never inspected by security officers. He brings whatever goods he likes into the country.

Furthermore, the army takes over government in *A Man of the People* through a coup with the intentions of eradicating thuggery and unwarranted deaths as well as bribery and corruption. The novel ends on the verge of the forceful occupation of state power by the military. *A Man of the People* and *Anthills of the Savannah* show civilians and the military as failures, who have used state power for corrupt purposes. A man like Nanga is not satisfied with earning over four thousand pounds a month as a minister. Yet he hitherto lived on a salary of eight pounds a month for several years. He now rides a Cadillac car and lives in a seven bedroom flat, but he insists on taking a ten percent bribe on every contract given out under the Ministry of Culture. Nanga's reaction against the dismissed ministers of state incidentally reveals the type of system of government adopted by the persons in power. It is a democratic government; persons have been elected into various positions of the state.

The Prime Minister reserves the veto power to dismiss his cabinet members as done in the novel. Dr. Makinde, a doctor of Philosophy in Public Finance, is dismissed irrationally for having advised against printing more currency notes weighed against the prevailing market situation. Fifteen million pounds are printed by the national bank to pay coffee farmers, who form the bulk of the population so as to bring back the People's Organization Party into power. The Minister of Finance is dismissed from office by the Prime Minister. He is blackmailed with the stigmatic remark of collaborating with "foreign saboteurs to destroy the new nation" (3).

The corrupt democratic system of government makes it easy to win elections through thuggery, bribery and blackmail. The absolute power of the Prime Minister aggravates the degree of corruption; the Minister of Finance and other Ministers are dismissed on the ground of sabotage without the democratic privilege of seeking redress. The people of Urua are ignorant of their rights as citizens. When the pipes kept in Urua are taken away overnight, owing to an initial declaration by the people for the candidature of Odili Samalu, they are incapacitated and compelled to declare Nanga as the only candidate without exercising their franchise or asking government to dismiss Nanga from government for unilaterally infringing on the communal rights of the people. Even the educated and well informed Odili is made to pay unwarranted tax levied against his father, owing to helplessness and the porous system that does not permit democratic procedures.

The refusal of people like the dismissed Minister of Finance, Odili and the people of Urua to fight against the ills of capitalism and capitalists make them to continue in power. Peasants can only benefit from the resources of government if they pressurize the capitalists to utilize the material resources to the profit of the masses or wrest power out of their hand. Power cannot be obtained without agitation. Those who seek to obtain power without agitation may be compared with those who want crops without plowing, or those who want rain without thunder or lightning and, those who want the ocean without the awful roar of it (wa Thiong'o 131).

Chief Nanga is returned unopposed. This is achieved through brutalizing, humiliating, beating, wounding, hospitalizing Odili and forcing him out of the election by denying him access to the nomination form. Max is knocked down by a car arranged by Chief Koko, the former Minister of Overseas Training, to prevent Max's party (the Common People's Convention) from protesting against the rigging of the election in question. This is the payment received by Max for accepting bribes from Chief Koko and promising to step down for him without doing so. The drama of corruption is intensified and compounded by the retaliation of Max's death by his girlfriend; Koko is shot dead by Eunice.

The greed for power and its slimy continuity by persons like Nanga and Koko symbolically represent raw, unprincipled and irresponsible Nigerians, who have Komson in Armah's *The Beautyful Ones Are Not Yet Born* as their Ghanaian counterpart. The peasants in Achebe's novels and Armah's *The Beautyful Ones* are unlike the peasants in Sembene Ousmane's *God's Bits of Wood*, who know their rights and insist on obtaining them despite the obstacles deliberately created by the capitalists to hinder them from wresting power from them and benefiting from the material resources.

In fact, within Umuaro, the traditional society created by Achebe, the dialectical conflicts between Ezeulu and Nwaka, and the traditional Igbo religious worshippers and Christians are caused by struggles to control power in the society. Nwaka argues that Ezeulu is ambitious for power; he acts as the antagonist of Ezeulu while the Christian church strives to invade the religious life of Umuaro.

The society presented by Achebe in *Arrow of God* is governed by a three-tier hierarchical government – each village has her own Council of Elders; Umuaro has her confederation of elders' council and the British has imposed her autocratic government disguised as democracy on the people.

Umuaro is a confederation of Umuachala, Umunneora, Umuagu, Umuezeani, Umuogwugwu and Umuisiuzo. Each village has its own god which is the deity worshipped by the citizens. The confederation has been fostered owing to threats from raiders from Abam. This confederation has also been responsible for its political power structure.

Ezeulu is from Umuachala, the weakest of the confederation. He is the one who wields the greatest and most awesome religious power in the novel. This is in conformity with true federalism. The villagers have come to form one polity in which the goals of each village are subordinated under own purposeful union. According to Enekwe, the balance of power in Umuaro has been attained by giving the spiritual mantle of leadership to Ezeulu, a man from the weakest village (34).

Nwaka's political ambition to curb Ezeulu's power is responsible for his argument against Ezeulu on the piece of land in dispute between Umuaro and Okperi. The aftermath of the war between Okperi and Umuaro is used by Ezeulu to illustrate the proverbial paradigm of power in the novel. The failure of Umuaro is compared with the failure of the best wrestler to win a crucial battle. This is illustrated by the story of the best but arrogant wrestler, who being dissatisfied with is success among men is finally defeated by a little wiry spirit. Power which is not tamed by reason, as this story illustrates, may lose luster and probably fail when needed most. The people come to realize too late that Ulu, their own powerful god, does not fight irrationally; he does not fight a war of blame.

The same proverbial paradigm of power hold true for Sam, the military dictator in *Anthills of the Savannah*, who being unsatisfied with becoming Head of State, attempts to become President-for-life. This same proverbial power paradigm holds the key to the life of Okonkwo in *Things Fall Apart* whose achievements have had communal support but, whose failure is explicable in the light of his refusal to follow public opinion.

Ezeulu's complexity of character is shown in his rejection of Warrant Chieftaincy offered him by Winterbottom. The rejection is froth with ironies of arrest, detention, misunderstanding and the demand for religious and civil privileges. Ezeulu knows that Oduche shall be among those who will wield civil power in the future. Achebe has accomplished this by creating the character of Obi Okonkwo in *No Longer at Ease*.

The society presented by Achebe in *Arrow of God* is well ordered. The manner of speaking in public shows the emphasis placed on obtaining permission or power to address the council or assembly as expressed in the words: Umuaro Kwenu (speaker's animation), Hem (response of assembly). The implicatures show an ordered society, which does not permit the misuse of the power of speech; the society can refuse to consent positively and withhold power from an addresser to the assembly.

Achebe's characters, language, traditional and modern settings of his novels all buttress the nature of power within a synchronic framework of time. According to Dan Izevbaye, Achebe's business in his narratives transcend his concern with artistic form; he is also concerned with the effective power of art (24).

Although Izevbaye says Ikem and Chris are the principal witnesses in *Anthills of the Savannah* against their friend, Sam the Head of State (32), their being witnesses also evoke the atmosphere of a fair hearing in a law court. This is the impression we are given until the relationships between Sam and Ikem, Sam and Chris deteriorate as the plot of the novel progresses towards the end. This style reinforces the degeneration of the character of Sam from an initial state of a gentleman to that of a brute beast without sympathy and a sense of mission. Fair hearing is denied Ikem unlike Obi Okonkwo in *No Longer at Ease*. The circular plot of the latter, at least, shows completion – the sense of mission and the failure of Obi Okonkwo. Sam's life has no holistic mission about it; it is like a parallel line which begins in the deceptive illusion of handing over power to civilians but ends with a hidden motive of retaining power as President-for-life.

Achebe has skillfully placed his characters at various angles from where they interpret Sam's life. He is like a masquerader dancing before his citizenry. Chris discusses the necessity of providing useful programmes and implementing them in Kangan with Sam against steering the wheel of governance aimlessly. Ikem, as Editor of the *National Gazette*, enlightens government on relevant matters of State, but he informs on the Head of State to the world through the British Broadcasting Corporation, when the former becomes despotic. Beatrice is the central voice that dines and dances ticklingly with the Head of State but, warns him and Chris on possible futuristic inauspicious occurrences. She is the prophetic voice unheeded in the novel. Achebe achieves a holistic vision, a pluralistic objective rendering of fictional truth through the shifting voice in *Anthills of the Savannah*.

Echeruo remarks that the style of rendition in *A Man of the People* is that of the first person narrative account. This has the advantage of giving the illumination of intimacy to the events created (160). This style also illuminates the relations between Odili and his love for Edna, Odili and his political ambition. His quest for political power is clouded with revenge but pretentiously hidden under the motive of wrestling power from Nanga the heartless capitalist. We believe his own personal reports on Nanga, Edna and himself and, we are relieved by his inability to win the election. Selfish ambition and malice have never yielded positive results for the progress of man as Sam's life in *Anthills of the Savannah* has been fictionally created to demonstrate.

Almost all aspects of Achebe's style in *A Man of the People*, *Arrow of God*, *No Longer at Ease*, *Things Fall Apart*, and *Anthills of the Savannah* buttress the different modes of power in traditional societies of Umuaro and Umuofia and, the modern societies like Odili's Nigeria and Sam's Kangan. Civilians as well as solders have failed to use the advantages of democracy and militarism for the progress of the masses. Characterization, language and setting have all been used to demonstrate dangerous machiavellian traits in selfish men like Nanga, Koko and Sam, and how well meaning persons like Ikem, Chris and the dismissed Minister of Finance in *A Man of the People* suffer, when they refuse to use the most effective means of combating corruption.

Works Cited

Primary Sources

Achebe, Chinua. *A Man of the People*. London, Heinemann, 1978 ed.

———. *Anthills of the Savannah*. Ibadan: Heinemann, 1987.

———. *Arrow of God*. London, Heinemann, 1974 ed.

———. *No Longer at Ease*. London, Heinemann, 1980 ed.

———. *Things Fall Apart*. London, Heinemann, 1958.

Secondary Sources

Abiola, Irele. "The Conflict in Achebe's Novels," *Introduction to African Literature*. Ed., Ulli Beier. London: Longman Group Limited, 1979.

Bassey, Celestine O. *The Structure of Black Revolution in South Africa*. Owerri: Executive Publishers, 1996.

Echeruo, M.J.C. "Chinua Achebe," *A Celebration of Black and African Writing*. Eds. Bruce King and Kolawole Ogungbesan, Zaria: Ahmadu Bello, 1975.

Enekwe, Onuora. "Chinua Achebe's Novels," *Perspectives on Nigerian Literature 1700 to the Present*. Vol. Two. Ed. Yemi Ogunbiyi. Lagos: Guardian Books Limited, 1988.

Izevbaye, Dan. "History's Eye Witness; Vision and Representation in the Works of Chinua Achebe." *Okike: An African Journal of New Writing*. Ed. Onuora Ossie Enekwe. Nsukka: Okike Magazine, no. 30, November, 1990.

wa Thiong'o, Ngugi. "The Robber and the Robbed." *Homecoming: Essays on African and Caribbean Literature, Culture and Politics*. London, Heinemann, 1972.

Chapter 18

Revisiting Their Visions: The African Writer and the Question of Commitment

Osita Ezeliora

Amongst the basic issues that dominated the criticism of contemporary African literature in the first quarter of its inception (1950–1975), was that of the writer's aesthetic and social commitment. In a way, the issue of the writer's commitment raised some fundamental questions which add to the numerous canons aptly described by Oladele Taiwo (1986:1–114) as "Vital Issues in the Criticism of African Literature". Some of the basic questions raised by scholars at the time greatly brought a renaissance of the ancient concerns about the place of art in man's socio-psychological ambience, the purpose of the writer in society and, in Africa's peculiar situation, whether the artist should be contented with the European bourgeois aesthetic sensibility which confines art to the basic attribute of providing beauty and aesthetic pleasure to the audience, or whether the artist should embrace a more utilitarian position and aspire to make his product speak for, and to his community.

In rudimentary essays, radical writings of cultural nationalism and the general revolutionary ethos that greeted the gradual liberation of African literature from what Chinweizu et al (1980:7–9) describe as Eurocentric criticism, the process of decolonization began, and the criticism of African literature was soon to move from the issue of language and the basis of Africanity in African literature to one of the writer's commitment. Marxist scholars of African literature were to see this issue from the point of view of the writer's ideological commitment, especially his sensitivity to the harrowing and traumatic experiences of the average, the common, the "Wretched of the Earth", in the hands of the new political elite whose greed, corruption and outright nonchalance to the predicaments of the overtly exploited masses needed to be challenged. To this class of scholars, the continent was on the brinks of collapse, and the entire society needed total conscientization. Hence, the literary artist should stop at nothing in creating a literature that must challenge the injustice emanating from such socio-economic imbalance. We revisit, in the brief discussion, the issue of the writer's commitment in African Literature. Our adventure becomes necessary because of the salutary manifestations of this dynamic literary tradition. We hope to "survey" these developments with a view to identifying additional relevant patterns for the reading of our literature.

But then, perhaps, we are confronted with a more difficult question than we ever conjectured. What is commitment? Must commitment only be seen from the point of view of the Marxist ideological stance? Suppose a writer remains eternally fascinated with the aesthetic sensibility of the pursuit of pleasure, and chooses to be committed to this art form, are we justified in our choice of condemning his sense of commitment to Art-for-Art's sake? The encounter with the colonialists had by the end of the 1960s left for Africa a legacy of Modern Literature in European Languages. The nature of the encounters had occasioned the regional characters of what later constitute the bulk of Written African Literature. In spite of the difference in the colonial experiences of the Francophone, Anglophone and even Lusophone African countries, the similarity in their concern for cultural liberation and assertion of black identity is evident, and the difference – only a matter of degree. Except, perhaps, for the North African writings with the predominantly Arabic cultural influences, lamentations and aggressions in varying virtuosities delineate the writings of East and South African Blacks as a result of the Settler's monopolization of fertile land amongst others, and the question of racial supremacy respectively.

The problems elicited by this regional bias in African Literature are legion. For instance, if in the context of the dominant socio-political realities in West Africa at the turn of the colonial encounter, novelists from this region wrote like the South Africans of the Apartheid era, could they have made the impacts we now identify with their earliest fiction? Moreover, could Ezekiel Mphaplele, Alex La Guma, Peter Abrahams, Andre Brink, Athol Fugard or Bessie Head have written in the relaxed atmosphere of Achebe, Soyinka, Armah and Ousmane's West Africa? Can a writer reasonably block his mind and creative intelligence to the socio-political realities of his immediate vicinity? Perhaps, yes, after all Jane Austen, the Romantic novelist, wrote during the Napoleonic wars. Yet, she centered her themes on domestic issues of love and marriage.

For the African literary intelligentsia, however, a response in the affirmative could only come from a Faustian character. Chinua Achebe in "The Novelist as Teacher" (1975:42–45), Wole Soyinka in "Ideology and Social Vision", Kofi Awoonor in "The Beast of the Earth" (1975:353–6), Emmanuel Obiechina and several other scholars and artists attempted to provide answers to the relevant questions of the writer's commitment especially as it affects the African peoples and their culture. To many, commitment is placed antithetically to alienation. Commitment in Literature, here, cannot be isolated from the definition of literature and the role of the artist to his society. We conceive of literature, again, as an artistic portraiture of a people's experience, mores and sensibilities.

Eric Bentley (1968:197) is his very influential book, *The Theatre of Commitment*, puts a finger to an insightful decoding of our discourse. In his words,

> Relative to the general social situation, the literature of commitment is radical.
> It is a literature of protest, not approval, of outrage, not tribute.

If we embrace the logic that literature is human experience in a contrived artistic whole, we may still observe that societal perception of certain beliefs is culture-bound and, consequently, relative. Thus, African regions with their defining features and the many ideological persuasions would, in a way, anticipate functional literature. The medium of the artist thus becomes of tremendous relevance to the intellectual and social development of the people. "In Africa," Emmanuel Obiechina observes, "the artist uses his medium to affirm those values that give fullness to the quality of life as perceived in time and space and, by the same token, to attack those negative values that undermine the sense of fullness of life and the realization of man's full potential". For Soyinka, "The artist (in Africa) has always served as a voice of vision", and the artist in our time should make his work relevant to his immediate society rather than merely chronicling the past for its own sake.

The experience of Africans since the advent of the Europeans is couched in the socio-political life of the people. This is often depicted in Modern African fiction in particular and the rest of our literature in general. The degree of the European influences on African regions determines the relevance of the artist within the region. It is in the timeless statement, "The Duty and Involvement of the African Writers", that Chinua Achebe captures the need for the African writer to demonstrate sufficient sensitivity to the dominant realities of his/her universe.

Listen to him:

> It is clear to me that an African writer who tries to avoid the big social and political issues of contemporary Africa will end up being completely irrelevant like that absurd man in the proverb who leaves his burning house to pursue a rat fleeing from the flames.

In a similar line of argument, Emmanuel Obiechina (1988:2) sums up the issue of commitment in his very interesting essay, "The Writer and His Commitment in Contemporary Nigerian Society", by pointing to a clearer direction for the visionary and sensitive artist. For Obiechina:

> The writer – today has to take his position against the oppression of the people,
> all forms of brutalities and of unwarrantable violence against the masses.

The East African experience is no less fascinating. The issue of the writer's commitment was the stimulating basis for Ali Mazrui's "*The Trial of Christopher Okigbo*", in which the author wonders whether the late Christopher Okigbo was right in his abandonment of the literary art for a more pragmatic commitment to alleviating the injustice and marginalization against his people through the barrel of the gun. A novel of ideas though, Mazrui's "… trial of Okigbo" leaves the perceptive reader surprised as to the wisdom of abandoning literary commitment. Yet, the reader venerates this sense of commitment associated with sacrificing one's life in seeing the psychological and socio-political emancipation of one's community. The Pan-Africanism of Mazrui's idiosyncracies was followed by a more assertive kind of cultural nationalism couched in some writers' desire to liberate the minds of the people through the medium of language. This was the forte of the Marxist revolutionary ethos of Ngugi wa Thiong'o and Micere Mugo. This was carried forward in creative writing by Ngugi wa Thiong'o and Ngugi wa Miiri in *Ngahika Ndenda* which was later translated as *I Will Marry When I Want*. Here, the liberated artist is reminded of the need to be truly African by adopting a language which is purely indigenous to Africa.

In addition, in the prefatory note to their highly captivating *The Trial of Dedan Kimathi*, the duo of Ngugi and Mugo affirm a position of totally decolonizing the African mind from the overwhelming influence of European imperialists and their new African surrogates. For Ngugi and Mugo,

> … All African literature and its writers is on trial. We cannot stand on the fence.
> We are either on the side of the people or on the side of imperialism.

This sense of commitment which seems to echo Okigbo's practical approach to confronting the problems of his society manifests, more than anywhere else, in the issue of commitment in South African literature. Here, we feel more comfortable to speak of the bulk of literature written within the apartheid era. In the introduction to his edited *Apartheid*, Alex La Guma defines the peculiar nature of South Africa when he awakens our curiosity to the knowledge that "the combination of racialism, capitalism and international imperialism has made South Africa a colony of a special type". From another South African artist, Andre Brink, we get an idea of commitment when he says that a literature which does not constantly and instantly confront, affront, offend – and thereby explore and test and challenge – the reader and the world is moribund. Brink's experiences as an artist in the claustrophobic environment of apartheid South Africa is quite instructive. In *Mapmakers: Writing in a State of Siege*, he argues:

> The writer is never really 'at home' in the world. Sometimes his presence is tolerated; sometimes he is patronized; often all the weapons in the arsenal of state are used against him: house arrest, detention, imprisonment, torture, exile, death (192).

For writers who are confronted with these apparent problems of state oppression, the possibility of their ever attaining total commitment to art would be analogous to that proverbial camel in Christian mythology in its process of passing through the needle's eye. But the South African exile has been identified as a fine instance of the committed artist in contemporary African writing. Arguing for this class of writers as the concrete epitome of committedness, Keorapetse Kgotsile (1985:81) says:

> I am talking about people who are forced into exile because they are commit-ted enough to hold certain views, to believe in certain orderings of economic, social, political and cultural relationships on this planet; they are prepared to function past the typewriter, to see to it that those things will be done or can be put into practice....
>
> In a situation of oppression, there is no choice beyond didactic writing; either you are a tool of oppression or an instrument of liberation.

This opinion is shared by writers and critics in Africa. Whether it is in Cairo or Johannesburg, Abidjan or Kampala; Tripoli, Accra, Younde or Nairobi, one impor-tant fact remains transparently clear and indisputable: Many African writers are agreed that the literary artist must not be alienated from his society, – "not even in anger". Achebe, Soyinka, Ousmane, Ngugi, Abrahams, Mphaplele, Farah, Armah amongst others, point to varying degrees of commitment to art and social change in their regions of Africa.

If we present Achebe as a fine representative of the genuine African novelist, we feel the sense of commitment which manifests both in his creative writing, his scholarship and essays of national relevance. The transitions in African literature, particularly the novel, point to Achebe as the teacher who would go the whole hog to remind his fellow Africans that the black man had not lived in a long night of primordial darkness prior to the advent of the white man; a writer who would remind the world that Africans had a sense of political administrative structures, forms of entertainment, marriage institutions, strong religious beliefs, a sense of communal ethos and judicial system in which there were no lawyers and no liars.

It is sad enough that the disintegration of this harmonious system – "with all its imperfections" – was to be catalyzed by the advent of the colonialists and their apostles of evangelism. This was the forte of Achebe's earlier fiction, as we witness in *Things Fall Apart* and *Arrow of God*. It is not without cause, therefore, that Achebe debunks the image painted of pre-colonial Africa by Joseph Conrad, in *Heart of Darkness*, as "a monumental untruth unsaved by ornate turgidity". The writer's awareness that the withdrawal of the white overlords does not necessarily lead to Nigeria's attainment of "political irredentism, social equality and economic emancipation" was the basis for the challenge of the high scale corruption and thuggery in Nigeria's political life. Achebe's involvement of the military in Nigerian politics has been two-dimensional, one coming as the "awaited messiah", while the other points to the painful truth that the "awaited messiah" is, in fact, worse than his predecessors – military and civilian alike. *A Man of the People* and *Anthills of the Savannah* present these aspects of Achebe's interest in re-shaping the sordid socio-political reality of his society.

His new image of the African woman is indicative of the transformations which modernism and Westernism have brought to bear on Africa, as against the essentially patriarchal Africa's pre-colonial past. Yet, before *Anthills of the Savannah*, Achebe had in *The Trouble with Nigeria* lamented the degree of senselessness which seems to rule the Nigerian nation. Irrespective of the fact that the slim volume is non-fictional, Achebe, in his characteristic bluntness, declares that "The trouble with Nigeria is one of leadership". His description of the "insanity" of a unit of the security agencies on the highway points to his aversion to the kind of madness which delineates all leadership in Nigeria.

But Achebe is not alone. Some other African writers have gone beyond the intellectual rationalization in the Ivory Towers to actual involvement in governments. Some have lived in exile; some have left their home countries either in frustration or in protest. Wole Soyinka, Ngugi wa Thiong'o, Ayi Kwei Armah, Kofi Awoonor, William Conton, Ferdinand Oyono, Mongo Beti, Nuruddin Farah, Kole Omotosho, Chukwuemeka Ike, are amongst the many writers whose publications or actions have shown commitment to the course of social change in their societies.

The trends in the novelistic genre and, indeed, the gamut of literary productions by Africans equally point to one form of commitment or the other. Some of the artists we still curiously describe as "new" in spite of the fact that they have spent over two decades in the field are of immense interest here. The poets, Niyi Osundare, Tanure Ojaide, Ezenwa Ohaeto, Ossie Enekwe, Odia Ofeimun, Tunde Fatunde, Femi Fatoba etc, are good examples of artists whose sense of commitment to a better Nigerian nationhood cannot be reasonably impugned. Chukwuemeka Ike's recent novels, especially *Our Children are Coming*, and *The Search* show a sense of commitment which is by every standard, as universal as the novels are genuinely local. Festus Iyayi, whose Marxist bent and irrepressible iconoclasm find parallel in Ngugi wa Thiong'o and Sembene Ousmane, belong to the "new" Nigerian novelists whose ideological commitment is directed at improving the painful reality of the average Nigerian worker and the underprivileged.

From *Violence, The Contract, Heroes* and his latest work, *Awaiting Court Martial*, Iyayi's interest in challenging hypocrisy at the top echelons of power marks him out as one of the most committed of contemporary African novelists.

In recent times, writers who have demonstrated sufficient sensitivity to gender discourses have channeled the struggle for social equality, psychological and economic emancipation of the citizenry to the domestic front. Unfortunately the lack of coherence in sensibility and nomenclature, and especially the pejorative image which women's struggles have generated in some parts of the world have left some African women writers so confused that even those who proclaim to be core feminists appear not to have demonstrated sufficient understanding of the fundamental tenets of the feminist cause. Women, at the global level, have – some genuine, some propagandistic – alleged that they are marginalized in practically every aspect of human endeavor. They point to the phallocentric male chauvinist as the cause of their problems because he employs every paraphernalia at his disposal, including religion and culture to subjugate the woman to nothingness.

Hence women, they argue, lack identity and live in the shadows of men. Of the numerous women writers of African descent, Flora Nwapa, Buchi Emecheta, Bessie Head, Mariama Ba, Aminata Sow Fall, Efua Sutherland, Ama Ata Aidoo, Catherine Acholonu, Molara Ogundipe-Leslie, Mabel Segun, Grace Ogot, Zainab Alkali, Ifeoma Okoye, Tess Onwueme, Theodora Akachi Ezeigbo, amongst others, have agitated for the proper entrenchment of the female figure in issues affecting their homes and societies.

While Catherine Acholonu's study, *Motherism: An Afrocentric Alternative to Feminism* (1995) has helped in the elucidation of that off-shoot of Marxism which many have wrongly come to identify with lesbianism, extreme stubbornness and conjugal irresponsibility in creative writing, Buchi Emecheta's exploration of pathos and the consistency of her interest in the womanist cause in her novels mark her out as the most vibrant, indeed, the leading African female artist. The Nigerian female writer has particularly been visible in this quest for the liberation of women. Some of the writers have gone into a cultural poetics which allows them the opportunity of recreating history and reconstructing the image of the noble African woman in the pre-colonial days. In a way, they respond to the earlier fictional works of Achebe, Soyinka, Ekwensi, Aluko and other first generation African novelists. Adopting a theory of New Historicism, these women artists claim that even in the midst of oppression, the African woman had in pre-colonial times contributed immensely towards community development. We observe a shift in their tone from mere lamentation to some level of aggression, perhaps signifying and are of empowerment.

Many of these writers have not made significant progress in the novel genre. But some are simply marvelous in the genre of the short story. Akachi Adimora-Ezeigbo's *Echoes in the Mind* with such surrealistic stories as "The Blind Man of Ekwulu", "The Verdict" and "Agaracha Must Come Home" is easily one of the best short story collections I have read in recent times. Be these as they may, these women writers have shown a willingness and sense of commitment towards improving the general human condition. In this regard, matters concerning the home front cannot be considered irrelevant in the plethora of problems facing mankind in contemporary society.

It is probably because of the genuine tears of artists like Emecheta, Nawal El-Sadaawi, Bessie Head and other women writers that the Nigerian male artists have begun to devote both serious scholarship and creative writing on the contribution of women to national development. Again, Achebe's *Anthills of the Savannah*, Ola Rotimi's *Our Husband Has Gone Mad Again*, Rotimi Johnson's *The Court of the Queen*, J.P. Clark's *The Wives' Revolt* and Timothy Jide-Asobele's *Ogu-Umunwanyi: Aba Women Riots*, are all relevant inputs to this development. In a way, it would appear, therefore, that the result of the African women writer's commitment to matters concerning her, is beginning to manifest.

The entry of Ben Okri into the African literary scene is yet to be fully acknowledged, in spite of his well-deserved Booker-laurel. Okri's novelistic form which has come to be seen as marvelous or magic realism is a surrealistic pattern which combines the socially realistic with the outrightly fantastical. Okri, to a substantial extent, re-echoes Amos Tutuola's fabulous tales and the Latin American Nobel Laureate, Garcia Marquez's fictional art. Except, perhaps, for his first work, *Flowers and Shadows*, most of Okri's later writings are attuned to this form. It becomes difficult to accuse a writer who explores the mythopoeic assumptions of his nativity of lacking in social commitment when one observes that beyond the profound Africanness of his setting and subject-matter, the artist mildly alerts the audience of the semblance of the mirage-political freedom of his country to the stubborn reincarnating child whose physical aura is shrouded in the mystery of death and rebirth. This is the preoccupation of much of Okri's writings. *Landscapes Within*, *The Famished Road*, *Stars of the New Curfew*, even *Flowers and Shadows* and his later writings all feature the metaphysical reality of death and dying, – but not as a finality of man's experience. To what, then, must the writer be specifically committed?

If we proceed to post-independence South African fiction, we are confronted with the salutary trend which jettisons the former hysterical voices of the apartheid era. Much of the new works present a mood and atmosphere which is quite relaxed. The problem of disillusionment which manifested in the literature of post-independence West African countries, for instance, is yet to surface here. Writers are still satisfied with the accomplishments of the new leadership, and the citizenry appear to open up fresher relationships which are inter-racial and globally acceptable. It is probably for this reason that most of the writers try to write nostalgically about their childhood experiences, the nightmare of writing within the old censorial system and, at the same time, celebrating their new-found freedom. Andre Brink's *On the Contrary, Imaginings of Sand, Devil's Valley*, Nadine Gordimer's *House Gun*, J.M. Coetzee's *Boyhood*, Jo-Anne Richard's *The Innocence of Roast Chicken* or Pamela Jooste's *Dance With a Poor Man's Daughter* are all recent South African fiction which point to the movement away from the literature of protest which had hitherto defined the basis of commitment of the South African writer.

In view of the experimental slant of some of the emergent writers, the attainment of political liberty by the hitherto protesting black writers in some racially prejudiced African countries, the new wave of militarism, ethnic wars, national and international conflicts that pervade most independent African countries, what should be the new basis of the writer's commitment? In addition, the deliberate impoverishment of the academia in some African countries has led to an exodus of most of the writers to the more appreciative countries in Europe, Asia, America and Canada. What claims would such writers make to commitment to social justice in Africa when they are almost completely immuned to the traumas of the ordinary citizens? In any case, what genuine claims to aesthetic responsibility would some of the writers make with their over-leanings on politics in their supposedly imaginative works? We return to the old argument of what constitutes pure aesthetics as against the political pamphlets and propaganda slogans that are often flown about as committed works of literature, and which has led Solomon Iyasere (1982:203) to aptly argue that:

> To programme writers, and to legislate for them what view they should champion is to encourage a rigid stereotyped mode of perception and sameness in articulation – culminating in the tyranny of uniformity and the consequent castration of the literature.

Cosmos Pieterse at the Texas symposium on Contemporary South African Literature, – the proceedings that later appeared as Contemporary Black South African Literature, edited by Bernth Lindfors, – had equally tried to point at the danger of combining politics and literature. If the artist must avoid a sheer dereliction of his responsibility, he necessarily must be seen as an artist whose interest in politics must not be the overriding concern of his art. Using the premise of drama, he argues (1985:135):

> Theatre is theater and politics is politics. Theatre should be seen and be discussed as theatre and not a politics. Unless this is done there will always be confusion as to what is theatre and what relevance it plays.

African literature has grown substantially. Five decades in the life of any entity is indicative of longevity, although it could still be considered very short in historical terms. Africa in the twenty-first century has to concretely identify the canons for the criticism of its literature since the experimental writings of the twentieth century *fin-de-siecle* appear to be immuned from the earlier frameworks of the first quarter of our writings and criticism. Theo Vincent's categorization of these standards in his brilliant study, "Africanity in Modern African Literature" as well as Fredrick Akporobaro's equally percipient structuralist approach in "African Identity and the Issue of Form and Originality in the African Novel" would remain enduring in the study of African literature. Beyond the simple paraphrase of the thematic preoccupations of the given work, both scholars profoundly examined the issue of what the African novelist has done with the foreign language and what new form and freshness such a writer has achieved, the rhythm of plot movement and character delineation and the spatio-temporal settings of the work.

In line with the positions of these foremost scholars, we re-assert, here, that the issue of identity in terms of African aesthetic sensibilities and what the African literary artist has done with it; the germane issue of aesthetic responsiveness with respect to basic humanistic ideals of universal concern, amongst others, be addressed with untrammeled eloquence. To these must be added the stream-lined new developments of the womanist readings, mythopoeic assumptions and general readings that must subsume the diverse African presence from the metaphysical, the fantastical and quotidian realities.

The writer's commitment, therefore, must not be seen from the point of view of the dominant politicization of a given literary text. Instead, it should be read in terms of a sustained, ratiocinative, aesthetic responsiveness in the diverse intellectual and imaginative creations of the artist. Whatever the situation, and for whatever ideological persuasion to which a writer is inclined, priority attention must not only be given to satisfying his professional conscience, but must also be done with a view to improving the standard of humanity in general.

Thus, a committed artist is not necessarily a sycophant who sings the song the people would like to hear, but a quintessence of truth who is aware of his responsibility as a guardian and promoter of a progressive morality. A committed artist is not the coward who preaches the dictates of the oppressors, or scared of incurring the wrath of the exploiter. The committed artist combats all forms of oppression and exploitation and, in the process, suggests a solution to societal predicaments.

It is in this respect that commitment to art and social justice shall remain a central canon upon which African literature would be read in the twenty-first century.

Works Cited

Achebe, Chinua. *Morning Yet on Creation Day; Essays*. London: Heinemann, 1975.

Achebe, Chinua. *Hopes and Impediments: Selected Essays*. London: Heinemann, 1983.

Achebe, Chinua. *The Trouble with Nigeria*. Enugu: Fourth Dimension, 1983.

Acholonu, C.O. *Motherism: An Afro-centric Alternative to Feminism*. Owerri: Afa Publications, 1995.

Akporobaro, F.B.O. "African Identity and the Issue of Form and Originality in the African Novel." *Lagos Review of English Studies*. Vol. VIII, 1986.

Awoonor, Kofi. *The Breast of the Earth: A Survey of the History, Culture and Literature of African South of the Sahara*. New York: NOK Publishers, 1975.

Bentley, Eric. *The Theater of Commitment*. London: Matheun & Co., 1968.

Brink, Andre. *Mapmakers: Writing In a State of Seige*. London: Faber & Faber, 1983.

Chinweizu, et al. *Toward the Decolonization of African Literature*. Enugu: Fourth Dimension, 1980.

Iyasere, Solomon. "A Review". *African Literature Today* 12. Ed. Eldred Durosimi Jones. London: Heinemann, 1982.

Kgosile, Keorapetse. "Literature and Commitment in South Africa." *Contemporary Black South African Literature: A Symposium*. Ed. Bernth Lindfors. Washington D.C. Three Continent Press, 1985.

La Guma, Alex (ed) *Apartheid: A Collection of Essays on South Africa by South Africans*. International Publishers, 1971.

Ngugu & Mugo. "Preface" *The Trial of Dedan Kimathi*. London: Heinemann, 1976.

Obiechina, Emmanuel. "The Writer and His Commitment in Contemporary Nigerian Society." *Okike* 27/28, 1988.

Pieterse, Cosmos. "On South African Theater", *Contemporary Black South African Literature: A Symposium*.

Taiwo, Oladele. *Social Experience in African Literature*. Enugu: Fourth Dimension, 1986.

Vincent, Theo. "Africanity in Modern African Literature." *The Arts and Civilization of Black & African Peoples, Vol. 3: Black Civilization and Literature*. Eds. Okpaku, J.O. Opubor, A.E. & Oloruntimehim, B.O. Lagos: CBAAC, 1986.

Part Four

Visions of History

Chapter 19

The Spirit of History in Chinua Achebe's Trilogy

Okey Ndibe

Each generation must out of relative obscurity discover its mission, fulfill it, or betray it.
– Franz Fanon, *The Wretched of the Earth*

The new school shares at the same time the characteristics of cannon and of magnet. From the cannon it draws its efficacy as an arm of combat. Better than the cannon, it makes conquest permanent. The cannon compels the body, the school bewitches the soul.
– Cheikh Hamidou Kane, *Ambiguous Adventure*

Take up the white man's burden –
Send forth the best ye breed –
Go bind your sons to exile
To serve your captive's need.
To wait in heavy harness,
On fluttered folk and wild –
Your new caught, sullen peoples,
Half-devil and half-child …
– Rudyard Kipling's *"The White Man's Burden"*

Born in November, 1930, Chinua Achebe's birth was a mere generation and a half removed from the most profound ferment in the history of his Igbo people. Europe's unbridled scramble for Africa, consecrated by the Berlin Conference of 1884, had begun in earnest in the last decade of the 19th century, and the consolidation of this imperialist intrusion continued well into the first decade of the 20th century. Of course Africa had had a relationship with Europe spanning several centuries and conducted sometimes on the basis of legitimate and mutually beneficial interests but often on terms that imperiled the human and material resources of Africa. Even so, the Berlin Conference and the record of imperial greed it unleashed upon Africa represented a new calamitous phase in the uneasy circuit of Euro-African intercourse. Kofi Awoonor, a Ghanaian Poet, novelist and critic, has stated that prior to the Conference:

> the European political map of Africa was a cartographic confusion of indeterminate settlements concentrated in forts, trading posts, and factories (12).

But following the Conference, Awoonor writes in his brilliant multi-disciplinary book, *The Breast of the Earth*:

> the features of colonialism became more clearly defined in terms of European imperialism and economics all over the globe. What had been a sporadic historical phenomenon became systematic and well defined by the end of the nineteenth century with the implementation of the conclusions of the Berlin Conference in 1884 (150).

The path to Europe's expansionist adventure was paved by missionaries who proselytized Africans for the Christian God and served as the advance party for the inevitable military machinery that followed. The penetration by the Christian church – described by Achebe in an essay as "the handmaiden of Empire" – and, later, colonialism into the African heartland was not without resistance, which was often severe, bloody and drawn out. It was into this contentious situation that Achebe was born. In a rare autobiographical essay titled "Named for Victoria, Queen of England," Achebe underlines the sharp divisions of his childhood world:

> The line between Christian and non-Christian was much more definite in my village forty years ago than it is today. When I was growing up I remember we tended to look down on the others. We were called in our language "the people of the church" or "the association of God." The others we called, with the conceit appropriate to followers of the true religion, the heathen or even "the people of nothing" (65).

But as sharply Manichean as this picture seems, Achebe's immensely complex sensibility was nevertheless able to recognize the allure and dignity of the traditional experience that Christianity so mindlessly maligned. With a courage remarkable for a fledging Christian, Achebe, then ten, often took his younger sister to "[partake] of heathen festival meals. I never found their rice and stew to have the flavor of idolatry." Rather than experience visceral revulsion at the ways of those heathens, Achebe felt, he informs us, "a fascination for the ritual and the life on the other arm of the crossroads" (68).

This is as clear a statement of a writer's early serendipitous awareness as we are likely to find. The prescience of this awareness in Achebe was only to grow and mature with age, experience and education, finally equipping him with the intellectual resources – a deep mastery of the dignity and beauty of Africa's pre-colonial past; an unsurpassed grasp of the accents with which his ancestors celebrated their existence; a firm grounding in the traditional techniques and immemorial idioms of storytelling – necessary to interrogate his history, to plumb the ironic interstices of his past. Achebe's five novels, several short stories and numerous essays, taken together, amount to a sustained exploration of the meaning of this history, a deployment, in other words, of his creative intelligence in the task of probing the rich, sometimes debilitating, sometimes enriching, paradoxes that have marked Africa's history since the epochal event of Europe's intrusion. Achebe's fascination for the experience that lay "on the other arm of the crossroads" points us to the early, perhaps earliest, source of what, years later, would inform the emergence of a remarkable creative talent eager and able to contest European ethnocentric malice against Africa.

In order to fully grasp the nature of Achebe's achievement, we must, it seems clear, draw attention to the stature of his challenge. An important facet of the experience of people in Achebe's generation was the monopoly enjoyed by a certain convention of African scholarship – if the term scholarship may be perorated by a phenomenon of such singular deformity, enormity and distortion. In Achebe's formative years, European ethnocentrism still spoke its opinions and couched its literature of Africa in the boldest, most uncouth and meretricious accents – emboldened in its haughty claims of the superiority of European civilization and of Africa's spiritual wretchedness, no doubt, by the absence of a viable countervailing outlook. What kind of statement was Europe making about Africa in the 19th century and even before?

Hegel, one of the most notorious deniers of African humanity and history, excluded Africa from any serious consideration in his book, *The Philosophy of History*, quoted by Ngugi in "The Writer and His Past." For Hegel, Africa was a space for ravenous snakes and beasts, and the African could only be improved – to the lower ranks of humanity – by undergoing European enslavement. In a cartographic sleight of hand, Hegel even contrived to excise Egypt out of Africa and argued that North Africa was part of Europe. Then the *coup de grace*:

> Africa proper, as far as history goes back, has remained for all purposes of connection with the rest of the world – shut up; it is the Gold-Land compressed within itself – the land of childhood, which lying beyond the days of self-conscious history, is enveloped in the dark mantle of the night.
>
> The negro as already observed exhibits the natural man in his completely wild and untamed state ...
>
> At this point we leave Africa never to mention it again. For it is no historical part of the world; it has no movement to exhibit. Historical movement in it – that is in its northern part – belongs to the Asiatic or European world ...

> What we understand by Africa, is the unhistorical underdeveloped spirit,
> still involved in the condition of nature … (42).

We have quoted Hegel at such considerable length not, as might be suspected, in order to offer a fringe, laughable perception of Africa but because his words are quite representative of a genre that was prevalent at one time in Europe's view of Africa. This attitude, exemplified in Hegelian reductionism, undermined the humanity of Africans and saw the continent that was man's first home and the center of the first important civilization as, in Achebe's words, "a place of negations at once remote and vaguely familiar, in comparison with which Europe's own state of spiritual grace will be manifest" (*Homecoming* 41–42).

This tableau of Africa has been hawked by European social philosophers, historians, novelists, poets, missionaries, colonial officers, diarists and journalists, all of them refining, according to their own peculiar lights and individual talent, the notion of darkness, recycling the idea of Africa's historylessness. Joseph Conrad, in his much celebrated novel, *Heart of Darkness*, chose the motif of Africa's inscrutable darkness for a novel conceived to lay bare the hypocrisy, profit motive and moral equivocations that fuel the imperial undertaking. Close on Conrad's heels was Joyce Cary, a British colonial officer in Northern Nigeria, who alchemized his superficial experience and racist notions into fodder for his several novels of Africa. *Mister Johnson*, the most widely known of these, and the most notoriously offensive, was hailed by an American critic, Charles R. Larson, as "one of the most highly original and fully realized characters in the entire realm of African fiction" which made other African novels "seem shallow and underdeveloped" (cited by Thelwell 11). But Achebe and other critics saw, instead, a most jaundiced and caricaturist picture. Michael Thelwell, a Jamaican novelist, essayist and critic, has offered a sharply different reading of the novel's main character:

> Poorly educated, deracinated, thoroughly pathetic and alienated, Mr. Johnson
> is a very shallowly drawn figure of paternalistic parody, however well meant. I
> recently reread Mr. Johnson. The portrait is even more reductive and offensively
> stereotypic than I had remembered (11).

The South African critic, Eskia Mphaphlele, was even less patient with Cary's book:

> I flung away Mr. Johnson with exasperation when I tried to read it for the first
> time in South Africa. I had seen too many journalistic caricatures of black people
> and 'bongo-bongo' cartoons showing Africans with filed teeth and bones stuck
> in their hair – too many for me to find amusement in Johnson's behavior, always
> on the verge of farce (161).

Kofi Awoonor has also described Cary's Johnson as an "African *deracine*, the product of colonial illogicality, and a buffoon ... a rebel for whom no code of honor exists. And blissfully, his innocent rebellion leads him to the colonial gallows (252).

Cary did not limit his defamation of the African character to the subjective realm of the novel; in a prefatory note to *The African Witch*, another of his so-called African novels, whose theme is conflicting religious beliefs, Cary contends:

> Basic obsessions, which in Europe hide themselves under all sorts of decorous scientific or theological or political uniforms, are there seen naked in bold and dramatic action (310).

Elsewhere in the same preface, Cary, seeking both to justify his practice and to pre-scribe a formulaic schema for those who might follow his example, suggests that:

> The African setting is dramatic, (it) demands a certain kind of story, a certain violence and coarseness of detail, almost a fabulous treatment, to keep it in its place (311).

Another colonial novelist, John Buchan, kin to Cary in more than one sense, invites a character in his novel, *Prester John*, to trot out the following epiphany:

> That is the difference between white and black, the gift of responsibility, the power of being in a little way a king, and so long as we know and practice it we will rule not in Africa alone but wherever there are dark men who live only for their bellies (202).

Cary, Conrad and Buchan belonged in the tradition of novelists for whom the African character is hopelessly mute, gleefully innocent and boundlessly exotic. It is a tradition exemplified in Daniel Defoe's *Robinson Crusoe*. But even Defoe and these other European versifiers of African experiences had Shakespeare as their ultimate narrative ancestor and provenance. In *The Tempest*, Shakespeare had created a model of the prototypical colonial subject, Caliban, who is invested with all the unflattering attributes that Shakespeare's later-day students found so irresistible. Caliban goes from being sovereign in his land to being a bumbling fool, incapable of intelligent speech or even utterance. Prospero, the imperial stranger on the island, slowly recreates Caliban in a new image, appropriates his land, and turns him into a slave. When Caliban objects to this treachery, Prospero responds in a blistering rage:

> *Thou most lying slave,*
> *Whom stripes may move, not kindness! I have used thee*
> *(Filth as thou art) with humane care; and lodged thee*
> *In mine own cell till thou didst seek to violate*
> *The honor of my child ...*
> *I pitied thee,*
> *Took pains to make thee speak, taught thee each hour*

One thing or other: when thou didst not, savage,
Know thine own meaning, but wouldst gabble like
A thing most brutish, I endow'd thy purposes
With words that made them known: but thy vile race,
Though thou didst learn, had that in't which good natures
Could not abide to be with; therefore was thou
Deservedly confined into this rock, who hadst
Deserved more than prison (1173).

Caliban's disinheritance presages by many years the experience of Africa under colonial subjugation. Ngugi wa Thiong'o, the Kenyan novelist and playwright, has rightly noted in his first collection of essays, *Homecoming*, that "In the story of Prospero and Caliban, Shakespeare had dramatized the practice and psychology of colonization years before it became a global phenomenon (7). Ngugi goes on to underline the parallels between the imaginatively fabricated world of *The Tempest* and Africa's lived experience. "Like Prospero," he states,

> the European colonizer instinctively knew and feared the threat posed by men with confidence in their own past and heritage. Why else should he devote his military might, his religious fervor, and his intellectual energy to denying that the African had true gods, had a culture, had a significant past? (9).

Since Shakespeare, this deeply supine arrogance – the idea that the native lacked the gift of language until the beneficence of the colonizer gave him one, that he was a congential rogue and an unredeemed naif unworthy of nature's providence – this arrogance has appeared again and again in the life and literature of Europe. In his slim but extremely important polemical work entitled *Discourse on Colonialism*, the Martinican poet, Aime Cesaire, offers a quick roll call of Europe's more infamous treatises, opinions and (at one time) certitudes. There is, for example, the French idealist philosopher, Renan, who argued that "The regeneration of the inferior or degenerate races by the superior races is part of the providential order of things for humanity (16). Or M. Albert Sarraut, a former French governor-general of Indochina, who, in a language and ideological outlook uncannily echoing Prospero's, told an audience of students that it was wrong to object to colonialism on the grounds of "an alleged right to possess the land one occupies, and some sort of right to remain in fierce isolation, which would leave unutilized resources to lie forever idle in the hands of incompetents" (Quoted by Cesaire 17). Or Reverend Barde who, summoning God's will to his side, pronounced that if the resources of the world "remained divided up indefinitely, as they would be without colonization, they would answer neither the purposes of God nor the just demands of the human collectivity (In Cesaire 17). Or, to indulge another clergy, a Reverend Muller: "Humanity must not, cannot allow the incompetence, negligence, and laziness of the uncivilized peoples to leave indefinitely the wealth which God has confided to them, charging them to make it serve the good of all" (Quoted by Cesaire 17).

The late art historian Robert M. Wren, in his book, *Achebe's World: The Historical and Cultural Context of the Novels*, has excavated a prelate whose views were, speaking literally, nearer to Achebe's home. Wren states that G.T. Basden, a missionary who was Achebe's father's "one-time teacher, supervisor, and friend" and "whom Ogidi honored with a carved ivory tusk" had quite an expansive view on the African's metaphysics. A free sample:

> ... the black man himself does not know his own mind. He does the most extraordinary things, and cannot explain why he does them.

Or:

> [The black man] is not controlled by logic: he is the victim of circumstance, and his policy is very largely one of drift.

Or, finally:

> A further result, and one which must always be borne in mind by the foreign inquirer into primitive customs, is that the ideas of the native are indefinite. He has no fixed thought (18–19).

"Alas!" we exclaim before turning from priests, those bewitchers of the soul, to paraphrase Cheikh Hamidou Kane, to survey the exploits and pronouncements of military men – whose words are even more coarse, inelegant, and brutally to the point. First, the glee of Saint-Arnaud who declaimed: "We lay waste, we burn, we plunder, we destroy the houses and the trees" (In Cesaire 18). Or Marshall Bugeaud: "We must have a great invasion of Africa, like the invasions of the Franks and the Goths" (In Cesaire 18). There is, of course, the barbarous record of General Gerard in his capture of Ambike, an Algerian village:

> The native riflemen had orders to kill only the men, but no one restrained them; intoxicated by the smell of blood, they spared not one woman, not one child ... At the end of the afternoon, the heat caused a light mist to arise: it was the blood of the five thousand victims, the ghost of the city, evaporating in the setting sun (Quoted in Cesaire 19).

On a scale of bestiality, did Colonel de Montagnac, "one of the conquerors of Algeria," fare as well as General Gerard? Said the colonel:

> In order to banish the thoughts that sometimes besiege me, I have some heads cut off, not the heads of artichokes but the heads of men (In Cesaire 18).

This genocide and unprovoked savagery were possible, in large part, because the whole machinery of Western philosophy had systematically underwritten, indeed sanctioned, the subtraction of Africa from the sum of humanity. The idea of Africans as *homo erectus*, as aberrants in the evolutionary chain, was widespread and widely held years before Europe set sail for Africa. Even the Christian church, which now sanctimoniously advertises itself as the upholder of the sacredness and sanctity of all life, was once embroiled in the question, as Achebe notes in his seminal essay, "African Literature as Celebration": "Did the Black man have a soul?" (53). It is worth quoting the words of M. Jules Romains, one of France's intellectual luminaries, as a way both of summing up the vulgarity of European ethnocentrism and underlining its appeal both to raw emotions and a neo-rationalist ethos. Monsieur Romains writes:

> I once had opposite me a row of some twenty pure blacks ... I will not even censure our Negroes and Negresses for chewing gum. I will only note ... that this movement has the effect of emphasizing the jaws, and that the associations which come to mind evoke the equatorial forest rather than the procession of the Panathenaea ... The black race has not yet produced, will never produce, an Einstein, a Stravinsky, a Gershwin (In Cesaire 30).

The reason one has recalled such an extensive menu of European racist attitudes to Africa – and other parts of the non-European world – is in order to bring to bold relief the monumental disorder that Achebe, as story creator and intellectual, has had to wrestle against. Besides, the background enables us to grasp the essentially historical nature of the burden Achebe was invited to bear. In a sense, that burden consisted of a return to the much maligned world of the heathen which had held such fascination for his childhood eyes, to examine its contours with brave but balanced eyes, finally emerging to bear witness that things were not as the white man had told it.

But if history was the tool with which the Africans erasure as a dignified human being was effected, if history was, therefore, central to Achebe's restorative mandate, the question is: What kind of history? Would Achebe attempt to engage the distorters and devaluers of his heritage on their own terms – a clearly ruinous and futile option? The European had, after all, forged a certain aesthetic of history – as a series of recorded "heroic" events, acts or movements bounded by time – and foisted this arbitrary notion on the rest of the world as a catechumenical verity. History was then reductively seen as epochal, and the job of historians was to document and compose panegyrics to the martial exploits of exemplary European individuals and their armies. What was not documented in a book was, by that fact, unhistorical – outside the purview of history. This Hegelian concept has continued to impress the contemporary imagination of Europe – so that Sir Hugh Trevor-Roper, a distinguished historian at Oxford, could say as recently as 1963 (and without any self-irony) that pre-colonial African history was a cipher, consisting entirely of darkness, which could not be a legitimate subject of history

(871). In this judgement, he fared worse than Edward Gibbon who grudgingly conceded some burst of history in Ethiopia which, said Gibbon, had by the seventh century slipped back to somnolent stillness, "forgetful of history by whom she was forgot" (Cited by Achebe, "Literature as Celebration" 53).

Derek Walcott, an award-winning poet from St. Lucia, has suggested an alternative frame for the apprehension of history. He contends that the:

> bravest, most hermetic writers ... can reject the pragmatic rational idea of history as time for the aboriginal concept of history as fable and myth (In Jeyifo ix).

Improving on this formulation – and extending it – Achebe, in an essay titled "Continuity and Change in Nigerian Education," rebuked the Roperian idea of history as "a catalogue of events and opinions printed in books." In opposition to this vision, Achebe proffers that:

> there is also a history which a people – every people – derive from wrestling with their own peculiar fate, and engrave in their hearts and memory – in their culture (4).

Seeking to elaborate on this enlarged spirit of history, Achebe dwells on a buttressing aspect of traditional communication and epistemology:

> When our fathers seemingly broke the flow of their discourse to interject a proverb they were linking the present with the past, the problem of now to the wisdom of all time. In that way they are saying to you: Don't despair or Don't rejoice (or whatever was appropriate), because whatever you are seeing now is not only not new; it has happened often enough in the past for your ancestors to sum up the constellation of its infinite variations in the unified and elegant form of its essence and meaning ("Continuity and Change ..." 4).

Which is Achebe's elegant way of stating that something as effortlessly available to the Igbo as the proverb, described by Achebe in his first novel, *Things Fall Apart*, as "the palm oil with which words are eaten" (7) is indeed a channel of history, a rather unprepossessing repository of historical consciousness. At any rate, Achebe – prepared by exposure to Western education for a total alienation from the experience of his heritage or, at best, a career as one of those freak creatures who are neither fully European nor at peace with their tradition – managed the miracle of emerging with a sensibility deeply steeped in the lore and history of his ancestors. As he told Awoonor in an interview in the *Breast of the Earth*, his first novel was conceived with the desire "to set the score right about my ancestors" (252). This inspiration is more religiously rendered in his essay, "Named for Victoria, Queen of England." In it Achebe testifies that *Things Fall Apart*:

> was an act of atonement with my past, the ritual return and homage of a prodigal son (70).

Achebe soon became, as a novelist and essayist, both a product and creator of history. He graduated from University College, Ibadan, in South-Western Nigeria almost a decade after the end of the Second World War, a cataclysmic even that, apart from taking thousands of African lives, catalyzed a new nationalist fervor in the colonized countries of Africa. The demand for independence and the struggle for liberation from the yoke of colonial humiliation meant that more and more Africans were calling to question the racist superstructure upon which imperialism rested. In the introduction to *Critical Perspectives on Chinua Achebe*, their encyclopedic collection of Achebe scholarship, the editors, C.L. Innes and Bernth Lindfors, draw attention to the larger political context that shaped Achebe's creative flowering:

> Chinua Achebe grew up at a time when Africans were not only opposing Euro-pean rule through political action, but also beginning to question with increasing vigor and clarity the cultural assumptions used to justify that rule (3).

In *African Writers Talking: A Collection of Radio Interviews* edited by Cosmo Pieterse and Dennis Duerden, Achebe named Joyce Cary's *Mister Johnson* as an immediate impetus in his decision to write:

> I know around '51, '52, I was quite certain that I was going to try my hand at writing, and one of the things that set me thinking was Joyce Cary's novel, set in Nigeria, *Mister Johnson*, which was praised so much, and it was clear to me that it was a most superficial picture of – not only the country – but even of the Nigerian character, and so I thought if this was famous, then perhaps someone ought to try and look at this from the inside (4).

He was well equipped. At Ibadan he had taken classes in Literature, History and Religion, a quite fortuitous conjunction as it turned out, since some of the invidi-ous rationale for the dehumanization of Africans had been developed within that disciplinary triad. But there was also a major problem. When Achebe set himself the task of fictionalizing the epic confrontation between Africa and Europe, and the dramatic impact of that encounter on Africa, no African writer had labored in that particular vineyard. Even so, he went ahead and succeeded so inimitably that of all who have followed in his wake none has been able to achieve a portraiture nearly as warm or to emerge with any insights remotely approaching the level of his. From the moment he began to write he exhibited a subtle sense of the rhythm of history; whether it be in his choice of theme, slant of statement, or the delectable balance which he brings to the evocation of his world, Achebe has been a true pioneer in the formulation of an African poetics.

Things Fall Apart which, approaching the fifth decade of its publication, re-mains the best selling African novel, was described by *Times Literary Supplement* in 1965 as:

probably as big a factor in the formation of a young West African's picture of his past, and of his relation to it, as any of the still rather distorted teachings of the pulpit and the primary school (791).

This is as concrete an independent verification of Achebe's success in his self-set task as is possible. For Achebe himself did state early in his career, in a much quoted essay titled "The Role of the Writer in a New Nation," his desire to demonstrate in his fiction and fact:

> ... that the African peoples did not hear of culture for the first time from Europeans; that their societies were not mindless but frequently had a philosophy of great depth and value and beauty, that they had poetry and, above all, they had dignity. It is this dignity that many African peoples all but lost in the colonial period, and it is this that they must now regain ... The writer's duty is to help them regain it by showing them in human terms what happened to them, what they lost (8).

It is a duty best approached, as Achebe's example has shown, with the transformative tools of creative fiction rather than with a traditional historian's *modus operandi* consisting of cataloguing, documentation, a faithfulness to sequentiality – all informed by the need to achieve an ultimately illusory posture of detachment and objectivity. In a brilliant essay, "The Truth of Fiction," Achebe offers a quick but defining hint of his confidence in the claims of literature over history:

> ... human societies have always attempted to sustain their cultural values by carefully preserved oral or written literatures which provide for them and their posterity a short cut now and again to the benefits of actual experience. What about history, you might ask, does it not vouchsafe the same enlightenment? The lessons of history are important, of course. But think how many aeons of history will be needed to distil the wisdom of Shakespeare's *King Lear* (145–146).

But even as Achebe set out to write, he was rendering a story forged by and deeply impregnated with history; in other words, he was sifting a historical experience through the crucible of fiction. Many fellow writers and critics have applauded the uncommon flair with which he has used the form of the novel (and, to a much lesser degree, the short story and poetry) to mediate history. Elizabeth Isichei, a historian and author of *A History of the Igbo People*, some of which dwells on themes explored in Achebe's novels, has written that Achebe's "historical novels are notable, not only for their literary qualities, but for their historical accuracy and perception" (253). In his Catholic book of criticism, *Tasks and Masks: Themes and Styles of African Literature*, the South African writer, Lewis Nkosi, suggests that "Achebe is more of a 'realist' in his treatment of African history than some rigorously trained historians" (39). Margaret Laurence, a Canadian critic, though writing specifically of *Arrow of God*, makes a point whose validity extends to the totality of Achebe's *oeuvre*:

> Achebe, in *Arrow of God* follows the course of history with accuracy, and at the same time manages to confirm that fiction is a great deal more true than fact (113).

But however unanimous the acclaim for Achebe's feat in a historical task, it would be wrong to regard him as a historical novelist in the ordinary sense of the term – that is as one who merely chronicles real events or traces faithfully from the demonstrably exact phenomena of lived history. He has instead sought to adopt the large frame of historical experience while imaginatively inventing the events which lend tension and dramatic force to the larger canvas. In 1987, following the publication of *Anthills of the Savannah*, Achebe was asked by a reporter if he conceived his novels in a historical order; in other words, if he had a schema moving from the past into the present. His answer on that occasion is instructive and should be quoted in full. "The correct answer," said Achebe:

> would be no, because what it implies is that when I was writing *Things Fall Apart* I already had the others in mind. The only thing I had in mind was the next two generations of Okonkwo, his son and his grandson. I had that kind of history in mind but I didn't think beyond that to *Arrow of God* and *A Man of the People*. The true interpretation is that I worked with the material as it evolved.
>
> My idea was to study in fictional terms the African story. So perhaps it was inevitable that one would move on historically to the present, and I have moved front and back. For example, in *Arrow of God* you can see a deeper reflection on the same kind of story as we had seen in *Things Fall Apart*, using different kinds of characters (33).

In all his fictionalizing of Africa's story, the need "to look back and try to find out where we went wrong, where the rain began to beat us," (44) has been central. The nature of Achebe's backward glance at the past is revealed most compellingly in his two novels of traditional Africa, *Things Fall Apart* and *Arrow of God*. The title for the first is adopted from W.B. Yeats' poem, "The Second Coming":

> *Turning and turning in the widening gyre*
> *The falcon cannot hear the falconer;*
> *Things fall apart; the center cannot hold;*
> *Mere anarchy is loosed upon the world (89).*

The very title – evocative of a cosmos in upheaval, a world turned on its head – is an apt shorthand for Achebe's total attitude to the debilitation wrought on Africa by Europe's imperial thrusts. The phrase – things fall apart – disembodied and pressed into epigrammatic service – achieves a horrific deepening of a sense of chasm, of a dark, unbridgeable gulf in African history. Things fall apart; an order passes; a dispensation dies; chaos ascends; terror triumphs. The eschatological echo of the title is matched by Achebe's apprehensions of the rapid and ruthless unraveling of an organic and intricate way of life – a desuetude compelled by the machinations of alien forces. In his book, *Culture, Tradition and Society in the West African Novel*, Emmanuel Obiechina suggests that the action of *Things Fall Apart*, "falls between the last ten years of the nineteenth century and the first ten of the twentieth, when Christian missions and the British administration first established their influence in the groups of villages north of Onitsha (201). Umuofia, the fictional locale of the novel, owes much to Achebe's natal village of Ogidi. In fact, Achebe once explained to an interviewer that, "There's actually no place called Umuofia, but its customs and its people are clearly those of Ogidi in Eastern Nigeria, which is where I'm from" (Achebe's Interview by Cott 186–187).

Achebe's strategy in *Things Fall Apart* may be said to depend, broadly, on three levels of treatment as well as three phases of dramatic portrayal. On a social plane, the first part offers us a privileged peep into the pristine world of Umuofia in the days preceding the white man's presence. The picture is one of a community with a settled, time-tested and self-contained way of life. The second part encompasses heraldings and intimations of an approaching alien force – contained in the news of how the white man sacked the Abame people – and culminates in the appearance of this presence. The third part deals with the dramatic changes wrought by that encounter. If we choose to view the story through the prism of its implications in the life of its central character, it should be possible to glean a tripartite pattern flowing from the shameful legacy of Unoka, Okonkwo's improvident father, through Okonkwo's acts of willed transformation of fate, to the reincarnation in Nwoye of traits that are, for Okonkwo at any rate, so unbearably borrowed from Unoka. At yet another quasi-religious level, *Things Fall Apart* details the development of Okonkwo's ascendancy in the social hierarchy of Umuofia, his exile in order to expiate a grave transgression against the earth goddess, and his less than heroic return.

As the novel opens we are introduced to Okonkwo who "was well known throughout the nine villages and even beyond" (3). In light of what happens subsequently, the compass of Okonkwo's world – the delineation of the territorial reach of his fame – may appear pathetically claustrophobic. Certainly Okonkwo's perception of the world could never approach the cosmopolitan playfulness of the hero of Achebe's first children's book, *Chike and the River*, who exults,

> So this is me, ... Chike Anene, alias Chiks the Boy, of Umuofia, Mbaino District, Onitsha Province, Eastern Nigeria, Nigeria, West Africa, World, Universe (46).

But Okonkwo's world was adequate to his apprehension of himself – an apprehension shared by his fellows – as a person of heroic stature. By the norms and standards of his society and within its autonomously determined parameters, Okonkwo's extraordinary greatness is beyond question. Achebe comes up with concrete proof of this greatness:

> His fame rested on solid personal achievements. As a young man of eighteen he had brought honor to his village by throwing Amalinze the Cat. Amalinze was the great wrestler who for seven years was unbeaten, from Umuofia to Mbaino (3).

But what makes his social stature truly spectacular are the odds he had to transcend in order to take his seat among the elders of the tribe. Unoka's bequest to Okonkwo was a most wretched and unenviable one. Unoka had taken no titles in the community – which meant that his stock was quite low – and compounded his laziness by being a bad debtor. As a result, Okonkwo's life was dominated by fear, the fear of failure and of weakness. It was deeper and more intimate than the fear of evil and capricious gods and of magic, the fear of the forest, and of the forces of nature, malevolent, red in tooth and claw. Okonkwo's fear was greater than these. It was not external but lay deep within himself. It was the fear of himself, lest he should be found to resemble his father (13).

The characters in *Things Fall Apart* are products of the mores, values and compulsions of their society. Unoka, the most unredeemed failure in the social landscape of Umuofia, might be a different character altogether given a society with a different outlook and measure of success. He was after all a very gifted musician who invested his whole being whenever he had the opportunity to indulge his vocation. His hard luck was to be born in a society in which prowess in farming and bravery in war defined manliness. Beyond excelling in music, Unoka, we are also told, had a way with words. In fact, his comforting words to Okonkwo following the disastrous harvest in what Achebe describes as "the worst year in living memory" turn out to be not only wise but – in view of the fate that finally overtakes Okonkwo – ironically prescient. Unoka says to his son:

> Do not despair. I know you will not despair. You have a manly and a proud heart. A proud heart can survive a general failure because such a failure does not prick its pride. It is more difficult and more bitter when a man fails alone (24–25).

When a man fails alone is a phrase that captures Unoka's own utter failure, and as Okonkwo, in time, will discover, it is his lot to do. Okonkwo's contempt for the habit of sustained introspection blinds him to the occasional wisdom in his father's utterance. His attitude owes to the rather narrow limits of his sensibility which moves him to seek to evince only those qualities and emotions consistent with strength, masculinity and courage. For a man who has come as far as he has, there is something to be said for his hauteur and pride. From being the son of a weakling and shiftless cheat – one who, moreover, dies of the swelling disease, thus forfeiting his right to a proper burial by his fellows – Okonkwo rises to become an outstanding wrestler and a great farmer, a man with three wives and several titles. We are meant to understand Okonkwo's crude brashness as a compensatory mask for a deeply embedded internal weakness. But the same society that won't hold his father's sins against him expects from him a measure of modesty and an acknowledgment of the dualistic complexity of things.

In a sense, Okonkwo represents an aberrant phenomenon in the pantheon of characters within his own society. Achebe has addressed the limitations of Okonkwo's world view in an interview published in Jonathan Cott's *Pipers at the Gate of Dawn: The Wisdom of Children's Literature*. Said the novelist:

> To my mind, one of the worst and most unimaginative of states is that of single-mindedness. This is the state of a man like Okonkwo in *Things Fall Apart*. In certain limited and restricted spheres this is admirable. But beyond that it becomes a real liability – he cannot see that things come in twos, and in that respect he resembles the British missionaries more than his own people (191).

While Okonkwo himself may have been too obsessively fixated on his father's weakness and his own manliness as exhausting the character types, Achebe offers us a varied array of other models. Okonkwo's friend, Obierika, rather than Unoka, is a more interesting contrast to Okonkwo's ultimately neurotic perception of the posture appropriate to a man of good standing in the community. But – enormous as he may seem to many readers – Okonkwo is an exquisitely drawn character who has triggered recognition in many a reader including one as distinguished as the late James Baldwin. At a forum at the African Literature Association Conference in Gainesville, Florida in 1980, where he appeared with Achebe, Baldwin noted,

> When I read *Things Fall Apart* in Paris ... the Ibo tribe in Nigeria ... a tribe I never saw; a system, to put it that way, or a society the rules of which were a mystery to me ... I recognized everybody in it. That book was about my father ... How he got over I don't know but he did (See *Teaching* TFA).

Reflecting on that response, Achebe has written in an essay entitled "Teaching *Things Fall Apart*" and published in a book of the same title that he did not expect

> that every reader or indeed that many readers of *Things Fall Apart* should come up with similar recognitions. That would make Okonkwo Everyman which he certainly is not; he is not even Every Igbo-Man (See *Teaching* TFA).

Part of Achebe's triumph in *Things Fall Apart* is to introduce us to a world in which various forces and tendencies – good and evil, spiritual and temporal, conservation and change, stasis and dynamism – exist side by side. Contrary to the pet notion of imperialist literature, the African inhabited an ordered, complex and self-regulating space. It was a space in which man had a considerable scope for drawing up the principles by which quality of his social existence could be enhanced. Man was in healthy communion with the gods – and could debate the gods if the occasion called for it, or even commit deicide when a particular god shirked his mandate or otherwise injected a malevolent spirit into man's social domain. It was a world in which each community had conventions determining its external relations with its neighbors on a number of issues. These included procedures for making war, a process in which the exigencies of man were often subordinated to the sanctioning authority of gods. It was a society that had an internal mechanism for changing any rules that tried its soul. For example, following Okonkwo's breach of the Week of Peace, Ogbuefi Ezeudu, the oldest man in Umuofia, tells two visitors "that the punishment for breaking the Peace of Ani had become very mild in their clan:"

> "It has not always been so," he said. "My father told me that he had been told that in the past a man who broke the peace was dragged on the ground through the village until he died. But after a while this custom was stopped because it spoiled the peace which it was meant to preserve" (31).

A society that evinced this dynamic disposition could have, in time, evolved to eschew, to take one example, the killing of twins. In the traditional society, stories were central to the process of change. In an essay titled, "What Has Literature Got to Do With It?," delivered as the 1986 Nigerian National Merit Award Lecture, Achebe, referring to a Fulani creation myth, made the following point:

> So important have such stories been to mankind that they are not restricted to accounts of initial creation but will be found following human societies as they recreate themselves through vicissitudes of their history, validating their social organizations, their political systems, their moral attitudes and religious beliefs, even their prejudices ... but they also serve to sanction change when it can no longer be denied. At such critical moments new versions of old stories or entirely fresh ones tend to be brought into being to mediate the changes and sometimes to consecrate opportunistic defections into more honorable rites of passage (163).

A major source of Okonkwo's problems arise from his inability, indeed unwillingness, to be a questioner of what he perceives as a static communal will, an unquestioning reverence proceeding, in part, from the fact that this will has been the bestower on him of such generous benediction. This habit is exemplified by Okonkwo's refusal to excuse himself from the duty of killing the doomed lad, Ikemefuna, who lived in his household for three years. Ezeudu is clear in his advice to Okonkwo:

... The Oracle of the Hills and the Caves has pronounced it. They will take him outside Umuofia as is the custom, and kill him there. But I want you to have nothing to do with it. He calls you father (57).

Okonkwo, of course, does not heed the counsel; what is worse, he is the one who strikes the fatal blow. Later, we see him querying Obierika for absenting himself, suggesting that his friend contested the authority of the gods. The debate that ensues is an occasion for the two friends to reveal their different outlooks:

"I do not [question the authority of the gods]. Why should I? But the Oracle did not ask me to carry out its decision."

"But someone had to do it. If we were all afraid of blood, it would not be done. And what do you think the Oracle would do then?"

"You know very well, Okonkwo, that I am not afraid of blood; and if anyone tells you that I am, he is telling a lie. And let me tell you one thing, my friend. If I were you I would have stayed at home. What you have done will not please the Earth. It is the kind of action for which the goddess wipes out whole families."

"The earth cannot punish me for obeying her messenger," Okonkwo said. "A child's fingers are not scalded by a piece of hot yam which its mother puts into its palm."

"That is true," Obierika agreed. "But if the Oracle said that my son should be killed I would neither dispute it nor be the one to do it" (66–67).

The exchange underlines Obierika's far more complex perception of his relationship to the gods – a perception profoundly rooted in the theological percepts of his and Okonkwo's society. In the story of Abraham, Christian theology advances the view that filial sacrifice represents the apotheosis of devotional virtue. Igbo traditional religious thought recoils from this view. Obierika, while excusing himself from killing Ikemefuna, can nevertheless claim to be in compliance with the oracle's order. The Igbo always permitted themselves some elbow room for the exercise of the human will in their transactions with their deities. It would be heresy, however, were Obierika to cross the boundary and contest the oracle's instruction. Paradoxically, Okonkwo, through his literal compliance, places himself at considerable peril. Although Achebe does not make the point explicitly, it may be plausibly suggested that Okonkwo's *hubris* in striking down Ikemefuna is partly responsible for unleashing a metaphysical curse that dogs him, accounting for his inadvert fatal shooting of a sixteen-year-old boy at the father's funeral (an offense for which he is banished into exile), and ultimately for his own suicide.

Okonkwo's hubristic temperament also renders him incapable of pausing to contemplate the cosmic conundrum introduced into his society by the arrival of the white man. To the bitter end, he clings to the position that the new assault could be handled by a recourse to Umuofia's martial might. As an exile in Mbanta, he tries but fails to persuade his mother's people to rout the Christians in retaliation for the killing of a royal python by an overzealous Christian convert. When one of the villagers makes the point that "It is not our custom to fight for our gods," Okonkwo condemns what he sees as cowardly reasoning:

> If a man comes into my hut and defecates on the floor, what do I do? Do I shut my eyes? No! I take a stick and break his head. That is what a man does. These people are daily pouring filth over us, and Okeke says we should pretend not to see? (158–159).

At the end of his seven year exile, Okonkwo returns to a vastly changed Umuofia. He discovers that the white man, Christianity, and the British judicial system have staked out a corner in the community's social arena. The despised figure of the District Commissioner has become the arbitrary and corrupt arbiter of disputes and dispenser of sanctions and punishments. Okonkwo discusses the untoward development with Obierika, wondering what has happened to Umuofia's power to fight:

> "Have you not heard how the white man wiped out Abame?" asked Obierika.
> "I have heard," said Okonkwo. "But I have also heard that Abame people were weak and foolish. Why did they not fight back? Had they no guns and machetes? We would be cowards to compare ourselves with the men of Abame. Their fathers had never dared to stand before our ancestors. We must fight these men and drive them from the land" (175–176).

Again it is Obierika who is able to comprehend the complexity of Umuofia's dilemma, one arising from the white man's seduction of some Umuofia citizens. He is aware of the fact that the community is now divided and weakened, since the white man, "has put a knife on the things that held us together and we have fallen apart." (176). In fact, once the white man factored himself into Umuofia's social space the moral atmosphere became ambiguous. This ambiguity explains in some measure Umuofia's loss of the will to fight, despite the persuasion of one as eloquent as Okika. Even though the tradition forbade the spilling of the blood of a clansman, Okika drags an extenuation into the argument:

> Our fathers never dreamed of such a thing, they never killed their brothers. But a white man never came to them. So we must do what our fathers would never have done... (203).

It is an ironic measure of Okonkwo's obsession with the vision of martial deportment that he is not detained by contemplation of the possible implications of willfully shedding the blood of a kinsman; and this despite the harsh exaction of his exile for a similar, albeit inadvertent, transgression.

Many perceptive critics have drawn attention to the even-handedness with which Achebe approached the execution of his poetic homage to his past. Dan Izevbaye, a Nigerian scholar, has pointed out in an essay titled "History's Eye-Witness: Vision and Representation in the Works of Chinua Achebe," that "the novels were also concerned with the internal contradictions of the traditional societies in which they were set." Awoonor has noted that Achebe's Africa:

> is full of contradictions. Its dynamics are too often determined by rigidity and an overextended system of masculinity (252).

Writing in the same vein, Lewis Nkosi makes the point that:

> Christianity wins out because Christianity probes and exploits real weakness in the old social order which has begun to crumble internally from its own contradictions (36).

Nkosi goes on to speculate on the nature of forces impelling the disintegration of the social fabric of African society:

> Although rooted in an understandable moral rationality, some of the cruelties of African society had deteriorated so uncomfortably into reflexive gestures of accidental crime and mechanical punishment that an internal revolution or change brought about by external forces had become an inevitable certainty (34).

In the end what is clear is that a number of internal fissures and external pressures conspired to enable the new dispensation to triumph. At a basic level, the struggle was one for power and the white man had a more menacing arsenal. Secondly, the white man insinuated himself sometimes with the most insidious and seductive cunning. Achebe himself has written in "Named for Victoria" that

> the bounties of the Christian God were not to be taken lightly – education, paid jobs, and many other advantages that nobody in his right senses could underrate. And in fairness we should add that there was more than naked opportunism in the defection of many to the new religion. For in some ways and in certain circumstances, it stood firmly on the side of humane behavior. It said, for instance, that twins were not evil and must no longer be abandoned in the forest to die (65).

That humane dimension – "the poetry of the new religion ... [the] hymn about brothers who sat in darkness and in fear ... the question of the twins crying in the bush and the question of Ikemefuna who was killed" (147) – is what finally impressed Nwoye, Okonkwo's first son. And we must suspect that Unoka, were he still alive, would also have been drawn to the new way.

The wryly ironic ending of *Things Fall Apart* invites the reader to confront, finally, the reductionist predilection of the would-be colonial historian. The District Commissioner, having presided over the perplexing matter of a man who killed an officer of the administration and then committed suicide, turns to ponder the practical question of how much space to devote to that particular drama in the book he proposes to write to be titled *The Pacification of the Primitive Tribes of the Lower Niger*. If the proposed title suggests a story whose trajectory will be different from the inimitable one we have just heard from Achebe, the D.C.'s decision that Okonkwo's saga can be compressed into "a reasonable paragraph" (209) reveals to us a man in the throes of a monumental amnesia. In the essay, "Teaching *Things Fall Apart*," Achebe asks the question: "Did Okonkwo fail?" His answer is remarkable for the way in which it rebukes the dismissive levity of the District Commissioner:

> In a certain sense, obviously, yes. But he also left behind a story strong enough to make those who hear it even in far-away Korea wish devoutly that things had gone differently for him (23).

Arrow of God, Achebe's other novel of traditional Africa, if considered in terms of the evolving pattern of the history that has animated his fiction, may be seen as his second novel even if it is the third one in actual execution and manufacture. The connectedness of the two stories is underscored by references in the two novels to similar events. The unnamed District Officer in *Things Fall Apart* with a proposed book titled *The Pacification of the Primitive Tribes of the Lower Niger* has emerged in *Arrow of God* as George Allen, the author of a book of the same title. Besides, there are several references in *Arrow of God* to the destruction of the Abame clan by the white man, an event touched upon in the first novel as well. Set some twenty years after the events of *Things Fall Apart*, *Arrow of God* is the most grandly conceived and magisterially wrought of Achebe's novels, which accounts for its being the favorite of a good number of literary scholars. Obiechina has praised the "composite grandeur" of the novel. Awoonor regards it as Achebe's "most controlled and balanced work artistically" (231). Achebe himself, speaking with characteristic circumspection in the preface to the second edition of the novel, describes *Arrow of God* as "the novel which I am most likely to be caught sitting down to read again." But in a 1976 interview with a Nigerian journalist, Achebe was less indirect when he confessed that "[*Arrow of God*] may be my favorite novel. I have to make that admission" (33).

What is beyond debate, at any rate, is that *Arrow of God* represents a far grander homage to the world that fell apart, and plumbs the story of Africa's encounter with Europe from more angles than in *Things Fall Apart*. Achebe has presented in the novel, to a far greater degree than in the first, compelling parallel visions of history as its consequences unfolded both in the lives of individual characters and within the social economy of the entire community. There are several levels of tensions operating within the social space and moral universe of this novel, and Achebe examines the implosion at greater length, carefully delineating the internal fissures waiting to be exploited, diligently portraying the chicanery of men and gods, the disruptive force of a foreign presence, and exploring the specific ways in which the interplay of human duplicity and divine complicity led to the collapse of a whole cosmology. The Nigerian critic, Abiola Irele, in an essay titled "The Tragic Conflict in the Novels of Chinua Achebe" emphasizes the layeredness of the tensions impinging on events in *Arrow of God* and yet cautions against isolating the forces into their discrete parts. Writes Irele:

> Achebe has woven the two movements of the individual and social drama into such unity that it would be artificial to separate them: the lives of individuals meet with a combination of events to force a tragic issue. Yet the tensions at the heart of this pattern are clearly schematized. On the one hand, the internal division in the village of Umuaro is polarized around the person of Ezeulu, the chief priest of Ulu, and that of his ambitious rival, Nwaka; and on the other hand, the conflict of cultures represented by the misunderstanding that opposed Ezeulu to the colonial administration in the person of Captain Winterbottom (17).

In *Arrow of God* what Obiechina calls "the tripartite forces: ranged against the traditional system – "the Christian missions, the British administration and the introduction of European-type trading stores" – have gained a cumulative impetus capable of destabilizing the foundations of traditional sovereignty. Consequently, the incipient disruption of the ideological perspectives welding Umuofia together in *Things Fall Apart* has, in *Arrow of God*'s Umuaro, grown into "chasms" – to use Obiechina's apt word. But Obiechina notes that:

> a good deal of the action [in *Arrow of God*] is concerned with the attempt by the chief character to build a bridge over the widening chasm. Ezeulu fails because his grasp of the situation is inadequate and so he is constantly surprised (242).

Ezeulu's failure encapsulates the inexorable doomed fate spelt by the advent of a Euro-Christian dispensation. The sources of his failure are remarkably different from the circumstances that account for Okonkwo's own tragic end; in fact Ezeulu is in many respects as temperamentally opposed to Okonkwo as it is possible to be – even if they share a certain streak of stubbornness and ultimately a fascination with the outer reaches of their own power. (An important difference is that while Okonkwo seeks to keep his power in constant physical display, Ezeulu exults in his sense of power mostly within a contemplative context). Ezeulu is, in a quite deliberate way, Achebe's attempt to portray a different facet of a robustly constituted sensibility responding to the seminal event of Europe's intrusion. Achebe confesses as much in the interview in *Pipers at the Gate*:

...I had to do Ezeulu because I had 'done' Okonkwo, if I may put it that way. ...
I wanted to say something deeper about the community itself, not through
the eyes of a simple-minded defender like Okonkwo, or of a simple-minded
opponent like the district commissioner, but of a man of title and importance
within the community – a ruler in fact, a priest, an intellectual ... Ezeulu's failing – his priestly arrogance – could apply to any priest, and it's really not very
harmful or fatal. But the situation he was dealing with couldn't have been solved
by anybody anyway. So the important thing was to have a complex sensibility
tackling that crisis, that's all. Not to have him succeed. And that's part of our
history (191–192).

The differences between Okonkwo and Ezeulu are so significant that the two
characters must be seen as embodying two different, if not polarized, impulses in
the African posture toward the alien presence of the white man and his elaborate
spiritual, economic and administrative paraphernalia. Where Okonkwo's opposition
to the new dispensation is deeply visceral, Ezeulu is moved by a healthy curiosity for
the white man's outlook. When Mr. Brown, a missionary in Umuofia, pays Okonkwo
a visit, the latter, Achebe tells us in *Things Fall Apart*, "had driven him away with the
threat that if he came into his compound again, he would be carried out of it" (182).
Ezeulu, on the other hand, not only welcomes Captain Winterbottom; he responds
to Winterbottom's appeal and sends Oduche along to learn the ways of the white
man. While Okonkwo sees Nwoye's defection to Christianity – and the prospect
of his other children also abandoning their ancestral gods – in apocalyptic terms,
Ezeulu regards symbolic gestures of accommodation to the white man as a deft
strategic maneuver. Ezeulu offers two kinds of rationalization for sending Oduche
to the white religion. The first is akin to the modern phenomenon of espionage – the
need to have Oduche as his eyes, a reporter on the motions and progress of the new
religion. Secondly, he summons ancestral wisdom to his side – recalling the proverb
that one does not stand in one place to watch a mask dancing; what Ezeulu yearns
for, then, is to preserve his interests and ensure his continued participation in the
widening gyre of history in the event that historical initiative is completely seized
by the new dispensation, "as many oracles prophesied" (43). Finally – talking about
the contrasts between Okonkwo and Ezeulu – while Okonkwo cannot conceivably
place himself at cross purposes with Umuofia's war will, Ezeulu not only withholds
Ulu's good offices from Umuaro in its unjust war with Okperi over land but also
testifies against his people in the dispute.

While much of the springs for Ezeulu's actions proceeds from a moral
outlook – the duty to tell Umuaro, and, later, the white man, the truth about the
disputed land – or enlightened self-interest – as in his gesture toward the new
religion – he is thwarted by the combative forces of other centers of power within
Umuaro and also by what Achebe calls "the powers of event" (229). In his futile

attempt to come to reasoned terms with the Christian religion, Ezeulu has no way of knowing that the new religion seeks not accommodation but assimilation, not dialogue in the spirit of ecumenism but conversion, not co-existence but conquest. Consequently, Ezeulu's act of pragmatic opportunism backfires: Oduche, who went in as a reluctant spy, becomes a fervid acolyte of Christianity. He imprisons a python in his box, thus precipitating the intensification of the hostility between his father and Ezidemili, custodian of the shrine of Idemili whose totemic figure is the wronged python. By sending Oduche to the white man Ezeulu ends up imperiling the traditional order and undermining the numinous realm from which Ulu, his deity, derives its central importance. When he testifies against Umuaro's land claims he must be understood to be acting in a manner consistent with his calling as a priest who must divine and proclaim the true will of his god. And yet – especially given the already momentous changes in Umuaro's world – his testimony ironically aggravates the centrifugal tendencies in Umuaro and weakens the corporate cohesion of the amalgam of six villages. The depth of this breach is grasped by recalling that the villages were federated and Ulu brought into being primarily to achieve a security end – the warding off of the mercenary soldiers of the Abam. Ulu is therefore at the core of the founding principle of the clan – a product of the people's federating impulse as well as a source of the town's creative energy.

The earnest forces of the European administration step into the uneasy context of Umuaro's threatened unity. Two important events in *Arrow of God* underline the plenary ascendancy of British power. The first is Winterbottom's brusque intervention to stop Umuaro's war with Okperi. The war lasts for four days, then:

> The next day, *Afo*, saw the war brought to a sudden close. The white man, Wintabota, brought soldiers to Umuaro and stopped it. The story of what these soldiers did in Abame was still told with fear, and so Umuaro made no effort to resist but laid down their arms (27).

In the next paragraph, Achebe limns the symbolic castration of Umuaro and the assertion of the singular authority of the colonial administration:

> The white man was not satisfied that he had stopped the war. He gathered all the guns in Umuaro and asked the soldiers to break them in the face of all, except three or four which he carried away. Afterwards he sat in judgement over Umuaro and Okperi and gave the disputed land to Okperi (28).

In *Culture, Tradition and Society in the West African Novel*, Obiechina refers to the breaking of the guns as "a symbolic act indicating the passing of traditional independence and free action." Besides, the conflict "provides the first occasion of the breach between the clan and the Chief Priest" (134–135), encapsulated in the words of Akuebue, Ezeulu's good friend, who tells him in rueful tones that "Umuaro will always say that you betrayed them before the white man" (131).

The other event that reinforces the stability of British power is the new road linking Umuaro and Okperi, two former bitter enemies. The road not only marks the extent and permanence of the British colonial presence and its transformative impact; it also symbolizes the inauguration of new political relations between hitherto autonomous, self-regulating communities. The white man's ability to commandeer Umuaro's unpaid labor for the construction of this road dramatizes the British administration's unchallenged control. Moses Unachukwu, speaking to members of the Otakagu age grade considering how to respond to the uncompensated conscription of their labor, highlights:

> Yes, we are talking about the white man's road. But when the roof and walls of a house fall in, the ceiling is not left standing. The white man, the new religion, the soldiers, the new road – they are all part of the same thing. The white man has a gun, a matchet, a bow and carries fire in his mouth. He does not fight with one weapon alone (85).

Ezeulu is a student of power, a man who considers as insultingly inadequate the conception of his role vis-à-vis his deity as parallel to "the power of a child over a goat that was said to be his" (3). His extension, even within the anonymity of his mind, of the limits of his own power, leads him, says Awoonor, to appropriate "for himself the attributes of his deity" (272). Obiechina points out that, in Ezeulu's mind, "he has already begun to assume for himself vast illegal powers" (237). Nwaka contents Ezeulu's authority in the secular sphere while Ezidemili personifies the challenge to Ezeulu's spiritual dominance. When Winterbottom invites Ezeulu to Okperi to offer him the position of warrant chief over Umuaro it is a development that could decisively resolve the power tussles within the clan. But the process is attended by much clumsiness, miscommunication and mutual incomprehension concerning the procedural protocol of the two traditions. As a result of which Winterbottom feels his good faith mocked and Ezeulu feels abandoned by Umuaro. Ezeulu's contemptuous refusal of the offer of warrant chieftaincy – "Tell the white man that Ezeulu will not be anybody's chief, except Ulu" (174) – is a stunning blow to the imperial pride of Britain. Tony Clarke, the British officer who made him the offer, is livid: "A witch-doctor making a fool of the British Administration in public!" (174). For his effrontery Ezeulu is detained for two months in Okperi. In that time he is, of course, unable to carry out the ritual mandate of his office as the regulator of the seasons. As a result of his detention he does not eat two of the sacred yams that mark the progression of the seasons and determine when the harvest must begin. But rather than shudder at the cataclysmic consequences of this state of affairs, Ezeulu sees it as his god's way of censuring Umuaro for abandoning its chief priest. Back from detention Ezeulu and Umuaro confront the dire implications of the uneaten yams. The harvest is to wait another two months;

the crops will start to rot in the ground, and famine of unprecedented proportions will befall the clan. The very material jugular of Umuaro is in jeopardy. In the face of this threat, Ezeulu is delirious about the prospect of acting as "an arrow in the bow of his god" in what he perceives as Ulu's impending fight with "the jealous cult of the sacred python" (191).

When it dawns on Umuaro that Ezeulu intends to delay the New Yam Festival for two moons, the clan sends a delegation of elders to him. They entreat him to approach Ulu in order to find ways by which the clan might make amends and resolve the dilemma. But Ezeulu's attempt to engage his god in vatic communication becomes, instead, an occasion for him to be haunted by his decision to send Oduche to the Christian faith:

> As Ezeulu cast his string of cowries the bell of Oduche's people began to ring. For one brief moment Ezeulu was distracted by its sad, measured monotone and he thought how strange it was that it should sound so near – much nearer than it did in his compound ... Ezeulu's announcement that his consultation with the deity had produced no result and that the six villages would be locked in the old year for two moons longer spread such alarm as had not been known in Umuaro in living memory (210).

Wole Soyinka, the Nigerian dramatist, novelist and essayist has underscored the poignant paradox in the situation. In *Myth, Literature and the African World* Soyinka observes that "The priest calls upon his deity but is answered by the bells of the Christian church" (88). Ulu's silence bodes ill – for the community as well as for Ulu and for its chief priest. Ezeulu's insistence on exacting vengeance on his enemies becomes a doubly jeopardous gamble. Ulu's *raison d'etre*, after all, is to secure the corporate security of Umuaro. In an agrarian economy, anything that threatens the food supply is mortally disruptive of corporate cohesion. In a sense, then, Ezeulu's inability to negotiate a compromise out of the crisis sets the stage for the dissolution of Umuaro's federal order. The death of Obika, Ezeulu's son, in the middle of the stand-off muddies the picture very much. Perhaps it is, as Ezeulu's enemies speculate, the deity's harsh rebuke to a chief priest whose defiance of the communal will amounts to a breech of the social compact which Ulu incarnates. But, as Achebe indicates, the ultimate winners are the predatory Christians lurking in the corner who inherit the prize forfeited by the feuding and exhausted forces of the traditional order.

Published in 1960, *No Longer at Ease* is Achebe's second novel. It is set in the mid-1950's, the period immediately preceding the euphoric attainment of independence by a number of African countries. The hero of *No Longer at Ease* is Obi Okonkwo, the grandson of Okonkwo of *Things Fall Apart*. As the novel begins, we see Obi Okonkwo standing trial for the crime of taking a bribe. Then we are quickly introduced to a typically superficial European perspective on this mini-tragedy. Mr. Green, Obi's boss and a man who reflects all the airs of the uppity colonial in his judgment of the African, is offering a sociological profile of the African to a friend of his who had wondered aloud why Obi Okonkwo had done what he did. "The African is corrupt through and through," pronounces Mr. Green. He then spells it out:

> "They are all corrupt," repeated Mr. Green. "I'm all for equality and all that. I for one would hate to live in South Africa. But equality won't alter facts."
>
> "What facts?" asked the British Council man, who was relatively new to the country. There was a lull in the general conversation, as many people were now listening to Mr. Green without appearing to do so.
>
> "The fact that over countless centuries the African has been the victim of the worst climate in the world and of every imaginable disease. Hardly his fault. But he has been sapped mentally and physically. We have brought him Western education. But what use is it to him?" (4).

The quasi-liberal accent of Mr. William Green's self-righteous denigration of Africans parallels, in its generalized tone, the naiveté of Obi Okonkwo's theory that "the public service of Nigeria would remain corrupt until the old Africans at the top were replaced by young men from the universities" (44). What renders Obi Okonkwo's thesis far more interesting is that, while Green is voicing opinions that are neither original nor surprising – given his counterparts that we had encountered in Achebe's earliest novel – Obi Okonkwo's view transcends the frontiers of the hackneyed concept of generational conflict. His view works to heighten the ironic texture of his own wretched downfall. But at an even more disturbing level, his theory advertises the position, perhaps unwittingly, that one's greater socialization in the ways of the white man improves one. It is a position that the elite of emergent ex-colonial countries are wont to embrace, almost reflexively, but one that Europeans like Green are quick to deny. For Green, education for the African vouchsafes little in the face of nature's prior, unalterably harsh, verdict. Speaking with his friend from the British Council, Green articulates the Africans' immutable ecological curse as consisting of the worst climate in the world and every imaginable disease.

But however sanctimonious his tone, Green's insight is impressive only as an earnest utterance of a cliché learned by rote – from his ancestors who plied the trade of defining the African mind (or, more likely, lack of it) from afar. Alternatively, in the case of George Allen, Winterbottom, Wade and Clarke, they try to define the African mind from merely superficial engagement with the African. (In which connection we may recall Chinweizu's statement in a terse, two-line poem entitled "Colonizer's Logic": "These natives are unintelligent – (We can't understand their language)" (63). But *No Longer at Ease* is, in the end, the story not of opinionated

Europeans but of Africans caught in an uncommon existential predicament. *Things Fall Apart* portrays the intricate rhythm of traditional life, by no means flawless, but adequate for the transactions which those who inhabited the world had the need to make. We saw Europe intruding on this settled way of life armed with a new theology, a new secular vision and a new administrative system. We saw Africa's combative response reflected both in Okonkwo's suicidal defiance and Ezeulu's calculated deployment of political cunning and intelligence in the spirit of pragmatism. *No Longer at Ease* takes up the story several decades later – to examine what has happened to a culture for long apprenticed to the values of Europe.

This examination centers around the only son of Isaac Okonkwo who, when we last saw him in *Things Fall Apart* is Nwoye, Okonkwo's apostate son, seduced by Christianity. Some critics have pointed to Obi Okonkwo's deficiency in what Awoonor refers to as "tragic grandeur" (268). It is true that, measured against his famous grandfather, Obi Okonkwo desires something as a domineering symbol of his epoch. Certainly, old Odogwu stretches credulity when he suggests that Obi is the reincarnation of Okonkwo; but he also has it right when be buttresses the different historical contexts inhabited by Okonkwo and his grandson:

> ... Today greatness has changed its tune. Titles are no longer great, neither are barns or large numbers of wives and children. Greatness is now in the things of the white man. And so we too have changed our tune. We are the first in all the nine villages to send our son to the white man's land ... (62).

He very perceptively places Obi's achievement in context – and within that specific context, there is grandeur. He has gone to England and returned with a degree which qualifies him for a job in Nigeria's Senior Civil Service. The Umuofia Progressive Union that paid his fees was actuated by self-interest. They wanted him to train as a lawyer in order to assume the burden of handling their land cases – since the days of acquiring land through martial valor are long gone. But he studies English instead, a discipline that lacks the aural power of Law or even the rarefied air of Classics. Even so, he becomes a *bona fide* member of Nigeria's elite – a tiny, much pampered breed, to whom, as independence drew close, the Europeans open the hitherto exclusive clubs, Senior Service jobs, and the affluent living quarters of Ikoyi. Obi Okonkwo becomes an interesting character precisely because he symbolizes the tensions between a resilient African sensibility and the ethos of nascent modernism – with its industrial luxuries, intellectual affectations, social leisures, elitist pomposities and the conflation of a multitude of interests. Some of Obi's problems proceed from his inability to balance the raucous claims of his community against those of his self-willed individualism. He does not properly perceive or welcome his role as the representative of Umuofia's stake in the new scheme of things. In contemplating his relationship to the Umuofia Progressive Union – the umbrella association which taxed its members to pay his school fees in London – Obi's perspective is too narrowly focused on his own comforts:

> Obi admitted that his people had a sizable point. What they did not know was that, having labored in sweat and tears to enroll their kinsman among the shining elite, they had to keep him there. Having made him a member of an exclusive club whose members greet one another with "How's the car behaving?" did they expect him to turn around and answer: "I'm sorry but my car is off the road. You see I couldn't pay my insurance premium?" Almost as unthinkable as a masked spirit in the old Ibo society answering another's esoteric salutation: "I'm sorry, my friend, but I don't understand your language. I'm but a human being wearing a mask." No, these things could not be (113).

The above contains the capsule of several themes dramatized in *No Longer at Ease*. One is the narcissistic self-absorption of the new elite whose robust exaltation in the privileges of their station blinds them to the responsibilities of their socially determined identities. But such abdication is quite tempting if not altogether irresistible in the cosmopolitanism of a city like Lagos marked by a pervasive moral ambiguity. The small communities – like Umuofia and Umuaro – had clearly defined moral principles which in a city that holds millions of people and a melange of cultures become untenable. Instead, some tentative, mostly opportunistic, loosely articulated principles – like the ritual of salutation of car-owning elites – are adopted. To be sure, the communities themselves also embrace this ambiguous moral outlook, exemplified by the prayer of an elder of the Umuofia Progressive Union during Obi Okonkwo's trial:

> "We are strangers in this land. If good comes to it may we have our fair share." Amen. "But if bad comes let it go to the owners of the land who know what gods should be appeased." Amen. "Many towns have four or five or even ten of their sons in European posts in this city. Umuofia has only one. And now our enemies say that even that one is too many for us. But our ancestors will not agree to such a thing." Amen. "An only palm fruit does not get lost in the fire." Amen (7).

The elder invokes the forces of the ancestral patrimony to come to Obi Okonkwo's defense, even though Obi and his father have long abandoned the gods of the homestead. (In Obi's case, even his loyalty to the Christian God is in serious question). The idea advanced in the invocation points to what Frantz Fanon aptly described as the pitfalls of national consciousness (148). For Umuofians living in Lagos, the city does not represent the capital of a country with whose fortunes their interests are bound up. Instead, Lagos is an artificial construct, good only for the opportunity it affords them to make money.

When it suits their purposes, the new elite, like Christopher and Obi, are not beyond making an effete appeal to the traditional order – as when Christopher tells his girlfriend:

> Look here, Bisi, we are not interested in what you want to do. It's for Obi and me to decide. This na Africa, you know (125).

Besides, their effort to weave proverbs into their discussions underlies the way in which traditional lore still impinges on their modern consciousness.

Obi Okonkwo, a man uneasily bestriding two worlds, comes to peril as a consequence of the contradictions of his situations. His initial idealism and refusal to be corrupted shows that Green's thesis is too simple-minded, indeed outrightly false. It is, on one level, the accumulation of several small impediments that finally trip Obi. Achebe shows us what he himself describes as "a succession of messy, debilitating ambushes" that mark Obi's agonized struggle and eventual fall. But Obi's weaknesses also lay deep within him. His idealistic posture is not served by a commensurate moral fuel or strength. In his insistence on marrying Clara Okeke, an *osu*, he exaggerates both his own power of will and the extent to which his parents' Christian ideology has transformed their outlook on what the traditional sensibility held profane. Following his argument with his father over Clara, Obi withdraws to quietly ponder his performance:

> ... His mind was troubled not only by what had happened by also by the discovery that there was nothing in him with which to challenge it honestly. All day he had striven to rouse his anger and his conviction, but he was honest enough with himself to realize that the response he got, no matter how violent it sometimes appeared, was not genuine. It came from the periphery, and not the center ... (156).

Ultimately his lack of central convictions will spell the slow collapse of his idealism especially in the aftermath of his mother's death. In the face of his rapidly accruing financial problems, Obi's chastening idealism yields place to the immediate exigency of paying bills and settling debts and leads to his arrest and trial for bribery. His fall does not resound with the power of his grandfather's demise. Even so, it is true that, in his own right, Obi has wrestled with his history – however limited his impact on it.

No Longer at Ease, set a few years before Nigeria's independence, presages with an uncanny clarity the shape of things to come in *A Man of the People*. Chief the Honorable Nanga, for example, is Honorable Sam Okoli writ large in the fullness of cupidity and vulgarity. The dissonant voices heard in *No Longer at Ease* become the divisive forces in *A Man of the People*. In the interview in *Pipers at the Gate*, Achebe addressed the problem posed by the kind of nation-state bequeathed to Africa:

... we have to find a way of dealing with the problems created by the fact that somebody says he's speaking on your behalf, but you don't know who he is. This is one of the problems of the modern world (171).

It is a theme which Achebe explores tentatively in *No Longer at Ease* but elaborates in *A Man of the People*. His trilogy constitutes, as Abiola Irele so elegantly put it, a revelation of "the intimate circumstances of the African Becoming" (21). And in doing this Achebe also developed a kind of software – a linguistic apparatus, so to speak – appropriate to the narration of Africa's story. He has consistently tasked the English language to bear the weight of his people's history. In a paper entitled, "Truth, Achebe and the African Novel," Michael Thelwell sums up the scale of Achebe's total achievement:

> Out of the vast resources of African linguistic tradition and values, the poetic styles and idiom of proverbial expression, riddle, parable and song, sacred and secular myth and ritual, Chinua Achebe, appropriating to his purposes the medium of the English language, was forging a prose universal in its reach while remaining uniquely African in image, reference and tonality. It is a language appropriate to the experience and organic to the sensibilities of the culture it represents (4).

Achebe's achievement in a profoundly historic task lies, then, both in the importance of the stories he has told – stories written in the spirit of setting the score right about his embattled past – and the African-inspired idiom in which they have been rendered.

Works Cited

Achebe, Chinua. "Teaching *Things Fall Apart*." *Approaches to Teaching Things Fall Apart*. Ed. Bernth Lindors. New York: MLA, 1991.

———. "An Image of Africa." *Hopes and Impediments: Selected Essays*. New York: Doubleday, 1989.

———. "What Has Literature Got To Do With It?" *Hopes and Impediments: Selected Essays*. New York: Doubleday, 1989.

———. "The Truth of Fiction." *Hopes and Impediments: Selected Essays*. New York: Doubleday, 1989.

———. "African Literature as Celebration." *African Commentary*. Vol. 1., Issue 2. Nov. 1989.

———. "Continuity and Change in Nigerian Education." A Public Lecture at the University of Lagos, Akoka. Nov. 24, 1976.

———. *Morning Yet on Creation Day: Essays*. London: Heinemann, 1975.

———. "Named for Victoria, Queen of England." *Morning Yet on Creation Day: Essays*. London: Heinemann, 1975

———. "The Novelist as Teacher." *Morning Yet on Creation Day: Essays*. London: Heinemann, 1975.

———. "The Role of the Writer in a New Nation." *African Writers on African Writing*. Ed. G.D. Killam. London: Heinemann, 1973.

———. *Chike and the River*. London: Cambridge University Press, 1966.

———. Preface to Second Edition. *Arrow of God*. New York: Doubleday, 1964.

———. *Things Fall Apart*. London: Heinemann, 1958.

Achebe's Interview by Jonathan Cott. *Pipers at The Gates of Dawn: The Wisdom of Children's Literature*. New York: McGraw-Hill, 1985.

Agetua, John. Ed. *Critics on Chinua Achebe: 1970–1976*. 1977.

Author's Interview of Chinua Achebe. *The African Guardian*. Lagos. Sept. 24, 1987.

Awoonor, Kofi. *The Breast of the Earth: A Survey of the History, Culture and Literature of Africa South of the Sahara*. New York: Anchor Books, 1976.

Basden, G.T. Quoted by Robert M. Wren. *Achebe's World: The Historical and Cultural Context of the Novels*. Washington, D.C.: Three Continents Press, 1980.

Buchan, John. *Prestor John*. Middlesex: Penguin Books, 1956.

Cary, Joyce. *The African Witch*. New York: Harper Colophon, 1963.

Cesaire, Aime. *Discourse on Colonialism*. New York: Monthly Review Press, 1972.

Deurden, Dennis and Cosmo Pieterse, Eds. "Finding Their Voices." *Times Literary Supplement*. Sept. 16, 1965. *African Writers Talking*. London: Heinemann, 1972.

Innes, C.L. and Bernth Lindfors, Eds. *Critical Perspectives on Chinua Achebe*. London: Heinemann, 1979.

Irele, Abiola. "The Tragic Conflict in the Novels of Chinua Achebe." *Critical Perspectives on Chinua Achebe*. Ed. C.L. Innes and Bernth Lindfors. Isichei, Elizabeth. *A History of the Igbo People*. London: Macmillan, 1968.

Izevbaye, Dan. "History's Eyewitness: Vision and Representation in the Works of Chinua Achebe." *Okike: An African Journal of New Writing*. No. 30. Ed. Onuora Ossie Enekwe. Nsukka, Nigeria, Nov. 1990.

Laurence, Margaret. *Long Drums and Cannons*. London: Macmillan, 1968.

Mphahlele, Ezekiel. "The White Man's Image of the Non-White in Fiction." *The African Image*. New York: Praeger Paperbacks, 1964.

Nkosi, Lewis. *Tasks and Masks: Themes and Styles of African Literature*. Essex: Longman, 1981.

Obiechina, Emmanuel. *Culture, Tradition and Society in the West African Novel*. London: Cambridge University Press, 1975.

Skakespeare, William. *The Complete Works*. Eds Stanley Wells and Gary Taylor. Oxford: Clarendon Press, 1988.

Thelwell, Michael. Cited in "Truth, Achebe and the African Novel." A Keynote Presentation at the University of Nigeria, Nsukka, at a Symposium: "*Eagle on Iroko*" in Honor of Chinua Achebe, February 12, 1990.

Trevor-Roper, Hugh. "The Rise of Christian Europe." *The Listener*. London. Nov. 28, 1963.

wa Thiong'o, Ngugi. "The Writer and His Past." *Homecoming: Essays on African and Caribbean Literature, Culture and Politics*. New York: Lawrence Hill and Company, 1972.

Walcott, Derek. Cited in Biodun Jeyifo. "Wole Soyinka and the Tropes of Disalienation." Introduction to Wole Soyinka's *Art, Dialogue and Outrage: Essays on Literature and Culture*. New York: Pantheon, 1993.

Yeats, William Butler. "The Second Coming." *Selected Poems and Four Plays*. New York: Scribner.

Chapter 20

History and Changes in Chinua Achebe's Fiction

Ada Uzoamaka Azodo

To RAISE THE QUESTION OF personal moral probity is to revisit the dilemma of Nigerians in a postmodern world, striving to be steadfast and clean in a world gone mad with materialism at the expense of spiritualism and decorum. It is clearly the problem of a people who have been dispossessed for a long period of time by the culmination of slavery, colonialism and neo-colonialism. The situation is comparable to that of a hybrid in an ambiguous world, neither here nor there, seeking to tilt the balance one way considered morally just or justifiable, as opposed to the other way that is seen as morally bankrupt. The individual struggles to please self according to one's conscience, and at the same time mindful of the environment and desirous not to displease those around, hence the struggle in the first place. Caught in the middle and not wanting to be buried in the process of making a choice between two difficult options, the personality is constantly torn. Daily living becomes a chore nearly impossible to cope with. The personal moral struggle arises then from the efforts of the self to escape the overwhelming urge to be and do like everyone else for personal and material gratification, rather than abide by the dictates of one's conscience to do the right thing even at the expense of personal comfort and ease.

If moral struggle arises from conflicting messages to self to be upright or to be corrupt, then societal conflicts arise from the uneven, unbalanced levels of societal structures and the dictates of divergent views of life brought about by historic time and its attendant changes generated both from the inside and from the outside. The very nature of a conflicting situation in the face of changes allows us to be rather self-questioning about it. For example, how does one stave off hunger when one is not making enough to take care of one's daily needs and still be able to withstand the easy way out of embezzlement, bribery and corruption? How does one, as an elite, live up to the expectations of society when the same society has placed undue demands on the individual without adequate provisions to make ends meet? What does it profit one to continue to struggle to do the right thing, when all have been condemned as corrupt, without exception, and no case made for the clean and upright? How do you, and for how long, remain the loner in the face of such dictum as: "When you are in Rome, do as the Romans?" How do you resist the temptation to take advantage of a person in spite of the power you have over him or her? How do you begin to engender democracy in the face of so much corruption and nepotism? Faced with a challenge to do the right and carry others with you, how do you begin when you are overwhelmed, in the minority, and the rest of the population see you as a crazy idiot? All these questions refer to societal changes and history and require an appreciation of the psychology of the people when the dominant philosophy seems to be to live the day as best as one can and let the morrow take care of itself, *carpe diem* ...

Issues of morality vis-à-vis change and history, therefore, tend to define a people in the eyes of others as either caring and upright or as callous and corrupt. They tend to present a people in their daily lives as a people who have their own minds and think through their actions before they do things. They present us as a people who chew on our words before we proffer them, or on the other hand as mere imitators of others. They tend to judge us according to our innate qualities or lack of them to take care of our neighbors, our kith and kin, as haters of humanity and decency. They present us as a people who love truth for its own sake, as should be expected of beings of superior nature, or as beings of inferior intelligence, awareness and humanity.

In Chinua Achebe's trilogy, which approaches the dimensions of Greek classical tradition, *Things Fall Apart*, *No Longer at Ease*, and *Arrow of God*, we see a consistent exploration of the personal struggle of morally rich heroes who are faithful to tradition and the old ways, Okonkwo, Obi Okonkwo and Ezeulu, in their travails and struggles against their changing environment. Historic time wages a war against their desire to do the right thing. Often, Achebe's critics have come away with the notion that his heroes fail in their quests due to a fatal flaw or their *hubris*, (an innate disability) to cope with the times. In this paper, I argue that the hero fails because he is a victim of history and change, hence the tragedy and/or the tragic nature of his ordeal, for had he escaped from the moral dictates of his conscience and gone with everyone else there would have been no tragedy. In this instance, I also see the hero who succumbs half-heartedly and with a torn conscience, to the lure of pleasure and materialism, in this instance Obi Okonkwo, as a victim of the same historic time and change. There is only that much of an ordeal that a human being can endure. From this angle of vision, his punishment by incarceration becomes an instrument of tragedy that is elevating rather than degrading.

More specifically, in the "Preface" to the second edition of *Arrow of God*, Achebe deals with two significant issues, one arising from the other. The first is on the question of which of his novels he considers his favorite. We assume that this question, given its time, is with regard to his trilogy, which also are his first three novels. The second issue is on the question of crime and punishment as Achebe questions the common perception that suffering is necessarily a reflection of guilt. In regard to the first issue, after likening the question to "asking a man to list his children in the order in which he loves them" (Achebe 1989), Achebe conceded the "peculiar attractiveness of each child." But he also noted: "for *Arrow of God* that peculiar quality may lie in the fact that it is the novel which I am most likely to be caught sitting down to read again (Achebe 1989). In spite of what he considers to be "certain structural weaknesses" in *Arrow of God*, Achebe still sees this particular novel as the story of the "magnificent man, Ezeulu," a being of "high historic destiny as victim, consecrating by his agony." If we take this issue further, the discussion lapses into the second issue already mentioned above. And the relevant issue is this: even though Ezeulu is stricken with dementia at the moment when historical changes become overbearing for him in the face of his steadfastness to hand on to tradition and values handed down to him, he comes out as a winner. He is spared the knowledge that his environment and his defecting subjects have decided to overrule the dictates of the gods on the ordering of the universe. It is therein that lies the true tragedy in Achebe's world, a tragedy which continues for postmodern Nigerians today without resolution. The Nigeria of Ezeulu's days seems not to be different from the Nigeria of today. The point needs to be made therefore that what appears as punishment in the eyes of the world, may not necessarily be so in the eyes of higher spiritual beings. This is where confusion arises and where challenge can be issued. Many critics still hold that heroes who commit suicide, earn prison sentences or run mad are the same kind of people – social misfits who deserve their downfall. On the other hand, in my opinion, these people should be seen as victims of their circumstances, age and time, who deserve our pity. Such victims should be raised to lofty moral heights as heroes, especially if their ordeal is in the service of the people and/or their conscience. They are the stuff of which true tragedy is made. They ought to be seen as victims of marginality and hybridity, where the periphery rather than the center is the site of moral probity.

One of the major issues that the hybrid has to deal with is how to remain alone in the margin, and by extension, steady in his conviction and being able to withstand temptations and not swing to the other side. At times, the said temptation comes in the form of arrogant rivals who perceive one as an obstacle in their match towards what they deem as theirs because they deserve it, or as signs of progress. Such is the fate of Ezeulu in regard to his arch rival, Ogalanya (the Rich one), who is eternally envious of Ezeulu's status, influence and power in the community. Ogalanya sees him as the sole impediment in his ambition to add power and authority to his wealth. At other times, the hybrid finds himself or herself up against a whole institution or system. Such is the fate of Okonkwo before the machinery of British oppression through church and secular administration of his people in *Things Fall Apart*. All along, there is the overwhelming desire to survive without succumbing, yet one lacks the material means to survive without falling victim to strong desire. Sometimes, temptation comes in the form of opposition to one's declared moral stance. It could be one's superiors who hold the yam and the knife as the Igbo would say. It could be very troubling when it concerns one's means of livelihood, such as a job and promotion of the job, as was the case of Obi Okonkwo in *No Longer at Ease*. Temptations can also come from a family member – a father, wife or an older person – to whom one has to defer. Personal moral struggle comes to a head when the laws of the land condone an opposing viewpoint on the moral issue in question.

Speaking about the land and its laws leads naturally to the notions of insider and outsider in the social structure. An insider sees the land as his and, for all intents and purposes, wants to work to make it a better place in which to live. The better a country is, the more satisfaction and peace of mind one gets, even in poverty. One shares what one has with one's neighbors and kith and kin. It is exasperating, however, to see the self transform into the other, that is from the insider into the outsider, though all the time remaining the insider who is not quite the outsider. From this ambiguous position on the inside, he looks outside and acts like an outsider. From the outside again, he looks into the inside and the outside simultaneously, acting like an outsider in the inside. What could be more confusing, more incomprehensible, both for all those inside and the others who are outside? Achebe states, for example, that what draws Nigerians from the rural areas to the city (of Lagos) is not so much work, for they have an abundance of it at their base, as money – that instrument of modern easy living, but also of moral decrepitude and corruption (Achebe 1989). Colonialism, with its attendant autocracy and dispossession of the oppressed, had reversed the normal order of things, allowing people to expect gratification without work (Achebe 1989, 112). To this assertion, Achebe responds through his persona, Obi Okonkwo: "You (the colonialists) devised these soft conditions for yourselves when every European was automatically in the senior service and every African automatically in the junior service. Now that a few of us have been admitted into the senior service, you turn around and blame us" (Achebe 1989, 144).

Perhaps *No Longer at Ease* differs tremendously from the previous and first novel, *Things Fall Apart*, and from the later one, *Arrow of God*, due to the fact that the tragic hero does not meet his downfall from standing firm to the end. He rather dabbles into corrupt practices which he had earlier very vehemently opposed, even though he was inadequately prepared for that kind of living. The moment that the insider deviates from the narrow and safe path, carved out for him by destiny, into the road of the outsider in pursuit of what is in fashion, he steps out of the known terrain of the security of his conscience, into the evil forest or the wilderness of evil forces. He is no longer himself, nor is he for stepping into it, the other who knows his path. The insider stands exposed to the forces of judgment, the law and public scrutiny. Immediately, he sounds false to himself and becomes false in the eyes of others who seek his downfall. At one and the same time, he is saying discordantly: "I am who I know I am" and also "I am you who I am, but you indeed whom I do not really want to be." The whole situation is very unsettling both to self and the Other. Therein lies the tragic flaw. Following Obi Okonkwo's downfall, a fellow towns-man puts the situation very succinctly when he says: "It is lack of experience (on Obi Okonkwo's part). He should not have accepted the money (twenty pounds bribe) himself. What others do is tell you to go and hand it to their houseboy. Obi tried to do what everyone does without finding out how it was done" (Achebe 1989, 13). It is much like "the house rat who went swimming with his friend the lizard and died from cold, for while the lizard's scales kept him dry the rat's hairy body remained wet" (Achebe 1989, 13–14).

When the hero comes to a full awakening to his dilemma and the futility of his efforts to remain steadfast in the face of overwhelming odds, but fails to cross over to the side of change and history, he suffers the same fate as the insider who swings to the outside, but who does not do so completely and adequately enough to avoid personal retribution. In the eyes of the white man, for example, the native is seen as corrupt and mean to his kind. Yet, the white man seems oblivious of the fact that exposing the so-called native to corrupt practices in the first instance by his coming, has mitigated or compromised the native's ability to keep to his original way of doing things. The cultural shock which followed the encounter of the West and Africa has made the indigenous people "counter-feit coins," to use a very popular parlance in Nigeria, which is neither adequate for the old way nor the new. The reality of the new way is indeed at variance with his perceived new way of doing things. The parallel to Prospero's Caliban is very illuminating here,

We could further clarify this point by looking at the issue of African religion as given in Achebe's fiction. Without creed and distributing power to different gods in the pantheon of hierarchical powers, it recognizes the sanctity of all souls, both animate and inanimate. A citizen may not kill, maim nor exercise meanness on his neighbor without paying for it immediately. And transgression was promptly chastised by the instruments of community law to teach others a lesson. The Europeans came with the Christian God, swept aside the African gods, rendering them impotent and ineffective, yet their new God did not adequately replace that which it swept aside. How else can one explain the situation of Okoli in *Things Fall Apart*, Okoli who, despite his conversion to Christianity, stood in awe of the traditional African deities, to the point that he killed the sacred python to assure himself that he had given up his African religion for good? Today, independent churches proliferate in the effort to Africanize Christianity once again, but rather unsuccessfully. The creed meant to guide morality is often transgressed with impunity in modern Nigeria. Confused, the Nigerian finds himself abandoned in the middle with no real moral codes of conduct left to guide his actions. This translates in foreign mass media condemning Nigerians (read Africans) as corrupt to the core, having no moral codes of conduct (Achebe 1991, 48). They blame Nigerians for living in the present and harboring no serious thoughts, if any thoughts at all, about the future (Achebe 1991, 93). But the truth of the matter is that, in the past, one cared more for one's neighbor than is the case today. All surpluses were squandered by all to maintain harmony in the community, through feasts, festivals and title taking. The greatest power in the land, when it is even vested in one single individual as opposed to a group of individuals, was given to the weakest. The rationale was that the weak was less likely to abuse power than the strong. He would be least likely to use his power as an oppressive tool. It was mainly for this reason that Ezeulu became the chief of his community, even though quite poor compared to his followers. Moral values which ensured social cohesion were prized over physical power, oppression and vengeance.

As is evident in Achebe's fiction, in modern times and following colonization, Warrant Chiefs who are agents of foreign domination and power were imposed on the people without the usual dialogue and discussion that the people were used to. Office was given to the influential and powerful, in order the more to ensure the domination of the foreign power on the people. The conquest of foreign dominance and power through the system of indirect rule was made complete and water-tight. For failing to accept the "honor", a prospective Warrant Chief was clamped into jail and made to suffer for his recalcitrance (Achebe 1989, 56–57; 116–119). For accepting the post and becoming corrupt like his white masters, new Warrant Chiefs were also deemed corrupt and their conduct incomprehensible (Achebe 1989, 59). The nature of the system of indirect rule also put the British, in turn, yes!, in a hybrid position, for they are neither the natives they claim to understand very well, nor are they any longer their old British persons, ignorant of the ways of the natives. It is worthy of note that unlike the French who made a tabula rasa of all things native and sought to assimilate him into French civilization, the British always commissioned their officers to study the ways of impressing their system on the African without disturbing too much his world view. The end result is a confused system of governance which is neither truly African any more nor British, hence inadequate and confining (Achebe 1989, 106; 180). The Nigerian is the individual torn by this sense of neither being here nor there, a victim of the times.

This paper has tried to theorize the present predicament of many a Nigerian in postmodern times in regard to questions of personal morality and societal instability. The question of individual accountability could never be completely erased, no matter how eloquently we blame past colonial masters for the ills of the country. Yet, it is a truism that society maketh man and man society. It would appear that man is a victim of society's lapses and corruption, not of his own moral failing. I do believe that African literary studies in the new millennium should be about providing ideas that would guide society to think more about reform rather than criticism of its citizens. Therein lies salvation for the human race. The individual is a victim of his environment and desires that we study appropriately his predicament and environment in order to start a new change in the right direction, a new direction which will ensure the establishment of true democracy and humanity.

We hope that our followers will not only examine other works by Achebe, but also other African works of fiction, in order to bring up ideas that could help societal reform in the new millennium. We believe that such an academic exercise could result in in-depth analyses of our age and society and would be of benefit to the whole humanity.

Works Cited

Achebe, Chinua. *Things Fall Apart*. London: Heinemann, 1958.

———. *Arrow of God*. London: Heinemann, 1964.

———. *No Longer at Ease*. London: Heinemann, 1989.

McClintock, Anne, Aamir Multi and Ella Shohat. *Dangerous Liaisons: Gender, Nation and Postcolonial Perspectives*. Minneapolis: University of Minnesota Press, 1998.

Minh-ha, Trinh. "Not You/Like You: Postcolonial Women and the Interlocking Questions of Identity and Difference." In *Dangerous Liaisons: Gender, Nation and Postcolonial Perspectives*. Minneapolis: University of Minnesota Press, 1998.

Chapter 21

Achebe's Works and the Omnipresence of the Colonial Legacy: A Theoretical Study of the Relationship Between Literature and History

Alfred Ndi

THE POSITION OF TRADITIONAL RUSSIAN FORMALISTS was that literature is a self-contained world with its own rules and regulations, an intransitive structure which has nothing to do with our realistic world and material experience (Jameson 1975; Matejka *et al*, 1971). While this premise may be relevant for literature written for the sake of art, to exhibit linguistic competence perhaps, it does not apply completely to African literature: a committed and transitive literature written for a social purpose. The novels of Chinua Achebe are written not only for the delight of the reader; they also have a didactic purpose. They entertain but also teach. They teach about the momentous historical events that shaped the past of the African continent and which also explain why the present takes the form it has.

Things Fall Apart describes the first phase of Western encounter with Africa at the beginning of the Twentieth Century, leading to the advent of British Indirect Rule in Igboland. The period between 1884 and 1900 was marked by the arrival of missionaries, administrators, traders and soldiers. As Okonkwo's exile into Mbanta ends, he returns home to discover that:

> The missionaries had come to Umuofia. They had built their Church there, won a handful of converts and were already sending evangelists to the surrounding towns and villages (101).

The missionaries came "to preach the gospel" (105). To achieve this objective, "they asked for a plot of land to build their Church" (105). With the increase in the number of Christians who soon constituted a small community of women, men and children, an injunction is passed in Mbanta proclaiming "that the adherents of the new faith were thenceforth excluded from the life and privileges of the clan" (113).

The presence of British Indirect Rule was evidenced by a new system of governance and law and order. The narrator explains:

> ... the white man had also brought a government. They had built a court where the District Commissioner judged cases in ignorance. He had court messengers who brought men to him for trial. Many of these messengers came from Umuru on the bank of the Great River where the white men first came ... They guarded the prison which was full of men who had offended against the white man's law. Some of these prisoners had thrown away their twins and some had molested the Christians (123).

W.E.F. Ward (1966: 312) confirms this new situation, and reports that the British administration was naïve about the implications of culture practices in Igboland. He says that:

> The British people were ... very ignorant of African life and the ideas which lie behind it, but it was a genuinely kindly feeling which led them to think it their duty to stop the human suffering contained in such practices as human sacrifice and the exposure of twins.

The British colonial administration "built a trading store and for the first time palm-oil and kernel became things of great price and much money flowed into Umuofia" (Achebe, 1958: 126). They also "built a school and a little hospital in Umuofia" (128). The school institution was resisted by the indigenous people. Mr. Brown "went from family to family begging people to send their children to his school" (128). He prophesies that "the leaders of the land in the future would be men and women who had learned to read and write" (128). Soon, the indigenous world began to have faith in and to trust the intentions of the colonial order. The narrator confirms that:

> In the end Mr. Brown's arguments began to have an effect. More people came to learn in his school and he encouraged them with gifts of singlets and towels (128).

The British people knew that their mission which they considered civilizing, would not be easy to accomplish. E.A. Ayandele (1966: 137) observes that the Europeans "bribed ... with appropriate European goods such as umbrellas, looking glasses, biscuits, velvet cloth and chairs." Added to these inducements were the benefits that the school brought to learners, and Achebe notes that "a few months in it were enough to make one a court clerk. Those who stayed longer became teachers" (128).

Teachers and clerks were the first professional personalities that the British administration created in colonial Nigeria. They constituted the highly respected elite which the indigenous Nigerian admired and the administration relied upon to promote its mission. The Christian religion gained in strength and prestige, "because of it link with the new administration" (128).

Achebe's *Arrow of God* and *No Longer at Ease* portray the colonial epoch in Nigeria when British Rule was already well implanted. *Arrow of God* marks the phase in the process of social change when the indigenous world was governed both by the British administration and local Chiefs. E.A. Keay and H. Thomas (1965: 114) explain:

> One of the aims of the British Government in ... Nigeria was to rule as far as possible through the Chiefs and their Councils. The system of government in [this colony] ... was a mixture of direct and indirect rule ... the central government was in the hands of the Governor, who was assisted by an executive and a legislative Council. Local government was largely in the hands of the tribal authorities under the supervision of British District Officers.

Captain Winterbottom is one of the District Officers in *Arrow of God*. His personal and administrative experiences described by Achebe, tell of the advancement of British colonial tradition in Africa:

> Fifteen years ago, Winterbottom might have been so depressed by the climate and food as to have doubts about service in Nigeria. But he was now a hardened coaster. And although the climate still made him irritable and limp, he would now exchange the life for the comfort of Europe. His strong belief in the value of the British mission in Africa was strangely enough, strengthened during the Cameroon campaign of 1916 when he fought the Germans. That was how he had got the title of Captain but unlike many other colonial administrators who also saw active service in the Cameroon, he carried his into peace-time (30).

Captain Winterbottom thinks that native administration is not sufficiently developed to be independent and unregulated. But instructions from his hierarchy insist that he must work in collaboration with the local Chief. The memorandum sent by the Lieutenant-Governor to him spells out the conduct of his rule in these terms:

> To many colonial nations, native administration means government by white men. You are all aware that HMG considers this policy as mistaken. In place of the alternative of governing directly through Administrative Officers, there is the other method of trying while we endeavour to purge the native system of its abuses to build a higher civilisation upon the soundly rooted native stock that had its foundation in the hearts and minds and thoughts of the people and therefore on which we can more easily build, moulding it and establishing it into lines consonant with modern ideas and higher standards, and yet all the time enlisting the real force of the spirit of the people, instead of killing that

323

out and trying to start afresh. We must not destroy the African atmosphere, the African mind, the whole foundation of his race (55–56).

British Indirect Rule also prompted change in the cultural and political outlook of the Igbo people. Chief Ikedi of Okperi saw opportunity in the colonial order. He became cleverer and corrupt, by getting his people to make him a King, "this ... among a people who abominated Kings" (Achebe, 1958: 58). Achebe concludes:

> This was what British administration was doing among the Ibos, making a dozen mushroom kings grow where there was none before (58).

No Longer at Ease marks a period of the colonial history of Africa when former British dependencies were just about to attain independence as evidenced by Charles Ibe's letter to Obi Okonkwo dated 1957 (87). This period was characterized by the emergence of what may be referred to as the second generation of educated Africans who had not only gone to school in Africa, but had done university studies in Europe, and had returned just in time to criticize the class and status assumptions of colonial Africa with the egalitarian philosophies they had learned abroad, and to occupy posts of responsibility both in the colonial and post-colonial administrations.

Obi Okonkwo represents the enlightened African. He has come a long way from the age of the indigenous African who was afraid of the colonialist's gun such as the men in *Things Fall Apart* who "had broken into tumult instead of action" (144–5) when Okonkwo, Obi's grandfather, cuts down the District Officer's messenger, and the epoch of the semi-acculturated Africans such as houseboys and road-diggers in *Arrow of God*.

The colonial master is sensitive to these historical changes in the personality of the African. The changes induce transformations in the preconceptive attitude of Mr. Green, as the narrator highlights:

> It was clear he loved Africa, but only Africa of a kind: the Africa of Charles the messenger, the Africa of his garden-boy and steward-boy. He must have come originally with an ideal – to bring light to the heart of darkness, to tribal head-hunters performing weird ceremonies and unspeakable rites. But when he arrived, Africa played him false. Where was his beloved bush full of human sacrifice? There was St. George horsed and caparisoned, but where was the dragon? In 1900, Mr. Green might have ranged among the great missionaries; in 1935 he would have made do with slapping headmasters in the presence of their pupils, but in 1957, he could only curse and swear (96–7).

A Man of the People and *Anthills of the Savannah* written in a bitter satirical style, mark the epoch of neo-colonial Africa; an epoch assessed by Achebe in *A Man of the People* as "the beginning of a phase for me in which I intend to take a hard look at what we in Africa are making of independence" (119). Neo-colonial Africa is the contemporary period of the continent characterized by political dictatorship and degeneration, administrative incompetence, repression of liberties, military brutality and permissive immorality. Achebe witnesses the birth of an African political system characterized by totalitarian regimes run by providential personalities and presidents-for-life, such as Ngongo in *Anthills of the Savannah* (53). He portrays African leaders ruling like domineering chiefs. They use methods such as panegyric verses to immortalize their influence in politics and to compel their subordinates to cower under them. The prime minister in *A Man of the People* is called by the names *the Tiger, the Lion, the One and Only, the Sky, the Ocean,* and many other names of praise (5). In *Anthills of the Savannah*, cabinet ministers keep their posts by "worshipping" and cringing in front of the president of Kangan (24). In *A Man of the People*, the single-party state setup requires that "loyalty to the party" (4) should be the only prerequisite that entitles one to a post of minister or to a high administrative position.

Anthills of the Savannah characterizes the post-colonial period as a time when presidents came to power without any preparation for political leadership (12). His Excellency, the inept President of Kangan seizes power through a *coup d' etat*; he gathers his collaborators and friends and asks them: "What shall I do?" (12). The African modern politician is "unable to re-establish vital links with the poor and the dispossessed" (141).

Although Honourable T.C. Kobina in *A Man of the People* is the minister of public constructions, he "hadn't been appointed for his expertise" (43). Chief Nanga is the minister of culture, but "he had never heard of his country's most famous novel" (65). In *Anthills of the Savannah* gangs of political supporters confront each other and create situations fraught with violence and death. The military President of Kangan lives in constant fear of a *coup d' etat*. He has a "constant nightmare ... of people falling into disaffection and erupting into ugly demonstrations" (13). His regime reacts to coup attempts with "secret trials and executions in the barracks" (14). Public executions are "such a popular sport" (43); railway workers and demonstrating students on strike are shot. Any official who challenges government authority loses his post or life.

Liberties of the press and association are confiscated and intellectuals are emasculated in *A Man of the People*. The mass media are used as instruments of manipulation to keep the African in ignorance and out of touch with reality. The Prime Minister dismisses Dr. Makinde, the technically-competent Minister of Finance and two-thirds of his cabinet members because their demands for economic reform would cause him to lose forthcoming elections. But during his evening broadcast on the national radio station, he announces that:

> ... the dismissed ministers were conspirators and traitors, who had teamed up
> with foreign saboteurs to destroy the nation (3).

After the announcement, the newspapers carry the Prime Minister's version of
the story. Manipulated student unions call for "a detention law to deal with the
miscreants" (4). Although Dr. Makinde presents a prepared speech on his economic
program, the Hansard newspaper carries a garbled version of it.

Chief Nanga declares privately that only European corporations should tar
roads in his country. To ensure that newspapers do not publish this information
which may scandalize him, he corrupts the press by giving a dash of five pounds
to the Editor of the Daily Matchet. He explains his motives:

> If I don't give him something now, tomorrow he go and write rubbish about
> me. They say it is the freedom of the press. But to me it is nothing short of the
> freedom to crucify innocent men and assassinate their character (66).

The press is presented as contributing to the tradition of dictatorship by fueling the
antagonism between politicians and intellectuals. It is characterized by nationalistic
ideologies and propaganda. After the dismissal of the Western-trained Minister of
Finance, Dr. Makinde, the Daily Chronicle carries an Editorial which reads:

> We are proud to be Africans. Our true leaders are not those intoxicated in their
> Oxford, Cambridge, or Harvard degrees, but those who speak the language of
> the people. Away with the damnable and expensive university education which
> only alienates an African from his rich and ancient culture (4).

Chris Oriko in *Anthills of the Savannah* is Commissioner for Information in Kangan, and in the words of His Excellency the President, he "owns all the words in
his country-newspapers, radio, and television stations" (6). News is announced by
half-literate and pretentious journalists and sometimes, the British Broadcasting
Corporation in London has a fuller story in the African news than local radio
stations in Kangan (164).

The African elite is also shown as a voiceless and subservient personality
prostrating before the official establishments of his country. His lack of courage causes him to betray social causes. His condescending silence and affairism
characterize his relationship with government institutions. Intellectuals criticize
anything government does:

> But when they are put in positions where they are supposed to influence gov-
> ernment policy, they acquiesce and start politicking because they want better
> positions (79–80).

Nationals with skills and university graduates are distrusted by the uneducated
politicians who prefer to work with European expatriates in *A Man of the People*.

They award public road contracts to foreign experts (42), although in the words of General Lango in *Anthills of the Savannah*, the roads break up … as they are being laid" (79). Graduates from universities in search of jobs must stoop to lick any Big Man's boots as a way of getting favors.

Essentially, there is no accountability by the management of the Kangan state economy. In the electricity corporation chaotic billing procedures are used to cover up massive fraud whenever the audit department suspects inquiries are underway. Alhadji Abdul Mahmoud is Chairman of the Kangan/American Chamber of Commerce. He uses his political position to monopolize the importation of fertilizers into the country. No custom officer dares to inspect his imports. His possessions include eight ocean liners, three private jets, fifty companies and a bank (117).

In *A Man of the People*, ministers snatch the girlfriends of poor intellectuals. As an era of favouritism and personal influences, Odili reveals that a common saying in the country after independence was that it didn't matter what you knew but who you knew (17). In an era of intellectual dishonesty and mediocrity; an era when the new African elite looks with contempt at the activities of the new class of political leaders who promote dictatorship and intolerance, the very ills that motivated the nationalists to fight against the colonial legacy. Odili underlines their preoccupations:

> The trouble with our new nation … was that none of us had been indoors long enough to be able to say 'To hell with it.' We had all been in the rain together … Then a handful of us – the smart and the lucky and the hardly ever the best – had scrambled for the one shelter our former rulers left, and had taken it over and barricaded themselves through numerous loudspeakers, that the first phase of the struggle had been won and that the next phase – the extension of our house – was even more important and called for new and original tactics; it required that all argument should cease and the whole people speak with one voice and that any more dissent and argument outside the door of the shelter would subvert and bring down the whole house (37).

It is an epoch when the high hope soon after independence is dashed by the corruption of politics. Max's father is so embittered by the mismanagement of independence of their country that he regrets: "We should never have asked the white man to go" (81).

Chinua Achebe's novels, *Things Fall Apart, Arrow of God, No Longer at Ease, A Man of the People*, and *Anthills of the Savannah*, are historically-committed works of literature. They describe in artistic and structural form, the pre-colonial, colonial and post-colonial epochs of Africa. They show in a chronological fashion the processes of transformation to which our ancestors were subjected and they account for the status-quo in contemporary Africa. In this way, Achebe has shown great expertise in amalgamating art and reality, creation and history.

Works Cited

Achebe, Chinua. *Things Fall Apart*. London: Heinemann, 1958.

———. *Arrow of God*. London: Heinemann, 1964.

———. *No Longer at Ease*. London: Heinemann, 1960.

———. *A Man of the People*. London: Heinemann, 1966.

———. *Anthills of the Savannah*. London: Heinemann, 1987.

Ayandele, E.A. "External Influence on African Society." In Joseph Anene and Godfrey Brown, eds. *Africa in the Nineteenth and Twentieth Centuries*. Ibadan: IUP and Nelson, 1966: 133–148.

Jameson, Fredric. *The Prison House of Language: A Critical Account of Structuralism and Russian Formalism*. Princeton and London: Princeton University Press, 1972.

Keay, E.A. and H. Thomas. *West African Government for Nigerian Students*. Ibadan: Ibadan Univ. Press, 1965

Matejka, Ladislav and Pomorska Krystyna. *Readings in Russian Poetics: Formalist and Structuralist Views*. Mass: MIT Press, 1971.

Ndi, Alfred. "Social Commitment in African Modern Literature: A Comprehensive Overview." 1977.

Ward, W.E.F. "Colonial Rule in West Africa." In Joseph Anene and Godfrey Brown, eds. *Africa in the Nineteenth and Twentieth Centuries*. Ibadan: IUP and Nelson: 308–325.

Part Five

African Womanhood

Chapter 22

Achebe on the Woman Question

Sophie Ogwude

FLORENCE STRATTON IN HER BOOK *Contemporary African Literature and the Politics of Gender* (1994) summarizes the popular view of female critiques as regards Achebe's portrayals of women in art. Of *Things Fall Apart* (1958), Stratton writes that in this novel Achebe "legitimizes this process whereby women were excluded from post-colonial politics and public affairs through its representation of pre-colonial Igbo society as governed entirely by men" (27). Echoing the same sentiments, Kerz Okafor states that in "Achebe's works [women] are mere echoes and voices, and [that] they unquestioningly acquiesce to the status quo" (142). In her own paraphrase of an earlier study she had done, Ezeigbo lists Achebe as one of the "notable male novelists who had formerly relegated women's experience to the background" (53). Unfortunately, Ezeigbo attributes what she, deems Achebe's welcome departure from this trend to his comment that the Nigerian society has "created all kinds of myth to support the suppression of the woman and … that the time has now come to put an end to that…" (Interview with A. Rutherford, quoted in *Feminism* (53). A resolution now believed to have been implemented in *Anthills of the Savannah*. I find this conclusion unsettling. In the first place, it is my conviction (and I propose to show this in the present study) that what Achebe has done in *Anthills of the Savannah* especially in the female portraitures is consistent with what he has always done. He has done nothing here organically different. The principles informing his female characterizations are unchanged. Notably also, Rutherford's interview with Achebe was published in 1987, the same year as the novel in question was first published in the United Kingdom. Therefore, it becomes difficult to accept the novelist's words as a declaration of an action plan for a novel which may in fact have been written, if not as a whole, then definitely to a great extent, even before such a declaration. Finally, needless to add that authorial statements are usually divorced from the appraisals of works of art and for good reasons.

However, if we leave all this at this point and re-focus attention on the concern of this paper which is to show that Achebe has not been anti-feminist and that his character portraitures, both male and female remain authentic within the specific periods in our history in which they are situated, then I should say upfront that I am not as presumptuous as to imagine that I could take on the role of an apologist for Chinua Achebe. Luckily for me, Kenneth Harrow sets the course of this paper in his observation that the artistic representation of social reality should not be equated to a legitimization of the same. He writes thus:

> What Achebe resists in *Things Fall Apart* is the romanticizing of the African past. Even though he constructs a male-centered gaze when depicting desire, he is critical of all that is human in that past society of the Igbos. And his criticism has remained powerful, in part because he does not flinch before the horrific. *Babies and the elderly ill are cast away into the forest, children are sacrificed, and manly heroes are reduced to insecure defensive chauvinists whose aggressive actions lead to the opposite of the intended consequences.* That is true of Christians as well as traditional believers, to whites and blacks, to men and women. If there is Ikemefuna, there is Nwoye, and their stories hardly legitimize oppressive divisions of power or exclusions of women in post – Independence Nigerian society (177–8; emphasis mine).

I have quoted Harrow at length because his is an apt summary of all the major issues in the novel. Ironically, although maligned by feminists, there are in fact very strong pointers to Achebe's feminist sympathies/leanings in this novel. In Ekwefi, the novelist depicts a woman who to all intents and purposes is a thorough feminist:

> Ekwefi's mind went back to the days when they were young. She had married Anene because Okonkwo was too poor then to marry. Two years after marriage to Anene she could bear it no longer and she ran away to Okonkwo (76).

In feminist parlance, it is said that until a woman can have freedom enough over her body to decide what sexual or marital roles, if any, she can be subjected to, she could forever remain a man's "vassal, the creature of another's will, frustrated in his transcendence and deprived of every value" (*The Second Sex* 21). The primary goal of womenfolk, feminists note, is the freedom to exercise personal rights unfettered by all human imposed restrictions. Marriage and other matters concerning a woman's right over her sexuality, are the proper contexts within which to fight for "the repossession by women of our bodies as Rich contends (292). Of all the social activities in Umuofia, Ekwefi loved wrestling best and predictably, she chooses to live with the best and most successful wrestler of the village.

In the period of our history when prudery was often equated with acceptable female decorum we find Achebe's Ekwefi jettisoning societal restrictions and expectations, and even under what native sense will call questionable circumstances, she is able to forge a meaningful relationship with Okonkwo. In fact, the novelist tells us that of all his wives she alone has "the audacity to bang on his door" (54). That Okonkwo will in a fit of male chauvinism beat her for killing a banana tree which was very much alive (27) and even proceed later (in response to further provocation) to test the firing ability of his gun on her, does not change the fact that had she died as a result of this "defensive chauvinism," it would simply have added to those "actions of a defensive chauvinist whose aggressive actions lead to the opposite of the intended consequences" as Harrow has intimated.

About Ekwefi's motherhood plight, Okonkwo is also responsive. About their encounter with Chielo, Achebe writes:

> Okonkwo was also feeling tired and sleepy, for although nobody else knew it, he had not slept at all last night. He had felt very anxious but did not show it. When Ekwefi had followed the priestess, he had allowed what he regarded as a reasonable and manly interval to pass and then gone with his matchet to the shrine, where he thought they must be. It was only when he had got there that it had occurred to him that the priestess might have chosen to go round the villages first. Okonkwo had returned home and sat waiting. When he thought he had waited long enough he again returned at the shrine. But the Hills and the Caves were as silent as death. It was only in his fourth trip that he had found Ekwefi, and by then he had become gravely worried (78).

Clearly, the images of female domination and oppression are absent from this work. Ekwefi, the wife who has not borne Okonkwo a son, is unquestionably, his favorite. Even the most casual reading of his novel reveals also that he favors his daughter, Ezinma, more than his first son, Nwoye. Again, the social function as well as the status of Chielo, the priestess of *Agbala* is undeniably equitable to that of the masquerades. Also, it is of significance that Chielo in this capacity is cast as being in a superior position to even the male members of this society. Even the status quo of which Okafor writes is a vexed issue and especially so in this novel. Embedded in this status quo are clearly defined duties and responsibilities for men as well as for women, distinct and separate duties often times complementary.

Frankly, I find it a trivialization of very serious concerns when feminists begin to look for loop-holes where there are none. Even in this very first novel, Achebe cannot be rightly accused of "relegating women's experience to the background" (Ezeigbo 53). Perhaps, the critic's real quarrel is with the traditional roles of the sexes and it is clear that there is a divide over this issue among feminists. Even in far-away France and fourteen years after the first appearance of *Things Fall Apart*, the celebrated feminist Simone de Beauvoir describes as the destiny of women in the society the female properties of marriage and motherhood. Is concern with such issues not really legitimate to women, even though feminists? We may decide what role we play in these areas if any; we have the right to refuse to be circumscribed by these concerns; we should, if we have to, be able to relegate marriage and motherhood to the background in pursuance of an incursion into the "man's world of adventure." But in the final analysis, marriage and motherhood are the domains of womanhood and we should not be less women for being feminists.

Achebe's first three novels at least are tragic. And *Things Fall Apart* is the tragedy of one man, worked out of his personal conflicts – his neurosis, almost – as well as out of the contrariness of his destiny" (Irele 1967: 27). Kirsten Holst Peterson (1995) has drawn attention to the fact that Okonkwo is sanctioned not for beating his wife but for doing so in the week of peace. But Okonkwo's tragedy is such that if judged on the male/female polemics, he can hardly be found any more guilty by one than by the other. "The meaning he attaches to 'manliness' amounts to fierceness, violence," writes Irele as he comments on the violation of the week of peace:

> His influence is such that he becomes a menace to his society even within the limits of its code ... he contravenes a sacred custom by beating his wife during a sacred week – he was 'not the man to stop beating somebody half way through, not even for fear of a goddess.' And one of the elders commenting on his action remarks: 'The evil you have done can ruin the whole clan. The earth goddess whom you have insulted may refuse to give us her increase, and we shall all perish.' (26, emphasis mine).

In *No Longer at Ease* (1960), the major catalysts against whom the hero Obi Okonkwo must contend are two female figures who loom large in the novel: his mother Hannah and his girlfriend, Clara. Obi Okonkwo emerges only as a wilting puppet at both their hands, a weakling of whom we are told that the death of one and the exit from his life of the other, combined to "dull his sensibility and left him a different man" (2). Hannah Okonkwo is "the woman who got things done" (150). Whereas Isaac Okonkwo, her husband was more the man of thought, she was the person of action and courage as her single-handed slaying of Udo's he-goat proves. On her own part, Clara is a British trained Nursing Sister – a feat even in these more recent times. Certainly, she is not the kind of person to be classified as an "echo". Against the backdrop of a listing of the great men of the past we learn that:

> Today greatness has changed its tune. Titles are no longer great, neither are barns or large numbers of wives or children. Greatness is now in the things of the white man. And so we too have changed our tune. We are the first in all the nine villages to send our son to the white man's land (49).

In direct competition with the village of Iguedo, the Mbaino village had also sent off their child to the white man's land. But a daughter and not a son. Whereas in the past it was possible to list only men as achievers, the current trend is different. Clara is painted in relative positive light as against the near despicable sketch of Obi, "a pathetic figure without any grain of nobility" (Irele 29).

Obviously, Achebe's heroes in these texts are largely pathetic. But rather than take up issues with Achebe on account of this, many critics have in examining such portraitures within the general socio-political contexts of the individual works reached the reasonable conclusion that the tragic medium of his exposition explains his characterizations. Irele who I must quote one last time provides characteristic insight where he writes that:

> Tragedy implies that working out in men's lives of a vigorous fatality that transcends the individual's ability to comprehend or to arrest its pre-ordained course of events (24).

What Achebe has done in *Anthills of the Savannah* particularly with female characterization is the same as he has done in the earlier novels. The Nigerian society like any other society is dynamic, continually changing in response to social realities and expectations. This means that the social truth or reality of the Nigerian domestic social scene in 1958 can only now be a far cry from the present day social scene. And for a writer as interested in social realism as Achebe is, this difference cannot but be reflected in his works.

Ezeigbo has hailed this novel as one in which female characters are "highlighted as achievers, women who dominate the action of the novel in more positive and constructive manner" (1988). But then the title of the relevant paper: "Reflecting the Times," underscores her point. Even as early as with *No Longer at Ease*, Achebe had realized that whereas it was possible in the past to list achievers and giants only in terms of male figures, all that had now gone and greatness could only now be measured in the things of the white man. Perhaps "more positive and constructive manner" is taken to mean roles antithetical to traditional women roles. However, for many, these traditional roles are also positive and constructive. Take the belabored issue of productive labor for instance. Engels, and later, Lenin in their contributions towards western feminism, had argued that "the first premise for the emancipation of women is the re-introduction of the entire female sex into public industry" (50) and that "in order to achieve the complete emancipation of women we must have social economy and the participation of women in general productive labour" (52). From the earliest of times, female labor has been an integral part of subsistence as well as economic production in Africa. With this in mind, it becomes hardly surprising that many African women fighting the feminist cause, are often-times unable to support feminists of other culture backgrounds who argue passionately about the need for female productive labor. Female engagement in productive labor *per se* cannot even provide much meaningful emancipation for women in Africa essentially because right from the earliest times as Angelika Bammer points out:

> Our bodies have been the nexus of the spheres of reproduction and production. The interlocking systems of economic and sexual exploitation within patriarchal culture ..." (153).

Wholesome as Engels' and Lenin's solution to the woman question may sound on account of the goals and meaningful life engagement and the economic independence possible with it, this solution is fraught with shortcomings. A woman's femininity has determined, and will determine, to what extent she participates in productive labor. Even Marxist feminists have since reconsidered their position and have argued that:

> a narrowly economic model of revolution based on the concepts of class and production that ignore the significantly different conditions of men and women in society is both insufficient and imprecise (Bammer 150).

Women need much more than engagement in productive labor for their advancement and emancipation. The proper starting point for the realization of these goals is a genuine attempt at understanding femininity. Many feminists have realized this and have worked at providing better alternatives to the large prescriptive solutions of Engels and Lenin. Women have seen that their lives and experiences and hopes and desires, provide the relevant avenues and answers. Writers who have as their immediate concerns authentic lives as Achebe does, have shown that it is from these that answers to the woman question may be found.

Okonkwo and his fellow men do not dominate the action of *Things Fall Apart* any more than Christopher Oriko, Ikem Oshodi, His excellency and all the other male characters do the action of *Anthills of the Savannah*. Neither can Beatrice fit into any of the female roles of the earlier work. Her education and exposure, some of the more positive consequences of our encounter with a colonial power have combined to widen her attainment landscape and we all know from experience that the job opportunities assured by Western education ill afford women the time to engage in long social activities as was possible in the past. At the present time, such activities, if at all, can now only be possible in the rural setting from which our education human-fold has fled. So that in the final analysis, we can legitimately conclude that Ekwefi, Hannah, Clara and Beatrice are all products of their times.

In reaction to the concerns of the present, Achebe goes further though to make some pronouncements on the woman question in *Anthills of the Savannah*. The salient point he makes is that the role of women should be determined by women and not prescribed by men. And so although the role of the woman in the women's war of 1929 served its purposes, "it is not enough" that women should be the court of last resort because the last resort is often "too late" (92). Thus, the womenfolk in this text are visibly involved all through in the socio-political drama it unfolds. Nnolim has dismissed feminism, especially in the African context, as "a house divided." Indeed, feminism can in a sense be deemed "a house divided" if we are to consider the different mainstream ideologies within the movement. But what remains an inalienable truth is that women must learn to tolerate their differences and forge common grounds. Thus, the working out of an acceptance between Beatrice and Agatha especially and these two together with Elewa, Aina and Adamma remains significant. These are all women but of different social/economic/educational backgrounds and in putting them all together in comradeship, Achebe makes the point that for women to be able to move forward in any meaningful manner, they must successfully combine their areas of strength.

On the basis of our discussion so far, it is believed that there is a need for African critics interested in African literature to redefine for themselves and their followers the term feminism in such a way as to take into account the peculiar parameters which might be admissible and even expected of the African feminist. The African feminist is a strong character even though her femininity belies this fact. She is a matriarch; she is home-proud and respects the man who is mindful of the need for the survival and preservation of family life. She is economically productive within and if need be, outside the home. Like her Western counterpart, she is also oriented towards self-preservation and employs all resources available to her in safeguarding all she holds sacred. Many of Achebe's heroines meet these standards.

Works Cited

Achebe, Chinua. *Things Fall Apart*. London: Heinemann, 1958.
———. *No Longer at Ease*. London: Heinemann, 1960.
———. *Anthills of the Savannah*. Ibadan: Heinemann Educational Books, 1988.
Bammer, Angelika. "Women and Revolution: Their Theories, Our Experiences" In *Literature and Ideology*. Lewis-bury: Bucknell University Press, 1982.
Beauvoir, S. *The Second Sex*. Harmondsworth: Penguin Books, 1972.
Engels, F. "Origin of the Family, Private Property and the State" In Marx and Engels *Selected Works*. London: Lawrence and Wishart, 1968.
Ezeigbo, T. "The Dynamics of African Womanhood in Ayi Kwei Armah's Novels" In H. Chukwuma ed. *Feminism in African Literature*. Enugu: New Generation, 1994: 53–71.
Harrow, K.W. "I'm Not a [Western] Feminist But…" A Review of Recent Critical Writings on African Women's Literature. In *Research in African Literatures*. Vol 29 (3). 1998: 171–190.
Irele, A. "The Tragic Conflict in Achebe's Novels." *Black Orpheus*. 17 June 1967: 24–32.
Lenin, V.I. *The Woman Question*. New York: International Publishers, 1951.
Nnolim, C. "A House Divided" In *Feminism in African Literature*. Enugu: New Generation, 1994: 248–261.
Okafor, K. "Ngugi's Women: Positive Factors of Social Regeneration" In *Feminism in African Literature*: 131–143.
Peterson, K.H. "First Things First: Problems of a Feminist Approach to African Literature" In Ashcroft, B., *et al* ed. *The Post Colonial Studies Reader*. London: Routledge, 1995: 251–3.
Rich, A. *Of Women Born*: Motherhood as Experience and Institution. New York: Bantam Books, 1977.

Chapter 23

The Changing Female Image in Achebe's Novels

Ngozi Ezenwanyi Umunnakwe

THIS PAPER POSITS THAT CHINUA ACHEBE, the distinguished and renowned Nigerian novelist gave the woman peripheral and marginal treatment in his early novels set in traditional Africa. Influenced by tradition and patriarchy, and obsessed with the glorification and deification of the man in traditional Igbo society, Achebe abysmally relegated the woman to the background.

However, with growing awareness and sudden realization of the potentialities and relevance of the woman in modern society, Achebe consciously begins to craft women with some measure of prominence and individuality in his *Anthills of the Savannah*. This welcome development and commitment to feminist ideals is the focus of this paper. The paper x-rays the changing female image in Achebe's works with focus on *No Longer at Ease*, *A Man of the People*, and *Anthills of the Savannah*. It highlights Achebe's changing perspective in the exploration and re-definition of the female psyche from his earlier to the later novels and commends the novelist for his flexibility and amenability to positive and realistic criticism.

Chinua Achebe, author of five full length novels, namely *Things Fall Apart* (1958), *No Longer at Ease* (1960), *Arrow of God* (1964), *A Man of the People* (1966) and *Anthills of the Savannah* (1987) has been variously accused of treating his female characters with levity. A hard look at his novels that deal with traditional Igbo society namely *Things Fall Apart* and *Arrow of God* reveals that no woman is given prominence. The women in these novels are marginally and superficially delineated. They are seen in the shadow of the men, as wives and mothers, which are roles traditionally assigned to them in patriarchal societies. We have glimpses of Okonkwo's three wives, Ezeulu's wives, Ogbuefi Ndulue's nine wives, among others. Most of these women have no names, they lack individuality and cannot assert their selfhood even in their homes. They are often mindless and intimidated into cowed silence. For instance, in *Arrow of God*, Ogbuefi Ndulue's nine wives are called upon to demonstrate their respect and loyalty to their husband. They come in turns, kneel down before him, respectfully take the wine gourd from his hand and drink the wine. Such condescending roles were gleefully highlighted to depict the subservient role of the woman in tradition and patriarchy.

In *Things Fall Apart*, Okonkwo's fiery anger is directed on his helpless and frightened wives. He beats up one of them during the Week of Peace and shoots at another, nearly killing her because she dares retort when he, Okonkwo, talks. Achebe's women are neither supposed to be seen nor heard. No woman therefore, in his traditional novels, could feature as a major character. Acholonu (312) succinctly buttresses this point when she writes that:

> the women are invariably made to live, be seen and appreciated essentially through their husbands, lovers or children. The resultant artistic invisibility, coupled with the disability of inferiorized and stereotyped characterization, is a necessary technique for proving [the] man's undisputed superiority and masculinity.

However, this situation begins to change slightly as Achebe crafts his urban novels, *No Longer at Ease* and *A Man of the People*. In these two novels, some measure of recognition and prominence, albeit infinitesimal, is accorded the woman. Clara, Obi Okonkwo's girlfriend is a British-trained nurse. This is a rare feat for a woman whose traditional role is circumscribed in the home and precisely in the kitchen. Achebe begins to recognize the potentials of the woman from this point. The woman is capable of acquiring education like the man, so our expectations for Clara becomes quite high.

Obi meets Clara first in London at a party. Both travel back home on board the ship Sasa and there Clara practices her profession, prescribing avomine tablets to fellow passengers as antidote for sea sickness but that is as far as her nursing profession goes. As soon as Clara returns to Nigeria, we are never again given the privilege of seeing her practice nursing. She is presented as Obi Okonkwo's girl-friend, who keeps busy shopping and cooking for him, accompanying him to films and night parties. Clara makes no impact whatsoever on the society in spite of her profession. Sadly therefore, our hopes for Clara as one who will elevate the status of the woman is dashed and all her education abroad squandered.

It is also pertinent to note that one never really knows what Clara looks like. Is she tall or short, dark or fair, slim or plump? Neither her physique nor her character is properly delineated. All we know is that "Clara is very beautiful" as corroborated by John Macmillan and Mrs. Tomlinson. However, almost immediately this beauty is marred by the knowledge that is forced on the reader – Clara is an *Osu* – born into the family of slaves:

> 'I am an *Osu*,' she wept ... 'So you see that we cannot get married ...' Clara declares to Obi (*No Longer at Ease* 64).

It is significant that when Achebe decides to create a female character of some prominence, he quickly destroys her with attributes that mar that position of prominence. Clara, in spite of all her potentials to transcend the barriers set against women in patriarchal society, is destroyed by labeling her a pariah. Instead of being a major character in that novel, Clara dwindles to a stereotype who quickly disappears from the novel even before Obi Okonkwo's story ends.

In *A Man of the People* the situation is much the same. We encounter Chief Nanga's "illiterate and complacent wife," Edna, who Odili saves from becoming Chief Nanga's second and "parlour wife" and Elsie, Odili's girlfriend, who was snatched from him by Chief Nanga himself. Hezekiah Samalu, Odili's father, had acquired five wives, the last of them being as young as his own daughter. In this novel, as in others before it, Achebe's preoccupation is with the men because, as far as he is concerned, it is a man's world. These women are disgustingly portrayed as sex objects, used at the whims and caprices of the men. Elsie John, the American, seduces Odili, making love with him in her matrimonial home; Barrister Mrs. Aliko breezes into town and sleeps with Chief Nanga in a hotel for twenty-five pounds; Elsie, Odili's girlfriend, gives in to Chief Nanga in his palatial mansion while Odili painfully listens to her moans and cries as Nanga ravishes her. The list is endless. The only enduring female character in that novel seems to be Eunice, Max's girlfriend who trained as a lawyer. She solidly stands behind Max during the turbulent campaign period and when Max is shot dead, she does not crumble and weep hopelessness, but calmly produces a gun from her hand bag, and pumps bullets into Chief Koko's chest, avenging Max's death instantly. Acholonu posits that "among these corrupt and wasted women, Eunice, the intellectual revolutionary, stands out like a star" (313).

By the time Achebe's fifth novel is written, his attitude and disposition towards women take on a more positive outlook. He begins to realize the full potentialities and capabilities of the woman hence in *Anthills of the Savannah* one is shocked into the realization that Achebe could craft a woman of such tremendous relevance, a woman with remarkable intellectual and moral strength to transform society, a society that used to be purely the man's preserve. Beatrice Okoh, the heroine of *Anthills of the Savannah*, like Clara, studies abroad but she reads English, the white man's own language, and graduates with a first class. Mad Medico introduces her in the following words:

> that girl there, sitting meekly and called Beatrice, took a walloping honours
> degree in English from London University. She is better at it than either of us,
> I can assure you (*Anthills* 62).

His Excellency introduces Beatrice thus:

> This is one of the most brilliant daughters of this country, Beatrice Okoh. She
> is a Senior Assistant Secretary in the Ministry of Finance, the only person in
> the service, male or female, with a first class honours in English and not from
> a local university but from Queen Mary College University of London. Our
> Beatrice beat the English to their game. We're very proud of her (75).

What an eloquent testimony coming from the Head of State himself. Thus Beatrice
is elevated well above the men – intellectually. She rubs shoulders with intellectuals
like Chris Oriko – Minister of Information, Ikem Osodi, Editor of the *National
Gazette* and even Sam, His Excellency. She is Chris' ideal woman:

> Beatrice is a perfect embodiment of my ideal woman, beautiful without being
> glamorous. Peaceful but very strong. Very, very strong. I love her and will go at
> whatever pace she dictates (*Anthills* 64).

In *Anthills of the Savannah*, Achebe, the master craftsman who hitherto had relegated women to the background of history, springs an astonishing surprise. Not
only does he recognize the potentialities of women, but he also tries to elevate them
far above the men in this novel. This astonishing novel with positive artistic vision
portrays Achebe as a socially committed writer who is sensitive to the socio-political changes in modern Nigerian society. Because the modern Nigerian woman has
proved her mettle in the educational, political, and socio-economic sectors of the
society, Achebe sees the need to delineate the woman with amazing potentialities.
Anthills therefore can be seen as an expression of faith and hope in the woman and
a recognition of the redemptive powers endowed in her.

Beatrice is Chris' girl-friend but she transcends the limitations of Clara in
No Longer at Ease or Elsie in *A Man of the People*. Beatrice asserts her individuality, taking initiatives even in sex relations and with her tremendous foresight and
insight, she alerts Chris of impending danger in the political scene. Chris calls her
the "priestess" or "prophetess" and Beatrice accepts these labels. She says:

> As a matter of fact, I do sometimes feel like Chielo in the novel, the priestess
> and prophetess of the Hills and the Caves (*Anthills* 114).

Following that lead, she unleashes a powerful prophecy:

> I see trouble building up for us. It will get to Ikem first … He will be the pre-
> cursor to make straight the way. But after him, it will be you. We are all in it,
> Ikem, you, me and even Him … (115).

This prophecy is fulfilled as the novel draws to an end. The "three green bottles" (Ikem, Chris and His Excellency) fall off the wall and are destroyed in the unfolding drama, leaving Beatrice, the prophetess to "gather the pieces of broken lives." Thus Beatrice is accorded redemptive powers even though she refuses to accept the role traditionally assigned to women. She says to Ikem:

> But the way I see it is that giving women today the same role which traditional society gave them of intervening only when everything else has failed is not enough ... It is not enough that women should be the court of last resort because that last resort is a damn sight too far and too late (*Anthills* 91–2).

Here, Beatrice advocates a power shift, suggesting that the men should give the women a chance to take charge believing that they would perform better. Since the "three green bottles" had failed in their bid to salvage the nation, the women, the likes of Beatrice and Elewa, should be given a chance to steer the ship of state. Who knows, the solution to the intractable societal problems may well lie in the hands of women.

Achebe also delineates Elewa as a female character with enduring qualities even though she is illiterate. She is a shop salesgirl who nonetheless rises to become Ikem's girl-friend. The educated, intellectual revolutionary and Editor of the *National Gazette* must have spotted Elewa's potentials to be so intimately associated with hers. Amadiume (148) asserts that Elewa "is not very schooled but ordinary, solid and sensible." She has "amazing potentials for linkage with the grassroots" (149). Even in her pidgin English, she makes very articulate and analytical contributions. She says to Ikem:

> But women don chop sand sand for this world o ... Imagine! But na we de causa m, na we own fault (*Anthills* 34).

She recognizes the oppression of women in the society and equally realizes the fact that the woman is her own worst enemy.

Beatrice's flat (house) becomes the rallying point for those who survived the political imbrioglio. She had earlier taken Elewa to her house after Ikem's death, protected and nursed her until she gave birth to a baby-girl. These humane and supportive gestures further heighten her personality and portray female solidarity in the face of threatening circumstances. When Elewa's baby is born, Beatrice organizes a naming ceremony contrary to tradition and proceeds to give the baby a name. She defends her action as she argues:

> In our traditional society ... the father names the child. But the man who should have done it today is absent ... What does a man know about a child anyway that he should presume to give it a name ... (*Anthills* 222).

Extending this logic, she names the baby Amaechina (may the path never close) a purely masculine name in Igbo land. However, Beatrice's justification for her action is sound and convincing to everybody.

Here, we see Achebe, the gynandrist fighting the cause of women, particularly, Igbo women. The men may see Achebe as a sell out; over-doing what he set out to do. They may wonder if it was necessary for Achebe to go to this length in an attempt to give the woman a pride of place in the society. Is Achebe advocating a power-shift from the men to the women?

Personally, I think Achebe is merely saying that any woman, who by dint of hard work, has achieved an elevated status in the society, should be recognized for her worth, irrespective of gender. Beatrice's achievements were no longer in doubt, she had risen far above the men so male prejudice and chauvinism should not bar her from enjoying privileges exclusively preserved for men. Achebe is merely subscribing to the proverbial adage which says that if a child washes clean his hands, he will eat with kings. Since Beatrice had tremendous potentials: strength of character, intellectual capabilities, insight etcetera, she should dine with Kings even though she is a woman.

According to Amadiume (155):

> Through the rebellious statements made and rituals demonstrated during the naming of Elewa and Ikem's baby, they over-rule 'outdated' customs and beliefs and propose new gender relations and a new society which should transcend sex, ethnic, religious and class divisions.

Idowu Omuyele in *West Africa Magazine* (347) reveals that Achebe had disclosed to Karen Vinkler that:

> his novels have steadily included more women's voices and that his next book will focus on women. From time to time in his culture, when things have gone wrong, women have risen up to take action ...

It is therefore quite commendable that Achebe has eventually realized the formidable role women play and have played even in traditional societies and it is a measure of the artistic sensitivity and maturity that he has decided to include more female voices. The fact that his "next book will focus on women" is refreshingly welcome. We eagerly await that new addition to the cause of feminism in African literature coming from the father of African literature himself.

Works Cited

Achebe, Chinua. *Things Fall Apart*. London: Heinemann Educational Books Ltd., 1958.

———. *No Longer at Ease*. London: Heinemann Educational Books Ltd., 1960.

———. *Arrow of God*. London: Heinemann Educational Books Ltd., 1964.

———. *A Man of the People*. London: Heinemann Educational Books Ltd., 1966.

———. *Anthills of the Savannah*. London: Heinemann Frontline Series. 1987.

Acholonu, R. "Outsiders or Insiders?: Women in *Anthills of the Savannah*" *Eagle on Iroko: Selected Papers from Chinua Achebe International Symposium 1990*. Ihekweazu Edith (ed). Ibadan: Heinemann Educational Books, 1996: 311–321.

Amadiume, I. "Class and Gender in *Anthills of the Savannah*". A Critique in *Okike: An African Journal of New Writing, Special Edition on Chinua Achebe at Sixty*. Enekwe, O.O. (ed). No. 30. November 1990: 147–157.

Idowu, O. "The Legacy of Chinua Achebe." *West Africa*. 16–29 March, 1998: 346–348.

Chapter 24

Achebe and African Womanhood in *Things Fall Apart*

Ifeoma Onyemelukwe

T HIS ESSAY IS A CRITICAL EXAMINATION of the depiction of African womanhood in *Things Fall Apart* (TFA), Achebe's first novel published in 1958, and described by Bernth Lindfors as the "first novel with unquestionable literary merit from English speaking West Africa" (3). The essay aims also to examine the perception of African womanhood by this committed, prolific and exceptionally gifted writer of international repute. Needless to say, Achebe's artistic output, by number and earned laurels, echo this well enough. Ironically, this genius whose works have constituted objects of uncountable literary researches, seems lamentably to be a victim or erroneous perception, by some critics, of his position *vis-a-vis* certain issues.

Significant to this study is that Achebe is labeled by some feminist critics (Chukwuma, Ogundipe) as a chauvinist more or less insensitive to the lot of the African woman. Whereas male writers like Isidore Okepewho, Ngugi wa Thiong'o, Sembene Ousmane and Mongo Beti, branded gynandrists by Charles Nnolim (252), are commended by feminists for championing, through the literary medium, the cause of subjugated, unprivileged and oppressed African woman. Achebe, for his part, is vituperated along with Cyprian Ekwensi, Wole Soyinka and some others for a sexist approach, painting women as helpless, dependent, disparaged beings destined in Ogunyemi's words "to carry *foofoo* and soup to men dealing with important matters" (66). Ama Ata Aidoo accuses Achebe of cavalier attitude to women in his works. TFA, in particular, lends Achebe to such biting criticisms. Aidoo castigates him for allowing his protagonist, Okonkwo, to batter his wives while his other wives hover around whimpering, "Okonkwo it is enough ..." (4).

It becomes pertinent to ask if these critics or interpreters are interpreting rightly Achebe's view of the African woman in his works, and specifically *Things Fall Apart*. Is Achebe's style deceptive in this novel? Is Okonkwo's view of womanhood mistaken for Achebe's? Is Achebe's depiction of the social reality of that ancient time vis-a-vis societal view of the African woman taken to be his own personal views in TFA.

What is womanhood? Let it be noted right away that womanhood is distinct from womanism, a term purely theoretical which, to our mind, is what Rosemarie Tong tags postmodern feminism, a perspective among others (1–2). Thus it is a matter of nomenclature. Womanism like postmodern feminism is an attempt to better the lot of the woman through institutional changes in a patriarchy. Both advocate a complementary relationship between man and woman. They emphasize tolerance for the couple, both partners accommodating each other's weaknesses and forming a complete whole. The term, accommodationist is, sometimes, used to describe an adherent of womanism or postmodern feminism.

Controversies stem from the existence of various shades of interpretation of the two concepts. Where critics like Rosemarie Tong could distinguish different perspectives of feminism, others like Ama Ata Aidoo, Chikwenye Ogunyemi, Marie Umeh and E.E. Ogini, tend to perceive feminism as synonymous with radicalism. But radicalism is only a streak of feminism. This explains why most African feminist writers reject the feminist label. The ideological misconception is implied in the following comment by Aidoo:

> Feminism, you know how we all feel about that embarrassing Western phi-
> losophy? The destroyer of homes. Imported mainly from America to ruin nice
> African women" (40–41).

Ogini posits that "womanism needs man" while "feminism shuns man" (82). However, not all brands of feminism shun man, radical feminism does. Marie Umeh is of the opinion that feminist plots end with the separation of the man and woman whereas womanist novels are committed to the survival and unity of males and females (265). But what Umeh and her likes call womanist novels, to other critics, are postmodern feminist novels. The fact of the matter is that whether they are labeled womanists, accommodationists or postmodern feminists, one is saying essentially the same thing. For man and woman to have any meaning fulfillment in life, the notion of fundamental dichotomous couple must be jettisoned, and man and woman viewed as partners in life, complementing each other rather than living as separate entities or pair of polar opposites with man as "self" and woman as "other".

Postmodern feminist writers like Mariama Ba and Sembene Ousmane (also Marxist), labeled womanist writers by Ogini and Nnolim are saying in essence that man should jettison all behavior patterns and socio-cultural practices that predispose woman to being treated as the "other". Woman, for her part, should avoid divorce or prostitution (one engendering the other) which purport to augur well for attainment of her independence and freedom but in the final analysis only further degrade her and leave her in the threshold of immorality, unacceptable to society.

Aderemi Bamikunle has rightly pointed out that "the subject matter, rather than the method of analysis is the most valid qualification for determining feminism" (9). Bamikunle also cautions against unduly narrowing the scope of feminism. Feminism, popularly known as women liberation or women rights movement which advocates legal equal rights for man and woman; a global movement for the advancement and emancipation of women, without doubt, has numerous brands significant among which are liberal, marxist, radical, psychoanalytical, socialist, existentialist and postmodern.

Womanhood, for its part, refers to the state or attributes of the being called a woman. *Chambers Twentieth Century Dictionary* defines womanhood as the state, character or qualities of a woman. It defines woman as an adult female of the human race, the female sex. Woman does not men "woe-man" or "woe-to-man" or accursed being. The Biblical origin of woman comes to mind here. ... And the rib, which the Lord God has taken from man, made he a woman and brought her unto the man. And Adam said, this is now bone of my bones, and flesh of my flesh. She shall be called Woman, because she was taken out of man (Genesis 2:22–23). Woman, therefore literally means she-man, womb-man, man with the womb of female-man given that she was taken out of man. Man and woman in this context refer to the biological sexes, male and female. This does not imply superiority or inferiority as upheld by male chauvinists in traditional patriarchy. We wish to stress that man and woman were originally made equal at creation and to complement each other. "So God created man in his own image, in the image of God created he him; male and female created he them" (Genesis 1:27).

As long as no dichotomy is placed on the two sexes, male and female, man and woman, all seems well. However, conflicts or problems emerge with patriarchal labels, binary oppositions or traditional boundaries between man and woman. Sociologically man and woman have perceived character or personality traits as well as gender/sex/social roles. It is in this sense that the determinants feminine/femininity and masculine/masculinity are ascribed to woman and man respectively. Similarly, psychological traits such as submissiveness, empathy and supportiveness are associated with woman while assertiveness, aggressiveness and rationality became, as it were, the exclusive reserve of man. This clear demarcation is a bone of contention of some feminists. They argue that any human being regardless of the sex can display any of the attributes. Who says only men can reason or only woman can cry? For the adherents of certain brands of feminism, it makes no sense talking of gender/sex/social roles since whatever a man can do a woman can also do or even do better. One is not ignorant of the Moremis, Aminas and Dauramas of old. Women achievers have been noted over the centuries.

With this background in mind the stage is set for our appraisal. What can be said of the image of woman in Achebe's world of TFA? Is she liberated or still a patriarchal creation playing the second fiddle? What is Achebe's view of womanhood? Is he really a male chauvinist as claimed by some critics? Does he show any feminist bent? These are some of the questions that will, hopefully, be answered in the course of our analysis.

Even a cursory reading of TFA leaves one with the sullen impression of a male hegemonous patriarchal society or gerontocracy where the woman is relegated to the background. The picture that emerges of the African woman and typically the traditional Igbo woman (since the novel is set in pre-colonial Igbo cultural area), is a faceless, voiceless being. Though called a being because she breathes, the African woman could compare favorably with an object or thing or a man's personal effect. Furthermore, it strikes the reader that this is a society, which prior to missionary incursion and colonial implantation, thrives on subsistence economy and seemingly justifiably adopts polygamy as a way of life: Okoye has three wives, Okonkwo three wives and Nwakibie more. It would seem that marrying several wives is a useful venture to the man whose principal occupation is farming. It enables him to possess many children (Nwakibie has thirty children, for example), who together with the individual's string of wives are very necessary for the farm work. This is one of the reasons put forward by the sociologist, Georges Balandier, for African men's leaning to polygamy (10). However, a thorough scrutiny of the characters in the novel, particularly, the macho central character reveals that polygamy as practiced in *Things Fall Apart*, reflecting the social reality of that ancient time, is predicated on some other motives which far from being altruistic, are selfish and egotistic. In the first place, men of Umuofia possess many wives as a symbol of affluence. Secondly, polygamy becomes a vehicle for procurement of social alliances. Okonkwo, for whom the desire to be one of the lords of the clan of Umuofia, has become an obsession, contemplates towards the end of his seven-year exile in Mbanta, his mother's village, marrying more wives and also having his two beautiful daughters. Ezinma and Obiageli married not to suitors from Mbanta but prospective and prosperous husbands in Umuofia, on return to the town. To buttress the point made here, it becomes necessary to contrast Okonkwo's polygamous marriage with the monogamous marriage of his "loafer" of a father, Unoka whose wife and children had barely enough to eat.

It would seem that Okonkwo's monomania for male dominance also predisposes him to accumulate women as one would of other personal belongings; to possess, admire, desire, dominate, despise, reject and possibly destroy at will. Nwoye's mother, Ekwefi and Ojiugo, the three wives of Okonkwo as shown in TFA could not raise any voice of protest against polygamy as would Mariama Ba's and Zaynab Alkali's victims of doomed illusion of marital bliss caused by their husbands' taking of second wives. Polygamy is thus depicted in TFA as an instrument of subjugation of the African woman; the man, head of the family declaring himself the self and the woman "the other." Through the practice of polygamy, man (representing the dominant or ruling class) relegates the African woman (representing the dominated or unprivileged class) to the background.

The writer of TFA, further lets the reader perceive the inferior position of the woman from the infrastructural arrangement of Okonkwo's compound with the man's *obi* or residence located in front behind the only gate in the red walls enclosing the large compound. On the contrary, the huts of the various wives are distributed in a semi-circular form behind the *obi*. The third person omniscient narrator refers to these huts as "out-houses". According to his account, "when he (Okonkwo) slept his wives and children in their out-houses could hear him breathe" (3). As if keeping them at the background is not enough, this macho man uses his heavy breathing to intimidate his unsuspecting wives and children. Even in his sleep he dominates them.

It could be argued that their abode is structured thus for security purposes. Okonkwo thereby avails himself of the entrance to fight any intruder and protects his wives and children in their "out-house". However, a more plausible explanation of Okonkwo's special architectural design appears to be his burning passion to possess and dominate the woman.

It is significant to note that the African man symbolized by the tragic hero, Okonkwo, is extremely jealous and would not want any male intruder into his wives' huts. Ironically, the same man could have illicit affairs with women (mistresses) in his "*obi*" without the legitimate wives or society frowning upon such acts. This is the case of Okonkwo's love escapade with Ekwefi, the village belle, prior to his possessing her fully as a second wife. Ekwefi deserts Anene, her husband, for the famous wrestler, Okonkwo. The third person narrator relates, "Ekwefi was going to the stream to fetch water. Okonkwo's house was on the way to the stream. She went in and knocked at his door and he came out. Even in those days he was not a man of many words. He just carried her into his bed and in the darkness began to feel around her waist for the loose end of her cloth" (76).

Nothing is said in TFA of Ekwefi's husband, Anene's reaction. Does it mean he is not aggrieved by Okonkwo's snatching of his wife? Achebe, perhaps, in his characteristic application of attention/interest retention techniques of suspense and economy of words and narrative stops at that. The reader is to extrapolate the rest of the story. Anene, the poor husband of Ekwefi, of course, dares not challenge Okonkwo, the renowned warrior and one of the greatest of his time. In that case, the jungle law seems to have taken hold. A pertinent question however, "Is it an acceptable code of conduct for a married Igbo woman to run to another man and begin to live with him as a wife; without *ikwu nga*, the refund of the bride-price and the payment of bride-price by the new husband?

A disturbing question here is whether Ekwefi was forced into marriage with Anene since the narrative makes it abundantly clear that she was in love with Okonkwo. If Okonkwo had the financial disposition he could well have married Ekwefi at that time for he was equally in love with her and still is, the love which he transferred to Ekwefi's only child, Ezinma. Compelled to lose her heart throb and marry Anene whom she does not love she could only bear it for a while and . soon escapes from her hell of a marriage to settle into marriage with Okonkwo. This time, she becomes a second wife. It is important to note the implication of Ekwefi's marriage experience; forced marriage becomes an instrument of oppression of the traditional African woman.

Significantly, in spite of the mutual love between Ekwefi and Okonkwo, this impulsive, tyrannical and short-tempered husband does not hesitate to beat her up mercilessly just for cutting a few banana leaves to wrap some food, in innocuous act. As if that is not enough, for daring to mock his poor skill at hunting, Okonkwo fires a shot at her which narrowly stops short of killing her. Is it love or madness that compels Okonkwo to treat his beloved wife like this? He had earlier beaten Ojuigo, his third wife, for failing to return in time to prepare his lunch. A justifiable anger, one might say. But should he allow his anger to overstep bounds to the point of beating his wives and damning the consequence as in desecrating the week of peace? Have his wives become yam to be pounded into *fufu*? Has he conquered Ekweki to dehumanize and possibly kill her at will?

Amazingly, in spite of Okonkwo's deplorable acts of firing at and beating Ekwefi, the "New Yam Festival was celebrating with great joy" in his household. None of his wives could raise dust. Chinua Achebe has, indeed portrayed these women (representing African women) as faceless and voiceless creatures. One could hardly visualize these women. These characters are not developed, unlike Okonkwo who is well rounded. They are not living but flat before our eyes. Not until much later in the plot does the reader get to know the age of Ekwefi and her peculiar plight. This is a woman who has suffered terribly because of recurrent infantile mortality which is attributable to sickle cell anemia in the offsprings following the undesirable genetic combination in couples of AS + AS. The writer feigns ignorance of this scientific/medical explanation of that phenomenon and allows the narrator impute to it one of these African superstitions: *Ogbanje,* that is a child billed to die and come again. Certainly, Achebe is well informed but deliberately exposes this superstitious belief and some others to hold them in derision even as he tactfully stifles characters not as an artistic weakness but to show to what extent the African woman is marginalized and degraded. It is incredible that an outrageous act of this magnitude by Okonkwo could attract no clear negative reactions in his home. The first wife could at least have raised a voice of protest. It would seem that these women have been tyranised by their chauvinistic husband, Okonkwo, to the point of never daring to wag a tongue no matter the situation. Is it not Ekwefi's ironic comment "guns that never shot" that almost sent her to her grave? Ekweki was "very much shaken and frightened," by the shot fired at her. A few minutes earlier she was subjected to fierce beating at the hands of Okonkwo who left her and her only daughter, Ezinma, weeping. Is Okonkwo misogynous or a woman hater? Why such dehumanization or depersonalization of the women? The novel presents us with wives subjugated with fear as evident in this passage:

> Okonkwo ruled his household with a *heavy hand*. His wives, especially the youngest, lived in *perpetual fear* of his *fiery temper* and so did his litter children (9, My emphasis).

It becomes obvious from this passage that Okonkwo is given to terrible temper which leads him to terrorize his wives and paralyze them with fear. To conceive Okonkwo's ill-treatment of his wives as an index of his misogyny is erroneous. At the surface level he may appear cruel but the deeper structures of the text reveal that he is not wicked and he does not really hate women. What he does is a device to cow them not really to oppress them but to maintain them in subjugation for fear of being perceived as weak and not able to control his household. The omniscient narrator has rightly observed: "Perhaps down in his heart Okonkwo was not a cruel man but his whole life was dominated by fear of failure and of weakness" (9).

Okonkwo reminds us here of Medza's father in Mongo Beti's *Mission to Kala* who is dubbed "papa omnipotent," "a dictator at home," "a tyrant at home." A home where terror reigns is a hell on earth. It may have everything but definitely not a conducive environment for proper upbringing and development of children. It is, therefore, not surprising that Nwoye is maladjusted and flees from home like Beti's Medza in *Mission to Kala*.

Things Fall Apart shows that Okonkwo is not alone in this practice of wife-battery. One of the cases presided over by the highest village judiciary, the *Egwugwu* cult, is a marital problem compounded by wife battery. Let us examine an excerpt: Odukwe was short and thick-set. He stepped forward, saluted the spirits and began his story. 'My in-law has told you that we went to his house, beat him up and took our sister and her children away. All that is true. He told you that he came to take back her bride-price and we refused to give it to him. That also is true. My in-law, Uzowulu is a beast. My sister lived with him for nine years. During those years no single day passed in the sky without his beating the woman. We have tried to settle their quarrels time without number and on each occasion Uzowulu was guilty. 'It is a lie!' Uzowulu shouted. 'Two years ago,' continued Odukwe, 'when she was pregnant, he beat her until she miscarried ...' (64–65).

Wife-battery is depicted here as a very common phenomenon in Umuofia so much so that Uzowulu beats his wife on a daily basis regardless of whether she is pregnant or sick. Strikingly, Achebe uses the character Odukwe as his mouthpiece to condemn this inhuman act which turns the African woman into a punch bag leaving her at the threshold of misery, shattered hope of marital bliss, frustration and dehumanization. By dubbing Uzowulu "a beast," Achebe is in fact, using this animal imagery to make a biting criticism of wife-battery and its advocates. Moreover, Odukwe and some other relatives beat up Uzowulu to teach him the lesson of his life if only that would purge him of the wicked propensity for battering his wife. Finally, the leader of the *Egwugwu* rules that Uzowulu should go and beg his in-laws with a pot of wine adding that "it is not bravery when a man fights with a woman." One can sense the novelist's voice behind the masquerade's denouncing wife-battery. Through the eyes of the masquerade, the writer makes us see wife-battery as a reprehensible act, something to be shunned.

Ironically, Okonkwo belongs to the *Egwugwu* cult and yet batters his wives, apparently, without any reproach. One would expect him to know better and behave better. What could be responsible for these gruesome acts unleashed on his wives? One thing is certain; Okonkwo is suffering from a psychological problem – the phobia of being dubbed weak and cowardly like his contemptible father. Unfortunately, that which he seeks desperately to shun constitutes his doom. As Eustace Palmer rightly notes. "This fear which dominates all his actions, contributes to his subsequent catastrophe" (11).

Things "fall apart" not only for the village but in particular for the tragic hero who was banished from his fatherland, for inadvertently committing a fratricide (female crime), to his mother's clan. Mbanta (meaning small clan) which as the name connotes represents for Okonkwo "women's clan," and he ends up committing suicide, a shameful death, an abomination. This amounts to dying like a fly or fowl. As a result, he attracts for himself a burial not apt for a great hero that he always aspired to be but one suited for a dog or an outcast. At death, he is not fit to be touched or buried by his clansmen but by aliens. Note that Okonkwo, even in brutally beating his wives, as in firing a shot at Ekwefi, did not do so out of innate rabid cruelty or callousness. The narrator states that "deep inside him, Okonkwo was not a cruel man." Indeed he is not when one considers that he is really caring, and through his sweat, provides his family with enough food. The same analysis holds true for his killing of Ikemefuna. It is, indeed, out of his monomania of domination of others to remain as it were, always, "a colossus" to borrow Shakespeare's term for Julius Caesar; while other "petty men peep under his huge legs to find themselves dishonorable graves." According to the narrator Okonkwo's "life had been ruled by a great passion to become one of the lords of the clan." Whatever will militate against the attainment of this noble goal he is ready to eliminate at all costs.

This monomania of male dominance is rooted in fear. Okonkwo must not be seen at any point, under any circumstance, as a lily-livered man for that is tanta-mount, in his eyes, to being a woman and a subjugated person. Ironically, Okonkwo is shown in *TFA* to have everything in a hero, except emotional stability/maturity. The extroverted, dynamic and irascible protagonist allows fear and fierce rage to lead him by the nose. Fits of short madness lead Okonkwo to act devoid of sanity and decorum. His killing of Ikemefuna, who called him father, is the height of absurdity. If he had emotional stability he would have left the killing to the other clansmen in line with the advice given to him by Ezeudu, "the oldest man in their quarter of Umuofia." After all, Ikemefuna would still have been killed whether Okonkwo participated in the killing or not.

The devastating psychological impact of this killing on Okonkwo (anorexia, insomnia, depression) goes to buttress the point of the incongruous and absurd nature of the act. Obierika rightly points out:

> If I were you (Okonkwo) I would have stayed at home. What you have done will not please the Earth. It is the kind of action for which the goddess wipes out whole families (46).

Adamant Okonkwo wonders why a great warrior who could drink with the human skulls of those he bravely killed (5 human skulls) will panic for killing Ikemefuna. This is evident in his introspection:

> 'When did you become a shivering old woman, Okonkwo asked himself, you who are known in all the nine villages for your valour in war? How can a man who killed five men in battle fall to pieces because he has added a boy to their number? Okonkwo, you have become a woman indeed (46).

Thus, we are free to think what we wish. As for the sexist/male chauvinist, Okonkwo, the killing of Ikemefuna is a mark of manhood, his latest show of manhood, and to tremble after killing him just as failing to kill him, will only betray him as a woman, or an effeminate man. He quickly purges himself of this perceived weakness.

One may ask, "what crime has Ikemefuna committed to deserve this capital punishment?" It is not foolhardy for Okonkwo to give uncritical deference to mon-strous prescriptions of the so-called *Egwugwu* and ancestral customs and traditions, retrogressive, obnoxious and unproductive as they may be. Okonkwo's tragic end may well be linked to this fratricide following the law of retributive justice. One may think that Achebe endorses Okonkwo's uncompromising attachment to the dictates of his culture which marks him (Achebe) out as a conservative. But does he? Okonkwo, to our mind is far from being the writer's model African man. He is not an autobiographical central character. In other words, what Okonkwo stands for is not quite Achebe's.

Notice that not all men in the narrative are blind adherents of ancestral traditions. Obierika, unlike his friend, Okonkwo does understand that the society is not static but dynamic and as such things are bound to fall apart to accommodate the new wind of change. Even some Ozo titled men have also turned Christians. But the monomaniac of male dominance will not bow to the authority of either white missionaries or colonial administrators as that will be tantamount to becoming a woman. Manhood for Okonkwo must not be compromised. He would rather take his life than live to see the reversal of roles where weak-minded men (the so-called black converts tagged "women") dominated, while great men of valor become the ruled, the subverted. Obierika realizes that his friend is deluded, that his is a sad misconception that things must not change. Obierika's view seems to be that of the author of TFA. In this sense, Achebe is not a conservative. While recognizing that the African has a culture distinct from the white man's he is receptive to positive change in society while condemning obnoxious elements of the indigenous culture such as the killing of innocent twins. The ambivalence in Umuofia society; acceptance of change versus conservatism is a reflection of the tragic hero's ambivalence of bravery versus weakness, success versus failure, manhood versus womanhood. As a result of Okonkwo's myopic view, the split personality ends up as a victim of unflinching attachment to ancestral norms and values unlike Ezeulu in *Arrow of God* who adapts promptly to change.

Okonkwo, manhood personified, hates anything that will link him to his father, Unoka dubbed *agbala*, the Ibgo word for woman. In short, Okonkwo dreads like leprosy anything that will link him to his despicable father or make people perceive him as a woman. This is because of his resentment for womanhood which, in his eyes, Unoka embodied. Thus as the omniscient narrator puts it: Okonkwo never showed any emotion openly, unless the emotion of anger. To show affection was a sign of weakness, the only thing worth demonstrating was strength (20). Rarely does it occur to Okonkwo that great men seldom betray any emotion at all. His susceptibility to tantrums makes him behave immaturely "as a woman" the same image which he persistently tries to shut out.

The plot shows Okonkwo as treating his family members especially his beloved wife, Ekwefi and Nwoye with iron hand. He must not be seen as hen-pecked, which he finds reprehensible in Nduluo who is endeared to his wife, Ozoemena, both having "one mind." For a man to consult his wife before doing a thing is a womanly act in Okonkwo's view but not Nduluo's. This, probably, explains in part, why Okonkwo dictates to his wives, shouts at them and resents their views. For example, he turns down Ekwefi's suggestion for them to kill two goats for the feast at Mbanta. Consider this conversation between Nwoye's mother and Okonkwo: "When Okonkwo brought him (Ikemefuna) home that day he called his most senior wife and handed him over to her. 'He belongs to the clan,' he told her. 'So look at him.' 'Is he staying long with us?' she said. 'Do what you are told, woman;' Okonkwo thundered and stammered 'when did you become one of the *ndichie* of Umuofia?' And so Nwoye's mother took Ikemefuna to her hut and asked no more questions" (10). The typically subservient African woman is silenced by the macho male protagonist. As far as Okonkwo is concerned, the woman has no business with decision-making processes at home or in the larger community. She is there to take orders, defer to the authority of the men, husband, *ndichie*, (elders or patriarchs) and the *Egwugwu* cult into which she remains uninitiated. Okonkwo believes firmly that a man must be in charge all the time. The narrator leads us through Okonkwo's eyes to see that "no matter how prosperous a man may be, if he was unable to rule his women and his children (and especially his women) he was not really a man" (37). Is it any surprise that at Ekwefi's mockery of his poor skill at hunting Okonkwo fires a shot at her and luckily narrowly misses killing her? Ekwefi unwittingly throws a challenge at him. Okonkwo cannot take a challenge from any man let alone a woman, an *agbala*!. Womanhood, therefore, as portrayed in TFA, is generally treated with disdain and resentment.

A dichotomous relationship appears, on the surface, to exist between manhood and womanhood in the world of Achebe's *Things Fall Apart*. Everything in Umuofia and the satellite villages seems to revolve around manhood. Manhood becomes the frame of reference. It is the hallmark of excellence and achievement. It also signifies ability to reason, have rational thinking, make wise choices and decisions. Thus, Okonkwo keeps wishing that Ezinma, endowed with great reasoning faculty, were a boy. It is conceivable that if TFA were created at the dawn of the 21st century, Okonkwo would have subjected Ezinma to a sex transplant only to turn her into the boy he wishes she were!

On the contrary, womanhood is used to qualify irrationality, inferior beings/ human endeavors. Take for example, a corn-cob with only a few scattered grains is called *Eze-agadinwanyi* in the novel. In reality in Igboland, that is what it is called. One wonders why it should be given such an appellation. Why not *Ezegadinwoke* meaning the teeth of an old man. Is it not because of the societal inclination to ascribe inferiority to womanhood? A more suitable metaphorical name for such corn-cob would be *Eze-agadi* meaning an old person's teeth. This will admit the fact of equality of man and woman both undergoing similar changes/deterioration with advancement in age. A human being regardless of the sex (male or female) may be left with a few scattered teeth when old. Furthermore, Okonkwo writes off his son, Nwoye as a "woman" for his perceived gullibility and acceptance of Christianity. All Umofian converts he tags women.

Achebe in his rich style draws the reader's attention to constant opposition in the narrative between manhood and womanhood, most often through the eyes of his central character, Okonkwo, who is obsessed with the show of masculinity. Thus, he talks of men's crops (yam, the king of crops which he cultivates) as opposed to women's crops (such as coco-yams, beans and cassava which his mother and sisters grow); men's stories (masculine stories of violence, wars, and bloodshed) versus women's stories (stories of tortoise and his wily ways, and the bird *eneke-nti-oba* in short, cock and bull stories); men's duties (bringing father's chair to a meeting place, roofing, splitting wood or pounding *foo-foo*) versus women's soft duties; men's abode (*Obi*) versus women's abode ("out-house"); men's town/village/clan (e.g. Umuofia prior to the coming of the white man – the clan of warlike men) versus women's town/village/clan (e.g. Umuofia after the advent of the white missionary; Abame and Aninta where titled men climb trees and pound *foo-foo* for their wives; and men's sitting posture (any how) versus women's sitting posture (sitting with the two legs together; men's ceremony (settlement of bride-pride, *Egwugwu* cult) versus women's ceremony (wine carrying and feasting for Umunna referring to the extensive group of women where the bride and her mother constitute the central figures). The series of opposition include partrilineal versus matrilineal systems; men's songs versus women's songs; men's burial versus women's burial, male crime (deliberate fratricide) versus female crime (accidental fratricide or manslaughter).

The series of binary oppositions are there not only to give relief and aesthetic beauty to the masterly creative work, TFA, but also to symbolize the existing internal conflicts or dialectics even in the traditional patriarchy long before the missionary incursion. Two classes emerge: the ruling class or the men (what Okonkwo will refer to as real men) and the ruled consisting of women, children, slaves and "she men" like slothful Unoka, men without titles. Womanhood, in Achebe's TFA, thus, clearly stands for the dominated, subjugated, repressed, non-privileged, excluded, and shunned. It represents the inhibited, cowed, frozen out, rejected and unwanted. It also implies the abandoned and dislocated, marginalized, depersonalized or reduced to nothing.

Paradoxically, womanhood as depicted in *Things Fall Apart* is the symbol of all the powerful fetishes/oracles which regulate the affairs of the people of Umuofia and its environs. Take, for example, *Ani* is female. This is the earth goddess and the source of all fertility. As reported: *Ani* played a greater part in the life of the people than any other deity. She was the ultimate judge of morality and conduct. And what was more, she was in close communion with the departed fathers of the clan whose bodies had been committed to earth (26). Also, the Oracle of the Hills and the Caves was called *"Agbala"* which as earlier remarked means woman in Igbo language. This Oracle is attended to by women. Chika and Chielo are two of such priestesses. Interestingly, *Agbala* is referred to in the novel as a god and not as goddess. According to the narrator, "no one had ever beheld *Agbala*." This powerful god (supposedly male) bears a female name *"Agbala"*. Furthermore, in order to hold in derision men in Umuofia (Igboland) who are slothful, mediocres and weaklings who have not taken up any title, they are dubbed *agbala*. This paradox does not fail to strike us.

It is only legitimate to ask why woman that is looked down upon in Umuofia is the same woman that is the Executive Director of most shrines and fetishes in the novel. And men, the so-called he-men bow to them. Why couldn't Okonkwo stop Chielo, the priestess of *Agbala* who whisks off his darling daughter, Ezinma at night at the request of *Agbala*? Perhaps, in not stopping her, little does it occur to the macho man that he is deferring to the authority of a woman, authority vested on her by the god she is serving. Why should a man obsessed by the singular passion to dominate now bow to a woman the least, in his view, to attract such attention? We take exception to Uhumwangho's assertion that "Okonkwo could have acted decisively" but keeps his distance (12). That Okonkwo who shows uncritical deference to ancestral tradition, as aptly declared by Killam cannnot be the same: Powerful as he is, the embodiment of the male principle, Okonkwo is subservient to the female principle as he follows the course of Chielo with his beloved daughter Ezinma with a terror equal to that of his wife, utterly powerless to alter the course of events (13).

In addition, as the oldest man in Mbanta explains philosophically, in spite of the patrilineal system, the Igbo people still declare in the name, Nneka that "Mother is supreme," that a child when beaten by his father seeks solace in its mother's hut and in time of "sorrow and bitterness," including banishment a man "finds refuge in his motherland" (94). By implication, when all is well a child belongs to its father but when the going is bad or the child misbehaves its father rejects it. The child then seeks and finds succor in his/her mother or the mother's people. It is important to highlight here that in real life a person can abuse an Igbo man's father or other relations and get away with it but not his mother or wife. The Igbo say that "you know the strength of a man when you touch his wife." In essence, the old man's thesis here can be summed up in the innate supremacy of motherhood or womanhood. In short, the woman takes the bitter pill. Who is stronger the person who takes honey or the one who takes bile? When it comes to the crunch the woman takes over. Yet she is treated as inferior, as the weaker sex. The old man's analysis shows that, in effect, the woman is by no means inferior to the man. Achebe apparently uses the old man to debunk the myth of the superiority of man. Biting irony is patent here.

It is important, however, to point out that even in TFA not all women have the kind of master-servant marital relationship as typified by Okonkwo's marriage. The author brings in Nduluo and Ozoemena a couple whose warm and friendly rapport, in spite of polygamous marriage, is worthy of emulation in the context of modern marriage albeit ridiculed by traditionalists. Achebe has a message for his readers by bringing in the example of Nduluo who although a great warrior like Okonkwo still listens to his wife as opposed to Okonkwo.

TFA shows the Igbo man symbolized by Okonkwo as very industrious, ensuring that he provides enough food for his wives and children. The Igbo man, in real life, is reputed as a most caring husband. That however, does not rule out instances of lazy weak men like Unoka.

It is also important to note that Chinua Achebe somewhat exaggerates Okonkwo's show of masculinity in TFA. The exaggeration is, nonetheless, a satiric device aimed at throwing into relief the natural inclination of Igbo men to rule or dominate their wives/women. It would seem that Achebe is subjecting this behavior to a satirical stint. Irony emerges in Achebe's skillful balance between the macho man's strength and weakness, bravery and fear. Okonkwo who personifies the Igbo man inspires the reader with a mixture of admiration and mild mockery. Okonkwo is ambivalent as his society is eating deep into his hard-earned personality and all he stands for. He finally cracks up under the force of his environment which, in turn, is falling apart.

To our mind, what Achebe does in TFA is that he subtly condemns some cultural elements such as wife-battery and excessive show of masculinity which tend to predispose women to oppression. Furthermore, he encourages women to remain in marriage, seemingly subscribing to patriarchal system of marriage albeit devoid of excessive show of masculinity. In his type, the man is leader of the relationship with the woman carefully fulfilling her traditional roles as a wife and mother. Needless to say that if Achebe were to rewrite TFA in this era of intense economic and political advancement, he would most likely depict womanhood in the role of the woman making valid contributions towards the economic and political development of her country. In this regard, Theodora Ezeigbo's remark calls for attention: As I stated in an earlier study, some notable male novelists who had formerly relegated women's experience to the background are now focusing their creative lens on women to the extent that some of them are delineating female characters who are highlighted as achievers, women who dominate the action of the novel in a more positive and constructive manner (14). The earlier part of Ezeigbo's assertion is at variance with the findings of this research. Achebe is not in any way relegating women's' experience to the background in *TFA*, for instance, but is reflecting the social reality of that ancient time. In making macho Okonkwo his central character around whom all things revolve, he is also aiming to blow out of proportion the excessive show of masculinity manifested in the societal relegation of womanhood to the background, as a way of holding it up to derision and ridicule. Okonkwo thus becomes the butt of the satirist. That Achebe is neither a male chauvinist nor conservative like Okonkwo, becomes more obvious in his latest novel, *Anthills of the Savannah*, where the female protagonist, Beatrice, is depicted as a sensitive leader of a budding group of patriots in an oppressed nation. Achebe admits himself that his society has "created all kinds of myth to support the suppression of the woman and that the time has now come to put an end to that" (15). Achebe's female characters are the products of the society from which they emerge.

In conclusion, we wish to submit that Achebe's view of womanhood has been more or less misconceived by earlier critics (for example, Ama Ata Aidoo, Ezeigbo). What Achebe does in *Things Fall Apart*, this anti-colonial novel, is to expose with some measure of exaggeration the people's (Igbo people's) concept of womanhood which without doubt, is not in consonance with his own personal views; debunk misconceived notions in the Igbo culture and leave the reader to deduce his, Achebe's own personal stand. The plot is woven around Okonkwo, the symbol *par excellence* of manhood, who from his humble beginning inherited nothing from his *agbala* father, to his rise to greatness by sheer dint of personal industry and laudable achievement; his great fall induced by his accidental murder of Ezeudu's son (a female crime), his banishment, miserable life in exile in Mbanta, his mother's clan (a kind of psychological death); his return to Umuofia, now transformed to "women's clan" where things have fallen apart with white missionary movement and colonial implantation; his failure to accept the change; his orchestrated but isolated anti-colonial struggle, his suicide and burial like a dog. What a tragic hero! What an embodiment of contradiction; between good and evil, strength and weakness, courage and fear, greatness and failure, overt self-confidence a covert insecurity, superiority and inferiority, manhood and womanhood; a paradox that reflects that of his society – Umuofia torn apart by the conflict of cultures – traditional and imported. The paradox appears to throw into relief the futility of gender discrimination, of making clear boundaries between manhood and womanhood seeing that they are not mutually exclusive but exist concomitantly in individuals and groups with acceptable complementarity.

Finally, far from being a male chauvinist, a sexist with "cavalier attitude" to womanhood, Chinua Achebe is a postmodern feminist subtly condemning male dominance, woman subjugation and oppression in a patriarchy. His postmodern feminist bent may not be obvious in TFA party because of his close attachment to the development of the central theme – collapse of an old order as a result of invasion by an alien and dominant system, and partly because at the historical time represented in his fiction, Igbo women had not attained the socio-political awareness of gender recognition, struggles and empowerment that is now the order of the day. Such development in women is beautifully reflected in *Anthills of the Savannah* published in 1987 reflecting the social reality of that time. *Better Life for Women, Family Support Program, Women in Nigeria*, are among the women's associations crusading for women liberation and the betterment of the lot of women. A Ministry of Women's Affairs has been created. We now have female ministers. Needless to say that the image of the woman has greatly improved in Igboland and Nigeria as a whole, thanks to implicit and explicit feminist commitment in writing. Is the time ripe for Nigerians to welcome a female Governor or Head of State?

Works Cited

Achebe, Chinua. *Things Fall Apart*. London: Heinemann, 1958.

Aidoo, Ama Ata. "Unwelcome Pals and Decorative Slaves: The Woman as Writer in Modern Africa." *Afa: Journal of Creative Writing*. 1982.

Balandier, Georges. *Sociologie Actuella de l'Afrique Noire*. Pair: Presses Universitaries de France. 1955.

Bamikunle, Aderemi. "Feminism in Nigerian Female Poetry." *Feminism in African Literature*. Ed. Helen *Chukwuma*. Enugu: New Generation, 1994.

Ezeigbo, Theodora. "Reflecting the Times: Radicalism in Recent Female-Oriented Fiction in Nigeria." Presented at the 8th Annual Conference on African Literature and the English Language. University of Calabar. May 1998.

Killam, G.D. *The Writings of Chinua Achebe*. London: Heinemann, 1969.

Lindfors, Bernth. "The Palm Oil with which Words are Eaten." *African Literature Today*. Nos. 1–4. Ed. Eldred D. Jones. Oxford: James Currey, 1970.

Nnolim, Charles. "A House Divided: Feminism in African Literature." *Feminism in African Literature*. Ed. Helen Chukwuma. Enugu: New Generation, 1994.

Ogini, E.E. "From Feminism to Womanism: An Instance of Sembene Ousmane and Mariama Ba." *Ekpoma Journal of Language and Literary Studies*. Vol 8. 1995/96.

Ogunyemi, Chikwenye. "Women and Nigerian Literature." *Perspectives on Nigerian Literature*. Vol. 1. Lagos: Guardian Books Ltd., 1988.

Palmer, Eustace. *An Introduction to the African Novel*. London: Heinemann, 1972.

Rutherford, Anna. "Interview with Chinua Achebe in London." Nov. 1987. Reproduced in *Kunapipi*. Vol. ix, No. 12, 1987.

Tong, Rosemarie. *Feminist Thought: A Comprehensive Introduction*. London: Routledge, 1993.

Chapter 25

The Changing Faces of the African Woman: A Look at Achebe's Novels

Grace J. Malgwi

Introduction

SINCE THE WHITE MAN SET FOOT on the African soil, the black man and certainly the black woman have not been the same again. All changed. Cultures were challenged, beliefs were questioned, values vanished and systems disintegrated.

The historian could not record these happenings satisfactorily as they were more than dates and events. They happened ever so slowly. They were not things one could feel, touch or see. The African writer has been more successful in recording this. For he, through his art, has been able to recreate these happenings allowing us entrance into the thoughts, fears, frustrations and disillusions of the actors on both sides.

Chinua Achebe in his novels has tried to portray this incursion on the African society in an as authentic a light as is artistically possible. In his first three novels, *Things Fall Apart, No Longer at Ease* and *Arrow of God*, he shows the reader a traditional society on the verge of collapse, a society in a flux grappling with the influence of a foreign culture and the clash between two cultures respectively. The eyes however beget more than the obvious: the African woman, sitting quietly and soberly looking on, was not spared the onslaught of the unfolding events. Achebe in his characteristic way painted the picture as he saw it. In *A Man of the People* and *Anthills of the Savannah*, we see an African woman so different from the Ezinma of *Things Fall Apart* and the wives of Ezeulu in *Arrow of God*. So different yet inwardly the same. Where, when and how did this change occur?

Before we begin a discussion on the transformation, so to say, of the African woman, it is important to clear the misconception about what Achebe did or did not do in his portrayal of female characters.

The Misconception

In most discussions on the place of women in Achebe's writings, the deduction has usually been that, the female characters were relegated to the background or portrayed as having inferior status. Such discussions have even gone on to suggest that *Anthills of the Savannah* was Achebe's way of righting the wrongs done to women in his earlier works. This apart from being untrue is grossly unfair not only to Achebe but also to the African woman. There has been no time in African history that the woman was inferior or relegated to the background.

Everything in African society had its place which neither man nor woman had a right to question: the gods, man, woman, animals, seasons and crops all had their places in the scheme of things.

When Okonkwo's wives and the other women noticed that one of the *egwugwu* had the "springy walk" of Okonkwo and also noticed that Okonkwo was not seated with the other titled men, they did not question it.

The *egwugwu* with the springy walk was one of the dead fathers of the clan (*Things Fall Apart* 64).

Yam is regarded as the king of crops. Does pounded yam fill the belly more than cassava *foofoo*? The superiority of yam is as sacred as the sacred python and is not to be questioned. So yam always came first. To say, therefore, that the African woman in *Things Fall Apart* or *Arrow of God* is given an inferior status or relegated to the background is to look at the African society with a foreign eye. Achebe, therefore, did not wake up one morning and decide to write a story in which a woman was the heroine. The African woman got there by an alienation of history and Achebe just recorded it as he saw it.

The Transformation

The legend of Idemili has it that in the beginning, power rampaged through our world naked so the Almighty ... decided to send his daughter, Idemili to bear witness to the moral nature of authority by wrapping around power's rude waist a loincloth of peace and modesty (*Anthills of the Savannah* 102).

Any man seeking the highest title of authority and power, the *ozo*, knows the importance of a daughter. He needs a young woman to hold his hand like a child and stand between him and the Daughter of the Almighty before he can be granted hearing.

The African woman was therefore an embodiment of peace, modesty and humility. In *Things Fall Apart*, we see Okonkwo trying to instill what he regards as manly qualities into Nwoye by refusing him to listen to his mother's stories. Okonkwo encouraged the boys to sit with him in his *obi* and he told them stories of the land – masculine stories of violence and bloodshed (*Things Fall Apart* 37).

The African woman of the pre-Christian and pre-colonial era was a woman satisfied with her place in society, content with her role as a wife, a mother and a helper for her husband. Okonkwo's wives helped in planting the yams and weeding the farm for that was a woman's job but covering the outer wall of the compound with palm branches and leaves was a job for men. This contentment with her position in society made the unalienated African woman more accepting of the polygamous society in which she lived. We see unity in Okonkwo's house not jealousy or rivalry. When Nwoye's mother asked Ekwefi to send Ezinma with some fire for her, Ezinma not only took the fire to her stepmother, but offered to make the fire. "Let me make the fire for you" Ezinma offered. "Thank you Ezibgo" she said. She often called her Ezibgo, which means "the good one" (*Things Fall Apart* 30).

In *Arrow of God*, we see Ezeulu accusing Matefi of being a wicked woman when she complains about not having cassava to cook for Akueke's husband and his people. "I have noticed that you will not do anything happily unless it is for yourself or your children … if Akueke's mother were alive she would not draw a line between her children and yours and you know it." (*Arrow of God* 61). Polygamy therefore was accepted. Chief Nanga's wife in *A Man of the People* is not overjoyed at her husband's new wife not because she was a wicked woman like Matefi but because of her exposure to the new life. The food is cooked and the smell of the soup is around. Let nobody remember who toiled and starved when there was no money (*A Man of the People* 88).

Chris, in describing Beatrice whom he regards as the perfect embodiment of an ideal woman, says she was like a tastefully produced book, easy on the eye. No pretentious distraction. Absolutely sound … beautiful without being glamourous. Peaceful but very strong. Very, very strong. (*Anthills of the Savannah* 63).

In this description we see an added quality of the ideal African woman, the quality of strength. In the days of Okonkwo and Ezeulu, the African woman was not required to be strong because she was amply protected by the African man and by the society. But with the weakening of the powers of the African man and the disintegration of society, the African woman had to be strong. Obi's mother had to be strong because Isaac Okonkwo was not. When faced with a problem under normal circumstances, he (Isaac Okonkwo) was apt to weigh it and measure it and look it up and down, postponing action. He relied heavily on his wife at such moments (*No Longer at Ease* 150).

Clara had to take care of herself when she found out she was pregnant and realized Obi was not strong enough to do right by her. There was something I wanted to tell you, but it doesn't matter. I ought to have been able to take care of myself (*No Longer at Ease* 130).

We see Comfort, Beatrice's friend stand up for herself when her fiance was not strong enough to shield her from the insult of his relatives. The insult did not bother her half as much as her young man's silence ... Then she told him she had always suspected he was something of a rat (*Anthills of the Savannah* 89). She then threw him out of her flat. Beatrice accused Chris of not caring enough about her safety and welfare when he encouraged her to attend the President's party and to keep all options open. She didn't feel right about it and told Chris she wants a man who cares enough to be curious about where his girl sleeps. That's the kind of man this girl wants (*Anthills of the Savannah* 113).

These kinds of men who cared where their girls slept were there in *Things Fall Apart* and *Arrow of God* and so the woman of that time could afford to relax and sit back because she knew she was protected.

When a daughter of Umuofia was murdered by the sons of Mbaino, the whole clan swung into action to ensure that justice was done (*Things Fall Apart* 8). When a difficult and obstinate man, Uzowulu, made it a habit to always beat up his wife, Mbafo, in *Things Fall Apart*, we see the *egwugwu*, the highest and most powerful decision making body in the clan being brought in to protect Mbafo. "I don't know why such a trifle should come before the *egwugwu*" said one elder to another. "Don't you know what kind of man Uzowulu is? He will not listen to any other decision," replied the other (*Things Fall Apart* 66).

We see a similar situation in *Arrow of God* when Obika beats up his half-sister. Akueke's husband, Ibe, tied him to a bed and set him down under the *Ukwa* tree because Ibe had beaten up Akueke. In justifying Okiba's action, one of the kinsmen of Ibe says: "Why do we pray to *Ulu* and to our ancestors to increase our numbers if not for this thing?" said their leader. "No one eats numbers. But if we are many nobody will dare to provoke us and our daughters will hold their heads up in their husbands' houses" (*Arrow of God* 12). Ezeulu was disgusted by Obika's drunken behavior because he was concerned about Obika's ability to protect his bride when she arrived. A man who could not watch his hut at night because he was dead with palm wine. Where did the manhood of such a husband lie? A man who could not protect his wife if night marauders knocked at his door (*Arrow of God* 79).

The traditional African woman had to change because her man had been weakened and the clan no longer acted as one. The African woman may have gained a virtue from the disintegration of her society but she also lost her sense of decency, high morality and pride in her womanhood.

In the traditional society, a woman was given away in marriage to a man who had the strength to care for her. The woman we see in *No Longer at Ease* is a woman who has lost her moral values and begun to see something as inconsequential as dancing as important to a relationship. As Joseph tells Obi, dancing is very important nowadays. No girl will look at you if you can't dance (*No Longer at Ease* 12).

This dancing girl goes into brief immoral relationships and sews pillowcases with strange words on them for her lovers. She engages in meaningless imitation of alien practices because she has no one to tell her better. She was tall and dark with enormous pneumatic bosom under a tight-fitting red and yellow dress. Her lips and long fingernails were painted a brilliant red and her eyebrows were fine black lines. She looked not unlike those wooden masks made in Ikot Ekpene. Altogether she left a nasty taste in Obi's mouth like the multicoloured word OSCULATE on the pillows (*No Longer at Ease* 13).

This dark maiden contrasts sharply with the young maiden described in *Things Fall Apart*. She wore a coiffure which was done up into a crest in the middle of the head. Cam Wood was rubbed lightly into her skin and all over her body were black patterns drawn with *Uli*. She wore a black necklace which hung down in three coils just above her succulent breasts. On her arms were red and yellow bangles, and on her waist four or five rows of *jigida* or waist beads (49).

Apart from this change in physical appearance, the issue of being "found at home" which was the pride of every young bride was thrown to the winds. Virginity, we are told by Joseph, was rare (*No Longer at Ease* 13). Clara got pregnant for Obi even before the "conversations began." This loose woman is typified by Elsie, the nurse in *A Man of the People*. She goes to bed with Odili barely an hour after meeting him. Elsie was, and for that matter still is the only girl I met and slept with the same day – in fact within an hour (*A Man of the People* 24).

We see her doing the same thing with Chief Nanga (69). This loose African woman tried to show she could rise to the height of immorality reached by the American Elsie and the American Jean. This woman has indeed really gone far, far away from the young bride in *Arrow of God* who was so worried about not being "found at home" on her wedding night because of a moonlight play when Obiora had put his penis between her thighs. True, he had only succeeded in playing at the entrance but she could not be too sure (*Arrow of God* 122).

The young bride in *Arrow of God* had to worry about her virginity because she knew the consequences of being found otherwise not only on herself but also on her family. With the new way of life, the African maiden now carries a highway between her thighs. She has become a plaything for the likes of Chief Nanga who had lost all decency. His suggestion to get girls for Odili to make up for his sleeping with Elsie showed the level to which the African woman's dignity had sunk. If you like I can bring you six girls this evening. You go do the thing *sotay* you go beg say you no want again (*A Man of the People* 72). And Chief Nanga, a Minister of culture, laughs finding humor in the degeneration of African womanhood.

Apart from this loss of moral values and pride in her womanhood caused by this new civilization and perpetuated by the African man, the new African woman was forced to take on responsibilities which were hitherto borne by men. In the traditional society depicted by Achebe in *Things Fall Apart* and *Arrow of God*, the African woman had no need for wealth, for a man took care of his wives and children. The man brings out the yams and each wife goes and takes her share (*Things Fall Apart* 30). In the new dispensation however, the woman is forced to fend for herself and for her children because the man has acquired new habits. In *A Man of the People*, we see Odili talking about his father's problems. He says that his father doesn't even make any pretence of providing for his family nowadays. He leaves every wife to her own devices ... (they) have to find their children's school fees from farming and petty trading (*A Man of the People* 30). The woman struggles while the man buys himself a jar or palm wine every morning and a bottle of schnapps now and again and talks politics.

Beatrice in *Anthills of the Savannah* was determined to make her career her major pre-occupation and if need be the only one rather than end up in the house of a worthless man (88).

The African woman changed as a result of the happenings around her. Is the African woman in *Anthills of the Savannah* of a superior status than the one in *Things Fall Apart*? She has grown some, she has degenerated some, but as Beatrice says you can't blame her: She didn't make her world so tough (88).

The Hope

The Igbo say that when a house collapses it is sheer stupidity to ask if the roof fell with it. Ikem in discussing the political oppression of women draws a parallel between the biblical fall of man in the Old Testament and the traditional version of the story. In both cases, the woman was said to have caused God to move away from man and so deserved whatever suffering man inflicted on her. Man, however, felt guilty and decided to uplift the woman. He called her Nneka "mother is supreme," and assigned her the "fire brigade" role of swinging into action whenever there was a fire and the world was crashing around the man (*Anthills of the Savannah* 98). Ikem admits that this might have been true of the woman in the past but in the present dispensation, where society was standing on its head, it is good for everybody to "know who is now holding up the action."

This role of holding up the action and picking up the pieces is a role foreign to the African woman but which she must of necessity perform to save society from total collapse. Beatrice, the symbol of this new African woman has to be two different people fused into one to be able to succeed. Beatrice Nwanyibuife is described as the village priestess who will prophesy when her divinity rides her abandoning if need be her soup-pot on the fire, but returning again when the god departs to the domesticity of kitchen or the bargaining market-stool behind her little display of peppers, dry fish and green vegetables (*Anthills of the Savannah* 105).

Ezinma in *Things Fall Apart* broke her visit to her future husband's family when she heard that her father had been arrested by the white man and was going to be hanged. We see her trying to make sure something was being done. As soon as she got home she went straight to Obierika to ask what the men of Umuofia were going to do about it (*Things Fall Apart* 139).

Okonkwo had always wished Ezinma were a boy. In the times of *Things Fall Apart*, only the men of Umuofia could do something about her father's predicament. Had Okonkwo lived in the times of *Anthills of the Savannah*, he would not have kept wishing, for a girl also became something.

Eunice, Maxwell Kulamo's fiancée in *A Man of the People* did not wait for the men to do something about the brutal murder of her fiance, she just "took out a pistol and fired two bullets into Chief Koko's chest (143). For had his (Maxwell's) spirit waited for the people to demand redress, it would have been waiting still, in the rain and out in the sun (*A Man of the People* 148).

Beatrice dared to challenge the shameless actions of a brutal president to his face when his cabinet of grownup enlightened men applauded him like mindless puppets.

The African woman, therefore, has come a long way from the quiet bystander looking on from the outside to a woman who wines and dines with dictators and tells them to their faces what she thinks of their actions. As has been seen earlier, the journey was not an easy one and the woman never wanted to come this far. She was not ambitious. She never sought attention. She was happy living in the "world inside a world inside a world, without end" her *Uwa-t-uwa* (*Anthills of the Savannah* 84).

She never asked to be noticed. She never embarked on anything that would call attention to herself. Her involvement was purely an accident of history (87). When Beatrice performs the naming ceremony of Elewa's baby, it was not planned. A baby was there, she had to be named but those to perform the rites were not there. "In our traditional society," resumed Beatrice "the father named the child. But the man who should have done it today is absent … The man is not here although I know he is floating around us now, watching with that small-boy smile of his" (*Anthills of the Savannah* 222).

Although the African woman has changed, the hope for Africa, however, lies with that African woman who has not lost touch with her African background.

Works Cited

Achebe, Chinua. *Things Fall Apart*. London: Heinemann, 1958.

———. *No Longer at Ease*. London: Heinemann, 1960.

———. *Arrow of God*. London: Heinemann, 1964.

———. *A Man of the People*. London: Heinemann, 1966.

———. *Anthills of the Savannah*. London: Heinemann, 1987.

Gillam, G.D. (Ed) *African Writers on African Writing*. London: Heinemann, 1973.

Taiwo, O. *Culture and the Nigerian Novel*. London: Macmillan, 1976.

Yankson, K.E. *Chinua Achebe's Novels: A Sociolinguistic Perspective*. Unuowulu-Obosi: Pacific Publishers, 1976.

Chapter 26

In Fairness:
The Female in Two of Chinua Achebe's Novels

Tanure Ojaide

Introduction

IN THE WEST, ESPECIALLY AMONG FEMINISTS, there is the tendency to see the African woman as more or less a chattel slave. The practice of polygyny, paying bride-price, and the abnormal case of Okonkwo beating his wives at little provocation are some of the points used to support the case of the subjugated African woman. African traditions differ from Western ones and there are no universal canons of judging the rightness of male-female relationships. Every judgement made in this area is bound to be highly subjective and relative culturally. Besides, there is great diversity in Africa, a continent that is seen by the uninformed outsider as monolithic. African myths and history are replete with females, goddesses and humans, who are revered and whose roles and status in the society contradict the idea of the marginalized and subservient female. Women may be in the background in some occasions but they are in the forefront in others. They may not go to war, but the judgement of the priestess is sought before a war can be fought. The Igbo woman is not portrayed as inferior or marginalized.

I intend to discuss the female in two of Chinua Achebe's novels with a view to bringing out the nature of the female, her relationship with the male, her role and status and, drawing from myths, characters and principles, show that the female or male has a stature depending upon individual performance. The excess of either male or female is rejected as extreme. There is the need for a blending of both male and female into an androgynous personality. The female is never in

Achebe presented as inferior but as a necessary partner to the male. She is equal to and sometimes superior to the male.

Patriarchy

The Igbo society is a patriarchy. Uchendu, Okonkwo's maternal uncle, says, "we all know a man is the head of the family" (*Things Fall Apart* 94). It is among other ethnic groups, not among the Igbo, that a man's children belong to his wife and her family. Despite the existing patriarchy, the place of the female in Igbo society is recognized and appreciated as most important.

Among the Igbo people, the woman is a traditional regent. Tess Onwueme's *The Reign of Wazobia* is based on an actual political practice of an Igbo group in which a female acts as a Prime Minister, the *Omu*. Igbo women initiated the Aba Revolt of 1929. Igbo women are some of the most industrious and best educated in Africa. Despite cases of women subjection in Buchi Emecheta's works, Igbo women in traditional and modern times fully actualize themselves as great achievers. Once in a while an author's individual unpleasant experience interferes with the reflection of reality as in Buchi Emecheta's case.

The Male

In Achebe's works, the female can be defined indirectly as one that is not male. In *Things Fall Apart* masculinity is touted by Okonkwo as a superior virtue. A great wrestler and warrior, he is physically strong. In addition, he has a big farm, many wives, and children and some of the highest titles of his society. To Okonkwo, he is the embodiment of manhood. As a result of his father's poverty and material failure resulting in indebtedness, Okonkwo's whole life is to live the opposite of his father. Thus he is disdainful of people who have no titles. He does not show any human emotions and sentiments so as not to be seen as weak. He gives the killing blow to Ikemefuna (who calls him father), because he "was afraid of being thought weak." The masculinity represented by Okonkwo lacks human sentiments and thoughtfulness. He is portrayed as having a rough exterior and sometimes rash gust. He is aggressive and violent. These qualities are not universally accepted in the Igbo society. The fact that Obierika, perhaps the most intellectual man in Umuofia, and Ezeudu, the oldest man, did not approve of Okonkwo's killing of Ikemefuna is a testimony of their rejection of Okonkwo's type of masculinity. Achebe uses the character of Obierika as a foil to Okonkwo and to criticize the concept of masculinity as ideal or superior.

The Female

The female is, among other qualities, peaceful, gentle, caring and emotional. These qualities are deduced from what the Okonkwo type of man is expected not to be. Though men without titles are called *agbala* for not being distinguished, Igbo myths do not support the view of this blanket denigration of the female (Amadiume 28–9). Though men are generally more visible, they are among failures, *Osu* caste and the *efulefus*. Women planted melons, beans, maize, cocoyams, and cassava, but not yams, the so-called king of crops. This should not be construed as a mark of inferiority but a matter of distribution of labour in a traditional subsistence economy.

Females in various roles perform most important functions in the society. They are goddesses, priestesses, mothers, wives and daughters. The female, in spite of her so-called weakness, is ironically the refuge for all humans. The mother is biologically more intimate with the child and the relationship between Ezinma and Ekwefi confirms this. Both *Things Fall Apart* and *Anthills of the Savannah* emphasize the special place of the mother and in both novels is mentioned the commonest name given to children, Nneka, "Mother is Supreme." As Uchendu explains, "when a father beats his child, it seeks sympathy in its mother's hut. A man belongs to his fatherland when things are good and life is sweet. But when there is sorrow and bitterness he finds refuge in his motherland. You mother is there to protect you" (94).

Equally important is the spiritual guardianship of traditions assigned females. *Ani*, the Earth goddess, is the ultimate judge of morality and conduct. In addition, she is the source of fertility and creativity. The Week of Peace and New Yam Festival are both dedicated to *Ani*, and an abomination against her is strictly avoided by the community. In *Anthills*, Idemili, God's daughter, is sent to earth to be the savior of mankind. The Almighty sends his daughter "to bear witness to the moral nature of authority by wrapping around Power's rude waist a loincloth of peace and modesty" (102). Man cannot get his cherished title of *ozo* without being sanctified by the goddess and the title-seeker's daughter. In Achebe, the female exemplified by *Ani* and *Idemili* is a symbol of purity. *Idemili* has to find the *ozo* title seeker worthy to save her sacred hierarchy from contamination and scandal. In *Things Fall Apart* Okonkwo is fined for violating the Week of Peace when he beats one of his wives, an affront against *Ani*. And again when he inadvertently kills Ezeudu's son during the old man's funeral, his house is razed and he flees into exile to atone for the contamination of the purity of the earth.

The female is not limited to goddesses, priestesses, mothers and daughters. There are male and female crimes. Okonkwo's accidental murder is a female one, which demands a seven-year exile, unlike the intentional male murder which would require life exile.

Also there are male and female crops. Yam is the king of crops and is cultivated by males. It requires a lot of physical labour to produce, and women, though they bear a lot of physical responsibilities in other spheres, are exempted from cultivating it. Instead they cultivate so-called female crops such as beans, maize and cassava. These crops are thought to require less physical labour to do well.

There are women stories and other social roles. Women have the responsibility of telling folktales to their children. Since most are moral tales, women are the educators of children towards good social behavior, ethics and morality. It is when it comes to disciplining that the father is called upon. Though male children could follow fathers out carrying their stools to meetings, the major responsibility for good upbringing in the Igbo society rests with mothers. Women's stories could be disparaged as "silly" by men, but they serve their etiological and moral purposes. In contrast to stories told by Ekwefi to Ezinma and Okonkwo's mother to him when young are "stories of the land – masculine stories of violence and bloodshed" (37). The effect of the two kinds of stories can be seen in Nwoye's response; he "knew that it was right to be masculine and to be violent, but somehow he still preferred the stories that his mother used to tell, and which she no doubt still told her younger children" (37). Nwoye's knowing that "it was right to be masculine and violent" is an effort to be politically correct in his father's house.

Women sometimes enforce disciplinary codes of the community like when they chase away the stray cow and fine its owner. Women may be in the background during settling of disputes, going to war, and at bride-price paying ceremonies, but they have their important roles in the community.

Female Male

In the Igbo world of Achebe's fiction, there are in-between the real male and real female men and women who have qualities traditionally attributed to the opposite gender and sex. They are the female males and male females.

Unoka and, to some extent, Nwoye are examples of the male with female attributes. Unoka was called *agbala*; he took no titles all his life. He was weak and considered a failure. He was talkative, unlike Okonkwo, a man of action who stuttered. Heavily indebted, he could not take care of his family. However, he was an artist, a poet and a musician. Epicurean, unlike the general grain of stoicism among Igbo people, he enjoyed drinking and playing on his flute. His happiest moments were the months after harvest when Okonkwo was restive for work. The female male, therefore, is soft and tender and enjoys the good things of life, unlike Okonkwo's rigid, harsh and industrious personality.

Another female male in *Things Fall Apart* is Nwoye. Rather cleverly, Achebe makes Okonkwo's father and son similar but different from the warrior. Nwoye prefers the "silly" women stories that his mother told him to Okonkwo's stories of bloodshed. He is alienated from his father because of the harsh way he is treated. He is later drawn to Christianity because it is not only a refuge but there is something femininely soothing in the hymns which attract his soft nature. Christianity is presented as a mother who draws all her children to her breast. Achebe sees Christianity in a tender feminine light. Nwoye does not care about the mysteries of the Holy Trinity, but is moved by the beautiful music. In a way, he has an artistic disposition like his grandfather, Unoka. They are devotees of *Ani*, the goddess of creativity and art. It seems the lack of recognition and acceptance of the female principle makes Christianity draw a lot of converts and directly lead to the collapse of traditional culture.

Male Female

Okonkwo often laments that his daughter by his favorite wife is not a boy: "she should have been a boy" (44–5). This is because he considers his first son, Nwoye, to be lazy and Ezinma more robust in behavior. However, it is in *Anthills* that the ultimate male female is introduced in the character of Beatrice. Ironically for her Igbo name, Nwanyibuife (a female is also something), she is imbued with male qualities. She is unconventional and rebellious, unlike her stereotypical gender kind. Hence her father always reminded her of her being female with such expressions as: 'Sit like a female!' or calling her a "female soldier" the day she fell off a cashew tree. "Female soldier" shows that she is physically stronger than the average female is expected to be. The mother who had prayed for a boy got a "boy" without knowing!

Beatrice is intelligent and her First Class Honors degree in English from a British university is vivid testimony. She is bold and independent. She knows what she wants and places her career first before other things that include marriage. Her relationship with Chris is based on equality. She gives Ikem insight into women. Ikem calls her writing "muscular" and "masculine" (91). She is the new woman, an intellectual who is assertive. If Amadiume says women lost their power in colonial times, Beatrice shows that the modern Igbo woman has regained her rightful place in society. Beatrice says "giving women today the same role which traditional society gave them of intervening only when everything else has failed is not enough" (91). After Chris' death, she carries herself remarkably well and cares for Elewa and her baby. She presides over the naming of Elewa's daughter and gives the male name of Amaechina to the baby. In other words, she effectively plays the traditional role men assign to themselves, and everybody, including Elewa's mother and Unoka-like uncle, accepts her authority.

Despite all her masculinity, Beatrice is a woman portrayed as having the mystical and physical attributes of a goddess, being indirectly presented as the modern-day Idemili sent as savior to the earth. While the goddess side of Beatrice may look bothersome, her new woman side with qualities for long attributed to men is most impressive.

Androgyny

In Achebe, there seems to be a tacit acceptance of the androgynous personality as the one that best suits society. Having qualities of the opposite sex appears to bring balance and intensity to the personality, especially in the case of Beatrice. The only male attribute as in Okonkwo is too extreme in his rigidity. The excess of the male in Okonkwo makes him beat his wife during the Week of Peace and kill Ikemefuna and somehow challenge his *chi*. This apparently leads to his tragedy. Also by not giving room to the female principles to flourish freely, Umuofia opens itself to Christianity. At the same time the purely female is too submissive and ineffectual. Though a priestess, Chielo has courage, energy and decisiveness, qualities many might attribute to males.

To affirm an androgynous viewpoint, Achebe makes Beatrice name Elewa's daughter "Amaechina", a name commonly given to males. This child, symbolic of a hopeful future in spite of current setbacks, blends male and female virtues that will lead to a progressive society. The exclusive male or female is not enough; only through the coming together of both can society's full potentials be exploited for its good. Ikem seems to be androgynous in his being a poet inspired by *Ani* and a revolutionary. To him the dual forces of nature blend.

Often unnoticed in *Things Fall Apart* and in real life among the Igbo people is the practice of gods having priestesses and goddesses having priests. Chika was the priestess of *Agbala*, the Oracle of the Hills and the Caves, who tells Unoka the bitter truth about his laziness. Conversely, Ezeani is the priest of *Ani*, the Earth goddess, who exacts a sacrifice from Okonkwo for beating his wife during the Week of Peace. The harmony between Ndulue and Ozoemena is a tribute to the equality of male and female.

Myth

Myth is the imaginative projection of reality in the past but which has remained in the psychic memory of a people. As already mentioned, myths about the female place her on a high pedestal. *Ani* is the goddess of the Earth, who is in charge of spirituality, morality, fertility and the purity of the land. Reared immensely, the Week of Peace and the New Yam Festival, the most important Igbo festivals are dedicated to her. An offence against her without prompt penitential sacrifice could bring disaster to an entire community. Similarly, the priestess of the Oracle is portrayed as fearless and the custodian of truth. Both Chika and Chielo excel in their roles as priestesses and earn respect from every member of the Umuofia community.

In *Anthills*, the myth of Idemili reinforces the primacy of women in spiritual and moral matters. The savior sent by Chukwu, she watches the morality of the Igbo people. The death of the pretender *ozo* seeker tells the power of Idemili. Achebe seems to suggest that Beatrice is a reincarnation of the goddess, and since myth is a projection of a people's reality, she becomes the redeemer of Kangan. At the end of the novel, her authority is generally accepted. Achebe seems to be saying that if in the olden days, women were hampered by cultural circumstances, in modern times, it is not so much the sex and gender that matter but the personality of the individual.

Irony and Paradox

There does not seem to be understanding of Achebe's position on sex and gender. He uses irony and paradox copiously to deflate a seeming male superiority, while simultaneously asserting the primacy of the individual personality.

Okonkwo might be very masculine but ironically his father and son are unlike him and give expression to their softer instincts. Okonkwo is portrayed as the extreme of masculinity which leads, to a large extent, to his tragedy. It is also ironical that Okonkwo as one of the justices of Umuofia dons the ancestral mask to judge the case of Udo's abuse of his wife. He is himself guilty of wife-beating. In any case, Udo's fine shows that wife-beating is not approved by the people's tradition but the practice of some unbalanced males.

Irony also informs Okonkwo's inadvertent murder. The man who prides himself as masculine commits a "female" offence, which mitigates his punishment from life exile to a mere seven years. In spite of his masculinity, he is "rejected" by his male side. His house is ritually destroyed and he takes refuge in Mbanta, his mother's home. In Achebe's subtle portrayal, the more Okonkwo asserts his maleness, the more the suppressed female side pops up to save him. Again, while all his life trying to avoid being like his father who is not properly buried, he ends by hanging himself and so can not be buried by his own people it would be an abomination to the Earth goddess.

The more the male side is deflated, the more the female is proved strong. There is the paradox of the women being seen as weak and yet the principle of power is based on a myth about a woman. The active principle of Umuofia's war medicine in *Things Fall Apart* is "an old woman with one leg" (8–9). Of course, though men are warriors, Umuofia does not fight a war of blame. This is a moral stance effected by the female principle. Only the priestess behold the Oracle. Chika was "full of the power of her god, and she was greatly feared." Power does not manifest itself only in physical and political forms; it also does in spiritual ways. Chielo, another priestess, is also fearless when possessed. Man may cultivate yam, the king of crops, but it is *Ani*, the Earth goddess, that gives fertility and her approval is sought through the New Yam Festival before fresh yam is eaten. Through *Ani*, Chika, Chielo and Idemili, Achebe shows that man may have physical brute force, but moral and spiritual powers lie with the female. He succeeds in using irony and paradox in deflating a male superiority and establishing a dual force of physical and spiritual powers, a balance of which is necessary for the individual and society. It is for this that individual androgyny and pulling together of male and female forces in society become necessary.

Status and Role of the Female

As already discussed, the female is not marginalized in social status as the examples of priestesses and highly educated Beatrice show. Women have roles in the traditional set-up which confine most to the kitchen and growing vegetables, beans, maize, melon and cassava, but that is neither what Achebe accepts in his works nor the myth and history of the Igbo people affirm. Status tends to be more important in feudal societies than in democratic societies in which role is highly regarded. Modernity is in several ways affecting what Igbo myths have long held: the importance of the individual in a communal system.

Conclusion

In conclusion, in Achebe's works, all excesses of male or female are rejected for an androgynous personality. Strength is not only physical but also spiritual and the two types are needed by both the individual and the society. Laziness is not a gender attribute as there are lazy men and strong women. The novelist uses irony and paradox to deflate the claim of a male superiority and to assert the indispensability of the female. Igbo myths which Achebe uses and interprets reinforce the importance of the female. There is opportunity for everyone in the Igbo society, irrespective of gender and sex. In patriarchy, women may not have a head-start, but like minorities generally can only prosper by asserting their will. Chika, Chielo and Beatrice do this and succeed. And *Ani* and *Idemili*, archetypes of the female force, show they are superior, if not equal, to the male. As Africa moves from traditionalism to modernity, the female will firmly establish herself as an equal and respectable partner to the male, a relationship necessary for progress. This may come about the process of modernity, but really a re-affirmation of the validity of a people's myths in the flux of their history.

Works Cited

Achebe, Chinua. *Things Fall Apart*. London: Heinemann, 1958.

———. *Anthills of the Savannah*. Ibadan: Heinemann, 1988.

Amadiume, Ifi. *Male Daughters, Female Husbands: Gender and Sex in an African Society*. London: Zed Books, 1987.

Diop, Cheik Anta. *The African Origin of Civilization: Myth or Reality?* Chicago: Lawrence Hill, 1974.

Innes, C.L. and Bernth Lindfors. *Critical Perspectives on Chinua Achebe*. London: Heinemann, 1979.

Onwueme, Tess. *The Reign of Wazobia*. Ibadan: Heinemann, 1988.

Parpart, Jane L. and Sharon B. Stichter. *Patriarchy and Class: African Women in the Home and Workforce*. Boulder: Westview Press, 1988.

Chapter 27

Mother is Supreme:
A Semiotic Reading of Motherhood and
Womanhood in Three of Achebe's Novels

Victoria A. Alabi

ONE OF THE TRICHOTOMIES WITHIN THE sign system as postulated by C.S. Peirce is made up of a *qualsign*, a *sinsign* and *legisign*. The *qualisign* which is relevant to our present study is a quality which acts as a sign and it is instantiated in iconic resemblance of which Peirce distinguishes three types: the image, the diagram and the metaphor. It is the metaphor that is of direct relevance in this paper.

Metaphor derives from the Greek word *metapherein* (*meta* 'beyond, *pherein* 'to bring') and among the most widely held theories of metaphor are the *comparison*, the substitution and the *interaction* models. Although, Peirce is the fore-runner of the interactionist theory of metaphor, its development seems to lie with his followers notable among whom is Parmegiani (1987–88).

For Parmegiani, in the interactionist theory of metaphor are two distinct subjects – Principal and Subsidiary, which are each "system of things" rather than "things." A metaphor works by applying to the principal subject a system of "associated implications" characteristic of the subsidiary subject. This, according to Parmegiani (1987–88:3), implies "a system of relationships that are active in our mind and which force us to locate the ground of the metaphor through the system of associated relationships and associations." To therefore comprehend the metaphor *Marriage is a zero-sum game*, according to Parmegiani (1987–88:3), depends on:

the simultaneous activation of the associated implications of the *frame* (*marriage*) [the principal subject] and the *focus* (*zero-sum game*) [the subsidiary subject] through a projection of one unto the other. The end result is an interpretation complex which relates marriage to game-theory.

It is metaphor "mother is supreme" that is mentioned in most of Achebe's novels in various ramifications that we wish to explore in this paper following Parmegiani's interactionist theory. We shall therefore, simultaneously activate the associated implications of the "frame" – "motherhood" and its "focus" – "is supreme" through a projection of one onto the other. The approach aims at obtaining an interpretation complex which gives us new insight into motherhood or womanhood in Achebe's *Things Fall Apart* (abbreviated after quotations as *TFA*), *No Longer at Ease* (abbreviated after quotations as *NLAE*) and *Arrow of God* (abbreviated after quotations as *AOG*). It is hoped that this interpretation will provide a new insight into Achebe's women above the level of marriage and procreation, cooking the family meals, honoring their husband's bed on invitation, and merging with the home environment peacefully (see Chukwuma 1989: 2).

It should be noted that our notion of womanhood in this paper is not limited to human beings but includes spirits and goddesses. This is so because in Achebe's world, there is a strong interaction among the living, the ancestral spirits of the clan, gods and goddesses. For example, on the night of *Akwu Nro* every widow in Umuachala prepares *foofoo* and palm-nut soup and puts it outside her hut. Before morning each dead husband comes up from *Ani-Mmo* to eat the food. The dead also come from the underworld to act as the highest and final court for the living and to attend the funeral of old men. According to Achebe:

> The land of the living was not far removed from the domain of the ancestors. There was coming and going between them (*TFA*, 111).
>
> People come from far and near to consult *Agbala* when misfortune dogged their steps or when they had a dispute with their neighbors. They came to discover what the future held for them or to consult the spirits of their departed fathers (*TFA*, 15).

Spirits of the drums or spirits of gods or goddesses, for example, *Agbala*, possess human beings. Indeed, certain festivals bring gods and men together in one crowd in which:

> a man might look to his right and find his neighbor and look to his left and see a god standing there – perhaps Agwu whose mother also gave birth to madness or Ngene, owner of a stream (*AOG*, 202).

In *Things Fall Apart*, Umuofia is feared by all its neighbors and one of the reasons for this is its power in war. No neighboring clan would go to war against it without first trying a peaceful settlement. The active principle in its most potent war-medicine is an old woman with one leg. The medicine itself is called *agadi-nwayi*.

> Ani, the earth goddess, the owner of all land, the source of all fertility is identified with motherhood. She plays a greater part in the life of the people than any other deity. She was the ultimate judge of morality and conduct. And what was more, she was in close communion with the departed fathers of the clan whose bodies had been committed to earth. (*TFA*, 33).

It is the law of the fathers of Umuofia that before any crop is put in the earth each person sacrifices a cock to Ani. New yams cannot be eaten until some are first offered to *Ani*. The principal and ultimate value of womanhood as seen in *Ani* is buttressed by the Gikuyu who, according to Kenyatta, (1979:21) also "considers ...the earth as the 'mother' of the tribe...it is the soil that feeds the child through a life time, and again after death it is the soil that nurses the spirit of the dead for eternity...the earth is the most sacred...the soil is especially honored, and an everlasting oath is to swear by earth."

In commerce, womanhood is metaphorically prominent. The people of Umuike want their market to grow and swallow up the markets of their neighbors. The powerful medicine they make stands on the market ground in the shape of an old woman with a fan on every market-day before the first cock-crow. With her magic fan she beckons to the market all the neighboring clans "in front of her and behind her, to her right and to her left" (*TFA*, 103) and brings everybody to the market. The men of Okperi also make a powerful deity and place their market in its care. The deity which is called *Nwanyieke* is an old woman. Every *Eke* day before cock-crow she appears in the market place with a broom in her right hand and dances round the vast open space beckoning with her broom in "all directions of the earth and drawing folk [sic] from every land" (*AOG*, 19). Indeed, the old woman of the market in Umuru "has swept the world with her broom, even the land of white men" (*AOG*, 19).

Although it is believed the Earth has declared that twins are an offence on the land and must be destroyed, it is also a woman, Nneka, whose four previous childbirths of twins have been thrown away that first takes a decisive step against the killing of twins in Mbanta. She is the first woman convert in Mbanta and true to her name, motherhood is supreme in the grievous suffering of mothers of twins and in the wastage of children's lives.

Womanhood is an absolute metaphorical force in the fall of Okonkwo in *Things Fall Apart*. During the Week of Peace, a sacred week in honor of the great goddess, Okonkwo severely beats his youngest wife on account of his uncooked afternoon meal. The Week of Peace is a week during which no man says a harsh word to his neighbor. It is unheard of to beat somebody during the sacred week and it is the first time for many years that a man has broken the sacred peace. Even the oldest men can only remember one or two other occasions somewhere in the dim past. Okonkwo thus commits a great evil which according to Ezeani "can ruin the whole clan" (*TFA*, 28). The earth goddess whom Okonkwo insults may refuse to give the clan her increase and without her blessing their crops will not grow and the whole clan will perish.

It is also because a woman, a daughter of Umuofia is killed in Mbaino that Ikemefuna comes into Okonkwo's house-hold. When Okonkwo kills this boy who calls him father, he displeases the earth goddess. Obierika tells Okonkwo:

> What you have done will not please the Earth. It is the kind of action for which the goddess wipes out whole families. (*TFA*, 60–61).

Okonkwo's contempt for and his displeasing the earth goddess result in calamity when he inadvertently commits a female crime against her. At Ezeudu's funeral Okonkwo's gun explodes and a piece of iron from it kills Ezeudu's sixteen-year old son. The confusion which follows "was without parallel in the tradition of Umuofia" (*TFA*, 112–113). Okonkwo is cast out of his "clan like a fish on to a dry, sandy beach, panting" (*TFA*, 119). He flees into the "embrace" of his mother in Mbanta. Her spirit is there to protect him. According to Uchendu:

> A man belongs to his fatherland when things are good and life is sweet. But where there is sorrow and bitterness he finds refuge in his motherland. (*TFA*, 122).

It is no wonder then, the fugitives from Abame, most of whom are the sons of Umuaro whose mothers have been buried there, also find refuge in Umuaro.

When Okonkwo returns to Umuofia after seven "wasted and weary" years in exile and he turns the fight of the earth goddess he has so sorely grieved into a personal fight, he is finally crushed. On an annual worship of the earth goddess which falls on Sunday, Enoch "kills" an ancestral spirit by tearing off his mask. That night:

> the Mother of the Spirits walked the length and breadth of the clan, weeping for her murdered son. It was a terrible night. Not even the oldest man in Umuofia had ever heard such a strange and fearful sound... (*TFA*, 168).
>
> The next day all the masked *egwugwu* in Umuofia take their revenge to pacify the spirit of the clan. Okonkwo and five other leaders of Umuofia are detained and maltreated. On the night of their release as Okonkwo lies on his bamboo bed he swore vengeance. If Umuofia decided on war, all would be well, but if they choose to be cowards he would go out and avenge himself (*TFA*, 179).

It is at the meeting of that morning that Okonkwo confronts the head messenger and beheads him. He then hangs himself thereby again committing an offence against the earth. Only strangers can bury him after which sacrifices would be made to cleanse the desecrated land. Ironically, Okonkwo who detests womanly persons and a womanly clan has the tide of his life absolutely charted by the supremacy of womanhood – both spirit and human. The metaphorical absolutism of Womanhood in Okonkwo's life may be shown diagrammatically thus:

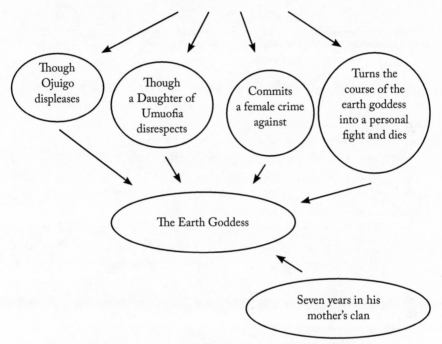

Fig. 1: Metaphorical Absolution of Womanhood in Okonkwo's Life

In *No Longer at Ease*, womanhood is again metaphorically portrayed. The two forces in Obi Okonkwo's life in the battle ground of a changing world are his mother and Clara. There is a special bond between Obi and his mother and of all her eight children Obi is nearest to her heart. When Obi turns about ten years old, an incident gives this special bond a concrete form in Obi's young mind. He forgets his rusty razor-blade with which he sharpens his pencil or sometimes cuts a grasshopper in his pocket. The blade cuts his mother's hand very badly when washing his clothes on a stone in the stream. She thus returns with the clothes unwashed and her hand dripping with blood. Achebe says:

> For some reason or other, whenever Obi thought affectionately of his mother, his mind went back to that shedding of her blood. It bound him very firmly to her (*NLAE*, 68–69).

On Obi's return from England he finds his mother so old and frail on account of long periods of illness and from then "he wore her sadness round his neck like a necklace of stone" (*NLAE*, 50). It is this Christ-figure whose sadness hangs around Obi's neck, like a necklace of stone, who cannot be "handled" on the matter of Clara being an *osu*, even when Obi's father seems to be giving in. Obi's mother is resolute and she tells her son:

> I have nothing to tell you in this matter except one thing. If you want to marry this girl, you must wait until I am no more. If God hears my prayers, you will not wait long…But if you do the thing while I am alive, you will have my blood on your head, because I shall kill myself (*NLAE* 123).

Unlike the woman in Christopher's story who could not fall into the well as she threatens after her two children have fallen into a well and drowned, Obi knows his own Christ-figure mother means every word she has said. Motherhood thus triumphs and Clara's pregnancy is aborted.

With the death of Obi's mother he "too had died" and for him "Beyond death there are no ideals and no humbug, only reality" (*NLAE*, 151). The two events of his mother's death and Clara going out of his life "following closely on each other had dulled his sensibility and left him a different man" (*NLAE*, 2).

Unlike Okonkwo's multilayered metaphorical pull by women in *Things Fall Apart*, Obi Okonkwo is only metaphorically wedged between two women, his mother and Clara. It is noteworthy that the traditional spiritual realm of the goddess in *Things Fall Apart* is replaced in *No Longer at Ease* by the Christlike image of Hannah Okonkwo who sheds her blood for her son. The metaphorical supremacy of womanhood in *No Longer at Ease* may be diagrammatically represented as follows:

Fig. 2: Metaphorical Supremacy of Womanhood over Obi Okonkwo

The metaphorical value of womanhood or motherhood is also prominent in the conflicts and struggles in *Arrow of God*. The last part of Nwaka's speech which utterly destroys Ezeulu's speech against fighting an unjust war is significant:

> …Elders and Ndichie of Umuaro let everyone return to his house if we have no heart in the fight. We shall not be the first people who abandoned their farmland or even their homestead to avoid war. But let us not tell ourselves or our children that we did it because the land belonged to other people. Let us rather tell them that their fathers did not choose to fight. Let us tell them also

that we marry the daughters of Okperi and their men marry our daughters, and that where there is this mingling men often lose the heart to fight (*AOG*, 16).

The hint that Ezeulu's mother comes from Okperi is the "last glancing blow" that Nwaka uses against Ezeulu's counsel. Although it is not only Ezeulu whose mother comes from Okperi, according to Achebe "none of the others dared go to his support" (*AOG*, 17). This commission, of not taking the matter of Umuaro's men marrying Umuaro's daughters into account is a grave mistake. *Ulu* or no *Ulu*, historical record or no historical records, borrowing from Obi in *No Longer at Ease*: "Did not the elders say that a man's in-law was his *chi*, his personal god?" (42). The Umuaros by thus sending an emissary to Okperi are asking their *chi* to choose peace or war.

Akukalia who is chosen to carry the white clay and the new palm frond is also a man of Umuaro whose mother comes from Okperi. At the meeting where he is chosen, the oldest man from his village says: "From the way Akukalia spoke I saw that he was in *great anger* (*AOG*, 17, emphasis mine). It is ominous that a man *in great anger* accepts to carry a message to his motherland when Okonkwo in *Things Fall Apart* who only brings to his mother a heavy face and seem not comforted is warned by Uchendu to be careful or he may displease the dead. On the way to Okperi Akukalia reminisces about the greatness of his mother's people:

> "My mother's people are great medicine-men." There was pride in his voice... "Umuru is no match for my mother's people in medicine" (*AOG*, 19).

Concerning their ways Akukalia says:

> They are very difficult people; my mother was no exception. But I know what they know. If a man of Okperi says to you come, he means run away with all your strength. If you are not used to their ways you may sit with them from cock-crow until roosting-time and join in their talk and their food, but all the while you will be floating on the surface of the water. So leave them to me because when a man of cunning dies a man of cunning buries him (*AOG*, 20).

In Okperi, Akukalia and the two other emissaries refuse kolanut and the piece of white clay from Uduezue, the nearest living relation to Akukalia's mother. This way, Akukalia symbolically refuses his mother's "welcome." Although on their way to Otikpo's house Akukalia "felt strangely tender" towards his mother's land and he "felt tender even towards" his mother, he again refuses "welcome" in Otikpo's house. Akukalia is thrice referred to as *Son of our Daughter* and twice Akukalia refers to the men as *Father of my Mother* but he ignores the "tenderness" of his motherland. He not only fights and spits into the faces of his mother's "fathers," but he also "passed shit on the head of his mother's father" by breaking Ebo's *Ikenga* and making him a corpse before his own eyes.

Akukalia is killed and "Umuaro might have left the matter there, and perhaps the whole land dispute with it as Ekwensu seemed to have taken a hand in it" (*AOG*, 25). However, Okperi merely returning the corpse without saying anything is a mark of contempt in Umuaro. But what else may be said for a people who choose to wrestle with their *chi* or for a man who passes shit on his mother's father? In the war occasioned by Akukalia's death, Umuaro is thrashed "enough for today and for tomorrow!" and the land is given to Okperi.

The hovering presence of Ezeulu's mother, a daughter of Okperi, around Ezeulu is significant in our metaphorical consideration of the supremacy of motherhood. As soon as the novel opens, in the fourth paragraph, we are told that although Ezeulu is now an old man, "the fear of the new moon which he felt as a little boy still hovered round him" and this fear is none other than "moments when his mother's feet were put in stocks, at the new moon" (*AOG*, 223). Thus, this priest, who has announced the arrival of the moon for eighteen years must have continually re-lived his mother's madness, month after month and year after year.

Indeed, Ezeulu is constantly linked with his mother's insanity. When Nwaka hears the story of Ezeulu's rejection of the white man's offer to be a Warrant Chief, his explanation is that "The man is as proud as a lunatic'... 'This proves what I have always told people, that he inherited his mother's madness'" (*AOG*, 176). When Ezeulu refuses to call a new yam festival, Ogbuefi Ofoka also says "sometimes I want to agree with those who say the man has caught his mother's madness" (*AOG*, 212). In Ezeulu's strange dream in Umuaro, the voice of the python ends as the voice of his mother when she is seized with madness and at the end, Nwanyi Okperi metaphorically exemplifies the supremacy of motherhood by claiming him for her own. In his last days we are told, Ezeulu lives "in the haughty splendor of a demented high priest" (*AOG*, 229).

The metaphorical supremacy of womanhood and motherhood in *Arrow of God* may be diagrammatically shown thus:

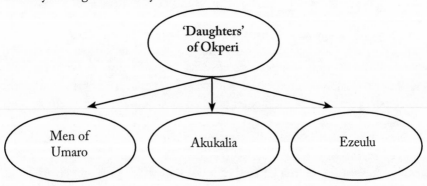

Fig. 3: Metaphorical Supremacy of Womanhood and Motherhood in *Arrow of God*

This paper has attempted a simultaneous activation of the associated implications of metaphorical "frame" "motherhood" or "womanhood" and the metaphorical "focus" of "supremacy" in three novels of Achebe. As a result of this activation, *agadi-nwayi*, *Ani*, the old women of the market, the mother of twins, Ojiugo, the daughter of Umuofia, Okonkwo's mother, Hannah, Clara, and the daughters of Okperi collectively become the movers and shapers of men and the society. By being supreme in war, by being the source of fertility and the ultimate judge of morality and conduct, by also being supreme in commerce, in taking a step against the grievous suffering of mothers and twins and wastage of children's lives, and in the lives of Okonkwo, Obi Okonkwo and the men of Umuaro, the woman or her metaphorical expression seem to provide a new insight into the place of the female gender in the male-dominated mores of traditional African aesthetics.

Works Cited

Achebe, Chinua. 1958. *Things Fall Apart*. London: Heinemann.

———. 1960. *No Longer at Ease*. London: Heinemann.

———. 1964. *Arrow of God*, Rev. Ed. London: Heinemann.

———. 1966. *A Man of the People*. London: Heinemann.

———. 1972. *Girls at War and Other Stories*. London: Heinemann.

———. 1987. *Anthills of the Savannah*. London: Heinemann.

Black, Max. 1981 [1955]. "Metaphor." In Johnson M. Ed. *Philosophical Perspectives on Metaphor*. Minneapolis, MN: University of Minnesota Press. pp. 63–82.

Chukwuma, Helen. 1989. "Positivism and the Female Crisis: The Novels of Buchi Emecheta." In Otokunefor Henrietta and Obiageli Nwodo. Eds. *Nigerian Female Writers*. Lagos: Malthouse Press Ltd. pp. 2–18.

Hawkes, Terence. 1977. *Structuralism and Semiotics*. London: Methuen & Co. Ltd.

Kenyatta, Jomo. 1979. [1938]. *Facing Mount Kenya*. London: Heinemann.

Parmegiani, Mariavittoria. 1987–1998. "A Critical Review of Traditional Theories of Metaphor and Related Linguistic Issues." In Danesi M. Metaphor, *Communication and Cognition*. Monograph Series of the Toronto Semiotic Circle, no. 2. pp. 1–7.

Savan, David. 1987–1988. "An Introduction to C.S. Peirce's Full System of Semiotic." Monograph Series of the Toronto Semiotic Circle, no. 1.

Zeman, J. Jay. 1976. "Peirce's Theory of Signs." In Sebeok Thomas. Ed. *A Perfusion of Signs*. Bloomington: Indiana University Press. pp. 22–39.

Chapter 28

Chinua Achebe's Legacy to His Daughter(s): Implications for the 21st Century

Marie Umeh

Human development if not engendered is endangered.
— Mahbub ul Haq

*What we need now are not just a few women who make history,
but many who make policy.*
— Geraldine Ferraro

THE MAJOR CHALLENGES FOR AFRICA in the 21st century include African women in national development schemes, policy making, grass-roots mobilization programs, as well as active participation in politics. The rescue of African nations from the leaking boats they have become will take place only when there is genuine power sharing between the two halves of the Black World, male and female. Since independence from British colonial rule in 1960, no president of Nigeria, in particular, or commander-in-chief of its armed forces has taken action to prevent gender apartheid – the atrocious rape of the fundamental rights of African women to realize their rights and responsibilities in their respective countries' national progress – which is preventing the "best" life for women and men.

Considering the dearth of women at the helms of power in many African countries, many postmodern theorists such as Ifi Amadiume, Carole Boyce Davies, Filomena Steady, Ayesha Imam, Obioma Nnaemeka, Chikwenye OkonjoOgunyemi, Molara Ogundipe-Leslie, Kamene Okonjo, Nawal El Saadawi, and Mamphela Ramphele, have concurred that the specific nature of women's gender problems in its various forms, internal and external, is grasped only by women and that freedom from the prisons of retrogressive cultural norms will be engendered only by women. Politically conscious African women no longer live under the illusion that freedom from patriarchal tyranny will come as a gift from their male kith and kin. In the present day whirlwind of economic political and social crisis in which Africa is embroiled, they understand that the road to their empowerment is through a united female front, straddling all classes, cross-culturally, and powerful enough to liberate all women from the injustices and oppression exercised daily against them.

Chinua Achebe's idea of centering women in his latest literary masterpiece, *Anthills of the Savannah*, is problematic as his positionality of the African woman as girlfriends, goddesses and "sweet mothers" is anachronistic. Chinua Achebe in this novel does not advance the discourse on gender imbalance in Africa nor does he appear to have any idea of what today's African women want or need. The problematics of Achebe's "gender intervention," to show allegiance with women against claims of sexism, revolves around his one-dimensional, stereotypical perceptions and (mis)representation of African women. This leads one to ask, "Is Achebe's literary cross-dressing a fashionable risk that is merely chic and trendy?" "Is his admission that 'woman is something,' the result of his genuine belief that the restoration of the African woman to her rightful place in her society also means the restoration of human values in the whole society?" Put differently, "Is Chinua Achebe truly committed to gender reform and the inclusion of African women today in the corridors of power?"

Chinua Achebe, the father of African Literature, the first great African writer in the English Language, has earned his space as one of the great masters in World Literature. Achebe is best known today for his role in the commencing of the Nigerian Literary Canon which inspired other writers to reclaim their African heritage, to make known the unique African world view, and to attempt to redress the injuustices of colonialism in the past and corruption in the present. Not only is Achebe a star in the literary sphere, but he has also distinguished himself as the first African editor of Heinemann Publishers African Writers Series founded in 1962. According to Alan Hill, the then Heinemann Educational Books Editor:

> For the next ten years Chinua Achebe edited the series. We published 100 titles in ten years, an average of ten per year. His name was the magnet that brought everything in, and his critical judgement was the decisive factor in what we published. And in addition to that, the fantastic sales of his own books selling by the millions provided the economic basis for the rest of the series ... Chinua read them all, commented on them, said whether he thought they were worth publishing or not and in addition to the hundred, there were many more that we didn't accept ... in many cases he did major editorial work, recommending to authors important improvements to their work.

Chinua Achebe as General Editor of the African Writers Series recommended to William Heinemann for publication the manuscripts of young writers such as Ngugi wa Thiong'o and Flora Nwapa. Thanks to Achebe's good judgement, both Ngugi wa Thiong'o and Flora Nwapa became prolific writers. Chinua Achebe included and supported rather than effaced new and talented women writers: a move which is partly responsible for Flora Nwapa becoming Africa's first female writer in the English language of international repute, with the publication of her novel, *Efuru* in 1966. Obviously Achebe respected her views of female empowerment in a specific African community, and did not hold her gender-specific insights and renditions of Ugwuta women against her.

After Achebe's initial encouragement, Nwapa went on to publish more books: novels, short stories, children's literature and prose-poems. In 1976, she launched a publishing company, Tana Press, Ltd., in Enugu. At various stages in her life, Nwapa excelled in other professions. She was an educational administrator at Lagos University, a Comissioner of Lands in the South Eastern Region of Nigeria, a university professor and the President of the Association of Nigerian Authors. Flora Nwapa proved that African women are capable and competent, in spheres beyond the domestic and spiritual. Certainly, Achebe's greatest legacy to African women was paving the way for women writers such as Flora Nwapa, Mabel Segun, Adora Ulasi, Ifeoma Okoye, Zaynab Alkali, and Buchi Emecheta, as well as his first daughter, Chinelo Achebe.

However, despite advancements that African women have made generally as literary artists, educators, business entrepreneurs, anthropologists, historians, industrialists, lawyers, medical doctors, and social scientists, few African women are found in positions of authority. According to a recent survey conducted by the United Nations, women's representation at the highest level of government in sub-Saharan Africa is approximately 4% (*The World's Women* 152). Hence, Ogundipe-Leslie rightly points out that "African women are not only written out of constitutions, commissions and committee reports, but they are often erased out of the national canvas of power broking and resource sharing" (248).

In view of the effacement of African women in nation-building, it is not surpising that the portrayal of extraordinary women in Achebe's literary world is yet to arrive. Achebe's attempt to shift the status of women from the peripheries to the center is depressing. This has led Patricia Alden to assert: "Achebe's portrait of Beatrice Okoh betrays a significant failure of imagination – a failure to take seriously, as part of the contemporary political struggle, the feminist challenge to patriarchal authority and a corresponding failure to create convincing, interesting women characters" (67). An examination of *Anthills of the Savannah* as an attempt to create gender balance and paint a true picture of the role of African women at the turn of the century reveals that the author assumes the natural right of men to leadership positions even though history teaches us otherwise. For example, Nigeria can boast of many dynamic women who made their mark: Inkpi of the Igala, Moremi of the Yoruba, Lady Oyinkan Abayomi, Daura of the Hausa, Queen Amina of Zaria, Queen Kambasa of Bonny, the heroines of the Aba Women's War and the awesome Olufunmilayo Ransome-Kuti of Abeokuta, are only a tip of the iceberg. Indeed, *Anthills* masks women's contributions to the socio-cultural, economical and political development of the nation-state. Other contemporary authors offer many examples of multi-dimensional and extraordinary female characters: Amos Tutuola in *The Brave African Huntress*, Peter Abrahams in *A Wreath for Udomo*, Ngugi wa Thiong'o in *Devil on the Cross* and Nuruddin Farah in *Sardines*. Yet in *Anthills of the Savannah*, patriarchal thought patterns which pigeonhole women in mystical and domestic spaces loom large.

The paradox is that three decades after the publication of *Things Fall Apart*, Achebe's attitudes toward the roles of women in African society are no different from what they used to be, thus creating a feeling of *déjà vu* and promoting a legacy of "otherness" to the stillborn struggling to be born anew. Rhonda Cobham observes in *Things Fall Apart*:

> We never really see Okonkwo's wives interacting with one another the way we see the men interacting among themselves or even Okonkwo interacting with his children … The only women we see acting with any authority is the priestess, Chielo and she is represented, in terms consistent with Western practice as a witch – a force for good or evil who is separate of a chain of ritual and social female authority.

Beatrice Okoh, a main character in *Anthills of the Savannah*, is primarily portrayed as Chris's "girl", despite her sound educational background and her position as Senior Assistant Secretary in the Ministry of Finance. In fact, none of the women in *Anthills* is described as a doer and actor, in the modern sense of the word. The women remain passive and mysterious beings. Chinua Achebe subconsciously subscribes to the Manichean view that man embodies strength and wisdom while woman remains man's plaything and servant. Conspicously absent from his novels is the androgynous nature of human beings celebrated in the Yoruba proverb, "If a man sees a snake and a woman kills it, it doesn't matter as long as the snake is dead." African philosophy, in this case, the Igbo world view, recognizes no rigid, absolute truth. There is no complete state; there are no hard-and-fast categories of cosmic and human realities; hence the belief that "when something stands, something stands beside it."

Particularly disturbing is Achebe's patronage of his male characters at the expense of his female characters. Emmanuel Obete, the President of the university's student union, is an activist who becomes Chris's savior. It is Emmanuel, who improvises the celebrated story that the "Commissioner for Information, Mr. Chris Oriko ... had left the country in a foreign airliner bound for London disguised as a Reverend Father and wearing a false beard" (196). Emmanuel's clever story printed in the daily newspaper, the *National Gazette*, serves as a decoy and enables Chris to escape from the claws of His Excellency Sam and his henchmen. On the other hand, Beatrice, whom Achebe apparently misnames, "female is also something," throughout the chase, passively awaits Chris's telephone calls with tears of loneliness streaming in her eyes. Furthermore, Beatrice is (mis)represented as a naive and sexually frustrated woman. When the two lovers meet while Chris is in hiding, her desire to stay with him overnight in threatening circumstances makes her look irrational and spoiled. For instance, she is willing to displace Braimoh's five children so that she and Chris can be alone in Braimoh's single, windowless room which accommodates him and his family (197). Even when her demands are met and she is alone with her man, she's more concerned with the bedbugs and mosquitoes, the general squalor of the place, than making the best of her last moments with Chris. Achebe's female character is thus politically incorrect. By attributing this false consciousness to Beatrice, Achebe reduces her to his female concept.

The reality of the situation is that within the Nigerian body politic, women are not perceived as having agency, taking action in their own lives, making decisions, dealing with problems or holding positions of leadership. Nevertheless, African women, finding ways to mobilize themselves and better their conditions, individually or corporately, are not a new phenomenon in Nigeria specifically or Africa generally. There is a long history of women organizing to improve their communities, on whose experiences many contemporary organizations draw. For example, at the grass-roots level the *umuada* (an association of all married or unmarried daughters of a lineage) and the *nwunyedi* (all wives of a lineage), in every village, town and city and at the middle class [elitist] level, Maryam Babangida's *Better Life for Rural Women Programme* and *Women in Nigeria* (*WIN*), are only a few organizations that have been effective in planning strategies and projects for the empowerment of women generally, and the amelioration of the lives of rural women. Similarly, women writers of Africa such as Flora Nwapa, Buchi Emecheta, Mariama Ba, and Lauretta Ngcobo, to name only a few, have no problems depicting dynamic female characters in their creative works as noble national subjects.

The present situation in the Nigerian body polity where women are shut out from political power is totally a western concept introduced by the British. In pre-colonial Africa, African women wielded power. Chinua Achebe, coming from Igboland where daughters' and wives' village associations exercise power, is aware of this fact through oral histories as well as the written accounts recorded by anthropologists, historians and sociologists. By interfering with the traditional balance of power in many parts of Nigeria, the British reduced female power and programmed African women to adopt the values of Victorian England (Allen 165). In this vein, the political world in *Anthills* is far from democratic. It merely reflects the wishes of the status quo which Achebe appears to condone, in this instance. African national-states must indeed do better than the Egyptians who excluded women from the helms of power (the case of Queen-Pharoah Hatshepsut) and even 20ᵗʰ Century Americans who are not thinking about women (Hillary Rodham Clinton's dilemma and Shannon Faulkner's predicament). The challenge of Africa in the 21ˢᵗ Century is to make women's *de jure* equality a reality rather than a rarity. And that is exactly the intention of the new female voices on the Nigerian literary scene.

Chinua Achebe's first daughter, Chinelo Achebe, has joined the vanguard of contemporary African women writers who have created a space for themselves to incorporate women's concerns in the predominately male centered literary canon. In her first collection of short stories, *The Last Laugh and Other Stories*, the lead story, "The Last Laugh," calls to question the male's point of view and debunks the idea of the natural inferiority of women and superiority of men. The story details the troubled marriage of Mike, a Nigerian student enrolled at an American university, and Terry, an African-American girl pursuing a law degree: in essence, a family divided against itself, symbolically a nation dis-eased. After ten years of marriage, Mike initiates their divorce by abandoning his family. The author situates the factors contributing to the marital collapse to the "battle of the sexes: Gender war transcends race, class and geophysical spaces. Except for a few Native American communities of the Western Hemisphere and the few matrilineal societies throughout the world, women cross-culturally share a heritage of effacement. As Simone de Beauvoir puts it, "woman is Other." Vivain Gornick explains:

> A look at culture and literature will confirm that the life of woman, like the life of every outsider, is determinedly symbolic of the life of the race; that this life is offered up as a sacrifice to the forces of annihilation that surround our sense of existence, in the hope that in reducing the strength of the outsider – in declaring her the bearer of all the insufficiency and contradiction of the race – the wildness, grief, and terror of loss that is in us will be grafted onto her, and the strength of those remaining within the circle will be increased. For in the end, that is what the outsider is all about; that is what power and powerlessness are all about; that is what the cultural decision that certain people are 'different' is all about (128).

Hence, the author is quite appropriate in locating sexual politics as a major political force to be reckoned with in African society. As a "daughter-of-the-soil" she speaks from experience and as a "been-to" educated in America, England and Canada, she speaks from an insider's point of view, as she participates in the controversy surrounding gender relationships globally. Her displeasure with gender and other inequities that is causing Nigeria (Africa) to flounder is manifested in her subtle attempts to destroy the status quo.

Chinelo Achebe's "The Last Laugh" is an attempt to promote the concept that men are in need of liberation from ingrained sexist attitudes. The sex-role reversal the author employs with the virilized (confident) Terry and the feminized (weak-minded) Mike is crucial in dismantling the patriarchial marriage institution where men are regarded as born leaders and women blind followers. For example, when Terry and Mike visit his village in Nigeria, Terry departs after two days, unable to cope with the "groveling poverty" she finds herself amidst. It is obvious that Mike did not inform her about the realities of village life. Because Terry returns to America and leaves his family in shock, Mike interprets her actions as insulting to his kith and kin, rather than looking inward and taking responsibility for his inability to prepare his foreign-born wife psychologically for the hardships of Nigerian rural life. He sees her actions as a rebellion, a hatred for his people, a blunt disregard for "his image." And similar to the Persian King Ahasuerus, who vanishes Queen Vashti for listening to her individual truth, rather than heeding his command, Mike loses all respect for Terry. Her assertiveness takes its toll in their marriage as it becomes a hard pill for Mike to swallow.

In retaliation, he heaps insults on his wife and her people upon his return to the States. Chinelo Achebe writes:

> It's always been easy for you, Terry, S ... You're a 'white' lady. You've never had problems; you've got the money, prestige, what more could you want? H ... you don't even need me, do you? But you know what you don't have, can never hope to have anymore?
>
> 'What?' she asked, in spite of herself, hating him.
>
> 'My respect, that's what,' he spat, and added. 'And I'll tell you one thing. I'm proud of my country, my colour. Even with all its problems, Nigeria will always be more vibrant, more real to me, then anywhere else. It belongs to Nigerians. We don't have to do any 'Uncle Tomming,' either. And, you dare compare it with your so-called 'developed' country ... It's home to me' (22–23).

Despite the stress in her life, Terry attains her degrees, secures a good job and tries her best to maintain her home. Mike, on the other hand, continues to harbor a grudge against his wife and her parents, who are successful lawyers and to have a defeatist attitude until he finally decides to strike out on his own.

The author continues to address the problems of rabid sexism that claims that anatomy is destiny. Terry is the breadwinner, while Mike is the perennial student. Frustrated and disoriented, Mike heads for self-destruction as he returns to Nigeria with only a first degree and lands in a country where only bribery or IM (*Ima mmadu* translated into English as "It's who you know") can get him a position with a good salary. Unsuccessful in all his attempts to acquire employment, he later decides to return to the States, with the mad idea of kidnapping his two sons and to revenge on his estranged wife because he is convinced that "Terry had gained the upper hand in [the] relationship ... and now ... I'm having the last laugh ... Now, I'm getting my own back" (27, 34). The truth of the matter is that Terry has resigned herself to a life alone as a single parent.

The couple's self-limiting problems and inability to communicate are a microcosm of a nation at war with itself. They represent the breakdown of communication throughout Nigeria between males and females, between ethnic groups, between civilians and the military and so on. As the celebrated author Audre Lorde aptly writes in one of her poems, "Among Ourselves": "We must stop killing/the other/in ourselves/the self that we hate in others ..." It means the exposure of self and the recognition of the terror we have for particular difference. It means to struggle with those with whom we might have much in common, with whom we might have differences. Such a stance means that most of us must give up something, whether it is class privilege or self-absorption to empower ourselves and other (Christian 209).

The exclusion of women from the material and mental resources at the top echelons of their respective societies is not to the advantage of the whole African body politic. In fact, the devastating effects of the present sex-role socialization practices where boys are favored while girls are denied their inalienable rights are severe enough to mobilize every man, woman and child to engender massive reforms in their societies. Buchi Emecheta explains in a conversation with Oladipo Ogundele:

> Our men don't realize that they are weak because they hide behind the women and at the same time, they put women down by not acknowledging the type of addition the women make to our daily living ... When you see [my] characters in black and white you will realize that our men need to reeducate themselves or reexamine their actions because it is overflowing from individual families to our government. You can see their weaknesses in the way they run our government. The funniest thing about it is that everybody is talking about it and there is nothing they can do to change it (453).

Men often develop the selfish attitude that leadership positions are their natural right. And when they are not in control of a situation, no matter how insignificant, they feel demoralized, enraged and diminished. Women are also disadvantaged in societies which cripple their imaginations. They often adopt subservient behavior and seek recognition through the limited spaces society has mapped out for them. Indeed, Mike lacks the courage, maturity and spirituality to view his problems in the proper perspective and realize that Terry is not the enemy and that she poses no real threat to him. His madness centers on the fact that he is not in control and rather than cooperate with his wife, he competes with her. The author writes:

> For one reason or the other, he seemed unable to complete work on his thesis ...
> And she was left thinking rather bitterly, after seven years, that perhaps she had
> not made the right choices ... Mike had become over-sensitive and withdrawn,
> refusing to confide in her, and blaming her and her parents; that they had helped
> to undermine his own confidence in himself, he had complained bitterly (25).

Apparently, Mike suffers from what psychoanalysts call the "castration complex."
He would not have resented Terry's forthrightness and success if she were a man.
Oftentimes when men fail or are unable to achieve, their egos become bruised. So,
Mike's lost self-esteem results in this self-inflicted depression, the warped attitude
that men alone must rule women and children, administer laws, judge cases and
distribute rewards or punishment. Man is the doer: woman, the receiver. Woman
is to remain a person defined not by the struggling development of her brain or
her will or her spirit, but rather by her childbearing properties and her status as
companion to man. Hence, in his failed attempt to "teach those white-skinned
negroes a thing or two," by taking his two sons back to Nigeria with him, Terry
has "the last laugh."

Collaboration between male and female is *sine qua non* to any nation's survival, stability and success. African artists can be a powerful force in anchoring the
leaking boats our African nations have become safely to shore. African literature
has a crucial role to play in "reversing the marginality of the invisible and silent
majority." African artists have to pay more attention to the use of language and its
diminishing and transforming powers. As Mamphela Ramphele insightfully puts
it: "[They] need to focus on the hidden text, conveying not only sexist undertones,
but also structural hierarchical values imbedded in language, which reflects past
and present inequalities" (12). Okonjo assets that African writers have the social
responsibility to provide a bird's eye view of legislative assemblies with parity
representation between men and women – a modernized dual-sex system – rather
than legislatures which bypass women or include a token sprinkling of women.
Article 2 of the *Convention of the Elimination of All Forms of Discrimination Against
Women* proscribes gender-based discrimination in all societies and warns African
nation-states to promote "the principle of the equality of men and women in their
national constitutions or other appropriate legislation if not yet incorporated therein,
and to ensure, through law and other appropriate means, the practical realization
of this principle" (249).

In the final analysis, Achebe's (re)presentation of women in *Anthills* elides
the power of African women. By eclipsing the rich female tradition of confident
and self-empowered women such as Idia of Benin, the most famous Iyoba, who
successfully commanded troops during her son's war with the people of Idah in the
sixteenth century Nigeria, or Nwanyeruwa, who triggered off the Aba Women's War
of 1929, is he not cheating the women? Conversely, Chinelo Achebe in "The Last

Laugh" symbolically severs the umbilical cord that wants to strangle the "Other". Rejecting the phallocratic socialization that is "enough ... to last [her] seven reincarnations," she crafts a story of strong women, who with or without a man, hold their own. For example, whereas Beatrice in *Anthills* is confirmed to "erotic cum spiritual vitality," the reverse takes place in "The Last Laugh" as Mike is housebound, while his wife Terry "swims with the sharks." Gender theorists at the *fin de siecle* believe that within this neglected half lies the savior(s) of the nation-state that the privileged half, cloning the colonizers is bent on destroying.

To conclude, the father-daughter dyad's perceptions of the roles of men and women in the new nation-state must be what Africa needs. Images of gender imbalance, rather than gender integration, sketched out in both dramas do not appeal to many scholars although both Nadine Gordimer and Chimalum Nwankwo concur that Beatrice is "one of the most extraordinary, attractive and moving women characters in any contemporary novel." However, with women largely absent from the decision-making process, little if any legislation will be passed in their favor despite the proclamation of the African Charter on Human and Peoples' Rights that the "State shall ensure the elimination of very discrimination against women" (Article 18: 9). What Africa really needs in fiction and in reality are characters who can lead the nation-state to its greatest potential with the participation of women and men at the helm truly representing gender diversity and gender balance. Chinua Achebe must come down to earth, talk with the women and work with them from the rural and urban sectors, to institute a new dispensation to eradicate gender stereotyping in the 21st century so as to be considered a serious contestant as the male "stiwanist" of the year. After all, literature is both a mirror and a hammer: it not only reflects, it shapes.

Works Cited

Achebe, Chinelo. *The Last Laugh and Other Stories*. Ibadan: Heinemann Educational Books, 1988. (All subsequent references to this edition will be referred to by page numbers).

Achebe, Chinua. *Anthills of the Savannah*. Ibadan: Heinemann Educational Books, 1988. (All subsequent references to this text will be referred to by page numbers).

African Charter on Human and Peoples' Rights. In the *International Law of Human Rights in Africa*. Comp. M. Hamalengqa, C. Flinterman and E.V.O. Dankwa. Boston: Martinus Nijhoff Publishers, 1981.

Alden, Patricia. "New Women and Old Myths: Chinua Achebe's *Anthills of the Savannah* and Nuruddin Farah's *Sardines*." Matatu. No. 8, Editions Rodopi B.V. Amsterdam, 1991: 67–80.

Berrian, Brenda F. "The Afro-American-West African Marriage Question: Its Literary and Historical Contexts." *Women in African Literature Today*. 15. 1987: 152–159.

Boyce-Davies, Carole and Molara Ogundipe-Leslie, Eds. *Moving Beyond Boundaries: International Dimensions of Black Women's Writing*. Volume 1. New York: New York University, 1995.

Boyce-Davies, Carole. "Writing Off Marginality, Minoring, and Effacement." Women's Studies International Forum. 14.4, 1991: 249–263.

Christian, Barbara. *Black Feminist Criticism. Perspectives on Black Women Writers*. New York: Pergamon Press, 1985.

Cobham, Rhonda. "Making Men and History: Achebe and the Politics of Revisionism." In *Approaches to Teaching Chinua Achebe's Things Fall Apart*. Ed. Bernth Lindors. New York: Modern Language Association of America, 1991.

Convention on the Elimination of All Forms of Discrimination Against Women. In *The International Law of Human Rights in Africa*. Comp. M.C. Hmalengwa, C. Flinterman, and E.V.O. Dankwa. Boston: Martinus Nijhoff Publishers, 1988.

El Saadawi, Nawal. *The Hidden Faces of Eve*. London: Zed Books, Ltd., 1980.

Ferraro, Geraldine. *Women: Challenges to the Year 2000*. New York: United Nations, 1991.

Freyer, Bryna. *Royal Benin Art*. Washington, D.C. Smithsonian Institute, 1987.

Gordimer, Nadine. "A Tyranny of Clowns." *New York Times*. February 21, 1998.

Gornick, Vivian. "Woman as Outsider." In *Woman in Sexist Society: Studies in Power and Powerlessness*. Eds. Vivian Gornick and Barbara K. Moran. New York: Basic Books, 1971: 126–144.

Hill, Alan. "Working with Chinua Achebe: The African Writers Series." In *Chinua Achebe:*

A Celebration. Ed. Kirsten Holst Petersen and Anna Rutherford. Oxford: Heinemann, 19990: 149–159.

Nwanko, Chimalum. "Soothing Ancient Bruises: Power and the New African Woman in Chinua Achebe's *Anthills of the Savannah.*" *Matatu* No. 8. Editions B.V. Amsterdam. 1991: 55–65.

Oyoke, Pat. U. *The Better Life Programme: Meteor or Monument.* Onitsha: Africana-Fep Publishers, 1993.

Ramphele, Mamphela. "Do Women Help Perpetuate Sexism? A Bird's Eye View from South Africa." *Africa Today.* 37.1 (1990): 7–17.

Rutherford, Anna. "Interview with Chinua Achebe." *Kunapipi.* 9.2 (1987): 1–17.

Ogundele, Oladipo. "A Conversation with Dr. Buchi Emecheta." *Emerging Perspectives on Buchi Emecheta.* Ed. Marie Umeh. Trenton, New Jersey: Africa World Press: 1955: 445–456.

Ogundipe-Leslie, Molara. *Re-Creating Ourselves: African Women & Critical Transformations.* Trenton: Africa World Press, 1994.

Ogunyemi, Chikwenye Okonjo. "The Invalid, Dea(r)th, and the Author: The Case of Flora Nwapa aka Professor (Mrs.) Flora Nwanzuruaha Nwakuche." *Research in African Literatures.* 26.2 (Summer, 1995): 1–16.

Okonjo, Kamene. "Reversing the Maginalization of the Invisible and Silent Majority: Women in Politics in Nigeria." *Women and Politics Worldwide.* Barbara J. Nelson and Najma Chowdhury. New Haven: Yale University Press, 1994: 512–26.

Part Six

Influences

Chapter 29

The "Sons of Achebe":
Example of John Munonye

Charles E. Nnolim

THERE IS NO ORGANIZED ACADEMY of writers known as "the sons of Achebe," although the term has been used quite often by literary critics. But for the purposes of this study, I identify as "sons of Achebe" all those first generation of African men and women who took to their literary calling in the footsteps of *Things Fall Apart*.

The sons of Achebe are those early post-Achebe writers who were so fascinated with the subject matter and technique which Achebe so admirable perfected that they set out consciously or unconsciously to imitate him. Outside Nigeria, Ngugi we Thiong'o and Ayi Kwei Armah are Achebe's novels identified as "archetypal" and which describes the impact of the coming of Europeans on African societies as a result. And they are not absolved from writing another brand of novels inaugurated by Achebe and identified by Larson as "the situational novel" which exists to present a group-felt experience so that whatever happens to the protagonist is felt by all the people involved in the story because the individual identifies with this society and acts as that society's consciousness. Armah and wa Thiong'o also follow in Achebe's tradition by their treatment of post-independence African societies displaying a "colonial" mentality, and full of "imperialist" stooges who collaborate with the imperialists to milk their countries dry for the benefit of post-colonial masters. Armah's *The Beautyful Ones Are Not Yet Born* and *Fragments* and Ngugi wa Thiong'o's *Weep Not Child, The River Between,* and *A Grain of Wheat* are in the Achebe tradition.

Within Nigeria, John Munonye (*The Only Son, Obi, A Wreath for the Maidens, Bridge to a Wedding*); Elechi Amadi (*The Concubine, The Slave, The Great Ponds*); Onuora Nzekwu (*Wand of Noble Wood, Blade Among the Boys*); T.M. Aluko (*One Man, One Wife, One Man, One Matchet, Chief the Honourable Minister*); Flora Nwapa (*Efuru, Idu*) are writers that must be identified as the "sons" of Achebe in more ways than one.

Beyond trying to copy Achebe in subject-matter as mentioned above, the "sons of Achebe" try, like Achebe to weave the local proverb into their narrative, to use our native myths, rituals, ceremonies, and legends unashamedly in their stories, and to promote awareness of what is really great and dignified in our culture. On a more subtle level, the "sons" of Achebe reel like him in ancestor worship and follow his tradition of cultural nationalism by trying, like him, to rehabilitate the dignity of the black man bruised and denigrated by the colonial master. This study intends to demonstrate that in writing *The Only Son* and *A Wreath for the Maidens*, Munonye could not have ignored Achebe's *Things Fall Apart* and *A Man of the People*, and did not ignore him in the least; in fact he did set out, perhaps unconsciously, to imitate Achebe, if not in those quirks and mannerisms called style, at least, in setting, subject matter, and narrative point of view. Let us then begin with *Things Fall Apart* and *The Only Son*.

To begin with, Achebe set his *Things Fall Apart* in Umuofia (children of the forest) and set out to record the rise of Okonkwo who, through a mischance ran to Mbanta (his mothers' place) for protection. In his absence, the white man came to Umuofia with his destabilizing religion and civilization. Munonye set *The Only Son* in Umudiobia (children of strangers) and set out to record the precarious life on an only son, Nnanna, who (after a fight) escaped to Nade (his mother's place) where he met the coming of the white man with its destablising religion and civilization. But while Okonwko returns to die in resisting the white man, Nnanna stays on to embrace and prosper from the allure of the white man's religion and civilization. The ending of each of these first novels at once reveals the philosophic outlook of each writer: while Achebe's story wears the face of tragedy in its record of a collective loss, Munonye's story wears the face of comedy in its record of progressive gain for the protagonist, in spite of the disappointment expressed by Nnanna's mother, Chiaku. Characteristically, Achebe's *Things Fall Apart* is a closed novel ending with the death of Okonkwo, while Munonye's is an open novel, ending in pregnancy for Chiaku (with the hope of a new life) and further adventures for Nnanna who joins Father Smith at Ossa, to chart a new course for himself. We must immediately observe that while Achebe sketches the cosmic implications of the colonial intrusion in Umuofia which ends in the death of a way of life for the Igbo, Munonye paints the picture of a seemingly minor impact of the same colonial intrusion on the household of a widow who, instead of succumbing to her own discomfiture and committing suicide, chooses a better alternative that leads to new life and happiness through remarriage. Although there is no room to discuss it in detail here, we must bear in mind that Achebe is essentially a writer of the tragic vision is, for the most part, comic.

In writing *The Only Son*, Munonye used Achebe's *Things Fall Apart* as his obvious quarry. In the latter, we remember that missionary activities provided the ammunition for many a do-or-die confrontation between the natives and the zealous converts. In *Things Fall Apart*, the natives looked at the misguided missionaries with benign amusement and allowed them to establish their church in the evil forest if that was where their demented sensibilities wanted to domicile their headquarters. This was the point of the greatest interest for Munonye and the main area of artistic indebtedness to Achebe. As in Umuofia, Nade was equally accommodating. Following Achebe, Munonye says that "when bald-headed Francis Osita, alias Ositason, arrived in Nade to start the church, hardly anybody took him seriously. The rulers merely left him at the mercy of the most prominent witch doctors of the land" (72). But soon the point at issue in both works centered around the Christian defiance of the sacred sanction and the breaking of the taboo and the consequence of such brazen behavior. In *Things Fall Apart*, it was Okoli who killed the sacred python out of zeal, and the consequence:

> He had fallen ill on the previous night. Before the day was over he was dead. His death showed that the gods were still able to fight their own battles (145).

Compare the above with Munonye. In *The Only Son*, it was the same category of people we have in *Things Fall Apart* who first embraced the Christian religion – the *efulefu*, outcasts, and cult slaves – and they were the most zealous, and the same fate awaited those breakers of the sacred sanction. Munonye says:

> Take the two friends, David and Dominic. Throughout Nade, these two men were better known as ex-slaves than as anything else. Slavery had been abolished; but that did not mean that a freed slave was equal to a free-born...Over the years, David and Dominic had fretted under jibes of this nature. Then the church arrived and preached, among other things, equality of all human beings, great or small, man or woman, slave or free, before the maker. Taking advantage of the teaching, they rebelled against their status. They were the very first converts George made in the town...Unknown to him, they proceeded to Igwe's shrine which was about three hundred yards away. About twenty minutes later, a mournful cry arose from there. "Igwe has been assaulted!" the voice said. Nade seldom acted in a hurry, and they did not in this case. Full twenty-eight days passed. On the morning of the twenty-ninth, David and Dominic were both reported dead. The story went that each of them had died quietly, and in his own house. It was the Igwe that did it (74–75).

Several facts from Achebe come together in the above passage: The status of the converts, their overzealous impudence, their iconoclastic tendencies, and the residual powers of the traditional gods which still mustered enough powers to demonstrate their continued potency against breakers of the taboo. Achebe had said in *Things Fall Apart* that none of the converts was a man whose word was heeded in the assembly. None of them was a man of title. They were mostly the kind of people that were called *efulefu*, worthless, empty men…Chielo, the priestess of *Agbala*, called the converts *the excrement of the clan* and the new faith was *a mad dog that had come to eat it up* (128). Now, Munonye's David and Dominic also share the same social status with Achebe's Enoch. While the former were freed slaves, the latter was an *Osu*, a cult-slave, since "his father was the priest of the snake cult" (159). Any wonder that Enoch's zeal knew no bounds. The zealous Enoch that unmasked the *egwugwu* (an act that caused the destruction of the church by enraged masked spirits and precipitated the imprisonment of important men in Umuofia, including Okonkwo) was the same zealot that "had killed and eaten the sacred python" (159). And the fate of Okoli in *Things Fall Apart* which resembles the fate of David and Dominic in *The Only Son* is extended in a watered-down fashion to show the continued power of the old over the fledgling adherents of the new. When bald-headed Francis Osita, alias Ositason, in *The Only Son*, defied the masked spirits, "then, before him, the masquerade waved the small, black idol in its hand, after which it ran away, the attendant following closely behind. A few days later, Francis discovered big leprous patches all over his body. He left Nade before the story spread" (73). This recreates the activities of zealous converts in the first novels of the two authors under study.

Munonye published his novel eight full years after Achebe, and it would be instructive to see how both novelists represented the missionaries themselves, their characters, and their proselytizing techniques. What Munonye did was a simple inversion of Achebe's mode of presentation. In Achebe, Mr. Brown, the first missionary in Umuofia, was a tactful, cautious man who was on the side of compromise and accommodation, in order to give his church a firm footing in a hostile environment. Mr. Brown was replaced by the no-nonsense hard-liner, Mr. Smith, under whose tough stand the neophyte church came to grief in Umuofia. According to Achebe, "there was a saying in Umuofia that as a man danced so the drums were beaten for him. Mr. Smith danced a furious step and so the drums went mad" (165). Naturally, under Mr. Smith's lead, characters like Okoli and Enoch emerged. And Enoch's devotion to the new faith "seemed so much greater than Smith's that the villagers called him the outsider who wept louder than the bereaved" (165). Munonye in *The Only Son* inverted the order of the appearance of the missionaries – all protestants in the two novels. While in Achebe, the tactful Mr. Brown is followed by the heedless zealot, Mr. Smith, whose fanaticism fuelled the events that brought grief to the church, in Munonye, the first to arrive were the fanatics bringing along their sound and fury before a wiser, more tactful missionary came to Nade to give the church a firm footing. Mr. Ositason had foolishly confronted a masked man who afflicted him with leprosy. On his leaving Nade, Mr. George, more fanatical and ear-clouting, next arrived. Some of his audience…called him a lunatic orator; some just snapped their fingers in their horror at the things that were coming out of the lunatic's mouth (73).

When George left Nade, blinded in one eye by his jealous wife for ogling the girls in his church, he was succeeded by Joseph who was quite cool-headed and calculating in his ways. Francis had offended the masquerade world and that had ruined him, he told himself George had been too aggressive in his approach. He was going to move cautiously…he would start a school…Joseph's successes was phenomenal (75–76). Achebe's *Things Fall Apart* draws attention to Okonkwo's reaction when his son joined that miscreant crowd, the Christians. Munonye's *The Only Son* equally re-creates Chiaku's reaction when Nnanna joined the church. To each parent, each son's conversion signals that part of the break-up of the cohesiveness of the old order which the coming of the white man was a harbinger. But while in Achebe, the cosmic implications of the break-up of the older order lends sublimity to *Things Fall Apart*, in Munonye, the ripples of that break-up seem to be confined to the discomfiture of a widow who in a swift reaction, charts for herself a new, more comforting course through re-marriage. This underlines the basic philosophic outlook of each writer. For Achebe, his tragic vision shows itself through loss; for Munonye, his comic vision is seen through regain. But in both Achebe and Munonye, no matter the opposition from the natives, the new order prevailed and gained a firm foothold in the societies mirrored.

In *Things Fall Apart*, Nwoye's callow soul drinks in the poetry of the new religion, as he abandons the harshness of his father's aggressive ways for the pacific ethos of the new religion. With his eyes on Achebe, Munonye creates Ibe as the tempter, who dazzles Nnanna with the magic of the new alphabet and the new literacy which the church and the school had brought in their train. We recall that when Okonkwo's brother, Amikwu, told Okonkwo that Nwoye had joined the new religion, Okonkwo awaited Nwoye's return, and then "sprang to his feet and gripped him by the neck…He seized a heavy stick that lay on the dwarf wall and hit him two or three savage blows" (136), as Nwoye tried to free himself from the choking grip. Compare this to Munonye. When Chiaku learnt from her brother, Oji, that Nnanna had joined the new religion, she "leapt up and pounced upon Nnanna. A second later, she had wound her hands round his neck, crushing it and choking him with her masculine strength" (112).

Munonye continues to be faithful to Achebe's method. After the savage blows from his father, Nwoye "walked away and never returned…He went back to the church and told Mr.Kiaga that he had decided to go to Umuofia, where the white missionary had set up a school to teach young Christians to read and write" (136–137). After Chiaku, following what she considered Nnanna's treachery, announced she was going to marry Okere, Nnanna goes to his teacher, announcing: "Master I want to leave our house…You told us something last week about the Reverend Father who will visit here soon…Master, I would like to follow him" (175–176).

Now the pathos surrounding the aftermath of the confrontations between father and son (in *Things Fall Apart*) and mother and son (in *The Only Son*) bears close resemblance, showing Munonye's fidelity to his source. After Nwoye's departure following the savage blows from his father, Okonkwo brooded:

> Why, he cried in his heart, should he, Okonkwo, of all people, be cursed with such a son…Now that he had time to think of it, his son's crime stood out in its stark enormity. To abandon the gods of one's father and go about with a lot of effeminate men clucking like old hens was the very depth of abomination. Suppose when he died all his male children decided to follow Nwoye's steps and abandon their ancestors? Okonkwo felt a cold shudder run through him at the terrible prospect, like the prospect of annihilation. He saw himself and his fathers crowding round their ancestral shrine waiting in vain for worship and sacrifice and finding nothing but ashes of bygone days, and his children the while praying to the white man's god (137).

The same touch of pathos surrounds Chiaku's knowledge of Nnanna's conversion. What one may call "the lament of Okonkwo" becomes "the lament of Chiaku", though Chiaku's is more attenuated and restricted in its cosmic implications:

> Chiaku broke into tears, sobbing spasmodically. But the load in her heart could not be washed out by tears alone. She opened her mouth…"Why should I continue to weep in this life where every broad road seems to end in bush…I've labored and labored to obtain our living. What did I not suffer from Amanze and his wives! That was at Umudiobia from where we fled. And yet, I had to bear everything because of my child. That's the child that has gone mad now…I fled to Nade, to my father's land. Here to start life afresh and live in peace. Suitors have come and I have turned them out. I tell them I have a son who is my husband. Just because I don't want to live away from him. That's the child that has gone mad now" (115).

To sum up, then, one must assert that John Munonye found Achebe's *Things Fall Apart* an irresistible quarry. As he was trying to find his feet as a fledgling novelist he could not resist looking closely and hard at Achebe's subject matter and technique in pulling off so resoundingly his first famous novel. He found the pre-colonial setting of *Things Fall Apart* irresistibly fascinating. But Munonye moved beyond merely finding Achebe's work fascinating. The impact of Christianity and colonialism for both authors, however, provided the ammunition for different visions of life. For Achebe, it was tragic, as he created Okonkwo who perished while he blindly opposed the new order, and his death signaled the collective collapse of a way of life. For Munonye, it was not so tragic for while a few souls like Chiaku suffered the pangs of this new order, the ultimate outcome provided fresh challenges for self-improvement. Hence, at the end of the trilogy in *Bridge to a Wedding*, Nnanna (now Mr. Kafo) has profited from his encounter with the white man; has offered education to all his children; has his daughter, Rose, married off to a graduate; and returns to Umudiobia (now Mudi) with its own modern network of roads, pipe-borne water, and electricity.

A few more examples and we round off Munonye's indebtedness to Achebe in *The Only Son*. Okonkwo's power-name is "the roaring flame", while Nnanna's (after many coaxing names called him by his adoring mother) is "the lion" – given to him by the teacher, after he scaled the wall to catch a truant classmate. Furthermore, in *Things Fall Apart*, Achebe waxes lyrical on the magic and power attendant on a dreaded masked spirit:

> A sickly odor hung in the air wherever he went, and flies went with him…Many years ago another *egwugwu* had dared to stand his ground before him and had been transfixed to the spot for two days. This one had only one hand and with it carried a basket full of water (108–109).

Again, compare this to a similar passage from Munonye on the powers of Ezedibia's fetish as narrated to Chiaku during her efforts to stop Nnanna from following the ways of the white man. Ezedibia, in the manner of Achebe's masked spirit, had transfixed thieves to the spot so that they were easily caught the next day, and at one time or the other, he had also carried a basket full of palm wine:

> "While they (the thieves) were gathering the yams in the dark night, something which Ezedibia planted there in the barn commanded them to stand still. The next morning they were all apprehended…He had done some incredible things. I remember the day he filled a small basket with palm-wine and carried it about, from one end of the market to another, without a single drop escaping" (135–136).

It is significant that the two incredible doings of Achebe's masked spirit narrated in one passage, metamorphose into two similar doings in Munonye, accomplished by one medicine man, and equally in one passage.

In moving beyond the two works just discussed, one notes that Achebe, the writer of the tragic vision, pursues Nwoye's son, Obi Okonkwo, to an ignoble and disgraceful fall from grace, to a prison term in *No Longer at Ease*, while the optimistic Munonye, by the end of his trilogy in *Bridge to a Wedding*, paints the picture of a glorious return of Nnanna (now, Mr. Joseph Kafo) to Umudiobia from Sankia where he has prospered. We must, of necessity, skip *No Longer at Ease* and *Obi* for a larger fish in *A Man of the People* and *A Wreath for the Maidens*. Munonye might continue to deny that he set out to imitate Achebe, but cleavages both in style and subject matter of the two novels are self-evident. Achebe published *A Man of the People* in 1966, while Munonye's *A Wreath for the Maidens* appeared in 1973, after the Nigeria-Biafra war. Both novels are topical in the sense that each chose a political-historical epoch in Nigeria and made scathing and scurrilous remarks about the operators of the system through the agency of imaginative literature. The lament of misrule is Achebe's major part of Munonye's theme in *A Wreath for the Maidens*.

Both *A Man of the People* and *A Wreath for the Maidens* read like a *roman a' clef* in which actual historical events are documented in a vaguely fictionalized form, but while Achebe chronicles the failings of Nigeria's first Republic and prophesizes its demise through a *coup d'etat* which actually takes place, Munonye recreates events leading to the Nigerian civil war and the mismanagement of the war by corrupt officials who turned a war of self-defence into a war of mutual self-destruction through greed, corruption, and selfishness.

We remember that Achebe, the intellectual, uses Odili as his mask, and the narrative point of view "I" as witness or "I" as minor character; Munonye, following this narrative vein, uses another intellectual, Roland Medo, whose narrative point of view is also "I" as witness. Three parties vied for election in *A Man of the People*: The POP (People's Organisation Party led by Teacher Nanga in Anata); the PAP (Progressive Alliance Party); and the CPC (Common People's Convention – a party of intellectuals led by Odili in Urua but which carried the fight right to Chief Nanga's doorstep). Compare these to the four major parties in Munonye's *A Wreath for the Maidens*: the PIP (People's Independence Party – led by Eduado Boga in Oban Constituency and to which Chief Lobe also belongs); PNDL (People's National Democratic League, led by Sunday Umelo); NIP (National Independence Party – led by Michael Ebo); and the RDP (The Real Democratic Party – led by Ubakile and which Mr. Roland has joined to oppose Chief Lobe who has just snatched his girl-friend, Ruth Aniedo).

Odili, the intellectual, moves from observer of the political scene to an active involvement in party politics in order to fight Chief Nanga of POP who had just snatched his girl, Elsie; Roland Medo, the intellectual, also goes from the position of observer of the political scene to active involvement in party politics in order to oppose Chief Lobe of PIP who has snatched his girl-frield, Ruth Aniedo. But while

Odili could not defeat Chief Nanga although he won the latter's intended second wife, Edna, Roland Medo has the satisfaction of his party defeating Chief Lobe although he did not win back Ruth who already had five children for Chief Lobe.

A Man of the People dwells on the state of anomy in politics caused by a vacuum created by the fact that knowledgeable intellectuals who should be involved in piloting the affairs of state have culpably left the stage for illiterates and uncouth practitioners like Chief Nanga who tells Odili: "Leave the dirty game of politics to us who know how to play it" (113). Achebe tells us: "But what else can you expect when intelligent people leave politics to illiterates like Chief Nanga" (73). Likewise, in *A Wreath for the Maidens*, resons are advanced why the uncouth and the illiterate have a field day in the political arena while the soft, educated intellectual is relegated to the background. Now, in *A Man of the People*, Chief Nanga was appointed the Minister of Culture in spite of his near illiteracy, and his sordid display of ignorance provided the reader with many a condescending chuckle as Chief Nanga "announced in public that he had never heard of his country's most famous novel and received applause" (62). He went on to cap this embarrassing announcement with a greater *faux pas* when, lifting his eyes off a prepared speech on great literary figures of the world, he added extemporaneously "Michael West and Dudley Stamp" (62). Munonye equally found this episode irresistible. He creates Chief Eduado Boga, the "uncultured Minister of Culture" (31) who is among those "not quite in a position to discuss affairs of state with good understanding" (17–18), and who is also made to read from a prepared speech he did not understand, and from which he received "frequent applause," until he also came to the last paragraph over which he stumbled until he abandoned the speech altogether in midstream complaining that the speech-writer, the Permanent Secretary, "had composed the heavy speech purposely to embarrass him before the public, and before the constituency" (32).

It is also interesting to note that in *A Man of the People*, Chief Nanga came to bribe Odili to step down for him by offering him a scholarship to study overseas, garnished with a personal cash gift of two hundred and fifty pounds sterling. This Odili turned down (112). In *A Wreath for the Maidens*, Chief Lobe had come to offer a similar bribe to Roland Medo through Biere Ekonte. Roland Medo equally turned this offer down and his party went on to defeat Lobe.

It is also instructive to note that in *A Man of the People*, Chief Nanga and his ilk collude with foreign companies to rape the nation. We are informed that the British Amalgamated made a free gift of ten luxurious buses to Chief Nanga, each costing six thousand pounds sterling, while "the European building firm of Antonio and Sons whom Nanga had recently given the half-million-pound contract to build the National Academy of Arts and Science" (92) had given him a modern four-storey structure as "dash." In the same vein, we learn in *A Wreath for the Maidens* that the

Honourable Minister of Local Government and Chieftaincy Affairs had directed that for the construction of a new market "only well-established contractors should be considered; and that expatriate firms must be given a chance" (35). The reason for this directive soon becomes clear: "there had been some firm understanding already between the Honourable Minister and the monopolistic firm of Shaws and Sharp Limited, Civil Engineers" (35), whom we soon learn "are going to finance the elections for the PIP" (37).

One easily notes, too, that while Odili resigns his teaching job and was assigned a Volkswagen car as a candidate for the CPC (Common People's Convention), Medo also resigns his teaching job and was assigned a Volkwagen car as the Publicity Secretary of the Real Democrats. And while in *A Man of the People*, Max compromises the moral stance of the CPC by accepting one thousand pounds sterling from Chief Koko (intended to bribe Max to step down for him) and bought a minibus for running their campaign, the chairman of the Real Democrats, Mr. Ubakile, compromises the moral stance of his party by accepting a red Volkswagen car from Mr. Lukter of the Premier Oil Company, also fur running their election campaign, in spite of Medo's demurral that it was a "dangerous gift" (44).

There is a point where both Odili and Medo display their youthful idealism. Odili, the idealist thinks elections can be won without dirtying one's hands (hence, his rebuke to Max for accepting Chief Koko's money and using it to fight him), plus his expecting a man like Chief Nanga or a junior Minister to resign "on a matter of principle" (79). Medo, on the other hand thinks elections could be won simply by sticking to the rules and principles and by not spending money on the electorate, because "the party has enough spontaneous goodwill to carry it through" (49).

Finally, we should note the pervasive corrupt political practices in the two works under study. In both novels, massive election rigging (Achebe) and census fraud (Munonye) and the confusion attendant on the violence let loose in the body politic ended with a *coup d'etat* by the army. Achebe ends his novel on this note, while hinting that "a coup might be followed by a counter coup and then where would we be?" (139), while Munonye goes further to enact the counter coup, the massacres and the civil war which inevitably followed. But the same irony that informs *A Man of the People* reveals itself in *A Wreath of the Maidens*. Independence which promised freedom and political utopia to the societies examined in both works, actually brought ethnic rivalry, exploitation of the masses, election rigging, census fraud, and fratricidal bloodletting.

Munonye admits that he admired Achebe and that he "was very encouraged" by Acehbe's success. The extent of his admiration and how far Munonye went in following in the footsteps of Achebe I have tried to sketch in this study although, I admit, all this may have been unconscious on Munonye's part. The rest is for scholars and critics to judge.

Note

In an interview with Munonye, Nnolim had asked him whether he was "one of what they call 'the sons of Achebe,'" or if he had "consciously set out to imitate him." Munonye's reply: "No, no, no…I don't think my style in any way resembles his." For the interview: See Okike 24 (June, 1983): 77–90

Works Cited

Achebe, Chinua. *Things Fall Apart*. London: Heinemann, 1955.
———. *A Man of the People*: New York: Anchor Books, 1967.
Munonye, John. *The Only Son*. London: Heinemann, 1966.
———. *A Wreath for the Maidens*. London: Heinemann, 1973.

Chapter 30

The *Author* Biography of Chinua Achebe: An Autobiographical Charting of an Experience and a Biographer's Tracking of a Life

Ezenwa-ohaeto

AUTOBIOGRAPHIES AND BIOGRAPHIES POSSESS common boundaries, literary interstices and layers of similar source material. A biography is often enriched by autobiographical incidents and events while an autobiography is enhanced by references to encounters and relationships encapsulated in biographical reflections concerning other people. Biography "connotes a relatively full account of a person's life, involving the attempt to set forth character, temperament and milieu, as well as the facts of the subject's activities and experiences." On the other hand, autobiography "is a biography written by the subject about himself or herself," (Abrams 14–15). These definitions indicate the interwoven nature of the two literary terms. However, this relationship does not obliterate some of the peculiar dilemmas that may arise from the narration of a personal story by a self as against the narration of that same story by another.

Related to this dilemma of what an individual narrates and what another person narrates about that individual is what Opoku-Agyemang regards as "a dramatic confirmation of the ephemeral circumstances of human existence. He asserts that "no autobiographer is given to see his or her work through. Every finished autobiography remains unfinished for the reason that the life which gave it life is itself unfinished at the work's completion; and the end of the writer's life is also proof that the work remains incomplete and will remain so forever" (Opoku-Agyemang 5). However, the biography of a living person could equally imply that the work is not complete because a biographer may decide not to proceed further on a published biography even when events and time indicate otherwise. But a much more problematic aspect is the fact that the self narrator in an autobiography is aware of the "truth" while the narrator of a biography can only vouch for what has been "corroborated as the truth." Thus there is an unconscious tension in the biography between facts and fiction. But the biographer could resolve that tension through the collation and analysis of the facts confirmed in the various "autobiographies" or narratives of those who have interacted with the subject. The problematics of this tension as well as the diligent excavation of the facts are part of the charting of this experience and the tracking of Chinua Achebe's life that culminated in writing his biography which necessitates this essay. Thus the essay revolves around the two angles of tracking Achebe's life through available facts, the interrogation of those facts and the inevitable experience in research and writing.

Nevertheless the two dimensions are not mutually exclusive especially since the subject of the work is both a writer and a person. Actually it is this idea that is implicated in the title: aut(hor)biography. It reflects the autobiographical and biographical dimensions of this discussion because Chinua Achebe is an author whose biography could be linked to his work as a creative writer in order to indicate an author-biography as well as reflect the inherent autobiographical elements in such writings. That author-biographical dimension is clearly emphasized by the literary importance of Chinua Achebe whose *Things Fall Apart* in 1958 marked a rupture in World Literature generally and African literature particularly. That novel has been widely accepted as presenting the most coherent and incisive picture of the pre-colonial and colonial experience in Africa. The lack of a common interpretation of the term "post-colonialism" and its contemporary multiple implications, as well as the Heinemann African literature library that Achebe edited, combined to signify a new perspective on modern literature in the world. It became possible to make new definitions of the ever present and constantly modified "colonial reality." This possibility is part of what has led to the emergence of new perceptions on African literature, society and life. Thus African writers and writers from societies with similar colonial experience have come to define themselves according to those landmark novels by Achebe. These issues constitute the major impulse for this biography, and also made the research and writing proceed from 1983 (when the permission was sought) to 1994 (when the research and writing was completed), a period of eleven years.

Within that period of research and writing it became clear that the work required not only interviews and research in institutions associated with Achebe but also a great deal of detective work. The detective work became inevitable after the identification of several incidents and events through the hints, comments and facts that are found in the essays of Chinua Achebe. This became a fortunate development because many of those incidents and events had receded in the minds of several people acquainted with Chinua Achebe. For instance, it took about three hours of prodding questions and general discussions to elicit some facts from an elderly Mr. Obiakonwa who was one of Chinua Achebe's teachers in the primary school. Contrastively another teacher who taught Achebe earlier on in the primary school, S.N.C. Okonkwo, had clear recollections of the events and incidents related to that period. Essentially, the facts that led to the diligent search for those retired teachers emanated from the insights derived from Chinua Achebe's essays. Such insights were possible because Achebe adheres to the features of the personal essay that the Indian novelist R.K. Narayan describes as capable of making the reader "see something of the author himself apart from the theme." Narayan adds that the personal essay "was enjoyable because it had the writer's likes, dislikes and his observations, always with a special flavour of humor, sympathy, aversion, style, charm, even oddity" (Narayan 8). Achebe's inclusion of those features in his essays are meant to clarify as well as indicate the experiential imperative to the ideas he is espousing. In consequence, the personal angles to his essays enabled the biographer to discover leads to other incidents that would have not been unearthed under normal circumstances. Furthermore, they provided opportunities for comparative interpretations between Achebe's autobiographical perspective and the vision of the biographer as well as the views of other people.

All the same an important aspect of such comparative interpretations hinges on what Mitchell calls the fascination of biography because it attempts "to authentically recreate the life and personality of an actual person" (Mitchell 170). Mitchell adds "in trying to chip and shape his raw material the biographer is in continual danger of shattering his base. Yet, if the biographer wishes to explore and present those more evanescent, intangible aspects of his subject's life and personality and their relationship to his work, he must chip and shape because "the biographer is a creative interpreter and shaper as well as gatherer of facts and must turn to some of the fiction writer's techniques (171). What emerges from this injunction is the dilemma of the writer of a biography who is placed between two extremes. Mitchell, therefore, further cautions against either an obsessive factual objectivity that prevents him (the biographer) from knowing his subject that he is unable to stand aside and be critical.

The implication of that caution means that in writing Chinua Achebe's biography the writer has to balance the presentation delicately between the two extremes. As a former undergraduate and graduate student of Achebe as well as a much younger colleague of his on the executive council of the Association of Nigerian Authors for some years, this writer had access to a human perspective on the subject of the biography. But the writer of a biography cannot depend solely on his own impressions. It is also helpful to solicit and procure the views of former fellow students and even fellow Nigerian writers who do not shy away from indicating their impressions, views and knowledge concerning Chinua Achebe. Thus the present writer in the biography draws his material from both a personal autobiographical perception and also from a general angle incorporating the autobiographical perceptions of other people. This technique makes it possible for the writer to stand aside and be critical without distorting reality by presenting a one dimensional portrait. The writer of a biography clearly has to be conscious that he does not impose himself on the material, not in terms of vision but in terms of writing his own self into the work rather than writing about the other who is the subject of the work. Obviously, it is this view that makes Mitchell insist that "a good biography, as well as presenting the facts, will manifest implicitly, if not explicitly, the biographer's particular vision of his subject and his work. This vision should grow out of and be defined by the researched material. But it will also be defined by what the biographer is, by his own presuppositions and world view. Here again the biographer faces a delicate balancing act. He interprets and arranges as well as shows his facts" (173).

In interpreting Chinua Achebe as the facts are elicited and his life unfolds it is this emergent vision that ultimately contributes towards the presentation of a rounded picture of the subject. Quite helpful to the writer of the biography are the varied visions of other people who have made periodic interpretations as a result of their encounter with the subject in the course of his life. In the case of Chinua Achebe, the memories of those momentous encounters spanned various countries in America, Africa, Europe, Asia and Australia. Fortunately, the encounters were not one-way affairs because while the people were assessing Achebe, he was also assessing them. That two-way activity enables the writer of his biography to juxtapose both reactions and arrive at reasonable and justifiable conclusions. In addition, at many of those cities that Achebe visited he had to address varied groups of people and audience which meant that his statements provide another vista through which his individual notions, feelings and reactions could be elicited and related to his life. These constant interlocutions featuring greatly in Achebe's life helped to authenticate the various significant dates in his career and life. They also made it possible to document the extent to which he had proceeded to highlight the values of literature and the unique contributions of African literature.

The documentation of a writer's life is clearly aided by the examination of that writer's works as well as the reactions to them. Since the literary works of Achebe are literary events, such reactions even when they are related to single articles or poems or speeches helped in tracking his life, career and feelings. That aspect of the research made it clear that size does not determine the substance of a literary contribution for his book *The Trouble with Nigeria* apart from the novels, and his articles on "The Novelist as Teacher" and "Racism in Conrad's *Heart of Darkness*" became the most quoted and misquoted. However, such emotional reactions made it inevitable that very strong views are expressed either in appreciation or dislike and these feelings even seeped into other areas like literary criticism. The assemblage and examination of these records and reactions to Achebe's literary works presented what could be regarded as the intrusion of the recorder into the record. The biographer has to examine them from as many dimensions as possible. Clearly, the intrusion of the biographer in the life of his subject not only exposes the essentially literary nature of his enterprise, correcting the false impression of readers that biography is scientific, objective, historical and comprehensive, but sometimes limits the over identification of the biographer with his subject. This excessive sympathy between author and subject produces adulatory lives, uncritical and distorted in their presentation of material (Nadel 28). Actually it is impossible to present the biography of Chinua Achebe through the extreme positions of either excessive sympathy or excessive distaste because many of his achievements have passed through the crucible of both foreign and local assessments. Those assessments also confirm Nadel's view that there is a persistent "awareness of audience" (29) in the construction of a biography and that awareness emanated quite early in Achebe's life and career.

All the same the fact that Achebe has been identifiable in the eyes of the local and foreign public means that his existence is documented. This fact eliminates the opposition between "facts" and "fiction" which Schipper highlights when she comments that "sometimes authors pretend to speak the truth while in fact they are telling lies or producing fantasies. Others pretend to be writing fiction while they are telling the story of their own life" (113). In Achebe's case, that distinction between his use of personal facts and fiction emanating from his imagination became clear quite early as the documented aspects of his life were made public through his education records, interviews and career in public service. Recognizing that "the autobiographical continuum" ranges "from the most private personal revelation to the most austere, historical narrative where the self exists only as it relates to the political or religious issue being presented" (Davies 183–4), then the autobiographical experience in the research and writing of Achebe's biography becomes a subsumed autobiography within the covers of this biography.

That the autobiographical experience is an essential part of an individual's writing experience and equally relevant to the tracking of Achebe's life is delineated by several issues. The first is that the biographer has to interview several associates of the subject since it is only through such wide ranging impressions that the facts have to be corroborated and interpreted objectively. In pursuance of that objective a long list of the names of individuals who have featured in Achebe's life was compiled. It became clear as the research and interviews were conducted that many of those people who were expected to narrate stories concerning the subject had gaps in their memories, and sometimes the past could not be effectively recollected. But an interesting development is that in the search for one individual, the researcher suddenly stumbled on another person who not only recollected significant details but also highlighted another relevant direction. Five incidents illustrate this aspect of the research.

I met Frank Okwuofu Achebe, Chinua's elder brother, shortly before his death and my interview with him elicited some information and few memorable incidents concerning the Isaac Achebe (the father of Chinua and Frank) family. But the wife of Frank Achebe known as Agnes who was present volunteered to narrate several incidents that helped put the story of Chinua Achebe's life in its proper perspective. In the same way I had trailed Chike Momah from New York to Lagos to Nnewi and Enugu in the bid to interview him extensively (2). We had had snatches of those interviews in some of those cities mentioned and the final comprehensive interview was scheduled at Enugu. On that day I could not travel with my car which was in a very bad shape and when I arrived at the venue I had to wait for many hours for Momah and his wife. They arrived in the evening and the interview proceeded in the presence of his host Edwin Nwogugu, a Professor of law, and another man who turned out to be Godwin Momah, the elder brother of Chike Momah. Both Momahs were Chinua Achebe's classmates at Government College, Umuahia, for Achebe had double promotion at one stage. It turned out that Godwin Momah had his own story to tell which enhanced Chike's recollection. My journey that day was memorable from another angle. I had not planned to spend the night in Enugu and I had to depart late in the evening. It was difficult getting public transport to Awka and I was forced to hitchhike from a lorry conveying goods after much plea at a police checkpoint. I arrived at Awka late in the night. The third incident concerning the encounter of an unanticipated informant occurred when I trailed Chijioke Abagwe, a retired broadcaster to Owerri at the Imo Broadcasting Services offices. Abagwe had left some hours before I arrived but I was directed to Manilla Chemists in the heart of Owerri town where I found him in the company of other retired gentlemen. He willingly answered my questions but it turned out that one of his companions there known as Mbah was hired by Chinua Achebe in 1960 at Enugu for the then Nigerian Broadcasting Corporation. Mbah helped in situating some of Abagwe's recollections.

On another search for a man at Ogidi I stumbled onto another contemporary of Achebe and the recollection of the two men, though slightly contrastive, enabled one's correct interpretation of both Achebe and his cultural roots. The two men between them painted memorable pictures of the thirties and forties scene at Ogidi as Achebe and his contemporaries were growing up. There was the fifth incident when I managed to track down an ex-soldier who would provide information concerning the war activities of Chinua Achebe. Pleasantly the man gave me some additional information concerning his relationship with Achebe from the fifties as a staff member under Achebe at the Broadcasting Service Enugu, through the period of the civil war. During that period, the ex-soldier was the Chairman of the Biafran Organization of Freedom Fighters with Achebe as a member of the organization until the days of the Nigerian second republic when he and Achebe were members of the People's Redemption Party of the late Aminu Kano. Such encounters that were unexpected but useful made it possible for the researcher to overcome the few impediments created by the deaths of some of those one would have chosen to interview. In actual fact, there was a man I had arranged to interview who died some weeks before that date.

The research and writing of Chinua Achebe's biography clearly portrayed the difficulties and the impediments to research work in societies that are still struggling with sociopolitical problems (3). The twin issue of research and writing made the tribulations of that reality definite. But the fact that the research proceeded inspite of those odds, is a testimony to the fact that this research work was destined to be carried out to its logical conclusion. It will be for others to say if it is written and researched with ingenuity, tenacity and objectivity but for the biographer a completion of the work portrays a completion of one major aspect of the necessary documentation through research and writing that African literature requires now and always.

The work had its trying moments but also its exciting moments especially when letters of inquiries received the expected responses. But there were times when responses to inquiries sent to the researcher failed to arrive. For instance, two recorded audiocassettes of reminiscences sent from London to Nigeria and from Australia to Germany never reached the researcher. Perhaps that was part of the hazards of dealing with unreliable and corrupt postal agents in Nigeria and Germany, who must have thought those were cassettes of disco music.

Nevertheless the fact that Achebe's life was tracked and that the tracking elicited an experience worth sharing are part of the dividends of this exercise. The implication is best encapsulated in Robert Fraser's image that "an autobiography may perhaps then be compared to a pond. There is a thin plop called birth followed by widening ripples which stretch out in every lateral direction" (87). That comparison can equally be made with a biography and the subsequent ripples that stretch out in every direction are part of the fact that this biography inevitably stretches out in the direction of history, culture, literature, politics, religion, philosophy, economics, biology and sociology.

Notes

1. The author is grateful to the Alexander Von Humboldt Foundation, Bonn, the University of Mainz and the University of Bayreuth, Germany for research facilities between 1993 and 1995. This biography was published by James Currey Publishers, London in collaboration with Indiana University Press, Bloomington, Indiana, U.S.A. and Heinemann, Ibadan, Nigeria.

2. It has to be noted that Chike Christian Momah and the distinguished Nigerian novelist Chukwuemeka Ike had documented memories of their school days at Government College, Umuahia, which they made available to me.

3. This research work which would have benefited from research grants and writing awards or grants could not receive such facilities in Nigeria because there does not exist a reasonable process and avenue for soliciting for such things.

Works Cited

Abrams, M.H. *A Glossary of Literary Terms*, 6th edition. Forth Worth: Harcourt Brace Java-novich College Publishers, 1993.

Davies, Carole Boyce. "Private Selves and Public Spaces: Autobiography and – The African Woman Writer," *Neo Helicon*. Vol. XVII, No. 2 1990: 183–210.

Fraser, Robert. "Dimensions of Personality: Elements of the Autobiographical Mode" in Doirean MacDermott, ed. *Autobiographical and Biographical Writing in the Common-wealth*. Barcelona: University of Barcelona and Editorial AUSA, 1984: 83–87.

Mitchell, Orm. "Rainbow and Granite: The Biographer's Charybdis and Scylla" in Diorean MacDermet, ed. *Autobiographical and Biographical Writing in the Commonwealth*. Barcelona: University of Barcelona and Editorial AUSA, 1984: 169–174.

Nadel, Ira B. "The Biographer's Secret" in James Olney, ed. *Studies in Autobiography*. New York and Oxford: Oxford University Press, 1988: 24–31.

Narayan, R.K. *A Writer's Nightmare Selected Essays 1958–1988*. New Delhi, India: Penguin Books, 1988.

Opoku-Agyemang, Kwadwo. "African Autobiography and Literary Theory," *Asemka*. No. 6. September 1989: 5–18.

Schipper, Mineke. *Beyond Boundaries: African Literature and Literary Theory*. London: Al-lison and Busby, 1989.

Epilogue

Chinua Achebe's Vision of Writing in Indigenous Nigerian Languages: The Example of Literary Creativity in Igbo Language*

Ernest N. Emenyonu

TWO THINGS EMERGED FROM THE ANNUAL ODENIGBO lecture given by Chinua Achebe on September 4, 1999 in Owerri, lmo State, Nigeria. First, the lecture brought Achebe into a head-on collision with Igbo linguistics scholars. Second, it forced scholars of Igbo Language and Literature to start debates again on the problematics of creating literature in an indigenous language in a multicultural, multilingual situation where a foreign language as official language has gained national currency even at the grassroots level and marginalized the status of mother tongues, as is the case in Nigeria today. The controversy surrounding the Igbo Oral-Written interface is an age-long conflict dating to 1841 when a concerted effort was made by European missionaries to create a standard written Igbo from a wide variety of spoken Igbo dialects. What gives the present controversy a different posture is that it is a clear-cut battle between scholars of Igbo linguistics led by 'Nolue Emenanjo, currently Rector of the Institute of Nigerian Languages, Aba, Abia State and creative artists led by Africa's leading novelist, Chinua Achebe. Furthermore, the present controversy is more clearly defined in linguistic terms, what Donatus Nwoga appropriately labeled "the legislative dogmatism of grammarians versus the creative experimentation of creative artists." Sadly however, the effect is the same now as in 1841. Writing in Igbo language has for more than a century stagnated as each phase of the controversy creates fresh impediments not only for the development of Igbo Literature but of Igbo Language Studies in general.

The purpose of this paper is to come up with workable solutions that will move Igbo Studies forward in the 21st century. In four stages, the paper will discuss: (a) the origins and substance of the controversy in which the Igbo OralWritten interface is engulfed; (b) Chinua Achebe's 1999 ODENIGBO lecture and the dimensions of the controversy it has engendered; (c) analysis of the key issues and, (d) proposals towards a lasting resolution of the critical issues.

A. The Origins and Substance of the Controversy

The Igbo language has a multiplicity of dialects, some of which are mutually unintelligible. The first dilemma of the European Christian missionaries who introduced writing in Igbo land in the mid-19th century was to decide on orthography acceptable to all the competing dialects. There was the urgent need to have in native tongue essential instruments of proselytization: the Bible, hymn books, prayer books, etc. The ramifications of this dilemma have been widening and the complexity growing ever since. Since 1841 three proposed solutions have failed woefully. The first was an experiment to forge a synthesis of some selected representative dialects. This Igbo Esperanto, "christened" Isuama Igbo, lasted from 1841 to 1872 and was riddled with uncompromising controversies all through its existence. A second experiment, Union Igbo (1905–1939), succeeded through the determined energies of the missionaries in having the English Bible, hymn books, and prayer books translated into it for effective evangelism. But it too, fell to the unrelenting onslaught of sectional conflicts. The third experiment was the Central Igbo, a kind of standard arrived at by a combination of a core of dialects. It lasted from 1939 to 1972, and although it appeared to have reduced significantly the thorniest issues in the controversy, its opposition and resistance among some Igbo groups remained persistent and unrelenting. After the Nigerian independence in 1960, and following the exit of the European Christian missionaries, the endemic controversy was inherited by the Society for the Promotion of Igbo Language and Culture (SPILC) founded by F.C. Ogbalu, a concerned pan-Igbo nationalist educator who also established a press devoted to the production and publication of educational materials in the Igbo language. Through his unflinching efforts a fourth experiment, and seemingly the ultimate solution, Standard Igbo was evolved in 1973 and has since then largely sustained creativity and other forms of writing in the Igbo language until 1978 when Chinua Achebe hurled the first "salvo" challenging linguistic legitimacy and socio-cultural authenticity of Standard Igbo. At the launching of Ernest Emenyonu's, *The Rise of the Igbo Novel*, published by Oxford University Press, which in part "explored the influence of European Christian missionaries on the development of Igbo orthography and written Igbo literature", Chinua Achebe strongly criticized the way the early missionaries had designed an Igbo orthography, the Union Igbo, and imposed it on the Igbo people. Achebe blamed the near stagnation of creativity in the Igbo language ever since on that dictatorial missionary manipulation. Since then, whenever and wherever Achebe had a chance, he continued unsparingly his attacks on the Union Igbo. Matters came to a head when His Grace, Dr. A.J.V. Obinna, Archbishop of the Catholic Archdiocese of Owerri invited Chinua Achebe from the United States to deliver the 4th in the series of a pan-Igbo annual lecture, ODENIGBO, in 1999. ODENIGBO, a creation of Archbishop Obinna, began in 1996 as a deliberate interventionist initiative of the intellectually vibrant and philosophically astute scholar/prelate to foster and maintain an intra-ethnic discourse on matters of significance in Igbo socia-cultural development. By having the lectures delivered in Igbo before a pan-Igbo audience and simultaneously published in Igbo language, Obinna sought to emphasize the homogeneity of Igbo people despite dialectal differences in speech. Furthermore, the exclusive use of Igbo language in the highly celebrated lectures ensures grass roots participation in the discourse unlike any other lecture series in existence with similar goals and objectives. The choice of Chinua Achebe as the 1999 lecturer seemed also an ingenious move to arrest an incipient suspicion in some quarters that ODENIGBO was a religious rather than a socio-cultural event, which drew its resources and inspiration from Igbo scholars who were first and foremost Roman Catholics. Chinua Achebe is a professing Anglican. Thus this choice was significant in that it bestowed credibility on ODENIGBO as a pan-Igbo non-denominational cultural event open to all who have the survival, growth, and stability of Igbo language and culture at heart. And nothing could have been more appropriate than Achebe's chosen topic "ECHI DI IME: TAA BU GBOO" (literally, TOMORROW IS PREGNANT, TODAY IS TOO EARLY TO PREDICT...).

B. Chinua Achebe's Lecture.

In his lecture, Achebe traced the history of missionary influence on the evolution of orthography for the Igbo language, and the process of the creation of Union Igbo as the standard for written Igbo at the turn of the 20th century. He adversely condemned the way and manner in which the standard was devised and blamed the chequered nature of the development of Igbo Language Studies since then on Archdeacon T.J. Dennis, the missionary whom he identified as the brain behind the creation of Union Igbo and its imposition on the Igbo. To Achebe, Union Igbo was a mechanical standardization, and its use in the translation of the Bible into Igbo in 1913 was a legacy detrimental to the growth and development of Igbo language and culture. He charged Dennis furthermore with" tinkering" with the roots of Igbo language out of sheer ignorance of the natural process of language development in human societies. In that process, Achebe alleged that Dennis had in his missionary over-zealousness and colonial mentality done irreparable harm to Igbo language in particular and Igbo life and culture in general. And then, by extension, Achebe condemned and derided present Igbo linguistics scholars, who, it seemed to him, had followed Archdeacon Dennis' subversive linguistic approach by making and imposing dogmatic rules on Standard Igbo evolved in 1973. He called such scholars" disciples of Dennis" and alleged that they too had unwittingly done more harm than good to the development of contemporary Igbo Language Studies. He charged that their various dogmatic impositions on the Igbo language, when compared to the strides made in Yoruba and Hausa Studies, were responsible for the slow pace of Igbo Language Studies. Achebe pointed to the stability in Yoruba language development studies as a credit to another missionary, Samuel Adjai Crowther, who had a totally different approach in the process of selecting a standard for written Yoruba language. Achebe was convinced that Crowther owed his success to his sensitivity to the Yoruba language of which he was a native speaker. One dialect in the Yoruba model, the Oyo dialect, was selected early and nurtured into the standard for writing in Yoruba language.

Perhaps what was most revolutionary in Achebe's ODENIGBO lecture was not what he said but rather what he did. Two decades after his initial condemnation of Union as well as Standard Igbo, Achebe had not shifted from his position that Igbo writers should be free to write in their various community dialects unencumbered by any standardization theories or practices. He resented attempts to force writers into straitjackets, maintaining unequivocally that literature has the mission "to give full and unfettered play to the creative genius of Igbo speech in all its splendid variety, not to dam it up into the sluggish pond of sterile pedantry ("Editorial and Linguistic Problems ..." 95). In keeping with this principle, therefore, Achebe wrote and delivered his ODENIGBO lecture in a brand of dialect peculiar only to Onitsha speakers of the language and almost unintelligible to more than half the audience. He was making an unmistakable millennium statement which would be hard to miss by those Igbo linguistics scholars whom he had once referred to as "egoistic schoolmen who have been concerned not to study the language but to steer it into the narrow tracks of their particular pet allusions" (95). The organizers of the lecture were forced to do the unprecedented: print in the same booklet two versions of the 23-page lecture: one in Achebe's original version, and the other in the conventional Standard Igbo. The climax of Achebe's position on the Igbo Oral-Written Interface was his call for the total abolition and the scrapping of Standard Igbo in which the Igbo language has been written and accepted by scholars since its evolution in 1973. Nothing could be more divisive at a forum assembled to celebrate Igbo cultural and socio-linguistic homogeneity despite dialectal diversities. Nothing could be more devastating for concerned scholars of Igbo Studies who had looked forward to the early decades of the 21st century as the era for Igbo Renaissance after over a century of fratricidal acrimonious controversies, first over the choice of a pan-Igbo orthography, and then over the standardization of written Igbo. Reactions to Achebe's views in the lecture were predictably fast, especially from linguistics scholars devoted to the theory and cause of Standard Igbo.

Reactions to Achebe's Views: Innocent Nwadike

Achebe's lecture drew many reactions both positive and negative, but more the latter. The most detailed and indeed the most negatively extreme came from Innocent Nwadike, an Igbo language lecturer at the University of Nigeria, Nsukka, who is apparently totally dedicated to the cause of Standard Igbo, as evident in his tone and language. What strikes the reader about Nwadike's article, "Achebe Missed It," published in a Nigerian weekly magazine (THE NEWS, 27 March 2000), was not the substance of Nwadike's disagreement with the views of Achebe, or his right to do so, but rather his compunction to deride and insult, as can be seen in the following excerpts:

> "Achebe had nothing to offer his audience except throwing of sand... Achebe's lecture turned out to be real throwing of sand which ended in pronunciation of the heresy of the last century of the second millennium... ."
>
> "Achebe's tragedy and failure started when he descended
> from his Olympian to copy without verification... ."
>
> "Achebe was led astray and he marshalled out many historical fallacies. ..."
>
> "Though Achebe has persistently stressed his unalloyed love for Igbo language, he has done nothing towards its promotion and growth, except continued destructive criticism since the 1970's... ."
>
> "In the course of his lecture Achebe leveled many false accusations against Dennis and very heart breaking are the lies against the dead... ."
>
> "Anyone who reads Achebe's lecture will notice an air of superiority and worldly triumphalism exhibited by the author almost arrogating to himself transcendental power which belongs to God alone...."
>
> "Let him [Achebe] as from today, learn to respect his people and all constituted authority...."
>
> "Let not Achebe constitute himself a cog in the wheel of progress like one Chief Nwakpuda of the Old Umuahia who tried to stop a locomotive engine from passing through his village. ..."
>
> "Achebe should stop embarrassing himself, for a beautiful face does not deserve a slap as the Igbo say..." (Emphasis mine).

The danger in resorting to name-calling in the course of an important discourse is that it distracts from the main focus of the essential argument. The issue of deciding on a standard for writing Igbo so that Igbo Language Studies can move on is too paramount to be sacrificed at the altar of rhetoric and polemics. Although in the Igbo republican culture, freedom of expression is encouraged and cultivated, and a child who washes his hands could eat with kings, this is not an invitation to anarchy and the denigration of hierarchy. The critical method in literary criticism is as important and significant as the substance of the criticism. How one says something in an Igbo gathering is as crucial as what one has to say and perhaps more so. Nwadike's ungracious choice of words, his personal attacks on Achebe, and his apparent gloating in subjecting Chinua Achebe to public ridicule is, to say the least, most unfortunate and quite antithetical to the Igbo cultural norm which restrains a child from jesting at, ridiculing, or speaking in utter derision of an elder, no matter the facts of the case. The Igbo have a saying that the public ridicule or disgrace of a titled elder is more painful than his execution.

Chinua Achebe is not a reckless man, and not in the least a careless writer. If anything he is a man who thinks carefully about issues, a conscious artist who is quite cautious in his choice of words for public utterance. He would, as the Igbo say, look to his left and to his right before crossing the road. And Igbo wisdom admonishes the onlooker to carefully search the direction to which a weeping child is pointing, for the child's mother or father may well be there. We applauded when, on behalf of the African continent, Chinua Achebe single-handedly took on the obnoxious institution of European colonialism and flawed it. We fully concurred when Achebe, on behalf of African culture and dignity, reduced to size the egocentric, egoistic, and presumptuous early Christian missionary and colonial administrator. We applauded Achebe's heroic and altruistic vocabulary in his novel *Things Fall Apart* when he lashed at the irreverence and high-handedness of the early Europeans who came to Africa:

> Does the white man understand our custom about land?
> How can he when he does not even speak our tongue? But he says that our customs are bad; and our own brothers who have taken up his religion also say that our customs are bad. How do you think we can fight when our own brothers have turned against us? The white man is very clever. He came quietly and peaceably with his religion. We were amused at his foolishness and allowed him to stay. Now he has won our brothers and our clan can no longer act like one. He has put a knife on the things that held us together and we have fallen apart … (176).

In his lecture, however, Achebe seems to be charging not at the misshapen European bull but the lamb at the sublime shrine of his people's spiritual existence. He once declared that a language is more than mere sounds and words; that indeed a language is a "people's world view." A language is a sacred symbol of a people's humanity. A committed African writer carries the burden of the conscience of his community. Chinua Achebe has positioned himself at the forefront of the committed African writers who use art to better the lives of their fellow men and women; who use art to restore the lost dignity of the African past; writers who use art as a celebration of life in the present. So rather than dismiss Achebe's views arbitrarily or hastily, we should examine them thoroughly and inform ourselves whether the spokesman of African cultural realism and renaissance had in fact missed the point about what is best for his own people's language and culture; whether in the full glare of bright lights, Chinua Achebe had misread the colors of the garments in his innermost closet. Only then can we look him fully in the eye and say the novelist lied!

C. Analysis of the Key Issues

Two supreme facts have to be established unequivocally at the onset. First, there is a Standard Igbo in existence; it is a reality; it cannot be set aside. It is not perfect but it is the best framework we have in existence for further development and improvement. It is a major legacy left for Igbo Language Studies by the Society for the Promotion of Igbo Language and Culture (SPILC) and its inimitable founding president, the late F.C. Ogbalu. In an August 1974 seminar of the SPILC, a Standardization Committee was set up. It was allembracing in composition: "lecturers of Igbo Studies at institutions of higher learning, authors, publishers, broadcasters, teachers of Igbo language in secondary schools and teacher training institutions, representatives of the Ministries of Education and Information, State Schools Management Boards and the Mass Media" (Ogbalu and Emenanjo Vol. Two, 98–108, 102–114). Since 1974, substantial improvements have continued to be made on the final product of the Standardization Committee. There is now in existence a very useful supplement, Igbo Metalanguage, produced under the auspices of the Nigerian Educational Research and Development Council (NERDC) which also sponsored the production of Yoruba Metalanguage and Hausa Metalanguage. Igbo Metalanguage serves as a common reference for writers, teachers, and examiners. It is a useful glossary which is an invaluable guide for anyone who wishes to learn the application of Standard Igbo in creative or other writings.

The second incontestable fact is that Igbo Language Studies and development currently, as has been the case for almost half a century, lag behind the other two major Nigerian languages – Hausa and Yoruba. As Donatus Nwoga pointed out in his exceptionally brilliant study, "From Dialectal Dichotomy to Igbo Standard Development" (103), the National Language Policy in Nigeria has been a major catalyst in the development of educational materials in the three languages designated as major. Nigeria, which speaks 394 indigenous languages, has given up choosing an official language from amongst them, but instead settled for English, a colonial inheritance, as its language of business, education, and government. The National Language Policy has identified three languages-Hausa, Igbo, and Yoruba-as major and requires them to be studied in schools as a means of advancing the theory that "first language education is the best tradition in the early years of the educational process." This policy has greatly enhanced the production and publication of educational materials, texts, and literature in the three major languages. The population of the Igbo-speaking people is at least the third highest in Nigeria's estimated 120 million population. It is a fact, however, that Hausa and Yoruba scholars and writers have made greater and far more impressive strides in the development of teaching and reading materials in Hausa and Yoruba languages than their Igbo counterparts have done for the Igbo language. It is most likely also that, outside Nigeria, Igbo is the least studied of the three languages. The reason is not difficult to find. The endless squabbles over orthography, standardization, and the like, can hardly inspire interest and excitement in prospective learners inside and outside Nigeria. Igbo people have not put their house in order and people do not waste time on something in a state of chaos. It is, therefore, in the best interest of the Igbo people and Igbo Studies that the present crisis be resolved quickly and in the best possible manner so that Igbo Studies can take its rightful place in the academy.

Two other issues deserve close critical attention because of their centrality in any possible solutions of the issues under review. First, to what extent should we blame Archdeacon Dennis for the stagnation and tardiness in Igbo Language Studies because of his invention of Union Igbo as the medium for translating the Bible into the Igbo language in 1913? Second, can we set aside the work of the Standardization Committee of 1974 as a compromise for moving forward Igbo Language Studies in the 21st century?

It would be quite absurd to blame Archdeacon Dennis for the instability in Igbo Language Studies for an alleged error in linguistic judgment made almost a century ago. It would be like blaming the British for the misrule and instability in the Nigerian government since the attainment of independence in 1960. Nigerians have had half a century to right the wrongs, correct the anomalies, refocus the directions of the country, and stamp out unprogressive legacies planted by the British at their exit. To continue to blame Archdeacon Dennis for our woes would be tantamount to saying that the issues of orthography and standardization have been stagnant and unrevisited since 1913. Yet we know that some Igbo Language scholars have invested considerable amounts of time and energy, in the last three decades at least, into research in Igbo language and culture. Can we easily forget or afford to ignore the tremendous works of the late F.C. Ogbalu and Donatus Nwoga, or the continuing endeavors of Ebo Ubahakwe, Nolue Emenanjo, M.J.C. Echeruo, Chukwuma Azuonye, B.I.N. Osuagwu, and G.E. Igwe, among others? These scholars have in their studies made tremendous strides to move Igbo Language Studies forward. We must, therefore, reject any approach that negates gained grounds. Any new studies must build on the noble achievements of previous endeavors. So, instead of taking 1913 as our point of reference, we must turn to achievements since 1982 and build on them. Nor can we close our eyes to Archbishop A.J.V. Obinna's 1996 landmark action towards a renaissance of igbo Language Studies. It is regrettable to discuss the ODENIGBO Lecture Series as simply a "closed-door" religious and Roman Catholic event, or to see the prelate as seeking to upstage the paraplegic AHIAJOKU Lecture Series initiated by the lmo State Government in 1979. Obinna is nationally and internationally recognized for his ardent interest in, and commitment to the preservation of Igbo Language and culture in particular and the arts and humanities in general. It was not a surprise to keen observers that he initiated the ODENIGBO Lecture Series. He would have done no less if he were an Anglican, Baptist, or Methodist Archbishop, or for that matter if he held the sacred *ofo* of the traditional religion in his Emekuku village near Owerri. Many igbo scholars had greeted with overwhelming enthusiasm a similar vision by the late Gaius Anoka when his brain child, the AHIAJOKU Lecture Series, was initiated under the auspices of the lmo State Government and designated to be delivered annually in the month of November. By the early 1990's igbo scholars had begun to witness with dismay the derailment of the noble objectives of the AHIAJOKU lectures owing largely to self-defeating manipulations and in-fighting by government bureaucrats. The AHIAJOKU lectures simply became one more government event, and like many things in government and civil service, it became the community goat that always died of hunger. Archbishop Obinna's initiative came just in time to arrest total public disenchantment with what had started off as a dynamic and progressive renaissance in modern Igbo culture. Since the end of the Nigerian civil war in 1970, the Igbo people seem to have developed a bewildering self-destructive tendency, with a sharp instinct for killing their best. Progressive ideas are treated with levity and cynicism. Novel initiatives for development are scoffed at and opposed to the bitter end and, when they are crushed, we realize too late that the perpetrators had nothing much to offer and, in most cases, nothing at all. In the fifth year of ODENIGBO, the lmo State Government suddenly woke up from almost a decade of amnesia and slumber to remember AHIAJOKU and immediately picked one more lecturer who spoke to a pan-Igbo audience about sacred ancestral Igbo culture and customs, in the English language! If history is anything to go by, AHIAJOKU will sooner or later make another jay-walk into coma. It is on record that Archbishop A.J.V. Obinna and the retired Anglican Archbishop B.C. Nwankiti in 1998 stood unflinchingly firm against all odds in their opposition to the desecration of Igbo artifacts, historic sculptures, and other spectacular works of art by an Islamic-minded Military Governor-turned-born-again-Christian, in the name of presumed reverence for the sanctity of a new found Christianity. It is one thing to denigrate Archdeacon Dennis, who may deserve it;

it is another to try to undermine the heroic efforts of Archbishop Obinna, who does not deserve it at all.

If we may return to Archdeacon Dennis, one final word is in order. Saint or sinner, let us allow Archdeacon T.J. Dennis, his Union [gbo, and his tinkering with the Igbo language, to go down in history as among those sad and costly prices which Nigeria had to pay for being subject to an imperial overlord who rode roughshod over our God-given languages, sacred customs, and traditional cultures. And let's move on!

Let us now turn attention to the second issue: "Can we set aside the present Standard Igbo as a necessary compromise for Igbo social unity and cultural homogeneity, and attempt a fresh start?" What has been discussed so far is substantial enough to indicate that setting aside the present Standard Igbo will not only be retrogressive but indeed suicidal. What is happening to Igbo language today with its multiplicity of dialects, and strivings to find a standard, is not a peculiar phenomenon. Germany had its language problems. England had its own. Finland evolved Standard Finnish as the solution to her dialectal problems at the end of the 19th century. Can we learn anything from each model and each approach? The best model of Igbo written language will be the one that is accessible to, or has the potential of being accessible to Igbo people across the board.

Often it is simplistically assumed that the Yoruba next door achieved their Standard Yoruba without rancor and schism, and that the selection of the Oyo dialect by the missionary, Samuel Adjai Crowther, in 1842 has never been challenged to date. Nothing could be farther from the truth. The Yoruba had something which was lacking in the Igbo traditional society: the institution of royal paramouncy as a central authority which exercised political power of a controlling nature. The Igbo, instead, had a decentralized political system which put a central controlling authority out of the question. Establishing a Standard in any language is a political action and is often accomplished where there is political control along with economic initiatives. It becomes easier to establish and enforce a language policy relative to the language of the group with dominant political power. Often the dialect of the dominant political group became the Standard, and political and economic instruments were used to sustain and legitimize it. The decentralized nature and politics of the Igbo as a group have not made the standardization process easy. The fragmented Igbo set-up which was a source of strength in the past has become a liability in the present. What has worked for the Yoruba has not worked for the Igbo, but it was not only because the Yoruba had traditional rulers who exercised central authority. The Yoruba had their full share of controversies over orthographies and dialects. The Oyo, Ijebu, Ondo, Ekiti, Ijesha, Igbomina, and Kabba all staked their claims. But there was political intervention when, following the Nigerian Independence, Chief Obafemi Awolowo, then Premier of the Western Region, introduced Free Primary Education in the region and decreed that the Yoruba language to be taught in the schools would be the Oyo dialect. That was a major factor in the stabilization of Standard Yoruba. But standardization does not mean the death of sectional dialects. The spoken language need not be identified as synonymous with the written standard. Political intervention was a great catalyst in the creation of the modern Standard Yoruba but Yoruba linguistics scholars did not rest on their oars. They devised some linguistic mechanisms for solving the problems created in the process of standardization. They fished out words from other dialects to satisfy new demands which could not be met by the Oyo dialect. They created the policy of mutual give-and-take among the various dialectal groups for the purpose of enriching the Standard. Yoruba Linguistics scholars disagree (as will always be expected in academic circles), but they never lose sight of their collective responsibility to standardize the language in the interest of the unity and identity of all Yoruba people. This commitment to a collective goal has yielded immense dividends in Yoruba Language Studies. The Yoruba alphabet was introduced in 1842 by the early Christian missionaries, as was the Igbo alphabet at about the same time. The first novel in the Yoruba language was published in 1928 not too long before the first Igbo novel, *Omenuko*, in 1933. The father of the Yoruba novel, D.O. Fagunwa, began writing in 1938, the same decade as Pita Nwana, the father of the Igbo Language novel. But today the Igbo cannot boast of half the literary output that exists in Yoruba language: a corpus that includes over 185 novels, 80 plays and a large number of collections of poetry and translations of other works into Yoruba. In addition, there are in existence the volumes *Yoruba Metalanguage; A Glossary of Yoruba Technical Terms in Language, Literature and Methodology,* as well as several Yoruba grammar books and reference works. There are translations of the Nigerian Highway Code into Yoruba. Although Chinua Achebe's *Things Fall Apart* is a classic novel that incomparably depicts Igbo culture and its worldview, the only translation of it in a Nigerian language is the Yoruba edition published in 2000. The Yoruba Writers Association was established in 1982 and is still going strong and increasing its cultural and educational impact on the growth and development of Yoruba language and literature. Igbo linguists, scholars and writers can learn something from their Yoruba counterparts, at least their intellectual attitude of accommodation and commitment to the collectivist goal of advancing the development of Yoruba Language Studies from one generation to the next despite differences in the Yoruba dialects which they speak in their intra-ethnic forums.

It is important to stress again that standardization does not mean the elimination or invalidation of other sub-dialects or the marginalization of the people who speak them. For instance, I speak the Mbieri dialect of Igbo language. Nobody can force me to speak any other dialect. If I have to address an audience in my local community, I will speak to them in our local dialect. If, however, I decide that my address will be published, I will have to have it written out in a form that is accessible to all Igbo readers. At the moment, I do not know how to write flawlessly in that accessible Standard form. I might resort to writing my speech in English and then have someone proficient in Standard Igbo translate it for me, or I could write it in Mbieri dialect the best way I know how and then have an expert in Standard Igbo put it in the proper form and character until I learn to do so myself.

The linguistic issue is complex and cannot be resolved by resorting to rhetoric and polemics. Dialects may be mutually unintelligible, but that does not change the structural unity of the language from which they all emanated. Igbo language scholars must work hard at the problematic grammatical level of Igbo as a language. One regrets to say that some of the Igbo language scholars are investing their time and scholarship in the areas of cowering before Textbooks Selection Committees of the Ministries of Education, and examination bodies in search of script-markers, rather than in the areas of genuine language development research projects. There is an urgent need for proper language education in the Igbo-speaking areas of Nigeria. People need to be properly enlightened about the present state and future of their language. A language draws its source and strength from the grassroots. The greatest potency of a language is in the domain of its metaphorical usage which resides with the users of the language. A language can die by the way scholars structure, "unstructured" or deconstruct it. A language gains its currency by usage. Stale usages will invariably, with time, wear off, and the language and its owners will move on. Tinkering with the Igbo language as if it were a toy is unacceptable either in the hands of T.J. Dennis or in the hands of any contemporary Igbo grammarian out of touch with the owners of the language. Inventing new words is a common phenomenon in any language development process, but if it is misused it can stultify or stifle the growth of the language. Achebe had a point when he criticized the tendency by a few Igbo linguists who, acting like a cabal would invent new words and blame the populace to whom those words might sound foreign, for "being absent at the meetings where the new words were 'inducted' into the language" (ODENIGBO 1999, 46). A language is the property of its collective owners and those who do anything on their behalf must "seek their consent" before making radical changes in their usage. But Achebe was not correct when he accused Igbo language scholars of "wanting all Igbo people to speak the same dialect" (ODENIGBO 1999, 48). The call of the scholars is for a standard written Igbo, not spoken Igbo. The spoken language is not synonymous with the written standard language. A strong program of public enlightenment or mass language education is necessary to allay the fears of people who may think that the establishment of a written standard will compel them directly or indirectly to learn another group's dialect. In the absence of a central authority to decree the use of Standard Igbo in all primary schools located in the Igbo-speaking States of Nigeria, as was the case with the then Yoruba Western Region, the best hope is for a strong official language policy for primary and secondary schools. Igbo language has to be taught at all levels in the educational system. Children must read in Igbo before they read in English at the beginning classes, and what they read must be written in consistent Standard Igbo. The inconsistency from the Union Igbo to Central Igbo and then to Standard Igbo which Achebe complains of in his lecture (46) is, indeed, a concern, but it is part of the process of the development of the language. It will not be in the interest of either the children who constitute the future generations of Igbo writers and scholars, or the Igbo language itself, to adopt Achebe's suggestion that "the language must be allowed to sort itself out in due course" (48). After more than 150 years of waiting, a "hold-on" policy is not the best approach to stimulate the growth of Igbo language and literature. We must teach the Standard that we have now in our schools. And we must reject Mazi Obieze Ogbo's suggestion that two linguistic strands be developed whereby" all students in schools in the Old Onitsha Province can be taught the Onitsha dialect and all students in schools of the old Owerri Province can be taught in Owerri dialect" (104). This, in effect, calls for two parallel forms of Standard written Igbo. Donatus Nwoga had the best response when he dismissed that as a return "to the perennial tale of Igbo sectionalism, pride, and inability to yield to the common good (109). We need a uniform Standard Igbo to project Igbo language to the world. We need a Standard Igbo in which Igbo scholars, creative writers, philosophers, and scientists can give vent to their special areas of knowledge. We need a Standard Igbo in which reading and teaching materials can be developed so that Igbo language can be a subject of study for Igbo speakers as well as other Nigerians and nationals of other countries of the world.

All this has enormous challenges for Igbo linguistics scholars and writers. Igbo grammar books are necessary at all levels of the educational system. Igbo language texts need to be strengthened by the works of Igbo creative writers. Several volumes of Igbo dictionaries are needed to supplement the grammar books and works of fiction in Igbo. An Igbo Language Bureau and Igbo Writers Association are essential to define the directions of Igbo language development for the future. Policy issues can be dealt with even in abstract terms as long as a sense of direction is clearly stated and any form of linguistic imperialism avoided.

D. Proposals for Pragmatic Solutions

Workable solutions are necessary for the positive advancement of Igbo Language Studies in the 21st century. First and foremost, all Igbo linguists, writers, and scholars should fundamentally accept and authenticate the existing Standard Igbo as a framework for future actions towards the development of the language. Future actions should include feeding new ways and logistics into the development process such that successive generations can further improve the language to accommodate new concepts and experiences relevant to their age.

Igbo language scholars should be more flexible in their approaches to the expansion of the language. Impositions of illogical and unnatural forms should be avoided. It is not necessary to evolve every word in the Igbo language for the sake of linguistic purity. Words can be chosen from any dialect of the Igbo language to accommodate a new concept. Imaginative coinages by the masses themselves may be preferable to "tedious compositions of scholars." It will be beneficial to adhere to Donatus Nwoga's suggestion that "borrowings appropriately adapted to the phonology of the Igbo language would be a most satisfactory manner of solving the problem of lexical expansion" (Nwoga 1994). Words and concepts from other languages should be absorbed and rendered phonologically in Igbo. There is no need to evolve a new Igbo word for "telephone/" for instance, when it can simply be indigenized through an Igbo spelling and pronunciation instead of inventing a whole sentence to give it an Igbo name. Insisting on inventing a new word for every new concept may produce strange and inappropriate nomenclatures. An example is the word Mahadum for "university." Mahadum does not indicate in historic terms the institution known as university. A university is defined by its function. Mahadum is a statement of scope. In any event "university" is no longer a new concept anywhere in Igbo land, the rural villages included. Pronunciations may differ according to the age of the speaker in the village or urban setting. After all, the word matimatiki for mathematics has successfully made its way into Yoruba language. The Igbo minstrels and comedians have been vastly successful in this regard both in their metaphorical coinages and idiomatic usages.

The present Standard Igbo should be seen and used as a centralizing instrument and the framework for further development through the writing of texts and different types of dictionaries and metalanguage texts which provide meanings for new coinages and idiomatic expressions in different dialects of Igbo language.

Igbo language has to be taught in schools at all levels. Children in schools situated in Igbo land should read in Igbo before reading in English. Igbo language should also be used in teaching other subjects in the school curriculum including science and mathematics, as this will enable appropriate words to be devised for technological data and concepts. New words and expressions should be tested in controlled situations before formal incorporation.

Creative artists should, while writing in the existing Standard Igbo freely use the idioms of their particular dialects as a means of enriching their texts and characterizations. In spite of standardization, the survival of various dialects of the Igbo language should be encouraged strongly.

An Igbo Language Bureau should be set up for the effective harmonization and implementation of policies aimed at projecting the direction of a dynamic development of Igbo Language Studies.

All ramifications of Igbo Language Studies have suffered stagnation in the 19th and 20th centuries because of sectional differences over orthography and dialect. The 21st century should learn from the errors and build on the gains of the past. The responsibility of all Igbo language scholars should be, in the words of Donatus Nwoga, "to standardize for the Igbo people a language which unifies them and gives them an identity … a language that can be the subject of studies by non-Igbo people in Igboland, by other Nigerians in their own homes, and by other nationals of the world as one of the developed languages of thought and literature" (104).

Notes

An earlier version of this paper was published in Falola and Harlow, *African Writers and Their Readers*. New Jersey, Africa World Press, 2002: 255–275.

I am grateful to Prof. Emmanuel N. Obiechina and Prof. M.J.C. Echeruo for allowing me to discuss the complexities of this topic at the various stages of writing the paper. Their views and generous suggestions proved immensely helpful in my completion of the paper. I am also grateful to Prof. Akinwumi Isola of the University of Ibadan for useful information on the Yoruba language background.

Works Cited

Achebe, Chinua. *Echi Di Ime: Taa Bu Gboo.* Owerri, Nigeria: Assumpta Press, 1999.

———. *Things Fall Apart.* New Hampshire: Heinemann, 1996.

———. "Editorial and Linguistic Problems in Aka Weta: A Comment". In *Uwa Ndi Igbo* 1, 1984: 95.

Emenyonu, Ernest. *The Rise of the Igbo Novel.* Ibadan: Oxford University Press, 1978.

Nwoga, Donatus. "From Dialectal Dichotomy to Igbo Standard Development." In Kalu Ogbaa. *The Gong and The Flute: African Literary Development and Celebration.* Westport, Conn.: Greenwood Press, 1994: l03–17.

Obinna, Anthony. *Ujunwa: Anuri Uwa Nile.* Owerri: Assumpta Press, 2000.

Ogbaa, Kalu. *The Gong and The Flute: African Literary Development and Celebration.* Westport, Conn.: Greenwood Press, 1994.

Ogbalu, F.C and Emenanjo E.N. *Igbo Language and Culture.* Ibadan: Oxford University Press, 1975.

———. *Igbo Language and Culture.* Vol. Two. Ibadan: University Press Ltd., 1982.

Ogbo, Obieze. "Saving the Igbo Language," Uwa Ndi Igbo: *Journal of Igbo Life and Culture.* Number 1 (June, 1984).

The News. Lagos, Nigeria 27 March, 2000.

Uwa Ndi Igbo: *Journal of Igbo Life and Culture.* Number 1, Nsukka, Nigeria, June 1984.

ISINKA

Notes on Contributors

Victoria Alabi – teaches in the Departmnet of Modern European Languages at the University of Ilorin, Nigeria

Ada Uzoamaka Azodo – teaches African Literature and French at Indiana University, Northwest.

John Douthwaite – teaches in the Comparative Literature Department of the University of Torino, Italy.

Afam Ebeogu – teaches in the English Department at Abia State University, Uturu, Abia State, Nigeria

Ebele O. Eko – teaches in the Department of English and Literary Studies at the University of Calabar, Nigeria. She was formerly Deputy Vice-Chancellor of the University. She had been the Desmond Tutu Distinguished Professor of English at the University of North Florida, Jacksonville, Florida.

Sunday Osim Etim – teaches in the Department of English at the College of Education, Akamkpa, Cross River State, Nigeria.

Osita Ezeliora – teaches in the Departmnet of English at Ogun State University, Ago-Iwoye, Nigeria.

Claudio Gorlier – teaches Literature at the University of Torino, Italy.

Anthonia C. Kalu – is Professor of Black Studies and teaches African Literature at Northern Colorado State University, Greeley, Colorado.

Isaac B. Lar – teaches in the Department of English at the University of Jos, Nigeria.

Grace J. Malgwi – teaches in the Department of English at the Federal College of Education, Yola, Adamawa State, Nigeria.

Angela F. Miri – teaches in the Department of English at the University of Jos, Nigeria.

Alfred Ndi – teaches African and Black Literature at the University of Younde I, Bamenda, Republic of Cameroon.

Okey Ndibe is a visiting writer-in-residence and Associate Professor of literature at Simon's Rock College of Bard in Great Barrington, MA. He is the author of *Arrows of Rain* (Heinemann, 2000) and is finishing work on a second novel, "foreign gods, inc."

Barine Sanah Ngaage – teaches in the Department of English at the College of Education, Port Harcourt, Rivers State, Nigeria.

Charles E. Nnolim – is a Professor of English and former Dean, School of Humanities at the University of Port Harcourt, Nigeria. He is a renowned critic of African Literature and has been published extensively in leading literary journals in Africa, Europe, and the United States.

J.O.J. Nwachukwu-Agbada – teaches in the Department of English at Abia State University, Uturu, Abia State, Nigeria. He is the author of *The Igbo Proverb* (2002).

Sophie Ogwude – teaches English in the General Studies Division at the Federal University of Technology, Owerri, Nigeria.

Ezenwa Ohaeto – teaches in the Department of English at Nnamdi Azikiwe University. Awka, Nigeria. He is the author of *Chinua Achebe: A Biography* (1997).

Tanure Ojaide – teaches in the African American and African Studies Department at the University of North Carolina at Charlotte. An award-winning prolific Nigerian poet, Ojaide is the author of several collections of poetry.

Augustine C. Okere – was until recently a Reader (Associate Professor) of English at the Alvan Ikoku College of Education, Owerri, Nigeria. He has published in international literary journals in Africa, Europe, Canada, and the United States.

Odirin Omiegbe – teaches at the College of Education, Ekiadolor, Benin City, Nigeria.

Jasper A. Onuekwusi – is Head of the Department of English, Imo State Univeristy, Owerri, Nigeria.

Nicholas Pwedden – is Head of the Department of English, University of Jos, Jos, Nigeria.

Omar Sougou – is Associate Professor of Literature, Universite Gaston Berger, Saint Louis, Senegal.

Marie Umeh – teaches in the Department of English at John Jay College of Criminal Justice, The City University of New York, New York.

Ngozi Ezenwanyi Umunnakwe – was until recently with the English Department at Imo State University, Owerri, Nigeria. She is now with the College of Education, Botswana.

Index